WITHDRAWN W9-ADZ-498

The *Romance of the Rose* was one of the most important works of medieval vernacular literature, exerting a profound impact on subsequent French literature for the next two hundred years and influencing medieval English, Italian, and Dutch literature as well. This study addresses the reception of the *Rose* by French-speaking readers from the late thirteenth to the early fifteenth century. The main emphasis is on a study of the manuscript tradition as a guide to the variety of ways in which the poem was read, interpreted, and appreciated during this period. Such evidence as readers' annotations and glosses, textual variants and rewritings, and manuscript illumination is used to construct a picture of the milieux in which the *Rose* was read, the interests and concerns of its readers, and the different ways in which they reacted to and reshaped the poem. The discussions of the manuscript tradition are complemented by a detailed examination of the use of the *Rose* by two important French writers of the fourteenth century: the monastic author Guillaume de Deguilleville and the courtly poet Guillaume de Machaut.

The importance of the *Rose* has long been recognized, as have the interpretive difficulties it presents. This is the first study, however, to examine systematically the evidence of the manuscript tradition, offering analyses of individual versions of the poem. It brings to light much previously unpublished material. It also demonstrates the value of manuscript analysis for the study both of medieval literature and of the ways in which the medieval audience read and interpreted texts.

CAMBRIDGE STUDIES IN MEDIEVAL LITERATURE 16

The *Romance of the Rose* and its Medieval Readers

CAMBRIDGE STUDIES IN MEDIEVAL LITERATURE 16

General Editor: Professor Alastair Minnis, Professor of Medieval Literature, University of York

Editorial Board
Professor Piero Boitani (Professor of English, Rome)
Professor Patrick Boyde, FBA (Serena Professor of Italian, Cambridge)
Professor John Burrow, FBA (Winterstoke Professor of English, Bristol)
Professor Alan Deyermond, FBA (Professor of Hispanic Studies, London)
Professor Peter Dronke, FBA (Professor of Medieval Latin Literature, Cambridge)
Dr Tony Hunt (St Peter's College, Oxford)
Professor Nigel Palmer (Professor of German Medieval and Linguistic Studies, Oxford)
Professor Winthrop Wetherbee (Professor of English, Cornell)

This series of critical books seeks to cover the whole area of literature written in the major medieval languages – the main European vernaculars, and medieval Latin and Greek – during the period *c.* 1100–*c.* 1500. Its chief aim is to publish and stimulate fresh scholarship and criticism on medieval literature, special emphasis being placed on understanding major works of poetry, prose and drama in relation to the contemporary culture and learning which fostered them.

Titles published
Dante's Inferno: *Difficulty and dead poetry*, by Robin Kirkpatrick
Dante and Difference: Writing in the Commedia, by Jeremy Tambling
Troubadours and Irony, by Simon Gaunt
Piers Plowman *and the New Anticlericalism*, by Wendy Scase
The Cantar de mio Cid: *Poetic creation in its economic and social contexts*, by Joseph Duggan
The Medieval Greek Romance, by Roderick Beaton
Reformist Apocalypticism and Piers Plowman, by Kathryn Kerby-Fulton
Dante and the Medieval Other World, by Alison Morgan
The Theatre of Medieval Europe: New research in early drama, edited by Eckehard Simon
The Book of Memory: A study of memory in medieval culture, by Mary J. Carruthers
Rhetoric, Hermeneutics and Translation in the Middle Ages: Academic traditions and vernacular texts, by Rita Copeland
The Arthurian Romances of Chrétien de Troyes: Once and future fictions, by Donald Maddox
Richard Rolle and the Invention of Authority, by Nicholas Watson
Dreaming in the Middle Ages, by Steven F. Kruger
Chaucer and the Tradition of the "Roman Antique", by Barbara Nolan
The Romance of the Rose *and its Medieval Readers: Interpretation, reception, manuscript transmission*, by Sylvia Huot

The *Romance of the Rose* and its medieval readers: interpretation, reception, manuscript transmission

SYLVIA HUOT

Associate Professor of French,
Northern Illinois University

CAMBRIDGE
UNIVERSITY PRESS

Published by the Press Syndicate of the University of Cambridge
The Pitt Building, Trumpington Street, Cambridge CB2 1RP
40 West 20th Street, New York, NY 10011-4211, USA
10 Stamford Road, Oakleigh, Victoria 3166, Australia

First published 1993

Printed in Great Britain at the University Press, Cambridge

A catalogue record for this book is available from the British Library

Library of Congress cataloguing in publication data

Huot, Sylvia Jean.
The Romance of the rose and its medieval readers: interpretation, reception, manuscript
transmission / Sylvia Huot.
p.   cm. – (Cambridge studies in medieval literature: 16)
Includes bibliographical references.
ISBN 0 521 41713 9
1. Guillaume, de Lorris, fl. 1230. Roman de la Rose. 2. Jean, de Meun, d. 1305 – Criticism
and interpretation – History. 3. Guillaume, de Lorris, fl. 1230 – Parodies, imitations, etc. 4.
Literature, Medieval – History and criticism – Theory, etc. 5. Love poetry, French – History
and criticism – Theory, etc. 6. Authors and readers – France – History. 7. Books and reading
– France – History. 8. Manuscripts, Medieval – France. 9. Courtly love in literature. 10.
Transmission of texts. 1. Title. 11. Series. PQ1528.H86 1992 841'.1 – dc20 91–45887 CIP

ISBN 0 521 41713 9 (hardback)

Contents

List of illustrations	x
Acknowledgments	xii
List of manuscripts cited	xiv

Introduction 1

1 Perspectives on the *Roman de la Rose*: the text and its manuscript
transmission 16
    An erotic dream, a learned compendium: the polymorphous
    Rose 18
    Manuscript presentation of the *Rose* 27
    Reading and rewriting the *Rose*: the malleable text 34
    The personalized *Rose* of MS Bibl. Nat. fr. 25525 40

2 Intertextual readings of the *Rose*: marginal glosses and readers'
annotations 47
    The *Rose* and the *Auctores*: the MSS Bibl. Nat. fr. 1560 and
    Arsenal 3337 48
    The *Flores auctorum* and the *Roman de la Rose* 59
    Text and gloss in MS Bibl. Nat. fr. 24390 63
    The MS Dijon, Bibl. Mun. 525: an anthology built on the *Rose* 75

3 The profitable, pleasurable *Rose*: the remaniement of Gui de Mori 85
    Gui de Mori as an author of the *Rose* 89
    Rewriting the Art of Love 93
    The *Rose* and the *auctores*: Jean de Meun and Gui de Mori 106
    Sacred and erotic love in MS *Tou* 115
    Gui de Mori in the *Rose* manuscript tradition 124

4 Adapting Jean de Meun to Guillaume de Lorris: the *Rose* of the *B*
manuscripts 130
    The *B* remaniement: an overview 133
    "La maniere du chastel prendre": the *Rose* of MS *Bi* 139

Contents

Rethinking the conflict of love and reason 145

Truth, deception, and euphemism: language and meaning in
the *B* text 151

The *B* remaniement and the *Rose* manuscript tradition 157

5 Transforming the mirror of lovers: manuscripts of the second
group 163

The totalizing mirror of love: the *Rose* of the *KMN*
manuscripts 163

The expurgated mirror of love: a survey of partial
modifications 182

A mirror of princes: the *Rose* of Cambridge Univ. Libr. Add.
MS 2993 195

6 "Exposé sur le *Roman de la Rose*": rewriting the *Rose* in the
Pelerinage de vie humaine 207

Adapting the *Rose*: from erotic quest to spiritual pilgrimage 208

Transformations of Genius: Moses, Aristotle, and Guillaume de
Deguilleville 220

Rethinking the pilgrimage: Deguilleville's second recension 225

Recuperating the *Rose*: the MS Arras, Bibl. Mun. 845 231

7 Poet of love and nature: Guillaume de Machaut and the *Rose* 239

Echoes of the *Rose* in the *Fonteinne amoureuse* 242

The reconciliation of love and reason in the *Remede de Fortune* 249

Reliving the *Rose*: allegory and irony in the *Voir Dit* 256

Writer of love and nature: Machaut and Genius 267

8 Sacred and erotic love: the visual gloss of MS Bibl. Nat. fr. 25526 273

The notion of a visual gloss: analogs for MS *Mi* 274

The marginalia of MS *Mi*: an overview 285

The iconography of erotic passion in MS *Mi* 292

The iconography of divine passion in MS *Mi* 301

The literary context of MS *Mi* 313

The codicological *Rose*: the concentric structure of MS *Mi* 319

9 Conclusion: the protean *Rose* 323

Appendix A   The Remaniement of Gui de Mori 338

1. Excerpt from the God of Love's explanation of true love 338

2. Reason's description of love 339

3. Exemplary tales of justice and injustice 344

4. The discourse of Genius 349

Contents

Appendix B   The B remaniement   353
  1. The discourse of Reason in MS Bi   353
  2. Passages from Reason in MS Be   361
Appendix C   The "litany of love" in the discourse of Reason   365
Appendix D   Discourse of Genius in MS Lm (partial)   369
Appendix E   The Rose of Cambridge, University Library Add. MS 2993 371
  1. Interpolation of the mirror of Virgil in MS κυ   371
  2. Interpolation on ancient heroes in MS κυ   372

Bibliography   384
Index of manuscripts   396
General Index   398

Illustrations

PLATES

page

1 Illustration of the Heavenly Park in the discourse of Genius. New York, The Pierpont Morgan Library MS M 132, fol. 142r.   30

2 Nature on her knees before Genius. Paris, Bibliothèque Nationale MS fr. 1565, fol. 126v.   32

3 Nature displays a rabbit while Genius addresses the troops of Love. Paris, Bibliothèque Nationale MS fr. 1565, fol. 127r.   33

4 The *Rose* of Michel Alès, showing his marginal annotations. Paris, Bibliothèque Nationale MS fr. 25525, fol. 324v.   42

5 Manuscript page showing the text of the Susannah interpolation from the remaniement of Gui de Mori added in the margins, around a gloss citing the *Decretum*. Paris, Bibliothèque Nationale MS fr. 24390, fol. 40r.   64

6 The manuscript of Mathias Rivalli, showing marginal annotations in the story of Abelard and Heloise in the discourse of the Jaloux. Dijon, Bibliothèque Municipale MS 525, fol. 47r.   80

7 The *Rose* of Gui de Mori, with marginal signs identifying interpolations. Tournai, Bibliothèque de la Ville MS 101, fol. 6r.   88

8 Opening page of the *Rose*, with an image of a beaver castrating itself in the lower margin. London, British Library MS Stowe 947, fol. 1r.   276

9 Marginal doodles in Augustine's *De Genesi adversus Manicheos*. Dijon, Bibliothèque Municipale MS 139, fol. 148r.   278

10 Marginal illustration of the story of Pygmalion. Paris, Bibliothèque Nationale MS fr. 12592, fol. 62v.   281

11 Marginal doodle representing the character of Faux Samblant. Paris, Bibliothèque Nationale MS fr. 12592, fol. 32r.   283

12 Marginal representation of fox and wolf as emblematic of Faux Samblant. Paris, Bibliothèque Nationale MS fr. 25526, fol. 115r.   287

13 Miniature representing Faux Samblant, Contrainte Astenance, and La Vieille; these figures are parodied by the animals in the lower margin. Paris, Bibliothèque Nationale MS fr. 25526, fol. 94v.   288

Illustrations

14 Marginal representation of a naval battle during the storming of
the tower of Jealousy. Paris, Bibliothèque Nationale MS fr.
25526, fol. 116v.   289

15 Miniature representing the meeting of the Lover and Bel Acueil
after the discourse of La Vieille; marginal representation of
copulation. Paris, Bibliothèque Nationale MS fr. 25526, fol.
111v.   293

16 Marginal image of phallus tree during the discourse of La
Vieille. Paris, Bibliothèque Nationale MS fr. 25526, fol. 106v.   294

17 Marginal representation of combat during the discourse of La
Vieille. Paris, Bibliothèque Nationale MS fr. 25526, fol. 107r.   295

18 Marginal representation of Genius as a bishop holding a pen
instead of a crosier. Paris, Bibliothèque Nationale MS fr. 25526,
fol. 154r.   299

19 Marginal representation of the Annunciation and the Visitation
in the discourse of Reason. Paris, Bibliothèque Nationale MS fr.
25526, fol. 43v.   304

20 Marginal representation of Saint Margaret in prison, as the
Lover approaches the Rose. Paris, Bibliothèque Nationale MS fr.
25526, fol. 161v.   308

21 Marginal representation of illuminators. Paris, Bibliothèque
Nationale MS fr. 25526, fol. 77v.   322

FIGURES

1 Interpolations in MSS of the B group.   *page* 147

2 Layout of bifolium with marginalia showing the lascivious
sporting of a nun and a monk, and a phallus tree.   293

3 Layout of bifolium showing scenes from the Nativity.   296

4 Layout of bifolium containing hunting scenes and a phallus tree.   297

5 Layout of bifolium depicting ecclesiastical and royal forces in an
allegorical representation of the alliance of Love and Genius.   299

6 Layout of bifolium showing Saint Nicholas and Saint Christopher.   303

7 Layout of gathering juxtaposing scenes from the Passion of Christ
and the Passion of Saint Margaret.   305

8 Layout of two bifolia showing scenes from the Nativity, Saint
Margaret as shepherdess, and Venus' bagpipe dance.   307

9 Layout of two bifolia showing scenes from the life of Christ in
the discourse of Faux Samblant.   310

Acknowledgments

Research for this book was conducted at numerous libraries, and would not have been possible without the cooperation of librarians and other staff members at the Bibliothèque Nationale, the Bibliothèque de l'Arsenal, and the Bibliothèque Mazarine, Paris; the Bibliothèque Municipale, Arras; the Bibliothèque Municipale, Dijon; the Bibliothèque de la Faculté de Médecine, Montpellier; the Bibliothèque Universitaire, Rennes; the Bibliothèque Royale, Brussels; the Bibliothèque de la Ville, Tournai; the Royal Library, Copenhagen; the British Library, London; the Bodleian Library, Oxford; the Newberry Library, Chicago; the Pierpont Morgan Library, New York; Firestone Library, Princeton University; and Founders Memorial Library, Northern Illinois University, DeKalb. In addition, the following libraries gave permission for material from their collections to be reproduced in this volume: the Bibliothèque Nationale, Paris; the Bibliothèque Municipale, Dijon; the Bibliothèque de la Ville, Tournai; the British Library, London; and the Pierpont Morgan Library, New York. I would also like to thank the Institut de Recherche et d'Histoire des Textes in Paris, a branch of the Centre National de Recherche Scientifique, for the use of their research facilities; and the Center for Research in the Humanities at the University of Copenhagen for their assistance in facilitating my visit to the Danish Royal Library.

I have been fortunate in the course of this study to benefit from the insight and expertise of numerous friends and colleagues. Among these I wish especially to thank Kevin Brownlee, John Dagenais, David Hult, Mary Speer, Dieuwke van der Poel, Lori Walters, and Winthrop Wetherbee. The members of my graduate seminar on the *Roman de la Rose* at the Newberry Library – Karen Grossweiner, William Heise, Paula Moehle, Marilyn Reppa, and Barbara Swann – contributed to a series of stimulating discussions that enabled me to rethink my way through the poem as I completed the final draft of this study. Leo Krumpholz has been a constant source of moral support, and has provided me with new perspectives on the phenomenon of literary and artistic *mouvance*.

Chapters 3, 4, and 9 contain material that appeared in my essay,

Acknowledgments

"Authors, Scribes, Remanieurs: A Note on the Textual History of the *Roman de la Rose*," in *Rethinking the "Romance of the Rose": Text, Image, Reception*, ed. Kevin Brownlee and Sylvia Huot (Philadelphia: University of Pennsylvania Press, forthcoming). I am grateful to the University of Pennsylvania Press for permission to reprint this material in revised form. Part of Chapter 7 appeared as "Reliving the *Roman de la Rose:* Allegory and Irony in Machaut's *Voir Dit*," *Chaucer's French Contemporaries: The Poetry/Poetics of Self and Tradition*, ed. R. Barton Palmer, Georgia State Literary Studies, 10 (New York: AMS Press, forthcoming). I am grateful to the AMS Press for permission to reprint this material.

This project was funded by a fellowship from the John Simon Guggenheim Memorial Foundation; by summer research stipends from the Graduate School, Northern Illinois University; and by a grant from the Deans Fund for Humanities Research, Northern Illinois University. I am most grateful for this generous support, without which the book could never have been written. Publication was made possible by grants from the Guggenheim Foundation and Northern Illinois University, which I gratefully acknowledge.

Manuscripts cited

Roman de la Rose manuscripts

1 *Manuscripts with sigla*
On the sigla, see Introduction, p. 5.

Ac. φε/*Ac.* Chantilly, Musée Condé 686
Arr. [My siglum.] Arras, Bibl. Mun. 845
Ba. Ba | *Ba.* Paris, Bibl. Nat. fr. 1571
Bâ. Bâ | *Bâ.* Paris, Bibl. Nat. fr. 1576
Be. Be | *Be.* Turin, University Library L. III. 22
Bê. Ra | *Bê.* Arras, Bibl. Mun. 897
Bi. Gi | *Bi.* Paris, Bibl. Nat. fr. 25524
Bï. – | *Bï.* Fragment; identified by Langlois as belonging to Hermann
Suchier (*Manuscrits*, pp. 166–67)
Bî. Gu | *Bî.* Paris, Bibl. Nat. fr. 24389
Bo. Ge | *Bo.* Paris, Bibl. Nat. fr. 2195
Bó. Gé | *Bó.* Paris, Bibl. de l'Arsenal 2988
Bô. Gê | *Bô.* Paris, Bibl. Nat. fr. 19154
Bu. Go | *Bu.* Brussels, Bibl. Roy. 11019
Bû. Mon | *Bû.* Montpellier, Faculté de Médecine H 438
*Bü. [My siglum] Private collection. See *Astor Collection of Illuminated Manuscripts*, no. 51.
By. φα | *By.* Chantilly, Musée Condé 911
*Bco. [My siglum] Copenhagen, Royal Library NGS 63, 2° [formerly
Fr. LVI]
Ca. Ca | *Ca.* Dijon, Bibl. Mun. 526
Dij. Dij | *Dij.* Dijon, Bibl. Mun. 525
Eb. γo | *Eb.* Paris, Bibl. Nat. Rothschild 2800
Fa. Fa | *Fa* Paris, Bibl. Nat. fr. 799
Fe. Fe | *Fe.* Paris, Bibl. Nat. fr. 19157
He. He | *He.* Copenhagen, Royal Library GKS 2061, 4° [formerly Fr.
LV]
Jo. Jo | *Jo.* Paris, Bibl. Nat. fr. 1569

Ke. Ke | Ke. Paris, Bibl. Nat. fr. 24390
Ki. Ki | Ki. Paris, Bibl. Mazarine 3873
Lb. Lb | Lb. Paris, Bibl. Nat. fr. 1561
Lg. Lg | Lg. Paris, Bibl. Nat. fr. 1564
Lk. Lk | Lk. Paris, Bibl. Nat. fr. 1567
Lm. Lm | Lm. Rennes, Bibl. Mun. 15963 [formerly 243]
Lm³. Lm³ | Lm³. London, British Libr. Stowe 947
Lq. Fi | Lq. Paris, Bibl. Nat. fr. 9345
Lw. Je | Lw. Paris, Bibl. Nat. fr. 1574
Lx. Zo | Lx. Paris, Bibl. Nat. fr. 1566
Lz. λα | Lz. Paris, Bibl. Nat. fr. 12587
Maz. Maz | Maz. Paris, Bibl. Mazarine 3874
Me. Me | Me. Paris, Bibl. Nat. fr. 1560
Mi. Mi | Mi. Paris, Bibl. Nat. fr. 25526
Mo. Mo | Mo. Lyon, Bibl. Mun. 764
Mor. [My siglum] Paris, Bibl. Nat. fr. 797
My. μα | My. Paris, Bibl. Nat. fr. 802
Nd. Nd | Nd. Paris, Bibl. Nat. fr. 1565
*Npr. [My siglum] Princeton University, Firestone Library, Garrett 126
Ter. Ter | Ter. Lost; most recent known location was Maihingen, Öttingen-Wallerstein Library
Tou. Tou | Tou. Tournai, Bibl. Mun. 101
ζα. ζα | ζα. Paris, Bibl. Nat. fr. 803
ςα. ςα | ςα. Paris, Bibl. Nat. fr. 12594
θα. θα | θα. Paris, Bibl. Nat. fr. 378
κυ. κυ | κυ. Cambridge University Library, Add. MS 2993
κω. κω | κω. London, British Libr. Egerton 881

2 *Manuscripts without sigla*

New York, Pierpont Morgan Library M 132
Paris, Bibl. de l'Arsenal 3337
Paris, Bibl. Nat. fr. 380
Paris, Bibl. Nat. fr. 1563
Paris, Bibl. Nat. fr. 12592
Paris, Bibl. Nat. fr. 12595
Paris, Bibl. Nat. fr. 24392
Paris, Bibl. Nat. fr. 25525

Other manuscripts

Cambridge, Magdalene College, Pepys Library 1594. *Remede de Fortune*; treatise opening "Hughe de Saint Victor dit . . ."

Dijon, Bibl. Mun. 139. Works by Saint Augustine

Paris, Bibl. Nat. fr. 246. *Histoire ancienne jusqu'à César.*

Paris, Bibl. Nat. fr. 829. *Pelerinage de vie humaine* (second recension).

Paris, Bibl. Nat. fr. 1317. Treatise on dreams; treatise on the human body.

Paris, Bibl. Nat. fr. 1946. Old French translation of the *Consolation of Philosophy.*

Paris, Bibl. Nat. fr. 9197. Commentary by Evrart de Conty on the *Echecs amoureux.*

Paris, Bibl. Nat. fr. 24432. Miscellany.

Paris, Bibl. Nat. n. a. fr. 20001. Miscellaneous leaves, including some from MS *Dij.*

Paris, Bibl. Nat. lat. 1860. *Florilegium.*

Paris, Bibl. Nat. lat. 3893. Gratian's *Decretum*, with the gloss by Bartholomew of Brescia.

Paris, Bibl. Nat. lat. 8758. *De amore* of Andreas Capellanus.

Paris, Bibl. Nat. lat. 15155. *Florilegium Gallicum.*

Paris, Bibl. Nat. lat. 16708. *Florilegium* of Latin authors.

Introduction

This project falls into two major areas of study. One is that of textual criticism; the other is the study of the *Roman de la Rose* and its medieval reception. Both topics have provided the arena for considerable scholarly debate.

Textual criticism encompasses a variety of approaches that tend to be grouped as either "Lachmannian" or "Bédierist": that is, as to whether the editor seeks primarily to reconstruct, or at least to approach, the original authorial text from the various surviving manuscripts or to present, with as little intervention as possible, the text of the manuscript judged as best. In some cases editors have preferred to present a series of versions in parallel or sequential format, rather than to settle on just one version.[1] Given the very different sorts of manuscript traditions that obtain for different texts and the varying critical notions of textuality and authorship, it is unlikely that any one editorial method will ever emerge as dominant to the exclusion of the others; indeed it can be very useful for the same text to be edited according to different methods.

While textual criticism has never ceased to flourish, recent years have witnessed a significant renewal of interest in both the theory and the practice of text editing, including a re-examination of the debate between the Bédierists and the Lachmannians.[2] This renewed debate is fueled in part by the modern interest in the textual object and in the primacy of the reader. The situation of the medieval text oddly concretizes certain tenets of twentieth-century critical theory. The medieval scribe is the very embodiment of the modern notion of the reader who, in reading, constructs the text anew. The medieval author, frequently anonymous, at best a shadowy

---

[1] For a succinct discussion of different editorial methods, with examples of each, see Speer, "Textual Criticism Redivivus"; Foulet and Speer, *On Editing Old French Texts*, pp. 1—39.

[2] This interest in textual criticism is reflected, for example, in *L'Esprit Créateur* 27, 1 (1987), edited by Uitti and titled *The Poetics of Textual Criticism: The Old French Example*; and in the appearance of studies devoted to a critical examination of editorial practices, such as the essays assembled by Kleinhenz, ed., in *Medieval Manuscripts and Textual Criticism*; B. Cerquiglini's *Eloge de la variante*; Speer's "Textual Criticism Redivivus" and "Wrestling with Change"; Foulet and Speer's *On Editing Old French Texts*; and Hult's "Reading it Right."

figure whose words have been obscured by generations of copyists, may well seem little more than a hypothesis or a linguistic function. Indeed, such a claim has in effect been made with regard to the *Rose*: Roger Dragonetti has suggested that Guillaume de Lorris is only a fiction devised by Jean de Meun.[3] Yet the work of those scholars who have combined textual criticism and codicology with literary criticism shows that while the notion of authorship in a manuscript culture is significantly different from that which exists in a print culture, there is no need to reject the very concept. David Hult, for example, while stressing that we can know nothing of Guillaume de Lorris' life, has shown the integrity of Guillaume's *Rose* and presented the codicological evidence, admittedly slender, that argues for the independent existence of that poem.[4] Daniel Poirion has shown that certain textual variants in Guillaume's *Rose* point to a reworking of the text – whose prior existence is thus implicitly established – by readers familiar with Jean's continuation, or even by Jean himself.[5] The combined disciplines of textual literary criticism allow us to see that the two parts of the *Rose* do emanate from different authorial origins. And in the course of their history, the poems of Guillaume and Jean passed through the hands of numerous scribes and poets who produced the proliferating versions we know today.

As a result of this tireless activity on the part of medieval readers and writers, the *Rose*, like most medieval works, exists in a variety of texts; the object of study must be defined according to one's critical priorities. Do we wish to study a historical process of creation, continuation, adaptation; or to reconstruct two distinct moments of original poetic creation, to be preserved as such? Are we interested in a text as a reflection of its author or of the circumstances of its composition; or are we more concerned with its subsequent reception by medieval readers and its impact on later authors, who may never have known the text in its original version? There is, of course, no reason to view these possibilities as mutually exclusive. The field of medieval literary studies must include a full range of perspectives and the various approaches that each entails.

It has become commonplace to point out that in the medieval vernacular tradition texts were not fixed, and that their creation and recreation depended on the combined work of poets, scribes, and performers, whose activities often overlap. It has been some twenty years since Elspeth Kennedy called attention to "the scribe as editor," in a phrase that has since

[3] Dragonetti, *Mirage des sources*, pp. 200–25.
[4] Hult, *Self-fulfilling Prophecies*, especially pp. 10–55.   [5] Poirion, "From Rhyme to Reason."

become part of the critical vocabulary of medieval literary studies.[6] David Hult has shown the fine line dividing scribes, remanieurs, and authors.[7] Jean Rychner proposed that a scribe who reworked a fabliau might be considered as the author of the new version.[8] Many studies have examined the important role played by scribes in transforming a text or group of texts into a book, a role that authors assumed only gradually and never more than partially.[9] The study of Old French literature can never be divorced from the question of transmission. Whether we wish to focus on the work of the original author or that of subsequent scribal editors and remanieurs, it is necessary to examine the history of the text and to distinguish, as far as possible, the stages by which the various surviving versions were created. The remanieur's innovations cannot be evaluated if we have no knowledge of the earlier version on which he or she worked; a medieval author's use of prior texts cannot be gauged if we do not know which versions of those texts were in circulation during that author's lifetime.

Literary critics have devised various approaches to the phenomenon of textual variance, recognizing that they, no less than editors, must confront the variant, the interpolation, the remaniement; must learn – or at least attempt – to distinguish between scribal intervention and scribal error. Daniel Poirion has termed the writing of the Middle Ages "manuscriture," in an effort to differentiate it from the very different written traditions of print culture.[10] Poirion points out the necessity of studying the variants, both large and small, that characterize the different versions of a medieval text; these variants have their own history and their own meaning. More recently, Bernard Cerquiglini has stated somewhat flamboyantly that "l'écriture médiévale . . . est variance."[11] This formulation, of course, is really a restatement of Zumthor's by now standard notion of *mouvance*.[12]

---

[6] Kennedy, "Scribe as Editor." See also Huot, "Scribe as Editor: Rubrication as Critical Apparatus in Two *Roman de la Rose* Manuscripts"; Shonk, "Scribe as Editor: The Primary Scribe of the Auchinleck Manuscript"; Rosenstein, "*Mouvance* and the Editor as Scribe."

[7] Hult, *Self-fulfilling Prophecies*, pp. 25–93.

[8] Rychner states: "Le copiste responsable de ces variantes a fait le texte sien, se l'est approprié dans une certaine mesure, et il n'est sans doute pas absolument exacte d'appeler 'copiste' l'auteur de ce qui ressemble si peu à une copie," in *Contribution à l'étude des fabliaux*, vol. 1, p. 45.

[9] For an examination of the role of the scribe in a particular manuscript tradition, including a consideration of the affinities between the work of scribes and that of poets, see Walters, "Rôle du scribe." On the role of the late medieval poet in manuscript production, see Williams, "An Author's Role in Fourteenth-Century Book Production"; and Wimsatt and Kibler, "Machaut's Text and the Question of His Personal Supervision." I have traced the roles of scribes and poets respectively, and the thematization of writing and compilation, in a series of thirteenth- and fourteenth-century texts, in *From Song to Book*. [10] Poirion, "Écriture et ré-écriture au moyen âge."

[11] B. Cerquiglini, *Eloge de la variante*, p. 111.

[12] On *mouvance*, see Zumthor, *Essai de poétique médiévale*, pp. 65–75; Speer, "Wrestling with Change." Zumthor was not the first to acknowledge this aspect of medieval literature, but his term has become standard.

While *mouvance* may be most pronounced and its pace most accelerated in the more fundamentally oral genres of lyric and *chanson de geste*, the phenomenon certainly exists in written traditions as well.

Admitting non-authorial versions to the canon of medieval studies entails a liberal definition of the object of literary study. A text should not be excluded just because its author chose to embed it in another text originally written by someone else (the interpolation); or just because it is the work of more than one author in succession (the abridgment or remaniement). The question is admittedly complicated with the *Rose*. Not only do we have to distinguish between the *Rose* as written by Guillaume, and Guillaume's *Rose* in some possibly altered form as read or revised by Jean and used as the basis for his poem; but also we must account for the various revisions and corruptions to which the conjoined *Rose* was subject, including the life of certain interpolations that originated in one version of the poem and were later inserted into other versions as well. What would be seen as a corrupt text with regard to Guillaume must be seen as an original authorial text with regard to Jean; what would be seen as corrupt with regard to both Guillaume and Jean is an authorial original with regard to a later remanieur or interpolator; and so on. If we are willing to tolerate two authors, then why not three or more? As we will see, the notion of the *Rose* as a poem with two (and only two) authors was already well established in the fourteenth century: the names of Jean de Meun and Guillaume de Lorris were known to all, while those of interpolators, abridgers, and remanieurs were almost never recorded. But anonymity is hardly grounds of exclusion of a text from literary study.

In examining the different versions of the *Rose*, I have thus accepted the idea that each version has its own integrity as a literary text, and that the figures who produced these texts must be included among the poets of the *Rose*. In distinguishing between deliberate and inadvertent alterations, I have given the scribe the benefit of the doubt wherever possible. If the line is metrically and grammatically correct, if the rhyme is acceptable, and if it makes common sense, I accept it as authentic to that version of the poem. In relatively few cases, where the text is clearly corrupt, I acknowledge scribal error. Admittedly grammatical and metrical correctness are not necessarily an index of intentionality. But for the purposes of this study, in order that each version be examined as far as possible on its own terms, I have chosen to err on the side of acceptance rather than rejection of the reading found in the manuscript.

The *Rose* exists in three modern editions.[13] Those of Poirion and Lecoy,

---

[13] The editions are those of Langlois, Lecoy, and Poirion.

"best manuscript" editions, have the advantage of allowing the reader access to a particular version in its integrity; and due to the difference in base manuscripts, these two editions allow for some interesting comparisons. For more complete information about the textual history of the poem one must turn to the earlier edition by Langlois, which aims to reconstruct the original text of the poem's two primary authors while providing extensive critical apparatus. But even Langlois does not list all variants. His concern with establishing the original text, quite understandable at a time when there was no critical edition, led Langlois to discount manuscripts with a strongly altered text.

Langlois reported more fully on his study of the manuscript tradition in *Les Manuscrits du "Roman de la Rose": Description et classement*.[14] He shows that the two portions of the poem must be treated independently, since Guillaume's romance circulated prior to Jean's work and had already developed variant readings. Not only were different versions of Jean's continuation attached haphazardly to different versions of Guillaume's poem during the early years of the manuscript tradition; but also, since scribes often used more than one manuscript in copying the *Rose*, the two parts of the poem would not necessarily come from the same source even in late manuscripts. As a result Langlois assigned a double siglum to each manuscript. I have found it more convenient, however, to refer to manuscripts solely by the sigla for Jean de Meun. Most of my discussion is devoted to Jean's *Rose*, which was subject to far more revision and rewriting than that of Guillaume. In the manuscript list, all manuscripts cited are listed under the siglum pertaining to Jean, after which I give the complete double siglum devised by Langlois. An asterisk preceding a siglum indicates that the manuscript was not classified by Langlois, and that I have assigned it to one of his families.

With regard to Guillaume's poem, *Rose* manuscripts must be divided into two groups; with regard to Jean de Meun, the manuscripts again fall into two groups, but these do not correspond to the groups created by Guillaume's text.[15] In both parts of the poem, each group contains several families. In some cases the family resemblance among manuscripts is quite

---

[14] For descriptions of fourteenth-century manuscripts not included in Langlois's catalog, see *Astor Collection of Illuminated Manuscripts*, no. 51; Dean, "Un Manuscrit"; Fawtier, "Deux manuscrits"; Ham, "Cheltenham Manuscripts"; Hawkins, "Manuscripts of the 'Roman de la Rose'"; Pickford, "'Roman de la Rose' and a Treatise"; Walters, "Parisian Manuscript."

[15] For Guillaume, the groups are distinguished according to whether or not they include Fear as a fourth guardian of the Rose in vv. 2835–67 of Langlois's edition (ed. Lecoy, vv. 2819–51); see *Manuscrits*, pp. 241–43. For Jean, the groups are distinguished by the presence or absence of a couplet occurring between Langlois's vv. 8178–79 (ed. Lecoy, vv. 8148–49); see *Manuscrits*, pp. 351–52. Group I versions of Guillaume are not necessarily paired with Group I versions of Jean; likewise for Group II. For Guillaume's poem there is also a small third group of manuscripts with a mixed text.

clear cut. The *B* family, which I will discuss in Chapter 4, is an early remaniement of Jean's portion of the poem that survives in a large number of manuscripts, many of which present a fairly uniform version of Guillaume's portion as well. Langlois identified twelve *B* manuscripts and one fragment, making this the largest family in Jean's Group 1; and he provided a detailed analysis of the subgroups, representing different recensions, that exist within it. I have no argument with his conclusions concerning the relations among the *B* manuscripts. Langlois, however, did not attempt to analyze the *B* remaniement or its various manifestations as an interpretation of the *Rose*, or to determine the social and intellectual contexts that might have informed the redaction of the various manuscript versions. It is to these questions that my own study is addressed.

It is among the manuscripts of Group II for Jean's *Rose* that the greatest variety is found. The largest family by far is *L*, which accounts for thirty-one of the 116 manuscripts classified by Langlois and can be thought of as the vulgate text of Jean's *Rose*. Closely related to *L* are the *K*, *M*, and *N* manuscripts – with six, six, and fourteen representatives respectively among those classified by Langlois – which share interpolations and variants in common with *L* and with one another in different combinations. The other families in the second group have elements in common with one or more of those four families, sometimes with material from *B* as well, and sometimes also with deletions, interpolations, or other variants of their own. Some of Langlois's families thus derive from a recognizable common ancestor, a particular revision of the *Rose*; while others are mixed, clearly deriving ultimately from a combination of more than one source. The high rate of "contamination" often makes classification extremely difficult, resulting in "families" of only one or two manuscripts that are in fact composites of as many as three or four other families.

When a text had been strongly altered, Langlois generally assigned it a siglum based on the version that lay behind the alterations. MS *Tou*, the remaniement by Gui de Mori – the only remanieur whose name is known – was assigned its own siglum, probably because the changes are so extensive, as we will see in Chapter 3, and because the text has a named author. But although MS *He* is in large part Gui's work, Langlois did not place it in a family with MS *Tou*; in his eyes it was an altered version of the *H* text rather than an altered version of Gui's remaniement. In the same manner he assigned the heavily abridged MS *Lm* to the *L* family, focusing not on the unique elements of the text but on those that it shares with the other *L* manuscripts; and he perceived MS *κν*, which contains hundreds of lines of interpolations, as an altered version of the *κ* text rather than as a new version requiring its own siglum. He reports only partially on the textual abridgments of MSS *He* and *Lm*, and says virtually nothing at all about the interpolations of MS *κv* or the extensive changes wrought in MS *Tou*. Such omissions can be explained in part by the sheer quantity of data; as it is, Langlois's account of manuscript families and variant readings fills nearly three hundred pages, not counting the individual manuscript descriptions. But Langlois's selectivity is also determined by his bias towards the original text. Interpolations and deletions are later alterations that can be ignored if it is possible to identify the text used by the abridger or interpolator. Again, one certainly cannot deny the utility of knowing what version of the text inspired a given set of revisions, or of grasping, as far as possible, the network of inter-manuscript relations. But to discount the importance and the interest of scribal revisions and remaniements is to overlook a crucial aspect of medieval literary tradition, one from which we have much to learn.

Such criticisms are not meant to obscure in any way the immense debt we owe to Langlois for providing us with the first critical edition and manuscript study of this important text. If he was unable completely to control the bewildering forest of variants produced by a poem of nearly 22,000 lines, with a manuscript tradition stretching from the thirteenth to the sixteenth centuries and resulting in the survival of well over 200 manuscript and printed copies, manifesting significant differences ranging from single words to thousands of lines – let this not be viewed as a fault of his, but rather as an indication of the enormity of the task. In 1925, the Swedish scholar Werner Söderhjelm published a description of a fifteenth-century *Rose* manuscript in the Royal Library of Stockholm; having noted certain affinities of the manuscript with Langlois's *L* and *N* families, Söderhjelm explained his decision not to attempt a definitive classification of the manuscript: "Je renoncerai donc à pénétrer plus avant dans les broussailles de la filiation des manuscrits du *Roman de la Rose*, presque inaccessibles au commun des mortels malgré les voies frayées par les admirables efforts d'Ernest Langlois."[16] Anyone who has worked with the body of *Rose* manuscripts is sure to second Söderhjelm's opinion. The definitive, comprehensive study of the *Rose* manuscript tradition will be possible only through the combined work of many scholars; and it will certainly rest on the foundation established by Langlois.

The project that I have undertaken here thus builds on and continues Langlois's work. The questions posed by scholars of medieval literature have inevitably changed somewhat in the course of the twentieth century; and the very fact of having a critical edition invites us to go on to further

---

[16] Söderhjelm, "Un manuscrit du *Roman de la Rose*," p. 86.

7

studies of the manuscripts, aimed at different goals. I propose here to return to the manuscripts and to study individual versions of the *Rose*. My study is not exhaustive; it examines a few specific rewritings of the *Rose* in some depth. Rather than seeking the "origins and sources" of the *Rose*, as did Langlois, I am concerned with its afterlife, with its history as a text.

Three fundamental purposes inform this study. One, to have a better basis on which to study the reception of the *Rose* by medieval poets. Just what did a medieval reader find when he or she opened a copy of the *Rose*? We cannot assume that Machaut, or Chaucer, or Christine de Pizan, necessarily read the text that we find in the modern editions. Passages that we consider interpolations or corruptions may have been accepted by them as canonical, or at least known as interesting variations. I will suggest, in fact, that Machaut knew certain passages that are not now considered authentic, and that Deguilleville knew the *Rose* in one or another recension of the *B* text.

Second, to gauge the medieval reading of the poem written by Guillaume and Jean. How was it understood? What aspects of it were considered important, or shocking, or difficult, or superfluous? What kind of text did people think it was, or want it to be? In exploring these questions manuscripts are an invaluable resource, including – or even especially – those that preserve an altered version of the text. Kate Harris has shown the usefulness of what she terms "bad texts" for studying medieval approaches to the works of Gower.[17] Her insight is equally applicable to the *Rose* and, indeed, to any medieval text that survives in multiple manuscripts. Robert Ivy's study of the manuscripts of Manessier's continuation of *Perceval* is aimed at establishing the text, distinguishing interpolations or other modifications from the original.[18] Yet along the way he offers tantalizing insights into the character of the various redactions: remanieurs combined the text with material from other sources, scribes edited the different continuations in order to create a coherent whole, and so on. Studying the ways that different scribes or poets expanded or reshaped the texts and the aesthetic or ideological principles that guided them would shed light both on medieval poetics, and on the *Perceval* and its meaning for medieval readers.

This last point leads to the most general purpose underlying my study, which is to explore the ways that manuscript studies can enrich the field of literary criticism. Non-authorial versions of a text are interesting in their own right as medieval poems. Some are perhaps more interesting than

[17] Harris, "John Gower's *Confessio Amantis*: The Virtues of Bad Texts."
[18] Ivy, *Manuscript Relations of Manessier's Continuation of the Old French "Perceval"*.

others, but all deserve study. Medievalists are quite accustomed to texts that are anonymous, and to those that exist in only one or two manuscripts. We also accept texts that are adaptations of previously existing texts, whether Latin or vernacular, written or oral: for example, the *Roman d'Eneas*, Marie de France's *Fables* and *Lais*, and the various prose and verse versions of the Tristan material. In her study of a reworked version of the *Eneas*, Annie Triaud argues that remaniement was a way of expressing one's admiration for a great poem: to rework a text was to renew its vitality.[19] The activities of scribal editors and remanieurs are an essential part of medieval literature. In a fascinating study of the two redactions of the *Roman des sept sages*, Mary Speer has shown that each version has its own stylistic integrity, and each can be related to a different social milieu.[20] Jean Rychner's important study of the fabliaux similarly shows that individual versions can be characterized by both style and ethos; careful analysis of multiple versions contributes to our knowledge not only of the fabliau as a constantly evolving literary form, but also of the literary tastes of different medieval social classes.[21]

The work of Speer, Rychner, Ivy, and others shows that the *Rose* is far from unique in having inspired successive revisions. Nonetheless, the *Rose* was a particularly important text, both inside and outside of France. Its importance lies not only in its pervasive influence on subsequent medieval literature, but also in its encyclopedic scope. To study the reception of the *Rose* is not only to trace the transformation of literary motifs, but also to encounter the range of medieval ideas about love and marriage, gender and sexuality, about sin and free will, about language and power, about human society, nature, and the cosmos. And because the *Rose* manuscript tradition is so vast, it yields a rich variety of material: interpolations and abridgments, reworkings of the text on both a large and a small scale, extensive programs of rubrication and illumination, a significant body of marginal annotations.

Any study of *Rose* reception necessarily participates in the tradition of scholarly debate over the meaning of the *Rose* and its meaning for medieval readers, two distinct matters that have not always been adequately separated. Naturally, showing that a given medieval reader considered

---

[19] Triaud, "Une version tardive de l'*Eneas*."

[20] Speer, "Editing the Formulaic Romance Style." In "Wrestling with Change," Speer briefly discusses the three redactions of Branch 1b of the *Roman de Renart* (pp. 323–25), arguing that the *A* redaction is "qualitatively better . . . [and] more authentic, closer to the author's intention," and hence the version to be used in any study of the text "for itself" (p. 325). Nonetheless she acknowledges that the other redactions can be useful "to find out how these scribal revisers treated their models and went about compiling Renart's adventures for a new public" (ibid.).

[21] Rychner, *Contribution à l'étude des fabliaux*, vol. 1.

Reason a figure of divine Sapience does not prove that Jean de Meun considered her to be that, any more than finding another medieval reader who treated her as simply the enemy of erotic passion proves that to have been Jean's idea. Medieval reactions to the *Rose* are far too varied to be used as a guide to the authors' intentions. The study of medieval readings of the *Rose* does necessitate a close examination of the text, however, and the evaluation of a medieval reader's response entails decisions about what aspects of the poem triggered such a response. The study of *Rose* reception additionally teaches us about the medieval interpretation of vernacular literature, and about the central role played by the *Rose* in the development of French literature as a learned and versatile art form.

Pierre-Yves Badel has already laid the groundwork for the study of *Rose* reception in fourteenth-century France.[22] His *"Roman de la Rose" au XIVe siècle* is essential reading not only for *Rose* scholars but also, given the importance of the *Rose* both in and outside of France, for anyone working in the field of fourteenth-century literature. As Badel shows, the *Rose* was read in all literate circles of society. Identifiable owners of *Rose* manuscripts in the fourteenth century include members of the royalty, the aristocracy, the clergy, and the bourgeoisie. Copies of the poem appeared in the libraries of religious institutions and of the Sorbonne. Given this extremely diverse readership and the encyclopedic quality of the poem, it is no surprise that the influence of the *Rose* can be discerned in the most varied literary works.

However, although Badel's study is a model of thoroughness with regard to the presence of the *Rose* in literary texts and other documents of the fourteenth and very early fifteenth centuries, he does not attempt to evaluate the *Rose* manuscript tradition. This omission is certainly understandable given the wealth of material. Badel's work is concerned with borrowings from the *Rose* and with citations or evaluations of the great poem in the works of other writers, not with the textual tradition of the *Rose* itself. His interest in establishing the social and intellectual context in which the *Rose* was read led him to survey manuscript owners as well as the nature of texts paired with the *Rose* in anthology codices, and he does cite rubrics and colophons from time to time. But he does not offer analyses of individual manuscripts. As a result his study contains no account of

---

[22] Badel, *Le "Roman de la Rose" au XIVe siècle.* Badel's study goes through the *querelle* and its immediate aftermath, and includes a list of citations of the *Rose* in texts of the fifteenth, sixteenth, and seventeenth centuries. The influence of the *Rose* also extended outside of France to the Low Countries, England, Italy, and Byzantium; see Van der Poel, *De Vlaamse 'Rose'*; Sutherland, ed., *Romaunt of the Rose*; Richards, *Dante and the "Roman de la Rose"*; Vanossi, *Dante e il "Roman de la Rose"*; Kahane and Kahane, "Hidden Narcissus."

readers' annotations, or of programs of illustration or rubrication taken as a whole, nor does he devote more than a couple of pages to the phenomenon of remaniement; such was not his purpose. My study thus complements that of Badel. The detailed study of individual codices produces a different sort of evidence that the *Rose* was read in diverse milieux and adapted to the tastes and intellectual sophistication of different publics.

My findings also corroborate Badel's assertion that the widespread admiration of the *Rose* contributed instrumentally to the nascent concept of a French literature that could be seen as being on a par with Latin literature.[23] Readers' annotations as well as interpolations show that the *Rose* was read in a learned context, that it was compared to Latin texts, that it was deemed an appropriate framework for introducing adaptations of Latin material. We can also see that different copies of the *Rose* were frequently compared and that scribes actually made something akin to a critical edition, combining from more than one source.

Badel asserted that the *Rose* remained relatively stable, suggesting that this was due to the great esteem in which it was held.[24] While Badel is correct up to a certain point, it would be inaccurate to assume that the *Rose* was never subject to *mouvance* or remaniement. It is true that alterations were not common after the first few decades of *Rose* reception, when the text began to assume its place of importance as a master work; and there are hardly any examples of significant restructuring. The *Rose* does not show the kind of extreme variation, resulting in what would have to be called entirely different texts, that one finds in the *chanson de geste* tradition, for example, or the various romances of Tristan. Nonetheless both restructuring and abridgment did take place. And interpolations abound; indeed, the evidence suggests that scribes often compared manuscripts in order to arrive at the most complete text possible.

The *Rose* was considered learned and edifying by many medieval readers, and was probably used in part for educational purposes. There is considerable evidence that it either was seen as providing an ethical message, or else was reworked until it could be seen that way. In this respect my study bears out certain claims made by John Fleming in his studies of *Rose* reception.[25] But I depart from Fleming in seeing a considerable diversity in medieval readings of the *Rose* and in the interpretation of its moral agenda. As Fleming argues, it would be wrong

---

[23] Badel, *Le "Roman de la Rose" au XIVe siècle*, ibid., pp. 93–94, 502–5.

[24] Ibid., p. 144. Badel is correct in asserting that no remaniement circulated widely. Even the *B* remaniement, certainly the most successful in that respect, survives today almost exclusively in manuscripts to which most of the passages once deleted have been restored.

[25] Fleming, *"Roman de la Rose"*; *"Moral Reputation of the Roman de la Rose."*

to assert that the *Rose* was generally perceived as irreverent or heretical, for it was read and appreciated by such monastic writers as Gui de Mori, Gilles li Muisis, and Guillaume de Deguilleville. Nonetheless there was considerable variation in the interpretation of its message and in the level of tolerance for humorous, bawdy, and digressive material. For some readers the morality was more important than for others, who read the poem more as entertaining social satire or Ovidian love psychology: ultimately exposing human follies, to be sure, but more interesting for its exposition of those follies than for its presentation of a corrective program to overcome them. One even finds abridgments in which philosophical or moralistic passages are deleted.

On the other hand, one also finds the deletion of passages that contained obscene language or were explicitly erotic or of questionable orthodoxy. The expansion of Reason's humorous comments about obscenity in several manuscript families shows that many medieval readers were quite prepared to accept her remarks, although one cannot tell whether or not they interpreted them, as Fleming does, as orthodox Augustinianism;[26] but the deletion of this passage in other redactions shows that not all medieval readers were prepared to accept it. This passage was deleted in two early versions of the poem, the remaniement of Gui de Mori and the *B* remaniement; its widespread acceptance seems to have come only later, with the growing authority of the *Rose*. The addition of Biblical material to the discourse of Reason, apparent both in the remaniement of Gui de Mori and in the widespread "litany of love" interpolation, suggests in turn that some readers wished to see her, as Fleming does, as a figure for divine Sapience; but it also suggests that they felt Jean's portrait of Reason to be lacking in explicitly Christian material, and that they considered it important for her advice to the Lover to include an overtly spiritual message. Deguilleville, on the other hand, shows in the *Pelerinage de vie humaine* that Reason – explicitly identified with her counterpart in the *Rose* – is distinct from divine Sapience and that her authority is strictly sublunary and wholly dependent on Grace. It is hardly surprising that medieval readers would see Reason as an important moral authority and source of wisdom, but they did not always agree on the extent to which Jean's Reason fulfilled the requirements for such a role, or on the precise nature of the authority she should be granted or the wisdom she taught. In this respect medieval readers are no different from modern readers, who also

---

[26] Fleming argues for the Augustinianism of Reason's discussion of language and obscenity in *Reason and the Lover*, pp. 98–113.

cannot agree on Reason's status: Christian or classical, divine or sublunary.[27] Reason's character varies, sometimes substantially, in the different redactions of the *Rose*.

The *Rose*, in other words, may have been less straightforward, less clearly orthodox, to a medieval audience than Fleming allows. And medieval readers may have been more susceptible than he tends to acknowledge to the erotic suggestiveness of Jean's audacious language, and to the sheer entertainment value of an art of love. The interface of the erotic, the natural, and the divine is an important and immensely complex issue that pervades the *Rose*; a major theme of the study to follow will be the examination of this problematic and of the ways that it was interpreted, nuanced, or reformulated by the medieval poets who expanded, abridged, or rewrote the *Rose*. We will also examine the closely related question of the balance within the poem between entertainment – the love story, the sometimes bawdy humor, the parodistic treatment of figures like Nature and Genius – and moral teachings; as we shall see, some poets of the *Rose* sought to tip this balance in one direction, some in another.

Equally important if somewhat differently construed is the erudite quality of the *Rose*, particularly that of Jean de Meun, and the juxtaposition of learned and erotic discourses. As might be expected, we find that some versions of the poem have been adapted for a less learned public; in other examples, the remanieur has strengthened or otherwise adjusted the poem's relationship to Latin literary and philosophical texts. Similarly, some versions retain or even expand on erotic passages, while others delete such material. A learned reading, of course, is not necessarily one that focuses primarily on moral edification, any more than it necessarily exhibits a greater tolerance for erotic innuendos or Ovidian love psychology. Rather, the distinctions of edification versus entertainment, of serious teaching versus parody, and of erudition versus popular culture, are separate categories that may or may not overlap, and must thus be addressed separately. As we examine different versions of the *Rose*, then, we shall consider the treatment in each of love and sexuality, of the status of Reason and Nature and their relationship to eros on the one hand, divinity on the other; the importance that seems to have been placed, in a given version, on the *Rose* as a vehicle for moral or religious instruction; the way in which learned material is handled and the relationship established within a given version between the *Rose* and the Latin tradition. In this way we shall formulate a variety of perspectives on each of a series of texts, on their

[27] For a lively if partisan review of critical perspectives on Reason, see Fleming, *Reason and the Lover*, pp. 3–38. Vitz criticizes Fleming's views in her review of *Reason and the Lover*. Ott reviews the main lines of *Rose* criticism in *Rosenroman*.

respective authors' reading of the *Rose*, and on the audience for which each was prepared.

After examining several different versions of the *Rose*, representing various degrees of alteration, I turn to two important examples of literary response to the *Rose*. Guillaume de Deguilleville, writing in a monastic context, and Guillaume de Machaut, writing for aristocratic patrons, exemplify two very different facets of fourteenth-century *Rose* reception. I include these readings of Deguilleville and Machaut not only because these poets were both careful readers of the *Rose* whose works offer sustained treatment of many of the interpretive issues central to this study, but also because, in the final analysis, the separation of interpolation and remaniement from literary imitation and allusion represents an artificial distinction. Both Gui de Mori and Guillaume de Machaut rewrote the *Rose*, incorporating material from that poem into their own work; the difference is one of degree.

I close with a discussion of an iconographic program. *Rose* iconography, particularly in the fourteenth century, has not been extensively studied. Alfred Kuhn's study of the opening-page miniatures in *Rose* manuscripts provides a point of departure for subsequent study of the iconographic tradition, but his work has not been continued in any systematic way.[28] Simonetta Peruzzi's monograph on the MS Florence, Bibl. Laur. A. e D. 153 includes a detailed description of the program of rubrication and illustration and a brief discussion of the stylistic features of the miniatures in the context of northern French manuscript illumination during the first half of the fourteenth century, but does not attempt to place the manuscript within the context of the *Rose* iconographic tradition.[29] Most recently, Eberhard König has published a facsimile edition of what may be the earliest surviving illustrated *Rose* manuscript, the late thirteenth-century MS Vatican Library, Urb. lat. 376; his commentary focuses on the question of dating and on the early development of an iconography for the *Rose*.[30] One can hope that König's provocative claims for the origins of *Rose* iconography will stimulate further work on the subject. John Fleming and Rosemund Tuve have produced the only other major works in this area, and both of these scholars, Tuve in particular, devote much of their analysis to fifteenth-century examples.[31] Fleming has been criticized for choosing

---

[28] Kuhn, "Illustration der Handschriften des *Rosenromans*."

[29] Peruzzi, *Codice Laurenziano*.

[30] König, *Rosenroman des Berthaud d'Achy*.

[31] Fleming, *"Roman de la Rose"*; Tuve, *Allegorical Imagery*. Fleming supports his reading of the *Rose* with frequent recourse to its manuscript illuminations, which he sees as providing a visual gloss on the text. Tuve likewise alludes frequently to illuminations in her discussion of allegory in the *Rose*, pp. 232–83, 321–30. Other contributions to the study of *Rose* iconography include Braet, "Roman der

his examples selectively without providing information about entire iconographic programs, and for not sufficiently distinguishing between the viewpoints of the thirteenth-century *Rose* authors and the fourteenth- and fifteenth-century artists who illustrated their poem.[32] Nonetheless his study raises important questions and offers some very real insights, both about the meaning of the *Rose* for medieval readers and about the nature of manuscript illuminations as a visual gloss on the text. Unfortunately, Fleming's detractors have not been quick to provide the comprehensive survey of *Rose* iconography that would finally enable us to place individual miniatures in the context both of the complete manuscript where they appear, and of the iconographic tradition for the passage that they illustrate. In the absence of such a survey, any study of *Rose* iconography is necessarily somewhat selective. But the detailed examination of an individual manuscript can, as König has shown, lead to considerable insight into one artist's understanding of the *Rose*. My analysis of the marginal illustrations in MS Bibl. Nat. fr. 25526 will examine the nature of the illustrative program and, in addition, its place in the larger context of the textual tradition and literary reception of the *Rose*.

In a series of Appendices I have included a selection of unpublished interpolations and abridgments. In preparing these texts I have followed the base manuscript closely, amending only when sense required it, noting all rejected readings, and providing variants when these exist. Most of the texts in the Appendices appear in only one or two manuscripts, since the interpolations appearing in numerous sources have nearly all been printed by Langlois. However, the "litany of love" (Appendix c) is an exception. It is one of the most widespread interpolations, yet Langlois does not print it. For this text I have provided variants from an example of each of the major manuscript families containing the passage, as well as MS *Arr*, discussed in Chapter 6.

Rose, Raum im Blick"; Dahlberg, "Love and the *Roman de la Rose*"; Hult, *Self-fulfilling Prophecies*, pp. 74–89; Nichols, "Ekphrasis, Iconoclasm, and Desire"; Richards, "Reflections on Oiseuse's Mirror"; and Walters, "Illuminating the *Rose*." The index announced by Kelly and Ohlgren in "Paths to Memory" promises a first step towards a more comprehensive study of *Rose* iconography.

[32] See, for example, Hult, *Self-fulfilling Prophecies*, pp. 75–76. Richards, in questioning Fleming's iconographic interpretation of Oiseuse as a figure for Luxuria, points out that the basis for this interpretation – Oiseuse's mirror and comb – do not appear in all illustrations depicting Oiseuse; see "Reflections on Oiseuse's Mirror," p. 303.

Perspectives on the *Roman de la Rose*: the text and its manuscript transmission

> La verité, qui est coverte,
> vos sera lores toute overte
> quant espondre m'oroiz le songe.
> (Guillaume de Lorris, vv. 2071–73)

> Et se vos i trovez riens trouble,
> g'esclarcirai ce qui vos trouble
> quant le songe m'orrez espondre.
> (Jean de Meun, vv. 15115–17)

> Or escoutés sanz contremant,
> s'orras desclorre la sentence
> de la merveilleuse subtence
> que t'ai dite par parabole.
> (Interpolation following v. 2340)[1]

Both Guillaume de Lorris and Jean de Meun promise to explicate the dream of which they write, bidding the reader to await the apparently imminent, yet somehow endlessly deferred unveiling. Guillaume repeatedly presents the promised explication as a revelation of hidden truth, an illumination that will take effect "quant j'avré apost le mistere" [when I have explicated the mystery (v. 1600)]: the mysterious workings of the dream, whose truth is the equally mysterious nature of love. Jean in turn expresses concern that his poem may prove troubling or offensive for its readers. In addition to promising to clear up any such confusion, he acknowledges that the poem may contain "paroles / semblanz trop baudes ou trop foles" [words appearing too bawdy or too foolish (vv. 15131–32)].

---

[1] "The truth, which is covered, will be completely opened to you when you have heard me explicate the dream"; "And if you find anything troubling there, I will explain that which troubles you when you have heard me explicate the dream"; "Now listen without distraction, and you will hear disclosed the meaning of the marvelous material that I have told you as a parable." The last is an interpolation in MS κυ, to be discussed in Chapter 5. Citations of the *Rose*, unless otherwise indicated, are to the edition by Lecoy.

In words that seem to anticipate the literary *querelle* of 1401–02, Jean asks his readers to justify the text to its detractors:

> pri vos que le me pardoignez,
> et de par moi leur respoignez
> que ce requeroit la matire. (vv. 15141–43)

I pray you to forgive me [for any excesses], and to reply to them, on my behalf, that the material required it.

Only in the event of criticism from the Church does Jean acknowledge the possibility of emendation: "presz sui qu'a son vouloir l'amende" [I am ready to amend it according to its (the Church's) wishes (v. 15271)]. Once the reader has heard the gloss, Jean states, he or she will not only be able to debate about love, but will also understand the totality of the poetic work, "quant que j'avrai devant escrit / et quant que je bé a escrire" [whatever I will already have written and whatever I intend to write (vv. 15122–23)].

The reader of the *Rose* is thus led to expect that at some point – in some ever-receding future – all will come clear: the hidden truths of the seemingly illusory dream, the heretofore unfathomable mysteries of love, the dynamics of the poetic text, the rationale for its many surprises and potentially shocking passages. Yet although much of what Jean writes – the discourse of Genius in particular – does provide a gloss of sorts, there is nothing in the text of either Guillaume or Jean that fulfills the promise of this all-encompassing explication.[2] Just as Guillaume left the anticipated conquest of the Rose for his continuators, so Guillaume and Jean both left the matter of glossing and explicating, justifying and emending, to their readers and continuators. In the latter area as in the former there was no lack of enthusiastic response. Jean, of course, allowed the Lover finally to have his moment with the Rose; previous to Jean, an anonymous poet had already arranged, in the space of seventy-six lines, for the Lover to spend a night of bliss with the Rose when Jealousy fell asleep (ed. Langlois, note to v. 4058). Of the poem's later readers, some eagerly took up the challenge of defending and explaining the *Rose*; others did find the text disturbing and sought, in part or in whole, to alter or suppress it. The work of those who set out to explicate and emend the *Rose* is preserved in its many and varied manuscripts, which provide a record of the interests and concerns of the poem's medieval readers and copyists. As Jean predicted, for example, the discourse of Faux Samblant, with its biting satire on the mendicant orders, was viewed as dangerous by some scribal editors of the *Rose*, who occasionally inserted warnings that the passage was not for general

---

2 On Guillaume's narrator, and on ways in which the endless deferral of meaning works against poetic closure, see Hult, *Self-fulfilling Prophecies*, pp. 160–4.

dissemination or even deleted parts of the text. The defence of plain speech in the discourse of Reason, the virulently antifeminist discourse of the Jaloux, the sexual machinations of La Vieille, and the juxtaposition of erotic and sacred registers in the discourse of Genius also caused confusion or consternation for some readers and rewriters of the *Rose*; and different manuscripts reflect different attempts to clarify, alter, or omit passages seen as obscure or dangerous. Influenced by Jean's continuation, the redactor of the *K* text even revised Guillaume's characterization of his poem as an art of love. In an important intervention directly preceding the God of Love's teachings, Guillaume's narrator announces that the romance offers a complete exposition "des jeus d'Amors" [of the game of love (v. 2067)]; but in *K* manuscripts, the romance is said to teach "de bien et de mal" [of good and evil (from MS *Ke*, fol. 16v)], with the added caution directed to the reader or auditor: "Mes face [le] bien et let le mal / Ou il aura painne infernal" [but let him do the good and leave aside the bad, or he will experience the pains of Hell (ibid.)].

In the chapters that follow, we shall examine closely a series of abridgments and reworkings of the *Rose*, dating from the late thirteenth and fourteenth centuries. Each in its own way responds to the mysteries, the ambiguities, the controversies of this long and complex poem. The question of the text is of fundamental importance: if we do not know what medieval readers found when they opened a copy of the *Roman de la Rose*, we can hardly expect to know how they interpreted it. Moreover, it is in following the life of the text – as it is expanded by interpolations, abridged, reorganized; rubricated, glossed and annotated – that we can most directly witness medieval readers interacting with the *Rose*. A knowledge of the manuscript tradition is a necessary basis for any approach to the question of what the *Rose* meant to its medieval audience. Through an integrated study of the *Rose* manuscript tradition and the literary and critical responses it inspired, we can identify the social and intellectual milieux in which the *Rose* circulated, and discern the outlines of different medieval readings of the poem.

AN EROTIC DREAM, A LEARNED COMPENDIUM: THE POLYMORPHOUS *ROSE*

Much of the controversy as well as the appeal of the *Rose* can be attributed to its combination of divergent literary registers, ranging from discussions of the Incarnation and the blessings of eternal life, philosophical discourses on free will, and edifying discussions of such topics as friendship and Fortune, to social and political satire, the art of love and seduction, and erotic allegory. The poem could thus appeal to both learned and popular audiences; it could be read for both pleasure and edification, as love poetry, topical satire, philosophy. The poem takes on a different aspect depending on the context in which it is read and the expectations with which it is approached.

Even the erotic dream itself, the narrative foundation of the poem, is valued differently in different medieval traditions. Within a clerical tradition, the erotic dream is diabolical, an experience no less sinful for its involuntary nature. From this perspective the *Rose* can be seen as itself an exposition of the folly and danger of erotic desire. Yet within the popular tradition of dream interpretation, the erotic dream can have a positive significance. A treatise on dreams in the fourteenth-century MS Bibl. Nat. fr. 1317 glosses a kiss, for example, as an omen of good will between the dreamer and the woman he kisses:

Cil qui songe qui'il baise aucune femme pour cause de amour et congnoissance, signifie qui'il fera bien a celle qui'il a baisiée, selon le desir. Si'il songe que le baisier soit pour cause de luxure, signifie que la femme ara d'icelui aucun benefice ou bien.
(B.N. fr. 1317, fol. 70r)

Whoever dreams that he kisses a woman out of love and personal acquaintance, it means that he will do something good for the woman he kisses, according to the desire. If he dreams that the kiss is because of lust, it means that the woman will have some gain or good thing from him.

The same treatise explains that to dream of carnal relations with a woman has a different meaning depending on the status of the woman: if she is "honorable" the dream is an omen of coming sorrow; if she is married but a loose woman it means that the man will acquire wealth dishonestly; and if she is of the lower classes, it is an omen of joy.

A different version of this treatise in the fourteenth-century MS Bibl. Nat. fr. 24432 glosses erotic dreams as good omens as long as they do not involve holy women and recluses:

Et de tant comme l'omme git plus avec fole femme commune, de tant plus sera enrichis. . . . Qui gist avec belle femme, il aura joie en cel an et gaing, et s'il ne la connoist, il aura plus de bien. (fol. 297v)

And however much the man lies with a common prostitute [in a dream], by that much he will be enriched. . . . He who lies with a beautiful woman [in a dream], he will have joy and gain in that year, and if he does not know her, it will be even better for him.

For a reader accustomed to thinking of dreams in this manner, the sexual conquest described in the *Rose* need not be seen as a nightmare or a sign of youthful folly, but as a sign of personal prowess and coming good fortune.

Moreover, the poem itself contains conflicting signals as to its moral significance. Guillaume de Lorris invokes the authority of Macrobius in claiming prophetic truth for his dream, yet Macrobius himself condemns erotic dreams as meaningless.[3] While Guillaume may not have known very much about Macrobius' treatise, it was most likely known to Jean de Meun, in whose hands the poem took on considerably more complexity. Already within Guillaume's text, the God of Love warns the Lover that he will be deluded by erotic dreams that provide only frustration (vv. 2421–34). Jean in turn incorporates a comment on the mendacity of erotic dreams into the discourse of Nature, using terms that unmistakably evoke the very dream described in the *Rose* (vv. 18353–74). And Ami advises the Lover that the pretense of dreaming about one's lady may prove a useful tool of seduction:

> Si li doit faindre noveaus songes,
> touz farsiz de plesanz mençonges,
> que, quant vient au soir qu'il se couche
> touz seus en sa chambre en sa couche,
> avis li est, quant il someille,
> car poi i dort et mout i veille,
> qu'il l'ait entre ses braz tenue. (vv. 9853–59)

Thus he should invent for her new dreams, all full of pleasant lies: that, when he goes to bed at night, all alone in bed in his room, it seems to him, when he dozes off, for he sleeps but little and often lies awake, that he holds her in his arms.

In this way one is led to doubt not only the truthfulness of the dream, but also that of the narrator who claims to have had such a dream.

The *Rose*, however, is no ordinary erotic dream narrative. It contains lengthy philosophical and satirical passages that appear as digressions if one assumes that the poem is primarily the story of seduction, but which might also be viewed as the very essence of the *Rose* if it is seen as a learned compendium, written in the vernacular for the "profiz et delectation" [profit and pleasure (v. 15211)] of a general public. Towards the end of his interview with Reason, the Lover tells her that he is, at the moment,

---

[3] Macrobius categorized the erotic dream as an *insomnium*, having no prophetic value (*Commentary on the Dream of Scipio*, 1, 3:2). Critics have variously categorized the dream narrated in the *Rose* as *insomnium* (e.g., Dahlberg, "Macrobius and the Unity of the *Roman de la Rose*") or *somnium* (e.g. Pickens, "*Somnium* and Interpretation"). In *Self-fulfilling Prophecies*, Hult points out that Guillaume may not have been very familiar with Macrobius' treatise (pp. 120, 126) and argues that Macrobius' theory applies to Guillaume's *Rose* through an understanding of dreams as "a literary device" (p. 121) and "a mode of allegorico-narrative *prophetic* expression" (p. 126, emphasis his), subverted by Guillaume's use of an erotic dream. For a discussion of the *Rose* – that of Guillaume and even more so that of Jean – as a *dépassement* of Macrobius' interpretive categories, see Fleming, *Reason and the Lover*, pp. 161–65.

uninterested in studying poetry, but that he intends to get around to it as soon as he can:

> Mes des poetes les sentances,
> les fables et les methaphores
> ne bé je pas a gloser ores.
> Mes se ja puis estre gueriz
> et li servises m'iert meriz
> don si grant guerredon atens,
> bien les gloseré tout a tens.   (vv. 7160–66)

> But I don't wish to gloss the sentences, fables and metaphors of the poets just now. But if I can ever be healed, and the service granted me from which I expect such great relief, then I will certainly gloss them in due time.

The Lover, in other words, promises to undertake more serious literary work once he has succeeded in plucking the Rose. Might this refer to the composition of the *Rose*? After all, Jean's poem can be seen as a gloss in more ways than one. As Paul Zumthor has stated, its relationship to Guillaume's romance is less one of narrative continuation than of providing "an immense gloss": Jean takes up Guillaume's various poetic themes and expands on each in a variety of contexts.[4] Moreover, Jean's reworking of material from the Latin poets and philosophers amounts to a reinterpretation, a recasting of a number of important texts. His *Rose* could thus be seen as providing a gloss on the philosophical tenets, fables and metaphors of Latin tradition, in the sense of Marie de France's belief, expressed in the famous Prologue of the *Lais*, that readers of ancient texts should "gloser la lettre / E de lur sen le surplus mettre" [gloss the letter and add their own additional meaning (ed. Rychner, vv. 15–16)].

In short, as we attempt to unravel the signals embedded within the text, we remain uncertain as to whether this poem is to be read as the story of a dream that truthfully represents a young man's initiation into the mysteries of eros, offered perhaps as an example of youthful folly, or perhaps as a celebration of human love; as a mendacious story of a dream that never took place, created as a tool of seduction; or as a scholarly reworking of the Latin poets, produced by an older, wiser, and presumably successful Lover. It seems, indeed, to be all of these at once. The poem's medieval readers were no less sensitive to its composite nature than we are, and they reacted in various ways, some choosing to concentrate on one or another aspect of the poem, others contemplating the blend of materials with either joy or dismay.

---

[4] Zumthor, "Narrative and Anti-narrative," p. 195. Zumthor makes a similar point in *Essai de poétique médiévale*, p. 374.

The most striking evidence for medieval interpretations of the *Rose* is the collection of documents generally known as the *querelle*: the debate pursued by Christine de Pizan, Jean Gerson, Jean de Montreuil, and Gontier and Pierre Col over the meaning and moral value of the *Rose*.[5] Christine's primary objections to the poem are that it fosters antifeminist attitudes, perpetrates a negative image of marriage, and contains salacious passages and vulgar language that could only serve to arouse the passions of its readers. She argues that Jean portrays love purely as sexual conquest and marriage as a battleground in which the only alternatives are for one partner to deceive or exploit the other; the *Rose* is no better than Ovid's "livre mal nommé *L'Art d'amours*" [book improperly named *Art of Love* (ed. Hicks, p. 138)]. She points out that "a estre bien amoureux n'est point necessaire estre fol" [to be truly in love it is not necessary to be foolish]; that however irrational love may sometimes be, "c'est pis decevoir que estre bien amoureux" [it is worse to deceive than to be in love]; and that "maistre Jehan de Meung ne senti onques que fu honourable amoureux" [master Jean de Meun never knew what an honorable lover was (p. 130)]. In general, she finds that the poem's mixture of authoritative citations, worthy philosophy, and lascivious doctrines could only serve to confuse and mislead the reader, turning vices into virtues and virtues into vices. Its juxtaposition of sacred and erotic registers, far from providing an edifying conclusion to the poem, is only a deceptive tactic to add authority to the allegory of seduction: "Et pour ce mesle il paradis avec les ordures dont il parle: por donner plus foy a son livre" [and for this reason he mingles paradise with the filth of which he speaks: to give greater faith to his book (ibid.)].

Gerson, while agreeing overall with Christine's view of the poem, concentrates especially on what he perceives as Jean's denigration of marriage, chastity, and religion; on the use of overly explicit language; and on the juxtaposition of sacred imagery with a scabrous account of sexual conquest. He also condemns Jean's use of morally objectionable source texts, such as bawdy pagan myths and Ovid's *Ars amatoria*, and his deformation of worthy texts: the representation of Nature and Genius, for example, is "corrumpuement estraitte du grant Alain" [corruptly extracted from the great Alain (ed. Hicks, p. 80)]. In Gerson's view, Jean's linguistic and poetic transgressions are not essentially different from bodily transgressions. Moving effortlessly from words to things, Gerson states that to

---

[5] See *Débat sur le Roman de la Rose*, ed. Hicks; all citations are from this edition. Most of the scholarship on the *querelle* has focused on the arguments of Jean's detractors, especially Christine de Pizan. See for example Baird and Kane, "*La Querelle de la Rose*"; Brownlee, "Discourses of the Self"; Fleming, "Moral Reputation of the *Roman de la Rose*"; Huot, "Seduction and Sublimation."

defend the legitimacy of the words "coilles" [balls] and "viz" [prick] and to praise the nobility of the male sexual organs, as Jean's Reason does, is but one step removed from arguing that there is no shame in going naked: to name the body part in a public document is tantamount to exposing one's own body to the eyes of the world (p. 83). His analysis of Jean's mixture of sacred and erotic imagery similarly implies an equivalence of words and things:

il n'a point fait moins de irreverence a Dieu d'ansy parler et entouiller vilainnes choses entre les parolles divines et consacrees que s'il eust getté le precieux corps Nostre Seigneur entre les piés de pourcealx ou sur ung fiens . . . Il n'eust mie pis fait de getter le teuxte des Euvangilles ou l'imaige du crucefix en une grant fange orde et parfonde!   (p. 79)

He has committed no less irreverence for God in speaking thus and in mingling scurrilous things among the divine and sacred words than if he had thrown the precious body of Our Lord under the feet of pigs or on to a dung heap . . . He would not have done worse in throwing the Gospel or the image of the crucifix into deep, filthy mud.

And Gerson uses this tactic to reply to the claim that the *Rose* portrays vice as an object lesson, a negative exemplum of what must be avoided: this, he says, is as though one committed lewd sex acts before the eyes of a young maiden in order to show her what not to do (p. 73). For Gerson, the *Rose* is a vivid and powerful text, one that comes to life before the eyes of its readers, embodying behavior that cannot be tolerated.

Contrasting with these scathing attacks on the *Rose* is Jean de Montreuil's lavish praise of the poem. Although his detailed exposition of the *Rose* is unfortunately lost, we can judge its tenor from Christine's summary, in her reply, of Montreuil's characterization of the poem: "mirouer de bien vivre, exemple de tous estas de soy politiquement gouverner et vivre religieusement et saigement" [mirror of right living, example for all social classes of how to comport oneself politically and how to live wisely and religiously (p. 21)]. Montreuil's opinion of Jean's poetic greatness is further expressed in the opening lines of his Epistle 118 to an unknown acquaintance:

Quo magis magisque perscrutor . . . misteriorum pondera ponderumque misteria operis illius profundi ac memorie percelebris a magistro Johanne de Magduno editi, et ingenium accuratius revolvitur artificis.   (ed. Hicks, p. 28)

The more closely I attend to the depths of the mysteries and the mysteries of the depths of this profound work of illustrious memory due to Master Jean de Meun, the more clearly the genius of the artist is revealed.

For Montreuil, Jean's erotic discourse and his praise of procreation posed no problem; indeed, in his Epistle 154, he states that the continuation of the human species is the purpose (*finis*) of the poem, and suggests that the poem's detractors may be resentful because they are incapable – due to religious vows or, he insinuates, physical disability – of participating in that process. The seeming excesses of the poem are redeemed, in Montreuil's eyes, by the overall satirical program and the necessity fully to develop each of the characters that figure therein; to this end, "plura licent que aliis actoribus prohibentur" [many things are allowed him that are forbidden to other authors (p. 42)].

The most elaborately worked out defense of the *Rose* that has survived from the *querelle* is that of Pierre Col. Like Montreuil, Col argues that Jean's purpose was to write a satirical work, and that the seemingly lewd and irreverent words should not be understood as his, but as those of his characters. Thus for Col, while the poem may contain material directed against women, against marriage, or against chastity, these doctrines are being satirized and are not meant to be emulated. Indeed, Col claims to know from experience that the *Rose* instills firm moral standards in its male readers: "En verité je cognois home fol amoureux, lequel pour soy oster de fole amour a emprunté de moy *Le Ronmant de la Rose*, et luy ay oÿ jurer par sa foy que c'est la chose qui plus li a aidié a s'en oster." [Truly I know a man, a foolish lover, who in order to rid himself of foolish love borrowed the *Romance of the Rose* from me, and I have heard him swear by his faith that it was the thing that most helped him to do so (ed. Hicks, p. 106).] He even goes so far as to argue that the *Rose* provides a service to women by warning them of male seduction techniques: "car de tant come il recite diverses manieres d'assaillir, de tant advise il plus les gardes du chastel pour eulx en deffendre: et a celle fin le fist il" [for the more he narrates diverse manners of assault, the more he warns the guardians of the castle so that they can defend it: and it was for this purpose that he wrote it (pp. 105–6)]. In this way, according to Col, the *Rose* differed from the *Ars amatoria*, which had no moral purpose.

Arguing further that discourse about sex does not by its mere presence condemn a book, Col invokes an argument that has since become common in debates about pornography and censorship: that the Bible itself is replete with stories of sinful behavior, including crimes of both sex and violence. The moral value of such passages is not fixed, but depends on the context in which they appear and the overall meaning to which they contribute. Col argues further that it is legitimate for Reason to speak openly of the sexual members because she does so in the context of a philosophical discussion; he points out that in the more lascivious passages, Jean consistently uses euphemism or allegory to refer to the sexual members and to the act of sexual intercourse.

One's acceptance of this argument, of course, depends both on one's tolerance for erotic discourse and on one's interpretation of the poem's overall meaning. For Gerson, the mere presence of lascivious doctrine and bawdy tales was already enough to condemn the book. Not only does he deny that the explicit representation of illicit behavior can serve any instructional purpose, but also he rejects the notion that such language, such ideas are legitimized by being part of an allegory, or by appearing in the mouth of a character other than the author: it is as though one were to say to a prince or lord, "Vraiement, sire, je vous dis en la persone d'ung jaloux ou d'une vieille ou par .i. songe que vostre fame est tres mauvaise et forfait son mariaige" [truly, sir, I tell you in the persona of a jealous husband or of an old woman or through a dream that your wife is very bad and violates her marriage (p. 72)]. Christine in turn is willing to admit the argument that context and purpose are the determining factors in evaluating a literary text; she employs precisely this argument in replying to Col's claim that the Bible contains stories about lewd behavior. But Christine does not accept the assertion of Col and Montreuil that the overall context of the *Rose*, the governing purpose of the poem, is one of moral instruction.

Addressing the problematic discourse of Genius, finally, Col decides that Genius is not really exhorting sinful behavior: sexual intercourse is lawful within marriage for procreative purposes. Col further cites Genius' condemnation of the Garden of Delight as proof that he does not urge absorption in the vanities of human life; avoiding the issue of the potentially blasphemous proximity of sacred images and erotic discourse, he points to the descriptions of Heaven as a locus of worthy doctrine. Interestingly, Col does not attempt to argue that the discourse of Genius is satirical, his line of defense for La Vieille and the Jaloux. Nor does he respond to Gerson's assertion that this section of the *Rose* is a corruption of Alain de Lille by arguing that Jean intended to parody either Alain or the doctrine of courtly love. Modern critics have often read the discourses of both Nature and Genius in this fashion. For John Fleming, the discourse of Genius contributes to a parodic representation of "courtly love" as a religion, hence as idolatrous and perverse; it is thus no different, in essence, from the discourses of La Vieille, Ami, and Faux Samblant.[6] For Winthrop Wetherbee, it is a comic deformation of Neoplatonic doctrines, pointing up

---

[6] Fleming, *"Roman de la Rose"*, pp. 208–26. See also Tuve, *Allegorical Imagery*, pp. 275–78.

the paradoxes inherent in the reality of human sexuality in a fallen world.[7] Wetherbee and Fleming agree in seeing Jean's Nature and Genius as somewhat comic figures, but disagree in their identification of the object of Jean's humor. Pierre Col, however, is unwilling to argue for any comic intent in the discourse of Nature or Genius. Evidently, the traditional dignity of the figures in question, as well as the powerful presence of sacred imagery and allusions to the doctrine of salvation and damnation, preclude the possibility of parody or satire, at least in the context of a response to Jean Gerson. Gerson's accusation of sacrilege can be answered only by showing that such solemn icons of the faith are being used with serious and moral intent. Likewise, Col is unprepared to argue, as some modern critics have done, that Jean was proposing a naturalistic celebration of sexuality in and of itself.[8] Only Jean's detractors, Gerson and Christine, make that particular claim, with Christine going so far as to argue that Col himself, and others like him, did not consider fornication outside of marriage as a sin.

Perhaps Pierre Col did hold that opinion; perhaps he privately did read Jean's Genius as a humorous and somewhat irreverent parody. Montreuil's assertion that the point of the *Rose* was the perpetuation of the species suggests that, while he may not actually have believed Genius' rather improbable assertion that procreative activity will gain one entrance to Heaven, he was untroubled by the poem's representation of sexuality. His assertion that Jean's satirical purpose justified his seeming transgressions could certainly be applied to the discourse of Genius. Still, Col was unwilling to make such an argument public; Montreuil did not bother to preserve his analysis of the *Rose* for posterity. The range of opinions expressed on the discourse of Genius, as well as those left unstated, show just how difficult Jean's poetic creation was.

Nothing was "settled" by the *querelle*; none of the participants were persuaded to change their opinion of the *Rose*. Their various perspectives on the text and on poetry in general remained distinct. In the course of the debate, however, many important issues were raised, revolving around the hybrid nature of the *Rose*, its blend of discourses and its panoply of characters, its tendency to resist definitive interpretation. The issues of the poem's relationship to its sources; of proper and improper language; of the

---

[7] Wetherbee, "Literal and the Allegorical"; *Platonism and Poetry*, pp. 255—66. See also Hill, "Narcissus, Pygmalion, and the Castration of Saturn." Polak discusses Jean's parody of Alain de Lille in "Plato, Nature and Jean de Meun." For general background on ancient and medieval views of procreation and celibacy, see Cohen, *"Be Fertile and Increase".*

[8] See, for example, Paré, *Idées et les lettres* and *"Roman de la Rose" et la scolastique courtoise*; Payen, *Rose et l'utopie.* For a general discussion of possible readings of the text, see Bouché, "L'obscène et le sacré."

representation of sexuality; of the uneasy relationship between the natural, the erotic, and the divine; of the message expressed in Jean's social satire: these points are central not only to the *querelle*, but, more generally, to medieval readings and rewritings of the *Rose* throughout the late thirteenth and fourteenth centuries. Through a study of the *Rose* manuscript tradition we can see generations of medieval readers grappling with these very questions. When the evidence of the manuscripts is correlated with literary responses to the *Rose* and with the *querelle*, we arrive at a clear picture of the evolution and cultural impact of the *Rose* up to the beginning of the fifteenth century: how it was read and perceived, the questions that it raised, its very real importance as a mirror of the diverse social, literary, and cultural heritage of the French Middle Ages.

MANUSCRIPT PRESENTATION OF THE *ROSE*

A survey of the rubrication and decoration of *Rose* manuscripts, and of the selection of other texts bound with the *Rose* in anthology codices, reveals a variety of perspectives on the poem. Rubrics and colophons frequently stress its edifying value, as in this colophon appearing in the MS Arsenal 3337, copied at Sully-sur-Loire in 1390:

> Qui ce rommans voudra entendre
> Et les raisons en bon sens prendre,
> Nobles science y trouvera
> Dont sages hons se prouvera;
> Et qui ou droit sens l'entendra
> Pour vaillant clerc l'auteur tendra. (fol. 123r)

> He who will care to attend to this romance, and take its arguments in good sense, will find there noble science, by which a wise man can prove himself; and he who understands it in the right way, will consider its author to be a worthy clerc.

The opening rubric in the mid fourteenth-century MS Bibl. Nat. fr. 24390 (MS *Ke*) comments on both the learned content of the text and its quality as a love poem:

> Ici est li commencemanz
> D'un moult soutif et gay rommanz,
> Ou mainte soutive parolle
> Est trouvee par bonne escolle.
> Si est la Rose seurnommé
> Ce [rommanz] por sa grant biauté. (fol. 1r)

> Here is the beginning of a very subtle and gay romance, where many subtle words are to be found for edification. And this romance is named "the Rose" for its great beauty.

The *Rose* is "beautiful," an artfully crafted work of literature; it is "gay,"a word that carries connotations of love poetry, of high-spirited adventure, of the verbal playfulness designated in the *Leys d'amour* as "gay sabcr."[9] It contains many notable sayings. And it is "subtle," a word often used in medieval poetry to refer both to the delightful pains of love and to poetic ingenuity.[10] For the rubricator of MS *Ke*, the aesthetic, amorous, and educational values of the *Rose* formed a happy union.

A search through thirteenth- and fourteenth-century *Rose* manuscripts turns up numerous examples where the romance is cast as love poetry. In the MS Bibl. Nat. fr. 1564 (*Lg*), copied in the first half of the fourteenth century, the last two pages of the book (vv. 21573 to the end) are decorated with a red flourish at every line, and a swirl of red roses fills the lower margin at the end of the poem. Surely such exuberance reflects a delight in the erotic climax of the poem and not a sober reflection on the follies of youth. In the MS Bibl. Nat. Rothschild 2800 (MS *Eb*), copied in 1329, the scribe described the owner of the manuscript in these terms:

> Onkes ne se pot tenir d'amer;
> Et si vous fai bien asavoir,
> Et si le vous tesmoigne pour voir,
> Que volentiers s'esbanioit
> Et moult grant entente metoit
> Au ju dont le Rose parole,
> Car il n'amoit autre carole.   (fol. 138r)

> He could never keep from loving; and I tell you, I testify to its truth, that he liked to make merry, and he attended closely to the game of which the *Rose* speaks, for he liked no other dance.

In the background of MS *Eb*, we glimpse a patron who considered himself a *bon vivant*, and who delighted in the depictions of flirtation and seduction in the *Rose*; a scribe who chose to please his employer by playing up this aspect of both patron and poem. The manuscript is decorated accordingly. The scribe frequently decorated initials with little drawings. Sometimes the drawings relate directly to the text: a head and outflung arm for the description of the dancing girls at the carol (v. 755, fol. 6v); a young man pointing to a heart pierced by an arrow at the Lover's lament, "Sui livrez a duel et a poine" [I am condemned to sorrow and pain (v. 3921, fol. 27r)]. In other cases, drawings of young men offering their hearts, of clasped hands, or of hearts pierced by arrows simply emphasize the general amorous tenor

---

[9] See Dragonetti, *Gai Savoir*.
[10] On the term "soutil" or "soutif," see Badel, *"Roman de la Rose" au XIVe siècle*, pp. 138–41; J. Cerquiglini, *"Un Engin si soutil"*, pp. 7–11.

of the poem. And at the end, lest there be any doubt as to the nature of the "game" of which the poem speaks, two miniatures illustrate the final conquest of the Rose, each with a double image: the lover advancing his staff towards the rosebush, and a couple in bed.

In the MS Bibl. Nat. fr. 1574 (MS *Lw*), on the other hand, a series of rubrics glosses the poem as an exposition of the follies of youth, and stresses the sacred content of Genius' discourse.[11] The opening lines of the narrative proper, for example, are identified as explaining "Comment printemps esmeut jeunesce / En oeseuse et en folesce" [How springtime moves youth to idleness and folly (fol. 1v)]. The appearance of Oiseuse is heralded as "Comment Oeseuse qui n'est pas sage / A mal fere donne passage" [How Idleness, who is not wise, opens the way to wrongdoing (fol. 5r)]; the courtly participants in the carol are identified as the followers of Love, "qui jones gens souvent afole" [who often drives young people to folly (fol. 7r)]. The elaborate rubrication of Guillaume's allegorical construct prepares for Genius' review of the courtly garden towards the end of the poem: a passage that the designer of MS *Lw* must have seen as providing the long-promised gloss on the dream. Having already encountered the didactic gloss on the Garden of Delight, the reader of MS *Lw* is not surprised by Genius' condemnation of the garden as a locus of folly and spiritual death. And the rubrication of Genius in turn explicates the expanded moral and spiritual context in which erotic love is now placed. The *biaus parc* that Genius offers in place of the courtly garden is identified as "L'esta[t] de par[adis]" [the condition of Paradise (fol. 147v, v. 20199)]; his description of the triune fountain with its trifaceted carbuncle is glossed as "De la tri[nité]" [concerning the Trinity (fol. 149v, v. 20494)]. The comparison of the two gardens is headed with the rubric "La comparison de ce monde au parc de paradis" [the comparison of this world with the park of paradise (fol. 148r, v. 20249)]. The rubricator of MS *Lw* read the *Rose* in much the same manner as Pierre Col. In designing a set of rubrics to *espondre le songe* [explicate the dream], as Guillaume and Jean put it, he undoubtedly felt that he was illuminating the hidden truths alluded to by the poem's authors.

The discourse of Genius was, as I mentioned earlier, a particular point of controversy in the *querelle*, and the manuscript tradition shows that this passage had always been susceptible of divergent readings. MS *Lw* is not the only instance of rubrication critiquing the preceptors of love and presenting Genius as a moral authority. An elaborate series of rubrics in rhymed couplets in the MS Pierpont Morgan Library M 132 outlines a

---

[11] On the rubrics in MS Bibl. Nat. fr. 1574, see my "Scribe as Editor."

Plate 1 Illustration of the Heavenly Park in the discourse of Genius. New York, The Pierpont Morgan Library MS M 132, fol. 142r.

didactic reading of the *Rose*, noting philosophical points and clarifying the poem's moral framework. Like the rubricator of MS *Lw*, who identified La Vieille's teachings with the lies and tricks of "les maquereles" [procuresses (fol. 107r)], the rubricator of MS M 132 stresses La Vieille's negative character, terming her "L'orde vieille, que Dieu confonde" [the filthy old woman, may God confound her (fol. 95r, v. 12957)] and describing her teachings as "tout le hourt du monde" [all the filth in the world (ibid.)]. But he introduces Genius' sermon as "l'escripture / Haute, sage, bonne, alosee" [the noble, wise, good, praiseworthy writing (fol. 138v, v. 19475)]. The lamb who ushers the servants of Nature into Heaven is illustrated as the haloed and nimbused Lamb of God (Pl. 1), and identified as "li trés doulz

Jhesu Crist" [the very sweet Jesus Christ (fol. 142r, v. 19919)]. The rubricator makes sure we understand what the park is:

> Genyus, par son escripture,
> Le biau parc expose et figure
> A la gloire de Paradis
> Dont Lucifer chaÿ jadis.   (fol. 145r, v. 20339)

Genius, with his writing, glosses and describes the beautiful park according to the glory of Paradise, from whence Lucifer fell long ago.

Yet at the same time, this manuscript that so stresses the theological elements of Genius' sermon and his promises of eternal salvation does not shy away from the explicit sexuality of Nature's works: the miniature at the close of Nature's discourse represents a couple in bed (fol. 137v, v. 19409). The overall interpretation implied by the rubrics and miniatures is similar to that outlined by Pierre Col: the discourse of Genius offers morally edifying instruction about the place of sexuality in human life.

The relationship between the Garden of Delight and the Heavenly Park is also addressed in the rubrication of MS *Bü*, a manuscript made in southern France or Catalonia and probably deriving from a learned milieu, to judge from its unusual series of miniatures illustrating Nature's discussion of the cosmos.[12] Again the Park is identified as "paradis," and its relation to the Garden is that of spiritual truths to the illusory forms in which they are expressed here below. Genius' comparison of the images on the garden wall to the representation of Hell and the created world outside the park is marked not as a simple contrast, but as a movement from sign to signified: "Par les ymaiges pourtraites hors du jardin d'amours entendrez ceux qui sont en enfer" [by the images portrayed outside the garden of love you will understand those who are in Hell (fol. 170v, v. 20273)]. Two further rubrics contrast the illusory nature of the Garden with the absolute reality of Paradise. Genius' comments on the Garden are headed, "Que tout fu truffe dou jardin d'amours" [that everything in the garden of love was deception (fol. 171r, v. 20319)]; and his return to the description of the Park is heralded, "Ci revient a la verité" [here he returns to the truth (ibid., v. 20339)]. For the designer of MS *Bü*, the closing sections of the poem are an important revelation of truths heretofore hidden beneath the veil of allegory: first the mysterious workings of the natural world, then the spiritual truths of which this world below is but a shadow.

Other manuscripts, however, suggest a more humorous reading of Nature and Genius as figures of eros. The MS Bibl. Nat. fr. 1565 (*Nd*)

---

[12] MS *Bü* is in a private collection; see *Astor Collection of Illuminated Manuscripts*, no. 51.

Plate 2   Nature on her knees before Genius. Paris, Bibliothèque Nationale MS fr. 1565, fol. 126v.

introduces the figure of Nature with the rubric, "Ci devise l'aucteur de Nature qui est en sa forge et de ses oeuvres" [here the author tells about Nature, who is in her forge, and about her works (fol. 104v, v. 15863)]; these works are illustrated with the image of a couple in bed. Nature's absolution by Genius is portrayed in a decidedly humorous image of Nature kneeling before Genius, who displays a glowing wand (fol. 126v, v. 19381): the subservience of Nature to Genius, her link with divinity, is conflated with her submission to and adoration of the phallic instrument of generation (Pl. 2). And on the facing page, the beginning of Genius' sermon is illustrated with an image of Genius preaching, accompanied by Nature, who smilingly displays a rabbit (fol. 127r, v. 19475): the authority of Nature, invoked by Genius in the opening line of his address, is limited to sexual reproduction (Pl. 3). This emphasis on the erotic and procreative aspects of Nature and Genius suggests a greater ironization of Genius' "theology," a higher tolerance for Jean's parodic rewriting of Alain de Lille. As we will see in subsequent chapters, the manuscript tradition of the *Rose*, in which the discourses of Nature and Genius were alternatively expanded and abridged in different ways, confirms the existence of diverse fourteenth-century reactions to this portion of Jean's poem.

Another gauge of the reception of the *Rose* is the choice of texts with

Plate 3 Nature displays a rabbit while Genius addresses the troops of Love. Paris, Bibliothèque Nationale MS fr. 1565, fol. 127r.

which it is bound in anthology manuscripts. By far the most frequent occurrence is for the *Rose* to be followed by the *Testament* attributed to Jean de Meun, often itself followed by the *Codicille* or *Tresor ou Sept articles de la foi*. Among the fourteenth-century *Rose* manuscripts catalogued by Langlois, a total of twenty-five, or about one-fifth – all of them dating from the second half of the century – include the *Testament*; ten of these also include the *Codicille* and/or the *Tresor*.[13] This practice reflects the growing interest in Jean as an author. By the second half of the fourteenth century, the compilation of single-author manuscripts was becoming more common, and it is hardly surprising that the phenomenon should manifest itself for an author as much admired as Jean de Meun.[14] The association of these devotional works with the *Rose* also suggests that the *Rose* may increasingly have been appreciated for its didactic value.

Aside from the *Testament, Codicille*, and *Tresor*, works included with the *Rose* in thirteenth- and fourteenth-century manuscripts are many and

---

[13] For a list of works included in *Rose* manuscripts, see Langlois, *Manuscripts*, pp. 213–18. See also Badel, *"Roman de la Rose" au XIVe siècle*, pp. 63–66.

[14] On the phenomenon of single-author manuscripts in the fourteenth century, see my *From Song to Book*.

varied; no one text appears in more than four of the surviving manuscripts. Some, such as the *Chastelaine de Vergi* and the *Prise amoureuse*, point to an understanding of the *Rose* as love poetry. The MS Dijon, Bibl. Mun. 526 (*Ca*) presents a veritable encyclopedia of love doctrine: a series of prose treatises outlining the art of love – the *Commens d'amours, Poissanche d'amours, Bestiaire d'amour*, and *Response au Bestiaire* – is followed by the *Rose*.[15] The *Rose* is also joined with the *Bestiaire* in three other surviving manuscripts.[16] In the MS Bibl. Nat. fr. 1569 (*Jo*) the *Rose* is equipped with a series of verse rubrics stressing the beauty and the value of Love's followers, and followed by the *Jeu de Robin et Marion*.[17] This idyllic piece continues the theme of love; the pastoral setting, with its rustic food, simple games, and loving couples, echoes the nostalgic evocations of an amorous Golden Age within the *Rose*. One is not surprised to find that a later owner of this manuscript was moved to sign his name in this manner: "Robert des Esleu, bon garçon et qui faict la ribauderie" [Robert des Esleu, a good fellow, and one who engages in ribaldry (fol 144v)].

Other manuscripts, however, pair the *Rose* with satirical texts that relate most closely to the discourse of Faux Samblant, such as the *Roman de Fauvel*. Devotional works also appear: the works of the Reclus de Molliens are found in three manuscripts, and assorted prayers, *serventois Nostre Dame*, and moral poems appear here and there. In the late fourteenth-century MS Bibl. Nat. fr. 12594, the *Rose* is followed by the moralizing *Miroir de l'ame*, the *Testament*, the *Miserere* of the Reclus de Molliens, and Jean de la Mote's *Voie d'Enfer et de Paradis*. A context such as this strongly suggests a compiler who would have echoed Jean de Montreuil's judgment of the *Rose* as "a mirror of right living."

Given such different ways of presenting the *Rose*, it is hardly surprising that the text itself was subject to change, as scribes and poets sought to shape the poem according to their expectations of what it was or ought to be. Likewise, readers of the *Rose* had their perspectives on the poem, recorded in marginal annotations; and from these, too, much can be learned about the medieval *Rose*.

READING AND REWRITING THE *ROSE*: THE MALLEABLE TEXT

Pierre-Yves Badel has argued that medieval readers approached the *Rose* selectively, focusing on those lines or sections that seemed most relevant

---

[15] I have discussed MS Dijon 526 in *From Song to Book*, pp. 152–56.

[16] I have discussed one of these manuscripts, Bibl. Nat. fr. 12786, in *From Song to Book*, pp. 16–19.

[17] On the rubrics in MS Bibl. Nat. fr. 1569, see my "Scribe as Editor."

for a given interpretation, seeking entertainment or wisdom in maxims or episodes without placing a high priority on the overall fabric of the text as a whole.[18] Perhaps not all medieval readers behaved in this fashion, but considerable evidence does point to a medieval practice of singling out particular lines or passages. These patterns of reading are recorded in manuscript annotations, which allow us to study the interests of medieval readers of the *Rose* and the passages that drew their attention.

The thirteenth-century MS Turin, Bibl. Univ. L. III. 22 (MS *Be*) was annotated in the fourteenth century by a reader who must, to judge from his reaction to the poem, have been a cleric. One passage that caught his attention is Jean's Apology, crucial to an assessment of the poem's significance for a clerical reader. He placed a large "Nota" at Jean's assertion that he never intended to "parler contre home vivant / sainte religion sivant" [speak against any living man following holy religion (vv. 15223–24)]. He also noted Reason's condemnation of "devin qui vont par terre: / quant il preeschent por aquerre / honors ou graces ou richeces" [theologians who travel around: when they preach in order to acquire honors or favors or riches (vv. 5071–73)]; this passage received the gloss, "Nota predicatores et m[. . .]" [note preachers and m[onks?] (fol. 39r)].

The majority of this reader's annotations appear in the discourse of La Vieille. Her comments about the seduction of nuns attracted his attention, perhaps because, as a cleric, he felt personally touched by it; in any case, he noted, "Amor monialium sumptuosus est valde nec potest inde lucrum provenire" [the love of nuns is terribly costly and no profit can come of it (vv. 14392–98; fol. 99r)]. He also noted Ovidian analogues for her claims that lovers are free to lie and that it is always better to keep more than one lover, and marked with a "Nota" her assertion that "dons de fame, au dire voir, / ne sunt fors laz a decevoir" [gifts given by women, to tell the truth, are nothing but snares to deceive (vv. 14401–2)]. Several of his comments are overtly antifeminist. To La Vieille's statement that a woman's chastity can be protected only if she herself wishes it – "Nus ne peut metre en fame garde, / s'ele meïsmes ne se garde" [no one can place a guard on a woman if she does not guard herself (vv. 14351–52)] – he replied, "Le deable la gardera" [the devil will guard her (fol. 100r)]. And at La Vieille's confession that the only man she ever loved was a scoundrel – "Mauvés iert, onques ne vi pire, / onc ne me cessa de despire" [he was bad, I never saw worse, and he never ceased to abuse me (vv. 14455–56) – our reader commented, "Nunqam mulier dilexit nec diliget probum sapientem nec

[18] Badel, *"Roman de la Rose" au XIVe siècle*, pp. 142–44.

35

diligentem virum" [no woman has ever loved nor ever will love an upstanding, wise, or attentive man (fol. 100v)].

The same reader also commented on two antifeminist passages in the discourse of Nature. At the assertion that "riens ne jure ne ne mant / de fame plus hardiement" [nothing swears or lies as boldly as a woman (vv. 18097–98)], he registered enthusiastic agreement: "Par le saint sang que Dieu respandit, vous dites voir" [by the holy blood that God shed, you speak the truth (fol. 123r)]. He was equally impressed by the statement that "qui queur de fame apercevroit, / ja mes fier ne s'i devroit" [he who could see the heart of a woman would never place his faith there (vv. 18113–14)]; to this, he added the comment, "Ne plus que en .i. serpent" [no more than in a serpent (fol. 124r)].

Material wealth and sexual relations – both renounced by clerics, both central to ecclesiastical corruption – seem to have been major preoccupations of this fourteenth-century reader of the *Rose*. A large "Nota," for example, marks Male Bouche's song about female lechery (vv. 3885–90). Several other "Nota" signs appear in Reason's discussion of the evils of wealth and the conflict between wealth and love. The themes come together in the anti-matrimonial sentiment expressed by Ami: that the sages of old "ne donassent pas franchise / por l'or d'Arrabe ne de Frise" [would not have given up freedom (i.e. would not have gotten married) for the gold of Araby or Frisia (vv. 9467–68)]. Our reader marked these lines with a proverb: "Non bene pro toto libertas venditur auro" [freedom is not to be sold for any amount of gold (fol. 68r).[19] Material wealth is inconsequential compared to preserving one's freedom; freedom in turn is defined as the unmarried state. In sum, our reader has focused on passages that bear directly on the clergy; on moralizing statements about wealth and financial greed; and on those that provide erotic titillation while reinforcing antifeminist and anti-matrimonial stereotypes. His comments certainly bear out Christine's assertion that the *Rose* could foster antifeminist attitudes. And his reading patterns exemplify the selective process of mining the poem for passages that suit one's interests.

In a survey of "Nota" signs in twenty-five manuscripts, I found other readers as well who chose to mark the cynical and lascivious "maxims" of Ami and La Vieille.[20] The abuse of authoritative discourse by a character such as La Vieille, sententiously uttering such lines as "Fole est qui son ami ne plume" [she is a fool who does not fleece her lover (v. 13667, marked in four of the manuscripts surveyed)], has a high comic value, especially for

---

[19] See Walther, *Proverbia Sententiaeque Latinitatis Medii Aevi*, no. 17307.
[20] "Medieval Readers of the *Roman de la Rose*."

readers trained to respond to proverbs and dicta. Both Ami and La Vieille parody learned discourse, citing classical exempla and referring to the "text" and "gloss" of their teachings; scribes and readers who glossed these irreverent teachings in the same way that one would gloss a moral treatise had entered into the spirit of Jean de Meun's satirical game. Other readers, however, concentrated their annotations mainly in the morally edifying discourses, such as those of Reason and Nature. In all, the survey of "Nota" signs shows that many medieval readers focused their attention on certain portions of the poem – the bawdy parts, or the satirical representation of marriage, or the art of love, or the philosophical teachings – to the exclusion of the rest.

The evidence of the manuscripts shows, then, that medieval reception of the *Rose* was pluralistic rather than monolithic. The poem was transmitted in a variety of contexts, read from a variety of perspectives. A similar diversity characterizes the textual tradition itself: the habit of selective reading parallels the selective copying and editing to which the *Rose*, even more than many other medieval vernacular texts, was subject. Some scribes and readers were content to mark or gloss Jean's claim that his poem is not misogynistic; the redactor responsible for the abridged *Rose* of MS Bibl. Nat. fr. 25524 (*Bi*) actually removed antifeminist passages. A reader of MS fr. 378 (*θα*) marked the passages representing both the good and the bad of marriage; Gui de Mori, author of a late thirteenth-century reworking of the *Rose*, rearranged whole blocks of text and added extensive interpolations which, among other things, served to cast a more favorable light on love and marriage. Some readers focused on the *Rose* as social satire or art of love, others as a vehicle for political, philosophical, and even theological discussion; poets and scribal editors who reworked the *Rose* likewise concentrated on one or another aspect of the text, or sought to bring the poem's diverse themes into some sort of harmony. The changes wrought thereby affected the poem's representation of love, marriage, and sexuality; its juxtaposition of erotic, satirical, philosophical, and sacred registers; its discussions of language, poetry, and interpretation.

The fluidity of the manuscript text is an issue in one of Pierre Col's epistles to Christine de Pizan. Christine had attacked a particular dictum in the discourse of Reason, "Car adés vient il mieuz, beau mestre, / decevoir que deceüz estre" [for it is better, fair sir, to deceive than to be deceived (vv. 4369–70)]. Col tried to defend the logic of this statement, but, no doubt feeling himself on somewhat difficult ground, eventually opted for a different solution: the lines in question "sont adjoustés: dont ceux qui ce font mesprannent trop, car je ne voy pas c'on y peust adjouster n'y oster sans empirer" [are interpolated: and those who do that are committing a fault, for I don't see that one could add or remove anything without injuring the text (p. 99)]. The fact of scribal revision provides a convenient escape for any reader of the *Rose* who comes upon a line that he or she does not like: it must be a later addition. Although as a fifteenth-century humanist, Col regards the authority of Jean de Meun in such a way as to feel distressed at the alteration of the text, his attitude is not altogether different from that of a scribe who, in copying the poem, might simply omit the offending lines without worrying about whether they are "original," "interpolated," or simply inappropriate to his understanding of the *Rose*: for the very process of rewriting and revision is a part of thirteenth- and fourteenth-century vernacular literature.

Not only did the Rose undergo transformations at the hands of abridgers and remanieurs; in addition, scribes and owners of manuscripts studied the text, compared versions, and often took care to insert newly discovered passages into a less complete manuscript or to combine more than one version in making a new copy. Because of the difference in opinions about the poem, individual passages may be expanded in one manuscript, abridged or omitted entirely in another. The discourse of Faux Samblant is a case in point. Jean foresaw that this passage might provoke controversy, and presented a sixty-line justification of the passage as an attack not on the Church, but on hypocrites (vv. 15213–72). In spite of this disclaimer, the passage clearly was perceived as potentially dangerous by some copyists. Three manuscripts contain warnings at v. 11193, a natural breaking point where, after a brief tirade of only a little over 200 lines, Faux Samblant "se voust tere" [wanted to fall silent (v. 11193)], but is goaded into revealing himself more fully by the insistent questioning of the God of Love. In MS Brussels, Bibl. Roy. 11019 (*Bu*), the scribal notice runs as follows:

> Ce qui s'en suit trespasseroiz a lire
> Devant genz de religion et
> Mesmement devant ordres
> Mendiens; car il sunt sotif et
> Artilieus, si vous porroient
> Tot grever ou nuire;
> Et devant genz du sicle, que l'en les
> Porroit mestre en erreur.
>
> (Langlois, *Manuscrits*, p. 396)

Avoid reading what follows to churchmen and especially mendicants; for they are subtle and crafty, and they could quickly harass or injure you; and to laymen, for they could be led into error.

Similar notices in MSS Montpellier, Fac. Méd. H 438 (*Bú*) and Brit. Libr. Egerton 881 simply warn that the passage in question should be revealed to no one.[21] Other scribes were even more concerned about the potential dangers of the text: in Rennes, Bibl. Mun. MS 15963 (*Lm*), for example, the discourse of Faux Samblant is drastically abridged, with over 600 lines deleted between vv. 11193 and 11950; in the original state of the Chantilly, Musée Condé MS 686 (*Ac*), the entirety of vv. 11193–950 was omitted.

Yet the manuscript history of Faux Samblant bears witness to divergent medieval attitudes towards the poem. In MS *Lw*, the text of Faux Samblant's discourse is intact; misreadings are averted by an explanatory rubric only a few lines into Faux Samblant's sermon, at v. 10993:

> Faus Samblant dit que pas ne maint
> Ou bonne religion maint;
> Mais maint avec les orguilleus,
> Qui contrefont religieus. (fol. 82r)

> Faux Samblant says that he does not reside where true religion is; but he resides with the proud, who falsely imitate churchmen.

The cleric Gui de Mori, in his reworking of the *Rose*, not only left the discourse of Faux Samblant intact: he added hundreds of additional lines on the subject of mendicancy and monastic corruption. Still, Gui was not taking any chances. At the end of the discourse of Faux Samblant, he inserted the portion of Jean's Apology that explains how Faux Samblant is to be read: as an attack on corruption, not as an attack on the Church. In this way he ensured that any reader of the poem would encounter the author's clarification immediately upon reading the Faux Samblant section. A similar tactic was employed by the scribe who arranged a series of long extracts from the *Rose* in MS Arras, Bibl. Mun. 845 (MS *Arr*): he included much of Faux Samblant's sermon, followed directly by the appropriate section of Jean's Apology.

A desire to extend the anti-clerical polemic is reflected in an interpolation of nearly a hundred lines in which Faux Samblant gloats about his much-abused privilege of taking confession, and which appears with some variation in fifty-seven, or about one half, of the manuscripts collated by Langlois.[22] Like other interpolations, it was sometimes added after the fact by an owner who evidently felt a need to "complete" a manuscript that originally lacked the passage. One of the most interesting such examples is MS *Ac*, in which we can see the progressive restructuring of the text before our very eyes. Here, the original scribe, after having copied a greatly reduced version of the discourse of Faux Samblant – as stated above, vv.

---

[21] These notices are printed by Langlois, *Manuscrits*, pp. 396–97.
[22] The interpolation about privileges is printed by Langlois, and its textual history discussed, in *Manuscrits*, pp. 426–30.

11193–950 were omitted – either discovered the complete text in a different source, or else changed his mind about the need to eliminate it; in any case, he inserted a small gathering with the omitted passage and placed marginal notations to indicate where it belonged in the text. Finally, in a third wave of copying, he inserted an additional leaf with the interpolation about confession, adding more marginal instructions to guide the reader through the now rather piecemeal text.[23] Clearly, *mouvance* is not limited to oral transmission. It is equally a phenomenon of a highly literate manuscript tradition in which texts are studied and evaluated, sources carefully compared: in short, of the medieval equivalent of textual criticism.

Who were these medieval editors, these readers and rewriters of the *Rose*? Unfortunately, the vast majority remain anonymous, and even those who name themselves are shadowy figures at best; our primary source of information is the manuscripts themselves. In the following study we shall examine numerous examples of individual manuscripts and remaniements. Here, by way of introduction, I shall present one example illustrating the various ways that a manuscript can tell us about its scribe or owner – in this case the same person – and about his interaction with the text.

THE PERSONALIZED *ROSE* OF MS BIBL. NAT. FR. 25525

The MS Bibl. Nat. fr. 25525 was copied in 1402 by the cleric Michel Alès, originally of Avranches, at that time residing in Avignon and employed by the cardinal Nicolas Brancaccio, bishop of Albano. The amount of personal material in the manuscript, including a copy of the cardinal's letter admitting Michel to Avignon, indicates that he prepared this copy of the

---

[23] The interpolation about privileges appears on fol. 77r, a single leaf inserted in front of the gathering – itself a later addition – that contains vv. 11193–950 (fol. 78–83). A later fourteenth-century scribe, wishing to restore some order to the piecemeal text, crossed out vv. 11951–12058 on fol. 76r–v and retranscribed them in their proper place at the end of the addition, on fol. 83r–v. The interpolation ends in the middle of the first column on fol. 77v and is followed by the words "Et sequitur 'Ci se volt tere Faus Semblant'." This last, in effect, is v. 11193, with which fol. 78r begins. Langlois, *Manuscrits* (p. 357), states that the scribe inserted the interpolation about privileges and the other omitted verses all at once, in a single gathering. He interprets the phrase "Et sequitur" as a trace of the warning about the text to follow, presumably copied from the model used for the interpolation (in the Montpellier manuscript, the warning begins "Istud sequitur"). Langlois further asserts that the other half of fol. 77, being unused, was cut off and its stub, which should have appeared after fol. 83 as the final page of the gathering, was mistakenly placed after fol. 77 at the time of rebinding. If this was the case, however, it is difficult to see why the scribe would have left the rest of fol. 77v blank and continued the text on a new page. Surely fol. 77 was inserted separately as a later addition subsequent to the addition of vv. 11193–950, and always was a single leaf. Moreover, the term "Et sequitur" most logically functions to direct the reader to the next block of text; Langlois admits that the standard warning would have been out of place here, at the end of the polemical and certainly controversial passage about privileges.

Rose for his own use. From his marginal glosses, from a prologue, colophon, and two interpolated passages that he placed in and around the *Rose*, and from the additional material that fills the last several pages of the codex, we can construct a certain portrait of this clerical reader of the *Rose* and of the circumstances under which his copy was made.[24]

Michel's marginalia are of three types: Latin glosses serving to explain words or phrases that seemed to him unclear; Latin maxims or citations of Latin poetry; and a series of French replies to the treacherous woman conjured up in Genius' warning never to reveal secrets to one's wife. His prologue, characterized by Langlois as "extremely mediocre" (*Manuscrits*, p. 65), nonetheless tells us something of his attitude towards the poem and its authors. The colophon, together with a passage inserted to explain why the projected illustrations were never executed, allows us to glimpse the turbulent environment of early fifteenth-century Avignon and how it affected Michel's work on this manuscript intended purely for his own use. A short interpolation in the discourse of Nature, as well as the various short pieces copied after the *Rose*, show us more of Michel's personal interests and concerns. Finally, the manuscript as a whole demonstrates the extent to which the scribe felt free to insert himself into the book he was copying, so that a text that had been composed more than a century earlier could become, to a certain extent, a reflection of its copyist and owner: Michel Alès, engaging with the text, projects himself into the *Miroër aus amoureus*.

The seventy-two Latin lexical glosses are interesting primarily as a guide to words that seemed difficult or ambiguous to a cleric writing in 1402. In many cases the words in question are thirteenth-century forms that had become archaic by this time. For example, he glossed "gie" [I] as "ego" (v. 5216); "tout diz" [always] as "semper" (v. 11410); "eves" [waters] as "aquae" (v. 20288). Other glosses identify homonyms: "pinguitudine" (v. 7503) distinguishes "saing" [fat] from its homophonic counterparts meaning 'healthy', 'breast', 'sign', or 'blood'; "jejunium" (v. 10538) distinguishes "jeun" [fasting] from "jeune" [young]. A third type of gloss involves lines that Michel perceived as corrupt and in need of correction or clarification. For example, he originally wrote v. 10796 as "Quant elle voit ce que je veil" [when she sees what I want]. Evidently finding this unsatisfactory, he amended "je veil" [I want] to "j'esveil" [I am alert, watchful], and clarified the meaning of the word with the Latin gloss "vigilo" [I am waking, vigilant].[25] Similarly, he originally copied v. 11072

---

[24] On MS Bibl. Nat. fr. 25525 see Langlois, *Manuscrits*, pp. 63–71.
[25] In Lecoy's edition, v. 10796 reads "quant ele veut ce que je veill" [when she wants what I want]. Langlois gives the same reading with slightly different spellings (his v. 10826).

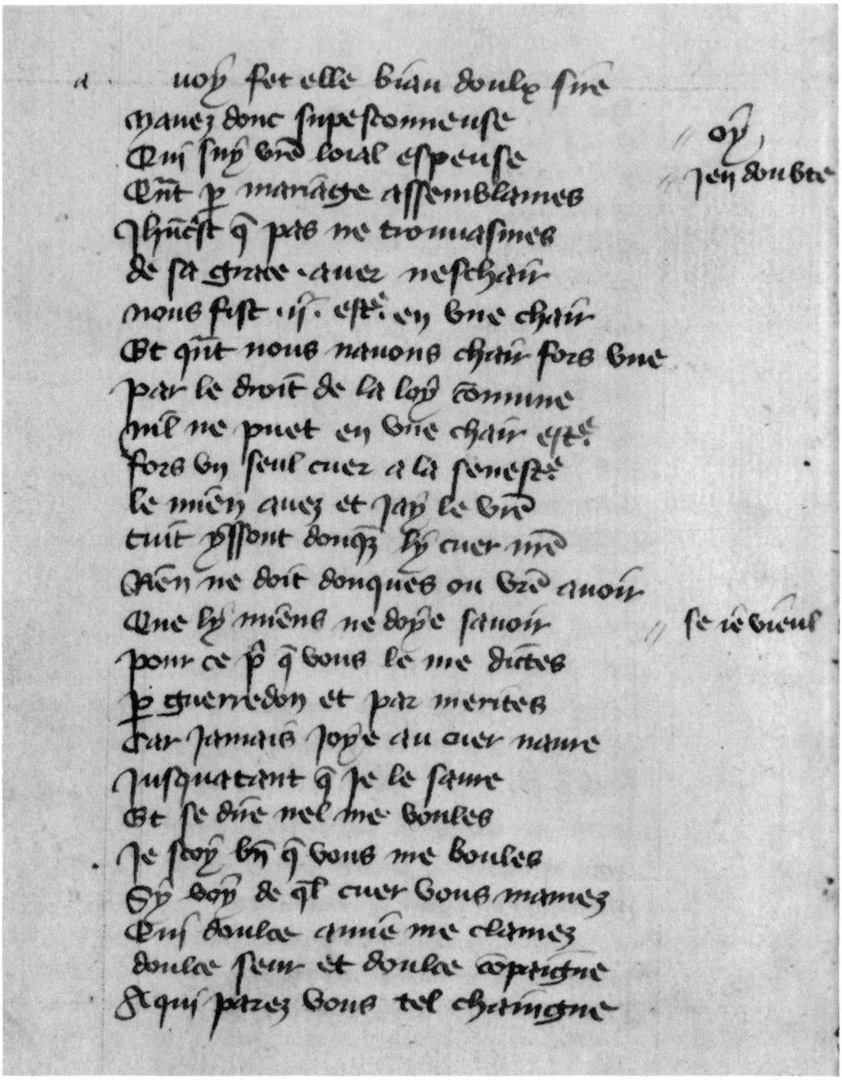

Plate 4 The *Rose* of Michel Alès, showing his marginal annotations. Paris, Bibliothèque Nationale MS fr. 25525, fol. 324v.

as "N'onques pour ce mains n'en sentirent" [they felt no less of it because of that], then changed the last word to "seintirent" – for the reading "they were no less holy because of that" – and added the clarifying gloss "sanctificare" [to sanctify]. In some cases, Michel's decisions about the text agree with those of its modern editors; in other cases they do not. Once again, *mouvance* takes place before our very eyes. One thing that is clear is that Michel studied the text and aimed for a coherent reading, whether or not he believed that it was the original reading. It is also clear that, for this clerical reader of the *Rose*, Latin was the preferred language of writing and study: although he was quite capable of composing verses – albeit mediocre ones – in French, explanatory notes to himself were automatically conceived in Latin.

Michel's poetic and proverbial glosses are typical of those found in fourteenth-century *Rose* manuscripts, and might even have been copied from his source, although his choice to include them still indicates that he considered them a useful "critical apparatus." At vv. 8231–32 – "car la vertu n'est mie mendre / de bien garder et de deffendre" [for there is no less virtue in guarding and keeping] – he inscribed the Ovidian source: "Non minor est virtus quam quaerere parta tueri. Ovidii" [nor is there less prowess in guarding what was won than in seeking. Ovid (*Ars amatoria*, 2:13; fol. 164r)]. At v. 9306 – "tele la mere, tel la fille" [like mother, like daughter] – he wrote: "De meretrice puta quod sit sua filia puta" [that from a lascivious whore there is a lascivious daughter (fol. 184r)]. Michel's glosses also include two comments on Fortune, no doubt a theme easily appreciated by one living through the Hundred Years' War and the papal schism. At vv. 6248–50 he wrote, seemingly in refutation of the argument advanced by Reason, "Honores mutant mores" [honors change human nature (fol. 132v)]. And at the description of the death of Croesus, he noted: "Ut Fortuna levis miseros facit esse beatos / Sic fortunatos destruit hora brevis" [just as fickle Fortune makes miserable ones happy, so she also quickly destroys the fortunate (fol. 137r; vv. 6481–506)].

The most interesting, and certainly the most unusual, of Michel's glosses are his replies to the arguments of the wife in Genius' bedroom scenario. Here Michel is no longer merely commenting on the text, clarifying it, or noting its sources; he has actually entered into its drama, and, taking the part of the henpecked husband, engages the wife in dialogue. The wife's protestations are undercut at every step through a series of thirteen replies (Pl. 4). For example:

> Vostre voiz ne puet estre oyee
> Fors que de moy tant seulement   // c'est trop
> . . .
> M'avez donc supesconneuse   // oÿ
> Qui suy vostre loial espeuse?   // j'en doubte
> (fol. 324r, vv. 16394–95; fol. 324v, 16403–4)

Your voice can't be heard here except by me alone. (– That's too much.) . . . Are you suspicious of me, then (– Yes), I who am your loyal wife? (– I doubt that.)

To the wife's claim that other men confide in their wives, "Tant que tout leur secrez leur dient" [so much that they tell them all their secrets (fol. 325v, v. 16456), Michel replies, "Comme folx" [like fools]; to her statement that she knows this because the other women have told her all about it (vv. 16463–68), he comments wryly, "Bien le croy" [I can well believe it (fol. 325v)]. After casting various doubts on the wife's moral character, Michel's final entry expresses the husband's regrets at taking a wife: when she invokes his marriage pledge (v. 16484–86), the marginal comment is "Je m'en repent" [I repent having done it (fol. 326r)]. In the hands of this early fifteenth-century reader, romance turns into dramatic farce.[26]

From a survey of the marginal glosses, then, we can already sketch a picture of Michel Alès as an educated man, well versed in Latin, and attracted particularly to the themes of Fortune, antifeminism, and erotic dalliance. It is not the refined courtly longing of Guillaume de Lorris that inspired Michel's pen, but rather Jean de Meun's Ovidian eroticism tinged with antifeminism. Ami's recommendation, derived from *Ars amatoria* 1:664–78, that the Lover use force to pluck the Rose, drew two "Nota bene" signs, placed at vv. 7661–62 and 7666–70, and the comment "Dum locus affuerit te precor esse virum" [when the opportunity presents itself, I pray you, be a man (fol. 158r), var. of *Pamphilus.*, v. 546)].

We can garner further insight into Michel as reader of the *Rose* from the prologue or "introïtte" that he composed to open his book. Here, he declares his admiration for "ly doulx Roumans de la Rose / Ou maint notable reppose" [the sweet *Romance of the Rose*, which contains much that is noteworthy (unnumbered folio; ed. Langlois, *Manuscrits*, p. 66)]. Michel recognizes that his own ability to discourse about love falls short of that of the poem before him, which "En parle mielx, les yeux touz clos" [speaks of it better even with its eyes closed (ibid.)] – perhaps an awkward allusion to the poem's claim to be the record of a dream. Indeed, Michel feels himself unworthy of entering the kitchen from which came the quill that wrote and illustrated the poem.[27] Had he heard about the *querelle* that was going on in Paris at the moment that he was making his copy of the *Rose*, it is clear which side he would have taken.

Michel also identifies himself with the "true lovers" who admire the *Rose* and "Souvent vont en leurs cuers clamant" [often appeal (to it) in their

---

[26] Thérèse Bouché comments on the dramatic qualities both of Genius' bedroom scenario, and of La Vieille's vivid evocation of a woman's manipulation of her lovers (vv. 14197–250), in "Ovide et Jean de Meun," pp. 82–85.

[27] Michel states that he is not worthy "d'estre en la cuysine / La ou fu la plume prise / Qui escript tout[e] la devise / Du roumans et la figure" [of being in the kitchen where the quill was taken that wrote the whole story and illustration of the romance (unnumbered folio; ed. Langlois, *Manuscrits*, p. 66)].

hearts (ibid., p. 65)]. He states that true lovers are those who honor all maidens and women, beautiful and ugly alike, although he cannot resist adding, "Non pour tant ne di ge mie / Qu'es plus belles n'en estudie" [nonethelesss I'm not saying that I don't concentrate on the more beautiful ones (ibid.)]. While such sentiments might at first glance seem contradictory to the antifeminist strains of Michel's glosses, the emphasis on desire and sexual conquest, coupled with a misogynistic distrust of marriage and mothers-in-law, is not at all unusual in clerical circles, among men whose vows prevent them from marrying if not from dallying. Indeed, it has been argued that it was for just such men – educated clerics in the lower orders, for whom a vow of chastity did not come easily – that Jean de Meun, not without humor and irony, wrote his exposition of sexual conquest and his defense of procreation and natural love.[28]

In addition to love, Michel was also concerned with the political situation that surrounded him, and commented on it both in a brief interpolation, and in a passage written to explain the lack of illustrations. The interpolation, inserted after v. 15936 during the discussion of death in the description of Nature, refers to the effects of the Hundred Years' War. The situation was grim in Michel's native Normandy:

> Quant cil qui se livre coppie
> Et ceste matiere estudie;
> Moult estoit il desconforté,
> Et disoit, Hé! mort, hé! mort, hé!
> Las! mort, maint as fait de Normans
> Petiz orphelins, qui de lor mams   //   mamila
> Devoient le lact sucier et trere,
> Dont aprés eulx les convient brere.
> En l'an mil. cccc. et un
> Tu fis tristres le bon commun,
> Et l'an devant et l'an apprés,
> Universel feis le grappés.   (fol. 315r–v)

When he who is copying this book, and studying this material; he was greatly distressed, and kept saying, "Oh! death, oh! death, oh! Alas! death, you have made many little Norman orphans, who should have been sucking milk from the breast, but they are forced to wail for it. In the year 1401 you turned the common good to sorrow, and the year before and the year after, you engaged in universal pillaging.

Michel's picture of life in Avignon is equally troubled. He comments on the pressures of his job that forced him to stay up far into the night in order to

---

[28] See the discussion by Badel, *"Roman de la Rose" au XIVe siècle*, pp. 32–64.

make this book for himself,[29] and explains that he was prevented from executing the illustrations he had planned because of "le temps dangereulx" [the dangerous times (fol. 32r)]. In Avignon, he relates,

> Mainte teste en fut couppee
> Et mainte mayson destruite,
> Et engins tenduz qui bruite
> Fesoient et grant derompement. (ibid.)

Many a head was cut off, and many a house destroyed, and contraptions built that made great noise and disruption.

It is not difficult to imagine that, in such an environment, the *Rose* might provide both a welcome escape from the dire matters at hand, and an agreeable philosophical discourse about confronting adversity.

In the closing pages of the book, Michel copied various short texts, including his letter of employment, a description of the comet of 1402, several prayers, a notice of the death of the canon Thomas Mulot, and a Latin poem about the papal schism, lauding Pope Clement and the king of France. In a book that already contains such diverse material as Reason's description of the battles of Manfred and Charles d'Anjou, meditations on the ravages of Fortune, Faux Samblant's exposé of clerical corruption, Nature's discussion of comets, and Genius' promises of spiritual absolution, Michel's entries are by no means out of place.

While Michel Alès did not provide us with an extended interpretation of the *Rose*, nor with a detailed self-portrait, his copy of the romance nonetheless enables us to witness one medieval reader engaging with the *Rose*, pondering its archaic language and sometimes corrupt text, enjoying its humor, identifying both with its praise of love and its criticism of marriage, and finding material relevant to his own troubled times. He boasts of having copied the text in a mere five weeks (fol. 421r), ambitiously plans several full pages of illustrations representing the garden and its allegorical inhabitants, then wistfully accepts that he simply does not have the luxury of carrying out those plans. The *Roman de la Rose* was for him both a cultural icon of great authority, a text he was barely worthy of associating himself with at all, and a curiously personal document into which he could insert himself at will. As we will see, Michel was far from unique in that respect; the *Rose* frequently provided the vehicle simultaneously for study, reflection, and personal expression, and a study of the manuscripts continuously turns up examples of unexpected, idiosyncratic responses to this encyclopedic, yet lyrical, poem.

---

[29] "Sovent tart couche et matinal, / Quer n'escrivioit pas a sa guise, / Ains luy convient faire servise; / Pour sa vie convient qu'ahenne / O son seigneur de Albenne." [Often he went to bed late, in the wee hours of the morning, for he did not write at his leisure, but was forced to perform his duties; he had to exert himself to earn his living with his lord of Albano (fol. 421v).]

2

Intertextual readings of the *Rose*: marginal glosses and readers' annotations

> And alle the walles with colours fyne
> Were peynted, bothe text and glose,
> Of al the Romaunce of the Rose.
> *(Book of the Duchess*, vv. 332–34)
>
> Je n'i faz riens fors reciter.[1]   *(Rose*, v. 15204)

Both authors of the *Rose* proclaim the relationship of their work to the Latin intellectual tradition. Guillaume cites Macrobius' commentary on the *Somnium Scipionis* as justification for his choice of the allegorical dream-vision as a literary form; and his claim that "l'art d'Amors est tote enclose" [the art of love is completely enclosed (v. 38)] in his poem is generally understood as an allusion to Ovid's *Ars amatoria* as one of the sources of the romance. Jean, far more steeped in the Latin tradition, cites numerous classical and medieval authors, including Juvenal, Cicero, Seneca, Boethius, and Guillaume de Saint-Amour; and he draws on still others that he does not cite, such as Alain de Lille. He claims – perhaps somewhat disingenuously – that he should not be held responsible for his words because he is only repeating what was said by the *auctores*.

It is hardly surprising, then, that the *Rose* should have appealed to educated readers, sensitive to its recasting of the Latin poets and philosophers. Of course, Jean's appropriation of anterior texts was not always viewed with admiration. We have seen that Gerson, railing against the *Rose* as a blasphemous work, describes it as a patchwork of immoral texts, inelegantly thrown together. Ovid's *Ars amatoria*, he points out, was considered so reprehensible even by pagans that its author was exiled; yet it is only one of many such texts incorporated into the *Rose*:

Car *L'Art d'amour*, laquelle escript Ovide, n'est pas seulement toute enclose ou dit livre, mais sont translatés, assemblés et tirés come a violance et sans propos autres livres plusseurs, tant d'Ovide come des autres, qui ne sont point moins deshonnestes et perilleux.   (ed. Hicks, pp. 76–77)

---

[1] "I do nothing there but cite [what the authors have said]," ed. Lecoy, v. 15204. I cite the *Book of the Duchess* in *Works*, ed. Robinson.

For not only is the *Art of Love* that Ovid wrote enclosed in the aforementioned book, but many other books, both by Ovid and by others, no less immoral and dangerous, are translated, assembled and dragged in with violence and for no reason.

As examples of the latter, Gerson cites the epistles of Abelard and Heloise, the poetry of Juvenal, and the "fables" of Mars and Venus, Pygmalion, and Adonis. Clearly, the *Rose* could not be appreciated by one who disapproved of the texts it so brilliantly blends and reworks.

For more sympathetic readers, however, the recognition of Latin texts in a vernacular format was one of the pleasures of reading the *Rose*, and the marginal glosses by which they noted Jean's various sources and analogues are eloquent proof that the creation of such a critical apparatus did not begin with modern editors. Citations of the *Ars amatoria* are most frequent among these glosses; meditation on the relationship between this text and the *Rose* is invited by Guillaume de Lorris' prologue allusion, itself picked up in standard incipit and explicit rubrication, where the poem is typically identified as "le Roman de la Rose / Ou l'art d'amours est tote enclose." Other Latin authors are cited from time to time: MS *Lw*, for example, contains marginal citations of Juvenal, Sallust, Ovid, and Virgil – along with various French and Latin maxims.[2] These annotations are of great importance, not only in establishing the circulation of the *Rose* in educated circles, but also in providing a guide to the literary and intellectual context in which medieval readers placed the *Rose*, and the interests and preoccupations with which they approached it.

THE *ROSE* AND THE *AUCTORES*: THE MSS BIBL. NAT. FR. 1560 AND ARSENAL 3337

One of the most varied assortments of *Rose* glosses that I have found to date appears in the mid-fourteenth-century MS Bibl. Nat. fr. 1560 (*Me*). The manuscript was probably copied in Normandy; a note on the flyleaf indicates that it was in Rouen by the late fourteenth century.[3] At some point not long after it was made, the pages were numbered and a table of

---

[2] The glosses in MS *Lw* identify the sources for various passages: Juvenal, *Satire* 6: 165 for vv. 8674–76 (fol. 65r); the opening lines of Sallust's *Catilina* 3 for vv. 15148–62 (fol. 111v); *Aeneid* 8: 220–24 for v. 15547 (Fol. 115r); *Metamorphoses* 10: 544 for vv. 15677–82 (fol. 115v). This manuscript, whose marginal "Nota bene" signs indicate a marked preference for philosophical and morally edifying passages (see my "Medieval Readers"), clearly belonged to a learned milieu.

[3] On the verso of the opening flyleaf is a memorandum: "Escript a Rouen ce lundi, troisieme jour de novembre. Le tout vostre en paiant." [Written in Rouen this Monday, the third day of November. The whole yours with payment.] Langlois dates the hand as late fourteenth century, and adds that the manuscript probably originated in Normandy, in *Manuscrits*, p. 18.

contents was added. The presence of this table, with 158 entries cataloging the narrative and thematic subdivisions of the *Rose*, shows that the manuscript belonged to someone who wanted to be able to refer to specific passages: someone who used it as a sort of anthology or reference book. There is no way of knowing whether or not this was the same person who was responsible for the glosses, but they too were probably entered not long after the manuscript was copied. Though few in number, the glosses suggest a university-educated reader. The range of authors cited is impressive: in addition to the Bible, we find Macrobius, Tibullus, Matthew of Vendôme, Ovid's *Metamorphoses*, Aristotle's *Physics* and *Ethics*, and the *Pamphilus*. The glosses are as follows:

Nota quod Scipio senator romanus, cum iret in Affricam ad destruendum Cartaginem, apparuit ei in sompniis Anchises, pater suus, qui multa ventura sibi revelavit et multa mistica sibi ostendit, quod sompnium postea Macrobius philosophus eleganter exposuit, interserendo multa de philosophia naturali et de scientia mathematicis in duobus commentariis. Et intitulatur liber ille Liber Macrobii sive Expositiones sompni Scipientis senatoris.

Note that Scipio the Roman senator, when he went to Africa to destroy Carthage, there appeared to him in his sleep his father Anchises, who revealed to him many things to come and showed him many mysteries, which dream Macrobius the philosopher later expounded elegantly, inserting a good deal of natural philosophy and mathematical science, in two commentaries. And that book is called "The Book of Macrobius or Exposition of the Dream of the senator Scipio."
(unnumbered folio, opposite opening-page miniature)

Tibullus. Libro ii° . Sompnia fallace ledunt temeraria mentes.

Tibullus, Book 2. Bold dreams afflict minds with deception.
(Pseudo-Tibullus, var. of 3, 4: 7)   (ibid.)

Salomon ecclesiastes v° . Ubi multa somnia, plurime vanitates.

Solomon, Ecclesiastes 5. Where there are many dreams, there are many vanities.
(Eccl. 5:6; RSV, Eccl. 5:7).   (ibid., opposite vv. 1–2)

Totum istud ponitur Matheis Vindenensis tractatu de loci placidi descripcione.

All this is laid out in Matthew of Vendôme's treatise on the description of the *locus placidus*. (*Ars versificatoria*, ed. Faral, 1: §109–13)   (fol. 1v, v. 47)

Nota quod ista vicia sive defectus non participant ad actum de delectione et ideo dicuntur esse extra murum.

Note that these vices or defects do not participate in the act of delight, and so are said to be outside the wall.   (fol. 2r, vv. 132–38)

iiii° phisicorum capitulo de tempore videbatur.

49

It is seen in the fourth book of the *Physics* in the chapter on time. (Aristotle's *Physics*, Bk. 4, ch. 10) (fol. 4r, v. 369)

In primo libro Ovidii metamorphoses, ii° capitulo de amore Phebu . . . de istis duabus arcubus invenies quid significat.

In the first book of Ovid's *Metamorphoses*, in the second chapter about the love of Phoebus . . . concerning these two bows you will find what it means. (*Metamorphoses*, 1:467–71). (fol. 8r, vv. 913–17)

In Ovidio metamorphoseos libro .iii. historiam plane invenies.

In Ovid, in Book 3 of the *Metamorphoses*, you will find the whole story. (*Metamorphoses*, 3:346–510)
(fol. 11r, v. 1437)

Primo ethicorum. Semper ratio deprecatur ad optimam.

The first book of the *Ethics*. Reason always urges to the best. (Aristotle's *Ethics*, 1) (fol. 29r, v. 4198)

In Pamphilo. Pulchrior esse putat vi perdere virginitatem / Quam dicat de me fac modo velle tuum.

In *Pamphilus*: She thinks it better to lose her virginity by force than to say, "Now do as you will with me" (*Pamphilus*, vv. 115–16) (fol. 52r, vv. 7664–70)

The three citations on the opening page provide an interesting frame of reference for the *Roman de la Rose*. The explanation of the dream of Scipio and Macrobius' commentary suggests a greater knowledge of the text than is reflected in Guillaume's passing reference. The glossator, for example, knows that Scipio was a senator and not, as Guillaume had said, a king. He also knows something of the circumstances of the dream, its content, and the nature of the commentary. Indeed, the pairing of Scipio the dreamer with Macrobius the commentator, who incorporated the dream into an "elegant" treatise drawing on science and philosophy, parallels the incorporation of Guillaume's dream into Jean's much larger work, which also draws on philosophical and scientific tradition. The opening note affirms both that dreams can have prophetic value, and that they can provide an appropriate vehicle for erudite commentary. Nonetheless, a reader of Macrobius would also know that erotic dreams were categorized as *insomnia*: dreams unworthy of interpretation or consideration.

The citations of Tibullus and the Bible provide examples of the "maintes gens" who claim that dreams are mendacious. Prophetic dreams are, of course, an important Biblical theme. But the dreams at issue here are of a different type, the trifling dreams of passion and fancy that include erotic dreams. Indeed, the condemnation of dreams in Ecclesiastes is applied explicitly to erotic dreams in a treatise that was widely read throughout the late medieval period, the *De miseria condicionis humane* of Pope Innocent III. In a section entitled "De terrore sompniorum" [Of the terror of dreams (1:23)], Innocent cites Ecclesiastes 5:6 in a discussion of the defilement caused by erotic dreams:

Multas curas sequuntur sompnia, et ubi multa sompnia, plurime vanitates. Multos errare fescerunt sompnia et exciderunt sperantes in illis. Apparent enim sepe in sompniis turpes ymagines, ex quibus per illusiones nocturnas non solum caro polluitur, sed et anima maculatur.

Many cares follow dreams, and where there are many dreams, there are many vanities. Dreams have caused many to go astray and have destroyed those who trust in them. For in dreams shameful images often appear, through the nocturnal deceits of which not only is the flesh contaminated but also the soul is defiled.

(ed. and transl. Lewis, pp. 132–35)

According to the medieval commentary tradition, the book of Ecclesiastes was about the vanity and mutability of all earthly things, a theme addressed in the *Rose* by Reason, Nature, and Genius. The Glossa Ordinaria relates Eccl. 5:6 to the preceding verse, "Ne dederis os tuum ut peccare facias carnem tuam" [do not allow your mouth to cause your flesh to sin], which is glossed, "Quasi ne dicas te ex infirmitate carnis tuae peccare" [that is, do not say that you sin because of the weakness of the flesh (*PL* 113, col. 1122)]. Eccl. 5:6 in turn is glossed, "Quasi, *Ne dederis os tuum*, etc., quia haec vita est quasi somnia, et multa videntur vera, quae sunt falsa; sic et excusatio tua" [like "Do not allow your mouth," etc., because this life is like dreams, and many things seem true which are false; just like your excuse (ibid.)]. The verse cited in MS *Me* thus not only comments on the potential vanity of dreams and the danger they bring of erotic temptation, but also warns more generally of the deceptive nature of this world. The specific example given is the human tendency to excuse sin as an inevitable consequence of the weakness of the flesh. Precisely this excuse is offered by the Lover in his rejection of Reason: he simply cannot give up his love for the Rose, because his desire is too strong and his commitment to winning it is irrevocable. The gloss suggests that the dream is to be read as an allegory for the illusions and self-deceptions of human life, with particular regard to sexual passions. In this way the erotic dream can, in fact, become the vehicle for important teachings.

The passage from Tibullus refers to dreams of rejection by one's lady: that, and not sexual arousal, is the Roman poet's idea of a nightmare. It is unlikely, however, that the glosser would have known the original context for the line. In the fourteenth century, the works of Tibullus were known almost exclusively from the florilegia, from which the erotic content of his poetry had been carefully expunged.[4] A reader of Tibullus in the florilegia would probably have assumed that the dreams in question were erotic dreams; he would have been free to decide for himself just what sort of dangers they posed. In the most widely disseminated florilegia, the line in question follows a passage on the evils of riches; it is accompanied by a second line stressing the terrors caused by dreams, and followed by an assertion that hard hearts can be won through soft prayers and a series of lines on the dangers of women. These are certainly all themes central to the *Rose*; it is logical that someone familiar with this version of Tibullus would see his comments as relevant to the dream recounted therein.

In all, these three glosses at the poem's beginning crystallize the conflicting views that emerge from medieval writings about dreams: dreams can present significant images, an allegory of an individual life or of the human condition; they can also be no more than a manifestation of the dreamer's own feverish passions, fears, and delusions, and can even lead to spiritual and bodily defilement. It is the genius of Jean de Meun that he made a dream of passion the vehicle for a learned commentary on human nature, society, and the cosmos. While we cannot tell from these three glosses precisely how the glosser understood this particular point, it is clear that he was profoundly interested in the paradox of a dream-vision at once erotic and moralistic.

The citation of Tibullus is interesting for another reason as well. If Tibullus was an obscure figure on the medieval literary scene, he does play a role, albeit a small one, in Jean's *Rose*. In an adaptation of Ovid's *Amores* 3, 9: 7–16, Jean has the God of Love describe the grief he and his mother felt at the death of Tibullus, who was one of the best "counsellors" Venus and Cupid had ever had (vv. 10478–91). Some readers of the poem, medieval and modern alike, have interpreted this passage as implying an identification of Guillaume de Lorris with Tibullus, or of Guillaume as the continuator of a tradition that includes Tibullus and the other Latin poets.[5]

---

[4] The textual history of Tibullus in the Middle Ages has been studied in some detail. Excerpts from his poems appear in a number of florilegia and in Vincent of Beauvais, but the only complete manuscript that can be documented is the one listed in Richard de Fournival's *Biblionomia*. By the fourteenth century, this manuscript was in the Sorbonne library. It is most likely that our glosser encountered Tibullus in one of the florilegia, since these circulated so much more widely. See Ullman, "Tibullus in the Mediaeval *Florilegia*"; Ullman's "The Library of the Sorbonne in the Fourteenth Century," in his *Studies in the Italian Renaissance*, pp. 41–53; Robathan, "The Missing Folios of the Paris *Florilegium* 15155"; Newton, "Tibullus in Two Grammatical Florilegia of the Middle Ages."

[5] Uitti, for example, interprets this allusion to the Latin poets as an identification of Guillaume and Jean as heirs to the Latin tradition, in "From *Clerc* to *Poète*." A fusion of Guillaume de Lorris with Tibullus is implied in a marginal gloss, perhaps by the scribe, in the thirteenth-century MS *By*: "Ci fenist Guillaumes Tybullus, et commance maistres Jehans de Meun" (fol. 90r, v. 10535). A similar note appears in MS *Bü* between the two parts of the poem.

Yet the God of Love explicitly states that Guillaume is not as wise as his Latin predecessors, hence not able to find his way to the end of the erotic quest. He needs help; this help is, of course, provided by Jean, who is thus more truly the heir to Tibullus, Ovid, and the other Latin authors.[6] The presence of Tibullus at the opening of the romance, as a voice warning about the deceptive torments of dreams, echoes his appearance at the poem's midpoint as an exemplar of amorous and poetic wisdom, whose advice would have enabled Guillaume to complete his quest more easily. Indeed, much of what remains of Tibullus' poetry in the florilegia – the blessings of the simple rustic life, the fine art of persuasion, the danger of feminine wiles – is echoed in the advice given by the Lover's chief counsellor in seduction, Ami. Along with the reference to Macrobius, the allusion to Tibullus looks ahead to Jean's continuation, where Guillaume's dream will be expounded, erotic love will be examined from various perspectives, and the quest ultimately fulfilled.

Other glosses reflect an interest in rhetoric (Matthew of Vendôme); in Guillaume's Ovidian material (the God of Love's two bows and the story of Narcissus); and in the poem's male-oriented treatment of women and sexuality (*Pamphilus*). The gloss on the wall-images makes it clear that the text is setting up a value system based on erotic pleasure, and is similar in spirit to the rubric appearing across the page-tops of MS *Lw*: "Des .x. images la portraiture / Dont le dieux d'amours n'a cure" (The portraiture of the ten images that the God of Love does not like [fol. 2r–v, 3r–v]). Also, like certain of the rubrics in MS *Lw*, the citation of Aristotle's *Ethics* in turn implies a critique of that pleasure-oriented value system, in stating that the advice of reason is always for the best. Along with the reference to Aristotle, the glosser added a couplet that appears in *Rose* manuscripts of the *B* family (see Chapter 4), stressing Reason's helpfulness: "Car selonc ce qu'elle porroit, / Moult volentiers me secorroit" [for insofar as she was able, she really wanted to help me (follows v. 4198; cf. Appendix B, 1, vv. 5–6)]. Moreover, the line chosen from the *Ethics* comes from a section in which Aristotle states that the power of the rational faculty is such that it can assert itself even in sleep, whereby the dreams of the virtuous are better than those of other people. Had the Lover only been strong enough, in other words, he could have listened to the voice of Reason even within his dream: the fact that he was asleep might explain his headstrong pursuit of erotic fulfillment, but does not in the end excuse it.

---

[6] Wetherbee proposes an ironic reading of Jean's juxtaposition of Guillaume de Lorris with the Latin poets, arguing that Jean, although clearly interested in a vernacular engagement with the Latin tradition, means to point out the incongruity between the *auctores* and courtly literature; see *Chaucer and the Poets*, p. 62.

The citation of Aristotle's *Physics* is interesting in the light of the earlier allusion to the "natural philosophy and mathematical science" in Macrobius. The glossator responds to Guillaume's question about the nature of the fleeting present moment, meeting-point of past and future:

> l'en ne puet neïs penser
> quel tens ce est qui est presenz,
> sel demandez a clers lisanz. (vv. 368–70)

> one cannot even imagine what time it is that is present; so ask learned clerks about it.

The glossator accordingly notes that the answer can be found in the *Physics*, where indeed Aristotle does address the question of whether or not the present can be said to exist and determines that it can. Aristotle goes on to define the experience of time's passage as a perception of difference. Interestingly, he uses the example of dreamers who, if they do not remember their dreams, will be unable to distinguish the moment of falling asleep from the moment of waking; the specific dreamers to which he refers are those who sleep in a temple where they can experience prophetic dreams and visions. The dream thus becomes a complex marker of time: at the moment of waking, memory of the dream establishes the difference between present and past, while a recognition of the dream's prophetic message further establishes the difference between present and future, when these events will have been realized. This configuration bears a striking resemblance to that set up in the *Rose*: at the moment of writing, the narrator looks back to a past time, marked by a dream that was itself prophetic, and which, at the hands of Jean de Meun, even comes to incorporate a record of the passage of time between the death of the first author and the birth of his continuator.[7] If indeed the glossator of MS *Me* had a direct knowledge of the *Physics* – and he did at least have enough familiarity to know that the discussion of time is in Book 4 – then he may have seen it as a useful commentary on the complex interplay between past, present, and future within the *Roman de la Rose*.

At some point in the mid fourteenth century, then, MS *Me* was read by someone who had at least a passing knowledge of the classics and an interest in both poetry and philosophy, and who often found cause to think of the classical authors when reading the *Rose*. The reading is sensitive to both ethical and aesthetic concerns. If the glossator saw the Garden of Delight as an allegory for the vanities of earthly life, for example, he

---

[7] On the temporal structure of the *Rose*, see Hult, *Self-Fulfilling Prophecies*, pp. 10–14, 127–60; Baumgartner, "Play of Temporalities" and "Temps linéaire."

nonetheless paused to admire the rhetorical tour de force of its description. And he had a considerable interest in the motif of dream, and in the ethical, temporal, and hermeneutic issues raised by this story of a prophetic erotic dream. The citation of the Bible in the midst of pagan writers need not surprise: it is a reflection of the interpenetration of scholasticism and humanism in the fourteenth century. Indeed, Nicholas of Lyra's commentary on Ecclesiastes, roughly contemporary with the glosses of MS *Me*, cites Aristotle's *Ethics* repeatedly, finding many parallels between the two texts. For the glosser of MS *Me*, the *Rose* is part of a learned textual network, and a reading of the *Rose* provides the occasion for a mental journey through numerous other texts. The fact that it is written in the vernacular poses no obstacle to its being studied in this way; indeed, equipped with its glosses, it begins to take on the appearance of a vernacular florilegium of the *auctores*. I will return to this point below; but first, let us examine the glosses in a second manuscript, Bibl. de l'Arsenal MS 3337. This set of glosses, somewhat different in nature, will expand our picture of *Rose* readership in the late fourteenth century.

A colophon, cited in the previous chapter, tells us that MS 3337 was copied at the castle of Sully-sur-Loire in 1390. It appears in an inventory of the library of Charles d'Albret, seneschal of France, that was drawn up in 1409.[8] It is possible that it was made for Charles's wife, Marie de Sully, from whom he acquired many of the books in his library. Here, then, the *Rose* is found in aristocratic rather than clerical circles. Aside from the psalter and breviary, the library inventory in which it appears lists only vernacular texts, such as the *Pelerinage* cycle of Guillaume de Deguilleville, the *Faits des Romains*, Christine de Pizan's *Avision*, a chansonnier, *La Dame a la licorne*, and the *Roman de Rou*. Even the Bible was in French translation. Not surprisingly, the glosses in this *Rose* manuscript, though entirely in Latin, reflect a less erudite background than those of MS *Me*. One set of twenty-eight glosses, entered by the scribe, consists mainly of proverbial sayings, with the occasional citation of Ovid. A second set of sixty entries consists almost entirely of citations of Ovid's *Ars amatoria*, sometimes rather extensive.[9] Finally, six more proverbial sayings are entered in a third hand.

---

[8] Stein, "La Bibliothèque du connétable d'Albret à Sully-sur-Loire (1409)." The manuscript is described by Langlois, *Manuscrits*, p. 76–77.

[9] Only three of the glosses entered by the second hand are not from the *Ars amatoria*: a line from Ovid's *Ex Ponto* (3, 1: 158; at vv. 7426–29); four lines of Latin verse concerning Daedalus and Icarus (at vv. 5199–203), printed in Langlois's description of the manuscript (p. 76); and a variant of a gloss found in Michel Alès' *Rose*, "Dum tempus affuerit monstra te esse virum" (at vv. 7661–62), which the glosser attributes to Ovid, but which appears to be a variant of *Pamphilus*, v. 546.

The scribal glosses appear in the margins, embellished with rectangular frames. It is quite unusual to find Latin glosses entered by the scribe in a fourteenth-century vernacular manuscript. The *Rose* of Michel Alès is a special case, since here the scribe was also the owner and reader of the book. But nothing suggests that the scribe of MS 3337 was preparing a book for his own use. The glosses may derive from the scribe's model; in any case, they were seen as a critical apparatus that, like rubrics or the commentaries often attached to Latin works, was an integral part of the text. This is, after all, the same scribe who stated in his colophon that the *Rose* contains much "noble science."

Interestingly, the glosses of the two main hands are clustered almost entirely in the teachings of the God of Love in Guillaume's section of the poem and in Jean's discourse of Ami, with only a few glosses turning up in the discourse of Reason, the discourse of La Vieille, and at occasional other points.[10] The noble science found in the *Rose* would seem to be largely one of love and seduction; one is reminded of the colophon in MS *Eb*, cited in the previous chapter, identifying its owner as one devoted to the "game" depicted in the *Rose*. The scribe does gloss certain standard tenets of medieval proverbs, such as the virtues of discretion:

> Gravis est culpa tacenda loqui.

It is a grave fault to speak that which should remain silent.

(Ars amatoria, 2:604; vv. 2075–77)

> Virtutem primam esse puta compescere linguam.

Consider the primary virtue to be holding one's tongue.

(Cato, Distichs, 1:3; vv. 7025–29);

the dangers of wealth:

> Dives divitias non congregat absque labore;
> Non tenet absque metu, non desinit absque dolore.

The rich man does not amass riches without labor; he does not keep them without fear or give them up without sorrow.   (vv. 5166–72);

and the blessings of friendship:

> Omni tempore diligit qui amicus est.

A friend remains true at all times.

(vv. 4900–1)

> Verus amicus omni prestantior auro.

A true friend is more valuable than gold.

(vv. 4917–18)

---

[10] The distribution of the glosses corresponds to the distribution of "Nota bene" signs outlined in Chapter 1, with some readers concentrating on the Ovidian teachings of Ami and La Vieille, others on the philosophical and morally edifying sections.

Some of the love teachings are also glossed in such a way as to make them of more general applicability, as in these comments on the virtues of monogamy and the power of erotic persuasion:

> Deficit ambobus qui vult servire duobus.

He fails both who wants to serve two.　　　(Werner, p. 19; vv. 2230–32)

> Qui patitur vincit.

He who endures conquers.　　　　　　　　　　(vv. 2613 and 3200)

> Acies in principio in fine frangitur.

What is steel in the beginning breaks in the end.　　　(vv. 3119–20)

Other glosses, however, focus more specifically on love and sexuality, either in the form of proverbial sayings:

> Casta quam nemo rogavit.

A chaste woman is one who has never been asked.　　　(vv. 3883–85)

> Qui plus castigat plus in amore ligat.

The more one chastises (lovers), the more he binds them in love.
　　　　　　　　　　　　　　　　　　　　　　　　(vv. 3988–90);

or by citing an Ovidian source:

> Non bene conveniunt nec in una sede morantur
> Majestas et amor.

Love and majesty do not go well together or remain in one seat.
　　　　　　　　　　　　　(*Metamorphoses* 2:846–47; vv. 1888–92)

> Promittas facito, quid enim promittere ledit?
> Polliciens dives quilibet esse potest.

Make promises, for what harm is in promising? By promising, anyone can be rich.　　　　　　　　　　　　(*Ars amatoria* 1:443–44; vv. 7416–19)

> Ad plures lupa tendit oves predetur ut unam.

The she-wolf draws near many sheep in order to prey on one.
　　　　　　　　　　　　　　(*Ars amatoria* 3:419; vv. 13553–55)

The lines glossed by the scribe, then, represent a mixture of moral sayings and worldly comments on seduction. For Christine de Pizan, this blend of the moral and the amoral made the poem more dangerous, since the unsuspecting reader, reassured by the moral tone of certain parts, would not be on guard against the subversive doctrine expressed elsewhere.[11] But for other readers, this mixture must have constituted, at least in part, the attraction of the *Rose*. The poem was funny, racy, erudite, moral; it depicted both the laudable wisdom and the amusing follies of the human race, and called for mental alertness in its readers.

The other major glossator, as I have said, concentrated almost entirely on tracing the presence of the *Ars amatoria* in the teachings of the God of Love and the discourse of Ami. In these sections, the poem is glossed quite heavily; the person responsible must have known the *Ars amatoria* extremely well, and may even have been comparing the two texts and copying the glosses directly from the source. One might expect such a reader to have similarly glossed the discourse of La Vieille, so much of which derives from Book 3 of the *Ars amatoria*; but, whether through lack of interest or lack of opportunity, this was not done. The two passages in question, however, are revealed to be a virtual florilegium of the first two books of the *Ars amatoria*: a total of sixty-three lines from Book 1 and forty lines from Book 2 appear in the margins of these pages.[12] The glossator even found an opportunity to cite the *Ars* in the discourse of Reason, hardly the most Ovidian portion of the poem. Her allusion to Daedalus inspired him to note in the margin: "Me pinnis sectare datis; ego praevius ibo / Sit tua cura sequi; me duce tutus eris." [Follow me on the wings I give you; I will go first; see that you follow; with me leading, you will be safe (*Ars amatoria*, 2:57–58; vv. 5196–97).] We might say that this reader was one who took seriously the claim that "l'art d'Amors est tote enclose" in the *Roman de la Rose*; he was prepared to find it everywhere. For him, the fascination of the *Rose*, at least in part, lay in decoding its relationship to this particular Latin text.

In the foregoing discussion I have referred more than once to the Latin florilegia. The relationship between the *Rose*, its glosses, and the florilegia bears closer scrutiny. To what extent might the *Rose* have been seen as analogous to the florilegia? In what way might the florilegia reflect – or help

---

[11] Christine states, "Nonobstant ce, je ne reppreuve mie *Le Rommant de la Rose* en toutes pars, car il y a de bonnes choses et bien dictes sans faille. Et de tant est plus gran le peril." [Nonetheless, I do not condemn the *Roman de la Rose* in all parts, for there are certainly things that are good and well said. And the danger is all the greater for it (ed. Hicks, p. 21).]

[12] For example, on fol. 44r alone, we find, in addition to the note "Dum tempus affuerit" (see above, note 9), the following glosses: *Ars* 1: 665–66 (vv. 7652–55); *Ars* 1:673 (vv. 7663–65); *Ars* 1:674 (vv. 7667–78); *Ars* 1:675–78 (vv. 7671–74); *Ars* 1:715–16 (vv. 7677–79); *Ars* 2:197 (vv. 7679–81); *Ars* 2:202 (vv. 7692–93); *Ars* 1:502 (v. 7698); *Ars* 2:201 (vv. 7701–2); *Ars* 2:199 (vv. 7704–5); *Ars* 1:769–70 (vv. 7730–32). For an overview of Jean's use of the *Ars amatoria*, see Bouché, "Ovide et Jean de Meun." Bouché provides a "Table de Concordance" of Jean's borrowings from Ovid (pp. 86–87), which does not always agree with the connections perceived by the reader of MS 3337.

shape – medieval attitudes towards poetry? After all, Jean de Meun, in what must surely have been a gesture towards the Latin encyclopedic tradition, retitled the complete poem "Miroër aus amoureus" (v. 10621); scribes occasionally translated this into Latin, calling the poem "Speculum amantum." Let us examine, then, the nature of medieval literary and philosophical compendia as a context for the reception of the *Rose*.

THE *FLORES AUCTORUM* AND THE *ROMAN DE LA ROSE*

Medieval compendia of Latin poetry and philosophy are of two basic types: those arranged according to author and text, and those arranged according to subject. An example of the former is the *Florilegium gallicum*, which presents excerpts from a series of Latin poets and philosophers.[13] An example of the latter is the *Speculum maius* of Vincent of Beauvais, in which each topic is treated by piecing together passages drawn from poets, historians, philosophers, and theologians. A poetic example of the latter type exists in the thirteenth-century MS Bibl. Nat. lat. 1860, where lines drawn from the Latin poets have been collated under various subject headings.[14]

A florilegium of the first type thus permits access to a given author, providing the reader with a selection of noteworthy lines. Each author is generally identified by means of a rubric, as is the title of each text. Sometimes rubrics also identify important themes within the works of a given author. The lines usually follow one another in the order in which they appear in the original text, though sometimes with slight reordering; passages chosen can range anywhere from one to fifteen or twenty lines. Lines are sometimes doctored to fit them into their new context or to remove objectionable content, such as erotic innuendos or references to pagan deities. Often, the collection is provided with a table of contents. Florilegia vary widely, reflecting individual tastes. For example, the late thirteenth-century MS Bibl. Nat. lat. 15155 has seventeen pages of lines from the *Ars amatoria* (fol. 67v–75v); the late fourteenth- or early fifteenth-century MS Bibl. Nat. lat. 16708, compiled by a Sorbonne master, has only two pages for the *Ars amatoria* (fol. 17r–v).

A compendium of the second type permits the reader to see what a whole range of authors have said about a given subject. Topics are identified by

---

[13] On the *Florilegium gallicum*, see Burton, *Classical Poets in the "Florilegium Gallicum"*; R. Rouse, "Florilegia and Latin Classical Authors in Twelfth- and Thirteenth-Century Orléans." On florilegia in general, see Sanford, "The Use of Classical Latin Authors in the Libri Manuales."

[14] On the florilegium in MS lat. 1860, see R. Rouse and M. Rouse, "The *Florilegium angelicum*."

rubrics and sometimes listed in an alphabetical index; authors and titles are identified either through marginal notations or by means of rubrics embedded in the text. Within each topical unit, lines may be arranged by author, with the lines from each author in turn grouped according to their text of origin; or, as in the case of Vincent of Beauvais, they may be incorporated into the compiler's exposition of his subject.

The florilegia, compendia, and preachers' manuals reflect an approach to canonical texts that is often characterized as typically medieval: texts are mined for moral lessons, wise sayings, examples of rhetorical figures. Of course medieval readers were also capable of appreciating a poem or treatise as a whole, and the existence of manuscripts devoted to the works of a single author, such as Ovid, Virgil, or Aristotle, shows that there was always an interest in compiling the literary or philosophical output of a given writer. But the florilegia, fruits of the medieval study of the Latin canon, do bear witness to a perception of these texts as vehicles for moral or scientific insights, social commentary, and rhetorical technique. In addition to the commentary tradition in which individual texts were studied in their entirety, there was also an impulse to reduce a text to its essentials; to commit to parchment, and memory, its most noteworthy lines; to index and collate the words of the *auctores* in what might be seen as medieval versions of the modern database. Armed with a florilegium of each type described above, a fourteenth-century reader could peruse a poet's most memorable verses and compare that poet's statements on a given subject to the words of other poets. Needless to say, such collections were invaluable tools for students, preachers, and writers.

The *Rose*, with its adaptations of such authors as Cicero, Boethius, Ovid, and Juvenal, could be compared to a vernacularized florilegium. Important texts like the *Ars amatoria*, the *Consolation of Philosophy*, and the *De amicitia* are presented in essence, interspersed with material adapted from other authors. Of course, the *Rose* presents this material in a narrative and dialogic framework. It is not literally a vernacular florilegium, in the manner of Alard de Cambrai's *Dits des sages* or the anonymous *Diz et proverbes des sages*. These works, which also date from the thirteenth century, are compendia of material drawn from the *auctores* and translated into French octosyllabic couplets. Like the Latin florilegia, Alard's *Dits des sages* is arranged according to author in some manuscripts and by subject in others.[15] While such compilations were widely read, surviving in numerous manuscripts, their success does not compare to that of Jean's hybrid

---

[15] See Payen, "Le *Livre de philosophie et de moralité* d'Alart de Cambrai."

text, at once florilegium, philosophical treatise, social satire, and love poem.

We have already seen evidence of selective reading of the *Rose* by its medieval audience: certain sections of the poem favored over others in a given manuscript, certain passages glossed or marked "Nota bene" for future reference. These reading patterns are not difficult to understand if we consider that the *Rose* was perceived in part as a verse compendium, and that its readers had been conditioned, in their approach to poetry, by the florilegium tradition. For readers who perused the Latin poets with an eye to picking out the "best" passages or those relating to a certain theme, and who also studied compilations of verse with an eye to identifying the various authors and works represented there, nothing could be more natural than to read the *Rose* in a similar way, marking pithy lines, noting important topics, and identifying source texts. In fact, the *Rose* was even dissected for use in vernacular compendia of didactic verse: among the many manuscripts of the *Diz et proverbes des sages*, there are four that include lines drawn from the *Rose*.[16] In the fourteenth-century MS Arras, Bibl. Mun. 845, to be discussed in Chapter 6, the *Rose* has been excerpted and expurgated in much the same way that the works of pagan love poets were bowdlerized for inclusion in florilegia. Similar reading habits prevailed in the study of both the Latin authors and the *Rose*, manifested both in marginal annotations and in the preparation of anthologies. Indeed, the process comes full circle in a fourteenth-century manuscript of the *Ars amatoria*, in which the scribe has copied passages from the *Rose*.[17]

Given the number and variety of medieval florilegia, it is difficult to say which one or ones the glossators of *Rose* manuscripts may have used, or even, for that matter, that they used florilegia at all. In the case of MS *Me*, however, the citation of Tibullus is very strong evidence, considering that only one complete manuscript of Tibullus' poetry is known to have existed in the fourteenth century: the manuscript that once belonged to Richard de Fournival, and which passed from him via Gerard d'Abbeville into the Sorbonne library.[18] The authors cited in MS *Me*, moreover, reflect an intellectual milieu very similar to that of surviving florilegia and compendia. The glossator of MS *Me* may have used Vincent of Beauvais as a

---

[16] See Morawski's introduction to his edition of *Les Diz et proverbes des sages (Proverbes as philosophes)*, pp. lx–lxi, lxiii.

[17] See Novati, *Attraverso il medio evo*, pp. 300–02; Badel, *"Roman de la Rose" au XIVe siècle*, pp. 142–43.

[18] On manuscripts of Tibullus, see Ullman as cited above in note 4. The Sorbonne library inventory of 1338 includes an entry for "Epymabaton Albii Tybullii elegoagraphi," identified as having come into the library "ex legato magistri G.": a reference to the legacy of Gerard d'Abbeville. See Delisle, "Bibliothèque de la Sorbonne – XIIIe et XIVe siècle," *Le Cabinet des manuscrits*, vol. 3, p. 68.

source. The line that he cites from Tibullus, for example, appears twice in Vincent's *Speculum doctrinale*.[19] Vincent also cites Book 4 of Aristotle's *Physics* in his discussion of the existence of the present as a point balanced between past and future (*Speculum naturale*, 4:58–71). In the same discussion, Vincent addresses the existence of time as a function of our perception, citing Aristotle's example of sleepers who cannot perceive the passage of time unless they recall their dreams. From the study of the *Speculum naturale*, then, our glossator could have been aware of the *Physics* as providing both a scientific definition of the present and a model for the special role of dream in determining the relationship of past, present, and future.

A poetic florilegium related in spirit to the glosses of MS *Me* is the late thirteenth-century MS Bibl. Nat. lat. 15155, which originally contained some lines from Tibullus.[20] It also contains passages from numerous other poets, including Ovid and Matthew of Vendôme, and from the *Pamphilus*. Among the lines from *Pamphilus* is the couplet cited in MS *Me*, with the marginal gloss: "Nota mulier vul[t] vinci" [Note that a woman wants to be conquered (fol. 16r)]. Nearly ten folios are devoted to passages illustrating rhetorical techniques for the description of places, headed "Bernardi Silvestris, loci descriptio" [Bernardus Silvestris, the description of place (fol. 45v)]; "Mathei Vindocinensis, loci descriptio" [Matthew of Vendôme, description of place (fol. 49v)]; and "Item brevis loci descriptio" [item, brief description of place (fol. 52v)]. If nothing else, we can say that MS lat. 15155 reflects interests similar to those of the glosser of MS *Me*.

But there may be more than just similar tastes involved. MS *Me* and MS lat. 15155 also share two variants for the line from Tibullus that do not coincide in any other known florilegium or in Vincent of Beauvais: 'ledunt' for 'ludunt' and 'mentes' for 'nocte'.[21] It is unlikely that such variants, which significantly alter the sense of the line, would arise independently. Could the glossator of MS *Me* have had access to MS lat. 15155? Though evidently compiled at Orléans, MS lat. 15155 was acquired by a Rouen

---

[19] On Tibullus in Vincent of Beauvais, see Ullman, "Tibullus in the Mediaeval *Florilegia*," pp. 154–58; Richter, *De Vincentii Bellovacensis Excerptis Tibullianis*. The line in question appears in Book 5, chap. 113 (an explication of fear) and Book 6, chap. 73 (on the vanity of material riches). In neither case is the line used in the context in which it appears in MS *Me*, namely the mendacity of dreams.

[20] MS lat. 15155 is missing several gatherings, but all of the missing pages have been found in other manuscripts. See Robathan, "Missing Folios"; and Pellegrin, "Manuscrits de l'abbaye de Saint-Victor et d'anciens collèges de Paris," pp. 74 and 96.

[21] Ullman provides a complete text and variants for the Tibullus passages in four florilegia in "Tibullus in the Mediaeval Florilegia," pp. 135–46. Variants from additional manuscripts are given by Burton, *Classical Poets in the "Florilegium Gallicum"*. Ullman reports on the variants of Tibullus citations in Vincent of Beauvais in the same article, p. 154, and in "Classical Authors in Certain Mediaeval Florilegia," p. 1, n. 1.

master in the mid fourteenth century;[22] MS *Me* was in Rouen by the late fourteenth century, and is probably of Norman origin. Circumstantial evidence thus indicates that the glosser of MS *Me* may have lived in Rouen and that he could have had access to MS lat. 15155 or to a copy made from it after its arrival in Normandy. MS lat. 15155 cannot have been our glossator's sole access to the Latin poets, for it does not include the account of Cupid's bows or the story of Narcissus. But it just may have been his source for the less widely disseminated verses of Tibullus; it could also have contributed to his interest in techniques of description.

The two *Rose* manuscripts we have examined so far have yielded examples of three different kinds of glosses: those that cite various source texts for the doctrine or the poetic techniques of the *Rose*, sometimes with the purpose of filling out a story or a scientific point that the *Rose* leaves incomplete; those that concentrate on identifying the presence of one particular source text throughout the *Rose*; and those that respond to the didactic content of the poem by summarizing its important points in Latin maxims. These are not the only possibilities, however. In order to explore still further the intellectual context in which the *Rose* was read and its relations to other texts, let us turn to a third example, the mid-fourteenth-century MS Bibl. Nat. fr. 24390.

TEXTS AND GLOSS IN MS BIBL. NAT. FR. 24390

The MS Bibl. Nat. fr. 24390 (*Ke*) contains the *Rose*, the *Testament* of Jean de Meun, and a stanzaic poem about death and salvation: a selection that suggests that the *Rose* was here conceived more as a didactic treatise than a tale of seduction. It was glossed by several different hands in the course of the fourteenth century. One hand, however, was responsible for the majority of annotations, and also added hundreds of lines of text, most of it from the late thirteenth-century rewriting of the *Rose* by Gui de Mori (Pl. 5). Gui's remaniement and its presence in MS *Ke* will be discussed in Chapter 3. Here, we will concentrate on the glosses, which are of several kinds.

---

[22] The associations of MS lat. 15155 with Orléans are already strongly suggested by its contents; in addition, a note in a mid-fourteenth-century hand on the last page reads, "Henricus Francisci Aurelianus vendidit h[. . .]. Henricus Ulid' de Rotomago emit" [Henri François of Orléans sold [this book]; Henri Ulid' of Rouen bought it]. Novati feels that the manuscript could not have gone to Rouen in the mid fourteenth century because of its acquisition, not too much later, by the abbey of Saint Victor; he transcribes the name of the buyer as "Henricus Vlid' Ceretomago," but admits that the 'Ce' is conjectural. See "Un Poème inconnu de Gautier de Châtillon," p. 267, n. 3. R. Rouse, however, accepts that the manuscript was purchased by "a Rouen master" in "Florilegia and Latin Classical Authors," p. 155.

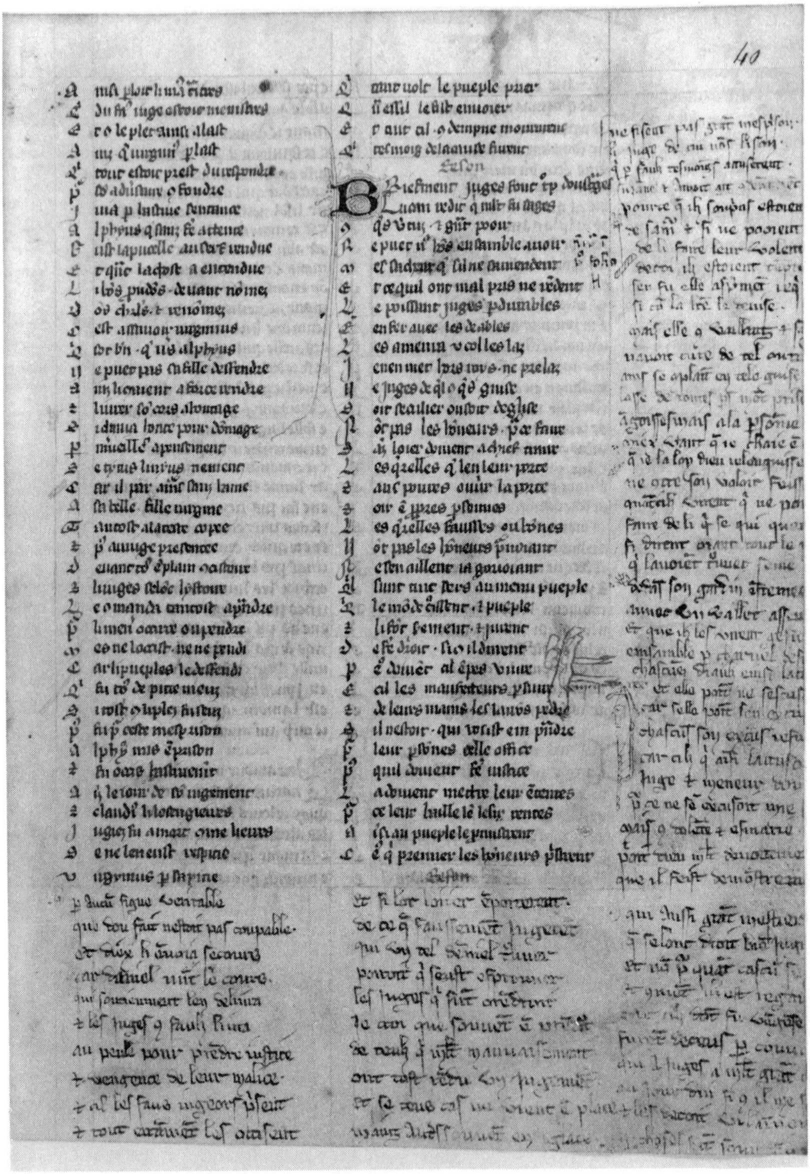

Plate 5 Manuscript page showing the text of the Susannah interpolation from the remaniement of Gui de Mori added in the margins, around a gloss citing the *Decretum* (*xxiii. q.v. rex*), now partially obscured by a crude doodle. Paris, Bibliothèque Nationale MS fr. 24390, fol. 40r.

The more minor hands are easily fit into categories we have already seen. One, for example, appears only on fol. 51r–53r (vv. 7379–7665), and, aside from the citation of *Pamphilus* that also appeared in MS *Me*, cites only the *Ars amatoria*.[23] Two others are limited almost entirely to the restoration of short passages (often a single couplet) originally omitted from the text, along with the occasional proverb or didactic couplet in French or Latin. One of these hands also cites Seneca during Ami's discussion of gift-giving, noting "Maledictum munus in quo dolus accipientis agnoscitur: Seneca, *De beneficiis*" [A cursed gift in which the guile of the receiver is known (variant of closing line of *De beneficiis*, 1:11)] at v. 8209 (fol. 56r). The use of the word 'dolus' [guile] is interesting: the standard text here reads 'vitium' [weakness, fault]. It is possible that the glosser either knew the text in a variant form, or misremembered the line. But one cannot help suspecting that he deliberately changed the wording in reference to the belief, elaborated at some length in the *Rose*, that women guilefully manipulate men's desire for sex in order to extract as many gifts as possible. Seneca had advised discretion in gift-giving, in order not to call attention to some fault in the recipient; the glosser of MS *Ke* notes that since the gift-giving recommended by Ami is nothing short of bribery, it cannot help but reflect on the wiles of those who solicit it.

The main glossator was much more prolific than any of the others; here I can cite only selected examples of his work. His hand appears not only throughout the *Rose*, but also in the *Testament* and the moral poem. Some of his annotations serve to mark important themes of the poem, such as: "De judice qui deberet suspendi" [Concerning the judge who deserved to be hanged (fol. 39v, across the top of the column containing vv. 5546–84)]; "Mulier est socia viri et par" [Woman is the companion and the helpmate (*or*: the equal) of man (at the top of fol. 63v, cued to v. 9397)]; "De principio regum et principum" [Concerning the beginning of kings and princes (fol. 65r, v. 9600)]; "De astronomia" [Concerning astronomy (fol. 117r, v. 17666)]. The assertion of companionship between the sexes on fol. 63r did not prevent the same reader from also noting, at La Vieille's characterization of feminine generosity as self-interested manipulation of men, "Natura mulieris" [The nature of woman (fol. 96v, vv. 14405–6)].

Other glosses fall into the category of proverbs or proverbial sayings, in both French and Latin:

---

[23] Besides the lines from *Pamphilus*, this glosser provided the following references: *Ars* 3:93, 90 (fol. 51r, vv. 7379–81); *Ars* 1:443–44 (v. 7415); *Ars* 1:633 (now mostly effaced [vv. 7419–20]); *Ars* 1:345 (fol. 52r, vv. 7547–49); *Ars* 1:389–90 (now mostly effaced [vv. 7573–74]); *Ars* 1:151 (fol. 53r, v. 7754).

> Temptalus in Stigiis nec aqua utitur neque pomo;
> Sic in divitiis eget avarus homo.[24]

Tantalus, in the Styx, has use of neither water nor apple; thus an avaricious man suffers in his wealth.

(fol. 126v, vv. 19252–56)

> Femina dum plorat, lacrimarum fraude laborat.[25]

When a woman weeps, she labors with fraudulent tears.

(fol. 90r, vv. 13351–54)

> Courtoisie de bouche assez vault et po coute.[26]

Courteous speech is worth much and costs little.

(fol. 110v, v. 16631)

Sometimes entire quatrains or sestets appear in the margins, and it can be difficult to know whether they were added as glosses or as insertions into the text. Perhaps this distinction would not have been meaningful to a fourteenth-century reader. As I said, the glossator did add numerous passages from Gui de Mori's reworking of the *Rose* (without, however, identifying them as such), some copied on the opening and closing flyleaves with cues indicating where they are to be inserted, and some written in the margins. For example, the following lines from Gui appear in the margin, cued to v. 4712:

> Que tant que li uns ait po[oir],
> Ne puet l'autre en grie[té voir],
> Que lues enns lui tant ne f[ace]
> Que sa mesaise li efface.

(fol. 34r)

As long as one of them has any power, he cannot abide seeing the other in need without doing whatever it takes to remove his suffering.

Since these lines can be found in a version of the *Rose* it seems safe to assume that they were intended as an addition to the text. But what about the following lines, cued to v. 4882:

> [Quant un]s hautz hons a nient vient,
> [Nullui] de lui ne souvient;
> [Et quant] Fortune l'a haut mis,
> [Chascun] vuet estre ses amis.

(fol. 35v)

When a powerful man comes to nothing, no one remembers him; and when Fortune has set him on high, everyone wants to be his friend.

---

[24] See Walther, ed., *Proverbia Sententiaeque Latinitatis Medii Aevi*, no. 31043.

[25] This line appears in a collection of sententiae titled "Contemptus mundi" in MS lat. 15155 (fol. 151r). Similar dicta circulated widely during the Middle Ages; cf., for example, "Femina dum plorat, hominem superare laborat" in the distichs of Cato (ed. Baehrens, 3:20). Lecoy gives several references in his note to vv. 13345–54.

[26] This saying is a variant of one found in Hassell, *Middle French Proverbs, Sentences, and Proverbial Phrases*: "Honnêteté de bouche petit couste et vault plenté" (H 57).

This quatrain does not appear in any version of the *Rose* that I have seen; nor was it invented by the glossator of MS *Ke*, for it appears in five manuscripts of the *Diz et proverbes des sages*.[27] Yet this need not prevent the glossator from seeing it as an appropriate addition to the *Rose*. After all, passages from the *Rose* were extracted and added to the *Diz et proverbes*, so why not the other way around?[28] With any manuscript text, and especially one that has the aspect of a compendium, the contours are never really fixed, and the boundary between text and gloss is never well defined. A similar question arises with this set of verses, cued to v. 14461: though the text is not in octosyllables, the glossator does seem to have adopted the voice of La Vieille:

> Je n'aimme pas celui
> Qui m'aimme en bonne foy,
> Tant que je fais celui
> Qui n'a cure de moy;
> Et aimme bien celui. (fol. 96v)

I do not love the one who truly loves me, as much as I do the one who doesn't care for me; and I really love him.

Like Michel Alès reacting to Genius' little domestic comedy, the glossator of MS *Ke* evidently became so caught up in the *Rose* that he could not resist entering into its dialectics.

The foregoing annotations, though certainly very interesting, are not qualitatively different from what we have already seen in other manuscripts. Other glosses in MS *Ke* are more unusual. For example, the glossator sometimes noted instances where the same motif appears in more than one place. Reason's discussion of the regrets caused by the vow of chastity reminded him of the similar discussion in the discourse of La Vieille. Accordingly, at the passage "la vit a grant mesese et pleure / la franchise qu'il a perdue" [there he lives in great discomfort and weeps for the freedom he has lost (vv. 4426–27, fol. 32v)] he placed the note, "Infra, la vieille, viii folio" [Below, La Vieille, eighth folio]. If we consider that the discourse of La Vieille begins at v. 12710 (fol. 86r), then the eighth folio of her discourse would be fol. 93. And it is on fol. 93v that we find her discussion of the vow of chastity, including a verbal echo of Reason: La Vieille's monk longs to recover "la franchise qu'il a perdue" [the freedom he has lost (v. 13945)]. Similarly, during Ami's discussion of poverty, the

---

[27] See Morawski, ed., *Diz et proverbes*, "Quatrains apocryphes," no. 103.
[28] In fact, a passage from the *Diz et proverbes* does appear among the excerpts of the *Rose* arranged in MS Arras, Bibl. Mun. 845, where it is fully integrated into the *Rose* text; see my discussion below, Chapter 6.

glossator refers to the related discussion in the discourse of Richesse, noting "Infra de richesce etc., Se" [Below, concerning Richesse etc., at "Se" (fol. 64v, vv. 9512–13)]. In effect, if we turn ahead to the discourse of Richesse, we find a mark placed at v. 10107 (fol. 68r), "Se Povreté vos eut baillier" [If Poverty can get you]. Again, the association is based on more than just a general topic. It is in v. 9512 that Ami introduces the personification of Larceny, son of Poverty; and v. 10107 is the beginning of a passage in which Richesse explains that Poverty hired Hunger as wetnurse for Larceny. As we will see, this reader was interested in law and justice; small wonder, then, that he noted this allusion to the relationship between poverty and crime.[29] His interest in legal and social issues is further reflected in his notation of the two passages where Faux Samblant is named *roi des ribaus*, the title of an officer in charge of regulating such matters as prostitution: at the line "Je te feré roy des ribaus" [I will make you king of ribalds (fol. 73v, v. 10903)] is the gloss, "Infra vii folio" [Below, seven folios (refers to fol. 81r, v. 11954)].

Our glossator was also interested in the *Rose* as a poem about love and sexuality. We have seen that he noted the allusions to the difficulties caused by the vow of chastity; and like Michel Alès he seems to have been attracted by both the denigration of marriage and the praise of amorous dalliance. With regard to marriage, for example, he added a six-line passage in the margins of the Jaloux, asserting the inevitability of cuckoldry (fol. 61v; v. 9101). Just before the discourse of the Jaloux, he noted the Ovidian source for the incompatibility of love and mastery, "Non bene conveniunt nec in una sede morantur / Amor et majestas" [Love and majesty do not go well together or remain in one seat (*Metamorphoses* 2:846–47)], at the lines "qu'onques amor et seigneurie / ne s'entrefirent compaignie" [never have love and mastery kept company (fol. 57r, vv. 8421–22)]. He then added the gloss, "Infra Amis" [Below, Ami]. In fact, the next time the rubric "Amis" appears is at the end of the discourse of the Jaloux, at v. 9391 (fol. 63v). We

---

[29] Medieval readers of the *Rose* – especially clerical readers – found it necessary to distinguish carefully between Holy Poverty, whose virtue could not be questioned, and the involuntary abject poverty that the text consistently holds up as negative. Gui de Mori's discomfort with the values assigned to Wealth and Poverty is clear from his reworking of the descriptions of Richesse and Povreté in Guillaume de Lorris: he inserts a complaint about the lack of regard for the poor into the latter, and a strongly worded criticism of the arrogance and spiritual bankruptcy of the wealthy into the former. Gui's remaniement will be discussed in Chapter 3. Evrart de Conty, in his early fifteenth-century commentary on the *Echecs amoureux*, specifies that the form of poverty criticized in the *Echecs* and the *Rose* is "la premiere maniere de povreté que j'ay devant miserable appellee" [the first kind of poverty, which I previously called "miserable" (Bibl. Nat. fr. 9197, fol. 275r)]. He further explains that this form of poverty can be considered among the vices because "miserable poverty" is conducive to criminal behavior. Evidently a similar interpretation prompted the annotations of MS *Ke* on this subject. On Evrart and his commentary, see Guichard-Tesson, "La *Glose des Echecs amoureux*."

recall that this page is headed with a gloss proclaiming companionship between man and woman in a Latin paraphrase of v. 9397. There is also a mark at the lines, "ja de sa fame n'iert amez / qui sires veust estre clamez" [he who wishes to be called "lord" will never be loved by his wife (vv. 9407–8)] and a series of flourishes marking vv. 9406–24. At v. 9400, the glosser wrote, "Qu'a bon droit doit cilz estre cous / Qui de sa fame est jalous" [for he who is jealous of his wife rightly deserves to be a cuckold]. The glossator was clearly attracted by Ami's ideal of extra-marital love, free of jealousy and constraint. For a clerical reader of the *Rose* – as our glossator surely was – attuned to the hardships of enforced celibacy, this idealization of erotic love outside of marriage, and the rather cavalier attitude toward the rights of the husband, could be an attractive fantasy.

One other comment on the text deserves mention because it indicates that the glossator of MS *Ke* was a serious student of the *Rose*. Just before the God of Love's teachings, Guillaume's narrator intervenes to comment on the poem's presentation of the rules of love:

> Bien les devise cist romanz;
> qui amer veut, or i entende,
> que li romanz des or amende.
> Des or le fet bon escouter,
> s'il est qui le sache conter,
> car la fin dou songe est mout bele
> et la matire en est novele. (vv. 2058–64)

This romance lays them out well; he who wants to love, now let him listen to it, for from here on out the romance improves. From now on it is good to listen to, for one who knows how to tell it, for the end of the dream is very beautiful, and its matter is new.

The passage is almost the same in MS *Ke*, with an important difference typical of this manuscript family: v. 2063 reads "livre" [book] for "songe" [dream]. The same variant appears in v. 2065. Struck by this comment on the nature of the poem, the glossator entered two comments: "Roman vocatur" [It is called 'romance'] cued to v. 2058, and "Liber vocatur" [It is called 'book'], cued to v. 2063. For our fourteenth-century reader, the distinction between "book" and "romance" was significant. To call the poem a book was to stress its learned qualities, its ties with the Latin tradition. Sensitive to the complexities of the *Rose*, interested both in its love intrigue and in its philosophical teachings, our glossator noticed this statement of the poem's dual nature, at once "roman" and "livre."

Before closing this discussion of the annotations of Ms *Ke*, there remains to examine one more set of glosses: a series of citations of Gratian's

Decretum, which extend throughout the *Rose*, the *Testament*, and the moral poem.[30] These glosses may have been entered by the same hand that was responsible for most of the other annotations in the manuscript.[31] Whoever wrote them knew both the *Decretum* and its commentary very well. Indeed, the glosses frequently make more sense if we assume that the reference includes not only the cited passage of the *Decretum*, but also the corresponding section in the gloss of Bartholomew of Brescia, which commonly accompanies the *Decretum* in the fourteenth century.[32] The glosses reflect an understanding of both the *Rose* and the *Decretum* as compendia, from which notable sayings can be extracted and appreciated in isolation from their context.

The glosses are by no means limited to what we would normally think of as points of canon law. They appear throughout the *Rose* and touch on all manner of topics. Sometimes the glossator made a straightforward association between the text of the *Rose* and that of the *Decretum*. During Reason's discussion of the duties of judges, for example, at the line "et cil les malfaiteurs [doivent] parsivre" [and they [must] pursue evil-doers (fol. 40r, v. 5654)], he placed a reference to Causa 23, q. 5, c. 40, which lists the law-enforcement responsibilities of kings: "Rex debet furta cohibere, adulteria punire, inpios de terra perdere . . . " [The king should suppress thieves, punish adulterers, drive the impious from the land]. In Genius' account of the fall of the Golden Age and the advent of the four seasons, at the couplet "estez, printans, autompne, ivers, / ce sunt li .iiii. tans divers" [summer, spring, fall, winter, these are the four seasons (fol. 132r, vv. 20163–64)], he cited Distinctio 76, c. 1, which explains the Church policy of fasting four times a year. And in Ami's account of the origins of private property at the end of the Golden Age, at the passage "que ce qui commun iert devant / conme le soleill et le vant / par covoitise aproprierent" [that which had formerly been communal, like the sun and the wind, they appropriated in greed (vv. 9629–31)], he entered a citation of Causa 12, q. 1, c. 2, which concerns the need for clerics to live communally without private

---

[30] I am grateful to Richard Rouse of the University of California, Los Angeles, for his assistance in identifying the citations of the *Decretum*.

[31] Since the Decretal glosses are largely in the form of numerals, it is difficult to be sure whether or not they are by the same hand responsible for the other glosses. In one instance, however, it is clear that the Decretal gloss pre-existed the addition of a passage from Gui de Mori, for the text has been transcribed in such a way as to leave space around the gloss (fol. 40r; see Pl. 5). If the main annotator of MS *Ke* did not enter the Decretal glosses, he nonetheless encountered them in his reading of the *Rose*.

[32] I have consulted the *Decretum* in the standard edition, *Corpus Iuris Canonici*, ed. Richter and Friedberg. In addition, I consulted the *Decretum* with the commentary by Bartholomew of Brescia in MS Bibl. Nat. lat. 3893, which was copied in Paris in 1314. For a general discussion of the development of the glosses on the *Decretum*, see Von Schulte, "Die Glosse zum Decret Gratians."

property. This gloss must have been motivated in particular by Gratian's citation of Plato on the communality of sun and wind: "Et sicut non potest, inquit, dividi aer, neque splendor solis" [and thus, he said, neither the air nor the sun's spendor can be divided up].

In other cases, the relationship between the *Rose* and the *Decretum* is less immediately obvious, turning on an idea that may not even be the main point of the *Decretum* passage. Faux Samblant, for example, mentions in passing that the members of the laity can often be holy:

> Il ne s'ensuit mie
> que cil maignent mauvese vie
> ne que por ce leur ames perdent
> qui aus dras du siecle s'aherdent.   (vv. 11061–64)

It does not follow that those who wear secular robes lead a bad life, or that they lose their souls thereby.

At v. 11064 (fol. 74v), the glosser placed a citation of Causa 22, q. 4, c. 23. This section of the *Decretum* is devoted to the problem of perjury in false or forced oaths, with a distinction between false oaths that the swearer knows to be false and those that he or she believes to be true. This may not seem particularly germane to the *Rose* passage in question, though the issue of perjury is relevant to Faux Samblant. But when the *Decretum* discussion turns to those forced against their will to take monastic vows, it refers to the fact that such vows are not actually necessary for personal holiness, since "nonnulli in laicali habitu sanctissimi et Deo delecti inveniantur" [plenty of very holy people, beloved of God, are found in secular habits]. The *Rose* gloss is now clear: we are reminded that the consciously fraudulent swearing of monastic vows, as exemplified by Faux Samblant, is indeed a serious offense; while moral integrity, whether or not accompanied by vows and monastic status, is always a virtue. We find an even more oblique use of the *Decretum* in a gloss appearing in Nature's discussion of inherited nobility, where it is noted that we should be neither praised nor blamed for the actions of our ancestors. At the line, "par vertu de persone estrange" [by virtue of some other person (fol. 123v, v. 18778)], is a citation of Distinctio 56. This section considers the legality of ordaining the illegitimate sons of priests. The discussion includes a citation of John Chrystostom: "Nunquam de viciis erubescamus parentum" [let us never blush for the misdeeds of our parents]. This more general point, rather than the specific question of ordination, clearly motivated the *Rose* gloss.

At times, the glosser even made his association on the basis of verbal parallels between the *Rose* and the *Decretum*. Genius' lengthy discussion of the need to withhold secrets from one's wife, for example, includes the dictum, "Mes parole une foiz volee / ne peut puis estre rapelee" [But speech once having flown off cannot be recalled (vv. 16515–16)]. These lines are glossed with a reference to Distinctio 43, c. 5, which addresses the responsibility of the priest to spread the word of God, while nonetheless withholding more subtle sacred mysteries from the uneducated. The issue of priestly speech and silence does relate, albeit tangentially, to the problem of communication between husband and wife. But what surely motivated the gloss is the particular wording of the condemnation of priestly indiscretion, the result of incautious loquaciousness "dum sine iudicio volat irrevocabile verbum" [when without judgment the unrecallable word flies out]. The verbal parallel with the *Rose* is strengthened in Bartholomew of Brescia's gloss on the term "irrevocabile verbum" (MS Bibl. Nat. lat. 3893, fol. 42v). He cites Horace: "Nam semel emissum manet irrevocabile verbum" [for once it is sent out, speech remains unrecallable (var. of Epistle 1, 18:71)] and, attributing it to Ovid, "Nescit vox missa reverti" [a voice having been sent forth is unable to return (Horace, *Ars poetica*, v. 390)]. A further line, "Vox semel emissa irreditura volat" [a voice once having been sent forth flies off, never to return] is also apparently attributed to Ovid, though I have found no trace of it in the Ovidian corpus. This thorough glossing of the irrevocability of speech is hardly necessary for an understanding of the doctrinal issue in question; indeed one might well question the authority of Horace and Ovid for a point of canon law. But the relevance of both the *Decretum* and its gloss for Genius' warning about "parole une foiz volee" that cannot be "rapelee" is indisputable.

This last example suggests that the person responsible for the glosses in MS *Ke* knew the *Decretum* and its commentary as a unit, without necessarily distinguishing between them when he cited a particular passage. Such an attitude recalls the earlier problem of how to tell whether lines written in the margins of the *Rose*, possibly by this very person, are intended as additions to the text or as commentary upon it. As I suggested, a fourteenth-century reader might not consider this an important distinction. One can find examples in other manuscripts where material that normally appears in the form of glosses has been absorbed into the text. To give but a single example: we have seen that citations of the *Ars amatoria* frequently gloss the discourse of Ami. In MS *He*, a common Ovidian gloss about the usefulness of promises has become a couplet within the text: "Ovides en sen art adjouste, / Proumettres vaut et nient ne couste" [Ovid in his *Art* adds that promising is useful and costs nothing (fol. 60v, following v. 7418)]. One can assume that the copyist of this manuscript or its ancestor found a citation of the *Ars amatoria* at this point in his model, and decided to incorporate it into the text.

Let us return to the glosses of MS *Ke*. In some cases, the glosses barely even make sense unless understood as referring to the commentary on the passage cited. In a discussion of evil, for example, Reason asserts that "li mauvès ne sunt pas home" [evil-doers are not human (v. 6292)]. The gloss (fol. 44r) cites Causa 7, q. 1, c. 5, a discussion of what to do when someone is ordained bishop without the prior death or dismissal of his predecessor. Of the would-be second bishop, the *Decretum* concludes that "non secundus ille, sed nullus est" [he is not a second (bishop), but rather nothing at all]. The relevance of this passage to the *Rose* becomes clear when we consult Bartholomew's gloss on "nullus"; here we are told "quod nullus est qui malus est" [because he who is evil is nothing (MS lat. 3893, fol. 161v)]. This lack of reality in evil was clearly an idea that appealed to the principal glosser of MS *Ke*, for he bracketed the formulation of that point in vv. 6265–68 and noted in the margin, "desit ad male faciendum etc." [is lacking for evil-doing etc. (fol. 44r)].

An even more clear-cut example of a citation based on Bartholomew of Brescia's commentary appears in the glossing of La Vieille's dismissal of the false oaths of lovers, "Dex se rit de tel serement" [God laughs at such an oath (v. 13095). Two glosses appear here, badly faded, but probably both by the same hand. One cites the Ovidian source of the line, "Jupiter ex altis periuria ridet amantum" [Jupiter from on high smiles on the perjuries of lovers (*Ars amatoria* 1:633)]. The other is a citation of Distinctio 86, c. 4, in which it is stated that doctrinal authority derives from the sacred scriptures, not from secular literature. The force of this point as a condemnation of La Vieille's Ovidian insouciance is established by Bartholomew's gloss, presumably meant to illustrate the dangers of taking one's moral guidance from the pagan poets: "Jupiter ex alto periuria ridet amantum" (MS lat. 3893, fol. 82r). Our glossator's familiarity with Bartholomew of Brescia, as well as his interest in the Latin poets, is proven by the fact that he would choose this passage to gloss La Vieille's words and not the seemingly more appropriate passage on perjury.

It is clear that, for this reader, the *Decretum* and its commentary formed a vast repertoire of knowledge, any individual part of which could be called upon for the confirmation or elucidation of otheɪ texts. Just as other readers may have relied on Vincent of Beauvais or on florilegia for their knowledge of Latin authors, so the glossator of MS *Ke* drew much of his knowledge from the *Decretum*: his concept of scriptural and patristic texts was derived from this conveniently accessible compendium. When Faux

Samblant states, "Et oncor devroit il tout vendre / et du labeur sa vie prendre" [and he should sell everything, and earn his living from labor (vv. 11298–99)], the gloss cites not the Gospel but the citation of the Gospel in Causa 14, q. 1: "Ait enim Dominus in evangelio: 'si uis perfectus esse, uade, et uende omnia, que habes, et da pauperibus.'" [For the Lord said in the Gospel: "If you want to be perfect, go, and sell all that you have, and give to the poor".] Similarly, when Faux Samblant alludes to Saint Paul's refusal to accept alms, the gloss refers not to the Bible but to the citation of the Biblical text in Causa 10, q. 3, c. 7. And in Nature's discussion of predestination and free will, the glossator identifies one of the arguments she offers as that of Augustine (fol. 114v, v. 17322). But the text that he then cites is once again not Augustine, but Causa 23, q. 4, c. 22, in which Augustine is quoted on the issue of predestination.[33]

To the modern reader, the idea of linking the *Rose* and the *Decretum* may seem strange; but for a fourteenth-century reader there was nothing strange about seeking points of contact between poetry, philosophy, theology, law. Even the study of love psychology could have its juridical side: a fourteenth-century manuscript of Andreas Capellanus' *De amore* has a series of glosses citing the *Codex Justinianus* and the *Digest*.[34] The glossator of MS *Me* cited Tibullus and Solomon as parallel authorities on the dangers of dreams; Nicholas of Lyra conjoined Ecclesiastes and Aristotle's *Ethics*; canon law itself is glossed with reference to pagan poets and philosophers. The study of the *Rose* participates in the same intellectual context that produced these other commentaries; its glosses, though sparse in comparison with those devised for Latin texts, are eloquent testimony to the importance of the *Rose*, a vernacular poem worthy of learned study.

In MS *Ke*, the *Rose* is expanded with expository passages from Gui de Mori, treating the importance of discretion, the nature of friendship, and the exercise of justice. Its didactic import is further elaborated through the medium of other texts that are brought to bear on it. These tend to be themselves compendia: proverb collections, the *Diz et proverbes*, the *Decretum*. For the readers of MS *Ke* – at least one of them certainly a *clerc* – the *Rose* takes its place among the Latin and vernacular compendia, all of which are linked through an intertextual network of shared ideas and shared text. The *Rose* found its way into the *Diz et proverbes*, which in turn

---

[33] Much of the material concerning Augustine's beliefs about free will actually occurs in c. 23; in medieval manuscripts, however, this section was often treated as part of c. 22.

[34] The manuscript is Bibl. Nat. lat. 8758. See Roy, "A la recherche des lecteurs médiévaux du *De amore* d'André le Chapelain," pp. 57–58. Since the glosses are in the hand of the scribe, Roy concludes that the manuscript was copied and studied by a man of law, and cites additional evidence for the circulation of the *De amore* in juridical circles.

found its way into the *Rose*; a line from Ovid, frequently found in florilegia, can gloss both the *Rose* and the *Decretum*; the *Decretum* itself can gloss the *Rose*, sometimes just by providing an alternate citation of the same text cited by the *Rose*. Text and gloss merge because both are an assemblage of references to other texts, grouped around some common theme. It is in MS *Ke* that the *Rose* is introduced as "un mout soutif et gai roman" [a very subtle and gay romance] containing "mainte soutive parole" [many subtle sayings (rubric, fol. 1r)]. During the fourteenth century the manuscript passed through the hands of various readers who appreciated the *Rose* both as an exposition of erotic love, and as an erudite and morally edifying treatise; and for whom the identification and exposition of its "soutive parole," and the discovery of parallel "parole" in other texts, were chief among the pleasures offered by a reading of the *Rose*.

THE MS DIJON, BIBL. MUN. 525: AN ANTHOLOGY BUILT ON THE *ROSE*

So far, we have seen examples in which the *Rose* is placed largely or exclusively in the context of Latin texts. In the present example, we find it in the company of mostly vernacular texts, though many of these are translations from the Latin. The scribe responsible for compiling the anthology certainly knew Latin, for he included the letters of Abelard and Heloise in his collection, and many of his marginal annotations are in Latin as well. But his interest was in compiling an anthology of vernacular texts and vernacularizations of Latin texts; had he known of Jean's translation of the correspondence of Abelard and Heloise, he would probably have used it instead of the Latin originals.[35] The *Rose*, a stunning example of vernacularization, is an appropriate starting point for such a collection.

The MS Dijon Bibl. Mun. 525 (*Dij*) was compiled during the 1350s and early 1360s by the scribe Mathias Rivalli, who left three colophons in the course of the collection.[36] From these we know that in 1361 he was working at the Parisian residence of the bishop of Amiens, Jean de Cherchemont (1325–73), and that he built the collection up over a period of several years. A colophon appearing after the *Roman de Fauvel* is dated 1355; the next one, entered after the letters of Abelard and Heloise, is dated 1361; the last one, after the *Consolation of Philosophy*, is dated 1362. The fact that

---

[35] Jean's translation of the *Historia calamitatum* seems not to have circulated widely, for it survives in only one manuscript. See Monfrin's introduction to his edition of the *Historia calamitatum*.

[36] MS *Dij* is described by Langlois, *Manuscrits*, pp. 122–25. Some of the missing pages appear among the fragments gathered together in MS Bibl. Nat. n. a. fr. 20001, where they form fol. 5–15; see Omont, "Notice sur quelques feuilles retrouvées."

Mathias worked on the collection for such a long time, coupled with the presence of numerous marginal annotations in his hand, indicates that it was most likely his own book. His colophon also appears in a copy of the *Histoire ancienne jusqu'a César* (Bibl. Nat. fr. 246) dated 1364, which eventually belonged to Jean, duc de Berry; whether Mathias originally made this book too for himself is unknown.[37]

Mathias began his anthology with a copy of the *Rose* that he acquired ready-made, for this portion of the manuscript is not in his hand. In its original state, the manuscript comprised the *Rose* (fol. 4r–112v) and several short pieces, all strongly antifeminist, that fill out the two folios remaining in the last gathering: the *Epître des femmes* (fol. 113r–v); the *Evangile des femmes* (fol. 113v–114r); a Latin motet (fol. 114); and the Latin *Centilogium magistri Johannis Maduno* (fol. 114r–v), a poem constructed of one hundred words beginning with 'F' and enumerating the many evil traits of women. Most of folio 114v remains blank.

Mathias began his collection with a new gathering; the first round of additions consists of Jean de Meun's *Testament* (fol. 115r–125r); the *Chaton en françoys*, a translation of the Distichs of Cato (fol. 125v–128v); the *Miserere* (fol. 129r–145r) and the *Roman de Charité* (fol. 145r*bis*–158v) of the Reclus de Molliens; and Book 1 of the *Roman de Fauvel* (fol. 158r*bis*–164r). At the end of *Fauvel*, Mathias transcribed a few verse maxims and left his first colophon (1355).

The second round of additions consists of Jean de Meun's *Codicille* (fol. 164r–65r); the *Advocacie Nostre Dame* (fol. 166r–177v; the end is missing); the *Doctrinal sauvage* and *Purgatoire Saint Patrice*, now both missing; the *Evangile de Nicodème*, identified here as *La Passion Nostre Seigneur* (fol. 178r–184v); Jean Ferron's version of the *Jeu des echecs moralisés* (fol. 185r–200v); and the correspondence of Abelard and Heloise, now missing. At this point Mathias left his second colophon (1361).

Finally, in 1362, Mathias added a French version of the *Consolation of Philosophy* (fol. 201r–221r), followed by his last colophon. Interestingly, he used two different translations. He began with the translation in verse and prose sometimes attributed to Jean de Meun; but near the beginning of Book 5, he switched to Jean's prose translation, explaining in a rubric:

---

[37] Mathias left a colophon in MS fr. 246, fol. 306v, identifying himself as "Mathiam Rivalli clericum pictavensem"; he gives the date 1364 and the location "in civitate et in vico novo beate Marie Parisius" [in the *cité* and in the new street of Blessed Mary, Paris]. The street in question, site of numerous booksellers and book-makers, was located near Notre Dame cathedral; possibly Mathias was still employed by the bishop.

Jusques cy souffist par tant come il en appartient aus lais, et depuis ci jusques a la fin
a esté pris de la translation que fist maistre Jehan de Meun, et est trop fort a
entendre, se n'est a gens bien lettrez. (fol. 217r)

This much [of the text] suffices insofar as the laity is concerned, and from here to
the end it has been taken from the translation that Master Jean de Meun made, and
it is very hard to understand, except for well-educated people.

This rubric recalls the notices sometimes found in the discourse of Faux
Samblant, warning against reading that section aloud to uneducated
persons; perhaps Mathias used his book for readings to aristocratic
patrons. It may also be that Jean's was the only translation he could find for
the difficult closing sections of Book 5, or that he considered it the most
reliable one.[38] As we will see, the marginal annotations indicate that
Mathias had a particular interest in Book 5 of the *Consolation of Philosophy*
and that he read it in tandem with the philosophical portions of the *Roman
de la Rose*.

The *Rose* thus provides the starting point for an anthology of didactic
and devotional works. Mathias provided his book with a detailed table of
contents, which facilitates access not only to particular texts, but also to
particular sections of a given text. The *Consolation of Philosophy*, for example,
warrants no less than fifty-three entries in the Table of Contents; the *Roman
de la Rose* is broken into 119 subdivisions. These entries are both thematic
and narrative, as for example:

Comme dame Venus et le dieu d'amours firent le serement. lxxvii
L'aucteur comme Nature euvre. lxxviii
De l'art d'arquemie. lxxviii
Comme Nature parle a Genius son chapellain. lxxix
Genius parle a Nature. lxxx
Comme les mariéz dient leurs secrez a leurs femes. La ou il dit, Mais li
fols. lxxx
Enseignemens pour soy garder des femes. La ou il dit, Beaux
seigneurs. lxxxvi. (fol. 2v)

How lady Venus and the God of Love swore the oath. fol. 77
The narrator, about how Nature works. fol. 78
About the art of alchemy. fol. 78
How Nature speaks to Genius, her chaplain. fol. 79
Genius speaks to Nature. fol. 80

---

[38] The closing sections of Book 5 were considered too difficult for the laity, and were not always
included in vernacular translations. See Atkinson and Cropp, "Trois traductions de la *Consolatio
Philosophiae* de Boèce," pp. 201–2.

How the husbands tell their secrets to their wives. The part where he says, "But the fool." fol. 80

Instructions on protecting oneself from women. The part where he says, "Fair lords." fol. 86.

An examination of the table of contents gives us a first impression of Mathias' interests in the texts he has compiled. The entries for the *Rose*, for example, indicate that he was not particularly interested in the poem's love teachings. The teachings of the God of Love are lumped under a single entry, "Les commandemens du dieu d'amours" [the commandments of the God of Love (fol. 2r)]. The discourse of La Vieille is similarly treated. The discourse of Ami, according to the Table, is mostly about poverty, friendship, the evils of marriage, and the origins of government. Of eleven entries, only two, concerning gift-giving and how to keep one's *amie*, relate to the long Ovidian lessons on seduction and courtship; while the origins of social comportment and government receive three entries:

Des amours et gouvernement de ceulz qui furent au commencement du monde. xxxix

. . .

Comme les roys et les princes furent créez. xlv
Comme les princes orent sergens premierement. xlv

(fol. 2r)

About the love and government of those who lived at the beginning of the world. fol. 39

. . .

How kings and princes were first created. fol. 45
How princes first had sergeants. fol. 45

An interest in the structure and governance of society is also apparent in the entries of the *Testament*, *Charité*, and *Fauvel*. Mathias' Table divides the *Testament* into sections on married men, the mendicant orders, prelates, priests, mendicants who follow the courts, and women, with closing sections on the seven deadly sins and a prayer to the Virgin. The *Charité* is introduced as a text "qui parle a touz les estaz" [which speaks to all levels of society (fol. 2v)]; the text is divided into sections addressed to the Pope, the cardinals, the emperor, kings, temporal judges, bishops and clerics, abbots and monks, and the lower classes. *Fauvel* in turn is a text "qui parle sur le gouvernement du siecle" [which speaks about the governance of this world (fol. 2v)]; it is similarly divided into sections on Church officials, mendicants and other religious orders, and the nobility. And of course Mathias' interest in the structure and government of society is also reflected in the *Echecs moralisés*, in which the game of chess becomes an elaborate exposition of the social and political order.

In addition to politics, Mathias was interested in various philosophical problems, such as the question of free will; he had a certain scholarly concern with the identification of classical allusions, expressed in his habit of highlighting in yellow the names of Latin authors in both the *Echecs moralisés* and the correspondence of Abelard and Heloise; he responded to the general didactic content of the texts he copied, including – in true clerical fashion – the antifeminist teachings. We can derive an impression of his intellectual and literary interests from the marginal annotations he left in MS *Dij*. These glosses, nearly always entered in red, are of two kinds: geometric symbols or "Nota" signs marking a passage he considered important, and a series of notes identifying shared motifs among certain texts in the collection. The texts cross-referenced in this fashion are the *Rose, Chaton*, the *Echecs moralisés*, the letters of Abelard and Heloise, and the *Consolation of Philosophy*. The cross-references are especially interesting, for they indicate that the book was actually studied as a whole, and not simply built up piecemeal. In particular, it seems that Mathias chose at least some of his texts with the *Rose* in mind, wishing to provide fuller treatment of certain topics that interested him and that the *Rose* did not adequately explain. We have already seen examples of scribes and readers who expanded on the *Rose* by noting related texts that could be referred to for more information, or by inserting passages into the *Rose* itself. Mathias chose a different method of adding his "surplus de sens." He brought other texts to bear on the *Rose*, and on each other, by combining them in a composite volume where each text could be studied both in its entirety, and in relation to the others.

The texts most directly linked to the *Rose* are the correspondence of Abelard and Heloise and the *Consolation of Philosophy*. Since the pages containing the letters are now lost – only two folios have since been recovered, among the fragments compiled in MS Bibl. Nat. n. a. fr. 20001 – it is impossible to verify the existence of annotations in these texts. In the *Rose*, however, when the story of Abelard is first introduced, Mathias noted, "Vide in suis epistolis ii^c iiii [see in his epistles, fol. 204r (fol. 47r, v. 8729)]. We can tell from the Table of Contents that this refers to the beginning of the *Historia calamitatum*. Mathias additionally provided references to the appropriate passages of the *Historia calamitatum* throughout the summary of Abelard's story (Pl. 6).[39] The brief account of Abelard

---

[39] References to specific passages in the *Historia Calamitatum* appear at 8730–31, 8732–33, 8737–57, 8759–62, 8763–65, 8766–68, 8769–70, 8771, 8773–74, 8775–76, 8777–95.

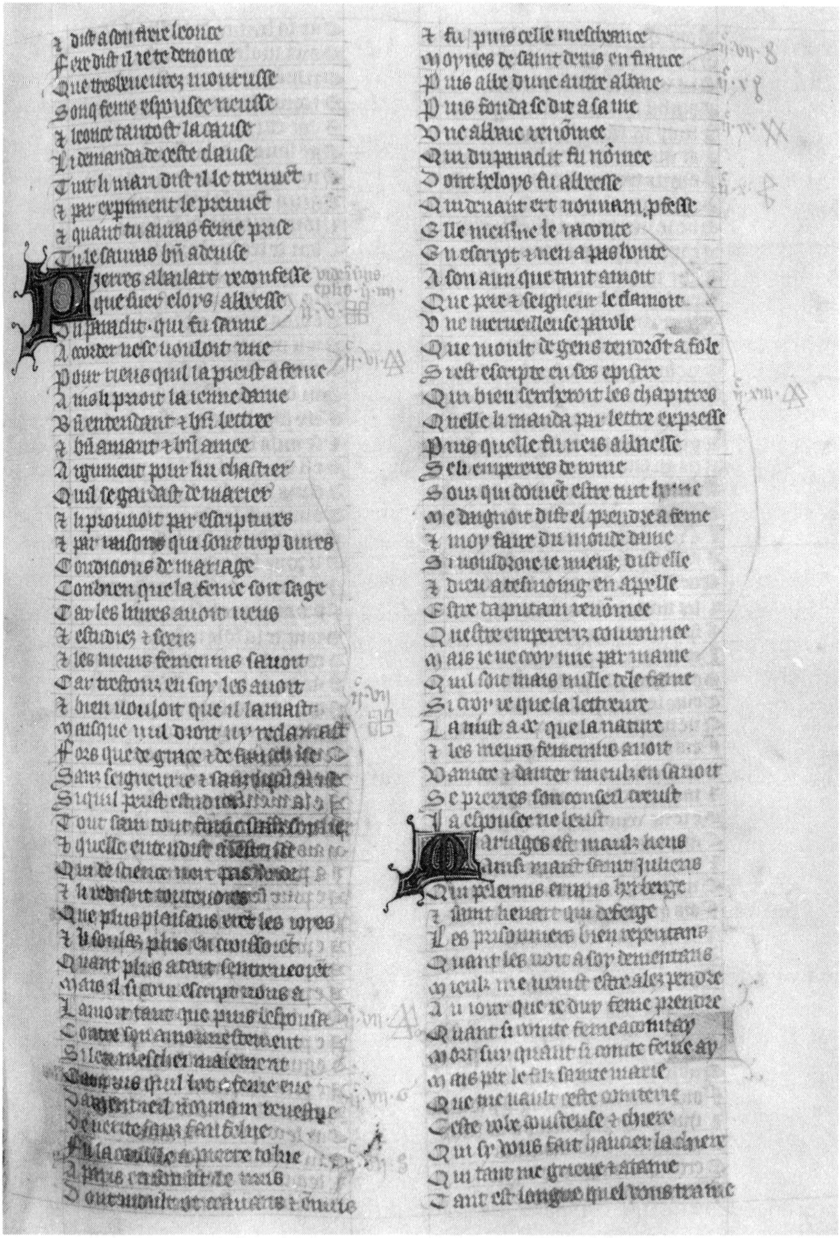

Plate 6 The manuscript of Mathias Rivalli, showing marginal annotations in the story of Abelard and Heloise in the discourse of the Jaloux. Dijon, Bibliothèque Municipale MS 525, fol. 47r.

and Heloise given in the *Rose* is thus expanded and linked directly to its full exposition in Abelard's own words.

The *Consolation of Philosophy* is also introduced to fill gaps in the *Rose*, as is shown by two notes in the discourse of Nature. Referring to the problem of free will, Nature comments that the topic is too long for full explanation and that the details can be found elsewhere:

> Bien est ailleurs determiné.
> Qui nou set a clerc le demande,
> qui leü l'ait et qui l'antande.   (vv. 17704–6)

It is all worked out elsewhere. Let him who does not know about it ask a clerk who has read and understood it.

At v. 17704 (fol. 92v), Mathias placed the reference "Boece ii^c xlviii." This leads to what is now fol. 217r; it is here, at Book 5, Prose 3 – where the reconciliation of divine foreknowledge and free will is explained – that the translation of Jean de Meun is substituted for the mixed version, with Mathias' comment that what follows is suitable only for the educated. Clearly Mathias, himself an educated man, wanted to supplement the philosophical discussions of the *Rose*; and he chose to do so in Jean's own translation of Boethius, which he probably saw as a companion piece to the less rigorously philosophical romance. Mathias also called upon Boethius to fill out the definition of "pardurableté" [eternity]. Nature defines the term in this way:

> car qui la diffinicion
> de pardurableté dellie,
> ce est possession de vie
> qui par fin ne peut estre prise,
> tretoute ansamble, san devise.   (vv. 17464–68)

For if you want to unravel the definition of "eternity," it is possession of life that can never come to an end, entirely whole, unconditional.

At v. 17466 (fol. 91v), Mathias placed the reference "Boece ii^c li." This leads to Book 5, Prose 6, to the section rubricated "Cy defenist qui est pardurableté" [here 'eternity' is defined (fol. 220r)]. Again, the sketchy definition given in the *Rose* is rounded out by the more complete discussion in Boethius.

Sometimes the cross-references are not so much for the purpose of completion as for that of source identification. The *Echecs moralisés*, for example, cites numerous Latin authors, whose names Mathias, like some other scribes of the *Echecs moralisés*, has highlighted in yellow. Whenever he noticed a citation of an author included in his anthology, he marked the spot: one citation of Boethius and three citations of the distichs of Cato.[40] Cato is also cited in the *Rose*, but Mathias did not explicitly mark these citations. Often, however, he did place a "Nota" or one of his geometrical signs next to a passage in the *Chaton* that is either explicitly cited in the *Rose*, or which corresponds to a point made in the *Rose*. Indeed, of the sixteen passages marked in the *Chaton*, five are cross-referenced to the *Echecs moralisés*; the other eleven are ideas found in the *Rose*.[41] Sometimes the corresponding passage in the *Rose* is marked with a "Nota." We can assume that Mathias did not get around to entering the full cross-reference with folio number every time he noticed a parallel; like that other clerical scribe, Michel Alès, Mathias did not necessarily complete the work on his manuscript.

Mathias had, as I said, a particular interest in classical allusions, and he often noted instances where an allusion is more fully explained, or even simply where it is repeated, in another text. In the *Rose*, for example, La Vieille refers briefly to the tale of Circe and Ulysses as an example of the fickleness of men:

> n'onq Cyrcé ne tint ansemant
> Ulixés qu'il ne s'en foïst
> por nul sort que fere en poïst.   (vv. 14376–78)

Nor did Circe retain Ulysses or keep him from fleeing, no matter what spell she was able to cast.

[40] In the *Echecs*, the passage, "Boece dit ou livre de consolacion, qui laisse a estre home en laissant vertu, il devient beste car dieu ne puet il estre" [Boethius says in the book of consolation, he who ceases to be a man by abandoning virtue becomes a beast, for he cannot be a god (fol. 196v)] is cross-referenced to the passage, "Ainsi avient que home qui par mauvaistié laisse boune vie, par qui il seroit diex, puis que ce ne veult, il est muez en beste" [Thus it happens that a man who by evil-doing abandons the good life by which he would be a god, since he does not want that, is changed into a beast (Boethius, book 4, prose 3; fol. 213r)]; the passage, "Chaton dit, ne croies pas gloutonie qui est amie au ventre" [Cato says, do not believe gluttony, which is friend to the stomach (fol. 196v)] is cued to the line, "Ne de trop mangier n'aies cure" [Nor should you wish to eat too much (*Chaton*, fol. 128r)]; the statement, "Chaton dit, acomplis et fay la loy que tu as faite et dounee" [Cato says, obey and keep the law that you have made and given (fol. 188v)] is cued to the lines, "La loy qu'auras faitte et dounee / Garde par toy ne soit faussee" [See that the law that you have made and given is not broken by you (*Chaton*, fol. 126r)]; and the dictum, "Chaton dit, puis que vifs bounement, ne fay force des paroles aus mauvais" [Cato says, since you lead an upright life, pay no mind to the words of the bad (fol. 197v)] is cross-referenced to an eight-line passage in the *Chaton* about ignoring slanderers (fol. 127v).

[41] Examples of passages marked in the *Chaton* that echo the *Rose*, or are cited in it, are: "Retien ta lengue et ta parole" [Keep a check on your tongue and your speech (cf. *Rose*, vv. 7023–27)]; "De la chose garder te poine / Que tu as gaaingné a grant poine" [Take care to keep that which you have earned through great effort (cf. *Rose*, vv. 14425–26, here marked "Nota")]; "Ne croire pas quanque tu oz / Je di que tu seroies foz / Car il n'est pas tout evangile / Quanque l'en dit aval la vile" [I say that you would be foolish to believe everything you hear, for not everything that is said around town is the gospel truth (cf. *Rose*, vv. 12187–88, here marked "Nota," and vv. 12247–48)]; "L'en dit que souef va la voie / Li homs qui d'autrui se chastoie" [It is said that the man who learns from others has an easy time of it (cf. *Rose*, vv. 7973–74)]; "Fame pleure quant elle veult" [A woman weeps when she wants to (cf. *Rose*, vv. 13351–52, here marked "Nota")].

A gloss here refers the reader to the *Consolation of Philosophy*, Book 4, Meter 3, where the story of Circe and Ulysses is told in more detail, and where its "true" moral significance is revealed: it is an allegory for the difference between mind and body, and demonstrates that what happens to the body is unimportant as long as the mind remains pure. Here, Mathias' gloss not only completes but also corrects the text of the *Rose*, ensuring that the orthodox moral lesson is not lost in the comedy of La Vieille's appropriation of the myth. In other examples, it is the *Rose* that provides the fuller account. This is the case for the allusions to Lucretia and to Nero's execution of Seneca in the *Echecs moralisés*, both of which are glossed in reference to the *Rose* (vv. 8578–612 and 6181–215 respectively). And in other cases still, the glosses simply link up two examples of the same allusion: the story of Zeuxis in both Abelard (Letter 7) and the *Rose* (vv. 16155–68); the story of the sword of Damocles, a reference to Xanthippe's shrewish treatment of Socrates, and a reference to Plato's school in the wilderness, in both the *Historia calamitatum* and the *Echecs moralisés*; a citation of Plato's assertion of the importance of wise governors in both the *Echecs moralisés* and the *Consolation of Philosophy* (Book 1, Prose 4).

Finally, some of Mathias' cross-references simply note motifs common to two of his texts. He found discussions of the effect of wine in both Heloise (Letter 5) and the *Echecs moralisés*; allusions to the self-castration of Origen in both the *Historia calamitatum* and the *Rose* (v. 17022); an exposition of the blessings of a good wife in both Abelard (Letter 2) and the *Rose* (vv. 18121–22). The two passages marked in *Fauvel*, concerning clerical corruption (ed. Langfors, vv. 843–46) and the mendicant orders (vv. 365–68), stress its thematic parallels with the discourse of Faux Samblant; although there is no gloss referring to the *Rose*, it is unlikely that a clerical reader would have failed to note this particular intertextual relationship. If the manuscript had not lost so many pages, we might be able to trace even more of Mathias' readings. The description of the earthly paradise in the *Purgatoire Saint Patrice*, for example, might have struck him as an interesting parallel to the earthly and heavenly gardens of the *Rose*; the accounts of divine justice and the torments of the damned might have reminded him of Reason's discussion of justice or of the descriptions of hell in the discourses of Nature and Genius.

But even without such speculation, MS *Dij* offers a remarkably detailed picture of the literary tastes and reading habits of this cleric living in Paris in the mid fourteenth century. Mathias was interested in the vernacularization of Latin texts, and in intertextual relationships among vernacular translations and between vernacular and Latin texts. He had an interest in classical literary and historical figures which included, but was not limited to, moral lessons that these figures illustrated. At the same time, he was a reader of texts like *Fauvel*, the *Charité*, and the *Testament* of Jean de Meun, that commented on contemporary French society. The *Rose* must have seemed to him the perfect starting point for his one-volume personal library. It contained everything that interested him: a reworking of the Latin tradition, moral and spiritual edification, an introduction to important philosophical problems, topical social commentary. On its Ovidian love teachings, Mathias is silent. This does not necessarily mean, of course, that he never read these portions of the poem or that he did not enjoy them. But it is safe to say that his main interests lay elsewhere. The one love story that he does include in his collection is that of Abelard and Heloise: an enigmatic story to be sure, but one which he may well have understood as illustrating the dangers of erotic love and marriage, and the triumph of spiritual purity and intellectual pursuits over the temptations of the flesh. His gloss on La Vieille's allusion to Circe supports such an interpretation of his attitude towards the erotic content of his book. Like Pierre Col fifty years later, Mathias appreciated the *Rose* as a compendium of learning and an affirmation of moral and spiritual values.

The foregoing survey of glosses on the *Rose*, while not exhaustive, has served to establish contexts for the reception of the *Rose* in the fourteenth century. It clearly reached an educated audience, one that included clerics and members of the university community; we recall that the *Rose* was among the very few vernacular texts represented in the Sorbonne library in the early fourteenth century.[42] It was also read by members of the nobility. It is to be associated with a lively interest in the Latin poets and philosophers and in the vernacularization of the Latin tradition; it could be read either as an edifying moral and philosophical treatise, or as an art of seduction – or as both at once. We have also seen that the limits of the text were somewhat fluid. Passages could be extracted or omitted; at the same time, the text easily absorbed new material. It is time now to turn to an examination of the textual history of the *Rose*, in order to see the ways in which the text was expanded, abridged, and rewritten.

[42] The "Romancium de rosa" is listed among the chained books in the 1338 inventory of the Sorbonne library; a note indicates that it was missing at the time of the inventory, which might be a sign of its popularity. Only three other vernacular books, all devotional texts, are listed among the chained volumes; an additional ten vernacular books, nearly all listed as missing, appear in the inventory of the non-chained volumes. The library as a whole numbered over 1700 volumes. See Delisle, "Bibliothèque de la Sorbonne," in *Cabinet des Manuscrits*, vol. 3, pp. 71, 72, 107.

3

The profitable, pleasurable *Rose*: the remaniement of Gui de Mori

> Tant i vaurai je dou mien faire
> C'aucune cose en osterai,
> Aucune cose y meterai:
> Si en sera plus entendables,
> Et a oïr plus delitables.
> (Gui de Mori, MS Tournai, Bibl. de la Ville 101, f. 5v)[1]

In 1290 the Picard cleric Gui de Mori completed his reworking of the *Roman de la Rose* as he then knew it: Guillaume's romance, completed by what is now referred to as the anonymous continuation, but which Gui perceived as an integral part of the text. Shortly thereafter he discovered Jean's continuation and incorporated that into his project of remaniement, thoroughly reworking Jean's text as well. Gui added a number of passages to Guillaume's romance, including an eleventh portrait on the wall of the Garden, that of Pride; a detailed exposition of the ten arrows of Love; expansions and reworkings of the portraits of the various allegorical personifications; a revision of the story of Narcissus that suppresses Echo and incorporates a reference to his mother, Liriopé, whose story is borrowed from the romance *Floris et Liriopé*; and long additions to the God of Love's teachings, enumerating such things as the distinction between true love and lust and an explication of the first four degrees of love (sight, speech, touch, and kiss). In addition to these long interpolations, Gui also added a number of short interpolations and minor modifications. Gui's work on Guillaume de Lorris has been studied in some detail.[2] His work on

---

[1] "I want to do my own work there, so that I will delete certain things, and add certain things; thus it will be more comprehensible, and more pleasant to listen to."

[2] On Gui de Mori, see Langlois, "Gui de Mori et le *Roman de la Rose*"; Fourez, "Le *Roman de la Rose* de la Bibliothèque de la ville de Tournai"; Jung, "Gui de Mori et Guillaume de Lorris"; Hult, "Gui de Mori, lecteur médiéval"; Walters, "Illuminating the *Rose*." Hult's study essentially reappears in *Self-fulfilling Prophecies*, pp. 34–64. Both Langlois and Jung publish important excerpts from Gui's work. Langlois gives Gui's prologue (pp. 259–62) and the passage that he inserted to announce himself as the third *Rose* poet (pp. 255–57). Jung, in addition to providing a detailed description of Gui's reworking of Guillaume, published Gui's version of the Narcissus story (pp. 120–22), the interpolation on the degrees of love (pp. 127–33), and the interpolation in the discourse of Ami in Jean de Meun on the impossibility of giving general rules in love (pp. 124–26).

Jean de Meun has been noted, but far less fully examined, although he effected even more considerable changes in this portion of the poem than in the first part: he added numerous interpolations totaling thousands of lines, deleted thousands more lines, and restructured entire sections of the poem. The chronology of Gui's work is explained in a rubric in the now-lost manuscript known as *Ter*, portions of which were fortunately transcribed by Méon and Langlois before it disappeared. Here Gui hypothesizes that Jean de Meun, provoked by Guillaume's boasts of having captured the Rose so easily, removed the original ending and added his own material in order to prolong the quest.[3] A somewhat similar statement appears in the MS Tournai, Bibl. de la Ville 101 (MS *Tou*), a reworked version of Gui's remaniement copied in 1330. MSS *Ter* and *Tou* both contain the anonymous continuation, followed first by Gui's explanatory statement and then by Jean's continuation.

Gui's contributions to Guillaume's romance have survived, in whole or in part, in ten manuscripts known today; a few passages even made their way into Molinet's prose version of the *Rose*.[4] His reworking of Jean, however, had less impact on the *Rose* manuscript tradition. Aside from the ill-fated MS *Ter*, only four surviving manuscripts transmit Gui's work on Jean. MS *Tou*, while offering a complete version of Gui's work, departs from the original by restoring thousands of lines that Gui had omitted; these restorations are indicated by marginal annotations that will be explained below. A second complete version of Gui's remaniement is preserved in the fifteenth-century MS Bibl. Nat. fr. 797, which I shall call MS *Mor*.[5] This text contains a number of long passages that are lacking

---

[3] Hult gives the text of Gui's statement about his work on the two parts of the *Rose*, based on the transcriptions by Méon and Langlois, in *Self-fulfilling Prophecies*, pp. 36–39. When Langlois published his catalogue of *Rose* manuscripts, MS *Ter* was in the Öttingen-Wallerstein library in Maihingen (*Manuscrits*, pp. 163–66); it has since disappeared.

[4] On Gui's presence in the *Rose* manuscript tradition, see Langlois, "Gui de Mori," pp. 270–71. Langlois lists five manuscripts, in addition to MSS *Tou* and *Ter*, that contain passages from Gui de Mori. He does not mention MSS *He* or *Ke*. An additional manuscript containing Gui's version of Guillaume together with the standard version of Jean was sold in 1988 by the firm of Ader, Picard, Tajan; see *Manuscrits et livres anciens*, no. 152. The version of Gui's remaniement in this manuscript is closer to MS *Tou* than to MS *Mor*; it does not include the interpolations given in Appendix A, 1. For all information concerning this manuscript, I am grateful to Heidrun Ost of the University of Kiel, who has studied it in connection with her doctoral dissertation on the *Rose* manuscript tradition. For a brief description of still another manuscript that contained Gui's work, at least in the first part of the poem, see Rouard, "D'un manuscrit inconnu." Rouard's description is not very detailed and the manuscript cannot be identified; I have not included it in the total.

[5] Of MS *Mor*, Langlois states that it is an amalgam of Gui's remaniement and the standard text, featuring Gui's "additions" and some of his "mutations," but not his "subtractions"; and that it is closely related to the MS Bibl. Nat. fr. 12590. He is wrong on both counts. MS *Mor* reflects nearly all of the deletions indicated in MS *Tou*; it is a recension of Gui's remaniement, not a combination of the latter with the standard text. And it is not related to MS fr. 12590, which features only a few passages from Gui in a text that is otherwise standard; for Jean de Meun, MS fr. 12590 belongs to the *B* family.

from MS *Tou*, and very few of the deletions indicated in MS *Tou* have been restored. MS *Mor* lacks the prologue that appears in MS *Tou*, as well as the anonymous continuation of Guillaume and the explanation of Gui's work; but it includes a passage inserted in the God of Love's discourse in which Gui announces himself by name as the poem's third author. Large portions of Gui's work are preserved, in turn, in the MS Copenhagen, Royal Library GKS 2061, 4° (*He*). As will be explained below, however, the text in MS *He* cannot be identified as that of Gui de Mori; rather, it is an independent version of the *Rose* into which some of Gui's interpolations have been inserted and from which many of his deletions – including some that have been restored in MS *Tou* – have been made. Many of Gui's most far-reaching changes, however, are absent from MS *He*. Finally, as noted in the previous chapter, a few of Gui's interpolations in the discourses of Reason and Ami have been added, after the fact, to MS *Ke*.

The presentation of Gui's work in MS *Tou* is truly extraordinary in the context of fourteenth-century vernacular manuscripts. The manuscript does not necessarily date from within Gui's lifetime; and as stated above, it contains a somewhat modified version of his remaniement, although this version certainly could be Gui's work. What makes MS *Tou* unique is its system of marginal annotations, explained in the prologue (fol. 5v): a horizontal bar ("une petite vergiele") indicates "k'ele aura bouté / Tout hors le superfluité" [that it has done away with superfluous material]; a star ("une estoilete petite") marks "ce que g'i ajousterai" [what I will interpolate], with marginal flourishes indicating the length of the interpolation (Pl. 7). Gui also notes that bar and star together indicate "risme noviele" [new rhyme]: the use of new words to express the original idea. He informs us that the technical terms ("propres nons") for these signs are "subtraction," "addition," and "mutation." Finally, he explains that a rose marks a "subtraction reprise," lines that were originally omitted but are now restored, again with marginal flourishes running the full length of the restored passage, and a second rose appearing at its end.

As a result of this system, the manuscript not only transmits a particular version of the *Rose*, but also provides a map of the ongoing processes of interpolation, abridgment, and restoration that characterize both the activity of remaniement and the *Rose* manuscript tradition in general. The

---

Although MS *Mor* dates from the fifteenth century, its language is compatible with a late thirteenth-century date for the text. One notes, for example, the scrupulous observance of subject and object case for masculine nouns and adjectives; pretonic vowels in hiatus before a tonic vowel, e.g., *meïsmes, veü*; the use of the ending *-iens* in the first-person plural conditional and imperfect. On the syntactic features that differentiate Old from Middle French, see Marchello-Nizia, *Histoire de la langue française*.

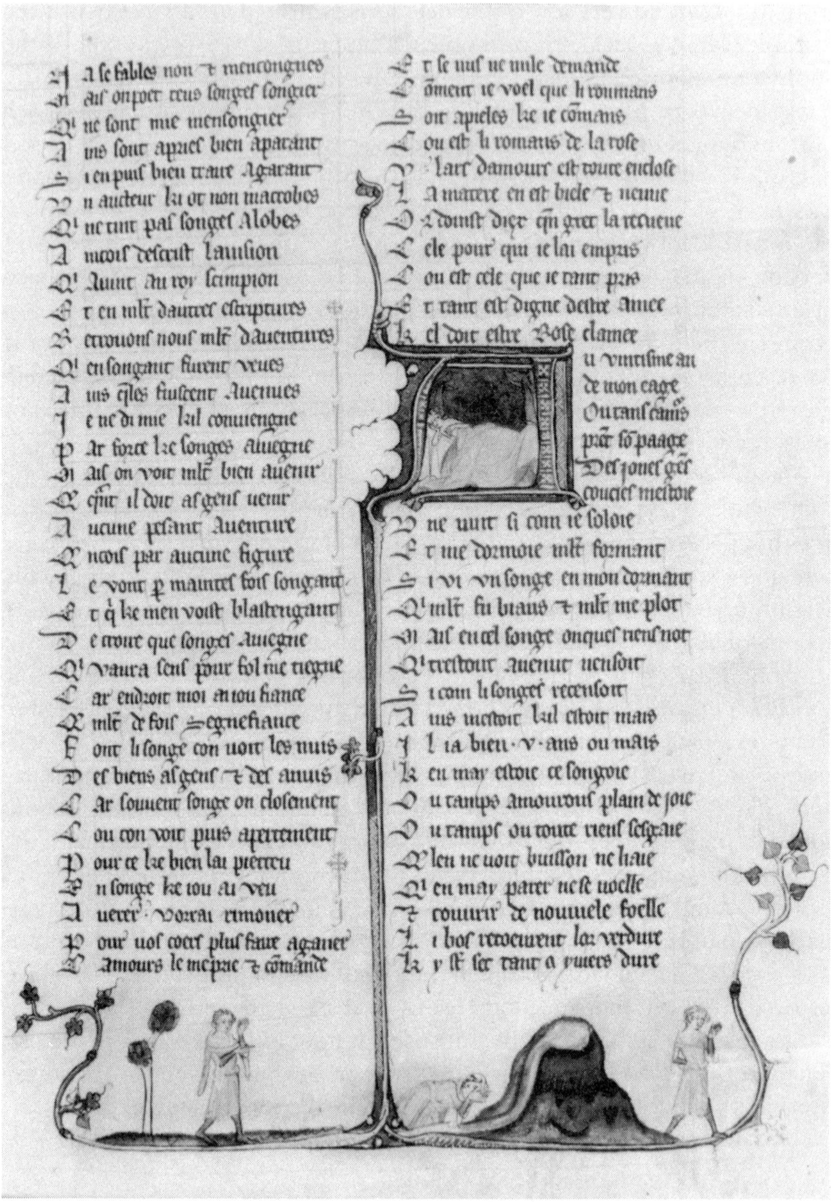

Plate 7 The *Rose* of Gui de Mori, with marginal signs identifying interpolations. Tournai, Bibliothèque de la Ville MS 101, fol. 6r.

marginal signs allow each reader or copyist to construct his or her own version of the *Rose*: interpolations can be kept or omitted, deletions can be left out or taken back. David Hult stated the case succinctly, pointing out that Gui "leaves himself open to an infinite number of future textual variants, all of which will depend on the viewpoint of each new reader."[6] This point, fully borne out in the manuscript tradition, is one to which I shall return.

In the lack of an edition, any examination of Gui's work must be carried out through simultaneous study of the three major surviving manuscripts, *Tou*, *Mor*, and *He*. Since MS *Tou* and *He* are chronologically closer to Gui and preserve his Picard dialect, I prefer to cite them when possible, using MS *Mor* for those passages that do not appear elsewhere. Since Gui's modifications of Guillaume de Lorris are better known, I shall largely concentrate here on his modification of Jean de Meun. In general, Gui has sought to impose a clearer, more linear structure on Jean's frequently – and brilliantly – digressive text; to achieve this, he not only adds and deletes verses, but also moves whole blocks of text to new locations, a type of alteration not identified by any marginal sign. The discourses of Reason, Ami, and La Vieille are restructured in this fashion, while those of Nature and Genius are tidied up largely through the deletion of material perceived as digressive. Gui further suppresses passages that were overly bawdy and reduces references to pagan mythology, though not to pagan history or philosophy. He has also added Biblical and patristic material, especially in the discourse of Reason. And he has sought to bring the *Rose* closer to certain Latin authors who loom large in its background: Macrobius, Boethius, Alain de Lille. In recasting the *Rose*, Gui clarifies the didactic aspects of the Art of Love, expanding on such topics as charity, jealousy, gift-giving, and the art of writing love letters; he elaborates a sort of middle ground where eros and friendship can meet.

GUI DE MORI AS AN AUTHOR OF THE *ROSE*

Nothing is known of Gui's life, beyond the few hints contained in his work. We know that he greatly admired the *Rose* and its authors, and hoped to join their ranks. In the prologue of MS *Tou*, Gui states that he has chosen to work on the *Rose* because he does not feel capable of creating a new text equal to that one; in the God of Love's discourse about the two *Rose* poets, he inserts a passage announcing himself as the third author.[7] Gui identifies

---

[6] Hult, *Self-fulfilling Prophecies*, p. 42. The notion that certain sections of the poem are "detachable" is not limited to Gui; see Van der Poel, "Over gebruikersnotities in het *Rose*-handschrift K. A. XXIV."

[7] For the complete text of Gui's prologue and self-portrait, see Langlois, "Gui de Mori et le *Roman de la Rose*," pp. 259–62 and 255–57.

himself as one who loved the *Rose* above all other literary works. He was a disciple of Love, but was prevented from following Love's commandments by the "prison" in which he lived. From this we can deduce that Gui was a priest or a monk, bound by a vow of chastity. It was probably for his fellow clerics that Gui prepared his version of the *Rose*: in his prologue, he states that he worked at the request of "cil ki sont de no couvent" [those who are of our convent/fellowship (MS *Tou*, fol. 5r)].

From Gui's self-portrait in the God of Love's discourse we can discern his attitude towards the *Rose* as an art of love and towards his own contribution to the poem. He deleted Cupid's assertion that Jean, in addition to completing the story of the erotic quest, would explicate it: "Puis vodra si la chose espondre / que riens ne s'i porra repondre" [then he will choose to expound the matter so well that there could be no argument with it (vv. 10573–74, deleted)]. Gui also omitted most of Jean's Apology, including his defense of the poem's daring language and his promise to explicate the material. Gui probably felt that although Jean did complete the narrative, he had not adequately explicated his material. Certainly Gui was not convinced that Jean's every word was justified, for he deleted thousands of Jean's lines. It was this need for explication and amendment that authorized Gui's own work on the *Rose*.

As the God of Love elaborates on Gui's persona, an interesting portrait emerges. Gui will be an honorable man, devoted to love; though unable to follow love's commandments himself, he will counsel other lovers. He also states that Gui will be a victim of Fortune and that he will suffer attacks from Male Bouche. Finally, the God of Love registers two complaints about Gui: he will teach Love's commandments,

> Fors tant que ja ne loera
> A personne ki amera
> Qu'en .i. soel lieu si son coer mete
> Que de legier ne s'en demete,
> Et vaura as amans aprendre
> Conment il devront les las tendre
> Por prendre autrui sans estre pris.
> (MS *Tou*, fol. 96r–v, interpolation following v. 10596)

except that he will never recommend to anyone who loves that he keep his heart in one place from which it cannot easily be moved, and he will want to teach lovers how they should lay their snares to catch others without getting caught themselves.

This image of the poet – that he will be heir to a well-established poetic tradition; that he will give advice about love, teaching both how to seduce and how to keep from succumbing oneself; that he will be a disciple of love;

and that he will be the victim of slander and misfortune – is modeled on Ovid's *Remedia amoris*. Gui's celibate state is of course not Ovidian, but like Ovid, he does stress his own commitment to love. In a digression at the approximate midpoint of the *Remedia amoris* (vv. 357–96), Ovid offers a brief excursus on Latin poetry, mentioning his elegiac predecessors – including Gallus and Tibullus – and comparing himself, as the leading elegiac poet, to Virgil, leading epic poet. He also complains that he has been the victim of envy and slander. It is shortly following this passage that Ovid suggests that amorous passion can be lessened by not limiting oneself to a single lover: "Hortor et, ut pariter binas habeatis amicas: / Fortior est, plures siquis habere potest" [and I urge that you have two girl friends at once: he who can have several is even stronger (vv. 441–42)]. And of course the guiding purpose of the *Remedia amoris* is to instruct lovers how to disentangle themselves from the snares of love.

Gui's decision to draw on the *Remedia* was no doubt inspired by Jean's own allusions to this poem. Jean's characterization of the two-part *Rose* recalls that of Ovid's *Ars amatoria* and *Remedia*. Cupid states that Guillaume will "conmancier le romant / ou seront mis tuit mi conmant" [begin the romance where all my commandments will be placed (vv. 10519–20)]; Jean will expand on love's teachings such that "ja mes cil qui les orront / des douz mauz d'amer ne morront" [never will those who hear them die from the sweet pains of love (vv. 10615–16)]. It is precisely the need to save unhappy lovers from suicide that Ovid cites in the prologue to the *Remedia*, stressing that his poetic oeuvre as a whole teaches both the cultivation and the healing of love: "Discite sanari, per quem didicistis amare" [learn to be healed from the one through whom you learned to love (*Rem.*, v. 43)]. And Ovid portrays himself as receiving the blessings of Cupid for his poetic enterprise: "movit Amor gemmatas aureus alas, / Et mihi 'propositum perfice' dixit 'opus' " [golden Love moved his jewelled wings and said to me, "finish your proposed work" (*Rem.*, vv. 39–40)]. The word "perfice" recalls the Old French "parfenir," used by Jean to refer to his work on the *Rose* (v. 10555), and even more closely the term "parfaire," often used by scribes to announce Jean's continuation.[8] The reference to Love's wings in turn is echoed in Cupid's promise to shelter the young Jean de Meun: "je l'afubleré de mes eles" [I will wrap him in my wings (v. 10607)]. Gui deleted this last line, transferring the associations with the Ovid of the *Remedia* to himself.

This conflation of the *Ars amatoria* and the *Remedia amoris* is in keeping

---

[8] On the word "parfaire" as applied to the continuation or completion of the *Rose*, see Hult, *Self-fulfilling Prophecies*, pp. 58–59, 78, 89.

with the medieval view of Ovid. The *Remedia* frequently follows the *Ars* in medieval manuscripts of Ovid's poetry; the *accessus* tradition identified it as a continuation of – sometimes as an atonement for – the *Ars*.[9] Gui would have recognized Ovid's *Amores* 3, 9 as the principal source for Cupid's discourse on Guillaume and Jean as the heirs to Tibullus, Gallus, Catullus, and Ovid; he would probably also have connected it to Ovid's hopes to enter literary tradition in *Ars amatoria*, 3:339–48. For his own self-portrait he drew on another Ovidian source, one equally relevant to the *Rose*. The *Rose* does contain the global art of love represented in Ovid's two-part work: the art of seduction and the antidote to erotic passion. Cupid, Ami, and La Vieille instruct the lover or courtesan in seduction techniques; Reason teaches how such passion is to be shunned, preaching reasonable love – friendship or conjugal relations for the purpose of procreation – in its place. Nature and Genius condemn the abuse of sexuality and promote lawful procreation; at Gui's hands, these two characters become less morally ambiguous. And Ami, in Gui's version, speaks more favorably of marriage and advises against succumbing to the desperate passions of jealousy.

Even the discourse of La Vieille can be seen as participating in the "remedy" aspect of the *Rose*. First of all, La Vieille's advice includes the two points identified in Gui's self-portrait: she teaches that a girl should never limit herself to one lover and that she should not let herself fall in love. In this respect, and in her citation of such unfortunate heroines as Phyllis and Dido, La Vieille's discourse does incorporate material from the *Remedia*; the clerical annotator of MS *Be*, discussed in Chapter 1, glossed La Vieille's stipulation always to have more than one lover with Ovid's advice in the *Remedia* (*Rem.*, vv. 441–42; at *Rose*, vv. 13134–42; fol. 92r). Moreover, Gui added a long interpolation in which La Vieille explains how to end a love affair gone bad. Secondly, the very presence of La Vieille's teachings in the *Rose*, ostensibly an art of seduction aimed at the education of men, raises interesting questions. Here, feminine secrets are revealed to the male reader: ploys and tricks, the deception of men so as to receive gifts and money while keeping as many lovers as possible, even feminine hygiene and tips about make-up and physical appearance. And it is precisely such feminine practices that, according to Ovid, a man should think of in attempting to end his amorous attachment. It is useful for the man to remind himself of how expensive his mistress has been, how she has lied to him and been unfaithful (vv. 301–6); it is quite effective to see her

---

[9] The medieval *accessus* tradition identified the *Remedia* as teaching how to extinguish the passions outlined in the *Ars*; the two poems formed a cohesive, all-encompassing doctrine of love. See Ghisalberti, "Medieval Biographies of Ovid," pp. 12–13 and 45–47.

putting on make-up, and thus to realize how artificial is her beauty (vv. 351–56). The discourse of La Vieille completes the adaptation of the *Ars* in the *Rose* by incorporating material from Book 3; its very presence also provides the male reader with the sort of material recommended in the *Remedia* for the cooling of ardor.

We can thus conclude that Gui saw the *Rose* as containing both the art and the remedy of love, with the latter accomplished both through the exposition of acceptable alternatives – love of God, friendship, reasonable courtship, marriage and procreation – and through the revelation of the sordid side of erotic pursuit. Gui no doubt felt that his modifications contributed to the status of the poem as a remedy to ardent passion. He does state in his prologue that his reworking of the *Rose* is meant to provide lovers with "consolation / De lors grans tribulations" [consolation from their great tribulations (MS *Tou*, fol. 5v)]. This manner of reading the *Rose* corresponds to that later described by Pierre Col, who, as we saw in Chapter 1, claimed to have cured a young man of *fol' amour* by giving him a copy of the *Rose*. In adapting the *Rose* so as to strengthen its value as an antidote to excessive passion, Gui attempted to resolve conflicts such as those that would be identified by Christine de Pizan, who expressed considerable skepticism at the idea that the *Rose* could have a salutary effect on an ardent young reader. As we will see, Gui frequently seems to anticipate criticisms that Christine and Gerson will make a century later. We could say that, in effect, he wanted the *Rose* to be what Pierre Col claimed it already was: a morally edifying commentary on the many aspects of human love.

REWRITING THE ART OF LOVE

One of the most interesting aspects of Gui's version of the *Rose* is his recasting of both the God of Love and Reason so as to bring these two figures closer together. On the one hand, Reason's definition of love is expanded to include divine love and Christian charity: her vision is far more inclusive than that of Cupid. Nonetheless, on the more limited topic of erotic love Cupid and Reason are virtually brought into agreement.

The exposition of love in the first part of the *Rose*, expanded in MS *Tou*, is even more profoundly altered in MS *Mor*, which contains interpolations appearing nowhere else. Gui's digression on the arrows of love, for example, now includes a long explication of fire as a metaphor for love and a defence of vision as more important than hearsay in the onset of love. Most important for our purposes here is a long passage inserted into Cupid's exchange with the Lover just before the series of commandments, in which the god explains that true love – the sort he fosters – involves more than mere sexual attraction (see Appendix A, 1). Many people, he states, believe that women are loved solely through carnal desire; but in reality, a woman should be loved for her own good qualities, "Pour ce qu'elle est ou belle ou bonne" [because she is either beautiful or good (App. A, 1:18)]. Echoing the Biblical commandment to love one's neighbor as oneself, and conflating erotic love with friendship, Cupid points out that just as a man would flee anything that might dishonor himself, so too he ought to avoid dishonoring his *amie*. The god does acknowledge that the ultimate goal of love is "vouloir joÿr de s'amie" [to want to take pleasure in one's beloved (MS *Mor*, fol. 17v)]; but he stresses that the love should continue unabated regardless of whether or not this consummation is attained. Indeed, a hallmark of false lovers is that their sentiments fade rapidly once their desire has been satiated. A true lover, however, experiences an ever-growing devotion to his beloved:

> Mais que cil joïrs ne port mie
> Au joant nul saoulement,
> Ne de desir refroidement,
> Mais com plus joira plus sera
> Desirans et miex amera,
> Et plus ert en grains de servir
> Pour ce guerredon deservir. (Ibid.)

But this pleasure should never bring satiety to the one taking pleasure, nor any cooling of desire; but the more pleasure he takes the more he will desire and the better he will love, and the more he will be inclined to perform service in order to deserve this reward.

Although the above passage appears only in MS *Mor*, a similar sentiment is expressed in Gui's exposition of the four stages of love, which appears in both MS *Mor* and MS *Tou*.[10] Here, the God of Love explains that "tous mes deduis est en cace" [my entire pleasure is in the hunt (MS *Tou*, fol. 29v)], that is, in the long process of flirtation and dalliance that precedes sexual consummation. Once the hunt has been completed, the only possibility of pleasure lies in starting anew; it is thus desirable for the hunt to be prolonged as much as possible. In this respect Cupid distinguishes himself from his mother, Venus, whose sole interest is in the moment of consummation: "Car ne voet longe cace faire; / Ses coers si se delite ou prendre, / C'au cacier n'a cure d'entendre." [For she does not wish to make a long hunt; her heart delights in the capture, and she has no interest in the

---

[10] The explanation of the four stages of love, including Cupid's preference for the protraction of the earlier stages, is published by Jung, "Gui de Mori et Guillaume de Lorris," pp. 127–33.

hunt (ibid.).] Once again, then, the God of Love declares his preference for love as an ongoing relationship rather than merely a means to sexual gratification.

The distinction between Venus and her son is already present in Jean de Meun's continuation, where Cupid explains that his mother "a pris mainte forterece . . . ou je ne fusse ja presanz" [has taken many a fortress . . . where I was never present (vv. 10736–38)]. Jean, however, focuses on the distinction between sex given for love and sex given for money:

> ne ne me plust onques tel prise
> de forterece sanz moi prise,
> car il me semble, que qu'en die,
> que ce n'est fors marcheandie.   (vv. 10741–44)

Nor am I pleased by such capturing of a fortress taken without me, for it seems to me, whatever one might say, that it is nothing but buying and selling.

Gui, however, deleted Cupid's remarks about use of money to win sexual favors (vv. 10743–84). Instead, he chose to elaborate an opposition between single-minded seduction and the protracted love affair. This is in fact the same distinction that he perceived as the guiding principle of Jean's long continuation, for, as we have seen, Gui believed that Guillaume's poem had originally ended with the so-called anonymous continuation, in which the Lover manages to spend a night with the Rose. According to Gui, Jean simply removed this ending and substituted his own "por ce ke maistre Guillaumes vint trop tost a fin" [because Master Guillaume came too quickly to the end (MS *Tou*, fol. 41v)]. Gui's reworking of the God of Love's teachings shows that for him, this phenomenon of dilatation and delay was not only a poetic principle, but also an important element of the courtly ethos of the art of love.

Reason in turn places human love, in its various aspects, in an all-encompassing framework. Asked by the Lover to define love, she initially responds with a very general definition of love as a "movement of the heart" that seeks to possess some object of desire, devoting "toute sa pensee . . . / Et s'entencion" [all its thought . . . and its intent (MS *Mor*, fol. 36v)] to this end. Reason then explains that just as there are many objects of desire, so there are many forms of love; she will begin with "la souveraine" (ibid.), the love manifested by God in the Incarnation:

> Dieux qui tout le monde fourma,
> Qui de vraie amour le fourme a,
> Nous volt monstrer apertement
> Le fourme d'amer vraiement

95

> Quant il prist fourme en char humaine,
> Pour nous desfourmer de la paine. (ibid.)

God who formed the entire world, who has the form of true love, wanted to show us openly the form of true love when he took form in human flesh, to reform us from torments.

Reason goes on to explain that the love of God transcends all human friendship: human love is proportional to the good qualities inherent in the love object, but the goodness of God is infinite, surpassing all human measure. The love of God must therefore be absolute, encompassing "Cuer, corps, force, ame, et pensee" [heart, body, strength, soul, and mind (MS *Mor*, fol. 37r)].

Proceeding to an explication of the origins of love, Reason describes love as a fountain flowing from God in two streams (see App. A, 2). One, Christian charity, passes through the world and returns to God; echoing 1 Corinthians 13, Reason stresses that this form of love is essential to all other virtues. The other stream, *convoitise*, dissipates itself in the world; under this heading are included the love of family members, sexual desire, and material greed, which form a hierarchy ranging from moral neutrality to depravity. The image of the fountain is most interesting, given the importance of the Fountain of Love in the first part of the *Rose*. Jean de Meun, in the discourse of Genius, had elaborated a comparison of the perilous fountain to the triune fountain of life; but this passage was deleted by Gui, along with all other references to the *biaus parc*. Gui clearly felt that it was more appropriate for Reason to explain the distinction between heavenly and earthly love. And while the distinction between charitable and cupidinous love is essential to his discussion, Gui did nonetheless choose to stress the ultimate oneness of the many forms of love, all of which flow from God and reflect, however dimly, the divine love that infuses the world.

Two points emerge from Gui's reworking of Reason's presentation of love. On the one hand, Reason is explicitly Christianized. Jean's Reason does not, of course, say anything incompatible with Christian doctrine; when she identifies herself as the daughter of God, it is certainly the Christian God that she means. Nonetheless, Jean's Reason never explicitly cites the Bible, and aside from Boethius, her authorities are all pagan: Cicero, Seneca, Lucan, Plato, Homer. Had the Lover accepted Jean's Reason as a love object, he would have been taking an important first step, learning to love his own rational soul as the image of God rather than to focus his desire on external objects. But from the Christian perspective, this is only the first step; the next step, equally crucial, is to ascend to the love of God. Jean's Reason, however, offers her love as an end in itself, inviting the

Lover to imitate Socrates. Indeed, it is one of the ironies of Jean's poem – a point noted, if unappreciatively, by Gerson – that Nature and Genius speak at far greater length and far more explicitly about theological matters than Reason does. In the modern era, scholars have disagreed on the precise identity of Reason. Fleming has identified her with Divine Sapience; Badel has stated categorically that in the *Rose*, to love Reason is to love God. However, the fact remains that Reason herself says nothing of such matters. Hence other critics, such as Wetherbee, Hill, and Vitz, have seen Reason as more strictly limited to human reason, as opposed to divine wisdom or faith.[11]

Such ambiguities are largely dispelled in Gui's version of the *Rose*, in which Reason repeatedly cites both Biblical and patristic sources, including among others Augustine, Gregory the Great, Psalms, and the book of Wisdom. Gui seems to have interpreted Reason in more or less the same light as Fleming or Badel; but he felt that Jean's text did not adequately develop Reason's identity as a link between the human and the divine. As will be discussed below, an important aspect of Gui's remaniement was the adaptation of the *Rose* to bring it closer to its Latin sources; the expanded discussion of love is a case in point, serving to link Reason more closely with Boethius' Philosophy and with the Ratio of Augustine's *Soliloquies*. The latter reminds Augustine that love is to be directed to the realm of the spirit, not that of the body; the former stresses the essential oneness of divine and human love, explaining that love governs the elements, conjoins in marriage, and determines the laws of friendship (Book 2, Meter 8). Philosophy's disquisition on cosmic harmony was understood in the Middle Ages as an explication of the divine basis of friendship and marriage, of the embeddedness of human love in the divinely ordained natural order: a theme of the *Rose* as well, and one that Gui chose to develop.[12] And Gui cites Augustine as authority for the notion of love as a

---

[11] Fleming, *"Roman de la Rose"*, pp. 112–21 and *passim*; Badel, "Raison 'Fille de Dieu'." This claim has been variously disputed or modified by other critics; see, for example, Wetherbee, *Platonism and Poetry*, pp. 258–59; Hill, "Narcissus, Pygmalion, and the Castration of Saturn." For Fleming's response to these and other criticisms of his characterization of Reason, and for an elaboration of Reason's sapiential identity and literary lineage, see Fleming's *Reason and the Lover*, pp. 3–63. Vitz critiques Fleming's reading in her review of the latter book, arguing among other things that Jean's Reason is classical rather than Christian.

[12] Gui's presentation of this motif is in keeping with the larger context of the vernacular reception of Boethius. The fourteenth-century translation of Renaut de Louhains, for example, elaborates on the continuity between human and divine love, as Philosophy, having explained the harmonious conjunction of the elements, states: "Or veuil löer amour mondainne / Qui vient de l'amour souverainne" [now I want to praise earthly love, which comes from sovereign (i.e. divine) love]. I cite from the edition in preparation by Béatrice Atherton for her doctoral dissertation at the University of Queensland (vv. 4279–80), based on MS Bibl. Nat. fr. 578. I am grateful to Ms. Atherton for making her text available to me.

process of spiritual formation. Echoing the play on "fourme" and its derivatives employed in the evocation of the Incarnation, cited above, Reason explains that "amours si est confourmable / Del amant a la chose amable" [love is conformance of the lover to the beloved (App. A. 2:103–4)]; citing both Augustine and Psalm 82 (Vulgate 81), she then states that self-love leads to death, while love of God allows for union with the divine. This view of love pervades Augustine's writings and derives ultimately from Saint Paul's statement in Romans 12:2: "Et nolite conformari huic saeculo, sed reformamini in novitate sensus vestri." [Do not be conformed to this world but be transformed by the renewal of your mind (RSV).] By having Reason express this doctrine, complete with a vernacular version of the play on *conformare* and *reformare* (App. A, 2:101–3), Gui further accentuates her aspect as the voice of divine wisdom.

Gui's Reason does not limit her teachings to spiritual love, however; she is equally concerned with worldly love, the other stream that flows from God. And in order to elaborate the relationship between human and divine love, Gui had not only to supply the context of spiritual charity, but also to distinguish human love from its purely cupidinous aspect; and it is here that we return to the altered version of the God of Love and to his affinities with Reason. Even Jean's Reason does allow for the possibility of sexual relations – presumably conjugal – as long as the purpose is procreation rather than pleasure or material recompense (vv. 4371–98, 4515–69).[13] Some of her remarks could also be applied to the pursuit of love relationships outside of marriage, provided these are kept within the limits of rational control. Indeed, Reason sums up her position in a line worthy of Guido Guinizelli, "Bone amor doit de fin cuer nestre" [good love should be born from a noble heart (v. 4567)]; and she assures the Lover that she has nothing against amorous relationships conducted properly:

> Ainsinc leur queurs emsanble joingnent,
> bien s'entraiment, bien s'entredoignent.
> Ne cuides pas que jes dessenble:
> je veill bien qu'il aillent ensanble
> et facent quant qu'il doivent fere
> conme courtais et debonere.   (vv. 4557–62)

Thus their hearts are joined together, they love one another well, they give to one another. Don't think that I want to separate them: I want them to come together and to do whatever they need to, behaving with courtesy and refinement.

---

[13] See Lynch, *High Medieval Dream Vision*, pp. 137–38. I cannot agree with Kaske that Reason's words imply an acceptance of pre-marital sex ("Getting around the Parson's Tale," pp. 152, 153); for a refutation of her argument, see Fleming, *Reason and the Lover*, pp. 14–15.

Gui retained these passages, introducing them with a short interpolation explaining that lovers are of more than one variety: those who love "purely" and those who love only for carnal pleasure. And it is in explaining the nature of "pure" love that Reason echoes the God of Love virtually verbatim, stressing that a noble lover would never seek to injure the reputation or the honour of his beloved (App. A, 2:126–31).

Most interesting of all, both Reason and the God of Love, as they appear in MS *Mor*, cite the tradition of vernacular love lyric as a source for human love properly conducted. Cupid, refuting the argument that women are loved only as a means to sexual gratification, states that "cil qui au pui ont chanté / Et qui mon mestier ont hanté / Sevent bien tenir le contraire" [those who have sung at the *puy*, and who have pursued my art, know how to maintain the contrary (App. A, 1:13–15)]. And Reason, arguing for a reasonable form of erotic love, informs the Lover that "pour ceste amour approuver / Sont fait li bel chant amoureux / Que li amant ont fait pour eulx" [the beautiful love songs that lovers have made for themselves are made in approval of this love (App. A, 2:123–25)]. Thus while Cupid and Reason occupy opposing sides – the former allied with Venus, the latter urging the Lover towards Christian charity – there is nonetheless a middle ground where both can meet, agreeing on a form of love that incorporates aspects of both eros and friendship. And this love is identified as that elaborated in the *trouvère* tradition and celebrated at the *puys*, the poetic and musical competitions held by the *trouvères*. The *puys* of Picardy and Artois, at which songs in honor of the Virgin were performed alongside those celebrating human love and where the pleasures and ethics of love were playfully debated in *jeux-partis*, are an important background for Gui's reception and rewriting of the *Rose*.[14] Gui may even have participated in the *puys* himself, at least as spectator. And the community of *trouvères* – many of them *clercs*, like Richard de Fournival and Adam de la Halle – no doubt constituted an important part of the early audience for the *Rose*. It is not hard to imagine that for such readers, as for Gui, the art of love elaborated in the *Rose* might seem incomplete, lacking an exposition of spiritual and divine love on the one hand, and of the more refined forms of human romantic love on the other.

Equally important to Gui's discourse of Reason is the *De amore* of

---

[14] On the *puys*, see Faral, *Jongleurs en France*, pp. 138–42. A connection between *Rose* readership and the *puy* is also implied by MS *Bé*, an anthology including the *Rose* and, among other things, two sirventes probably deriving from the *puy* competition, since both are built on the same series of stanza openings; see Langlois, *Manuscrits*, pp. 110–16. The topic of the two songs – the Incarnation, presented as a consequence of the fact that "love is more powerful than nature" – has a certain relevance to the *Rose*.

Andreas Capellanus. Gui's reworking of Reason's discussion results in a clear hierarchy of descending moral value: love of God and charity; friendship; "natureuls affections . . . par aliance ou par lignage" [natural affection . . . through alliance or lineage (MS *Mor*, fol. 38r)]; the "pure" love associated with the *trouvère* tradition; lustful passion; and material greed. This moral system is essentially the same as that outlined in the *De amore*, where the form of love designated as *purus* and *sapiens* occupies a middle ground between friendship and marital affection on the one hand and excessive passion on the other, and ultimately between the extremes of *caritas* and prostitution.[15] Like Andreas, Gui stresses the spiritual dangers of erotic love and extols the virtues of Christian charity and friendship, yet still acknowledges the possibility of an ennobling form of love between man and woman. True to her identity as daughter of God and image of Divine Sapience, Reason does clearly prefer the more spiritual forms of love. But her remarks about those who love "purely" and those who love for carnal pleasure serve to define a broad moral spectrum, allowing for a form of love service not incompatible with reason.

Reason's discussion of human love is continued by Ami, who, in Gui's *Rose*, expands on the possible integration of friendship and erotic love. Jean de Meun's Ami devotes a hundred lines to the description of true friendship (vv. 8025–124). Gui's Ami expands the discussion of friendship and love, reminding the Lover that the God of Love himself had recommended confiding in a friend, and even quoting the relevant lines (vv. 2672–74 and 2677–80) from the God of Love's commandments (MS *Tou*, fol. 82v). Gui's Ami points out that in love, five people are united in a network of mutual trust: the two lovers, each lover's friend and confidant, and the go-between to whom messages are entrusted, and who necessarily knows the lovers' secrets unless they are literate enough to manage a written correspondence. Erotic love, in other words, need not exclude friendship.

Ami does warn about the existence of women who deceive men for the sake of material gain, claiming to love when they do not. He tells the Lover to beware, for the power of love is such that even wise men have been known to fall in love with such temptresses. Ami cites Reason on this point, quoting lines (a version of vv. 4306–10) that Gui had deleted from the discourse of Reason:

> Et Raisons le dist en ses dis,
> Que si sage n'a l'en trouvé,
> Ne de force si esprouvé,
> Ne qui tant ait autres bontés,
> Qui par Amors ne soit dontés.   (MS *Tou*, fol. 79r)

---

[15] See Kelly, "Courtly Love in Perspective."

And Reason said it in her discourse, that so wise a man has never been found, nor of such proven strength, nor one so endowed with other virtues, that he was not conquered by love.

But while such women do pose a threat, this does not mean that love itself must be avoided; one simply has to find a woman "plaine de francise . . . vaillans et courtoise" [full of frankness . . . valiant and courteous (MS *Tou*, fol. 79v)]. Ami agrees with both the God of Love and Reason that such a relationship, marked by mutual generosity, will not necessarily include full sexual consummation:

> Et par amors vous habandonne
> Et son avoir et sa personne;
> Ou sans se personne, l'avoir
> Poés a vo voloir avoir;
>
> . . .
>
> Mais congiét avés dou closier
> D'aler auques priés dou rosier.   (Ibid.)

And out of love she abandons to you her belongings and her person; or without her person, you still have access to her belongings . . . But you have permission to go into the enclosure and closely approach the rosebush.

Gui's Ami then explains that the complexities of the feminine character are such that no general rules can be given for winning them over: "Lor acointance est arbitraire" [their acquaintance is arbitrary (MS *Tou*, fol. 80r)]. In an obvious allusion to the *De amore*, he states that he will not attempt to describe the manner of address appropriate for men of each social class to use with women of the various classes; one must simply learn to judge the particular situation at hand.

Gui does devote considerable space to the issues of jealousy and marital harmony. Gui's Ami distinguishes between "jalousie" and "langheur," explaining that while a certain languorous yearning is appropriate to love, jealousy is not.[16] Once again he cites Reason, drawing on her celebrated litany of the paradoxes of love (vv. 4263–300) in order to establish the distinction between these two states of mind. There Reason refers to amorous languor: "C'est langueur toute santeïve, / c'est santé toute maladive" [it is a healthy languor, it is a sickly health (vv. 4275–76)]. Ami

---

[16] Gui raises Andreas' claim that jealousy is necessary for love by having the Lover cite *De amore*: "J'oÿ dire, n'a pas granment, / Que cis par amors n'amoit mie / Qui n'estoit jalous de s'amie" [I recently heard it said that he who is not jealous of his girl friend does not really love her (MS *Tou*, fol. 84r)]. This prompts Ami's explanation of jealousy and languor, leading into the discourse of the Jaloux. The necessity of jealousy in love is the second of the rules of love given at the end of Book 2 of *De amore*.

reinterprets this statement, explaining that "langheur" is a form of love sickness from which one can quickly recover:

> Et pour cou Raisons la soutive
> Dist que c'est santés maladive,
> Car il n'est nus si langereus,
> Quant li jours vient bons eureus,
> Que il poet la joie saisir,
> Dont il a eü tel desire. (MS *Tou*, fol. 84v)

And therefore subtle Reason said that it is a sickly health, for there is no one so languorous that he cannot achieve joy when the happy day arrives that he has so desired.

But whereas the languorous lover is sustained by hope, jealousy is a form of despair:

> Mais jalousie la sauvage,
> Qui ne poet de son cuer la rage
> Oster, est par Raison clamee
> Esperance desesperee. (Ibid.)

But savage jealousy, which cannot remove the rage from its heart, is what Reason calls despairing hope.

Jealousy turns love to hatred, producing the violent emotions so contrary to Reason:

> Pour ce ensi Raisons le define
> Que c'est amoureuse haïne,
> Qui toudis est a li contraire. (MS *Tou*, fol. 85v)

Therefore Reason defines it as amorous hatred, which is always contrary to her.

Gui de Mori's Ami emerges as a figure strangely in agreement with Reason in his assessment of love. True, he does advise the Lover to use force and deception in outwitting the guardians of the Rose.[17] In an interpolation, he even recommends enlisting the help of a valiant man known as Faux Samblant (MS *Tou*, fol. 70v). Gui does, however, delete Ami's justification of adultery (vv. 7375–84). And as Ami's account progresses, and he distinguishes the different kinds of love affairs, the ideal that emerges is one based on friendship, generosity, and trust; the dark passions condemned by Reason are associated with jealousy and greed, neither of which, in Ami's opinion, can coexist with real love. Ami and Reason are still to be

---

[17] Gui does, however, add a brief interpolation in which Ami warns the Lover that force must be used with extreme caution.

distinguished; in Gui's reworking of Guillaume de Lorris, Ami tells the Lover, "Ne ja de Raison ne vous caille, / Car n'est riens que ses consaus vaille / En ce cas chi" [nor should you care about Reason, for her advice is worth nothing in this particular case (MS *Tou*, fol. 34r, follows v. 3110)]. Yet even there, Ami adds that the Lover should remember to seek Reason's advice in other matters. Just as Gui smoothed out the differences between Reason and Love, so here he aims at a reconciliation of sorts between Reason and Ami, Love's advocate.

Gui also modifies Jean's negative portrayal of marriage. The long discourse on jealousy makes it amply clear that the Jaloux is being held up as a wholly negative example: it is neither marriage nor the feminine character, but rather male jealousy that is the object of satire. Not that women are always blameless. In a move characteristic of his continuing effort to impose thematic order on Jean's poem, Gui transplants Genius' account of the wife who demands to know her husband's secrets (most of vv. 16317–666) into the discourse of Ami. This scenario directly follows that of the Jaloux, and is introduced by the rubric, "C'on ne se fie trop en feme" [that one should not trust a woman too much (MS *Tou*, fol. 91r)]: the evils of too little trust and of male domination are paired with an illustration of the dangers involved in trusting one's wife too much, and hence of female domination. But here too, Gui makes sure that the episode is seen not as a warning against love or marriage, but only as a call for discretion and balance. Jean's Genius had qualified his words:

> n'onc ne fu l'antancion moie,
> que les fames chieres n'aiez
> ne que si foïr les daiez
> que bien avec eus ne gisiez.　　　(vv. 16588–91)

Nor was it my intention that you not cherish women, nor that you should so flee them that you do not lie with them.

Gui amends this to read, "Ne que si fuir les doiiés / Que vous de riens les mesprisiés" [nor that you should so flee them that you in any way devalue them (MS *Tou*, fol. 92v)], and adds, "Car li hom ki feme n'onnoere / Ne doit estre honnerés nule oere" [for the man who does not honor women should in no way be honored (ibid.)]. Gui's Ami explains that women should assume household responsibilities and should have freedom to come and go, as long as the husband remains the head of the household: "Mais adiés humle et deboinaire / Doit estre a son mari sougite" [but she should be humble and good-tempered, subject to her husband (MS *Tou*, fol. 93r)]. Friendship and love, not tyrannical domination, are the substance of the marriage bond: men are urged to treat their wives as *amies*, so as to achieve "Loiauté, pais, et concordance" [loyalty, peace, and harmony (ibid.)].

Gui's treatment of marriage anticipates criticisms that will be leveled against Jean de Meun over a century later. Both Christine and Gerson attacked Jean's negative portrayal of marriage; Christine commented in the *Cité des dames* that she could not imagine any man allowing his wife to bully him so.[18] She further insinuated, in her epistle "Reverence, honneur avec recommandacion," that a man deceived by a woman has only himself to blame: "Et se tu dis que tu en es assotéz, si ne t'en assote mie" [and if you say that you're bedazzled by her, well then, don't get bedazzled (ed. Hicks, p. 18)]. Christine found it particularly incongruous that the priest of Nature, who presides over procreation and urges sexual activity, should be the one who warns men to flee women.[19] Such behavior on the part of Genius certainly has no precedent in Alain de Lille. Gui was clearly troubled by similar concerns. His revisions result in a more orderly treatment of marriage, appropriately located entirely within Ami's discourse about relations between the sexes. Genius is accordingly freed of his antifeminist and anti-marital associations, so that his exhortation to procreate can be understood in the context of marriage.[20] And marriage itself is portrayed more favorably: marital discord is a danger, but can be avoided if both parties are reasonable.

Finally, Gui's structural revisions of Ami parallel his treatment of the other major discourses. He replaced Jean's concentric "ring" structure with a linear order, moving all of the discussions of the Golden Age – used by Jean to frame the discourse of the Jaloux – into one place, and relocating Ami's closing advice about love into the first half of his discourse, along with the other recommendations for managing a love affair.[21] And as he had

---

[18] In the *Cité des dames*, Reason says, "For where has the husband ever been found who would allow his wife to have authority to abuse and insult him as a matter of course, as these authorities maintain?" (trans. Richards, p. 7). Gerson charges that Jean "vuelt deffandre mariaige, sans exepcion, par .i. Jalous souspessonneux" [wants to forbid marriage, with no exceptions, by means of a suspicious jealous husband (ed. Hicks, p. 61)].

[19] Christine points out the contradiction that Genius urges men both to lie with women and to flee them, in "Reverence, honneur, avec recommandacion," p. 17, and "Pour ce que entendeme humain," p. 132.

[20] Christine asserts that Genius, in exhorting procreation, "ne pansa oncques a marriage, le bon homme" [never thought of marriage, that fine gentleman ("Pour ce que entendeme humain," p. 143)].

[21] Poirion pointed out the use of *emboîtement* in the discourse of Ami in his *"Roman de la Rose"*, p. 125. Gui's changes include the insertion of vv. 8997–9008, along with much interpolated material, before v. 8252; the insertion after v. 8424 of most of vv. 9463–634, this followed by the discussion of friendship and love; after which come vv. 9823–38, somewhat rearranged and combined with interpolated material; vv. 9703–12 and 9696–702, along with the interpolations on jealousy and languor; and finally the discourse of the Jaloux, beginning with v. 8425. While these are not Gui's only structural changes in the discourse of Ami, the above examples are sufficient to demonstrate his efforts to transform Jean's concentric-ring structure into a linear progression.

done with Reason, Gui deleted certain pagan references, such as the description of Zephyrus and Flora (vv. 8383–92) and Juvenal's comment that a man who finds a chaste woman should make a sacrifice to Juno (vv. 8677–84). The marginal signs of MS *Tou* indicate that Gui had also once deleted the story of Abelard and Heloise, which might have offended him both as the story of a fallen cleric and as an argument against marriage. The story now appears, however, not only in MS *Tou* but also in MSS *He* and *Mor*. Popular interest in the story may have militated against its exclusion from the poem.

The poem concludes, in Gui as in Jean, with the plucking of the Rose; but Gui brought the action to a much more rapid close. He deleted the story of Pygmalion, and he removed the lengthy digressions in the concluding passage. The original state of the text is preserved in both MS *Mor* and MS *He*, which faithfully reproduce the deletions indicated in MS *Tou*. The single longest deletion in the poem's conclusion is that of vv. 21317–667, which include the Lover's praise of his own testicles, the metaphors of pilgrimage, relic, and sanctuary, and the graphic account of the penetration to the Rose. The transition from v. 21316 to v. 21668 is handled like this:

21316	Jou qui l'en rench mierci .c.^m,
xxx	Com cil qui pas n'iere courciés
xxx	Me sui lues mout bien escourciés,
xxx	Et passe avant pour la main tendre
21668	Au rainsiel pour le bouton prendre.

(MS *He*, fol. 149r)

I, who gave a hundred thousand thanks, like one who is not at all unhappy, betook myself and stepped forward in order to reach out my hand to the stalk and take the bud.

Gui does allow the Lover to reach the Rose, to impregnate it, and to express his pleasure. Less severe than Gerson, Gui held no objection to the consummation of the erotic quest, but only to a lascivious treatment of the climactic moments. His previous work on the poem had established the groundwork for a morally acceptable erotic relationship, one based on mutual love and trust and pursued within the bounds set by Reason and Nature. Gui's Lover remains an ironic figure, no closer to moral enlightenment than that of Jean. But Gui's version of the poem does more clearly show us the alternatives to the Lover's behavior; and the modified account of his folly makes for a more traditional moral exemplum. The removal of the more blatantly pornographic passages and pagan fables, along with the elaboration of a clearer didactic framework, rendered the story fit for consumption within Gui's clerical community.

THE *ROSE* AND THE *AUCTORES*: JEAN DE MEUN AND GUI DE MORI

One of the essential features of Jean's *Rose* is its blend of seemingly disparate materials: Ovidian love psychology, Boethian philosophy, Chartrian naturalism. Not only does Jean draw his material from a wide range of sources, but he freely adapts and distorts this material to fit its new context, such that it is often difficult to be sure whether a given author is being used seriously or parodically. We have already seen that Gui expanded on the Ovidian model in the *Rose* and that he adjusted its ethos of love in accordance with the teachings of Andreas Capellanus and the *trouvère* tradition of *fin' amours*. He was equally concerned with adapting the relationship of the *Rose* to its other sources. We have seen one example in the discourse of Reason, where Reason's comments on love are expanded in order to bring her closer to her Boethian model. I wish now to examine more closely the importance of both Boethius and Alain de Lille as guides to Gui's reworking of Reason, Nature, and Genius.

The principal deletions in Gui's version of the discourse of Reason fall into three categories: allusions to unorthodox sexual practices, passages involving the word 'coilles', and references to pagan mythology.[22] In Jean de Meun, Reason alludes to "cil de male vie / que Genius esconmenie" [those of evil habits whom Genius excommunicates (vv. 4313–14)]; this reference to homosexuality has been excised, as has most of Genius' description and condemnation of homosexuality. Reason's discourse contains a second reference to homosexuality, this time coupled with a reference to incest: Nero, she says, "bailla soi meïsme a home" [even gave himself over to a man (v. 6179)] in addition to having sexual relations with his sister. The story of Nero is retained by Gui, but the allusions to his sexual escapades are gone; instead, Gui states simply that "Moult fist d'autres maus grant plenté / Plains de malvaise volenté" [he committed many other evil deeds, full of ill will (MS *Tou*, fol. 63r)].[23]

The same bowdlerizing spirit is reflected in the omission of the word "coilles" in MS *Tou*. The story of the castration of Saturn is deleted

---

[22] The one major deletion that does not fall into one of these categories is that of the story of Charles d'Anjou and Manfred, removed through the deletion of vv. 6597–713. This omission is easily explained on political grounds. MS *Tou* was made for the Pourrés family of Tournai; as subjects of the Empire, they would hardly appreciate the pro-French bias of Jean's account. Indeed, of the manuscript's ornamental initials, four are decorated with the lion of Hainaut and Flanders; five with the German eagle; and one with the three leopards of England (see Fourez, "Le *Roman de la Rose*," p. 219).

[23] Gui was not the only medieval reader of the *Rose* who wished to suppress Nero's homosexuality. In manuscripts of the *K* family one often finds a variant of this passage saying not that Nero gave himself over to a man, but that he gave his sister over to his men.

entirely; since the offending word is thus absent, there can be no accusations of bawdiness and hence no debate about language. The removal of the debate about language posed a bit of a problem, since it does contain some useful material. Gui solved this dilemma by inserting Reason's statements about discretion into the discourse of the God of Love in Guillaume de Lorris: in an expansion on Love's "clean speech" commandment following v. 2102, we find vv. 7005–12 and 7023–30. In the area of language, at least, Gui wanted no conflict between Love and Reason.[24] The patron deity of love poetry, served by Guillaume de Lorris, Jean de Meun, and Gui de Mori alike, could not be perceived as instilling irrational linguistic values. Similarly, Reason, whose wisdom is needed if poetry is to retain its edifying function, cannot be allowed to violate the principles of poetic decorum; and as Gerson was later to point out, something is very wrong when Cupid appears more reasonable than Reason herself![25]

Gui's removal of Reason's plain speech – the fable itself and the ensuing discussion – is an example of his unwillingness to tolerate Jean's more adventuresome departures from the Latin authors. As Fleming has pointed out, the Lover's reproach that the word "coilles" does not belong "en bouche a cortaise pucele" [in the mouth of a courteous virgin (v. 6901)] is an echo of the *De planctu Naturae*, where Natura announces that she will describe human vice in euphemistic allegory, so that filthy words will not appear "in ore virginali" [in a virginal mouth (ed. Häring, p. 839)].[26] Jean's Reason thus takes a position on language and interpretation different from that of Alain's Natura. In a sense, she is more consistent. Natura is no slave to the literal sense of words; like Reason, she offers an explanation of poetic integument. In both texts, this explanation is occasioned by one character's objection to a bawdy pagan fable; but whereas in the *Rose* it is Reason who narrates the fable and the Lover who objects, in *De planctu Naturae* the situation is reversed. Natura laments the sexual crimes of humanity; the narrator asks why she has neglected to mention the similar crimes of the gods. Natura, shocked, replies that such fables are nothing more than poetic fictions, unfit for serious study.

[24] The story of the castration of Saturn and the ensuing debate about language and obscenity has been restored by MS *Mor*, in a version close to manuscripts of the first group, particularly MS *Eb*. However, the lines about discretion remain in the discourse of the God of Love. It is impossible to know whether the restoration of these passages derives from Gui or from a later scribe.

[25] Gerson complains that Cupid seems "plus chaste et raisonnables que dame Raison et Chasteté" [more chaste and more reasonable than Lady Reason and Chastity (ed. Hicks, p. 85)].

[26] Fleming, *Reason and the Lover*, pp. 106–7; see especially p. 106, n. 9 Quilligan addresses the different positions expressed by Jean's Reason and Alain's Natura, with regard to the dynamics of poetic allegory, in "Words and Sex."

In the ensuing brief discussion of poetry, Natura explains that poets may intoxicate their audience by presenting "sine omni palliationis remedio . . . nudam falsitatem" [naked falsehood without any protective cloak (p. 837)]; or, to make an even greater impression, "ipsam falsitatem quadam probabilitatis hypocrisi palliant" [they cloak the falsehood with a certain pretense of probability (ibid.)]. If poetry is to have value, the reader must look beneath the surface, "ut exteriore falsitatis objecto putamine, dulciorem nucleum veritatis secrete intus lector inveniat" [so that, the external rind being removed, the reader finds within the sweeter, hidden kernel of truth (ibid.)]. Bawdy fables about pagan gods, however, are not capable of containing any truth.

The three possibilities outlined here find their correspondence in the *Rose*, but with interesting modifications. The latter technique, of expressing truth through a cloak of allegory, is that proposed by Reason; the second possibility, that of hiding false or lascivious material under a euphemistic, deceptively inoffensive surface, is what the Lover wishes Reason had done: "ne sai con nomer les osastes, / au mains quant le mot ne glosastes / par quelque cortaise parole" [I don't know how you dared to name them, without at least having glossed the word with some courteous phrase (vv. 6903–5)]. Of course, the Lover is not worried about the truth or falsehood of Reason's fable, but only its language; he proceeds to "gloss" his own erotic tale in elaborate detail at the end of the poem. The first scenario – the naked presentation of fictions – is what he finally accuses Reason of having done. But Reason – surprisingly, if we expect her to follow in the footsteps of Natura – clings to her right to name sexual matters openly, and also argues for the philosophical worth of the story of primeval castration. An erotic tale about pagan gods can contain a moral point, and the lack of a euphemistic cover poses no obstacle to its pedagogical use: the tale itself is the allegorical veil, and does not need a veil of its own.

The Lover, in other words, understands integument as euphemism; Reason understands it as the packaging of philosophical truths in fictional form. The Lover shares Natura's preference for the "cloak of euphonious speech" while ignoring her concern for the truth; Reason shares her belief that poetic figures must express truths, but denies the need for euphemism. In effect, Jean dismantles Natura's arguments, showing that the distinction of acceptable and unacceptable fictions, as well as that between acceptable and unacceptable language, is erroneous: what matters is not the words or the stories themselves but the way they are used. The passage brilliantly prepares for the poem's conclusion, where we see that a text that is overtly spiritual can still be extremely erotic – and yet, correctly read, nonetheless a moral exemplum.

As we have seen, Gui was not alone among medieval readers in objecting to Reason's arguments. Gui had neither the daring spirit nor the comic flair of Jean de Meun: he wanted Reason to be morally unambiguous, truly the poetic sister of Alain's Natura and Boethius' Philosophy, just as he wanted the didactic structure of the poem to be clear. As his prologue states, his goal was to render the *Rose* "plus entendables / Et a oïr plus delitables" [more comprehensible, and more pleasant to listen to (MS *Tou*, fol. 5v)]. In this respect he was remaining true to the values enunciated by Jean himself, who states that "profiz et delectation" [profit and pleasure (v. 15211)] are the twin purposes of poetry. But for Gui, the occasional lapses into bawdy language and moral turpitude, and the labyrinthine ramblings that Jean sometimes indulges in, detracted from the pleasure and profit of the text.

The castration of Saturn was not the only myth that Gui deleted. He had nothing against pagan writers: his interpolations in the discourse of Reason are replete with allusions to Aristotle, Cicero, and Seneca. Mythology, however, was another matter. Not only did he delete the story of Jupiter and Saturn; the marginal signs of MS *Tou* indicate that at one point Gui had also deleted the allusion to Daedalus (vv. 5196–99); similarly marked, and still missing from MS *Mor*, are the stories of Mars and Venus and Pygmalion; Deucalion and Pyrrha are missing from MS *Tou* and MS *Mor*. This removal of pagan fables continues the spirit of Guillaume de Lorris, whose adaptation of the story of Narcissus and Echo omits Echo's encounter with Juno as well as the metamorphoses of both Echo and Narcissus; Gui adapted the tale of Narcissus even further, situating it in the world of medieval romance by incorporating material from *Floris et Liriopé*. His treatment of the story of Venus and Adonis is similar. He retained Venus' lecture to Adonis about which animals to hunt, perhaps because it echoed the theme of hunt that he had developed at some length in the first part of the poem: Venus' words show that she favors a quick and easy conquest.[27] But he deleted the account of Adonis' death – perhaps in the interests of narrative coherence, since Adonis is still alive at the moment described in the *Rose* (vv. 15647–68, 15735–37) – and its ludicrous moral lesson of never doubting the fidelity of one's *amie*.

[27] I have discussed the passage in which Cupid declares his preference for hunt over capture. In addition, Gui's description of the Garden includes the advice to hunt squirrels and rabbits rather than stags, boars, or foxes; the various animals are clearly allegories for different kinds of women (timid and harmless; dangerously resistant; deceivers). The story of Venus and Adonis is glossed as a warning not to pursue inappropriate women in the commentary on the *Echecs amoureux* (Bibl. Nat. fr. 9197, fol. 222r–v).

In reducing the poem's mythological program, Gui brought it closer in line with the literary values of Macrobius, whose authority is invoked in Guillaume's prologue. Macrobious stipulates that only a certain kind of fable is appropriate to philosophical treatises: the *narratio fabulosa*, built on "a solid foundation of truth, which is treated in a fictitious style" (*Commentary* 1, 2:9; tr. Stahl). But even these are unacceptable when "the presentation of the plot involves matters that are base and unworthy of divinities and are monstrosities of some sort (as, for example, gods caught in adultery, Saturn cutting off the privy parts of his father)" (1, 2:11). As Fleming has shown, Jean consistently undid Macrobius' categories: he wrote of an erotic dream, he employed bawdy fables in a learned context.[28] But such was not Gui's style; even the erotic dream, though preserved, undergoes modifications that render its conclusion less a tour de force of erotic allegory. As I have said, Gui consistently adjusted the relationship of the *Rose* to the Latin tradition. And just as he omitted a passage putting Reason in conflict with Alain de Lille's Natura, so also he sought to reinstate the literary standards of Macrobius.

The dangerous pagan elements of Reason's discourse, then, were to be suppressed. In an interesting move, Gui even deleted the allusion to Suetonius' characterization of Christianity as "fause religion novele / et malfesant" [a false and pernicious new religion (vv. 6430–31)]. Suetonius is cited as the source for the story of Nero; to identify him as an enemy of the faith would undermine his authority, destroying the delicate balance of pagan and Christian traditions. Preserving this balance was important to Gui; and to this end he expanded Reason's exposition with Biblical allusions. In an interpolation on friendship, for example, Gui's Reason cites not only Cicero, Seneca, and Aristotle, but also Sirach, adding the wisdom of the Old Testament to that of the philosophers. The doubling of pagan and Biblical authority is especially striking in the discussion of injustice, where the tragic story of Virginia, victim of a corrupt judgment, is followed by the tale of Susannah, saved from false judgment by divine intervention (Daniel 13).[29] Virginia and Susannah are similar characters: both are faced with a choice between sexual violation and death, and both – like that other pagan woman, Lucretia, whose story is told later on by the Jaloux – prefer death. For the two pagan women, however, death is the only possible solution, the only means by which they can dramatize their plight in the eyes of the populace, thus achieving posthumous redress through the imprisonment and suicide of Appius and the exile of Tarquin

---

[28] Fleming, *Reason and the Lover*, p. 165.
[29] The text of this interpolation is given in Appendix A, 3. It should be noted that the first-person voice in the interpolation is that of Reason.

respectively. The Biblical heroine, however, knows of a higher authority through whom she can be vindicated without having to die. The importance of this divine authority is reiterated as Gui's interpolation continues, citing the example of the pagan King Avenir, a ruthless persecutor of Christians, and the ex-courtier, now a Christian convert, who upbraids him.[30] Clearly, it is the convert's Christian faith that gives him the courage and moral authority to confront the evil king.

A similar juxtaposition of pagan and Biblical models appears in Reason's discussion of Fortune. Gui retains her accounts of the demise of Seneca, Nero, and Croesus, and adds an allusion to Joseph's imprisonment by Potiphar. While Gui does not mention the incident with Potiphar's wife, any medieval reader would know the story. The example of Joseph parallels that of Susannah, an innocent person falsely accused of sexual misconduct; and again the reader knows that unlike his pagan counterparts, Joseph will be saved and will rise to a position of power. Joseph's powers of dream interpretation, in turn, contrast with Croesus' inability to understand his dream or to accept Phanie's all too accurate reading of it. The story shows that although Joseph was subject to Fortune, his patience, faith and God-given powers ultimately enabled him to triumph over adversity. The addition of these Biblical exempla thus has a double effect on Reason's discourse. Not only is her authority expanded to include that of the Bible, but her teachings acquire a greater degree of optimism: powerful though Fortune may be, she can always be overturned by the greater power of divine Providence.

The discourse of Nature is similarly edited by Gui to conform to the models of Boethius' Philosophy and Alain's Natura. Although in MS *Tou* the discourses of Nature and Genius appear much as they do in the standard version of the poem, MSS *Mor* and *He*, as well as the marginal signs in MS *Tou* indicating a "subtraction reprise," show that Gui's original remaniement shortened these sections considerably. As with the discourses of Ami and La Vieille, that of Nature is simplified and a linear order imposed on its circular structure.[31] The single largest deletion – whereby 594 lines are reduced to a mere thirty-eight – is that of vv. 17891–18484, of which only vv. 17951–54, 17983–18012, and 18243–46 remain: in this way Gui deletes most of Nature's discussion of storms, and her entire treatment of optics, dreams, and visions. Many other shorter passages are removed as well.

---

[30] The story of King Avenir appears in the legend of Barlaam and Josaphat, which circulated in various Latin and vernacular versions; see Sonet, *Le Roman de Barlaam et Josaphat*, vol. 1. Gui's treatment of the episode is fairly close to that in the version by Gui de Cambrai, ed. Zotenberg and Meyer; the episode in question is pp. 7–10.

[31] On the structure of Nature's discourse, see Patterson, " 'For the Wyves love of Bathe'," pp. 672–73.

Predictably, the reference to the castration of Origen is gone, as are mythological allusions. Moral qualms no doubt also motivated the deletion of Nature's initial condemnation of Faux Samblant and Contrainte Attenance and her subsequent pardon, based on the acknowledgment that such "barat" [fraud] is necessary for the cause of Love (vv. 19315–38); indeed this passage is not among those restored to MS *Tou*. The lengthy passages on mirrors and optics, dreams, and storms – mostly restored to MS *Tou* – were presumably seen as irrelevant to Nature's main argument. And interestingly, Gui removed Nature's account of the Incarnation and its foretelling by pagan writers. What is left of the discourse of Nature, in this much-reduced version, is the description of the cosmos; the reconciliation of free will and divine foreknowledge; the account of rainbows and other heavenly signs; the discussion of nobility, contrasting the nobility of lineage with that of the heart; and the enumeration of human vices.

The discourse of Nature in this version is rendered much clearer, much more focused, and less frivolous. Nature is not distracted from serious philosophical issues by a rambling exposition of optical illusions, and from there by the story of Venus' adultery with Mars. Appropriately, Gui omits Nature's self-deprecating comment on her own loquaciousness, "Fame sui, si ne me puis tere" [I am a woman, so I cannot keep quiet (vv. 19188–90)]. Gui's Nature has had her dignity restored. She contributes to the moral framework of the poem, setting forth human vices and virtues and establishing the individual's responsibility for his or her actions. As was already suggested by Reason's various exempla, we are not mere victims of fortune or fate: we are free to choose in what way we will react to the course of events, and our choice of vicious or virtuous behaviour may even affect the outcome of those events. Gui creates a Nature much closer to her Latin models, Philosophy and Natura; once again, he undoes Jean's daring and humorous distortions of Latin texts.

A few examples will illustrate the ways in which Gui deletes digressions that detract from the impact of Nature's arguments. In a discussion of the role of free will in the pursuit of virtue and the avoidance of sin, Nature alludes to the influence of heavenly bodies on individual character and the power of free will to resist such influences. In Jean's texts this initiates a long digression (vv. 17549–672) in which Nature, moving from the psychological to the physical effects of the heavens, considers the benefits that would accrue to humankind if people were able to predict natural disasters such as droughts, storms, and floods: they would know whether to build houses or boats, whether to live in highlands or lowlands. The discussion of floods in turn leads to a digression within the digression, in which Nature recounts the story of Deucalion and Pyrrha (vv. 17568–615).

After returning to and concluding the topic of meteorology, Nature finally returns to the main line of her argument, noting that if people could so successfully avoid the physical discomforts caused by adverse weather conditions, then the soul – which everyone knows is much more powerful than the body – surely has the ability to overcome moral problems caused by the adverse influence of the stars (vv. 17673–84). This entire digression is deleted – and not even restored in MS *Tou* – to allow for an uninterrupted exposition of human responsibility for sin. Other, shorter deletions have the effect of reducing excess wordiness without changing the content of the argument. At one point, for example, Jean's Nature explains that constraints of time prevent her from offering a complete exposition of her topic, adding that it has all been worked out already in other texts; anyone wanting more information can ask a *clerc* (vv. 17697–706). She then states that she will offer a few more arguments, though, because her detractors, wishing to avoid personal responsibility and blame God, might still raise certain points that she has not yet sufficiently refuted. The twenty-line passage leading up to these new arguments (vv. 17697–716) is reduced by Gui to eight lines:

17697	Des destinees plus parlaisce,
17698	Fortune et cas determinaisce,
17701	Et mains exemples i preïsse;
17702	Mais trop longement i meïsse.
17707	N'encor se taire m'en deüsce,
17708	Ja certes parlé n'en eüsce.
17710	Mais mes anemis poroit dire
17716	Qu'il n'a pas franc voloir d'ellire.

(MS *Tou*, fol. 143r)

I would speak more about destiny, I would determine fortune and chance, and give many examples; but it would take too long. Yet if I had to keep quiet about it, I certainly would never have spoken about it. But my enemy might claim that he does not have the free will to make choices.

And as this new argument develops, Jean's Nature, in spite of her earlier disclaimer, multiplies examples of the various possible human acts that might be blamed on predestination; the catalog culminates in the ten-line evocation of a failed marriage, in which "cist soit fos ou cele fole" [he or she might behave foolishly (v. 17739)], and which would have been justified on the basis that "Ceste fist diex por cestui nestre" [God caused her to be born for him (v. 17734)] and "Destinee li estoit cete" [she was destined for him (v. 17737)]. Gui suppresses the enumeration of examples, including the marriage vignette, by summing up all possibilities with the words, "Et puis, quant a la cose faite / Soit boine ou male" [and then, as for the thing that was done, be it good or evil (ibid.; replaces vv. 17738–42)]. Gui's

Nature is indeed far less garrulous than that of Jean, and far more capable of sticking to the point.

Gui de Mori's Nature, as she appears in MSS *He* and *Mor*, is also largely de-Christianized. Her discourse still opens with an invocation of "Cil diex, qui de biautez habonde" [that God who abounds in beauty (v. 16699)], and she still speaks of an omniscient divine creator. But this deity remains vague. Gui deletes Plato's description of the supreme god (vv. 19033–88), the account of the Trinity (vv. 19103–14), the mystery of the Incarnation (vv. 19089–102, 19118–32), the prophecies of Virgil and Albumasar (vv. 19133–60), and the reference to the Crucifixion (vv. 19179–83). In this respect Gui once again reveals concerns similar to those of Gerson, who complained that Jean frequently "atribue a la persone qui parle ce qui ne le doit appartenir" [attributes to the person speaking that which is inappropriate], citing the example of "Nature parlant de paradis et des misteres de nostre foy" [Nature speaking of paradise and of the mysteries of our faith (ed. Hicks, p. 85)]. Gui's Nature may be an authority on heavenly bodies and human nature, but she knows nothing of sacred mysteries. Once again, she has been brought closer to Alain's Natura, who, while readily acknowledging the supremacy of the divine Creator, avoids detailed discussion of the Incarnation or the Trinity.

The treatment of Genius accords with that of Nature. Almost 90% of his sermon is deleted, including the discussions of homosexuality and castration, and most of the exhortations to sexual intercourse; the myths of the fall of the Golden Age and the founding of Thebes; the description of pagan Hell; the review of Guillaume's Garden of Delight; and the entire exposition of the *biaus parc* (see App. A, 4). These deletions are all quite predictable, given Gui's treatment of the rest of the poem. Genius does advise Love's troops to follow the works of Nature, to beget offspring, and to avoid sin. As in *De planctu Naturae*, he participates in the miraculous transmission of life through procreation; he is a spokesman for the possibility of sexual activity within a moral framework. But that is all that he is. He offers no cosmology, no story of civilization, no attempt to conjoin the erotic and the sacred in a vision of procreation as salvation. The juxtaposition of erotic and sacred imagery that so disturbed both Gerson and Christine is thus abolished. Gui's Genius plays a much more limited role than that of Jean de Meun; he has largely been turned back into the Genius of *De planctu Naturae*.[32]

---

[32] In *De planctu Naturae*, Genius delivers a very short pronouncement of anathema against those who violate moral law, including – but not limited to – those who go against the "law of Venus." By this Alain alluded to homosexuality, not chastity. Genius' anathema appears in the closing section (ed. Häring, pp. 878–79). On differences between Jean's Genius and that of Alain, see Paré, *Idées et les lettres*, pp. 283–85; Nitzsche, *Genius Figure*, pp. 88–125.

Why, then, were so many of the deleted passages restored in MS *Tou*? We do not know whether the version presented here derives from Gui or from a later redactor. The prologue, missing from MSS *Mor* and *Ter*,[33] can only have been drafted for use in a manuscript containing "subtractions reprises" – quite possible either MS *Tou* itself or its model. In any case, the *Rose* of MS *Tou* is a reshaping of Gui's remaniement. Let us now examine the Tournai *Rose*, considering the function of its prologue and colophon and the appropriateness of this new version to the aristocratic context in which the manuscript was made.

SACRED AND EROTIC LOVE IN MS *TOU*

As we have seen, the original version of Gui's remaniement, insofar as we can reconstruct it from the surviving manuscripts, reflects attitudes somewhat similar to those voiced a century later by Gerson. Gerson objected to Reason's use of the word "coilles"; to the denigration of marriage; to the use of pagan mythology and of material from Ovid and Juvenal, and to the corruption of the material taken from Alain de Lille; to the story of Abelard and Heloise; to the presence of religious mysteries in the discourse of Nature; to the mixture of the sacred and the erotic in the discourse of Genius and in the poem's conclusion; and to the generally lascivious tenor of the text. Gui had no objection to Ovidian love psychology, at least as a poetic device, and indeed proclaims his desire to compose an *art d'aimer*; he was less severe in his literary tastes than Gerson. Nonetheless he did remove the word "coilles," the mythological allusions, some of the Juvenal material, the story of Abelard and Heloise, and portions of Nature and Genius; he modified considerably the discussion of both love and marriage, deleted the use of sacred imagery in an erotic context, and greatly shortened the account of the plucking of the Rose. For all his admiration of Guillaume and Jean, Gui nonetheless found the poem to be in need of considerable reworking; and a common clerical spirit informs both his and Gerson's reactions.

By no means all of Gui's changes have been undone in MS *Tou*. Though the word "coilles" now appears in the discourse of Ami and Genius, it was not reintroduced into Reason's discourse, certainly its most problematic location; the discussions of marriage and the feminine character remain modified, to allow for a tempered, more optimistic view. But the myths

---

[33] Jung calculates that, based on its number of folios and number of lines per folio, MS *Ter* must have contained about 19,000 lines; this would be the approximate length of Gui's *Rose* without the "subtractions reprises." Jung also acknowledges, however, that we do not know whether any pages were missing from MS *Ter*. See "Gui de Mori et Guillaume de Lorris," p. 112.

have been restored, as have the story of Abelard and Heloise, many of the lengthy digressions in Nature and her references to sacred mysteries, the discourse of Genius, and the full conclusion of the poem. On the other hand, MS *Tou* is missing Reason's discussion of divine love, her explication of love as a fountain, Cupid's arguments against love as a means to carnal gratification, and various other passages found in MS *Mor*. The version of Gui's *Rose* found in MS *Tou* represents a different taste, a different orientation, on the part of either the redactor or the intended reader.

The restoration of pagan references is not complete; certain passages were more easily accepted than others. During the God of Love's address to his troops, for example, he swears an eighteen-line oath, beginning with his mother and his grandfather, Saturn. He then names his brothers, commenting that due to his mother's promiscuity, "nus ne set nomer les peres, / tant sunt divers" [no one can name (their) fathers, so diverse are they (vv. 10804–05)]. And finally, he swears by the "palu d'enfer" [marshes of Hell (v. 10808)], appending a brief explanation of the penalty attached by the gods for breaking such an oath as this. According to the marginal signs in MS *Tou*, confirmed by MS *Mor*, Gui originally reduced this passage to just four lines:

10797	Mais par sainte Venus, ma mere,
10798	Et par Saturnus, son viel pere;
10803	Par la foi que doi tous mes freres,
10804	Dont nus ne set nommer les peres.

(MS *Tou*, fol. 93r)

But by holy Venus, my mother, and by Saturn, her old father; by the faith I owe all my brothers, of whom no one can name the fathers.

Gui thus retained the allusion to Cupid's ancestors, but, in accordance with his suppression throughout the poem of references to the struggle between Jupiter and Saturn, omitted the comment on the manner of Venus' engendering. Similarly, he kept the allusion to Cupid's many brothers and their fathers, but discreetly omitted the lines that emphasize the reason for the diversity of these fathers. The remainder of the oath, with its polytheistic overtones, was also omitted. In MS *Tou*, the reference to Venus' engendering (vv. 10799–800) has been restored; the other deleted lines have not. It is as though, having decided to reinstate Genius' account of Jupiter's displacement of Saturn and the resulting decline of the Golden Age, the redactor of MS *Tou* – whether Gui or a later scribe – saw no reason not to include this other brief allusion to Saturn's demise, but still preferred to suppress the references to the promiscuity and the perjuries of the pagan gods.

One can discern a similar attempt to distinguish between acceptable and unacceptable mythological references in other sections of the poem. In the discourses of both La Vieille and Nature, for example, the story of Mars and Venus has been restored. Perhaps the important role played in the frame narrative by Venus provided some justification for including myths involving her; it is interesting to note that the other major mythological episode originally deleted and then restored in MS *Tou* is the story of Pygmalion, in which Venus also plays a decisive role. La Vieille's brief digression about Argus' inability to keep watch over Io (vv. 14357–62), however, was not restored. This myth, unlike that of Pygmalion, has no immediate bearing on the frame narrative. And, since it involves the transformation of Io into a cow, it is less easily rationalized than the story of Mars and Venus, which can be read as simply a tale of adultery. Similarly, the myth of Deucalion and Pyrrha was never restored: it bears less directly on the story than does the myth of Pygmalion, it has no characters in common with the frame narrative, and it involves a miraculous transformation wrought by pagan gods. The pattern continues in the deletion of Juvenal's advice to sacrifice a gilded cow to Juno if one is lucky enough to find a chaste woman (vv. 8677–86). The subsequent citation of Juvenal's argument against marriage (vv. 8705–14) indicates that it was neither the antifeminist tenor of the passage nor the identity of the author that inspired the deletion and the decision not to restore it, but rather the idea of sacrificing to pagan gods.

What might have inspired this cautious restoration of pagan mythology to Gui's expurgated *Rose*? The most likely explanation is that the changes introduced in Gui's *Rose* reflect the context in which the manuscript was made. Gui's original work was done in a clerical context. His remaniement was thus aimed at *clercs* who desired a little light reading in the vernacular, but who could not be allowed to stray too far from the path of Christian doctrine, or to read anything too lascivious. We have already seen that Gui's work, while undoubtedly still too frivolous for Gerson's exacting standards, does go a long way towards meeting the objections levied by that churchman.

Numerous details suggest that Gui's *Rose* was aimed at an educated audience. For one thing, he multiplies the literary allusions, both Christian and classical. And he deletes passages that are clearly for the benefit of a lay readership. In two different places, readers of the *Rose* are instructed to consult clerks for more information about a particular point: in Guillaume's discussion of time (v. 370) and in Nature's discussion of predestination (vv. 17705–06). Gui deleted both of these passages, probably because his intended readers were clerks themselves. He also omitted the definition of "pardurableté" [eternity (vv. 17465–68)], a similarly superfluous passage for his intended readership. The clerical milieu is further suggested in Gui's treatment of Faux Samblant. He added several hundred verses to the discussions of monastic corruption, and, in order to assure that this section of the poem was understood as attacking not ecclesiastics but ecclesiastical corruption, he inserted the portion of Jean's Apology dealing with Faux Samblant (vv. 15213–5, 15218–68) directly into the discourse of Faux Samblant itself, following v. 11938. Finally, one of his interpolations in the discourse of La Vieille, a discussion and ultimately a condemnation of the courtship of nuns, would also have a particular relevance for clerical readers.

MS *Tou* itself, on the other hand, was made for lay patronage. The marginal illumination on fol. 5r, showing a kneeling couple with a coat-of-arms, indicates that this manuscript was made for a member of the Pourrès family of Tournai, possibly on the occasion of a wedding, or at any rate for a married couple.[34] One can assume, then, that at least some of its departures from Gui's original plan would have been made with this lay readership, and this context of aristocratic marriage, in mind. The length and complexity of the *Rose*, and the extent of Gui's revisions, would make it difficult for any redactor to achieve a hundred percent consistency in transforming a "clerical" *Rose* into a "lay" *Rose*, especially if the redactor was himself a cleric. Still, the changes we have seen – the partial restoration of mythological material and the decreased concern with bawdy and irreverent passages, such as the unorthodox begetting of Venus and the sexual "pilgrimage" to the Rose – do suggest the more worldly tastes of a lay audience. Lay patronage would also explain the restoration of the above-mentioned definition of "pardurableté." The modified treatment of marriage and the acknowledgment of loyal and virtuous women make the *Rose* in MS *Tou* far more appropriate to a celebration of marriage than that of Jean. If MS *Tou* was made for a wedding, or if it was produced for a married couple, then it is no surprise that its redactor would have chosen to use Gui's remaniement.

One of the most interesting differences between the recensions of MS *Tou* and MS *Mor* is the treatment of sacred and sexual love in each. In MS *Mor*, it is Reason who explains the nature of divine love, who cites the Incarnation, and who employs the fountain motif as a means of elaborating the different forms of love. But in MS *Tou* it is Nature who invokes the Incarnation; and the task of explicating the relationship between sexual

---

[34] See Fourez, "Le *Roman de la Rose*," pp. 215–16, n. 5.

activity and spiritual salvation reverts from Reason to Genius, placing this crucial set of arguments in the context of procreation and natural law rather than that of Christian rationalism. In MS *Mor*, while both Reason and the God of Love allude to the possibility of sexual consummation, both also promote a form of human love grounded in mutual respect and affection; even Ami agrees that full sexual consummation is not really necessary in a love relationship. Reason does additionally stipulate that if such should occur, it must be for the purpose of procreation. In MS *Tou*, however, with its fully restored discourse of Genius, procreation is the all-important goal of all sexual activity. The distinction elaborated by Genius is between fertile and sterile love, not between love based on affection or *caritas* and that based on carnal desire. For the Reason of MS *Mor*, human love participates in the divine insofar as it partakes of charity, of love for another person grounded in love of God; for the Genius of MS *Tou*, human love participates in the divine insofar as it is fruitful and life-sustaining.

This emphasis on procreation would probably also be more acceptable in lay circles. Indeed, the sacralization of procreation is entirely appropriate to marriage, a sacrament of the Church established for the purpose of conjoining male and female and legitimizing procreation. Exegetical tradition also saw human marriage as a metaphor for the relationship of the soul to God and of the Church to Christ. The prologue of MS *Tou* juxtaposes spiritual and erotic love right from the outset. In the opening couplet, Gui alludes to Richard de Fournival's *Bestiaire d'amours*, in which a bestiary, normally a format used to present the natural world as an allegory of sacred history and redemption, becomes instead an allegory of erotic love.[35] Explaining that love is the most important field of knowledge, Gui then cites Hugh of Saint Victor's mystical treatise *De arrha animae*.[36] Here, Gui states, one can read that

> Amours est li vie dou coeur;
> Ne ce ne peut estre a nul feur

---

[35] Gui's prologue begins with a maxim derived from Aristotle: "Toute discrete creature / Desire a savoir par nature" [each and every creature naturally desires knowledge (MS *Tou*, fol. 5r)]. Richard begins the *Bestiaire d'amours* with the same statement: "Toutes gens desirent par nature a savoir" [all people naturally desire knowledge (ed. Segre, p. 1)]. On the relationship of the *Bestiaire d'amours* to both devotional bestiaries and the *Rose*, see my discussion in *From Song to Book*, pp. 135–48.

[36] Gui cites the opening section, in which the man says to his soul, "Ego scio, quod vita tua dilectio est et scio quod sine dilectione esse non potes" [I know that love is your very life and that without love you cannot exist (ed. Migne, col. 951)]. Citations of the Latin text will be to this edition; translations are from *Soliloquy on the Earnest Money of the Soul*, transl. Herbert. Since there is no proof one way or the other for the authorship of the prologue, and since its perspective agrees with that expressed by Gui elsewhere in the text, I shall assume that he did write it.

> Que nus coeurs sans amours demeure,
> Ki a vivre couvoite une hoeure.   (MS *Tou*, fol. 5r)

Love is the life of the heart; nor could it ever be possible for any heart that wished to live for even one hour to remain without love.

Yet Gui moves very quickly from this evocation of mystical *caritas* to a different sort of love:

> Et pour çou que jou, tres m'enfance,
> Me sui penés du maintenir
> Amours, ne me puis plus tenir
> Que ne face sa volenté,
> Dont j'ai le coeur entalenté.   (Ibid.)

And since from my childhood I have applied myself to the cultivation of love, I can't keep from doing love's will, which is my heart's desire.

With this language – "maintenir amours," "faire sa volenté," "le coeur entalenté" – we have unmistakably entered the realm of *fin' amors*. Gui's *Rose*, as it appears in MS *Tou*, is thus inscribed within a dual concept of love, that which joins man and woman and that which joins the soul to God.

Later, in his interview with Reason, the Lover reminds her of the importance of love by citing *De arrha animae* in very similar terms:

> S'ai veüe une auctorité
> Que je tieng bien por verité,
> Qui dist que li vie dou coer,
> Çou est amors, ne a nul foer
> Li coers ne poet sains amor vivre. (MS *Tou*, fol. 55v)

And I have seen an authoritative text, which I consider true, that said that the life of the heart is love, nor can it ever be possible for the heart to live without love.

The Lover also cites 1 John 3:14, arguing that 'cis ki sains Jehans se claime / Nous dist k'en le mort maint qui n'aime" [he who is called Saint John tells us that he who does not love, dwells in death (fol. 55v)].[37] The Lover's use of these texts is richly ironic, for he certainly is not clinging to a form of love more spiritual than that of Lady Reason – least of all in MS *Mor*, which also includes these passages. But Gui's repeated citation of *De arrha animae* casts in high relief one of the central problems of the *Rose*, namely, the integration of sexual desire and Christian love, and the role of eros in both the natural and the divine orders. In Hugh's treatise, the model of human marriage is a metaphor for the mystical union of the soul with God; yet in

---

[37] Gui cites the Vulgate almost verbatim: "Qui non diligit, manet in morte."

Gui's prologue, and even more strongly in the Lover's words to Reason, one feels that the union of the soul with God has become a metaphor, or at least a model, for human love. Much the same could be said for the conclusion of the *Rose*, especially in the less abridged MS *Tou*: religious veneration is a metaphor for sexual intercourse, itself identified as the path to spiritual salvation. The Lover has confused and perverted the normal function of allegorical language.

De arrha animae has several points of contact with the *Rose*; and by citing it Gui invites us to read the *Rose* against the backdrop of Hugh's mystical treatise. The treatise takes the form of a dialogue between a man and his soul, a format that parallels the dialogical structure of the *Rose*, especially those sections where the Lover is in dialogue with his own cupidinous or rational faculties. The man invites his soul to select a love object, proposing first that the soul should love itself: "O si faciem tuam videres, agnosceres certe quanta reprehensione digna fueras, cum aliquid extra te amore tuo dignum existimabas." [If you could observe your own countenance, you would surely know what great reproof you deserved in thinking some physical object external to yourself worthy of your love (ed. Migne, col. 953; tr. Herbert, p. 15).] To this the soul objects that self-love is folly: "illum non rectissime insipientem quisque diceret, qui ad pascendum amorem suum similitudinem vultus sui jugiter in speculo considerat?" [would not everyone rightly call that man foolish who for the purpose of nourishing his love should continually consider his likeness in a mirror? (col. 953–54; p. 15)]. It declares itself in need of "quoddam alterius generis speculum . . . in quo faciem cordis mei cognoscam et diligam" [a certain mirror of another kind, by which I can know and love the sight of my heart (col. 953, p. 15)]. The man counsels his soul to remember its inner vision, so clear-sighted that "nulla eum foris peregrina similitudo, vel adumbrata veritatis imaginatio fallere potest" [no foreign likeness nor empty shadow of the truth can deceive it (col. 954; p. 16)].

This exchange, when held up to the *Rose*, illuminates the Narcissus passage: we see that Narcissus is the very embodiment of a perverse self-love brought on by inner blindness, a soul deceived by an *ombre*, an empty shadow. And while the Lover may at least avoid the error of loving his own image, he nonetheless commits the closely related error of directing his love to an external object.[38] Does he not, after all, ignore Reason's claim that his only real possessions are within himself (vv.

---

[38] In the mythographic tradition, Narcissus is interpreted as a figure not only for pride and self-love, but also for the sin of loving the creature more than the creator, which Gui alludes to in MS *Mor* (App. A, 2: 112–15).

5300–01), and her offer of herself as a mirror – one that would allow him to see into his own heart (v. 5789)? Does he not reject her suggestion that he should love her, his own rational soul, his personal link to God?

Having first encouraged his soul to look within and to fix its love on the spiritual, the man in Hugh's dialogue then reminds his soul that it has a "sponsum" [betrothed] – God – who has given it innumerable gifts. These include not only life itself, but also the natural world, which was created to meet the needs of humanity: "Hoc coelum, hoc terra, hoc aer, hoc maria, cum iis, quae in eis sunt, universis, explere non cessant." [This the heavens, earth, seas and all things in them never fail to supply (col. 955; p. 17).] If we are to read *De arrha animae* in tandem with the *Rose*, this evocation of the natural world as a divine gift can be seen as parallel to Nature's review of the earth and the cosmos. The man reminds his soul not to love the world for its own sake, however, but "ut arrham sponsi . . . nec ista pro illo, nec ista cum illo, sed ista propter illum, et per ista illum, et supra ista illum diligat" [as the earnest money of your betrothed . . . do not prefer these gifts to the giver, but hold them dear because of him and through them and above them love him (col. 955; p. 17)]; to do otherwise would be to behave as a harlot. The motif of the harlot who exploits love for the sake of material gain is certainly prominent in the *Rose*. And human efforts to possess and exploit the earth are identified by Ami – and in MS *Tou*, by Genius as well – with the fall of the Golden Age, a naturalistic version of the Fall from Grace.

A final parallel between the *Rose* and *De arrha animae* occurs in the conclusion of each text. The Lover embraces his Rose; and the soul in Hugh's dialogue comes to know the embraces of its divine bridegroom: "Exhilaratur conscientia, in oblivionem venit omnis praeteritorum dolorum miseria, exsultat animus . . . cor illuminatur, desideria jucundantur . . . et quasi quiddam amplexibus amoris intus teneo." [My senses are exhilerated, all the misery of past sorrows falls away, my mind is exultant . . . my heart also is cheered and my desires are pleased . . . and as it were I hold someone within me in the embraces of love (col. 970; p. 35).] In the former we witness the consummation of erotic desire; in the latter, the mystical union of the soul with God.

In elaborating this comparison I do not mean to imply, of course, that the two texts are parallel in all respects; still less, that Guillaume or Jean modeled the *Rose* on *De arrha animae*. But Gui clearly had thought about the two texts and found Hugh's treatise a useful counterpoint to the *Rose*. On the one hand, then, his remaniement serves to strengthen the authority of Reason, Nature, and Genius, while also stressing the need for an integration of friendship and sexual love, and casting marriage – the obvious locus of such an integration – in a more favorable light. At the same time, he intensifies the folly of the Lover, who succeeds neither in attaining spiritual love nor in redefining his erotic desire in the context of either friendship or marriage. Indeed, a willing pupil of Faux Samblant, he uses the language of spiritual love to veil the sexual. The relationship of *De arrha animae* to the *Rose* is particularly intriguing in MS *Tou*, which contains the complete discourse of Genius, the story of Pygmalion's idolatrous passion, and the detailed "pilgrimage" to the Rose. In a version of the *Rose* prepared for aristocratic readers who had taken no vows of chastity, and especially if that version was intended as a wedding gift, Genius' enshrining of the commandment to be fruitful and multiply need not pose a problem; one could read the passage in the manner of Pierre Col, as a condemnation of vain pleasure, a celebration of conjugal relations, and a reminder of that higher love, of which human love is but a shadow. In such a reading, Genius would be seen as correcting the Lover's mistaken association of his own love for the Rose with that proposed by Hugh.

It is precisely the discourse of Genius, with its double vision of worldly and spiritual joy, that is invoked in the colophon of MS *Tou*:

> Explicit li livres del Rose,
> Ou l'art d'amor est toute enclose.
> Escris fu l'an mil et .ccc.
> Et .xxx.; porfitans as gens
> Est, li quel se voelent tenir
> Au siecle, por eaus maintenir
> En estat de parfaite joie
> Mondaine; ou d'ensievre le voie
> De venir a joie sans fin,
> Qui voet ensievre le chemin
> Des blances brebis desus dites,
> Que li dous paistres a eslites,
> Pour mener el biau parc joli,
> Ou tuit puissons jouer od li.   (fol. 171r)

Here ends the book of the Rose, where the art of love is completely enclosed. It was written in the year 1330; it is profitable to people who want to remain in the secular world, to keep themselves in a state of perfect worldly joy; or for following the way that leads to joy without end, whoever might want to follow the path of the above-mentioned white sheep, whom the good shepherd has selected, to take with him into the beautiful, lovely park; may we all play there with him.

As was established in the prologue – and as was already suggested, I might add, by the portrait of the Virgin Mary that heads the Table of Contents – the *Rose* of MS *Tou* represents an effort to come to terms with the poem's depiction of sexuality as a part of both the social and the cosmic orders.[39] The colophon is both syntactically and conceptually difficult to interpret, reflecting the complexity of the moral and spiritual issues involved. But it does state that the *Rose* offers advice about different kinds of love. With its advice about love, justice, friendship, and marriage, and its warnings about corruption and exploitation, it offers a moral program for the laity, those pursuing "perfect joy" in the secular world. But the *Rose* is not limited to matters of this world: it also suggests that human love can be integrated into a Christian framework of spiritual redemption. And as I have said, it is this latter possibility that is offered in the sacrament of marriage. MS *Tou* offers an extended meditation on the meeting of the natural and the sacred, on the difficult but crucial separation of carnal lust and divinely sanctioned procreation; most generally, on the place of human love in the divine scheme of things.

GUI DE MORI IN THE *ROSE* MANUSCRIPT TRADITION

As stated above, Gui's interpolations in Guillaume's *Rose* circulated more widely than his reworking of Jean's text, which survives today in only four manuscripts aside from the lost MS *Ter*. Of these, MSS *Tou* and *Mor* and the passages added to MS *Ke* are closely related; standing somewhat apart is MS *He*. The latter is not simply a copy of Gui's remaniement, but rather a copy of the *Rose* made from a manuscript of a different family and edited in consultation with Gui's remaniement: many of his interpolations have been inserted, and many of his deletions – especially towards the end of the poem – have been made. However, Gui's name appears nowhere in the manuscript. His prologue is lacking, as are the marginal signs described therein. The passage announcing Gui as the third *Rose* poet is also missing, as is the passage inserted between Guillaume and Jean. MS *He* clearly was not made by someone who wished to preserve Gui's work as such. It results rather from a comparison of at least two versions of the *Rose* – that of the *H* family and that of Gui de Mori – and a judicious effort to create a composite edition, drawing the best from both sources. In fact, yet a third version of the *Rose*, that of family *B*, lies somewhere in the textual history of MS *He*, for it contains as well two passages from that remaniement: the Lover's characterization of Reason as "commune amie" and the God of Love's account of the contest between Apollo and Marsyas.[40] As we have

---

[39] Jung argues that Gui's citation of Hugh need not indicate a Christian interpretation of the *Rose* and suggests that the Christianizing framework of MS *Tou* – the portrait of the Virgin and the colophon – is the work of a later redactor; see "Gui de Mori et Guillaume de Lorris," p. 113, n. 20.

[40] For these interpolations, see Langlois's edition of the *Rose*, notes to vv. 6916 and 10830–31. The *B* text will be discussed below, in Chapter 4.

seen, Gui's system of marginal annotations would encourage such a project of textual comparison and adaptation, facilitating as they do the identification of his various "additions," "subtractions," and "mutations."

The redactor of MS *He* took a number of Gui's modifications in Guillaume de Lorris: the portrait of Orgeuil, the discourse on the arrows of love, the portrait of Plaisance, and the discussion of the first four degrees of love. He also borrowed some of Gui's lines for the opening portion of Love's commandments, and, while retaining Guillaume's version of the story of Narcissus, inserted Gui's reference to Liriopé and Floris after v. 1504. In Jean de Meun, the redactor of MS *He* inserted Gui's interpolations on youth and old age (after v. 4514); on friendship (after v. 4672); on the corruption of judges, the judgment of Susannah, and the depravity of King Avenir (after v. 5558); on clerical corruption (after vv. 11102, 11128, and 11494); and on the means of ridding oneself of an unwanted suitor (after v. 14516). However, these passages do not always appear in the same place that they do in MSS *Tou* and *Mor*; in the discourse of Faux Samblant, for example, several different interpolations, totaling 420 lines, are lumped together following v. 11494. In addition, the redactor of MS *He* relied entirely on an unaltered version of Gui's remaniement from the closing portions of Nature's discourse through to the end of the poem, for we find here all of the deletions made by Gui, both those that are preserved as such in the Tournai manuscript and those that have been restored there.

As an example of the differences between MSS *He*, *Mor*, and *Tou*, we can take the long interpolation appearing in Reason's discussion of justice, and comprising the story of Susannah, the confrontation of King Avenir and his former courtier, and an expansion of Reason's tirade against judicial corruption in general (see Appendix A, 3). First of all, the manuscripts disagree on the exact location of the interpolation: in MSS *Mor* and *Tou* it follows the story of Virginia, appearing after v. 5628; while MS *He* places it just before the story of Virginia, after v. 5558. Secondly, the interpolation itself is arranged differently in each redaction. In MSS *Mor* and *Tou*, the passage begins with the tale of Susannah, moves on to the example of Avenir, and then leads back into Reason's discussion of judges with a more general treatment of the topic of judicial corruption, incorporating a few lines from Jean de Meun. In MS *He*, the interpolation begins with the general discussion of judicial corruption and then moves on to the examples of Susannah and Avenir, re-entering Jean de Meun's text with the example of Virginia. The version in MS *He* also includes a few lines that do not appear in the other manuscripts. In all manuscripts, the three exemplary stories – those of Virginia and Appius, Susannah and the elders, and Avenir and his courtier – are grouped together; the more general discussion is used in MSS *Mor* and *Tou* to lead back into Jean's similar discussion, while in MS *He* it is used to lead from Jean's opening lines on the topic of justice into the series of examples.

Each version of the interpolation has its own internal logic. MSS *Mor* and *Tou* bridge the transition from the series of examples to the more general discussion by commenting on the phenomenon of judicial corruption:

> Mais des juges qui ore keurent
> Comment les povres gens sekeurent,
> Moult d'exemples trouver poroie,
> Se ramentevoir les voloie.

> (MS *Tou*, fol. 59r)

> But as for the judges there are now, and how much they help poor people, I could come up with plenty of examples if I wanted to compile them.

In MS *He*, on the other hand, this passage serves as an introduction to the series of exemplary tales. The interpolation begins with the general discussion, culminating in the lines cited above; instead of the ironic "sekeurent" [help] one finds "deveurent" [devour]. There follows the example of Susannah, illustrating the plight of the victim saved only by divine intervention; then the tale of King Avenir, showing how to upbraid corrupt judges and rulers; and finally the story of Virginia and Appius, in which Virginius, though forced to sacrifice his daughter's life, does succeed in confronting the corrupt officials and bringing about their downfall. The emphasis in MS *He* is thus on the means by which corruption can be challenged, with Avenir and Appius appearing as parallel figures. MSS *Mor* and *Tou*, however, pair the stories of the two women, Susannah and Virginia: the emphasis here is on the contrast between human and divine justice, and – as is certainly relevant to the *Rose* – on the plight of women who are sexually exploited by men. It is interesting that this version of the interpolation appears in versions of Gui's remaniement that also include the stories of two other wronged women: Heloise, originally deleted but here restored, and Lucretia, whose story, though abridged, does include the fact of her suicide and the subsequent assertion that rapists must be put to death.[41] It is possible that the interpolation as it appears in MS *He* derives from a recension in which the figures of Heloise and Lucretia were absent, and the emphasis was less on the fate of women than on justice and governance.

---

[41] On Lucretia and Heloise as figures of feminine autonomy in the *Rose*, see Baumgartner, "De Lucrèce à Héloïse."

The passages selected by the redactor of MS *He* suggest a dual interest in the *Rose*: in its love teachings, and in its exposition of personal and political ethics. The other texts copied with the *Rose* in this manuscript reflect these interests. The redactor's borrowings from Gui's reworking of Guillaume de Lorris, as well as his inclusion of La Vieille's advice about ending a love affair, fall into the former category; this same interest is also reflected in a short poem on the power of love that appears later in the manuscript (fol. 154r–v). His concern with ethics, on the other hand, is reflected in his use of Gui's interpolations on youthful folly, friendship, justice – particularly in this version, emphasizing the individual's resistance to injustice and tyranny – and ecclesiastical corruption. The interest in clerical corruption in particular is reflected in the final piece of the manuscript, Brisebare's allegorical *Plait de l'Evesque et de Droit* (fol. 154v–161r). Finally, love and justice, nobility of spirit, the power of Fortune, and the circumvention of tyranny are all present in the *Dit de l'Empeureur Coustant*, which follows the *Rose* (fol. 149v–154r): in this poem, a king is unable to prevent a marriage between his daughter and a low-born but inherently noble man – the future Emperor Constantine, as it turns out. Since the entire manuscript is written in one hand, we can assume that its contents were assembled as a collection by its redactor.[42] This anthology built on the revised *Rose* illustrates, once again, that for medieval readers the *Rose* was both entertaining and instructive, addressing both serious social and political issues and the delights of personal love.

In its conclusion, as I have said, MS *He* follows Gui's text quite closely; and since it draws on Gui's *remaniement* as it existed prior to the restorations of MS *Tou*, it can provide a guide to ways in which Gui had altered the text in making his deletions. Together with MS *Mor*, for example, it confirms Gui's radical abridgment of the concluding sections of the poem. It is possible that certain variants unique to MS *He* also derive from Gui de Mori. In the discourse of the Jaloux, for example, the marginal signs in MS *Tou* indicate that vv. 9125–26 – "Toutes estes, serez et fustes, / de fet ou de volenté, pustes" [all of you women are, will be and were, in deed or in will, whores] – have been restored. Marc-René Jung noted this fact, citing the original deletion of these lines as an indication that Gui's antifeminism was at least less crude than that of Jean.[43] And indeed, these lines are missing from MS *Mor*. In MS *He*, we find that vv. 9125–26 are also missing; but what replaces them is hardly more flattering to women:

---

[42] For a description of these texts, see Langlois, *Manuscrits*, pp. 175–77.
[43] Jung, "Gui de Mori et Guillaume de Lorris," p. 126.

Toutes fustes, serés, ou estes,
De fait ou de volenté, prestes
D'avoecques tous hommes gesir,
Pour faire vo carnel desir.
Nulle, je croi, ne s'en gardast,
Se peurs ou hontes n'el tardast.   (MS *He*, fol. 72v)

All you women were, will be, and are, in deed or in will, ready to lie with any man, to satisfy your carnal desires. I don't believe that any woman would keep from doing this, unless she was stopped by fear or shame.

While Gui did, as we have seen, modify the poem's antifeminist tenor, this particular passage may not be a case in point. It is after all spoken by the Jaloux, whom Gui retained as a negative example. When judging the "subtractions reprises" of MS Tou, or even the deletions of MS *Mor*, we must bear in mind that there is no way of knowing what may have once taken the place of the excised material. Gui did not devise any marginal sign to indicate a deleted interpolation or an undone mutation; all that he tells us is that certain lines, once omitted, are now back in their place. While the evidence of manuscript readings must always be interpreted with caution, MS *He* does provide a control for our study of Gui's remaniement.

In MS *Ke*, finally, we can see the composite text taking shape, as Gui's additions to the *Rose* are grafted on to a text of the *K* family. We have already seen, in the preceding chapter, how the reader responsible for these additions studied and annotated the *Rose*. His borrowings from Gui are limited to certain interpolations in Reason and Ami, principally the stories of Susannah and Avenir, the discussions of friendship, and, in Ami, the advice about gift-giving and the warnings about avaricious women. He follows MSS *Mor* and *Tou* in placing the stories of Susannah and Avenir directly after that of Virginia. A note at the end of the Avenir episode indicates that the interpolation, written thus far in the margins, was continued on a now lost leaf at the beginning of the manuscript; one can presume that the passage continued, as in MSS *Mor* and *Tou*, with the more general discussion of judicial corruption.

The interpolation on friendship, on the other hand, does not follow the order that is seen in all of the other manuscripts.[44] The annotator of MS *Ke* transcribed this passage in piecemeal fashion, beginning with the description of the virtue of compassion – the last of the four virtues addressed by Gui – and moving from there to pick up the beginning portion of the

---

[44] The excerpts from Gui transcribed on the last page of MS *Ke* were printed by Morawski, who did not recognize them as the work of Gui de Mori, as "Fragment d'un *Art d'aimer* perdu du xiiie siècle." See my "Notice sur les fragments poètiques."

interpolation. Perhaps, as Morawski suggests, the annotator of MS *Ke* wanted to highlight the importance of compassion; or perhaps he did not decide until later that he wanted the remainder of the interpolation. The passage was transcribed on the last page of the manuscript, following the interpolation about gift-giving, itself incomplete. Clearly the annotator did not copy the passages from Gui de Mori in a systematic fashion, moving through the text in order, for the interpolation about friendship precedes the passage about gift-giving by thousands of lines. Rather, he compared the two manuscripts at his leisure, periodically coming upon passages that did not appear in MS *Ke* and copying out the lines that most interested him, sometimes in the margins, sometimes in blank spaces at the beginning or the end of the volume. Shorter passages may even have been entered from memory. MS *Ke* shows us one way that a text like that of MS *He* comes into being: as successive waves of annotation and interpolation add to the *Rose* material drawn from other manuscripts and even from other sources altogether, such as the *Diz et proverbes des sages*, a composite text is created; and when it is copied – especially if it is copied by a scribe who chooses to add his own emendations – a new manuscript family is born.

4

Adapting Jean de Meun to Guillaume de Lorris: the *Rose* of the *B* manuscripts

> Je ne say se le sussesseur le cuidoit honourer: s'il le creoit pour vray il fu deceu; car a ung commencement qui par aventure se porroit assés passer selond son fait – mesment entre Crestiens – il adjousta tres orde fin et moien desraisonnable contre Raison.   (Jean Gerson, "Traictié d'une vision")[1]

In his "Traictié d'une vision faite contre *Le Ronmant de la Rose*," Jean Gerson comments on the irony that Jean's Reason violates the "clean speech" commandment laid down by Guillaume's Cupid, resulting in a situation where Cupid appears "plus chaste et raisonnables" [more chaste and reasonable (ed. Hicks, p. 85)] than Reason herself. This leads Gerson to a short digression on the dual authorship of the *Rose*, in which it is clear that he views the portion of Guillaume far more favorably than that of Jean – indeed, that he considers Jean to have betrayed the very spirit of Guillaume's undertaking. Jean, as Gerson has already explained through the person of Dame Eloquence, committed the literary sin of plagiarism – vilely distorting the material he took from such worthy authors as Alain de Lille – as well as the crimes of foul language, attacks on the Church and on chastity, and generally lascivious discourse. Guillaume, however, had committed none of these errors:

> Piessà les fondemens estoient gettés par le premier, et de sa propre main et matiere sans mendier sa et la, et sans y assembler tel viltey de boe et de flache puante et orde comme est mise ou sommillon de cest ouvraige.   (ed. Hicks, p. 85)

> Long ago the foundations were raised by the first [author], with his own hand and his own material, without going begging here and there, and without mixing in such filth of mud and of polluted, stinking water as is used in the summit of this work.

---

[1] "I don't know if the successor thought he was honoring him: if he did, he was certainly deceived; for to a beginning that, perchance, could have proved acceptable enough – even among Christians – he added a very filthy ending and an irrational middle part contrary to Reason" (ed. Hicks, pp. 85–86).

Far from honoring Guillaume de Lorris with his continuation, Gerson argues, Jean merely rendered the romance as a whole unfit for decent company.

While Gerson's reaction is extreme, he raises points that had not gone unnoticed by early readers of the *Rose*. We have seen that Gui de Mori attempted to clarify certain potentially problematic passages, to reduce the erotic tenor of the conclusion, and to bring the figures of Reason, Nature, and Genius more into line with their models in Alain de Lille and Boethius; he deleted the bawdy language and fables unworthy of such exalted personae. Gui furthermore felt the need to justify Jean's decision to impose a new, much longer ending on Guillaume's romance. His tendency to dismantle the circular structure of Jean's major discourses in favor of a linear structure is a further step toward stylistic unity in the conjoined *Rose* of Guillaume and Jean.

Gui is the only medieval rewriter of the *Rose* who left us his name; but his is not the only remaniement. In this chapter, we will examine the family of manuscripts designated as *B*: a reworking of Jean's portion of the *Rose* which, while less extensive than that of Gui, is nonetheless a significant alteration of the text.[2] The *B* remanieur sought to remove discrepancies between the two parts of the conjoined *Rose*; his recasting of Jean de Meun is very much in the spirit of Guillaume de Lorris. In some cases his approach resembles that of Gui. For example, the different *B* recensions present various ways of adapting or suppressing entirely Reason's defense of plain speech. The *B* remanieur also modified or deleted the poem's more salacious passages; this tendency is especially marked in MS Bibl. Nat. fr. 25524 (*Bi*), where antifeminist passages have been deleted as well. The discourse of Faux Samblant has been reworked and, as in MS *Tou*, now contains allusions to Augustine's treatise on monastic life; but compared to the hundreds of lines added to Faux Samblant in MS *Tou*, the *B* interpolations, totaling a few dozen lines, are quite modest.[3] On the other hand, whereas Gui deleted mythological material, the *B* text retains such passages. In all but the heavily abridged MS *Bi*, it even adds a reference to Adonis in Cupid's account of the death of Tibullus, bringing that passage closer to its source in Ovid's *Amores*; it expands Cupid's account of his lineage, and follows that with the story of Apollo and Marsyas.[4] Overall, then, the approach to the *Rose* represented by the *B* text is related, but not identical, to that of Gui de Mori; the two remaniements reflect somewhat

[2] For a discussion of the *B* manuscript family, see Langlois, *Manuscrits*, pp. 359–405. Langlois considers, and rejects, the possibility that the abridged *B* text represents an early draft of Jean's own work.
[3] Langlois gives the *B* variants for the discourse of Faux Samblant in the notes to his edition.
[4] Langlois gives the Tibullus and the Apollo–Marsyas interpolations in the notes to vv. 10518 and 10830–31 respectively in his edition.

different notions of the edifice to be raised on the foundations laid by Guillaume.

The *B* remaniement, like that of Gui, took on different versions for different publics. It may have originated in a clerical or university milieu, given the insertion of Ovidian material; the allusions to Augustine's treatise on monastic life; a revision of Reason's discussion of language that focuses on the problem of truth and interpretation; and, in the discourse of Nature in MS Turin, Bibl. Univ. L. III. 22 (*Be*), a concern with establishing the proper relationship between Nature and God. But the *B* text was also adapted for a less sophisticated public. In MS (*Bi*), the *Rose* has become an allegorical romance, more in the courtly than the Ovidian or the Boethian tradition; and accessible to an audience with more conservative tastes, less interested in philosophy, less tolerant of bawdy double entendres and less appreciative of antifeminist and anti-matrimonial polemic, at least in the context of a poem that is supposed to be a romance, written in honor of a woman "worthy of being called Rose." Whereas Gui expanded the poem's examination of marriage, clarifying the arguments and setting forth an ideal of conjugal harmony, MS *Bi* avoids the issue altogether: the *Rose* is simply the story of a young man's initiation into love. The longer form of the *B* text, in contrast, appeals to a public – whether lay or clerical – with more liberal tastes, a greater interest in the integration of diverse literary and intellectual traditions, and a great appreciation for the transformation of the erotic allegory into a vehicle for moral, satirical, and philosophical material.

Because of the mutability of the vernacular text and the unceasing editorial activities of medieval scribes, illustrated so vividly in the annotation and multiple versions of Gui's remaniement, it is impossible to reconstruct exactly what the original *B* text may have been: here we lack the carefully annotated edition that we are so lucky to have for Gui de Mori. The comparison of *B* manuscripts shows that nearly all now contain many "subtractions reprises," as Gui put it. Variations among the *B* manuscripts also show that the *B* text has passed through a series of recensions, differing in their treatment of particular passages and in the extent to which the text is abridged. All of the *B* manuscripts, however, share enough common material that they can be considered to form a family, deriving ultimately from a set of revisions devised in the late thirteenth century on the text of Jean de Meun.[5] I will begin with an overview of the shared features of the

---

[5] Langlois suggests that the various *B* redactions "sortent toutes du même atelier, ou d'un même original dont les corrections, additions ou suppressions étaient indiquées en marge" (*Manuscrits*, p. 385). Given the way in which Gui's contemporary remaniement was annotated, and the versions that it gave rise to, this suggestion is most likely correct.

various *B* manuscripts, followed by a description of the more extreme abridgments in MS *Bi* and then by a closer look at the section of the *Rose* that was the most substantially altered in the *B* manuscripts: the discourse of Reason.

THE *B* REMANIEMENT: AN OVERVIEW

The existence of thirteenth-century manuscripts of the *B* text shows that this remaniement dates from a very early moment in the textual history of the *Rose*. As such it allows us to witness the response of a reader for whom Jean de Meun was not yet a figure of great authority, and for whom the *Rose* itself was not yet viewed as the master work of French literature. The most obvious index of this early approach to the *Rose* is that the entire discussion of the poem's authors is deleted, as is the identification of Gallus, Catullus, and Ovid as the poetic ancestors of the *Rose* poets.[6] In manuscripts preserving this early form of the *B* text, the *Rose* is thus presented as though it were the work of a single anonymous author. But the *B* text nonetheless manifests an interest in the figure of the poet through the inclusion of two interpolations in the discourse of the God of Love. One of these shows that the *B* redactor, in spite of having deleted the reference to Gallus, Catullus, and Ovid, was aware of Jean's use of Ovid's elegy on the death of Tibullus. Drawing on *Amores* 3, 9 (vv. 7–12, 15, 61–64), Jean portrays Cupid describing the grief he and Venus experienced at the death of Tibullus. In the *B* manuscripts, this account is expanded with an allusion to the death of Adonis. In reference to Venus' grief for Tibullus, the God of Love states:

10487	Por cui mort ma mere plora
10488	tant que pres qu'el ne s'acora.
xxx	N'onc pour Adonis n'ot tel peine,
xxx	Quant li senglers l'ot mort en l'aine,
xxx	Dont il mourut a grant haschiee.
xxx	Onques ne dut estre laissiee
xxx	La grant douleur qu'ele en menot;
xxx	Mais pour Tibullus plus en ot.

(ed. Langlois, note to his v. 10518)

---

[6] The discussion of authorship is missing from MSS *Be*, *Bi*, and *Lz* (Bibl. Nat. fr. 12587); the latter, in spite of its designation as a member of the *L* family, follows a version of the *B* text close to MS *Be* in large portions of the poem. According to Langlois, MS *Lz* has lost two folios between v. 10352 and v. 10672. This would mean that little or no text was originally missing. However, in my examination of the manuscript I found only one folio to be missing. This would mean that some 168 lines were deleted; we cannot know the exact number, of course, since we do not know if the text included miniatures or rubrics. However, the version of vv. 10353–671 present in either MS *Be* or MS *Bi* has approximately the right number of lines to fit on one folio of MS *Lz*. The discussion of the authors has been restored in all other *B* manuscripts, reflecting the admiration for Jean de Meun that quickly developed in the fourteenth century.

For whose death my mother wept so much that she nearly died. Never did she experience such pain for Adonis, when the boar fatally struck him in the groin, from which he died in great torment. The great sorrow she experienced was never to be abandoned; but for Tibullus she felt even more.

These lines are an expansion of Ovid's, "Nec minus est confusa Venus moriente Tibullo / quam iuveni rupit cum ferus inguen aper." [Nor is Venus less distressed at the death of Tibullus than when the wild beast ripped the youth's groin (*Amores* 3, 9:15–16).] Indeed, the medieval poet goes one better than Ovid, depicting Venus as grieving even more for Tibullus than for Adonis.

Even if the *B* redactor did not care to preserve the identities of the *Rose* poets or to highlight the process of poetic continuation, then, he did have an interest in the incorporation of Latin models into the *Rose*. The interpolation prepares for the subsequent appearance of Adonis, strengthening his presence as an exemplary figure. The interpolated lines also show that the *B* redactor was sensitive to Jean's strategy of exalting the figure of the poet as one who serves love.[7] By adapting his Ovidian source in such a way as to assert that Venus cared more for a love poet than for her own lover, the *B* redactor privileges poetry as the highest form of love service.

The figure of the poet is evoked once more at a later point in the God of Love's discourse. In an interpolation following v. 10800, Cupid describes his ancestry and professes his intense dislike for his Aunt Juno; he compares his feelings for Juno to those of Apollo for Marsyas, and proceeds to recount the musical contest of Marsyas and Apollo. The story of Marsyas and Apollo is modeled on the account in *Metamorphoses* 6, but, by making Midas the judge, conflates the story with that of the contest between Apollo and Pan. What is interesting for our purposes is the way in which Cupid associates himself with Apollo. He first sets up the analogy of the two rivalries, declaring his hatred for Juno and adding, "Bien l'ain tant com Phebus fist Marse" [I like her as much as Phoebus did Marsyas (ed. Langlois, note to line 10830, vv. 16–18)]. And as he tells the story, Cupid reiterates his disapproval of Marsyas:

> La satyreau tieng a coupable,
> Non pour ce que la buisine ot,
> Mais contre Phebus buisinot.
>
> (ed. Langlois, vv. 28–30)

I consider the satyr guilty, not because he had the flute, but because he played against Phoebus.

---

[7] See Brownlee, *Poetic Identity*, pp. 12–14; Uitti, "From *Clerc* to *Poète*."

The association of Cupid with Apollo is all the more striking since it reverses the traditional interpretation of the Apollo-Marsyas contest. Ordinarily, the opposition of Apollo and Marsyas is glossed as that of spirit or intellect and senses or folly: Marsyas is an exemplar of foolishness and sensuality.[8] One could thus reasonably suppose that Cupid, son of Venus and enemy of Reason, would be inclined to identify with Marsyas rather than Apollo. That this is not the case suggests that the *B* redactor wished to redefine the terms of the myth, providing thereby a mythographic basis for the *Rose* as learned love poetry. Cupid has, after all, just enunciated his concern for love poets and his intention to preside over the composition of the *Rose*. What we now encounter is an association of the patron of love poets with the frequently amorous god of poetry, expressed as a sort of common alliance against the enemies of love (Juno, rival of Venus in the Judgment of Paris) and art (Marsyas, rival of Apollo). This association assures us that the poetry fostered by the God of Love will be of the inspired, high style of Apollo and not the rustic low style of Marsyas. Such an assurance may have seemed necessary in light of the rivalry between Love and Reason: how can good poetry be written without the cooperation of Reason, inventor of language and proponent of literary exegesis? Apollo, in whom love, wisdom, and poetry are united, provides a convenient solution to this problem.[9] As we will see, the *B remanieur* acknowledges that the poetics of love are fundamentally different from those of Reason; nonetheless, he preserves the possibility of a love poetry that reaches intellectual heights of its own.

The redactor probably conceived the idea of introducing Apollo from the allusion to Apollo's song at the death of Orpheus in *Amores* 3, 9:21–24. Ovid established an analogy between Cupid, mourning the death of Tibullus, and Apollo, mourning the death of Orpheus. For Ovid, the important point would have been the identification of Tibullus with Orpheus; the *B* redactor, less concerned with Tibullus, chose instead to capitalize on the association of Apollo and Cupid. The idea may also have been suggested by Ovid's invocation of Apollo in the *Ars amatoria* and the *Remedia amoris*. Although Ovid begins the *Ars* with the claim that his poetry is inspired by love alone and not by Apollo (vv. 25–30), he later announces the intervention of Apollo, who interrupts the narrator to explain the relevance to love of his famous dictum "Know thyself": "Qui sibi notus erit, solus sapienter amabit" [only he who knows himself will

---

[8] For example, Arnulf of Orleans glosses the myth as follows: "Marsia i. insipientia disputavit cum Apolline i. cum sapientia, sed confutata per sapientiam fuit excoriata." [Marsyas, i.e. foolishness, disputed with Apollo, i.e. wisdom, but, confounded by wisdom, was flayed (ed. Ghisalberti, p. 217).]

[9] On the figure of Apollo in late medieval love poetry, see my "Daisy and the Laurel."

love wisely (2:501)]. Ovid's humorous twist on the notion that spiritual self-knowledge contributes to wise love – namely, that knowing one's physical allure enables one better to display it – is echoed in the advice of Ami and La Vieille, while the serious side of the dictum is implied by Reason and explicitly stated by Nature: "car cil seus aime sagement / qui se connoit antierement" [for he alone loves wisely who fully knows himself (vv. 17761–62)]. Moreover, Apollo and Cupid are the deities presiding over the *Remedia amoris* (vv. 39–40, 75–78, 251–52, 704–6); and as we have seen, Gui de Mori, whose rewriting of the *Rose* is roughly contemporary with the B remaniement, associated the *Rose* with this poem as well. Like Ovid's art and remedy of love, the *Rose* unfolds under the dual auspices of love and wisdom, figured by Cupid and Apollo; it explores wise and unwise love, amorous and philosophical wisdom.

Not only did the B remanieur remove all indications of the change in authorial identity part way through the *Rose*; he also effected changes in Jean's text that lessened the disparity between Guillaume's romance and its continuation. Somewhat like Gui de Mori, though less sweepingly, the B remanieur sought both to reduce the digressiveness of Jean's text and to delete passages of questionable morality. His alteration of the discourse of Reason, which survives today in different recensions, will be discussed below. The discourse of Ami is most significantly altered in MS *Bi*, which is more heavily abridged than the original B text; but the evidence of the B family as a whole does suggest that the original remaniement did at least reduce Ami's cavalier discussion of rape and deception.[10] Richesse's description and personification of Hunger, Poverty, and Larceny is deleted (vv. 10111–200), probably because it has no immediate bearing on the exposition of love. Interestingly, the God of Love's discussion of poor and wealthy lovers is also reduced through the deletion of vv. 10753–86 and vv. 10861–86. The enmity of Richesse is established, and Cupid's preference for love given freely is enunciated; but the comparison of a woman to a horse and the complaint that a man can never pay enough to own a woman outright are deleted, as is the vow that women are systematically to despoil their wealthy lovers. The B redactor seems to have wanted the God of Love to retain the courtly aura that surrounds him in Guillaume's poem, untainted by the mercenary ethos of La Vieille. In a similar spirit he omitted vv. 10311–16: that portion of the Lover's apology to Cupid in which he reiterates his refusal to follow Reason. While the enmity of Reason and Love is clear in the B text, the redactor nonetheless preferred not to belabor the point.

While unlike Gui, the B remanieur did retain mythological passages, he

---

[10] On the recensions of one important passage in the discourse of Ami (vv. 7579–688), see below, in the final section of this chapter.

nonetheless subjected them to the same kinds of revisions as the rest of the poem. The story of Pygmalion, which appears in a somewhat expurgated version, is a case in point.[11] Pygmalion no longer delivers his prayer to Venus, but to the gods in general; his thanksgiving to Venus after the "miracle" is similarly omitted (vv. 21143–44). Pygmalion's lengthy promise to abandon chastity is deleted (vv. 21055–66, 21071–78), and his prayer reduced to a simple request: that the beautiful one who has stolen his heart become his loyal beloved, and that she be given the body and soul of a woman. Venus' response to the prayer is rendered more acceptable through deletion of her delight at the prospect of Pygmalion doing penance "tout nuz antre les braz s'amie" [all naked in the arms of his beloved (v. 21085; MSS *Bi* and *Be* delete vv. 21085–86)]. And the incestuous coupling of Cynaras and Myrrha is passed over more rapidly, through the reduction of vv. 21157–66 to just two lines. Yet the *B* remanieur was not merely in a hurry to return to the frame narrative, for he also added some lines to the story, such as the detail that Pygmalion had lived his life hitherto in complete chastity and that he was an experienced carver of idols for the temple. Thus the story of Pygmalion retains its character as an entertaining narrative vignette, a pendant to the Narcissus passage at the poem's beginning and a gloss on the Lover's behavior; the deletion of digressive passages and overly explicit eroticism reflects the processes at work in the *B* remaniement as a whole.

The story of Mars and Venus has likewise been modified in accordance with the stricter moral standards manifested throughout the *B* remaniement. Even in the frequently lascivious discourse of La Vieille, the tale of Mars and Venus is recounted without the brief aside that "cil a mout po de savoir / qui seus cuide sa fame avoir" [he who expects to have his wife all to himself has very little knowledge (vv. 13821–22; MS *Be* deletes vv. 13817–22)]. And Venus' behavior is rendered more understandable through a small revision that makes Vulcan into the classic wife-beating *jaloux*: v. 13834, "car Vulcanus si lez estoit" [for Vulcan was so ugly] becomes "car Vulcanus si la batoit" [for Vulcan beat her so much; in MSS *Be, Ba, Bâ*]. When the tale is retold by Nature and Genius it requires even more careful revision, since these figures are meant to be moral authorities; it is after all precisely the adultery of Venus that troubles Nature in *De planctu Naturae*. MS *Be* accordingly deletes the suggestion, put forth in Jean's text by both Nature and Genius, that if Mars and Venus had seen Vulcan's net they could have gone elsewhere to take their pleasure, or even have cut the snare to pieces (vv. 18055–58, 18065–70, 18073–74 deleted). The suggestion that Venus could have invented excuses if the two were

---

[11] For a more detailed discussion of the Pygmalion passage in MSS *Bi* and *Be*, see Langlois, *Manuscrits*, pp. 392–93.

discovered by Vulcan is somewhat shortened (vv. 18083–88 deleted); and the explanation of this inventiveness by the fact that "Venus . . . mout est sage dame" [Venus . . . is a very wise lady (v. 18079)] is also excised. The tirade concerning feminine treachery, however, is retained as the moral lesson of the story; as we saw in Chapter 1, it even drew enthusiastic glossing from a fourteenth-century reader of MS *Be*.

The discourse of Nature has taken on a particularly interesting aspect in MS *Be*. Whether it derives from the original *B* text, from an intermediate ancestor, or from the scribe responsible for MS *Be*, this recension was certainly produced by someone working with a version of the *B* text who wished to adapt the discourse of Nature to fit the overall recasting of the poem. Not surprisingly, the text has been streamlined. The discussion of mirrors, for example, is retained, but in a shortened form from which many details and digressive elaborations have been deleted. The most interesting variants involve Nature's responsibility for the formation of the human race. Whereas in Jean's text Nature takes credit for creating humans, causing them to be born equal, and endowing them with living, sentient bodies, the Nature of MS *Be* attributes these acts to God. The principal examples are as follows:

Standard Text	*MS Be*
car ges faz touz samblables estre	Diex les fist tous samblables estre
(v. 18565)	(fol. 126v)
[for I make them all the same]	[God made them all the same]
Car quant ges faz semblables nestre,	Car Diex les fait sans blasme nestre.
s'il veulent donques gentis estre	S'il voloient donc ge[ntis estre]
d'autre noblece que de cele	D'autre noblesce que de cele
que je leur doing, qui mout est bele,	Que Diex lor [donne, qui mout est bele]
qui a non naturel franchise,	Qui a non naturele franchise,
que j'ai seur touz egaument mise . . .	Qu'il a sour tous [egau]ment mise . . .
(vv. 18839–44)	(fol. 128r)
[for when I cause them to be born the same, if they want then to be noble according to a nobility other than the one I give them, which is very beautiful and is called natural nobility, which I have placed equally in all of them . . .]	[For God causes them to be born blameless. If they want then to be noble according to a nobility other than the one God gives them, which is very beautiful and is called natural nobility, which he has placed equally in all of them . . .]
des biens qui de par moi leur vienent	Des biens qui de par Dieu lor vienent
(v. 18984)	(fol. 129r)
[by the good things that come to them from me]	[by the good things that come to them from God]

In addition, although MS *Be* includes Nature's account of having made human beings to look up towards the heavens, it does delete her statement that "bien puis dire, san mantir, / jou faz estre, vivre et santir" [I can well say without lying, I make them be, live, and feel (vv. 19007–8)]. The text of MS *Be* is the work of a redactor who wanted to clarify Nature's subservient role with regard to the divine Creator. Not surprisingly, MS *Be* includes Nature's discussion of the mysteries of the Trinity and the Incarnation. Clearly, the redactor of this text did not share Gui's need to exclude theological material from Nature's discourse; but he did attempt to adjust the text towards a more orthodox representation of the natural and the divine. Most likely the *Be* version of the *Rose* was created in the same clerical milieu where this manuscript was later read and annotated.

The alterations apparent in the *B* manuscripts as a whole – reduction of digression, bowdlerization, an effort to impose a greater unity on the conjoined *Rose* of Guillaume and Jean – are taken to an even greater extreme in MS *Bi*, sole surviving copy of a heavily abridged version of the *B* text. Before proceeding to a more detailed analysis of the discourse of Reason in the *B* tradition, let us pause to examine the characteristics of the "short form" of the *B* text.

"LA MANIERE DU CHASTEL PRENDRE": THE *ROSE* OF MS *BI*

In MS *Bi*, as in *B* manuscripts in general, the text of Guillaume de Lorris is almost untouched; but that of Jean de Meun has been reduced to some three thousand lines, or approximately one-sixth its usual length. The principal deletions are the discourses of La Vieille, Nature, and Genius, removed in their entirety; but many other smaller cuts were made as well. In fact, due to the extreme abridgment of Jean's portion, the midpoint of MS *Bi* is Guillaume's description of the kiss. There results a bipartite narrative structure: the first half moves through the Lover's encounters with a series of allegorical figures, building to a climax with the intervention of Venus and the kiss; the second half finds him once more on the outside of an enclosed space, moves through a second series of encounters, and reaches the final climax with the second intervention of Venus and the plucking of the Rose. The result is less an exposition of the many forms of love than an allegorical romance in the courtly tradition.

In effect, Jean's continuation has become exactly that: a continuation and resolution of the narrative begun by Guillaume. Most of the material that has no precedent in Guillaume's delicate poem is omitted entirely, leaving no trace. The major exception to this pattern is that most of the discourse of

Faux Samblant is left intact, though somewhat shortened and reworked[12] – a rather odd exception, considering that almost any other portion of Jean's poem has more bearing on love, seduction, or the quest for the Rose than do the words of Faux Samblant. It must be noted, however, that Faux Samblant could not be removed entirely since he is instrumental to the plot: it is he who vanquishes Male Bouche and paves the way for the Lover's reunion with Bel Acueil. Moreover, the confrontation between Faux Samblant and Male Bouche recalls the anxiety about *losengiers* and *mesdisants* that haunts the Old French lyric tradition. Faux Samblant's role was thus prepared not only by Guillaume's introduction of Male Bouche – and also, if indirectly, by his description of Papelardie on the garden wall – but also by the courtly tradition in which Guillaume's *Rose* and that of MS *Bi* are inscribed.

The discourses of Reason, Ami, Richesse, and the God of Love do remain, but all are significantly abridged. Reason's discourse, for example, is reduced from 3000 to a mere 300 lines (see Appendix B, 1). Reason becomes an authority on the nature of love and a rival for the lover's affections; she offers her arguments against the follies of love and begs him to love her instead, which he refuses. The debate as to whether or not she is counselling the Lover to hate and the discussion of the types of love remain for the most part. Gone, however, are the philosophical passages relating to youth and old age, wealth, fortune, and justice; the classical exempla, such as Nero, Seneca, and Croesus; and, since the word "coilles" has disappeared along with the reference to Saturn, there is no debate about language either. Rather than providing the occasion for an elaborate review of material adapted from Boethius, Alain de Lille, and others, the Lover's encounter with Reason is reduced simply to the opposition of amorous passion and rational restraint, recalling the debate between Reason and Love in Chrétien's *Chevalier de la charrette* (ed. Foulet and Uitti, vv. 369–81).

The discourse of Ami in MS *Bi* is abridged to include only those parts that are directly relevant to the art of seduction; the entire second half of Ami (vv. 8207–9972) is deleted. Not only is the Jaloux gone – after all, he is not meant as a model for the Lover to imitate – but also the discussions of the Golden Age and of the origins of private property, government, and

---

[12] MS *Bi* has the *B* interpolations given by Langlois in the discourse of Faux Samblant. In addition, it deletes vv. 11567–610 (the exposition of Matthew 23); 11687–756 (Faux Samblant's power); 11819–65 (the conflict of Jehan and Pierre); 11873–96 (Faux Samblant does not worry about God's judgment); and most of the allusions to Guillaume de Saint-Amour and to the disputes between the mendicants and the University of Paris (vv. 11269–72, 11395–466, 11761–64). The evidence of other *B* manuscripts, particularly MS *Be*, suggests that most of these deletions derive from the *B* prototype.

law. The folio that contained whatever there was of the text between vv.
7880 and 8189 is now missing; but since a folio of this manuscript holds
only sixty lines (thirty lines on each side), it is clear that most of the
intervening material – the discourse on poverty and true friendship – must
have been deleted as well. This, of course, is in keeping with the
modification of the discourse of Reason: only that which pertains directly
to the exposition of love is preserved.

The suppression of the second half of Ami's discourse results in the
removal of much of the poem's antifeminist diatribe. The redactor of the *Bi*
text must have found such material unsuitable to a poem ostensibly about
love, dedicated to a lady, and containing the commandment to honor and
serve women:

> Toutes fames ser et honore,
> en aus servir poine et labeure;
> et se tu oz nul mesdisanz
> qui aille fame despisant,
> blasme le et di qu'il se taise. (vv. 2103–7)

Serve and honor all women, strive and labor to serve them; and if you hear
any slanderer who goes around disparaging women, criticize him and tell him
to be quiet.

The *Bi* redactor took this piece of advice to heart, using his scribal powers
to silence the detractors of women within the *Rose* itself. The Jaloux is
excised; so, at a later point in the poem, is Genius' warning about disclosing
secrets to one's wife (omitted in the deletion of vv. 15774–20680), as well as
the entire discourse of La Vieille (omitted in the deletion of vv.
12511–14722); and so even are Ami's antifeminist comments. The omitted
second half of his discourse includes not only the Jaloux, but also such
topics as the insatiable greed of most women (vv. 8252–72, 8317–22) and
the inability of women to accept advice or chastisement, however sound
(vv. 9933–56). Some antifeminist material is deleted from the first half of
Ami's discourse as well. Gone are vv. 7579–7688, in which Ami complains
that women, while naturally eager to give themselves over to prospective
lovers, have come to expect gifts in exchange for such favors; warns against
the likelihood of losing one's beloved to other suitors; and urges the use of
force, explaining that women often prefer it that way. Thus, while Ami
does still counsel the Lover to placate the Rose's guardians through the use
of gifts and feigned innocence – in effect, to win his lady by masking the
sexual nature of his intentions and softening her heart with little love
tokens – he at least does so with a minimum of antifeminist commentary.
And he concentrates on allaying fears, wearing down resistance, and

capturing the allegiance of Bel Acueil, without suggesting that the Lover seek an opportunity for rape. In effect, Jean's Ami has been recast in the image of Guillaume's Ami, and his advice brought into line with the commandments of the God of Love, much as Reason's discourse was brought back within the parameters of her advice in Guillaume de Lorris, and her words censored to conform to the God of Love's linguistic predilections.[13]

The discourse of Richesse is kept in shortened form; but interestingly, all reference to her grievance against the Lover is omitted from Cupid's encounter with his barons, along with the discussion of wealth and poverty in the context of love service.[14] Clearly, the *Bi* redactor did not appreciate the opposition of wealth and love; and neither the terrors of poverty nor the association of material wealth with depravity and prostitution are themes of this version of the *Rose*. One must recall that the enmity of Love and Richesse is an invention of Jean de Meun; Guillaume had placed Richesse among the participants in the carol, identifying her as a follower of the God of Love. Her presence infused the Garden of Delight with an aura of opulence appropriate to the cultivation of love as an aristocratic pastime; as Guillaume tells us, the carbuncle in her hair shone so strongly "qu'a Richeice en replandissoit / durement le vis et la face / et, entor li, tote la place" [that it brightly illuminated Richesse's face and, around her, the entire place (vv. 1104–06)]. Again remaining as true as possible to Guillaume, the *Bi* redactor modified the negative role that Jean devised for Richesse, showing only that the Lover will not buy his way to the Rose – a rather uncourtly way of winning one's beloved in any case.

In light of the foregoing it is no surprise to find that the conclusion of the poem is greatly reduced, and while traces remain of the imagery of sanctuary, the passage is no more explicitly or elaborately erotic than corresponding passages in the works of Chrétien or other romance authors. Following Bel Acueil's agreement to grant the Lover the Rose, the poem ends like this:

21316	Je, qui l'en rent merci .c. mile,
21561	A genous vois sans demourer,
21562	Ausinc comme pour aourer
21563	Le bel saintuare honorable.
xxx	Puis m'en entrai sans nule fable,

---

[13] MS *Bi* appropriately omits most of Jean's Apology, deleting vv. 15123–272: it retains only his promise that, once he has completely expounded the dream and glossed the text, his readers will have a full understanding of love. The modification of the poem is such that the disclaimers are no longer needed. [14] The deleted passages are vv. 10659–88, 10753–86, 10791–856, and 10859–88.

xxx	Pour baisier le bele chassete
xxx	Dedans l'archiere petite[te].
21565	Mais toute iert ja tombé par terre:
	[MS: par guerre]
21566	Au feu ne puis riens tenir guerre.
21611	Entre les pilierés me mis,
21612	Mais je n'i entrai pas demis.
21613	Moi pesoit que plus n'i entroie,
21614	Mais outre pooïr ne poaie.
21745	Ains que d'ilec me remuasse,
xxx	En brisant la tres bele chasse,
21747	Par grant joliveté coilli
21748	La flour dou bel rosier foilli.
21749	Ainsinc oï la rose vermoille.
21750	Atant fu jours et je m'esvoille.

(fol. 108r)

And I, who gave a hundred thousand thanks, went down on my knees at once as if to worship the beautiful honorable sanctuary. Then I went in, it is no lie, to kiss the beautiful casket inside the little archway. But everything had already fallen down: nothing can stand up to fire. I placed myself between the pillars, but I didn't even get halfway in. I was sorry not to go in farther, but I couldn't do any better. Before moving from there, breaking the beautiful case, with great pleasure I plucked the blossom of the leafy rosebush. Thus I had the red rose. Then it was daybreak, and I awoke.

While in this version it is still clear what the Lover is doing, and the sexual act is still expressed in terms of religious worship, the many lascivious details of Jean's account have been omitted. The redactor made the best of a difficult situation, allowing the Lover to possess the Rose – Guillaume de Lorris himself, after all, had already strongly hinted that such was to be the outcome of the quest – while preserving decorum to an even greater extent than Gui de Mori.[15]

Two apparent digressions that remain in MS *Bi* are the stories of Adonis and Pygmalion. At first glance their inclusion might seem inconsistent with the otherwise evident desire to "stick to the story"; but instead, we must see this as evidence that these two mythological exempla were perceived by our redactor as important elements of the romance. Guillaume set a clear precedent for the use of mythological lovers with his strategic retelling of the story of Narcissus. The stories of Adonis and Pygmalion contribute to

---

[15] Guillaume looks forward to an eventual capture of the Rose in his allusion to "li chastiaus riches et forz / qu'Amors prist puis par ses esforz" [the rich and strong castle that Love later took through his efforts (vv. 3485–86)]. See Kelly, " 'Li chastiaus . . . Qu'Amors prist puis par ses esforz' "; Hult, *Self-fulfilling Prophecies*, pp. 171–74.

the exposition of successful and unsuccessful love, with the latter even comparing himself to Narcissus (vv. 20846–58).[16] Within MS *Bi*, so much shorter than the original poem, the three tales are in much closer proximity, and the mythological material takes up a greater proportion of the whole; it is thus of even more prominent importance. Missing, however, are the *B* interpolations about Tibullus and Apollo and Marsyas: the *Rose* of MS *Bi* is focused on the figure of the lover, not the poet.

Although no other manuscript of this recension survives, Langlois's catalogue includes the description of a single bifolium recovered from the binding of a book. This was the outermost leaf of a gathering, and as such is numbered. It is thus possible to compute the approximate number of lines that could have been contained in that gathering, as well as the approximate number of lines that could have been contained in the manuscript up to that point. As Langlois demonstrates, these calculations show that the length of the poem in this manuscript would have corresponded exactly with that in MS *Bi* if, like MS *Bi*, this one had neither rubrics nor miniatures.[17] We thus know that at least two copies of this recension did exist. And since the fragment dates from the late thirteenth or early fourteenth century, we can conclude that the *Bi* text, like the *B* remaniement itself, dates from a very early period of *Rose* reception: probably from a time in which Guillaume's romance still circulated without Jean's continuation, and affected people's views of what the *Rose* was. Consequently, remaining true to the romance set in motion by Guillaume de Lorris was a guiding principle for the redactor of the *Bi* text. In the prologue to his translation of the *Consolation of Philosophy*, Jean sums up his work as the continuator of Guillaume de Lorris: "Je Jehan de Meun qui jadis ou rommant de la Rose, puis que Jalousie ot mis en prison Bel Acueil, enseignai la maniere du chastel prendre et de la rose cueillir." [I, Jean de Meun, who long ago in the *Romance of the Rose*, after Jealousy had imprisoned Bel Acueil, taught how to storm the castle and pluck the rose (ed. Dedeck-Héry, p. 168).] As we know, Jean in fact contributed a great deal more to the *Rose* than simply the method for storming the castle and picking the Rose. But the shorthand

---

[16] Much has been written on the programmatic use of Narcissus and Pygmalion in the *Rose*, sometimes with reference to Adonis as well; for example, see Poirion, "Narcisse et Pygmalion dans le *Roman de la Rose*"; Brownlee, "Orpheus's Song Resung"; my *From Song to Book*, pp. 96–99; Fleming, The *"Roman de la Rose"*, pp. 231–32.

[17] The calculations show that the first nineteen gatherings would have been missing 6406 lines, and that gathering 20 reduced vv. 12507–15466 to 240 lines. See Langlois, *Manuscrits*, pp. 166–67. While one cannot be absolutely certain that the fragment in question, which Langlois designates *Bï*, derives from a manuscript that had the same lacunae and the same text as MS *Bi*, the existence of two independent remaniements, each deleting some nine thousand *different* lines from the first fifteen thousand and each independently reducing vv. 12507–15466 to 240 lines, would be a truly extraordinary coincidence. Langlois assumes that MS *Bï* did contain the same version as MS *Bi*.

characterization of his work could be applied to MS *Bi*: this concise, focused account truly is an exposition of the means by which the Rose was won.

RETHINKING THE CONFLICT OF LOVE AND REASON

We turn now to a more extended analysis of the discourse of Reason in the *B* manuscripts. This portion of the poem merits special examination both because its multiple recensions are particularly complicated, and because the changes wrought shed considerable light on this early reading of the *Rose*. In most *B* manuscripts, the first half of the discourse of Reason – that portion leading up to her offer of herself as *amie* – does not differ radically from the standard text. It is the second half, where Reason strays from the topic of love to discuss Fortune, wars, politics, history, and language, that shows the most signs of reworking; and here the modifications, as well as the variations among members of the *B* family, are considerable. MS *Be*, for example, is a fusion of at least two different recensions of the second half of Reason's discourse.[18] One version, similar in spirit to that of MS *Bi*, brought Reason's discourse to a rapid conclusion in only thirty-six lines, following v. 5816 (See App. B, 2, A): having offered herself as love object she asks the Lover to abandon the God of Love; he refuses, reiterating his devotion to the Rose; Reason acknowledges her defeat and gives him leave to love, though not without a final chastisement. Following this preliminary conclusion, however, the text of Reason's discourse has been restored, though still in a reworked form: either MS *Be* or its source represents a conflation of an abridged version of the text with a more complete recension of the *B* text.

MS *Be* is not the only manuscript that bears witness to this early abridgment of Reason. In the mid fourteenth-century MS *Fe* (Bibl. Nat. fr. 19157), various passages have been added in the margins and at the end, copied from one or more other manuscripts. Among these passages are Gui's description of Orgueil (fol. 2v, at v. 234) and the thirty-six line "conclusion" of the discourse of Reason, exactly as it appears in MS *Be*, inserted after v. 5816 (on fol. 124v, with a note indicating where it belongs). The MS Bibl. Nat. fr. 12587 (*Lz*) probably also had this shortened version of Reason in its original state, before the addition of

---

[18] See Langlois, *Manuscrits*, pp. 368–71.

supplementary pages bearing the missing text.[19] Furthermore, a thirty-
one-line passage that is almost the same as the thirty-six-line "conclusion"
found in MS *Be* appears in four other manuscripts (MSS *Bê, Bo, Bó,* and *Bô*)
after v. 6870, just preceding the argument about plain speech.[20] From these
manuscripts, one would assume that the quick conclusion was devised not
to replace the entire second half of Reason, but merely to avoid the
discussion of plain speech, which was nonetheless reinserted – in a *B*
recension – into our four exemplars or their ancestor. Is the text glimpsed
in MSS *Be* and *Fe* a further abridging of an original text represented in MSS
Bê, Bo, Bó, and *Bô*? Or do the latter simply represent the work of a scribe
who chose to insert the restored text – vv. 5817–6870, in which Reason
discusses Fortune – in a different place? The question is probably one that
cannot be answered without the discovery of more manuscripts. All that
we can say with certainty is that, in the transmission of the *B* text, the
second half of the discourse of Reason is more problematic than the first
half, and the most problematic part of all is the debate about language.

For the above group of manuscripts are not the only ones that point to an
early suppression of Reason's defense of plain speech. Nine other *B*
manuscripts contain a different interpolation directly preceding the
discussion of language or, in the case of MS *Bi*, replacing it. In this passage
the Lover informs Reason that he will never love her – not because of her
language, of which he says nothing, but because he realizes that she wants
all men to love her, and he is not interested in a "communal" girl friend (see
App. B, 1:265–90). The deletion of the language debate required the
rewriting of the Lover's final dismissal of Reason, and in this regard the *B*
manuscripts can be divided into two groups: those having the passage in
which he rejects the notion of a *commune amie* ("D'autre part, se je vous
amoie") and those with a version of the conclusion represented in MS *Be*
("Et laisse ta pensee fole"). No manuscript that I have found contains both
passages (see Figure 1). Yet the two groups are clearly related: a humorous
prolongation of the Lover's dismissal of Reason ("Tant l'ain, se vous le

---

[19] In MS *Lz*, the original pages containing the end of Reason and the beginning of Ami were replaced,
in the fourteenth century, with new pages. As the manuscript now stands, the last original page of
Reason ends with v. 5474; the first original page of Ami begins with v. 7284. The new pages – two
small gatherings inserted into the middle of an original gathering, in replacement of its third, fourth,
and fifth folios – supply the complete text that should lie between these lines. The three folios that
originally held the text between v. 5474 and v. 7284 could have held a maximum of 504 lines. Since
the manuscript is illuminated, and almost certainly had a miniature at the beginning of Ami's
discourse, it is likely that the pages held even fewer lines of text than that. This means that the
discourse of Reason came to a rapid conclusion after v. 5474, even though its first half is intact. The
version of MS *Be* has approximately the right number of lines to fit, making allowance for an
unknown number of miniatures and rubrics. See Langlois, *Manuscrits*, pp. 40–43, 480.

[20] See Langlois, *Manuscrits*, pp. 371–73.

Interpolations	Ba	Bâ	Be	Bê	Bi	Bî	Bo	Bó	Bô	Bu	Bû	By	*Bco	*Bü
D'autre part, se je vous aimoie . . .	(1)	(1)	—	—	(1)	(2)	—	—	—	(1)	(3)	(3)	(1)	(3)
Et laisse ta pensee fole . . .	—	—	(4)	(5)	—	—	(5)	(5)	(5)	—	—	—	—	—
Tant l'ain, se vous le saviez . . .	(6)	—	—	(6)	(7)	(6)	(6)	(6)	(6)	—	—	—	(6)	(8)

(1) Follows v. 6886.
(2) Follows an interpolation after v. 7198.
(3) Follows v. 6890.
(4) Follows v. 5816. Inserted here in MS *Fe* also.
(5) Follows v. 6870.
(6) Follows v. 7198; see Langlois's note to v. 7228 of his edition.
(7) Two lines only (App. B, 1:297–98).
(8) Follows v.7192.

Figure 1   Interpolations in MSS of the B group.

saviez") appears in examples of both groups, and both also share significant variants in the language debate as it now appears. There is evidence for the suppression of virtually the entire second half of Reason in both groups: the principal omissions in MS *Bi* are vv. 5815–6870 and 6897–7198; the ancestor of Ms *Be* omitted vv. 5817–7162. The evidence of MSS *Bi*, *Fe*, and *Lz* shows that neither of these abridgments was an isolated occurrence. Yet both groups also include manuscripts in which the second half of Reason's discourse is fully or almost fully present, and only the debate about language shows signs of significant reworking.

The *B* family, in other words, includes two abridgments of the discourse of Reason, quite different, yet each aimed at deleting approximately the same material: the debate about euphemism and plain speech. Both versions of Reason also existed in more drastically abridged recensions, in which virtually the entire second half of Reason's discourse was deleted: not only the language debate, but also the discussion of Fortune and the examples drawn from ancient and contemporary history. One can hypothesize that the workshop responsible for the *B* remaniement devised two different ways of abridging the discourse of Reason, each available in a "long form" that omitted only the discussion of language and a "short form" that omitted the discussion of Fortune as well; also devised a way of rendering the linguistic debate acceptable by reworking it; and combined this newly revised material with all of the abridged versions. This material in turn underwent further revision, and deleted passages may have been restored only in successive stages. One has the impression of enormous fertility, of constant reworking of Reason's problematic views on language, during the early years of *Rose* transmission. Such variety is there that no surviving B manuscript has all of the interpolations identified with the B remaniement; only MS *Bi*, by far the most extreme abridgment, makes all of the deletions.

The argument between Reason and the Lover over the issue of communality merits closer attention; though brief, it offers an important insight into the B remanieur's understanding of the conflict of love and reason. In this passage the Lover bases his rejection of Reason on the argument that "Il n'est hons a bourc ne a vile" [there isn't a man in city or town (App. B, 1:268)] that Reason does not want as her lover. If he accepted her as his *amie*, says the Lover, she would have "plus de .c. mile" [more than a hundred thousand (App. B, 1:267)] other lovers as well: "Trestout le mondë averiés! / Trop vous abondoneroiés" [you would have the whole world; you would give of yourself too freely (App. B, 1:273–74)]. The Lover complains that he does not want a common girl friend; he wants one all to himself. Although Reason taunts him for being "jalous" and insists that she would never cuckold him, the Lover remains unmoved, resting his case with the words, "Ne je ne vous en croirai pas: / Or avez gastés tous vos pas" [I will never believe you; you have wasted all your efforts (App. B, 1:299–300).]

The debate about communality and privacy illustrates the same clash of perspectives as that about plain speech and euphemism: in both cases, the Lover sees Reason as a bawd, while she sees him as small-minded, uncomprehending, and obsessed with sex. In the discourse of erotic love, it is love itself, and sexual functions, that must be "glossed," that is, veiled in linguistic euphemism, metaphors, and allegorical images. As the Lover comes to learn, and as is vividly illustrated by the intervention of Faux Samblant, the discourse of love must never acknowledge the real object of desire; Reason's assertion that a primary purpose of language is "por fere noz volairs entendre" [to make our wishes known (v. 7071)] is directly contradicted by the Lover's other advisers. This aspect of the love teachings of the *Rose* was observed by the late fourteenth-century commentator on the *Echecs amoureux*, who stressed the importance of Faux Samblant and Contrainte Astenance in conquering Male Bouche and Jealousy: "Car on ne puelt selon la verité ces deux grans ennemis d'amours mieulx decepvoir que par bien dissimuler et par bien sagement toudis celer s'amour." [For truly one cannot better deceive these two great enemies of love than by carefully feigning and dissimulating and by always prudently hiding one's love (Bibl. Nat. fr. 9197, fol. 422).] In the Lover's eyes, Reason's casual use of explicitly sexual language rends the carefully constructed mask of amorous discourse. From Reason's perspective, of course, the situation is reversed: the purpose of language (and of glossing) is not to hide but to reveal meaning, and the reader or listener is intended not to be distracted or lulled by the words and surface images, but rather to look beyond these to the higher truths that they imply.[21] The linguistic debate not only reveals the Lover's sexual anxieties, but also casts in high relief the problematics of erotic allegory and lays the groundwork for the poem's controversial conclusion, where the act of sexual intercourse is described in considerable detail without ever using the words "coilles" or "viz."

The debate about plain speech and the final plucking of the Rose stand in an interesting sort of opposition: in one passage explicitly sexual terminology is used in a fable about justice and in a discussion first of the sanctity of procreation, then of language and interpretation; in the other, a series of metaphors is used to describe sexual activity. A continuing exploration and exposition of the relationship between language and eros, and of the power of words to hide or to reveal, to arouse or to subdue, runs throughout Jean's *Rose*. It is hardly surprising that, as evidenced in MS *Bi*, a medieval reader disconcerted by Reason's plain speech would object to the poem's conclusion as well. Christine de Pizan, who was deeply offended by Reason's use and defense of obscenity, stated that the allegorical images used at the end of the poem are "six fois plus atisans et plus penetratis et plus delicteus a ceulx qui y sont enclins que se il les nommast par leurs propres nons" [six times more exciting and more penetrating and more arousing for those who are so inclined than if he had called them by their proper names (ed. Hicks, p. 125)]. Gui, who suppressed Reason's linguistic arguments as well as every instance of the word "coilles," also modified the end of the poem. The *Bi* redactor, who deleted all appearances of the word "coilles" as well as most of the concluding passage, thus fits into a recognizable pattern in medieval *Rose* reception.

Just as the redactor chose to modify the erotic allegory, keeping eros to a minimum, so he sought to redefine the terms of the debate between Reason and the Lover. The question of private ownership is briefly raised by Jean de Meun, when the Lover responds to Reason's condemnation of material wealth by asking "quels choses peuent estre moies / et se du mien puis riens avoir" [what things can be mine, and whether I can have anything of my own (vv. 5292–93)]. Reason replies that one's only real belongings are

---

[21] On the different meanings assigned the terms "glose" and "gloser" by Reason and the Lover respectively, see Paré, *Le Roman de la Rose et la scolastique courtoise*, pp. 26–30. The point is also raised by Fleming, *Reason and the Lover*, p. 105.

spiritual in nature, "touz les biens que dedanz toi senz" [all the goods that you feel in yourself (v. 5301)], since all else is transitory. The phenomenon of private property is evoked by Ami as one of the consequences of the fall of the Golden Age (vv. 9607–34). Just as erotic love in a fallen world entails a discourse of mystification and masked desire, so also it problematizes the ideal of communality; and the Lover's courtly ethos commits him to a view of love as strictly private and non-transferable, focused upon a single object to the exclusion of all others. He desires to possess the Rose, not to share it with all mankind. Reason's concept of "bone volenté commune" [communal good will (v. 4656; App. B, 1:150), of a community of philosophers joined by their common love of wisdom, is as foreign to the Lover as is her practice of plain speech about sexual matters for the purpose of conveying philosophical truths: he does not wish to "approprier commune amie" [appropriate a communal girl friend (App. B, 1:276)]. Communality of love violates the Lover's most cherished principles. His reactions show that he is unable to distinguish between Reason's communal good will and La Vieille's ideal – present in all B manuscripts except MS *Bi* – of sexual communality: "chascune por chascun conmune / et chascun conmun a chascune" [each woman common to each man, and each man common to each woman (vv. 13857–58)].

The Lover's accusation of ribaldry, be it linguistic or amorous in nature, prompts Reason to defend herself against charges of sinfulness and villainy. In Jean's text, she states:

> Mes chose ou peché se meïst
> n'est riens qui fere me feïst,
> n'onc en ma vie ne pechié.   (vv. 6923–25)

But nothing could induce me to do anything that involved sin, nor have I ever sinned in my life.

And in defense of the words "coilles" and "viz," she states: "Je fiz les moz, et sui certaine / qu'onques ne fis chose vilaine" [I made the words, and I am certain that I never made anything villainous (vv. 7089–90)]. Reason gives a similar response to the issue of communality in the B interpolation:

> Seroies tu jalous de moi,
> Que pechiés en moi se meïst?
> Certains seras, se Diex m'aïst,
> Que ja n'i aras vilenie
> Quant de t'amour m'aras saisie.   (App. B, 1:282–86)

Would you be jealous of me, [suspicious] that sin might be found in me? You will be certain, so help me God, never to experience any villainy once you have fixed your love on me.

In short, the redactor of this version of the B text expands on what for him must have been the essence of the confrontation between Reason and the Lover: the Lover is unable to grasp rational love, or to recognize it as a viable alternative to his current state. He sees it first as the absence of love, hence as hate; and then, in a comic reversal, as an alarming proliferation of love, a promiscuity that knows no bounds. Erotic love, as prescribed by Cupid in the fateful encounter beside the fountain, remains for him the defining context for all discourse and the moral standard against which all loves are measured.

The prolongation of the Lover's final dismissal of Reason ("Tant l'ain"), finally, is common to both recensions of the discourse of Reason. In this passage, the Lover continues to treat Reason like a lovesick maiden, telling her that, should she feel herself constrained to die if deprived of his love, "Mout seroit corte vostre vie." [Your life would be very short (ed. Langlois, note to line 7228, v. 5).] He is, he informs her, unmoved, no matter how much she may "Braire, crier, gemir, plorer, / Fondre en larmes" [bray, cry out, moan, weep, dissolve in tears (vv. 8–9)]. That the Lover could attribute such irrational behavior to Reason, believing her love to be of the only kind he understands, adds a humorous touch that is very much in the spirit of his complaints about both her ribald language and her promiscuity, although the passage is not limited to manuscripts that contain the latter. This spirit is continued in the next line, where the Lover adds that he would never desire Reason, "Et fuissiez fille a .iiii. deus" [even if you were the daughter of four gods (v. 10)]. Here the Lover's misunderstanding of Reason builds to a hilarious climax: he cannot even grasp that she is the daughter, not of some pagan god, but of God.

As with the confusion generated by Reason's ideal of communality, so here the B remanieur shows his appreciation for a certain aspect of Jean's humor: the Lover's distortion of Reason, whom he seems scarcely able to distinguish from La Vieille, through a consistent pattern of eroticization and literalization of the spiritual, the intellectual, the allegorical. In spite of his discomfort with Reason's defense of obscenity, the remanieur responsible for the longer form of the B text was clearly attracted to the issues of language and interpretation. Let us look more closely at his handling of the language debate itself, which appears, in reworked form, in all B manuscripts except MS *Bi*.

TRUTH, DECEPTION, AND EUPHEMISM: LANGUAGE AND MEANING IN THE *B* TEXT

The language debate opens in B manuscripts with a reworking of vv. 6915–26, in which Reason asserts that she is without sin and can speak freely. As Langlois has shown, all *B* manuscripts have more or less the same combination of original and interpolated lines here, but the lines are differently arranged in almost every manuscript.[22] Reading through the multiple versions, one can conclude that in the original *B* text, whatever its precise form, the terms of the language discussion were redefined to focus on issues of truth and hypocrisy, discretion, and interpretation, largely or wholly ignoring the question of obscenity. In MS *Be*, for example, Reason states:

> Je n'ai pas de voir dire honte
> Se verité n'est si cuisant
> Qu'el fust contre vertu nuisant.
> Mais quant la verité doit nuire
> Contre vertu, bon le fait fuire.
> Sans faille bien l'as oï dire,
> Tout voir ne sont pas bon a dire.[23]

> (App. B, 2, B:10–16)

I am not ashamed of speaking the truth as long as the truth is not so biting that it would injure virtue. But when the truth would injure virtue, then it is good to flee it. Surely you have heard it said, not all truths are good to say.

These lines introduce the notion that the truth is usually to be voiced, but occasionally, when discretion requires it, must be suppressed – a motif that recurs in a passage added to the discourse of Faux Samblant in the *B* text:

> Je n'aim pas ome qui ne ment
> Et qui dit voir, se n'est pour nuire. (follows v. 11873)

I do not like a man who does not lie and who speaks the truth, unless it is to cause injury.

---

[22] For a table showing the arrangement of lines between v. 6916 and v. 6927 presented by most of the *B* manuscripts, see Langlois, *Manuscrits*, pp. 379–80. One must bear in mind that for Jean's text, it is necessary to subtract 30 from Langlois's line numbers in order to determine the corresponding line number in Lecoy's edition: Langlois's table thus covers his vv. 6946–57. One inaccuracy in Langlois's table must be pointed out: he states (p. 380, n. 12) that MS *Be* features an interpolation of twenty-six lines in the midst of the passage in question, and admits that he failed to transcribe them; he supposes this to be the passage in which the Lover accuses Reason of promiscuity ("D'autre part, se je vous amoie"). This passage, however, does not appear at all in MS *Be*. The interpolation in question is actually a portion of Reason's discussion of poetic integument; see App. B, 2, B:25–52.

[23] By way of comparison, I give here the opening lines of Reason's reply in Bibl. Nat. fr. 19154 (MS *Bâ*): "Biaus amis, je puis bien nommer, / Sans moi fere mal renommer, / Chose qui a pechié ne monte; / Ne n'ai pas de voir dire honte, / Se verité fust si cuisant / Qu'il fust contre vertu nuisant; / Ne de nommer par prop[r]e nom / Chose qui n'est se bonne non. / Sans fa[i]lle bien l'as oï dire: / Touz voirz ne sont pas bons a dire." [Fair friend, I can certainly name a thing that has nothing to do with sin, without giving myself a bad name; nor am I ashamed of speaking the truth, as if truth could be so biting as to be injurious to virtue; or of naming by its proper name a thing that is nothing but good. Undoubtedly you have heard it said: not all truths are good to say (fol. 46v).] For the modification of vv. 6915–27 as it appears in MSS *Ba* and *Bâ*, see Langlois's edition, note to his vv. 6951–58.

In the B text, these two passages stress the opposition of Faux Samblant and Reason: the former is committed to fraudulence, admitting truth only if it can undermine virtue or stability; the latter is committed to truth and openness, making allowance only for the prevention of gossip or scandal-mongering. The Reason of the B remaniement goes on specifically to condemn hypocrites, stating, "Mes peres plus que nus les blasme, / N'il ne het tant nul autre blasme." [My father condemns them more than anyone; he hates no other crime so much (App. B, 2, B:53–54).][24] Reason's words here prepare both for Ami's casual defense of hypocrisy and for the intervention of Faux Samblant; the gulf between her perspective and that espoused by the followers of the God of Love is clear.

No manuscript survives in which the expanded version of vv. 6915–26 replaces the discussion of obscenity. But a close examination of the B variants shows that much or all of the latter passage was almost certainly absent from early recensions of the B text. The most important evidence for this is the deletion in several B manuscripts of the pardon the Lover grants Reason for the infamous "two words" (vv. 7171–74).[25] Moreover, Reason's defense of plain speech is no longer linked syntactically to her protestations of sinlessness. In Jean's text Reason's defense is introduced with the subordinating conjunction "se": "n'encor ne faz je pas pechié / se je nome les nobles choses / par plein texte" [nor do I sin if I name noble things with plain language (vv. 6926–28)]. In most B manuscripts, this transition is absent. Lines 6925–26 are reworked: "Et je qui onques ne pechié / Ne hé tant rien com tel pechié" [I who have never sinned hate nothing so much as a sin like that (App. B, 2, B:55–56)]. Moreover, these lines no longer precede v. 6927. In most B manuscripts, the lines preceding v. 6927 are: "Je ne tiens autre chose a lede; / Qui plaidier en voudra, s'en plede." [I consider nothing else displeasing; let whoever wants to dispute this, do so (App. B, 2, B:59–60).] There is thus no need, syntactically, to include Reason's defense of plain speech and her praise of the sexual members (vv. 6927–48). The later insertion of these lines necessitated the reworking of v. 6927 to make it an independent clause, opening "Bien puis nomer" [I can certainly name] rather than "se je nome" [if I name).

---

[24] In MS Bô, where Reason's words about truth and hypocrisy are not interrupted by the discussion of integument as in MS Be, the passage appears as follows: "Car verité quant vous la ditez / Por connoistre lez ypocritez: / Tel verité n'est pas a taire, / Ains la doit on adez retraire. / Mon pere plus que nul lez blasme, / N'il ne het plus nul autre blasme." [For truth, when you speak it in order to expose hypocrites: such truth is not to be silenced, indeed one should speak it continuously. My father criticizes them more than anyone, nor does he have greater hatred for any other misdeed (fol. 46v).]   [25] See Langlois, Manuscrits, p. 378.

All signs thus point to the discussion of euphemism and obscenity having been inserted into a text from which it had originally been written out: a version in which the closing discussion had focused on truth, discretion, and interpretation. This analysis allows us to identify three major recensions of the discourse of Reason. Two were wholly lacking the discussion of language; in one the Lover dismissed Reason over the issue of communality, while in the other he simply reiterated his refusal to give up the Rose. The third – an expanded version of either of the first two – included the discussion of language, but in a radically different form. It is possible that, as in MS *Bi* – and MS *Tou* – the very word "coilles" was missing from the first two of these recensions; it is likely, however, that it appeared in the third recension and that it was the Lover's objections to Reason's plainly worded fable that occasioned her disquisition on language and interpretation, with little or no further attention to the issue of obscenity. The evidence of the B family as a whole shows that the discussion of obscenity, euphemism, and the sexual members was restored to the text in piecemeal fashion, with different scribes choosing to insert different selections of lines in successive waves of copying. Indeed, comparison of the B manuscripts for this latter portion of Reason's discourse in fact reveals such bewildering variety, such endless reordering and rearrangement of lines, that Langlois was moved to use the versions of vv. 6916–27 as an exemplary case, illustrating "quel désordre une même interpolation peut introduire dans les différentes copies de cette famille extraordinaire" (*Manuscrits*, pp. 379–80).

One clue to earlier recensions of the B text lies in the placement of an interpolated couplet – "Mais quant la verité doit nuire / Contre vertu, bon le fait fuire" [But when truth would injure virtue, it is good to flee it (App. B, 2, B: 13–14)] – that appears sometimes in an interpolation following v. 6922, but more frequently follows v. 7122.[26] This state of affairs would result from an early B recension in which the interpolated lines formed the bridge between vv. 6922 and 7121, that is, one that omitted much or all vv. 6923–7122: the discussion of plain speech and euphemism, the praise of the sexual members, and the suggestion that the terms "coilles" and "reliques" might be interchangeable. When the deleted lines were restored in subsequent manuscripts, they were not always inserted in the same place – a common enough occurrence. In this early recension, the discussion of literary integument (vv. 7123–50) would have directly followed the rewritten version of Reason's assertion of her own sinlessness and her

---

[26] The couplet appears in the interpolation following v. 6922 in MSS *Bâ* and *Be*; it follows v. 7122 in MSS *Bê*, *Bî*, *Bo*, *Bó*, and *Bô*.

praise of truth.[27] Such a redaction would reduce Reason's defense to a simple statement: being without sin herself, she can speak freely of anything; she is an enemy of hypocri' y and a friend of the open truth in all cases except where it might be injurious to virtue; her words were meant as a parable, which one interprets by seeking the truth hidden within. It is not hard to imagine that a scribe wishing to preserve Reason's explication of language and interpretation without indulging in excesses might consider this a judicious compromise. MSS *Ba*, *Bâ*, and *Be*, for their part, place vv. 7103–4 after v. 7122, suggesting that they might derive from a common ancestor in which vv. 7105–22 were deleted: a less exacting compromise that would restore nearly all of Reason's words, while still drawing the line at her list of colloquial terms for the male member and her comment that in the act of sexual intercourse, women no longer think in euphemistic terms.

The *B* remanieur's attitude towards the issue of plain speech is further revealed in Cupid's description of the castration of Saturn, which occurs in the same interpolation as the account of Apollo and Marsyas; it was surely intended for a version of the *Rose* that included at least some hint of the Lover's dismay at Reason's use of the word "coilles" in her account of the same event. Regarding Jupiter's usurpation of Saturn, Cupid coyly states that the former "Copa li ce que vous savez, / Car maintes foiz oï l'avez" [cut off his you-know-what, for you have heard it many times (ed. Langlois, note to lines 10830–31, vv. 5–6)]. True to the principles he stipulated for his young disciple, Cupid refuses to name testicles; instead, he "glosses" them "par quelque cortaise parole" [with some courteous word (v. 6905)], in the manner suggested by the Lover to Reason. This circumlocution stands in direct response to Reason's plain speech and the Lover's challenge, extending the comedy of the confrontation and demonstrating the ultimate futility of such euphemistic efforts – since the phrase "ce que vous savez" invites the reader to supply the missing word anyway.

Indeed, the contrast between Cupid's narration of the castration of Saturn and that of Reason is quite telling. Reason had not intended the Lover to focus on the castration of Saturn as a literal, anatomical event, but rather as a parable for the corruption of justice through the birth of cupidinous desire. Chastising the Lover for his over-literal interpretation, Reason stresses that "En ma parole autre sen ot" [in my speech there was a different meaning (v. 7128)]. Cupid, on the other hand, does intend the

---

[27] Although the insertion of Reason's discussion of integument (vv. 7123–35, rearranged) into her discussion of hypocrisy in MS *Be* is awkward and ill-placed, resulting surely from scribal confusion or inattention, this reading does lend support to the idea that the discussion of truth and hypocrisy may once have led directly into the discussion on interpretation, skipping over the issue of euphemism and obscenity.

story to be understood literally as the historical account of his own ancestry. Reason has used a bodily image to incarnate an abstract philosophical precept; Cupid has used euphemism as a means of describing castration and, in the lines that follow, his own incestuous begetting through the *joliveté* of Jupiter and Venus. Both Reason and Cupid employ figurative language to express hidden truths: Reason to reveal the "secrets of philosophy" (v. 7140), Cupid to reveal the sexual secrets of his ancestors. The *B* remanieur has captured Jean's point that the refined language of love's disciples creates, in Maureen Quilligan's words, "a perfect inversion of the normal allegorical process of metaphor."[28]

The *B* remanieur continues the exposition of literal and figurative language in a brief interpolation in the Lover's exchange with Dangier on the occasion of his encounter with Bel Acueil after the discourse of La Vieille. Here, as in Jean's text, the Lover slyly suggests that if he has misbehaved, he should be put in prison along with Bel Acueil; Dangier instantly recognizes this proposition for the ploy that it is. In MSS *Ba*, *Bu*, and **Bu* – representing two rather distant branches of the *B* family – the Lover additionally makes an even more audacious proposal, in an interpolation following v. 14974: "Puis que ge me seré renduz / Bien soie a ses fourches penduz: / Autre amande ja n'en prenez." [Since I have surrendered myself, let me be hung at her (his/its) forking limbs: exact no other penalty (MS *Ba*, fol. 100r).] Dangier at once recognizes the sexual innuendo in the Lover's request, exclaiming, "Bien savons que vous demandez / Et quex fourches vous entendez." [We know very well what you are asking and what forks you have in mind (ibid.).] In this foretaste of the poem's conclusion, the Lover demonstrates that he is learning to "gloss" his expression of sexual desire; Dangier's clear-sighted response stands, indeed, as a comment on the entire concluding passage. Reason's comments about truth and hypocrisy are entirely appropriate, for the Lover's commitment to "clean speech" is indeed hypocritical, aimed not at avoiding erotic discourse but at obfuscating it. From this passage, as from the God of Love's coy designation of testicles, we can conclude that the *B* remanieur did appreciate Jean's play with implicit and explicit eroticism; if he was troubled, it was only by the presence of overly explicit language in an inappropriate context. From his reworking of this ongoing thematics, it is clear that he wished to bring out several points: the importance of both truth and discretion; the need to interpret correctly, whether literally or figuratively; the inability of euphemism to redeem a fundamentally mendacious or scurrilous proposal, just as the pious exterior of Faux

[28] Quilligan, "Words and Sex," p. 199. See also Bouché, "L'Obscène et le sacré."

Samblant does nothing to modify his evil nature. Less daring than Jean, however, he preferred to approach the issue through a humorous treatment of euphemism rather than of obscenity.

THE *B* REMANIEMENT AND THE *ROSE* MANUSCRIPT TRADITION

The *B* text circulated rather widely: of the 116 *Rose* manuscripts classified by Langlois, thirteen are designated as *B*, making it the third largest of his manuscript families. In addition, *B* material – especially the Lover's characterization of Reason as "commune amie" and the Apollo–Marsyas interpolation – is found in numerous manuscripts of other families. The former passage, for example, appears in manuscripts of the *K* family, while those of the *J* family have both; the latter passage even appears in the sixteenth-century printed version attributed to Clément Marot (ed. Baridon, vv. 11069–108). The *B* text was also used as the basis for a Flemish translation of the *Rose* dating from ca. 1290 – further proof of the early date of the remaniement – and contributed some passages to the Middle English *Rose*.[29] The editorial activities of medieval scribes produced extensive contamination – or cross-fertilization, depending on one's perspective – between manuscript families, thereby giving the modern textual critic a task of truly dizzying proportions. But by studying specific examples of textual "contamination," we can acquire a deeper understanding of the dynamics of the *Rose* manuscript tradition.

The transmission of the *B* text no doubt operated in a manner similar to that of Gui de Mori. The evidence suggests that there may have been no one original, authoritative version of Gui's remaniement, but rather an annotated copy of the *Rose* from which various versions could be produced according to the dictates of the given scribe or patron. The "prototype" or "original" of Gui's remaniement could reasonably be defined as a copy of the *Rose* in which all indicated changes were made. But Gui's prologue indicates that even he did not feel that all of his modifications needed to be included all of the time. A scribe making a copy of Gui's remaniement could study the array of possibilities and decide which relocations and

[29] The Middle English *Rose* was revised by someone using a *B* manuscript; see Sutherland, ed., *The Romaunt of the Rose and Le Roman de la Rose*, pp. xxviii–xxxiv. Sutherland's remarks about the relationship of the Middle English version of Faux Samblant to MS *Be* (pp. xxxiii–xxxiv) must be somewhat modified, since MS *Be* is not, as he supposes, missing a page, but rather lines of text. But the deletion of text in *B* manuscripts and the frequent practice of adding such text in the margins, sometimes without sufficiently clear indication of where it belongs, could certainly account for the disorder of the Middle English text, which involves passages commonly deleted from the *B* manuscripts. On the use of the *B* text for the Flemish translation of the *Rose*, see Van der Poel, *De Vlaamse "Rose" en "Die Rose" van Heinric*, pp. 64–75.

deletions he wished to make and which additions he wished to include, in part or in whole. The scribe's choices might be dictated by the prospective owner of the manuscript, or by his own tastes, which might in turn vary from one time to another. Thus even "originals" copied by the same scribe from the master copy could manifest considerable variety.

Passages spread easily from one manuscript family to another through the comparison of manuscripts and the insertion of passages thus discovered. We have already seen examples of this practice in MSS *Ke* and *Fe*. MS Bibl. Nat. fr. 1559 (*La*) also has numerous passages from the *B* text added in its margins, while MSS *Be* and *Lz* have had most of their deleted passages restored. One of the results of this practice was the creation of manuscripts in which lines composed to replace deleted material appear side by side with the passages they originally replaced. A scribe wishing to combine the two readings had to decide in what order the rival passages should appear. Needless to say, medieval scribes did not have access to the comprehensive manuscript analyses that would enable them to distinguish between original and reworked passages; nor should we assume that they would necessarily have considered this important. Most seem to have been motivated by a desire for textual completeness, and simply arranged the lines they found in their sources as they thought best. As a result, the lines show one order in some manuscripts and a different order in others.

The insertion of text in the margins or on supplementary pages is not the only way that different versions of the *Rose* could be combined. Sometimes it is clear that a scribe was copying from at least two manuscripts at once, in order to arrive at the most complete text possible. Such, for example, is the case with the early fifteenth-century MS Bibl. Nat. fr. 1563. In this manuscript the *Rose* is followed by the documents of the *querelle*; it was compiled by someone with a great interest in the *Rose*.[30] The text is profusely illustrated with an important series of miniatures whose amateurish quality leads one to wonder whether they might not be the work of the scribe himself, product of his close engagement with the poem. The numerous "Nota bene" signs in the margins of both the *Rose* and the *querelle* documents are a further indication that this manuscript was used for close study of the *Rose*. Little is known about the provenance of the manuscript, but it did belong during the fifteenth century to a Dominican friar who may also have been the copyist: on the flyleaf is the inscription "Frere Jehan de Merville, de l'orede de Perechue" [*sic*].[31]

[30] On MS Bibl. Nat. fr. 1563, see Langlois, *Manuscrits*, pp. 20–22; Hicks, *Débat sur le "Roman de la Rose"*, pp. lxxxi–lxxxiii.

[31] The inscription is obviously an awkward misspelling of "Ordre des Preecheurs." Langlois hesitates in his identification of the hand with that of the text, listing Jehan de Merville as "copiste ou possesseur" in his list of copyists (*Manuscrits*, p. 219). In any case, the hands are very close.

Given the scholarly milieu and the intense interest in the interpretation of the *Rose*, it is hardly surprising to find that the scribe was working from more than one model, creating a composite edition. For certain parts of the text, he used a *B* manuscript closely related to MSS *Bê*, *Bo*, and *Bô*; MS fr. 1563 shares a number of significant variants with these manuscripts. Yet the manuscript lacks the interpolations in the discourse of Reason and those about Adonis and Marsyas in the God of Love's discourse, and contains other variants not shared by the *B* text. But it is not only the presence of material from different manuscript families that suggests a plurality of sources for MS fr. 1563. One can actually see places where the scribe made corrections – usually with red ink – so as to insert lines from an exemplar other than the one he had been following. These lines are not written in the margins; they were copied at the same time as the rest of the poem. A few examples will illustrate.

A clear-cut instance of combining two manuscript families appears in the description of Venus' burning arrow. In the following passage, the lines here italicized have been crossed out in red ink:

20757	L'arc tant et le brandon encoche,
20758	*Et quant elle ot bien mis en coche,*
20759	*Jusqu'a l'oreille l'arc entoise,*
20760	*Qui n'est pas plus grans d'une toise.*
xxx	Dit que ne mengera de boche,
xxx	Tant que la tour avera arse.
xxx	Adonques l'arc forment embrase,
20759	Et jusqu'a l'oreille l'entoise,
20760	Ci n'iere pas lons d'une toise. (fol. 137v)

She draws the bow and places the torch in it, [*and when she has fitted it to the notch, she draws the bow, which is no more than six feet long, back to her ear*] and says that she will not eat a mouthful until she has burned the tower. Right then the bow is blazing brightly, and she draws it back to her ear; it was not six feet long.

What evidently happened here is that the scribe, having transcribed his text through v. 20760, discovered the variant lines following v. 20757 in his other source. Since the interpolated couplet would not make sense without the alternative version of v. 20758, and since that line in turn needed to follow v. 20757, the scribe simply expunged vv. 20758–60 and replaced them with the altered and lengthier reading of the other manuscript. A similar event transpired with Ami's advice to placate the Rose's guardians with gifts: the scribe copied vv. 7495–96 directly after v. 7486, then crossed them out in red ink and proceeded with vv. 7487ff., including vv. 7495–96 in their proper place. The mysterious appearance of vv. 7495–96 after v. 7486 is easily explained with reference to MSS *Bi*, *Bê*, *Bo*, and *Bô*: in all of these vv. 7487–94 have been deleted, so that v. 7495 does follow v. 7486. The scribe – who seems to have found his task a difficult one – did not notice the presence of the eight extra lines in his other source until after he had already transcribed vv. 7495–96.

Comparison of *B* and *B*-related manuscripts shows that certain passages passed through numerous recensions, as though especially problematic for medieval readers. I have stated, for example, that the *Bi* redactor omitted vv. 7579–7688: a particularly uncourtly passage, with antifeminist over-tones, in which Ami complains that women, contrary to their natural carnality, have been conditioned to expect gifts in exchange for sexual favors and counsels the Lover to press his case insistently, using force if he can find the opportunity. This passage is variously handled in the other *B* manuscripts. MS *Bê* replaces vv. 7579–7606 – the assertion that women would offer themselves freely had they not been led to expect gifts, and the condemnation of men who agree to pay for sex – with four lines:

xxx	Et se nulz les requeroit,
xxx	Saviés conment en averroit?
7582	Certainement, il requeroient,
xxx	Et leurz serviches offerroyent.	(fol. 43r)

And if no one asked them [for sex], do you know how it would happen? Certainly, they would do the asking, and offer their services.[32]

The same lines appear in MSS *Ba*, *Be*, and *Bo* as well, but there they are followed by vv. 7579–606. Ami's wistful speculation about a world in which women would offer sex freely is thus suppressed entirely in MS *Bi*; reduced to a four-line summary in MS *Bê*; and expanded to include that summary in MSS *Ba*, *Be*, and *Bo*. In still other *B* manuscripts, the passage appears as it does in the standard text. The recommendation to use force (vv. 7639–88), in turn, appears in all *B* manuscripts except MS *Bo* and, of course, MS *Bi*. That MS *Bê* would delete vv. 7579–7606, MS *Bo* vv. 7639–88, and MS *Bi* the entirety of vv. 7579–7688 suggests that, at the very least, both vv. 7579–7606 and vv. 7639–88 were deleted from the original *B* text, leaving at most the exhortation not to delay one's suit too long and the warning not to press a woman who is clearly distressed. MS *Bi* is a further abridgment of the *B* text; the other manuscripts are the results of various efforts to restore those portions of the standard text deemed acceptable by the scribe in question.

Yet another reworking of this vexed passage appears in MS fr. 1563.

[32] The "they" of v. 7582 does refer to women. Ami uses the masculine pronoun because he is referring to the "portiers" [gatekeepers]. Two of these, however – Fear and Shame – are personifications of feminine attributes, as is Dangier.

Following v. 7578, the scribe copied the four lines seen in MS *Bê* and a scattering of the other lines, some now crossed out in red ink, before returning to vv. 7579ff. (including the lines already transcribed):

xxx	Et se nus ne les requieroit,
xxx	Savés vous que il en seroit?
7582	Certainement, il requieroient,
xxx	Et leur servises offriroient.
7607	Mais onques pour ce n'atendés!
7608	Requierés les et leur tandés
7609	Les las pour vostre proie prendre,
7610	Car vous pouvés tant attendre [-1]
7611	Qu'autre si pouroient combatre,
7612	Ou ung ou .ii. ou .iii. ou quatre.
7615	Tost seroient ailleurs tourné,
7616	Se trop avoiés sejourné.
7617	Jamais atans n'y vandriés,
7618	Pour ce que trop attendiiés.
7631	*Mais quant courrencié le verrés,*
7632	*Ja de ce ne le requierés,*
7635	*Se la tristesce n'estoit nee*
7636	*De jalousie la desvee.*
7637	*Em les eüst pro vous batus,*
7638	*Donc courous s'i fust embatus.*
7579	Et si sunt tuit de tel maniere . . .

And if no one asked them, do you know how it would be? Certainly, they would do the asking, and offer their services. But don't wait for that! Ask them, and spread your snares to capture your prey. For you can end up waiting so long that someone else could conquer, one or two [others], or three or four. They would soon have turned elsewhere, if you had delayed too long. You would never get anything, because you waited too long. [*But when you see her upset, don't ask her then, unless her sadness is caused by that madwoman, Jealousy. They (the "gate-keepers") might have been beaten on your account, and thus Anger would have slipped in.*] For all of them are of such a nature . . .

The most likely explanation for this state of affairs is that the scribe was working from a *B* manuscript which, like MS *Bê*, replaced vv. 7579–606 with four lines; like MSS *Bo* and *Bô*, omitted vv. 7613–14; additionally omitted vv. 7619–30 and 7633–34; and, like MS *Bo*, omitted vv. 7639–88. Only after having copied v. 7638 did the scribe notice that his other source contained supplementary text. Comparing his sources, the scribe located the beginning of this material lacking from his *B* model at v. 7579. He thus expunged vv. 7631–38 and inserted the new material, failing to notice that it also contained the ten lines that he had copied preceding v. 7631.

The passage first copied by the scribe of MS fr. 1563 probably represents the original *B* text. The lines omitted – such as vv. 7613–14, in which Ami suggests that a lady could have fifty-two dozen lovers a year – might well have seemed excessive to a redactor seeking to restore to Jean's continuation something of the spirit of Guillaume de Lorris. In the version represented in MS fr. 1563, the essence of Ami's advice is preserved: do not wait for the woman to make the first move, or you risk losing out to more aggressive rivals; but do not press your case if the lady is clearly distressed. This version of the text provides a "missing link," a common ground for the various other *B* recensions: most likely, the *B* prototype.

Insofar as we can glimpse the original modifications that produced the various *B* texts, then, we can say that this version of the *Rose* simplifies Jean's enormously complex and frequently ambiguous work, but not without preserving certain features of the original. It is the work of someone familiar with Jean's Ovidian sources and sympathetic to the project of rewriting the Ovidian models, though not always with Jean's spirit of daring. The redactor appreciated Jean's humorous portrayal of the conflict of love, resistance, and reason and of the resulting clash of linguistic and ethical codes; at the same time, he sought to express this conflict in somewhat less flamboyant terms. And without going to the extent of Gui de Mori, he did reduce the digressive character of Jean's continuation by deleting what he perceived as repetitive or extraneous material. By all of these means he imposed a greater degree of unity on the conjoined *Rose* of Guillaume and Jean, even taking the step of suppressing allusions to the poem's dual authorship. It is probable that, like Gui, he was one who encountered Jean's continuation only after having already come to know and love the *Rose* of Guillaume de Lorris.

5

Transforming the mirror of lovers: manuscripts of the second group

Nature rit, si comme moi semble,
Quand hic et haec joignent ensemble.

(Explicit in *N* MSS)

Donc aime la vierge Marie,
Par amour a li te marie.
T'ame ne veult autre mari.[1]

(Interpolation in *KMN* MSS)

In the two preceding chapters we have examined two early remaniements of the *Rose* and their impact on the textual history of the poem. But while these may be the most extensive rewritings of the *Rose* dating from the first century of the poem's existence, they are by no means the only instances of interpolations or other modifications introduced into the text of the *Rose*. In this chapter we will examine several more examples of textual alteration: a group of interpolations largely shared by members of Langlois's second group, and some more extensive modifications wrought on individual members of that group.

THE TOTALIZING MIRROR OF LOVE: THE *ROSE* OF THE *KMN* MANUSCRIPTS

In his analysis of the tradition of Jean de Meun's *Rose*, Langlois placed twenty-six of his 116 classified manuscripts under the sigla *K* (six), *M* (six) and *N* (fourteen).[2] The families are closely related, sharing many variants. Each additionally has variants of its own; and the *K* text, as noted in Chapter 4, has absorbed some interpolations from the *B* remaniement. With the *KMN* group of manuscripts, we are again largely concerned with

---

[1] "Nature laughs, so it seems to me, when 'he' and 'she' join together" (see Langlois, *Manuscrits*, p. 448); "So love the Virgin Mary; wed her in love. Your soul needs no other spouse." (Appendix C: 99–101.)   [2] See Langlois, *Manuscrits*, pp. 425–87.

the *Rose* of Jean de Meun, for it is in his portion of the text that we find the most extensive interpolations. Because of the number of manuscripts and the enormous number of variants, many of which do not significantly affect the poem's argument and may simply derive from scribal error, I have not attempted an exhaustive survey of these three families. Rather, I shall focus on a series of interpolations occurring in the discourse of Reason, in the discourse of Genius, and in the concluding section of the poem. These passages cast a new light on the figures of Reason and Genius and on the status of, and relationship between, rational love, spiritual love, and procreation. These interpolations can be found in manuscripts of the late thirteenth and early fourteenth century; like the texts of Gui de Mori and the *B* remanieur, they date from an early period of *Rose* reception.

The first passage for consideration is the interpolation that Langlois designates "litany of love" (see Appendix C). Over a hundred lines long, it follows v. 4370 in twenty-eight, or nearly one-fourth, of the manuscripts collated by Langlois.[3] Most of these are members of the *KMN* group. The passage had an illustrious survival throughout the medieval and Renaissance periods, continuing to appear not only in fifteenth-century manuscripts, but even in early printed editions, including the sixteenth-century modernization attributed to Clément Marot (ed. Baridon, vv. 4413–516). Méon included it as a footnote in his edition of the *Rose*, but Langlois refrained from printing it, either in his study of *Rose* manuscripts or among the variants in his edition. At first glance, it is clear that these lines are not the work of Jean de Meun. The repetition of the same rhymes four and even six lines in a row, for example, is not consistent with his style. Nonetheless, the passage was widely accepted for some two hundred years, and deserves our attention as part of the medieval *Rose*.

In this passage, as in Gui de Mori's interpolations about divine love and Christian charity (see Chapter 3), Reason is made into a figure of Christian Sapience. The "litany of love" represents an independent response to the lack of explicitly Christian material in Reason's discourse; and like Gui, its author drew on 1 Corinthians 13:

> Amors est fors, amour est dure,
> Amors soustient, amor endure,
>
> . . .
>
> Amour loial, amour seüre,
> Sert et de service n'a cure.   (App. C:8–9, 12–13)

---

[3] See Langlois, *Manuscrits*, p. 425. An eight-line passage that is very close to the account of the Passion in the "litany" (App. A: 34–40) appears in the thirteenth-century MS Chantilly, Musée Condé 1942, fol. 6v, under the rubric "Hec sunt aliqua que Deus facit de se ipso amore generis humani" [these are some things that God did himself for love of the human race]. For this information I am grateful to Peter Allen of Pomona College.

Love is strong, love is firm, love sustains, love endures, . . . Loyal love, true love, serves and asks for nothing in return.

These words echo both the sentiments expressed by Paul and his use of anaphora: "Charitas patiens est, benigna est. Charitas . . . non est ambitiosa, non quaerit quae sua sunt . . . omnia suffert, omnia credit, omnia sperat, omnia sustinet." [Love is patient and kind; love . . . is not rude. Love does not insist on its own way . . . Love bears all things, believes all things, hopes all things, endures all things (rsv, 1 Corinthians 13:4, 5, 7).] Like Gui, the author of the "litany" invokes the Incarnation, citing the events of Christ's Passion as the manifestation of divine love. And returning to 1 Corinthians 13, he identifies love as the principal virtue, greater than "foi ne esperance, / Justice, force, n'atremprance" [faith and hope, justice, force, and temperance (vv. 49–50)], and stresses it as necessary to almsgiving, martyrdom, or any other virtuous behavior.

Finally, just as Paul concludes his praise of love with the hope of knowing God face to face (1 Corinthians 13:12), so Reason moves on to an evocation of the mystical ascent experienced when "fine amor d'amer est yvre" [true love is intoxicated with loving (v. 71)]:

> Lors dort en meditation,
> Puis monte en contemplacion;
> Ilec s'aboivre, ilec s'esveille,
> Ilec voit mainte grant merveille.   (vv. 77–80)

It sleeps in meditation, then ascends in contemplation; there it drinks deeply, there awakes, there sees many a great wonder.

And Reason concludes her account of this decidedly supra-rational love by offering not herself, but the Virgin Mary as object of devotion. Once again, Reason's exposition of love takes on a spiritual dimension, as she demonstrates that charitable love of one's neighbor, God's love for the human race, and the mystical union of human and divine are linked as manifestations of the same divine force. But unlike Gui's interpolations on the same topic, which survive today only in MS *Mor*, the "litany" became one of the most widespread of all *Rose* interpolations.

In addition to 1 Corinthians 13, the "litany" draws on the *Consolation of Philosophy*, in particular Book 2, Meter 8 – which, as we saw, was probably one of Gui's sources as well – and Book 4, Meter 1, describing the soul's ascent to the highest heaven. The ascent of Prudence in *Anticlaudianus* may also be a source; there, Prudence is conducted by Reason to the threshold of Heaven and led by Theology to the divine palace, where she experiences an ecstasy that is a kind of sleep: "sompnoque soporans / Extasis ipsa suo, mentem dormire coegit" [ecstasy bringing a slumber of its own, caused her mind to sleep (*Ant.* 6:7–8; cf. App. C:77)]. Indeed, the incantatory repetition of rhymes and of the word *amour* sets the "litany" off from its frame text, recalling the distinction between meter and prose in both the *Consolation* and *Anticlaudianus.* As in Gui's remaniement, Jean's poem is brought closer to its Latin models. The passage reminds us that Reason is not an end in herself, but rather serves as link between the human and the divine. As Philosophy states in the *Consolation*: "Quare in illius summae intellegentiae cacumen, si possumus, erigamur; illic enim ratio uidebit quod in se non potest intueri." [Wherefore let us be lifted up, if we can, to the peak of that highest intelligence; for there reason will see what it cannot contemplate within itself (Book 5, Prose 5).]

Vernacular translations of the *Consolation* are particularly close to the *Rose*, and provide an important context in which to examine the *Rose* as a locus for the vernacular reception of Boethius.[4] For example, the notion that the soul's ascent is due to love finds a precedent in the early thirteenth-century prose translation (Version I), which glosses the "wings" offered by Philosophy in Book 4, Meter 1 as the virtues, adding, "Dous sunt les vertuz principels: l'amor de Deu e d'ome crestien, que nos apeloms Charité." [There are two principal virtues: love of God and love of a fellow Christian, which we call Charity (ed. Bolton-Hall, p. 153).] The Anonymous Benedictine who revised the translation by Renaut de Louhans, in turn, expands on Meter 1 of Book 4 with language that hints at the mystical vision as a sublimated eroticism.[5] When the Latin Philosophy tells Boethius that, should he arrive at such a place, he will recognize it as his true home, her citation of his imagined words is introduced by a simple "dices" [you will say (4, 2:25)]. In the Old French text, in contrast, the soul speaks "d'un trés embrazé desire / Et en trés desireux plaisir, / Joieuse" [with a burning desire, and in very desirous pleasure, joyous (Bibl. Nat. fr. 1946, fol. 158v)]. And in a development that has no real precedent in the Latin text, the Old French text describes the visionary experience in terminology reminiscent of the *Rose* interpolation (cf. App. C:77–79):

> Ta pensëe or endormie,
> Par voler ainsy resveillie,
> Sera par contemplation
> Lors en grand consolation.　　　　　　　　　　(fol. 159r)

Your mind now asleep, thus awakened by the flight, will, through contemplation, experience great consolation.

---

[4] On vernacular translations of Boethius, see Dwyer, *Boethian Fictions*; Minnis, ed., *Medieval Boethius.*
[5] The revision by the Anonymous Benedictine is known as Version x. For advice concerning Old French translations of Boethius, I am grateful to J. Keith Atkinson and Béatrice Atherton, both of the University of Queensland.

The *Rose*, in the *KMN* text as in Gui's remaniement, is further exploited as a vehicle for the vernacularization of Boethius. The relationship between the reception of the *Rose* and that of the *Consolation* is clearly a significant factor; an in-depth comparative study of the *Rose* in its various manifestations and the translations of Boethius is much needed.

The addition of the "litany" thus expands the character of Reason in a manner similar to that of Gui, blurring the line between rationalism and mysticism. It intensifies the irony of the Lover's position when he accuses Reason of proposing an impossible love, one so unearthly as to require flying over the cloud tops and assailing Heaven like the Titans of old, thereby risking Jove's lightning bolt (vv. 5393–401). While in Jean's text the Lover's words already seem excessive and short-sighted, they become positively rich once Reason actually has proposed a type of love that allows for a spiritual ascent to heaven. Despite Reason's reliance on Greek and Roman authors, it is clear now who is the real pagan – a point brought home in many *B* MSS with the Lover's comment that he does not care how many gods Reason has in her ancestry. In the "litany," Reason clearly speaks as the daughter of the Christian God.

Reason's established Christian identity does not exclude humorous elements in her interactions with the Lover. In manuscripts of the *K* family, as noted above, he rejects Reason as a "commune amie." While mystical writings do address the human desire to be individually loved by God, the treatment of this issue in the *Rose* is decidedly comical, with the Lover accusing Reason of wild abandon and Reason assuring him that he will not be cuckolded. Similarly, Reason's defense of plain speech appears in manuscripts of the *KMN* group. In fact, in most of these manuscripts the passage is amplified by a six-line interpolation that Langlois identifies as having originated in the *L* redaction, a version quite close to what we think of as the standard text. In this passage, which follows v. 7090 or, in *K* manuscripts, v. 7088, Reason expands on her fantasy of what would happen if relics were called "coilles":

> E quant pour reliques m'oïsses
> Couilles nomer, le mot preïsses
> Pour si bel, e tant le prisasses,
> Que par tout couilles aourasses,
> E les baisasses en eglises,
> En or e en argent assises.
>
> (ed. Langlois, var. to his v. 7120)

And when you heard me use the word "balls" for relics, you would think the word was so beautiful, and would prize it so much, that you would worship balls everywhere, and kiss them in churches, enshrined in gold and silver.

From mystical union with God to a fabliau-like image of testicles on an altar: one might well say that Reason's discourse, in the *KMN* manuscripts, goes from the sublime to the ridiculous.

Nonetheless, Reason's words to the Lover are quite pertinent. If he is unprepared to worship relics while calling them balls, he is quite willing, by the end of the poem, to worship the feminine genitalia by calling them relics. For those who are not afraid of verbal daring, the interpolation delightfully captures the unbridgeable gap between Reason's linguistic orientation and that of the Lover. Since for Reason, words are used to communicate, the logical result of a switch of nomenclature is a transfer of associations to the new word. But for the Lover, words are used to mask. For him, the switch in names proves to be a brilliant strategy, for the word retains its old associations in its new context: rather than continuing to worship relics, calling them testicles, he continues to worship the object designated by the word "relics," having substituted for the original a very different sort of thing.[6] The effect, in the *KMN* manuscripts as in the *B* text, is one of consistent and perverse literalization on the part of the Lover. He turns Reason's mystical ascent into an image of himself winging his way towards some imagined Olympus; in *K* MSS, he additionally perceives universal charity as a form of promiscuity; and taking her suggestion about the interchangeability of sacred and sexual terminology, he ultimately worships at the altar of enshrined genitalia. The effect is very much in the spirit of Jean de Meun.

The Lover's moral failings are also expressed in a ten-line interpolation appearing after v. 21396 (*K* manuscripts) or v. 21398 (*N* manuscripts).[7] As the Lover approaches the Rose, congratulating himself on his victory, he considers the price of his refusal to follow Reason:

> Mais se je Raison creüsse,
> Sachiez que sages fait eüsse,
> De jour cler alasse et venisse,
> Ne en tel lieu ne me meïsse
> Que ne veïsse devant moi.
>
> (Langlois, *Manuscrits*, p. 447)

But if I had believed Reason, know that I would have acted wisely; I would have come and gone by daylight, and wouldn't have put myself in a situation where I couldn't see before me.

Nonetheless he reiterates that he will not believe her, explaining that "ele

---

[6] This point is raised by Quilligan, "Words and Sex," p. 207; Lynch, *High Medieval Dream Vision*, p. 128; Bouché, "L'Obscène et le sacré."

[7] For the complete passage see Langlois, *Manuscrits*, p. 447.

me veut arriere traire / La ou mes cueurs se veut plus traire" [she wants to pull me back from where my heart is most determined to go (ibid.)]. The Lover's backward glance at Reason already appears in Jean's text: "Mes de Reson ne me souvint, / qui tant en moi gasta de peine" [but I didn't remember Reason, who wasted so much effort on me (vv. 21730–31)]. The admission that believing Reason might have been a good idea, however, is new, and represents a short-lived glimmer of enlightenment – the Lover's first such moment since his brief regrets at the beginning of Jean's continuation. Also intriguing is the allusion to coming and going by daylight. The God of Love predicted that the Lover would experience considerable comings and goings at night, mostly for the purpose of visiting his lady and keeping vigil outside her door (vv. 2491–2533); and by the end of the poem, the image of traversing ditches in the dark, feeling one's way with the trusty staff provided by Nature, has become a decidedly bawdy joke (vv. 21369–97). In the *KN* interpolation, the Lover implies that if he had followed Reason rather than Cupid, he could have avoided these nightly peregrinations. As a disciple of Reason, the Lover would achieve moral enlightenment; and he would pursue relationships that would not require feeling about in the dark.

Nonetheless, the possibility does exist within the *KMN* text for sexual activity that is compatible with Reason and integrated into a divinely ordained natural order. It may seem odd to argue that it is in this version of the *Rose*, where Reason so explicitly emerges as an agent of divine grace, that she should also be seen as authorizing sexual activity. But let us examine closely the context for the digression on mystical love. Reason first condemns the irrational nature of erotic desire, stressing its deceptive methods, its lack of real love, and its lack of interest in the purpose of sexual relations, procreation (vv. 4347–70). At this point, she reveals the existence of "a different love," and launches into her exposition of Christian charity and divine love. Here, then, is one possible alternative to carnal desire: if the Lover feels the stirring of passion, if he wishes to be intoxicated by ecstatic love, he should turn to God.

At the end of her description of mystical love, Reason returns to the topic of sexual love: "De l'autre amour dirai la cure, / Selon la devine Escripture." [I will tell you the office of the other love, according to Holy Scriptures (App. c:107–8).] She proceeds to explain that anyone who does engage in sexual relations should do so not for the purpose of pleasure, but for that of procreation; lovers, while permitted to take their pleasure and to give one another small tokens of affection, must be bound by neither sexual desire nor material greed. In the *KMN* text, Reason offers two complementary alternatives to relationships motivated by lust or greed: love of

God and Christian charity on the one hand, and on the other, sexual – presumably conjugal – relations for the purpose of procreation, based on mutual love and friendship. Such positions are not contradictory at all, and even rest on Scriptural authority; Paul himself, in the text that underlies Reason's discourse of Christian love, also addresses the dangers of sexual desire and recommends marriage as a viable alternative for those who cannot live in chastity (1 Corinthians 7). The Reason of the *KMN* text did, after all, preface her remarks about proper sexual love by saying that she would explain such love "according to the Scriptures," a remark that could refer either to 1 Corinthians 7 or to Genesis 1:28. As Fleming so succinctly put it, "The Lover's problem is not sexuality but irrationality."[8]

In light of the foregoing, it is most interesting to note two further interpolated couplets. The first appears only in *K* manuscripts and in those, such as MS *κυ*, that have drawn directly on the *K* text; in a direct response to the issues outlined above, Reason's defense of legitimate sexual relations is made to refer explicitly to marriage:

4589	Ne cuidiez pas que j'es dessamble;
4590	Je veil bien qu'il voisent ensamble,
xxx	Et par mariage s'alient
xxx	Si com les loys leur certefient.

(MS *Ke*, fol. 33r)

> Don't think I would separate them; I want them to come together and to join themselves in marriage, as provided by law.

In the *K* text, it is finally explicit that lawful marriage is the context in which Reason envisages procreation. The stipulation can be extended to Genius' exhortations, given a second interpolated couplet that appears in the discourse of Genius in *K*, *M*, and *N* manuscripts:

20607	Pensez de Nature honorer,
20608	servez la par bien laborer.
xxx	Mais comment que il vous aviengne,
xxx	De Raison vueil qu'il vous souviengne.

(as cited by Langlois, *Manuscrits*, p. 453)

> Be sure to honor Nature, serve her by working well. But whatever happens to you, I want you to remember Reason.

With the addition of just two lines, Genius is transformed from an avatar of indiscriminate copulation to a proponent of the behavior jointly favored by Nature and Reason. Given the overall context, this can only mean a love based on friendship, leading to sexual relations for the purpose of

---

[8] *Reason and the Lover*, p. 24; see also pp. 23, 14–15.

procreation, and carried out in accordance with Reason, herself an agent of divine authority and, in the *K* text, explicitly a proponent of marriage.

The *KMN* couplet appears at a crucial moment, when Genius is summing up his advice in a series of commandments:

> Pensez de Nature honorer,
> servez la par bien laborer;
> et se de l'autrui riens avez,
> rendez le, se vos le savez;
> et se vos randre ne pouez
> les biens despanduz ou jouez,
> aiez en bone volanté,
> quant des biens avrez a planté.
> D'occision nus ne s'aprouche,
> netes aiez et mains et bouche.   (vv. 20607–16)

Take care to honor Nature, serve her by laboring well; and if you have anything belonging to someone else, give it back, if you know of it; and if you can't give back goods spent or gambled away, be good-willed about it when you do have plenty of goods. Let no one partake of murder, keep hands and mouth clean.

Marc-René Jung cites this passage as evidence that Genius is concerned with moral values extending beyond sexual activity; he concludes that Jean employs heterosexuality as a synecdoche for virtuous behavior, just as Alain used homosexuality as a synecdoche for vice.[9] I would qualify this assessment: it is not Jean but Genius for whom heterosexuality is a synecdoche for virtuous behavior. Indeed, the equation might better be reversed: that Genius uses virtuous behavior as a code for heterosexual activity. For Genius' seemingly innocent commandments have a source, one that strongly colors their moral significance: a passage in the *Ars amatoria*, devoted to a justification of falsehood and deception as long as such practices are reserved to the battle of the sexes. Ovid's narrator assures his readers that Jupiter himself is guilty of making false oaths to Juno; hence, "Juppiter ex alto periuria ridet amantum" [Jupiter from on high smiles on the perjuries of lovers (*Ars* 1:633)]. Such gods are extremely useful, and should therefore be honored:

> Expedit esse deos, et, ut expedit, esse putemus;
> . . .
>   . . . innocue vivite: numen adest;
> Reddite despositum; pietas sua foedora servet:
> Fraus absit; vacuas caedis habete manus.

---

9 Marc-René Jung, "Jean de Meun et l'allégorie," p. 32.

It is expedient there should be gods, and as it is expedient let us deem that gods exist; . . . live innocently, gods are nigh; return what is given to your keeping; let duty keep her covenant; let fraud be absent; keep your hands clean of blood.   (*Ars* 1:637, 640–42, transl. Mozley.)

Genius, who has moved steadily further from his model in *De planctu Naturae*, is now truly on the verge of turning into the old *lascivi praeceptor Amoris* himself, with Nature, his presiding deity, assuming the role of the god who smiles on the perjuries of lovers.[10] Did she not agree to pardon Cupid for associating himself with Faux Samblant (vv. 19335–38)?

The inserted lines help to redress this situation, bringing Genius back into line with Reason: if Nature is to be honored, it must be in a rational manner. Even so, the text requires close reading. The most logical supposition is that Genius has in mind that portion of Reason's discourse stating that the legitimate purpose of sexual activity is procreation (vv. 4357–90, 4515–32). Reason here explains that it was to ensure the survival of the species that Nature made sex pleasurable. But it is also in the course of this passage that Reason speaks of men who pretend to be *fins amanz*, deceiving women with "lies and fables"; she adds that such men are less deceived than real *fins amanz*, uttering her controversial maxim, "car adés vient il mieuz, beau mestre, / decevoir que deceüz estre" [for it is better, fair sir, to deceive than to be deceived (vv. 4369–70)]. And in a subsequent development of the motif of procreation, she alludes to the moral turpitude of women who deceive men, granting sexual favors only for financial gain. Strangely, Genius' citation of Reason seems only to relocate his Ovidian commandments in the context of sexual deception, as though she too accepted with equanimity the perjuries of lovers.

Have we, in fact, re-entered the Ovidian world, one in which men are advised to deal honorably with one another and to court the favors of indulgent deities while deceiving the crafty woman, "ut periuras merito periuria fallant" [that perjuries may rightly cheat the perjured (*Ars* 1:657)]? No doubt the Lover would approve such a reading; if he learns anything at all in the course of the poem, it is the value of deception. And a reader like Christine de Pizan, who strongly objected to Reason's words about deception (vv. 4369–70), would surely catch the intertextual play and find it in poor taste. Pierre Col, on the other hand, attempted to defend vv. 4369–70, arguing that Reason does not say that either deceiving or being deceived is good in itself, but only ranks them with regard to one another. And in fact, upon examination, we see that Reason does qualify her remarks: it is better to deceive than to be deceived, "quant le maien n'i

---

[10] Ovid refers to himself as "lascivi praeceptor Amoris" [preceptor of wanton love] in *Ars amatoria* 2:497.

sevent querre" [when they don't know how to seek the middle ground (v. 4372)]. Obviously, Reason does not mean to justify either of the two extremes: what she condones is affectionate sexual relations for the purpose of procreation. It is to this teaching that the interpolated couplet in Genius refers; its author was one who read the poem in a manner similar to that of Col or Montreuil. For such a reader, the resulting juxtaposition of texts would present another literary trick, source at once of profit and pleasure, of the sort that the *Rose* abounds with.

For Jean de Meun is a tricky poet. In continuing a poem that cites Macrobius as its authority, he intensifies the erotic aspect of the dream, omitting no details, and illustrates learned discussions with bawdy fables. Borrowing from *De planctu Naturae*, he produces one avatar of Natura – Reason – who feels no word to be inappropriate to her virginal mouth; and another – Nature – who, instead of deploring Venus' adultery with Antigamen, jokes about her adultery with Mars. Jean forces his readers to attend closely to the intricacies of his text and to its relationships, both subtle and overt, to anterior texts. The discourse of Genius is no exception, and the interpolated couplet enters fully into the richness of the text. We encounter a series of commandments that seem to be models of virtue, then – as we recognize their source – take on a much darker aspect; only to seem once more vindicated, purged of their former associations by their new association with Reason. But when we consult Reason, as Genius bids us to do, we find ourselves momentarily plunged back into the world where the best advice is "Fallite fallentes" [deceive the deceivers (*Ars* 1:645)]. What we finally realize is that the joke is on us, that the real target of the text is precisely those who misread it, unable to follow its labyrinthine movements, its transformations of literary models, its juggling with the categories of the meaningful and the trivial, the rational and the irrational. The *KMN* couplet is far from resolving all of the problems of Genius' discourse, to be sure. The reading of Genius that it implies may not even be the one envisaged by Jean, who showed no particular inclination to redeem Genius by linking him to Reason. Nonetheless, the text so amended has its own internal logic. In conjunction with the overtly Christian context provided for Reason's discussion of procreation, it suggests a reading of Genius' words as compatible with Christian doctrine: that by serving Nature in accordance with Reason, who in turn sees that we remain in accordance with God, we can engage in proper sexual activity within a Christian context and look forward to salvation in the afterlife.

Modern critical debate about the discourse of Genius tends to assume that his sermon reflects ideas incompatible with Christian orthodoxy – variously identified as Aristotelian, Averroist, idolatrous, or otherwise cupidinous – and to address the question of whether or not, or to what extent, these ideas are those of Jean de Meun: is the passage a celebration or a satire of natural sexuality?[11] But although textual and iconographic evidence does exist for a parodic reading of Jean's Genius in the fourteenth century, medieval readings often revolve around the question of whether or not Genius' words can be reconciled with Christian doctrine, without addressing the possibility of parody or satire. As we saw in Chapter 1, both Christine and Gerson rejected the possibility of any redeeming interpretation of Genius' sermon; Col's defense of Genius argues that the passage expresses important moral and spiritual values. He defends the discourses of Ami and La Vieille as satirical pieces, but not the discourse of Genius. It was evidently a delicate matter, in a public forum, to make jokes – especially bawdy jokes – about the Lamb of God.

Col's position is not a new one. While we have seen evidence in the textual history of the *Rose* for discomfort with the sermon of Genius, evidence also exists for a "straight" reading of the sermon as an unveiling of the poem's moral and spiritual significance. These contrasting approaches are reflected in MS *Tou*, which bears witness both to Gui's original deletion of most of Genius' sermon, and to the subsequent restoration of the missing text and its integration into a framework uniting conjugal and spiritual bliss. One must conclude that Col was speaking for a significant portion of medieval *Rose* readership when he defended the discourse of Genius. Indeed, Col specifically cites the discourses of Reason and Genius as evidence that Jean was no longer a *fol amoureux* when he wrote the *Rose*. No foolish lover could have such an obvious love of Reason, he says; nor would a foolish lover have said, as Jean did through the agency of Genius, that the Garden of Delight is sheer vanity and that the fountain of Narcissus brings death. Col offers this argument with some insistence:

Conment pouoit il mieux monstrer qu'il n'estoit pas fol amoureux et qu'il amoit Raison que en blasment le vergier de Deduit et les choses qui y sont, et en louant Raison et mettant ung aultre parc (ung autre parc ou vergier), ouquel il figure si notablement la Trinitey et l'Incarnation par l'escharboucle et par l'olive qui prant son acroissement de la rousee de la fontainne, etc.? (ed. Hicks, pp. 94–95)

How could he better show that he was not a foolish lover and that he loved Reason than by criticizing the Garden of Delight and the things that are there, and by praising Reason and positing a different park (a different park or garden), in which he so explicitly represents the Trinity and the Incarnation with the carbuncle and the olive that grows from the dew of the fountain, etc.?

---

[11] See the discussion of medieval and modern readings of Genius in Chapter 1.

Col argues further that Nature and Genius urge not foolish love, but rather "les euvres de Nature" [the works of Nature (p. 107)], and that these are legitimate for the purposes of procreation and of avoiding homosexuality. While as we have seen Col is unwilling to claim that indulgence in the work of Nature outside marriage is not a sin, he does point out that it is permitted within marriage. After arguing that Jean does not condemn marriage, Col concludes that since sexual activity is permissible in certain cases, it is not bad in itself; if Genius urges engagement in heterosexual relations for the two above-mentioned purposes, "je n'y voy point de mesprison" [I see nothing wrong with it (p. 108)].

Fourteenth-century scribes could gloss the discourse of Genius as an allegory of Christian Heaven and salvation; Pierre Col could link the discourse of Genius to that of Reason, arguing that Genius' defense of sexuality is a legitimate one, inscribed in a moral framework that contrasts the frivolities of erotic dalliance with the enduring realities of Heaven. Given this context, it should not surprise us to find, in the *KMN* manuscripts, that the text has been altered to bring the discourses of Reason and Genius closer together. Reason and Genius always had agreed in condemning hedonism – the pursual of *delit* for its own sake – and in promoting reproduction as the legitimate motivation for sexual activity. Jean's Reason cites Genius; now Genius in turn cites Reason.[12] Genius already contrasted the followers of Cupid with the followers of Christ, formulating his defense of procreation in the context of the divinely ordained cosmic order; Reason now does likewise. Whereas Genius focuses on achieving Heaven through pursuit of the works of Nature, Reason concentrates on the more intellectual, indeed mystical, approach. But medieval tradition had long acknowledged the existence of the active and the contemplative life as two complementary spheres. As in MS *Tou*, if less explicitly, the revised *Rose* of the *KMN* manuscripts addresses both earthly and heavenly joy, mapping out a space within which a fallen but redeemed humanity can partake of both.

In this respect, it is interesting to examine the other major variant common to the *KMN* group of manuscripts: the Medusa interpolation, inserted between the description of the silver feminine figure on the tower, at whom Venus fires her burning arrow, and the story of Pygmalion

---

[12] In the *MN* manuscripts, Genius' recounting of the castration of Saturn is linked to that of Reason through the insertion of vv. 5509–12 into Genius' account, following v. 20006. (Langlois cryptically identifies the inserted lines as his vv. 5999–602 – presumably the result of a misprint – in *Manuscrits*, p. 460.) The lines in question also appear in their normal place. Whatever may have inspired this transfer – and it seems pointless to entertain the many possible hypotheses – it is at least clear that the redactor of the *MN* ancestor had noted that Reason and Genius are the two characters in the poem who identify the castration of Saturn as the key event in the fall of the Golden Age.

(following v. 20780).[13] The narrator tells us that the image on the tower is more powerful than Medusa, and proceeds then to a brief account of Medusa's petrifying powers and Perseus' success in vanquishing her. Perseus accomplished his mission, we learn, with the aid of a shield that doubled as a mirror, given to him by his sister Pallas. He went on to use Medusa's head as a weapon against his various enemies. But the image sought by the Lover "les vertuz Medusa seurmonte" [surpasses Medusa's power (ed. Langlois, note to line 20810, v. 28)]: it resuscitates, bringing the petrified back to life and restoring the insane to their senses.

As I have argued elsewhere, Pallas provides a mythographic analogy with Reason in the *Rose* as a figure of chastity and intellect; Medusa, in medieval mythographic tradition, is a figure for feminine sexual attraction and its lethal effects on men.[14] The petrifaction induced by Medusa is hinted at in the God of Love's statement that his lovesick disciple behaves "come une ymage mue / qui ne se croule ne remue [like a mute image that neither shifts nor moves" (vv. 2275–76)]. Perseus, brother and disciple of Pallas and destroyer of Medusa, is thus an image of what the Lover could have been had he chosen to follow Reason. The mirror that protects Perseus by allowing him to glimpse the horrific eros of Medusa without being touched by it, echoes Reason's characterization of herself as a mirror in which the Lover could view, and correct, his folly: "te mire en mon cler visage" [behold yourself in my bright face (v. 5789)], she had urged him. And a reader familiar with the *Metamorphoses* might recall that Perseus, aided by Pallas, was able to fly – something else, as we have seen, that the Lover accused Reason of wanting him to do. At this highly charged moment – the lady represented by Bel Acueil, Dangier, and the Rose has just assumed feminine form for the first time, and the Lover is about to gain access to her hidden sanctuary – we are reminded of the dangers of erotic attraction and of the possibility of rational defense against it.

By inserting the Medusa interpolation where he does, the anonymous redactor juxtaposes the configuration of Pallas–Perseus–Medusa with that of Venus–Pygmalion–Galatea. Pygmalion, at one time chaste, becomes the opposite of Perseus when he commits himself to the worship of Venus. Smitten with love for a cold and unresponsive statue, Pygmalion reacts by bursting into song, dancing and cavorting about, and lamenting his mad passion, comparing himself favorably to Narcissus in the process. He, too, resembles the Lover of the Rose, who, in Guillaume's portion, joins the carol, indulges in considerable lamentation, and, of course, remembers the

---

[13] Langlois gives the Medusa interpolation as a variant reading for his vv. 20810–11, as well as in his *Manuscrits*, pp. 453–54.   [14] See my "Medusa Interpolation."

story of Narcissus, deciding that it does not apply to him. While Venus' intervention does allow Pygmalion to fulfil his duty to Nature by begetting a child, the incestuous culmination of his lineage shows that it is irreparably marred. In the *KMN* manuscripts, Perseus and Pygmalion represent two opposite poles: the warrior disciple of Pallas, immune to the bewitching powers of feminine sexuality, and the artist disciple of Venus, driven mad by the erotic feminine presence he has created.

Between these two extremes, the author of the Medusa interpolation hints at a possible middle ground. The image sought by the Lover is contrasted with both Medusa and Pygmalion's statue, suggesting that it represents a third alternative. Its curative powers would provide an antidote to either petrifaction or the madness suffered by Pygmalion:

> Car qui de ceste s'aprochast
> Et tout veïst et tout touchast,
> S'il fust ainz en roche muez
> Ou de son droit sen remuez,
> Ja puis roche ne le tenist,
> En son droit sen s'en revenist.
>
> (ed. Langlois, note to line 20810, vv. 39–44)

For whoever might approach this one, and see it all and touch it all, if he had ever been turned to stone or driven out of his mind, the rock would no longer hold him, he would return to his right mind.

The series of contrasts – "Cele nuist et ceste profite, / Cele ocit, ceste resouscite" [that one injures and this one profits, that one kills, this one resuscitates (ed. Langlois, vv. 35–36)] – recalls Genius' juxtaposition of the Garden of Delight with the Heavenly Park. The life-giving powers of the Lover's statue contrast with the lethal powers of Medusa and, implicitly, with the intoxicating qualities of Pygmalion's statue.

Within the *KMN* text, the mapping out of a life-sustaining middle ground between militant chastity and mad passion is a strategy familiar from the discourses of both Reason and Genius. As we have seen, Reason elaborates her ideal of "le maien" [the middle ground (v. 4372)] in juxtaposition with mystical love on the one hand, lustful and avaricious passion on the other; Genius argues for natural, procreative sexuality in accordance with Reason, within a framework defined by the contrast between the sterile and transitory Garden of Delight and the eternal joy of Heaven. The Medusa interpolation thus continues the general tenor of the *KMN* text.

The *Rose* of the *KMN* manuscripts is not the result of a thorough-going remaniement. Indeed, considerable unresolved tensions lurk beneath the surface of the retouched *Rose* of the *KMN* manuscripts: could Perseus possibly be a less than positive exemplum? Is Nature defending the adultery of Mars and Venus (vv. 18031–59)? And why should Genius have the authority to absolve anyone of their sins? The accumulated effect of the passages introduced into these copies of the *Rose* is to suggest a defense of reasonable procreative love – implicitly or explicitly conjugal – as would be later elaborated by Pierre Col; but the poem was not rigorously adapted to fit this particular view. In fact, it is unlikely that all of the interpolations examined here derive from the same redactor. Nonetheless, these interpolations generally occur together; and to some extent they are probably linked, the presence of one implying an interpretation of the poem that in turn inspired the addition of another.

The reworking of the *Rose* in the *KMN* manuscripts suggests an educated readership; as I have shown, the resulting text is compatible with the reading put forth by Col and Montreuil. It is not surprising that this version of the poem, one that calls for a close reading of the *Rose* in the context of Latin poetic and philosophical texts, should explicitly identify the poem as a book, a *livre*. Just before the God of Love delivers his explication of love, Guillaume intervenes to comment on the beauty and educational value of his dream; and here the *KLMN* manuscripts nearly all change "songe" [dream] to "livre" [book]. The narrator assures us that the romance explains all the rules of love, asserting that "la fin du livre est moult bele / Et la matiere en est nouvele" [the end of the book is very beautiful, and its matter is new (vv. 2063–64 in MS *Mi*, fol. 17r)]; whoever hears the end of the book will know all about love, provided he or she wait "Que j'esponne et que je rommance / Du livre la senefiance" [until I explain and put into vernacular the meaning of the book (vv. 2069–70 in MS *Mi*, fol. 17r)].[15] Guillaume's intervention originally involved a distinction between the dream that is the source of meaning, and the vernacular romance in which the dream is represented and opened up for interpretation. But the *KLMN* text presents a distinction between romance and book: between the written text, source of meaning and authority, and the process of narrating and presenting this material in the vernacular. The dream is not lost entirely, for the intervention still closes with the promise that the truth will be revealed "Quant espondre m'orrez le songe, / Ou il n'a nul mot de mençonge" [when you have heard me explicate the dream,

---

[15] Langlois notes the change of "songe" to "livre" in vv. 2063 and 2065 (his vv. 2065 and 2067) in MSS *KLMN* and *Tou*, but does not mention v. 2070 (his v. 2072), whose modification is less frequent; see *Manuscrits*, p. 311. In Lecoy's edition, the lines in question appear as "car la fin dou songe est mout bele" (v. 2063); "Qui dou songe le fin ora" (v. 2065); and "que je die et que j'encomance / dou songe la senefiance" (vv. 2069–70). Hult discusses the passage in *Self-fulfilling Prophecies*, pp. 165–69.

where there is not a single word that is a lie (vv. 2073–74, MS *Mi*, fol. 17r)].
Nonetheless, there is a shift of focus away from the dream itself – the
youthful experience of desire – towards the act of narrating and explicating.
Ultimately, it is the book, where narrative and explication coexist, that is
the locus both of aesthetic pleasure – the beautiful ending, the new material
– and of meaning, of "senefiance" and "verité." As we saw in Chapter 2,
one medieval reader of MS *Ke* was moved to comment on the reference to
the *Rose* as both "roman" and "livre": a written work, an object of study, in
the vernacular. And the edifying value of the *Rose* is stressed in the *K* text
variant, cited in Chapter 1, announcing the poem as an exposition not of
love but of good and evil.

The notion of the *Rose* as a learned text from which lessons can be drawn
is also expressed in the interpolation appearing at the end of the poem in *N*
manuscripts, as well as in some manuscripts of other families.[16] The
dreamer reviews the events of his dream, reveling in its successful outcome;
he closes with the following reflections:

> Fous est qui en Dieu ne se fie,
> Et quiconques blasme les songes
> Et die que ce sont mençonges;
> De cestui ne le di ge mie,
> Car je tesmoigne et certifie
> Que tout quanques j'ai recité
> Est fine et pure verité.
>
> (Langlois, *Manuscrits*, p. 448)

He is a fool who does not trust in God, and who criticizes dreams and says
that they are lies; I don't say that about this one, for I testify and certify that
everything I have recounted [or: quoted] is pure and utter truth.

The interpolator plays on the famous rhyme pair with which the *Rose*
begins, contrasting – or subtly linking – dreams and lies; after reiterating it,
he closes on an answering rhyme, one that links truth ("verité") with the
act of narration and the citation of textual authorities ("recité"). The verb
"reciter" can mean "recount" or "explain," as in Faux Samblant's refusal
to "reciter" all of the places where he resides (vv. 10922–23); it can also
refer to textual citation, as in La Vieille's announcement of her intention to
"reciter" the words of Horace (vv. 13887–90). It appears in the latter sense
in the Lover's comments on obscenity, when he explains that he can
pronounce ribald words as long as he is only quoting someone else: "Mes
des que je n'en sui fesierres, / j'en puis bien estre recitierres" [but as long as I

---

[16] The passage appears, for example, in MS *Mi*, and was added after the fact to MS *Me*.

am not the initiator, I can certainly cite them (vv. 5687–88)]. The Lover's meaning here is somewhat obscure, but most likely he means that he cannot use an obscene word to refer directly to obscene things or actions, but only to refer to the word itself by citing an anterior usage; this, at any rate, is what he does when he later complains, "Si ne vos tiegn pas a cortaise / quant ci m'avez coilles nommees." [Anyhow I don't consider you courteous when here you have uttered "balls" to me (vv. 6898–99).][17] "Reciter" thus implies a use of language that is less concerned with expressing the ideas of the speaker, or with representing the empirical world, than with citing the ideas of a previous speaker, or even with the representation of language itself as an object.

The word "reciter" also appears in Jean's Apology in the context of poetic truth and authority. Jean begins by asserting that the bawdy words in his poem were required by the subject matter, for, as Sallust tells us, "li diz doit le fet resambler" [the account should resemble the deed (v. 15160)]. This immediate grounding of the *Rose* in experience is undercut, however, by his subsequent assertion that what he says about the feminine character is true because it is derived from the authors "qui an leur livres ont escrites / les paroles que g'en ai dites, / et ceus avec que g'en dirai" [who have written in their books the words that I have said about it and those with which I will speak about it (vv. 15189–91)]. The lines that follow contain repeated juxtapositions in rhyme position of words relating to mendacity and delusion on the one hand, the production of literature on the other. Having alluded to the text he has yet to produce ("que g'en *dirai*"), Jean goes on to assure the reader:

> ne ja de riens n'an *mentirai*,
> se li preudome n'en *mentirent*
> qui les anciens livres *firent*.
> Et tuit a ma reson s'acordent
> quant les meurs femenins recordent,
> ne ne furent ne fos ne *ivres*
> quant il les mistrent en leur *livres*.
>
> (vv. 15192–98, emphasis mine)

Nor will I ever *lie* about anything, as long as the worthy men who *made* the ancient books did not *lie*. And they all agree with my argument when they record feminine behavior, nor were they foolish or *drunk* when they put that in their *books*.

---

[17] Fleming, attempting to unravel the Lover's cryptic distinction between the "fesierres" and the "recitierres" of a word, concludes that for the Lover, obscenity consists only of uttering a newly invented dirty word, but not in using one that anyone else has already used (*Reason and the Lover*, pp. 102–3). Such illogicality, however, strikes me as a bit much even for the Lover.

Jean himself had thus already shifted the opposition/pairing of *songe* and *mensonge* – the truth or mendacity of a dream experience, as measured against the experiences of waking life – to one focused on the truth or mendacity of poetic discourse and of books. The authors of old grounded their writings in experience, he states; but as for him, "je n'i faz riens fors reciter" [I do nothing but quote (v. 15204)]. This movement from a poetics grounded in experience towards one grounded in anterior texts and even in pure logic is reiterated at the end of the Apology, when Jean states that he has said nothing "qui ne soit en escrit trové / et par experimant prové, / ou par reson au mains provable" [that is not found in writing and proven by experience, or at least provable by reason (vv. 15265–67)].

These various meanings of "reciter" are all important in the *N* interpolation: to narrate; to explain; to cite; to present words, arguments, even language itself as an object of analysis and interpretation, a component part of some larger argument. The truth of the allegorical dream lies not in its revelation of an erotic conquest yet to be or of a sexual climax experienced at the moment of waking, but more generally, as Guillaume put it, in its "senefiance / des biens as genz et des anuiz" [signification of the good and the bad of human life (vv. 16–17)]; and this moral lesson in turn is a function not of the event dreamed about, but of the way in which this event is told. The dream itself, as a dream, might be mendacious as Macrobius claimed; it might, as insinuated by Ami, never even have taken place. Nonetheless, through its narration and incorporation into a larger literary context, the story of the dream becomes a vehicle for the truth. Similarly, the words spoken by the various personae of the dream are frequently mendacious and misleading; yet these discourses can be used, in the larger context of the poem as a whole, to express truths beyond the grasp of those characters. The *N* interpolation continues the ironic tenor of Jean's text down to the last line. From the Lover's perspective, the dream is true because it does, in fact, result in a sexual climax: the experience of desire and consummation provides the link between dream and reality. But read properly, it is true in a different sense: as a literary artifact, a dazzling and often daring review of classical and medieval authors; as a dramatization of reading and misreading; as a mirror of love, desire, and sexuality.

A final comment on the *Rose*'s representation of sexuality appears in the explicit found in many *N* manuscripts:[18]

---

[18] A longer version of the explicit appears in the MS Lyon, Bibl. Mun. 764 (*Mo*): "Nature y est ramenteüe, / Qui bien doit estre soustenue, / Qu'el rit tous jours, si com moi semble, / Quant hic et hec joingnent ensemble. / Qui Nature ne soustendroit, / Sachiez que li mondes faudroit. / Explicit le Romans de la Rose, / Ou l'art d'amours est toute enclose." [Nature, who should be well maintained,

Explicit le Romans de la Rose,
Ou l'Art d'Amours est toute enclose.
Nature rit, si com moi semble,
Quant hic et hec joignent ensemble.

(Langlois, *Manuscrits*, p. 448)

Here ends the *Romance of the Rose*, where the Art of Love is totally enclosed.
Nature laughs, so it seems to me, when "he" and "she" join together.

The second couplet is from Gautier de Coinci's *Miracles de Nostre Dame*, where it is part of a diatribe against homosexuality (1 *Miracles* 11, ed. Koenig, "D'un archevesque qui fu a Tholete," vv. 1239–40). Nature's laughter, her expression of joy at the moment of copulation, recalls Venus' laughter at the arrival of Genius (vv. 19454–56): sex is indeed delightful, and it is precisely for that reason that it is dangerous. But Nature's laughter contrasts pointedly with her earlier tears, as she contemplated the sins of humanity and wondered whether the species was worth perpetuating. Fruitful sexual coupling – and the Lover's encounter with the Rose is, in spite of everything, a fruitful one – is the antidote to Nature's woe: as Col said, it is lawful in the context of marriage, and should be pursued for the twin purposes of procreation and avoidance of homosexuality. It is by no means clear that either of these purposes is in the Lover's mind as he approaches the Rose, or that his feelings include either friendship or Christian charity. He is, after all, a *fol amoureux*. But the discourses of Reason, Nature, and Genius, the contrasting exempla of Perseus and Pygmalion, the Rose's pregnancy, and the *N* explicit, as well as the other discourses of the *Rose*, form a variegated backdrop against which the Lover's folly can be judged: a panoply of loves, natural and unnatural, sacred and earthly, noble and ignoble, sexual and asexual. That the book should close with Nature's laughter is a reminder that whatever solution we may devise takes place in the divinely ordained natural order, an order within which sexual activity has its rightful place.

THE EXPURGATED MIRROR OF LOVE: A SURVEY OF PARTIAL MODIFICATIONS

A truly exhaustive survey of the myriad of variant readings produced by the vast manuscript tradition of the *Rose* would be both cumbersome and

is given her due, for she always laughs, it seems to me, when "he" and "she" join together. If Nature was not maintained, know that the world would die out. Here ends the Romance of the Rose, where the art of love is totally enclosed (fol. 123r)]. See Langlois, *Manuscrits*, p. 130. The first four lines of this explicit appear in the late fourteenth-century MS Bibl. Nat. fr. 802 (*My*), fol. 143r; see Langlois, *Manuscrits*, p. 10. The additional lines do not derive from Gautier de Coinci.

bewildering in its sheer volume. It is my intention here to illustrate the range of variation found in manuscripts of the second group with a few selected examples of manuscripts in which specific passages are expanded, altered, or deleted. This survey will culminate in a more detailed analysis of the MS Rennes, Bibl. Mun. 15963 (*Lm*), in which a large portion of the poem has been substantially abridged, before moving on, in the next section, to the examination of a manuscript whose interpolations are so extensive as to require individual treatment.

Sometimes a manuscript that presents an otherwise complete text will have undergone the modification or deletion of just one passage, evidently deemed either indecent or irrelevant by the scribe or his patron. One such example is the MS Bibl. Mazarine 3873 (*Ki*), from which all trace of the Lover's argument with Reason over language and obscenity has been removed. MS *Ki* retains the passage in which Reason utters the word "coilles," but the Lover's two objections and Reason's long reply are missing entirely. His first objection is suppressed through the deletion of vv. 5667–732, which allows Reason to move without interruption from the discussion of justice to that of family love. A portion of the deleted text, in which Reason protests that she in no way counsels hatred and urges the Lover to seek the middle way (vv. 5697–732), is inserted into her exposition of what he will gain if he gives his love to her, between vv. 5777 and 5778: an awkward move that destroys the rhyme and evidently troubled the copyist, since he transcribed only the first three words of v. 5777 ("Lors te verras," fol. 39r). This particular state of affairs probably resulted from a misreading – whether by the scribe of MS *Ki* or by one of his forebears – of marginal indications that were meant to insert the block of text into a slightly different spot, or perhaps to include additional lines bridging the transition. In any case, the omission of the exchange regarding the word "coilles" is no accident, for the entire language debate is subsequently deleted through the omission of vv. 6897–7174. MS *Ki* thus offers one more piece of evidence for a medieval reader's difficulties in accepting Reason's defense of plain speech.

In other cases, a manuscript that otherwise presents a standard version of the text – whether that established by Langlois or that typically associated with a given manuscript family – will contain certain small variants that reflect a desire to fine-tune a particular passage, or perhaps to contribute a little joke or an aside. In MSS Bibl. Nat. fr. 1566 (*Lx*) and 1574 (*Lw*), for example, Genius' condemnation of castration is expanded by an interpolated couplet: "Car rien ne vaut cul sans coullez / Ne que sans sel fresces andoilles" [for an ass without balls is worth nothing, like fresh sausage without salt (MS *Lx*, fol. 121r; follows v. 20020)]. Clearly, the redactor of this little addition was not one to be troubled by the presence of bawdy language or humor in the words of Nature's priest, any more than he was by Reason's comments about testicles and relics, the expanded version of which naturally appears in these exemplars of the *L* text.

Ms *Lx* presents additional variants in the representation of Nero. The statement that Nero marked the end of a noble lineage – "que en Neron fu definee / des Cesariens la lignee" [that in Nero was ended the line of the Caesars (vv. 6433–34)] – has become "Qu'en Neron fu determinee / Des Sarrazinois la lingnie" (fol. 38v), which might mean either that the Saracen line was ended in Nero, or that in him it was fixed and established. In either case this reading bears no relation to historical reality, and one might be tempted to feel that the transformation of "Cesariens" into "Sarrizinois" was the result of a simple misreading. Yet this passage follows directly on the allusion to Suetonius, "qui la loi crestiene apele / fause religion novele / et malfesant" [who calls Christian law a false and harmful new religion (vv. 6429–31)]; and in a great many *Rose* manuscripts, through the simple transformation of "qui" into "que," this point of view is ascribed not to Suetonius but to Nero himself.[19] Such a perspective is hardly inappropriate to Nero; indeed the *K* text informs us that, along with his other crimes, Nero crucified Saint Peter (var. of v. 6162). Most likely, then, the identification of Nero with the Saracens, those powerful enemies of the Christian faith, is a meaningful detail.

A second variant in the account of Nero's life in MS *Lx* is equally interesting. Jean, describing Nero's seeming piety during the early years of his reign, cites his pretensions of regret at being forced to sign an execution warrant:

> tant sembla vaillanz et piteus
> li desloiaus, li despiteus;
> et dist en audience a Rome,
> quant il por condampner un home . . . (vv. 6441–44)

He seemed so valiant and merciful, the disloyal, the cruel; and he said publicly in Rome, when in order to condemn a man . . .

In MS *Lx*, the hypocritical Nero addressing the Romans has been associated with none other than Faux Samblant, whose opening gambit is here placed in Nero's mouth:

---

[19] The variant reading is easily understandable even aside from the wish to identify the blasphemous position with the evil Nero rather than the authoritative writer, for the scribal abbreviations for "Que" and "Qui" – differentiated only by the use of a small wavy line for the former and a small straight line for the latter – are not always easy to tell apart, especially at the hands of a scribe who wrote hastily.

6441 Tant sembla vaillant et piteux
6442 Li delloiaux, li despiteux,
10975 Et dist a tous en audience,
10976 "Baron, entendez ma sentence." (fol. 38v)

He seemed so worthy and merciful, the disloyal, the cruel, and he said to all publicly, "Barons, hear my teaching."

Following this, the scribe left six blank lines before continuing with v. 6449; probably he had intended to adapt the missing text, vv. 6443–48, to its new context. The association of Nero and Faux Samblant, while most explicitly invited by the characterization of Nero as a hypocrite, is appropriate in many ways. Within the *Rose*, Nero represents the absolute corruption of absolute power, including, in some versions, the persecution of the Christian faith. The copyist of MS *Lx*, or the redactor of its model, perceived these affinities between Nero and Faux Samblant and acted to create an explicit link between the two widely separated textual passages.

In other cases – to return to our survey – one finds manuscripts in which the modifications, while limited to particular sections, are nonetheless more extensive than the above examples. The MSS Bibl. Nat. fr. 799 (*Fa*) and 19157 (*Fe*), whose text is an amalgam of the *K*, *L*, and *M* families, have had several hundred verses deleted from the closing sections of the poem (Nature, Genius, and the conclusion).[20] Many of these are scattered – a couplet here, a couplet there – in such a way that they serve simply to shorten the poem without actually deleting any of its argumentation or its imagery. Certain sections, however, have been pared down more than others. For example, Nature's discussion of "out-of-the-body" night-time travel with Dame Habonde has been considerably reduced through the deletion of vv. 18421–30, 18439–56, and 18463–68; probably this passage, whose only point is to refute the existence of such travel, seemed an overly long or irrelevant digression. The excursus on nobility, and particularly the explanation of why clerks are likely to be more truly noble than aristocrats, has been similarly abridged, although its main lines still stand (the principal deletions are vv. 18635–46 and 18681–710). Perhaps this text derives from an aristocratic milieu less willing to look upon clerks as noble, or perhaps the scribe just wanted to get through Nature's many digressions and return to the quest for the Rose. And certain passages have no doubt been omitted for their questionable morality, such as Nature's emphasis on the sin of avoiding sexual intercourse (vv. 19293–304) and her acceptance of Faux Samblant's role in amorous pursuit (vv. 19325–38). In all, no specific interpretation of the *Rose* emerges from the examination of MSS *Fa* and *Fe*,

[20] See Langlois, *Manuscrits*, pp. 499–500.

but one might well suspect that it is the work of one who would second Christine de Pizan's characterization of the *Rose*: "Quel long procès! quel difficile chose!" [what a long process! what a difficult thing! (*Epistre au dieu d'amours*, ed. Roy, v. 390)].

An entirely different revision of Nature and Genius, finally, appears in MS Bibl. Nat. fr. 1567 (*Lk*). Far from abridging the discussion of the nobility of clerks, for example, MS *Lk* offers an expanded version of this passage with several interpolations, such as the following elaboration on the point that those who have performed no great exploits cannot derive nobility from their ancestry:

> Combien qu'aient soliers forez,
> Et aient leurs estriers dorez;
> Combien qu'il saillent detordant,
> Leurs chaperons tournez devant,
> Pour oysiaux seur leurs poings tenir;
> Ne pour leurs chastiaus soustenir
> Tailles ou mortemains avoir
> Ne fait gentillesce esmouvoir.
> Gentillesce en bon corage
> N'i fait richesce ne parage.
>
> (MS *Lx*, fol. 135v, between vv. 18728–29)

> For all their fur-lined shoes and their gilded stirrups, and for all that they unfurl their cloaks, turned towards the front so that they can carry birds on their wrists; nor do their seigneurial rights to levy taxes and dispose of property, for the maintenance of their castles, bestow nobility. Nobility in a good heart is the result of neither wealth nor lineage.

The notion of personal responsibility for one's character, for better or for worse, is similarly reflected in an interpolation in Nature's discussion of free will, stressing that "good Christians" know that their misdeeds could never have been caused or desired by God (fol. 130r; follows v. 17762).

If Nature's remarks about free will, nobility, and personal ethics are treated seriously, however, Genius' teachings about procreation are more problematical. The theological content of Genius' discourse is almost entirely omitted; instead, he appears as the voice of active and fruitful sexuality. In MS *Lk*, once again, we find evidence for a medieval reader who perceived Genius' words as being more in the spirit of Venus than that of the Immaculate Lamb, and who took steps to correct the jarring blend of material Jean had created. First of all, an amusing interpolation stresses the link between Nature and Venus and identifies Genius firmly with the erotic aspect of Nature's processes:

19470	Et cil cui les paroles plaisent
19471	S'entrejoingnent et s'entreboutent
19472	Et tant se taisent et escoutent
xxx	Les commandement de Nature,
xxx	Qui est seur toute creature.
xxx	Et chascuns bien y obeïst,
xxx	Selonc que sont grant et petit,
xxx	A ce que Nature requiert.
xxx	Et dame Venus, qui bien s'iert
xxx	Acesmëe moult cointement,
xxx	Tenoit son brandon flamboiant
xxx	Dont la chaleur vaut pis qu'arsure;
xxx	Entre les deciples Nature
xxx	Se fu mise pour labourer.
xxx	Tous les commance a sarmonner
xxx	Selonc son oevre et sa loy:
xxx	"Mi ami, entendez a moy,
xxx	Et mes euvres continuez;
xxx	De nuit et de jours labourez;
xxx	Ne pensez a autre mestier.
xxx	Vez ci qui le vous vient preeschier:
xxx	C'est Genius li bons preudon
xxx	Qui de Nature en ha le don,
xxx	Qui apporte les briez seellez
xxx	Si comme lire les orrez.
xxx	Par luy si vous mande m'amie
xxx	Que chascuns moingne bonne vie.
xxx	Ne pensez a autres douleurs
xxx	Fors qu'a bien amer par amours.
xxx	Ne n'aiez autre cusançon.
xxx	Je vous enseingne la leçon
xxx	Et la chartre qu'en vous envoie
xxx	Ou il ha tant et bien et joie.
19473	Par tels paroles s'encommence
19474	La diffinitive sentence
xxx	Que Genius si vous veult lire.
xxx	Or escoutez trestuit a tire. (fol. 139r–v)

And those to whom the words are pleasing join together and bump against one another, and fall silent and listen to Nature's commandment, which applies to all creatures. And each one, large or small, obeys Nature's requirements. And lady Venus, who had decked herself out very prettily, was holding her flaming torch, whose heat is worse than burning coals. She had gone among the disciples of Nature to do her work. She began to harangue them all, according to her work and her law: "My friends, listen to me, and continue my works; labor at it night and day; think of nothing else. Here is the one who comes to preach to you: Genius, the good gentleman, who is endowed by Nature, and who brings the sealed letters, just as you will hear them. By him my friend commands you that everyone should lead a good life. Have no cares, other than to fall in love; have no other concern. I teach you the lesson. And the charter that is sent to you, where there is so much good and so much joy, begins with these words the definitive teaching that Genius wishes to read to you. Now listen everyone, without interruption.

Genius is thus presented as illustrating the joint will of Venus and Nature; his audience is identified as "disciples of Nature," a humorous way of designating their devotion to active sexuality. It is hardly surprising, therefore, that his sermon is reduced almost exclusively to the condemnation of sodomites and the exhortation to engage in procreative sexual activity. That portion of the sermon is largely intact, though occasionally streamlined; Genius' wish to see sodomites castrated, for example, is reduced from twenty lines (vv. 19637–56) to just six, probably because it seemed inappropriate for Genius, of all people, to approve so heartily of castrating anyone. In spite of the occasional condensing of lengthy passages, however, Genius' exhortations and his excommunication are quite clear. He does touch on the issue of spiritual purity. In an expanded reminder of the need for confession after sexual activity, Genius urges his audience to love God, adding, "Et desprisiez fragilité / Et delit et charnalité" [and despise fragility, pleasure, and carnality (follows v. 19863, fol. 141r)]; he further suggests that they pray to the Mother of God for intercession with her son, the celestial king. The redactor of MS *Lk* must have felt that some gesture towards Christian ethics was needed, given that Nature is God's vicar, that sin is contrary to natural law, and that Genius is attempting to concentrate on the procreative rather than the pleasurable side of sexuality.

The above passage, however, is Genius' only explicit allusion to the Christian God. Jean's Genius, having delivered his exhortations, introduces the park where white sheep are kept by the Son of the Virgin (v. 19908); he stresses the immortality and timelessness of the park and, after a digression about the fall of the Golden Age and the reign of Jupiter, elaborates his detailed comparison of this celestial garden to the Garden of Delight. In MS *Lk*, however, the comparison of the two gardens is omitted; Genius' sermon breaks off shortly after his initial description of Jupiter's reign of pleasure (at v. 20166).[21] And even the initial description

---

[21] Following v. 20167 is an adaptation of vv. 20637–38: "Genius fu sus la bretesche: / En ceste maniere leur preesche" [Genius was on the podium: in this manner he preaches to them (fol. 142v)]. Genius' discourse breaks off so abruptly that one might be tempted to think its termination was due to an accident, such as missing pages in the model. Still, the reworking of the initial description of the *biaus*

of the Heavenly Park is no longer explicitly Christian: the allusion to the Son of the Virgin is absent, and the insistence on its eternal character is greatly abridged. Instead, having urged his audience to help spread the message of his sermon and to take the initiative in setting the example, Genius introduces the motif of the park in this fashion:

> Menez paistre vos brebiettes
> Es prez les petites florettes,
> Par la droite sente serie
> Qui toute est herbue et florie.
>
> (fol. 141r; follows v. 19904)

Lead your little sheep to graze in the fields on the little flowers, by the pretty little path that is decked with grass and flowers.

In this formulation, Genius' park sounds considerably less like Christian Heaven than like the Garden of Delight itself, and his metaphor of leading sheep down the little flowery path cannot but remind one of the Lover's declared preference for "les jolives santeletes" [pleasant little paths (v. 21402)] – that is, for young maidens rather than older women. Moreover, the figurative portrayal of sexual intercourse through the image of leading an animal to feed or to water in a field or garden is familiar from the fabliau tradition. The redactor of MS *Lk* was evidently unable to accept Jean's representation of earthly and heavenly delight, distinguished by their respective association with the pleasure or the fruit of sexual intercourse, as either literary parody or serious moral doctrine. In this version of the *Rose* Genius, though aware of divine authority, is completely contained within the sublunar world of Nature and Venus; and it is clear that it is through prayer and confession, not through procreation, that one obtains Salvation. Both the humor and the moral lesson of Genius' discourse are preserved, but potentially blasphemous material is deleted.

For a more sustained abridgment of the *L* text, finally, we turn now to the mid fourteenth-century MS *Lm*, which contains the *Roman de la Rose* and the *Chastelaine de Vergi*. It is a composite manuscript, part of which – gatherings 10–14, comprising vv. 10831–20637 of the *Rose* – is an abridged version of the text. The remainder of the text has not been abridged. Although the script and style of illustration are uniform throughout the manuscript, the central gatherings were made separately. The pages in gatherings 10–14 are ruled with only thirty-five lines to the column, as

---

parc certainly supports the idea that the elaboration of the Heavenly Park was deliberately deleted. The abruptness of the ending is most likely due either to a less than skillful editing job on the part of the scribal editor, or to an accidental omission of an interpolated passage meant to replace the deleted material.

opposed to forty in gatherings 1–9 and 15–16. Moreover, gathering 9 was constructed to fit in front of a pre-existing tenth gathering: whereas all of the other gatherings of the codex have eight folios, gathering 9 has only six. And towards the end of the gathering, a total of twenty-one verses are split between two lines, thereby stretching out the text so that v. 10830 will arrive at the bottom of the last page.

If the first nine and last two gatherings were made to replace the manuscript's original opening and closing portions – probably because these had been damaged – then they could also have been copied from a different source; this would explain why the abridgments occur only in the discourses of Faux Samblant, La Vieille, Nature, and Genius. In the original manuscript, the other discourses may have been abridged as well. No evidence exists, however, that would either confirm or disprove such a hypothesis. Since all that remains of the original text is vv. 10831–20637, our analysis must be confined to that portion.

Essentially, the deletions made in MS *Lm* are motivated by two impulses: to focus more closely on the exposition and critique of erotic love, and to modify or eliminate passages that might be politically or morally controversial. Either of these two motives could have resulted in the drastic abridgment of the discourse of Faux Samblant, from which 646 lines are omitted. The deleted passages include the entire section devoted to Guillaume de Saint-Amour and the *Evangile pardurable*, as well as much of the diatribe about mendicancy and labor; the two largest cuts are vv. 11239–522 and 11547–866. Surely no portion of the *Rose* has less direct bearing on erotic love than the discourse of Faux Samblant. Moreover, the events involving Guillaume de Saint-Amour were long past by the time MS *Lm* was written; if the manuscript was prepared for lay patronage, the issues addressed by Faux Samblant might have seemed an uninteresting intrusion, quite irrelevant to the "real" import of the *Rose*. This material might even have seemed dangerous: as we have seen, the warnings preserved in certain manuscripts indicate that the discourse of Faux Samblant was sometimes withheld from lay audiences.

The discourse of La Vieille is largely intact; this section is of course highly relevant to the exposition of erotic love in its various aspects, and in particular to the incorporation of Ovid's *Ars amatoria*. Nonetheless, numerous passages of varying lengths, totalling several hundred lines, have been excised. In addition to the deletions, which will be discussed below, the scribe introduced one very interesting change: he made Bel Acueil female. Instead of "filz" [son] or "biaus filz" [fair son], La Vieille now addresses Bel Acueil as "fille" [daughter] or "belle fille" [fair daughter] (e.g. fol. 82v, v. 13469; fol. 84r, v. 13855; fol. 85r, v. 14009). In v.

12863, "chiers filz" [dear son] has become "douce suer" [sweet sister (fol. 80v)]. Illustrators of the *Rose* sometimes represented Bel Acueil as a lady, no doubt seeing him as the logical stand-in for the lady figured by the Rose.[22] But I have seen no other example in which Bel Acueil was actually given a feminine gender within the text.[23] Indeed, Bel Acueil retains his masculine identity elsewhere in MS *Lm*, both in the original section and in the outer gatherings. But the redactor evidently found it unacceptable that the art of seducing men should be addressed to a boy, and for this section only he feminized Bel Acueil.

Some of the cuts in the discourse of La Vieille serve to streamline her speech, reducing digressiveness and extraneous details. The deletion of La Vieille's introductory remarks (vv. 12967–13007) and an early digression about flirtation (vv. 13027–64) decreases repetition and makes for a clearer, more concise opening to her teachings. She now begins with two precepts – "Puis dist, 'Ja larges ne soiés, / En plusieurs lieus le cuer aiez'" [then she said, "Never be generous, keep your heart in many places" (fol. 80v, vv. 13007–8)] – and proceeds to expound on the danger of generosity (vv. 13010–26) and the advantages of having multiple suitors (vv. 13065–180). La Vieille's words about male treachery are abridged through the deletion of the exempla of Phyllis, Oenone, and Medea (vv. 13181–234); the redactor must have felt that the focus of La Vieille was meant to be on the character of women, not men, for a later passage about male treachery (vv. 13601–48) was also omitted. In a similar vein, the redactor omitted an aside addressed to men, concerning the advantages of having lay women as lovers rather than nuns (vv. 14393–96): these lines have no place in the sexual education of a girl.

The passages relating to clothing, make-up, and table manners have been condensed somewhat, though not entirely removed; a total of 137 lines are excised from this section of La Vieille's discourse.[24] The redactor may have felt that the endless multiplication of beauty tips and advice about social comportment detracted from the central focus on love and seduction. He

---

[22] Tuve criticizes as inept the illustrators who represent Bel Acueil as a lady; see *Allegorical Imagery*, pp. 322–23. Fleming, however, points out that the allegorical abstraction of "Fair Welcome" can legitimately be considered either masculine or feminine in different contexts; see *"Roman de la Rose"*, pp. 43–46.

[23] A similar modification occurs in an anonymous Flemish translation of the *Rose* dating from ca. 1290: here, although Bel Acueil remains male, the translation introduces the female character of Florentine, who also accompanies the Rose and is imprisoned along with Bel Acueil. The Flemish poet thus circumvents the problem of Bel Acueil's masculine gender by creating a feminine personification of the lady. See Van der Poel, *De Vlaamse Rose en Die Rose van Heinric*, pp. 31–32, 34, 36, 48–49.

[24] The principal deletions are vv. 13289–98, 13345–48, 13365–70, 13381–94, 13405–18, 13495–502, 13505–6, 13510–22, and 13525–70.

thus prepared a more concise version of La Vieille's teachings, while still retaining her insistence on the importance of physical allure, a woman's chief source of power in the battle of the sexes.

La Vieille's own story is also shortened.[25] In particular, the redactor played down her admission of having had many different lovers, of having wronged especially those men who really loved her, and of having been brutalized by the one man she did love. While these cuts may have been motivated in part by a simple desire to shorten what is, after all, an extremely long poem, the redactor was surely guided by a certain bowdlerizing spirit. While La Vieille's advice about having many suitors is retained, her more specific comments about keeping one's various lovers apart are deleted (vv. 13571–86). The redactor also omitted the entirety of vv. 14111–350, probably the most "pornographic" portion of La Vieille's discourse. Here, La Vieille defends adultery, scoffing at male attempts to keep women under control; discusses love-making, noting a preference for simultaneous orgasms; describes the drama created when a woman has visits from two different lovers at once; and explains how to elude one's husband, drugging him if necessary. Finally, La Vieille's moral about her own life – that a girl must extract gifts while she is young (vv. 14511–16) – is deleted, leaving only the bitter words, "Cist miens estat vos soit examples" [let my condition be a lesson to you (v. 14510)]. As a result, the reader is free to draw his or her own moral lesson from La Vieille's teachings – a lesson which might in fact be quite different from the one La Vieille had imagined.

Even the Lover himself is freed somewhat from his direct association with the more cynical aspect of the quest as represented by Jean de Meun. In Jean's text, when the Lover promises gifts to La Vieille if she lets him meet with Bel Acueil, he offers an aside to the reader acknowledging the falseness of his promise: "car mout bien d'Ami me souvint, / qui me dist que bien promeïsse, / neïs se randre ne poïsse" [for I remembered Ami very well, who told me that I should go ahead and promise even if I couldn't carry through on it (vv. 14684–86)]. These lines are omitted in MS *Lm*. Similarly, while the Lover does express his gratitude to Faux Samblant and Contrainte Astenance, his recommendation that anyone who wished to be a traitor should follow these two figures (vv. 14719–22) is deleted. The omission of the allusion to Ami is tantalizing, raising obvious questions about the treatment of Ami's discourse in the original manuscript: was his more cynical advice deleted? As we have seen, it would not be the first time that objectionable passages were omitted from the discourse of Ami.

---

[25] The lines that have been eliminated are vv. 12870–76, 12883–90, 12899–904, 12907–12, and 12915–19; and vv. 14451–52, 14470–76, 14479–84, and 14486–92.

The battle between the forces of Love and those of Jealousy is left intact, as is the digression about Adonis. With the appearance of Nature and Genius, however, the deletions recommence. Surprisingly, Genius' long digression about the dangers of confiding in women is deleted (vv. 16313–676). One might think that this passage, bearing directly on the exposition of marriage and the feminine character, would have been retained. It was, moreover, a very popular passage with medieval readers, to judge from the number of "Nota" signs appearing in its margins in so many manuscripts.[26] Again, its absence raises a tantalizing question: could it have been moved, as in MSS *Mor* and *Tou*, to the discourse of Ami? This question, of course, must remain unanswered, but it is an intriguing possibility. In any case, the redactor may have felt the passage to be inappropriate to the context at hand: amusing though it may be, it has no bearing on the figure of Nature, and this kind of bourgeois farce is quite out of keeping with everything else that Genius has to say.

The discourse of Nature has been heavily abridged; like the redactor of MS *Bi*, the redactor of MS *Lm* or its source must have felt that her long philosophical ramblings had little relevance to the art of love. Most of the discussion of free will is gone, with the single largest deletion extending to 612 lines (vv. 17233–844). The redactor had little interest in the *Rose* as a learned compendium, incorporating vernacularizations of such texts as the *Consolation of Philosophy*, Guillaume de Saint-Amour's *De periculis*, and *De planctu Naturae* into the all-encompassing framework of love and desire. Rather, he sought to exclude material extraneous to his understanding of the *Rose* as an exposition of love and social comportment. Nature's philosophical teachings are reduced to the tenet that due to free will, human beings are responsible for their own actions and moral choices; failure to participate properly in the process of procreation is thus a punishable sin. Some of Nature's comments about the natural world do remain, such as her description of the heavenly bodies and portions of her accounts of optics and dreams.[27] Such material is of easier access than the difficult philosophical passages, and does also bear on the *Rose* as a dream-vision. Nature's remarks about true nobility are kept; again, these contribute to a didactic program of interest even to a less educated lay reader. Her discussion of the Incarnation also remains, though somewhat streamlined.[28] Clearly, the

---

[26] See my "Medieval Readers of the *Roman de la Rose*."

[27] In the sections on optics and dreams, the redactor eliminated vv. 18029–192, 18349–50, 18355–56, 18379–80, and 18389–90.

[28] From the "theological" portion of Nature's discourse, the redactor eliminated vv. 19041–52, 19089–114, and 19135–60.

redactor of MS *Lm* was guided by priorities quite different from those of Gui de Mori.

The Nature that emerges in MS *Lm* is thus less philosophical than that of Jean. She is also less indiscriminate in her approval of heterosexual activity. For example, her allusion to the story of Mars and Venus and her nonchalant attitude towards adultery are deleted, as is her acceptance of Faux Samblant and Contrainte Astenance as legitimate participants in the erotic quest (vv. 19329–38). In all, the treatment of Nature is in keeping with that of Faux Samblant and La Vieille: the poem is at once more focused on the art of love, and less open to sexually provocative and morally ambiguous material. The Nature of MS *Lm* oversees the running of the cosmos and, in particular, the endless replenishment of life on earth. She is the upholder of both physical and ethical principles. And she knows herself to be subject to a divine authority that she recognizes without fully understanding what it is. She thus contributes to the widening of the scope of the poem at this point: erotic desire is placed in cosmic perspective. But this is accomplished in considerably fewer words, with less attention to the philosophical principles involved and with less room for moral questions, than in Jean's text.

The treatment of Genius accords with this effort to incorporate the art of love into a larger moral and spiritual framework, one that provides a perspective in keeping with Christian doctrine. The very identity of Genius is modified through the deletion of Jean's description of his priestly functions (vv. 16243–54). Jean, following Alain, states that Genius transcribes the figures of the many perishable creatures produced by Nature: he is thus a figure of procreation. MS *Lm*, however, identifies Genius only as Nature's priest, without specifying his duties: his character is vaguer, less closely tied to procreation per se. Genius' sermon in turn is heavily abridged in its first half (see Appendix D). Most of the exhortations to sexual activity, along with explicit allusions to homosexuality and castration, are deleted. Genius simply calls for all to uphold the works of Nature through loyal love, reminding his audience to seek God's blessing after each embrace: certainly a much less controversial, less problematic lesson. He then introduces the reign of Jupiter, criticizing its emphasis on *delit*, and proceeds to his comparison of the Garden of Delight to the Heavenly Park. It is in the course of this that the original portion of the manuscript ends. But enough of the material concerning the Heavenly Park appears, unabridged, before the end of the gathering to suggest that this portion of Genius' sermon was left intact by the reader of MS *Lm*; at the very least, it was well represented.

The treatment of Genius in MS *Lm* is thus diametrically opposed to that of MS *Lk*, and consistent with the reading of Genius implied by the *KMN* manuscripts and outlined by Pierre Col; the difference, of course, is that the redactor of MS *Lm* felt the need to modify the text in order to bring this reading out. Genius condemns hedonism, which Reason had already opposed to the principle of procreation, and he reminds his audience of the Christian framework within which sexuality, and all moral actions, exist. In Jean de Meun, Genius' theological teachings collide with his obsessive urgings to engage in sexual intercourse; but in MS *Lm*, the erotic aspect of his sermon has been so thoroughly toned down that it no longer poses much of a problem. The redactor of MS *Lm* deleted Genius' negative comments regarding chastity, further clarifying the moral tone of Genius' sermon. It would certainly be interesting to know how other portions of the poem, such as the discourse of Reason and the conclusion, were treated. But even without this information, we can say that to all appearances, the *Rose* of MS *Lm* was prepared, probably for lay patronage, according to principles similar to those informing the *B* remaniement: a desire to make the poem less intellectually rigorous, less digressive, and also less provocative, less confusing in its ethical orientation. Though less drastically abridged than in MS *Bi*, the *Rose* of MS *Lm* has once again been adapted to the framework of Guillaume's original romance.

A MIRROR OF PRINCES: THE *ROSE* OF CAMBRIDGE UNIV. LIBR. ADD. MS 2993

The *Rose* of Cambridge University Library Additional MS 2993 (MS *κυ*) was copied in 1354. Langlois identifies it as a composite of the *K*, *L*, and *N* texts; it includes, in addition to numerous minor variants, Faux Samblant's discourse on the privilege of hearing confessions (see Langlois, *Manuscrits*, pp. 426–30), the Medusa interpolation, and Genius' exhortation to remember Reason.[29] This base text has been augmented by a series of interpolations ranging from hundreds of lines to a single couplet. The longest, a 376-line digression about Priam, Alexander, Pompey, and Caesar, amplifies Reason's discussion of great men laid low by Fortune; it presents material deriving from Lucan and Suetonius, though the poet's immediate source may well have been the *Fet des Romains*.[30] Also

---

[29] Langlois gives only a cursory account of MS *κυ*; see *Manuscrits*, pp. 148–49 and 501.

[30] As documented in the notes to Appendix E, 2, certain details of the passage appear to be the poet's own invention. Although it follows the *Fet des Romains* in its main outlines, the text contains numerous details that do not appear in the *Fet*, in its Latin sources, or in the Old French epic version of the *Pharsalia* (Bibl. Nat. fr. 1457). For advice regarding this passage, I am grateful to Olivier Collet of the University of Geneva and Gabrielle Spiegel of the University of Maryland.

substantial are a twenty-line augmentation of the description of Richesse, stressing the extent to which people are loved for their wealth rather than their personal characteristics (follows v. 1030); and a thirty-six-line interpolation comparing the mirror in the fountain of Narcissus to the mirror of Virgil (follows v. 1576).

The version of Guillaume de Lorris found in MS κυ appears in another manuscript as well, the late fourteenth-century Pierpont Morgan MS M 132. The version of Jean de Meun in MS M 132, however, is, as far as one can tell – several gatherings are missing – the standard text, without the interpolations of MS κυ or the B or KLMN manuscripts. This raises the possibility that the modifications in Guillaume and those in Jean are not due to the same redactor. However, as will be explained below, it is most likely that the Rose of MS κυ was revised throughout by the same person. MS M 132 is simply one more example of a composite manuscript: either by chance or by design, the copyist of MS M 132 or its source combined a reworked version of Guillaume with the standard text of Jean. The existence of MS M 132 does prove, in any case, that the reworked version of Guillaume circulated to at least some extent. The reworked version of Jean exists, to my knowledge, in no other manuscript. However, the interpolation on the great heroes of antiquity does appear in the late fifteenth-century MS Bibl. Nat. fr. 24392, a sumptuous codex that belonged to Anne of France.[31] Like so many of the interpolations that entered the Rose manuscript tradition, this particular passage was detached from its original context and copied into a different version of the Rose.

No one over-arching interpretation of the poem can be discerned from MS κυ, although an interest in classical history and legend is apparent. Nonetheless, MS κυ has its story to tell about medieval reception of the Rose. The account of Virgil's mirror is one of the most interesting additions. The perilous mirror in the fountain, we are told, is even brighter and reveals even more things than the mirror made in Rome by "Virgiles li nobiles clers" [Virgil the noble scholar (App. E, 1:3)]. That mirror served for the protection of Rome by showing all activity within a radius of seven leagues around the city.[32] But the mirror in the fountain is so powerful that no man, however wise, can look into it without being caught by Cupid. The comparison elaborated here thus involves two very different kinds of

---

[31] For a description of MS fr. 24392, see Langlois, Manuscrits, pp. 61–62. For the information that this manuscript contains the passage on Caesar and Pompey, I am grateful to Max Grosse of the University of Konstanz.

[32] The legend of Virgil's mirror was widespread during the Middle Ages; its earliest known vernacular source is the twelfth-century Roman des sept sages de Rome, ed. Speer, vv. 3979–4002. Speer provides information about the background of the legend in her note to v. 3931.

mirrors: one warns of danger, allowing for self-defense, while the other is itself a locus of concentrated danger against which no defense is possible.

The notion of mirrors that avert, transmit, or reveal danger is a recurring theme in the *Rose*. Reason offers herself as a corrective mirror, an antidote to the passion induced by gazing into the mirror of love. Nature, in her discourse on the properties of mirrors, comments that if only Mars and Venus had had a magnifying mirror, they could have seen the net spread by Vulcan and so escaped the humiliation of ensnarement. And of course the Medusa interpolation, which appears in MS κυ, contains a reference to the mirror of Perseus, which protected him against the lethal powers of Medusa by providing a mediated view of her. The mirrors of Reason, Nature, and Perseus all, in different ways, counteract the power of the perilous mirror of love: by dissolving amorous passion, by warning of imminent danger, by nullifying the powers of feminine sexuality. The interpolation of Virgil's mirror adds to the series of contrasts, highlighting the dangerous powers of the mirror of love right from the start.

The account of Virgil's mirror is of particular relevance to the story of Perseus and Medusa, affecting our understanding of this passage as a gloss on the Lover's precarious situation. Our hero has fallen in love by looking into a perilous mirror, more powerful than the defensive mirror at Rome; yet he feels no need for a defensive mirror, believing that the image he pursues is endowed with curative powers, unlike the deadly Medusa. MS κυ thus intensifies the initial negative portrayal of love as irrational passion, and suggests an ironic reading of the Medusa analogy. If the Lover believes himself to be in no need of Perseus' mirror of wisdom, it may be because he is unable to judge his situation accurately: his insight recalls that of Pygmalion, who judged his own passion more reasonable than that of Narcissus. The mirror of Virgil bears a striking resemblance to that of Perseus. The former was crafted by a "noble scholar," and served for the military defense of a great city, seat of the empire; the latter – literally a shield – derived from Pallas, goddess of wisdom and military strategy, and was used for the defense of a noble warrior, figure of virtue. At both the beginning and the end of the poem, the Lover is contrasted with figures of wisdom and of military prowess. Such comparisons hardly cast a favorable light on the erotic quest, the sophistical arguments it rests on, or the mighty "battles" it wages. As we will see, the *Rose* of MS κυ was most likely prepared for an aristocratic patron. These pointed contrasts between the Lover's passion and the military accomplishments of past heroes, informed by the wisdom of a Virgil or a Pallas Athene, are an important contribution to the didactic program of the *Rose* as a poem aimed at members of the ruling class, reminding them of their social responsibilities. The amorous fountain with its perilous mirror is opposed not only to the heavenly Fountain of Life, but also to the mirror of worldly wisdom and virtue.

The Lover's self-indulgent folly is heightened by several short interpolations in the discourse of Reason. Although MS κυ does not contain the "litany of love," it does elaborate on Reason's divine origins when she presses her suit with the Lover:

5768	Ne sui je belle dame et tendre,
xxx	Gente de corps et de visage?
xxx	Fille sui d'un preudons moult sage:
xxx	C'est Jhesu Crist, qui tout créa,
xxx	Qui le mont fist; quanqu'il y a,
xxx	Mist et forma, ce sai je bien.
xxx	Et ne vois tu com je sui bien
5769	Digne de servir .i. preudomme . . . (fol. 44v)

Am I not a beautiful and tender lady, noble in person and face? I am the daughter of a very wise gentleman: Jesus Christ, who created everything, who made the world; whatever is in it, he formed and placed there, this I know well. And don't you see that I am really worthy to serve a gentleman . . .

By stressing Reason's divine lineage, the redactor of MS κυ highlights her worthiness as a love object. The allusion to Christ is particularly interesting, given that in the theology of the Trinity the Son is identified with Divine Sapience, a possible analogue for Reason. As the daughter of God's Son, Reason is the image of Sapience found in every human being. Within the sublunary world of human life, Reason is thus the most reliable guide we can find and our closest link with divinity. To reject her love is indeed to turn away from God – as Gui de Mori said, echoing Saint Paul, to love the creature more than the creator (App. A, 2:114–15). The idolatrous nature of the Lover's passion is further stressed in an interpolation at the end of his conversation with Reason (following v. 7198). To emphasize his unreceptiveness to Reason's arguments, the Lover states:

> Car je vous promet, se la dame
> De paradis, qui est la jame
> Et l'esmeraude et l'escharboucle,
> Et en qui bontez reluit toute,
> Vouloit m'amie devenir,
> Pour li n'i pourroit avenir.   (fol. 58r)

For I promise you, if the Lady of Heaven, who is the jewel and the emerald and the carbuncle, and in whom all goodness sparkles, wanted to be my girl friend, it couldn't happen for her.

The Lover's rejection of the Virgin Mary accomplishes even more explicitly what is implied in the *KMN* manuscripts, where he ignores Reason's suggestion of devoting himself to the Virgin. One cannot help wondering if the redactor of the text in MS κυ had seen the "litany of love," and wished to create a similar effect.

The redactor of MS κυ also followed the *KLN* text in admitting and even expanding the discussion of plain speech. In chastizing Reason for not speaking euphemistically, the Lover had pointed out that even lower-class nurses use euphemisms for the sexual members of babies; in MS κυ he helpfully adds that these terms include "teches" [hooks], "pinectes" [little thorns or pine cones], and "hernas" [harnesses (fol. 56r, following v. 6912)]. Citing her God-given right to speak openly, Reason replies that it is the Lover who is being discourteous:

> Diex mon pere n'en parle mie.
> Et tu ne m'en espargnes mie
> A m'en dire outrage et folie.
> Vilain es, quant dis vilanie
> A pucelle de tel renon,
> Qui ne veult fors se t'amour non.
>
> (fol. 57r, following v. 7050)

God, my father, says nothing about it. And you don't spare me, uttering folly and outrage about it to me. You are a churl, to speak so crudely to a maiden of such renown, who wants only your love.

In these lines, Reason lampoons the Lover's courtly pretentions, suggesting that obscenity is in the mind of the beholder. Indeed, she accuses him of "outrage," a term commonly applied to male sexual aggression; Bel Acueil, for example, accuses the Lover of being "outrageus" when he plucks the Rose (v. 21709). In adding that she wants only his love, Reason slyly chastises him for responding to her use of the word "coilles" as though it were a sexual advance, the only kind of discourse he understands.

MS κυ includes the interpolation in which Reason elaborates on the consequences of calling relics "balls." The redactor evidently enjoyed the extended joke about sacred and sexual terminology, for he inserted a parallel passage expanding on the idea of calling testicles "relics":

> Et aussi com tu as despis
> Et es nons de couilles et de vis,
> Se couilles eüssent non reliques,
> Tu qui si vilment les depiques,
> Reliques moult fort desprisasses,
> Et nulle riens ne les prisasses,
> Et deïsses grans vilanies.

Ceste parolle ci ne nies,
Car Diex s'en pourroit courroucier,
Et fort ferir sans menacier.

(fol. 57v, following v. 7090)

And also, since you despise both the word "balls" and the word "prick," if
balls were called "relics," you who attack them so vilely would intensely
despise relics, and would not value them at all, and would say terrible things.
Don't deny this, for God could become angry, and strike a blow without
warning.

While this passage does not have the comic brilliance of its counterpart in
the *KLMN* manuscripts, it does continue the exposition of the Lover's
folly and Reason's inability to penetrate his linguistic biases. For of course
the renaming of the sexual members did not cause the Lover to revile those
words at all; still less the things so named. Instead, it provided him with a
euphemistic language for the extravagant praise of his own genitalia.

The above modifications in the text, then, were probably inspired by
various interpolations in the *KLN* from which the redactor worked.
Certain other interpolations, like the description of Virgil's mirror, reflect
an interest in ancient and modern history, particularly in royal or imperial
figures. We find a six-line reiteration of Nero's evil character after v. 6180;
and following v. 6486, a twenty-line account of Croesus' request to Phanie
for an interpretation of his dream, including an explanation of Phanie's low
opinion of her father. Phanie's words are particularly relevant to the moral
instruction of the aristocracy; and her authority is bolstered by Croesus'
own admission that she is "sage / Et par nature et par usage" [wise both by
nature and through study (fol. 50r)]. A positive model of Christian chivalry
is found in the account of Charles d'Anjou's victories, expanded by a brief
prayer for his soul:[33]

Le filz de Dieu, c'est Jhesu Crist,
Quant il trespassera du monde,
Le face pur et net et monde
De ses pechiés, et si le maint
U saint paradis ou il maint.

---

[33] The insertion of recent events into the *Rose* is not unique to MS *κυ*. In MS Bibl. Nat. fr. 803 (ζα), a
sixteen-line interpolation on the fate of Enguerrand de Marigny – who aided Philip the Fair in the
persecution of the Templars, and was himself executed after Philip's death – follows the account of
the conquest of Sicily (fol. 49r–v, after v. 6710); and in MS *Ac*, the death of Robert d'Artois is
recorded in four verses written in the margin next to his appearance in the discourse of Nature (vv.
17769–74; see Langlois, *Manuscrits*, pp. 93–94).

Amen, amen, ainsi soit il,
et nous garde tous de peril.

(fol. 51r–v, follows v. 6710)

When he passes away from this world, may the Son of God, that is, Jesus Christ, make him pure and clean and cleansed of his sins, and conduct him to blessed paradise where he dwells. Amen, amen, so be it, and may he protect us all from danger.

From this passage, we know that the *Rose* of MS κυ, unlike that of MS *Tou*, must have been prepared in France, probably for a patron who was nostalgic for the "good old days" of the Capetians.

The long interpolation about ancient heroes, finally, clearly indicates the historical and political interests of its redactor. The interpolation, which follows v. 6747, begins with an evocation of the tragic demise of Priam and his sons, and then describes the stunning victories and ignominious death of Alexander. Most of the passage, however, is devoted to a detailed account of the war between Caesar and Pompey, the murder of Pompey, the suicide of Cato, and the assassination of Caesar. Reason stresses the frequent treachery of political machinations and the fickleness of Fortune. The passage fits very well into the context of Reason's discourse, illustrating her points and rounding out her panoply of heroes. An interesting aspect of the passage is its negative portrayal of Caesar, not unprecedented but here particularly harsh. The war between Caesar and Pompey is presented as a tragic event, "aspre et dure, / Sans reson, sans nulle mesure" [bitter and harsh, without reason, without measure (App. E, 2:119–20)]; the envoys dispatched to murder Pompey are characterized as ".ii. faux gloutons" [two treacherous thugs (v. 145)]. The poet bemoans the ignominy of Pompey's death and praises the courage of an exiled Roman who secretly recovers and cremates Pompey's body.

As Caesar consolidates his power, the poet reiterates his evil character, terming him "Cezar, l'enpereur de Romme, / Qui a fet mal a maint preudomme" [Caesar, emperor of Rome, who did wrong to many a worthy man (vv. 203–4)]; Cato's suicide is motivated by his horror at having to serve a *vilain* (vv. 260–62). The Roman citizens accept Caesar as emperor only under duress:

Et li bourgois, li citoien
Virent que il ne valut rien,
Et qu'il escouvenoit par force
Qu'il fust leur sires . . .   (vv. 285–88)

And the bourgeois and the citizens saw that he wasn't worth anything, and that he would be their lord, because there was no help for it.

The poet details Caesar's shortcomings as ruler: when accepting the homage of his vassals, he offers no compensation for the damages they have suffered in his defense (vv. 293–95); he establishes games that are really nothing more than "Luites fors dont il vint tourmens / Et maulz" [harsh struggles from which came torments and pain (vv. 304–5)]; he is so arrogant that he wants to rule the birds and the beasts (vv. 310–13); in short, all his actions are "ennuieuses, / Pesans, chargans, et venimeuses" [annoying, heavy, burdensome, and venomous (vv. 307–8)]. The poet has here invented details giving Caesar an even more negative image than that found in Lucan or Suetonius or in the *Fet des Romains*. The ensuing assassination clearly stands as a warning to overbearing monarchs.

The accumulated effect of these interpolations, so many of which stress the duties and potential shortcomings of rulers and the importance of wisdom, nobility, prowess, and justice, is to increase the didactic value of the *Rose* for members of the aristocracy. In this light it is no surprise that of all the carol participants, it is Richesse whose portrait is the most reworked. Richesse is certainly the most problematic of the carolers, and the only one who refuses to join in the erotic quest. She embodies a moral dilemma that is never fully resolved within the poem: poverty is a horror to be rigorously avoided, but wealth is a ready source of corruption. Without attempting to confront such thorny issues head on, the redactor does pause to expand on the problem of hypocritical courtiers who fawn on the powerful purely for the sake of material gain. Guillaume already comments on Richesse's many followers; our redactor adds,

> Pour ce qu'elle ot assez argent,
> A elle service de gent;
> Mais s'el fust povre de deniers,
> Et que vuis fussent ses greniers,
> Tant fust bele ne savouree,
> Pour ce ne fust ja honnouree.[34]
>
> (MS M 132, fol. 10, follows v. 1030)

Because she had plenty of money, she has people at her service. But if she was without money, and her coffers were empty, no matter how beautiful or delightful she was, she would never be honored for those qualities.

The redactor goes on to comment on the eternal enmity between the rich and the poor, stating that "Riche vouldroit avoir geté / Li povres homs dedenz la boe" [the rich man would like to have thrown the poor man into the mud (ibid.)]. The aristocratic reader is thus reminded that wealth

---

[34] MS κυ is missing its first gathering, and what is now the first page of the codex begins with the ninth line of the Richesse interpolation. I have therefore taken the passage from MS M 132.

cannot form the basis for true loyalty, and also of the dependence of the poor on the rich.

Also contributing to the thematics of good and bad governance, finally, is a brief interpolation in Ami's account of the origins of government:

> 9578 Lors s'asemblerent pour eslire
> xxx Aucun sages hons qui sceüst
> xxx Entr'eulz droit faire, et bien peüst
> xxx Eulz maintenir et gouverner
> xxx Et loiauté entr'eulz mener. (fol. 75v)

Then they assembled in order to elect some wise man who would know how to do right among them, and who could maintain and govern them, and promote loyalty among them.

This thumbnail sketch of the wise ruler is aimed, once again, at the moral instruction of the aristocracy. In MS κυ the *Rose* has become in part a mirror of princes, reminding those who rule of the dangers, the privileges, and the responsibilities of their position. The *Pharsalia* material is well suited to such a purpose; as Eva Sanford has shown, Lucan's poem influenced late medieval ideas of the state.[35] The long interpolation in Faux Samblant about the privilege of hearing confession participates in this general commentary on the exercise and abuse of power. Like the Medusa passage, the Faux Samblant interpolation did not originate with MS κυ but it is certainly appropriate to this redaction.

As we saw in Chapter 1, the *Rose* is sometimes anthologized with texts providing political and social commentary. The association of the *Rose* with ancient history is less common, but one notable example, now lost, can be reconstructed from the library inventory of Jean, duc de Berry. According to the inventory, the duke acquired a codex in 1404 that contained, along with other didactic treatises, the *Rose*; the romances of *Thebes* and *Troie*; and the chronicle of Orosius and "livre de Lucan," probably the *Fet des Romains*.[36] Just fifty years after the copying of MS κυ, in other words, a royal prince acquired a manuscript in which the *Rose* was incorporated into a volume of educational treatises, some of which contained material strikingly similar to that added to the *Rose* itself in MS κυ. This extraordinary coincidence strongly supports the hypothesis that the *Rose* of MS κυ was prepared for aristocratic patronage. That the only other known occurrence of the interpolation on Alexander, Priam, and Caesar is in a manuscript that belonged to another member of the royal

---

[35] Sanford, "Manuscripts of Lucan," pp. 293–94.
[36] See Delisle, "Librairie du duc de Berry – 1402–1416," in *Le Cabinet des manuscrits*, vol. 3, pp. 170–194. The volume in question is no. 146.

family, Anne of France, is further evidence for the circulation of this redaction of the *Rose* in aristocratic circles.

One interpolation in the God of Love's discourse in Guillaume de Lorris stresses the educational value of the *Rose* in a different way, illustrating the use of poetic integument and parable. Describing the effects of erotic desire, Cupid uses the metaphor of a flame burning in a lover's heart. In MS *κυ* this passage is expanded with a comment on exegetical technique:

> Dit li diex d'amours a l'amant,
> "Or escoutés sanz contremant,
> S'orras desclorre la sentence
> De la merveilleuse subtence
> Que t'a dite par parabole:
> Riens qui i soit ne tieng a lobe."[37]
>
> (fol. 19r; follows v. 2340)

The God of Love said to the Lover, "Now listen without delay, and you will hear disclosed the meaning of the marvelous substance that I have said to you by means of a parable: I consider no part of it to be trivial."

The passage suggests that the redactor was writing for an audience with sufficient education to recognize the existence of literary figures and to appreciate their analysis – though one for whom such a process would still be something of a novelty, since the figure in question is a rather simple one. The passage prepares for Reason's discussion of exegesis in Jean de Meun. In view of the ensuing conflict between the rhetoric of love and that of Reason, the redactor may even have wished to point out that the God of Love himself speaks in poetic images: such discourse is not limited to the Latin poets. Implicit in MS *κυ* is a perception of the *Rose*, a vernacular poem about erotic love, as a text nonetheless both learned and ennobling.

Not all modifications are equally relevant to the redactor's didactic plan. Many interpolations simply elaborate on a particular point without altering the sense of the passage. For example, Ami's statement that a man should never wait for the woman to make the first move is emphasized through the addition of the couplet, "Et si vous di sans nulle fable, / Ce n'est pas chose resonnable" [and I tell you without making it up, it is not a reasonable thing (fol. 61v, follows v. 7620)]; Genius' recapitulative description of the Garden of Delight is augmented by the couplet, "Et tretoutes bestes sauvages / Qui pasturent par les boscages" [and all sorts of wild animals, who feed through the woods (fol. 154v, follows v. 20312)]. The temptation

---

[37] Ms M 132 has, for the third and fourth lines of this passage, "S'orra desclorre la substance / De la merveilleuse sentence."

to expand on the *Rose*, to add one's bit to its ongoing creation and re-creation, was seemingly irresistible.

Some interpolated lines, finally, serve no purpose beyond that of reiterating the diegetic speech situation, as for example, "Dit li diex d'amours Cupido, / 'Biaus amis, or entent .i. po' " [Cupid, the God of Love, said, "Fair friend, now listen a bit" (fol. 20r, follows v. 2450)]. Such couplets are little more than rubrics, incorporated into the body of the text. In most fourteenth-century *Rose* manuscripts, the long discourses are broken up not only by subject headings, but also by rubrics reiterating the identity of the speaker. Such rubrics appear in MS κυ also; the interpolations, inserted in places where confusion as to voice might occur, would clarify the rhetorical structure of the poem for a listening audience unable to see the rubrics.[38]

The reiteration of the identity of the speaker and of the relationship between the speaker and the addressee is a recognizable habit of the κυ redactor. It shows up in both parts of the poem, that of Guillaume and that of Jean; it is apparent in several places in the long interpolation on the heroes of antiquity (App. E, 2:1–2, 117, 278, 279–81). These passages are representative of a persistent inclination to multiply instances of narrator intervention, whether in the voice of the fictional narrators of the great monologues or that of the narrator of the poem as a whole, by addressing the audience, reiterating the identity of the speaker, summing up the arguments and noting transitions, often with the use of first- and second-person pronouns. This trait, coupled with the consistency of the didactic program present throughout the poem, confirms that the *Rose* of MS κυ is the work of a single redactor.

We can gather, then, that the *Rose* of MS κυ is the work of someone with a certain grounding in literary and historical studies, although the many points that distinguish his account of Caesar and Pompey from that of other known sources may be an indication that his recollection of the details was imperfect; and that it presupposes an oral presentation, clarifying the text, strengthening the voice of the presenter, and consolidating his or her bond with the listening audience. The redactor of MS κυ enjoyed and expanded on the humor of the *Rose*; he also understood it as a didactic treatise, whose teachings he sought to clarify. The folly of destructive passion – lust, greed, jealousy, pride – is illustrated; the importance of wisdom and moderation

---

[38] For example, couplets reiterating the identity of the speaker appear at moments when the God of Love is about to assume the voice of his lovesick disciple (at vv. 2451, 2287, 2425) and when Ami begins to quote words once spoken to himself (at v. 8034). In her analysis of the Brabantine translation of the *Rose*, Van der Poel notes a similar use of *inquit* formulae, which she also interprets as being aimed at a listening audience; see *De Vlaamse 'Rose' en 'Die Rose' van Heinric*, p. 99.

in those who rule is stressed, as are the dangers of absolute power; and since MS κυ frequently incorporates the K text, it contains the passage in which Reason explicitly designates marriage, a crucial institution in aristocratic life, as the appropriate context for sexual activity. All of this, together with the attention to political and military figures, suggests that the redactor had in mind lay, probably, aristocratic, patronage. Indeed, the anti-imperialist bent of the Caesar passage suggests that the text may have been prepared for a member of the aristocracy who was in conflict with the new Valois dynasty – perhaps for someone implicated in the power struggles taking place between Philip VI or John II and the nobility.

In many respects this approach to the didactic value of the *Rose* resembles that outlined by Pierre Col. For Col, the *Rose* has an all-encompassing didactic programme, embracing "toutes choses selonc leur estat au profit de creature humainne, tant a l'ame come au corps" [all things according to their status for the profit of humanity, as much for the soul as for the body (ed. Hicks, p. 106)]. For this reason the poem needed to portray folly as explicitly as widsom: "Pour ce parle il de paradis et de vertus: pour les suir; et des vices, pour les fouir" [therefore he speaks of paradise and of virtues, that they be pursued; and of vices, that they be shunned (pp. 106–7)]. In this assessment of the varied mix of the *Rose* Col echoes the sentiment expressed in MS κυ and again deriving from the K text: that the *Rose* offers a complete exposition of good and evil, and that the reader or listener must know which to follow and which to shun.

The rewritings and reworkings of the *Rose* that we have examined in the last three chapters show considerable variety. What one remanieur suppressed, another expanded; what one considered important, another ignored. The social values expressed in the poem were reconsidered; the complex relationship between the natural, the rational, and the divine, and the nature of human love and sexuality, were re-examined and redefined. But for medieval authors who admired the *Rose* there was also another way of engaging with the great poem: rather than grafting their work onto the *Rose*, they could incorporate motifs and constructs from the *Rose* into their own new texts. It is to this method of rewriting the *Rose* that we must now turn.

6

"Exposé sur le *Roman de la Rose*": rewriting the *Rose* in the *Pelerinage de vie humaine*

> En veillant avoie leü,
> Consideré et bien veü
> Le biau *Roumans de la Rose*.
> Bien croi que ce fu la chose
> Qui plus m'esmut a ce songier
> Que ci aprés vous veuil nuncier.[1]
>
> (*Pelerinage*, vv. 9–14)

The close relationship between Guillaume de Deguilleville's *Pelerinage de vie humaine* and the *Roman de la Rose* is proclaimed both by the rubrics introducing it and within the body of the poem. In the Prologue of the first recension, written in 1330, Deguilleville announces his intention to narrate a dream inspired by a reading of the *Rose*; at a later point, Reason cites the *Rose* as source for her arguments against erotic love. In fourteenth-century manuscripts, the *Pelerinage* is sometimes rubricated as "exposé sur le Roman de la Rose" [based on the *Romance of the Rose*]. The MS Arras, Bibl. Mun. 845 (MS *Arr*), an anthology that includes, among other things, Deguilleville's three-part *Pelerinage* cycle and some excerpts from the *Rose*, announces the *Pelerinage de vie humaine* as "uns biaux miroirs de sauvement ... fais par poeterie, comme li Livres de le Roze, qui est en grant partie de philozofie, mes cilz pelerinages est de theologie" [a beautiful mirror of salvation ... made by means of poetry, like the Book of the Rose, which is largely philosophical, but this pilgrimage is theological (MS *Arr*, fol. 103r)]. As these rubrics suggest, the *Pelerinage de vie humaine* is not an imitation of the *Rose* as an erotic allegory with philosophical digressions: it is a transposition of the allegorical figures and poetic imagery of the *Rose* into a theological framework, entailing a profound rethinking of the poem.

---

[1] "In waking I had read, considered and thoroughly looked at the beautiful *Romance of the Rose*. I really think that this was the thing that most moved me to dream the thing that I want to tell you next." I cite the edition by Stürzinger.

This reworking of the *Rose* touches on such fundamental issues as the role of Reason and Nature and the problems of language and interpretation.[2]

The relationship between the *Rose* and the *Pelerinage* is further complicated by the existence of an as yet unedited second recension of the *Pelerinage*, which Deguilleville produced in 1355. By this time he had evidently changed his opinion of the *Rose*, for instead of praising it as the inspiration for his dream, he now calls it the work of Venus. Other changes effected in the text also point to Deguilleville's desire to distance himself from this secular work. In assessing the *Pelerinage* as a rewriting and reinterpretation of the *Rose*, then, we will begin with the first recension, and then look at ways in which changes introduced in the second version reflect a different attitude towards the *Rose*.

But our examination of the *Rose* and the *Pelerinage* will not end there. In MS *Arr*, a series of excerpts from the *Rose* has been edited to conform to the spiritual context of the *Pelerinage*: it is as though the *Pelerinage* has been read back into the *Rose*. After examining the *Pelerinage* as a reworking of the *Rose*, in two phases, we will turn to this example of the *Rose* literally rewritten in the light of the *Pelerinage*. From source to adaptation to remaniement, to the adaptation of the source: this circular movement vividly demonstrates not only the fluidity of the medieval vernacular text, but also the importance of intertextual dialogue in the fourteenth century. The processes of commentary, gloss, adaptation, anthologizing, and remaniement all come together in MS *Arr*, a collection infused with the spirit of the theologized *Rose* in which texts comment upon and complete one another, and seem to rewrite one another.

ADAPTING THE *ROSE*: FROM EROTIC QUEST TO SPIRITUAL PILGRIMAGE

Deguilleville did not base his narrative framework directly on that of the *Rose*, but he did borrow numerous motifs and details, reworking them in the new context of spiritual pilgrimage. These motifs are selectively chosen and rearranged to arrive at a vision which, while constantly recalling the *Rose*, is of a very different sort. To begin with, just as Guillaume's Lover first glimpses the Rose in the crystal mirror within the Fountain of Narcissus, so Deguilleville's pilgrim catches sight of his goal, the Heavenly

---

[2] For a survey of the echoes of the *Rose* in the *Pelerinage*, see Badel, *"Roman de la Rose" au XIVe siècle*, pp. 362–76. For a general discussion of Deguilleville and his works, see Faral, "Guillaume de Digulleville, moine de Chaalis." Deguilleville's recasting of *Rose* material to fit his own moral agenda is discussed by Wright, "Deguilleville's *Pelerinage de Vie Humaine*."

Jerusalem, "En un mirour . . . / Qui sanz mesure grans estoit" [in a mirror
. . . that was immensely large (vv. 39–40)]. The pilgrim is dismayed to see
that the city is heavily fortified and guarded by cherubim, making it
extremely difficult to enter; he is relieved to discover that entrance is not
impossible, due to the help offered by various figures inside the city. Saint
Benedict lowers a ladder from the top of the wall; Saint Francis lets down a
knotted cord; Saint Augustine and other Church Doctors, scattering their
words like breadcrumbs, entice people to fly up like birds. The walled city
recalls both the walled and initially impenetrable Garden of Delight, and
the fortified and guarded castle containing the Rose, both of which the
Lover struggles to enter. The latter analogy is strengthened by a reference
to the "dangier" [resistance (*PVH*, v. 124)] of the cherubim; Dangier was
of course the primary obstacle between the Lover and the Rose.

The image of souls as birds flying up at the bidding of Augustine and
other theologians is a particularly ingenious reworking of several motifs
from the *Rose*. The Church Doctors are described as bird hunters [*oiseleur*
(*PVH*, v. 101)]:

> Quar pour les pasteaus qu'il tenoient
> Et la semence qu'espandoient,
> Pour leurs enmielés morsiaus
> Et leurs diz doucereux et biaus
> Maintes gens oysiaus devenoient
> Et en haut puis droit s'en voloient.
>
> (*PVH*, vv. 107–12)

Because many people became birds and flew right up on high, for the food
they held out and the seeds they spread, and for their honeyed morsels and
their sweet and beautiful words.

The *Rose* also speaks of a birdcatcher who sows seeds and hunts humans:

> Cupido, li filz Venus,
> sema d'Amors ici la graine
> qui toute acuevre la fontaine,
> et fist ses laz environ tendre
> et ses engins i mist por prendre
> demoiseilles et demoisiaus,
> qu'Amors si ne velt autre oisiaus. (*Rose*, vv. 1586–92)

Cupid, the son of Venus, sowed here the seed of Love, which completely
covers the fountain, and spread his snares all around, and set his traps to catch
maidens and youths, for Love wants no other birds.

The analogy between seduction and bird-hunting reappears at the end of
the *Rose*, where the seductive words of the would-be lover are compared to
the bird-calls of the hunter, enticing birds to their doom "par douz sonez"

[by sweet twitters (*Rose*, v. 21463)]. Thus the "foolish bird" is caught, not knowing how to "respondre au sofime / qui l'a mis en decepcion / par figure de diction" [respond to the sophism that has deceived it, through figures of speech (*Rose*, vv. 21468–50)]; even so are young girls deceived and captured by their seducers.

The quest for the Rose thus begins and ends with the image of bird-hunting. Humans, like birds, are ensnared by Cupid, trapped in the grasses he has claimed through his metaphorical sowing; inexperienced maidens, like birds, are deceived and trapped by the false words of sweet-talking hunters. The image recurs in somewhat different guise in the discourse of La Vieille, who compares a young man cloistered in a monastery – and by implication also the woman trapped in marriage – to a caged bird longing for its freedom (*Rose*, vv. 13911–36). The image derives from Boethius, who compares the human soul lodged in its body to a caged bird yearning for its homeland (*Consolation of Philosophy* 3, Meter 2). La Vieille's appropriation of the image stresses her carnality: the freedom she imagines is not spiritual release, but sexual promiscuity. And as we are shown in the other passages, those who devote themselves to erotic love are entering, not escaping from, snares.

Deguilleville has transformed this extended metaphor of seduction into one of salvation. Guillaume de Lorris, referring to the seeds of love, implicitly plays on the sexual overtones inherent in the concept of "sowing" and "seed." Jean exploits this image of procreative sowing at the end of the *Rose*, when the Lover, after hearing Genius' exhortations to "plow," eagerly parts the petals to find the Rose's seed, mingling with it his own. Deguilleville, however, plays on a different allegorical meaning of 'semence', one familiar from the exegetical tradition: the seed is the word of God, the sower is the preacher who spreads the word.[3] It is these seeds, not the seeds of procreation, that draw the bird-like souls beheld by the pilgrim; the sweet words that lure them are truth-bearing, not deceptive sophisms. The souls entering Heaven through the tutelage of Augustine have escaped the cages and the snares of earthly attachment.

The image of flight recalls another passage of the *Rose* as well. Annoyed at Reason's suggestion that he devote himself to a type of love he can barely imagine, the Lover asks rhetorically,

> Puis je voler avec les grues,
> voire saillir outre les nues,
> con fist li cignes Socratés?   (*Rose*, vv. 5393–95)

Can I fly with the cranes, indeed soar beyond the clouds, like the swan of Socrates?

---

[3] See Wailes, *Medieval Allegories of Jesus' Parables*, pp. 96–103.

In MSS *Bi* and *Bî*, Reason reiterates the Lover's image of flight in her response:

> 5404   Biaus amis, dit el, or m'escoute.
> xxx   Ja voler ne te convendra,
> xxx   Mais voloir a chascun vaudra.
>
> (App. B, 1:vv. 220–22)

Fair friend, said she, now listen to me. You won't have to fly, but to exert your will; that suffices for anyone.

Punning on "voler" [fly] and "voloir" [want], Reason makes fun of the Lover's hyperbolic protestations while reminding him that good behavior is a matter of free will, thus always within his capabilities. Deguilleville, who probably read the *Rose* in a *B* text or one containing *B* material, shows us that exercising our will in the pursuit of religion may enable us to fly after all. Indeed, in an amusing scene, Reason does help the pilgrim to fly briefly during a lesson on the distinction between soul and body. Of this out-of-the-body experience, the pilgrim says, "Bien me sembloit que (je) volasse" [it really seemed like I was flying (*PVH*, v. 6207)]; and he later reiterates, "Je voloie sur les nues / Plus haut que hairons ne grues" [I flew above the clouds, higher than herons or cranes (*PVH*, vv. 6303–04)]. Since at this point the pilgrim has barely begun his journey, the flight is short-lived; one presumes that he will not really fly until he reaches his celestial destination.

Deguilleville does also retain the image of the soul as a bird caught in the snares of temptation. When the pilgrim chooses to take the path of Oiseuse, thus clearly re-enacting the errors of the *Rose* protagonist, Deguilleville comments:

> Or me gart Diex par sa pitié,
> Quar prez sui de mauves marchié.
> Tant com l'oisel va coliant
> Et ça et la le col tournant,
> Souvent avient qu'au las est pris
> Qui li est en son chemin mis.
>
> (*PVH*, vv. 7023–28)

Now God protect me in his mercy, for I am close to a dangerous pass. Just as the bird goes looking around, and turning its neck this way and that, often it happens that it is caught in the snare that has been placed in its path.

This intervention, commenting in the present tense on the dangers faced by a protagonist representing the narrator's past self, recalls Guillaume's statement as the hero of the *Rose* explores the Garden, stalked by Cupid:

> Or me gart Dex de mortel plaie,
> se tant avient qu'il a moi traie!
> Je, cui de ce ne fu noient,
> m'alai adez esbanoiant . . . (*Rose*, vv. 1313–16)

Now God protect me from a mortal wound, should it so happen that he [Cupid] shoots me! I, unaware of all this, went along happily.

And just as the hero of the *Rose* is attacked by the God of Love, so Deguilleville's pilgrim soon falls into the snares of Sloth, and is subsequently assaulted by other vices. By echoing the *Rose* at this point, Deguilleville implies that the carefree dreamer's encounter in the Garden was with sinful, not virtuous, love. And unlike the authors of the *Rose*, Deguilleville takes it upon himself to present an unambiguous moral critique of sensuality and a model of the soul's spiritual conversion.

At a later point, the pilgrim even discovers that the devil himself is a hunter, fisher, and bird-catcher. In the latter capacity, Satan attempts to waylay the souls of mystics:

> De ceus que vois quë eles ont
> Et qui bons contemplatifs sont
> Oiselëur est devenu.
>
> (*PVH*, vv. 11709–11)

He has become a bird-catcher of those whom you see who have wings, and are good contemplatives.

By reiterating the imagery of hunt and flight in various contexts, Deguilleville reminds us that the bird-like soul must know which "oiseleur" to fly to, for one will lay snares, while the other will set it free; and that this freedom, this flight, this Christian love, is not at all impossible, whatever the Lover of the *Rose* may have thought in his folly.

As the pilgrim continues on his quest, numerous other figures and motifs familiar from the *Rose* appear, some of which will be discussed below: the allegorical personifications of Reason and Nature, for example, and various discussions about language and meaning. And imagery of the *Rose* appears, in its new form, as the pilgrim reaches his preliminary destination, the Ship of Religion. Repenting of his many follies, assaulted on all sides by vices, the pilgrim prays and, with the help of Grace, bathes in the tub of penance. This tub is filled by drops of water falling from a disembodied eye, set in a large rock. Grace explains to the pilgrim that the rock is the hardened heart of a sinner, and the water the penitential tears that he sheds when Grace enables him to see himself:

Et lors quant l'ueil a bien veü
La durté du cuer, esmeü
Tantost est a forment plourer.

(*PVH*, vv. 11267–69)

and then when the eye has really seen the hardness of the heart, it is moved at once to weep bitterly.

After bathing in the pool of tears, the pilgrim is sufficiently healed that he can continue on his path, though not without considerably more tribulations along the way.

This striking image, I submit, is a reworking of Guillaume de Lorris' perilous fountain. That fountain too was set in rock, the "piere de mabre" [stone of marble (*Rose*, v. 1430)] bearing the inscription about Narcissus.[4] While the Lover of the *Rose* does not go so far as to bathe in the fountain of Narcissus, it is certainly at the fountain that he undergoes his spiritual transformation, entering Love's service. The crystals that mirror the garden, revealing the rose and enrapturing the *Rose* protagonist, have often been compared to eyes; and with the powerful exemplum of Narcissus it is specifically gazing at oneself, into one's own eyes, that is at issue.[5] Deguilleville read this complex passage as an allegory of the "concupiscentia oculorum" [lust of the eyes (1 John 2:16)] and its power to move the soul to desire and passion, thereby hardening the heart.[6] By transforming the crucial fountain from a locus of bewitching vision to one of self-knowledge, penance, and tears, Deguilleville reminds us of the dangers of the senses and of the importance of inner, rather than outer, vision. And like Augustine, he stresses the proper use of tears: not for self-pity, as

---

[4] Evrart de Conty, in his commentary on the *Echecs amoureux*, glosses the marble basin of the Fountain of Love as representing "ceux qui sont endurcy" [those who are hardened] and pursue only "les desirs de leur coers" [the desires of their hearts (Bibl. Nat. fr. 9197, fol. 323v)]. Crystal is also associated with both hardness and coldness in medieval lapidary tradition; on the link between the crystals in the Fountain and the Lover's psychological state, see Roy, " 'Cristals est glace endurcie par molt d'ans'."

[5] Numerous modern critics have interpreted the crystals as eyes. Some see them as the lady's eyes: Lewis, *Allegory of Love*, pp. 125ff.; Frappier, "Variations sur le thème du miroir." Others see them as the dreamer's own eyes: Robertson, *Preface to Chaucer*, p. 95; Fleming, *"Roman de la Rose"*, pp. 93–95. For a survey of critical reaction to the crystals, see Hillman, "Another Look into the Mirror Perilous."

[6] The commentary on the *Echecs amoureux* glosses the crystals as representing all forms of perception, including "la vertu sensitif qui comprent les chinq sens forains" [the sensible virtue which comprises the five external senses (Bibl. Nat. fr. 9197, fol. 323v)]; the "internal senses," i.e. "la fantasie, l'ymagination, et la memoire" [fantasy, imagination, and memory (fol. 324r)]; and "l'entendement" [the intellect (ibid.)]. The gloss explains that the crystals show only half of the garden at a time because those who gaze into the mirror of worldly desire are blinded to such things as Heaven, Fortune, justice, and death. On vision and the erotic gaze in Guillaume de Lorris, see Nichols, "Ekphrasis, Iconoclasm, and Desire."

exemplified by both Narcissus and the Lover of the *Rose*, but rather for self-abnegation in the name of penance.[7]

The pilgrim's entrance into the castle of Cîteaux on the Ship of Religion is described in terms that both recall and subvert the climactic passages of the *Rose*: it is as though the Lover had entered the Tower of Jealousy under the auspices of Reason rather than Venus, wanting only to be the Rose's friend. Dangier has been replaced by Fear of God, whose blows must be sustained by anyone wishing to enter. Guillaume's carol is transformed into the pure song of chastity and the sacred music of Latria, who plays organ and psaltery "Si comme fust jouglerresse / Et de gent (une) esbaterresse" [as though she were an entertainer, a female jongleur (*PVH*, vv. 12699–700)]. Chastity is described as the châtelaine who defends the castle against attacks from arrows or darts: clearly it will not suffer the fate described in the *Rose*, where Cupid's foes were routed by Venus' burning arrow. The pilgrim even finds an "amie," though not of the sort acquired by the Lover of the *Rose*. In this case the "amie" is Chastity; Grace explains:

> Volentiers avec toi gerra
> Toutes les foys qu'il te plaira.
> Avec les autres souvent gist
> Et se repose toute nuit.　　　(*PVH*, vv. 12791–94)

She will gladly lie with you whenever you like. She often lies with the others, and stays there all night.

The pilgrim has accepted that which so upset the Lover of the *Rose* in the B remaniement: he has a "commune amie" (see App. B, 1:vv. 265–89). Deguilleville shows that his pilgrim has acquired the wisdom that the Lover of the *Rose* never came to understand: not only has he learned to fly, but also he has learned the value of chaste love, and the virtue of communal devotion to spiritual ideals.

In keeping with his transformation of the quest and the character of its protagonist, Deguilleville also restructures the hierarchy of authorities that populate the moral world of his poem. As in the *Rose*, Reason and Nature appear, and Deguilleville specifies that both are superior to the unnatural, irrational vices.[8] But unlike Jean, Deguilleville also makes it clear that

---

[7] Tears, both good and bad, are a frequently recurring image in Augustine's *Confessions*; see, for example, Book 3, chapters 2, 11, 12; Book 8, chapter 12. Visual concupiscence plays a particularly prominent role in Book 10, chapters 34–35.

[8] Some of Deguilleville's vices proclaim their alienation from Nature. Avarice, for example, states that "point ne sui de son lignage / N'onc ne fu de son ouvrage" [I am not of her lineage, nor was I ever of her making (vv. 10109–10)].

neither Reason nor Nature is the absolute authority. Higher than both of them is Divine Grace, the pilgrim's most important guide and helpmeet. The persona of Grace partakes of both Reason and Nature as they appear in Jean's *Rose*, while her supremacy is firmly established, both through her interactions with these two lesser authorities, and in the ways that she plays off Jean's figures of Nature and Reason. At the beginning of the *Pelerinage*, for example, the pilgrim attaches what might seem an inordinate importance to the *escherpe* and *bourdon* [pouch and staff] needed for his journey. He feels unable to set forth without them, and continues to worry about it until Grace finally provides the needed equipment. Both pouch and staff are then described in detail. The pouch is stained with the blood of Saint Stephen and covered with twelve little bells, each inscribed with an article of the Credo: it is identified as Faith. The staff, endowed with a mirror that reflects the Heavenly Jerusalem and a carbuncle symbolizing the Virgin Mary, is identified as Hope. The pilgrim's equipment, gift of Grace, is an allegory for the theological virtues that will sustain him on his journey through life.

While pouch and staff are normal accoutrements of any pilgrimage, one cannot help thinking of the pouch and staff that figure so prominently at the end of the *Rose*. In the final scene, the Lover has become a pilgrim; his pouch and staff, provided by Nature, are the tools with which he makes his way into the shrine housing the Rose. Jean's description of the Lover's equipment leaves no doubt about its anatomical nature: the staff is "roide et fort" [stiff and strong (*Rose*, v. 21324)], while the pouch is "d'une pel souple san cousture" [of a supple skin, without stitches (*Rose*, v. 21328)] and contains two hammers that impel the Lover onward in his assault, but which remain "dehors . . . pendillanz [dangling outside (*Rose*, v. 21620)] when the staff is finally inserted between the two pillars. As we have seen, this erotic pilgrimage is deleted by both Gui de Mori and the *Bi* remanieur. Deguileville borrows the motif, but, as with the imagery of bird-hunting, he transforms erotic allegory into spiritual allegory. His pilgrim will realize his desire not through the grace of Nature, but through the grace of God.

If Grace replaces Nature as outfitter of the pilgrim, she also takes over some of Reason's functions as instructor, companion, and bearer of divine authority. She supplants Reason as daughter of God (*PVH*, vv. 297–98), and offers herself as the best friend the pilgrim could have, presumably even better than Reason: "Tant com m'aras en compaignie, / N'aras ja meilleur amie" [as long as you have my company, you will never have a better friend (*PVH*, vv. 317–18)]. And it is she who explains to the pilgrim the value of a "commune amie." The pilgrim, who has been thinking of Grace as his friend and counting on her to provide him with pouch and staff, is dismayed when he hears her friendship being promised to some newly ordained canons:

> Veez cy Grace Dieu, prenez la!
> Je la vous doing en compaignie,
> Pour qu'en faciez vostre amie.
>
> (*PVH*, vv. 1018–20)

See here Divine Grace, take her! I give her to you as companion, that you might make her your friend.

Seeing the pilgrim's distress, Grace chides him for his misconceptions:

> Fol, que vas tu ainsi pensant?
> Me cuides tu tout seul avoir
> A amie? Tu dois savoir
> Que bien commun est le meilleur.
>
> (*PVH*, vv. 1032–35)

Fool, what are you thinking? Did you think you would have me all to yourself as friend? You should know that the common good is the best.

She explains that her wish is to bestow her love on everyone: "A toute gent vueil profiter / Et touz veul par amours amer" [I want to profit all people, and to be in love with everyone (*PVH*, vv. 1049–50)]. In borrowing this motif from the *Rose*, Deguilleville divests it of its sexual overtones – the pilgrim does not denigrate Grace, or suggest that she may cuckold him – but retains the lesson, offered with a touch of humor, that Christian love is universal rather than exclusive.

The shortcomings of Reason and Nature are dramatized in an amusing scene near the beginning of the poem. The pilgrim witnesses the ordination of several new canons, presided over by a bishop who is identified as a new Moses; Reason then preaches a sermon. As in the *Rose*, she offers herself as "amie" (*PVH*, vv. 846–47), adding that those who do not love her will never have any friends at all. She counsels against various vices, culminating in "amour charnel" [carnal love (*PVH*, v. 879)], and points out that the follies of this particular vice are explained in the *Rose*: "Ce verrez vous tout sans glose / Ou roumans qui est de la Rose" [you will see that entirely, without gloss, in the *Romance of the Rose* (*PVH*, vv. 881–82)]. And as in the *Rose*, Reason discusses the execution of justice; she is clearly an important guide through life.

For all that, Reason's wisdom and authority are limited. When Moses celebrates the Eucharist and the amazed pilgrim sees bread and wine transformed into the flesh and blood of a lamb, Reason is at a loss to explain what has happened. To the pilgrim's questions, she can only reply, "Cy me faut mon entendement / Et mon sens tout outreement" [here my under-standing and my sense fail quite utterly (*PVH*, vv. 1477–78)]. Whereas in the *Rose* it was the Lover's own obstinacy that caused Reason finally to leave him "pensis et morne" [pensive and sad (*Rose*, v. 7200)], here it is her inability to comprehend the miracle of transsubstantiation that causes her departure: 'Triste en la place me laissa / Et triste en sa tour s'en ala" [she left me there, sad, and sadly she went back to her tower (*PVH*, vv. 1501–2)]. When Reason reappears, she is bearing a written charter, in which Grace grants her the limited and very specific authority to aid the pilgrim against Rude Understanding. This having been accomplished, she answers a few questions and then vanishes; it is ultimately Grace who saves the pilgrim and guides him into the ship of Religion.

The question of transsubstantiation is not left at that, however. Alerted by Reason, Nature appears on the scene: she has come to inform Grace that she is tired of having her laws broken – bushes that burn without being consumed, water that turns into wine, wine that turns into blood – and she wants this nonsense to end at once. Nature acknowledges that the heavenly spheres are the rightful domain of Grace, but she claims the sublunary world as her own. Moving from the heavenly bodies to the world of wind and water, plants and animals, Nature echoes her own discourse in the *Rose*. There too she had a complaint, human sinfulness. Deguilleville offers a different complaint of nature, one also aimed at the unnatural; but instead of the sub-natural, Deguilleville's Nature laments the supra-natural. Grace, of course, successfully defends her supremacy, pointing out that without divine grace, the natural world would not even exist; in the end, Nature apologizes and withdraws her complaint.

In this way Deguilleville establishes a clearer and more complete hierarchy than Jean, one in which Nature and Reason occupy an intermediate position between vice and divinity. Jean did not, of course, deny the ultimate supremacy of God. His Nature invokes the Creator and expresses her wonderment at the mysteries of the Trinity, the Incarnation, and the Virgin Birth; Genius speaks glowingly of the joys of Heaven, which far surpass those of the earthly Garden of Delight. As we have seen, however, the theological elements in the discourses of Nature and Genius were not well received by such ecclesiastical readers as Gui de Mori and Jean Gerson. Deguilleville's attempt to set things straight suggests a similar discomfort: his Nature does speak of divine mysteries, but in a manner that reveals only incomprehension. The naturalistic world view portrayed in the *Rose*, whether seriously or satirically, is thoroughly dismantled by Deguilleville.

The *B* or *B*-related text in which Deguilleville read the *Rose* clearly

included some version of the debate over language between Reason and the
Lover. This debate about the literal and the figurative, about signification
and interpretation, about linguistic propriety and impropriety, is echoed in
Nature's argument with Grace, in the argument between Reason and Rude
Understanding, and in a second debate about the Eucharist between
Aristotle and Sapience, which will be discussed below. The argument
between Nature and Grace turns on an issue of propriety: Nature objects to
Grace's tendency to violate natural laws in performing miracles. She thus
presumes to accuse Grace, her superior, of illegal behavior. The Lover's
attack on Reason is similar: from his inferior position of irrational
lovesickness, he accuses Reason, inventor of all words, of misusing
language. Reason, like Grace, points out that she has a higher purpose, one
that her detractor cannot comprehend. Reason also assures the Lover that,
while she may chastise him, she is not so foolish "que je mesdie ne ne tence"
[that I would slander or quarrel (*Rose*, v. 6974)], for "tencier est venjance
mauvese" [quarreling is an evil vengeance (*Rose*, v. 6976)]. Similarly, Grace
tells Nature, "tencerresse point ne sui" [I am not quarrelsome (*PVH*, v.
1702)].

The argument between Rude Understanding and Reason is even closer
to that of the *Rose*, for it focuses on a linguistic issue. Rude Understanding,
having seen false grain measures known as *raison*, accuses Reason of being a
grain thief. Reason replies that one cannot necessarily trust in a name:

> Entre non et existence
> Vueil je bien faire difference.
> Autre chose est estre Raison
> Et autre chose avoir son non. (*PVH*, vv. 5291–94)

> I want to make a clear difference between name and existence. It is one thing
> to be Reason, and another thing to have her name.

Rude Understanding, however, scornfully retorts that when he hears
something called a cat, he knows that it is a cat and not a cow, concluding,
"A leur nons connois bien chascun, / Quar leur nons et eus sont tout un" [I
know all things well by their names, for they and their names are one
(*PVH*, vv. 5325–26)].

The linguistic debate in the *Pelerinage*, like that in the *Rose*, thus turns on
the literal and figurative use of words. But the terms of the debate are not
quite the same. Jean's Reason argues for plain speech, designating things
by their proper names rather than obscuring them with euphemisms; she
points out that the real significance of her words was not in their literal
meaning, but in the moral lesson taught by the fable. She adds that
euphemism does not change anything anyway, since the meaning is still the

same. The Lover, on the other hand, maintains that words are tainted by the things that they stand for, and that even if one must refer to objectionable things, one should do it with unobjectionable words. As I argued above, Jean here presents the conflict between a rational discourse that seeks to communicate meaning as fully as possible, and an erotic discourse that seeks to seduce by obscuring one's real intentions. In the *B* remaniement, this point is stressed in Reason's observation that the truth should be used to unmask hypocrites.

Deguilleville retains essentially the same basic point, but approaches it from a different direction. Instead of asking whether or not it is permissible to use words that refer literally to "unmentionable" things, such as the sex organs, he addresses the issue of euphemism, asking whether or not an evil is masked by being given a nice name, and whether or not the use of a given word as a euphemism taints it and renders it unfit for use in its original meaning. Reason reminds Rude Understanding that words are often abused for the purpose of covering up evil: "Du non faire couverture / Puet on pour couvrir s'ordure" [one can use the name as a covering, to cover up one's filth (*PVH*, vv. 5295–96)]. But this linguistic sleight of hand does not turn evil to good; nor does it contaminate the name or the thing that properly bears that name. Indeed, Reason professes to be flattered that her name is used as a cover for fraud:

> Et se de mon non cointoier
> Celle mesure et simploier
> Se vout, pour ce diffamee
> N'en sui je pas, mes honnouree.
>
> (*PVH*, vv. 5309–12)

> And if this measure wants to beautify itself and make itself seem honest by means of my name, I am not defamed by that, but honored.

Taking his cue from the *B* remaniement, Deguilleville investigates the linguistic abuse of fraudulent euphemism and hypocrisy, avoiding the question of just how far plain speech may be carried. In Chapter 4, we saw that there is evidence for recensions of the *B* text that deleted vv. 6927–56 – Reason's praise of the sexual members and the Lover's charge of obscenity – and vv. 7105–22, Reason's analysis of sexual euphemisms. If it was in such a manuscript that Deguilleville read the *Rose*, then he would not even have known the extent to which Jean's Reason focuses her discussion of language on sexual terminology.

Deguilleville also offers here an implicit critique of the allegory of sexual intercourse at the end of the *Rose*. The religious imagery used there, he suggests, does not change the nature of what is being portrayed; neither does it impugn the sanctity of that imagery. The inability to distinguish between the literal and the euphemistic is a form of dull-wittedness, as is the tendency to interpret everything according to one's personal preoccupations. Indeed, the Lover of the *Rose* is accused of rude understanding by none other than Dangier, on whom Deguilleville's Rude Understanding is modeled. Dangier is outraged when the Lover interprets Bel Acueil's courteous words as permission to pluck the Rose:

> quant ses paroles apreïstes,
> ou droit sen por quoi nes preïstes?
> Prandre les si vilenement
> vos mut de rude antandement.

(Rose, vv. 14831–34)

When you heard his words, why didn't you take them according to their proper meaning? Rude understanding causes you to interpret them so vilely.

And in the *B* text, it is Dangier who unmasks the Lover's true intentions in offering to be hung from the *fourches* of the rosebush. Obsessed with his longing for the Rose, the Lover sees the fulfilment of his desire as the goal of all communication with Bel Acueil; at the same time, he imagines that by not openly naming that desire, he preserves decorum. There is a delightful irony in the fact that it is Dangier the *vilain* who deflates the Lover's courtly pretentions and accuses him of rudeness. By identifying the obstreperous peasant that blocks the pilgrim's way as Rude Understanding, Deguilleville confirms that it is not resistance to seduction that is ignoble, but rather the inability to think, speak, and behave in a rational manner. In the pilgrimage of life, it is our own dullness and resistance we must overcome, not those of others; and in this we are aided, not by Venus or even Nature, but by Reason acting as the agent of Grace.

TRANSFORMATIONS OF GENIUS: MOSES, ARISTOTLE, AND GUILLAUME DE DEGUILLEVILLE

For a clerical reader of the *Rose*, the figures of Genius and Faux Samblant are likely to attract particular attention: Faux Samblant because his discourse focuses on ecclesiastical corruption, and Genius because he elaborates an explicitly theological framework for the erotic quest. Both are clerical figures of sorts. Faux Samblant is dressed as a mendicant friar and pretends to confess Male Bouche; Genius is the priest and confessor of Nature and bishop of Love, and pronounces an excommunication of those who work against Nature while extending a pardon and promise of eternal salvation to those who further her works. Both are also problematic, and

Deguilleville does not borrow either figure as such. Monastic corruption is addressed, however, especially in the second recension of the *Pelerinage*. Faux Samblant also lies behind some of the personifications of vices in the *Pelerinage*, particularly Avarice.[9] And the discourse of Genius informs the poem in several ways, not the least of which is the very idea of a theological rewriting of the *Rose*.

Genius in the *Rose* is an enigmatic and complex character, resembling little else in the corpus of medieval literature.[10] Genius as he appears in *De planctu Naturae*, Jean's immediate source, does not derive his authority from either Venus or Nature: Venus is subject to Nature, while Nature herself is subject to God. Alain's Genius opens his anathema, "Auctoritate superessentialis Vsye eiusque Notionis eterne, assensu celestis milicie, coniuncte Nature etiam" [by the authority of the supreme Being and His eternal Idea, with the accord of the heavenly militia and the agreement of Nature as well (ed. Häring, Prose 18, lines 141–43)]. This is a very different way of invoking the chain of command from that posited by Jean's Genius, who begins:

> De l'auctorité de Nature,
> qui de tout le monde a la cure
> comme vicaire et connestable
> a l'ampereeur pardurable.　　(*Rose*, vv. 19475–78)

By the authority of Nature, who has charge of all the world, as vicar and constable of the eternal emperor.

Jean's Genius does not deny the ultimate authority of God, but he is more concerned with the immediate authority of Nature than with its divine source. Rather than mediating between the natural and the divine, he appears to mediate between the natural and the passionate, providing the impetus whereby the Lover's desire can be channeled into procreative sexual activity. Or perhaps it would be more accurate to say that he conflates these two functions, infusing natural sexuality with the sanctity of natural law and linking the immortality of the species to that of the individual soul.

Deguilleville sorts out the various elements of Genius' character. As the embodiment of the natural sex drive, he is replaced by the personification of Luxuria, an unambiguously negative figure who temporarily impedes the pilgrim's progress. Genius the bishop and Genius the representative of

---

[9] For example, Avarice's tongue is called "Parjurement" [perjury], and her fingers have such names as Hypocrisy, Fraud, and Trickery. Like Faux Samblant, she proclaims her hatred of poverty and her power to manipulate rulers.

[10] On literary precedents for Jean's Genius, see Nitzsche, *Genius Figure*.

Nature are reflected in two other characters in the *Pelerinage*: Moses and Aristotle. Moses is the bishop in the church to which Grace first brings the young pilgrim. He is identified as successor to the original Moses, and presides over the sacraments of baptism, confirmation, and communion. He is allied with Reason – it is she who lectures his charges about their moral and judicial responsibilities – but his authority, like hers, derives from Grace. Moses appears only briefly in the *Pelerinage*, and is not a major character. But as bishop of Grace, he does implicitly offer a corrected version of Jean's priest of Nature and bishop of Love.

Genius' identity as priest of Nature also lies behind the figure of Aristotle in the *Pelerinage*, whom Deguilleville characterizes as a *clerc* of Nature (*PVH*, v. 2918). Aristotle's appearance is limited to a single scene, in which he is sent by Nature to argue with Divine Sapience about the miracle of the Eucharist. This time the controversy is not one of unnatural transformation, but rather one of logic: Aristotle refutes Sapience's claim that a tiny wafer contains enough food to sustain the entire human race. He argues that the natural laws of physics would prevent such a thing, for the container cannot be smaller than the thing contained. Furthermore, Sapience has claimed that any part of the Host, however small, contains as much as the whole: a contradiction of Aristotle's rule that the whole is always greater than any of its parts. He thus accuses Sapience of "grant mespresure / Encontre moi et contre Nature" [great misdoing against me and against Nature (*PVH*, vv. 2981–82)]. This "misdoing" is spelled out as sophistry (*PVH*, vv. 2942, 3076), fraud and deception (*PVH*, vv. 2968, 3077) and lack of discretion (*PVH*, v. 3078). As in the dispute between Nature and Grace, the argument of Aristotle and Sapience reveals the failure of pagan philosophy to account for sacred mysteries.

In Sapience's reply, the primacy of divine wisdom over nature and natural reason is clearly established. Sapience explains that she has established two schools. One offers teaching on "divers ars" [diverse arts (*PVH*, v. 3000)], and Nature herself was the first pupil here, learning "Nobles mestiers et bien soutis, / Si com de faire fleuretes" [noble and very subtle skills, such as how to make flowers (*PVH*, vv. 3006–7)]. The other school is devoted to logic and ethical philosophy:

> En l'autre escolle j'enseignoie
> L'entendement et l'enfourmoie
> A arguer et desputer
> Et a jugier et discerner
> Entre le bon et le mauves
> Et a faire canon et lais. (*PVH*, vv. 3011–16)

In the other school I taught and formed the understanding to argue and dispute, and to judge and discern between good and evil, and to make canons and laws.

It was at this school that Aristotle received his education, learning the "secrets of nature" (*PVH*, v. 3030). Thus all natural processes, as well as all human philosophy – Christian and pagan alike – derive from Divine Sapience. Having reminded Aristotle that his learning is dependent on her, Sapience demonstrates through a series of analogies that the relationship of container to thing contained, and of part to whole, is more complicated than he had imagined. Vanquished, he apologizes and withdraws his complaint.

The confrontation of pagan and Christian views is an issue in Jean's discourse of Genius as well. But whereas Jean presents – and does not explicitly refute – the sacralization of the natural, Deguilleville proposes, and then does refute, the naturalization of the sacred. The choice of Aristotle as a stand-in for Genius is not arbitrary. The idea of the primacy of the species over the individual, used by Jean's Genius to justify his condemnation of chastity and exhortation to engage in procreative sex, is a tenet of medieval Aristotelianism. Moreover, Aristotle was among the most important of the pagan philosophers whose works were alternately taught and condemned during the later Middle Ages. Deguilleville may well have seen the discourse of Genius as a head-on collision between Aristotelian and Averroist naturalism and Christian doctrine; in his reworking of the *Rose*, the conflict of philosophy and theology reappears in a less salacious form.[11] Deguilleville's strategy here is similar to that in his reworking of the linguistic debate with Reason: important issues raised in the *Rose* are re-examined, but in a less provocative format, and with less ambiguous conclusions. The question of erotic vocabulary and euphemism becomes, as in the *B remaniement*, an issue of truth and hypocrisy; the naturalistic attack on chastity as contrary to procreation is generalized into a perception of mystery and miracle as contrary to natural law.

Deguilleville makes his views on procreation clear in a passage where Reason explains to the pilgrim that his identity lies not in his body, which is in fact his enemy, but in his soul. Thus his true father is not Thomas de Deguilleville, from whom he received only the body that weighs him down, but rather God. This passage is an important reworking of material from the *Rose*. It recalls Jean's distinction between art and Nature, in which he stresses the latter's superiority: "mes par antantive cure / a genouz est devant Nature" [but with profound concern, (art) is on its knees before

---

[11] On doctrinal issues raised by Genius, see Paré, *Idées et les lettres au XIIIe Siècle*, pp. 279–97.

Nature (*Rose*, vv. 15989–90)]. No work of art can equal the works of Nature, for whatever art may produce, "ne les fera par eus aler, / vivre, mouvoir, santir, paler" [it will never make them go by themselves, live, move, feel, or speak (*Rose*, vv. 16033–34)]. And if Nature is the only true artist, we are also shown that it is through the agency of Venus that her art, procreation, takes place. Venus' privileged role in the creative process is stressed in the story of Pygmalion, where it is she who brings about the "manifest miracle" (*Rose*, v. 21130) of bringing the statue to life so that it can be Pygmalion's lover and bear his child.

For Deguilleville, however, the naturalistic creative process of forming the body is in no way exalted. He described it, in fact, as another form of human art; the body is, after all, created through the lowly human activity of sexual intercourse. And the body is subject to the same defects that Jean ascribed to art, being

> Un simulacre fait d'ordure,
> Une estatue de limon,
> Un espouentail a coulon.
> Par li ne se puet remuer
> Ne rien faire ne labourer,
> Quar impotent est et contrait,
> Sourt, avugle, et contrefait.   (*PVH*, vv. 5814–20)

A phantom made of filth, a statue of clay, a scarecrow. By itself it cannot move, or work or do anything, for it is powerless and paralyzed, deaf, blind, and counterfeit.

The only true artist, in fact, is God; and without any participation of natural or human agents, it is he who makes our souls. The human soul is described as a work of art representing its creator: "de Dieu la pourtraiture / Et l'ymage et la faiture" [the portrait and the image and the creation of God (*PVH*, vv. 5947–48)]. For Deguilleville it is not a question of Art being on its knees before Nature, but rather of Nature being on her knees before God – a point brought home when Nature literally gets down on her knees in contrition before Grace, once the latter has successfully refuted her objections to miracle.

By rewriting the *Rose* as he does – systematically transposing erotic allegory into religious allegory, replacing rationalism and naturalism with Christian doctrine – Deguilleville in fact becomes himself a Genius figure of sorts. For while every section of Jean's poem is in some sense a rethinking of and commentary upon Guillaume's *Rose*, the discourse of Genius contains the most explicit examination and transformation of

Guillaume's allegory.[12] Genius offers a step-by-step recapitulation of the Garden of Delight; at every point, the features of the Garden are contrasted with the vastly superior corresponding features of the Heavenly Park. The Park indeed is a translation of the Garden into theologically charged imagery. Thus the pine tree and Fountain of Love are replaced by the olive-bearing Tree of Life and the trinitarian Fountain of Life; the two reflective crystals by the tri-faceted carbuncle, source of light; the frivolous song and dance of the carolers by the sacred music of heaven. Venus' son Cupid, presiding deity in the Garden, is replaced by the Lamb, son of the Virgin. As we have seen, medieval readers did not doubt that this Park was indeed the Christian Heaven. In many ways Genius does seem to offer Love's followers a more noble goal, a higher quest. The problem, of course, is Genius' insistence on heterosexual coupling as the means of reaching this goal.

For a reader with Deguilleville's proclivities, the discourse of Genius would thus be both profoundly interesting and profoundly disturbing. The idea of recasting the *Rose* as a religious vision may even have been initially inspired by Genius' elaborate rewriting of Guillaume de Lorris. But Deguilleville set out to do the job properly. A poetic quest for spiritual bliss, a reinvestment of religious significance into the elements of erotic allegory: what could be more appealing for a monastic reader enamoured of the *Rose?* Like Gui de Mori, Deguilleville found a way to justify his study of a controversial secular poem, and he offered other would-be readers of the *Rose* a more ennobling text with which to satisfy their desire for allegorical entertainment in the vernacular.

RETHINKING THE PILGRIMAGE: DEGUILLEVILLE'S SECOND
RECENSION

The *Pelerinage de vie humaine* enjoyed considerable success. No doubt this very success was one of the reasons for Deguilleville's decision to rework his poem and to continue it through the addition of the *Pelerinage de l'ame* twenty-five years later, in 1355.[13] In the prologue to the second recension, Deguilleville complains that his poem was circulated against his will, before it was ready for public consumption. The first draft, he claims, was written immediately upon awakening from his dream, when he was still "sommeilleux" [sleepy (Bibl. Nat. fr. 829, fol. 1r)], and was intended only

---

[12] See Smith, "In Search of the Ideal Landscape"; Brownlee, "Jean de Meun and the Limits of Romance."

[13] Faral describes the changes introduced in the second recension in "Guillaume de Degulleville, moine de Chaalis." Since there is no edition, I cite the second recension in the MS Bibl. Nat. fr. 829.

as a means of committing the dream to memory for later revision, "Quant plus esveillié seroye / Et pensé plus y auroie" [when I would be more awake, and would have thought about it more (ibid.)]. But the poem got out into the world; and now, he says, it has spread so far and wide that he can never hope to track down and correct all of the extant copies. Deguilleville also claims to have forgotten much of his dream in the intervening years. Nonetheless, he vows to revise it as best he can, and to replace copies of the first draft with the new, improved version. In this last effort it must be said that he was singularly unsuccessful; the first recension survives today in an impressive fifty-three manuscripts, while the second survives in only eight.

It is unlikely that Deguilleville really did try to prevent his first version of the *Pelerinage* from circulating. It is clear, however, that by 1355 he had changed his mind about the kind of poem he wished the *Pelerinage* to be. The first version was aimed at all people, 'Riche, povre, sage et fol, / Soient roys, soient roynes, / Pelerins et pelerines" [rich, poor, wise, and foolish, be they kings or queens, male or female pilgrims (*PVH*, vv. 4–6)]. It was not aimed at a clerical audience: "En francois toute mise l'ai / A ce que l'entendent li lai" [I have done it in French, so that the laity will understand it (*PVH*, vv. 23–24)]. And the poem was divided into four books, each presented as a day's sermon, and each ending with an exhortation to return the following day for the next instalment. The second recension, in contrast, contains several lengthy passages in Latin, and is not divided into sections for oral presentation. Whereas the first recension was aimed at a general public expected to receive the text orally, the second recension was aimed at an educated audience who would in all likelihood read the text themselves. It may be that the poem circulated more widely than Deguilleville had expected, and in view of its growing fame he wished to make it a more serious and more learned work.

Deguilleville's new attitude towards his poem is paralleled by his revised opinion of the *Roman de la Rose*, no longer seen as an appropriate source of inspiration for a religious vision. The prologue reference to Deguilleville's bedtime perusal of the *Rose* is deleted; instead, the only explicit allusion to the *Rose* is a condemnation of its moral failings, or perhaps of its moral ambiguity. Of course, the *Rose* does still remain an important intertext for the *Pelerinage*. Even in criticizing the *Rose*, Deguilleville cannot resist imitating it as well. The critique of the *Rose* is placed in the mouth of Venus, who has been relocated to appear at the approximate midpoint of the poem.[14] Deguilleville thus echoes and subverts Jean's tactic of placing a

---

[14] The complete text of Venus' exchange with the pilgrim on the topic of the *Rose* is printed by Badel according to MS Bibl. Nat. fr. 12466, in *Roman de la Rose au XIVe siècle*, pp. 368–69.

laudatory statement about his own authorship of the *Rose*, spoken by the God of Love, at the midpoint of the *Rose*. The God of Love had promised to shelter the young Jean with his wings and to inspire his poetry. Deguilleville's Venus now proudly asserts that she has done just that, in effect "ghost-writing" the *Rose* through the agency of Jean de Meun. She refers to it as "mon Rommant dit de la Rose" [my *Romance of the Rose* (fol. 66r)]:

> Car je le fis et il est mien.
> Et ce puis je prouver tres bien,
> Car du premier jusques au bout,
> Senz descontinuer par tout,
> Il n'y a fors de moy parlé. (fol. 66v)

For I made it and it is mine, and I can prove this very well, for from beginning to end, without ever stopping, it speaks of nothing but me.

Since in the context of the *Pelerinage* Venus is a wholly negative character, there can be no doubt that Deguilleville means to criticize the *Rose* as a frivolous, even dangerous, text. He assimilates Venus and Jean to Male Bouche for their attacks on chastity, on religious orders, and on Normans:

> Male bouche ot ton escrivain.
> . . .
> Et tu male bouche as aussi,
> Quant contre Chasteté menti
> As, et ton clerc fait mentir
> Pour faire bonnes gens haïr. (Ibid.)

Your writer had an evil mouth . . . And you have an evil mouth also, when you have lied against Chastity and caused your clerk to lie, in order to make good people be hated.

This last line also implicitly assimilates Jean to Faux Samblant, who boasts both of his own mendacity and of his power to injure others.

Deguilleville's admission of the *Rose*'s shortcomings – its potential to arouse, rather than subdue, its readers' passions – is nonetheless counter-balanced by his acknowledgment that the poem does contain worthy material. This praise of the *Rose* is humorously placed in the mouth of Venus as well, in the form of her complaint that Jean did not quite keep his promise to write a poem entirely devoted to her:

> Il n'y a fors de moy parlé,
> Ce tant seulement excepté
> Que mon clerc escrivain embla
> Et en estranges champs soya. (Ibid.)

Nothing is discussed there other than me, except for what my clerkly writer stole and got from other fields.

One can only assume that Venus has in mind Jean's use of such authors as Cicero, Boethius, and Alain de Lille – in other words, precisely those passages of the *Rose* that could redeem it in the eyes of a reader like Deguilleville. In Venus' complaint we catch an echo of the assessment that would be made fifty years later by Christine de Pizan: "Non obstant ce, je ne reppreuve mie *Le Rommant de la Rose* en toutes pars, car il y a de bonnes choses et bien dictes sans faille." [In spite of that, I don't criticize the *Romance of the Rose* completely, for there are certainly things in it that are good and well said (ed. Hicks, p. 21).] Nonetheless, Christine's follow-up comment probably reflects Deguilleville's ultimate opinion as well: "Et de tant est plus grant le peril: car plus est adjoustee foy au mal de tant comme le bien y est plus auttentique." [And the danger is therefore all the greater: for the more authentic the good is, the more faith will be placed in the evil as well (ibid.).] Such an attitude – an admiration for Jean's poetic craftsmanship, a recognition of the *Rose*'s literary merits and potential for edification, coupled with an uneasiness for its seeming glorification of the erotic quest and its prolonged attention to the more sordid aspects of "love" – would explain Deguilleville's desire to recast the *Rose* as a story of spiritual conversion. His greater uneasiness in 1355 might even be explained by his having encountered the *Rose* in an unexpurgated, non-*B* manuscript.

Deguilleville introduced extensive changes in the second recension of the *Pelerinage*; here I can cite only a few examples, focusing on elements that reflect his view of the *Rose* and its implicit presence throughout his own poem. He goes even farther in defining the limits of rationalism, expanding Grace's role to include the pilgrim's flying lesson. This passage was in all probability associated with Reason in the first recension because of its direct inspiration from passages in the *Rose* where Reason and the Lover argue about flight and about bodily as opposed to intellectual pleasures. But in the second recension, Deguilleville wanted to downplay the role of Reason in spiritual contemplation, stressing the dependence of all such inward flights on Grace. Grace herself is also slightly changed to be less like a courtly lady. The word "amie" is no longer applied to her. Instead of exhorting the new canons to make her their friend, Moses now tells them to receive her in joy and to stay with her always. Nor does Grace refer to herself as the pilgrim's "amie" (*PVH*, v. 1034), or state that "touz veul par amours amer" [I want to be in love with everyone (*PVH*, v. 1050)]; this last wish is reformulated as "tous bons pelerins amer" [to love all good pilgrims (fol. 6v)]. These subtle revisions serve to distance Grace from the rhetoric of courtly love, making her a more exalted figure.

The more spiritual orientation is also reflected in Deguilleville's use of Ovid in the second recension of the *Pelerinage*. Ovid does not figure at all in the first recension, but in the second version he puts in a brief appearance. Towards the end, when the pilgrim is suffering at the hands of his enemies, he meets "un vieil clerc" [an old clerk (fol. 126v)] who expresses sympathy and offers to help him by pronouncing a curse on his enemies. The clerk turns out to be Ovid, and the curse is a sixteen-line segment from the maledictory poem *Ibis* (vv. 107–18, 123, 120, 125–26). But the pilgrim, though grateful for Ovid's kind intentions, explains that he cannot accept the curse; he prefers to await the judgment of God. Ovid departs in words reminiscent of Reason's departure in the *Rose*: "Ainsi Ovide s'en rala / Et la tout pensif me laissa" [So Ovid went away and left me all pensive (fol. 126v)]. Considering that Ovid is the poet most explicitly enshrined in the *Rose* – and marginal annotations show that this point was not lost on medieval readers – the pilgrim's rejection of his verse is also an implicit critique of that enthusiastic appropriation of the classical literary tradition that the *Rose* exemplifies. One is reminded of other ecclesiastical readers of the *Rose*: Gui, who excised references to pagan mythology; Gerson, who condemned Jean's use of Ovid and Juvenal.

Deguilleville expands on the various dangers faced by the pilgrim in his journey through the Sea of Life, and some of the figures that he introduces or develops further reflect on the *Rose*. In the first recension, for example, Syrena is described in only eight lines (*PVH*, vv. 11963–70): he is "worldly solace" and attracts seafarers, particularly young ones, by means of "chant et deduit vain" [song and vain delight (v. 11964)]. In the second recension, however, Syrena, also referred to as Esbatement [entertainment], is described in more detail, and has an actual encounter with the pilgrim. The pilgrim first becomes aware of Esbatement when he hears his song:

> Une voix bien mellodieuse
> Si tres doulce et si gracieuse
> Que tout le cuer m'en resjouÿ,
> Et mes douleurs mis en oubly.   (fol. 114v)

A very melodious voice, so sweet and so gracious that my whole heart rejoiced, and I forgot my sorrows.

Upon investigation, he finds Esbatement at the water's edge: a curious figure with the head and torso of a man and the legs and feet of a bird, playing a fiddle. Esbatement offers to provide entertainment on any musical instrument, to sing, to dance, or to play games. Off shore, the pilgrim notices a floating tower, "trestoute quarree" [completely square (ibid.)], with smoke and flames issuing from its windows. This is the ship of Satan, who, Esbatement explains, "Fait tout fumer et embraser / Ceulx qui de lui veulent jouer" [makes those who want to play with him smoulder and burn (fol. 115r)]. Even this warning does not dissuade the pilgrim from lingering to hear Esbatement play the fiddle; and with the pilgrim thus distracted, Esbatement suddenly seizes him with one of his bird-claw feet and drags him under the water. Only with difficulty does the pilgrim escape.

The entire scene is made up of imagery familiar from the *Rose*. Esbatement recalls the carol which so pleased the hero of the *Rose* and provided his first initiation into Cupid's court. Indeed, Esbatement's unceremonious grabbing of the pilgrim is a distant echo of Courtoisie's compelling invitation, "ça venez, / et aveques nos vos prenez / a la querole" [come here, and join us in the carol (*Rose*, vv. 783–85)]. Esbatement's bird-like features also recall Guillaume's Garden, for it was the melodious sounds of birdsong that first attracted the dreamer:

> Quant j'oï les oisiaus chanter,
> forment me pris a dementer
> par quel art ne par quel engin
> je porroie entrer el jardin. (*Rose*, vv. 495–98)

When I heard the birds sing, I began to think very hard about some means or some device by which I could enter the garden.

And once the dreamer has entered the garden, he reflects that the birdsong resembles the "chanz des seraines de mer" [song of the sirens of the sea (*Rose*, v. 670)]. Deguilleville's Syrena/Esbatement is a conflation of the bewitching birds and the seductive song and dance that set the scene for the *Rose* hero's fateful encounter with erotic desire. The flaming tower, in turn, derives from the culminating passage of the *Rose*. Like the Garden itself, the tower built by Jealousy to enclose the Rose is "de droit quareüre" [perfectly square (*Rose*, v. 3797)]. When the Rose is well protected, it obviously does not smoke; but once Venus has fired her flaming arrow, the tower is on fire. The square burning tower is thus an image of chastity overcome by passion; and just as Satan in his tower seeks to capture souls, so the Lover of the *Rose* was all too eager to rush into the still-burning tower as soon as its guards had fled.

While Deguilleville no longer explicitly acknowledges his debt to the *Rose*, he continues to mine it for striking imagery. And in every case, he uses this imagery in such a way as to make an unambiguous moral statement, implicitly undermining the *Rose*'s celebration of erotic love. Such was the power of the *Rose* in the imagination of this fourteenth-century poet that even in writing a spiritual treatise, he continually returned to the beautiful, troublesome, endlessly compelling masterpiece of Guillaume de Lorris and Jean de Meun.

RECUPERATING THE *ROSE*: THE MS ARRAS, BIBL. MUN. 845

We turn now to a codex that bears witness to a fourteenth-century interest in the *Pelerinage* cycle and in the moral and spiritual revision of the *Rose*. MS *Arr* is dominated by Deguilleville's three poems: the first recension of the *Pelerinage de vie humaine*, followed by the *Pelerinage de l'ame* and *Pelerinage de Jesus Christ*. In addition, the manuscript contains other devotional texts, including discourses on the Ten Commandments, the *Dit des trois morts et des trois vifs*, the *Testament* and *Sept Articles de la foi* attributed to Jean de Meun, the *Doctrinal aux simples gens*, extracts from a French verse translation of the *Consolation of Philosophy*, and assorted shorter poems. It also contains lengthy excerpts from the *Rose*, introduced as "partie du livre de la Roze, scilicet le capitle de Raison, de Nature, de Faux Samblant et de Viel Amy" [part of the *Book of the Rose*, namely the chapters of Reason, Nature, Faux Samblant, and Old Friend (fol. 250v)].[15]

The collection is thus fairly homogeneous, addressing matters of both morality and faith, and presenting the human condition both on earth and after death. All of the contents can be seen as glosses or expansions on the material in the three *Pelerinage* poems. But the *Pelerinage de vie humaine* is a glossing and reworking of the *Rose*, explicitly so in the first recension; and the rubric in MS *Arr*, cited above, stresses the identity of the *Pelerinage* as a theological counterpart to the philosophical *Rose*. The *Rose* itself has been adapted in accordance with the moral and spiritual values of the *Pelerinage*, as will be discussed below. Many of the texts in MS *Arr* relate not only to the *Pelerinage*, but also to the *Rose*, and to the project of rewriting and adapting the *Rose* in a moral and spiritual context. The two devotional texts attributed to Jean de Meun, for example, establish that poet's reputation as one working within the framework of Christian orthodoxy. The *Consolation of Philosophy* is an important source for the *Rose*, addressing the topics of Fortune, self-sufficiency, and free will that figure in the portions of Reason and Nature included in MS *Arr*.[16]

MS *Arr* opens with a full-page representation of the Ten Commandments as ten arrows aimed at the human soul (fol. 1v). On the facing page is an exposition of the Commandments (fol. 2r). On the following page (fol. 2v), the drama of sin and salvation is represented in a miniature, extending across both columns. On the left, an old man kneels before God, holding a

---

[15] For a description of MS *Arr*, see Langlois, *Manuscrits*, pp. 98–110. The *Consolation* passages are from Version 10, the revision by the Anonymous Benedictine (ca. 1380) of the earlier fourteenth-century Version 9 by Renaut de Louhans.

[16] The *Consolation of Philosophy* was reworked in the same way as the *Rose*: it is divested of its narrative framework and of all references to pagan mythology, leaving only a series of edifying discourses.

scroll with the inscription "Quel cose faut il faire pour avoir paradis" [what must one do to achieve Paradise?], while God extends a scroll inscribed, "Mes .x. commandemens que je donnay jadis"[my ten commandments that I gave long ago]. On the right, a young man holds a scroll that says, "Les commandemens de dieu sont trop fort" [the commandments of God are too difficult]; he converses with the devil, whose scroll is inscribed, "Fay mon conseil, il a grant tort" [take my advice, he is very wrong]. Underneath the miniature, filling the left column, is a version of the Ten Commandments in octosyllabic verse; on the right are the ten command-ments of the devil, each of which counsels the opposite of the correspond-ing commandment of God. For example, the first commandment on the left is, "Dieu deseure tout ameras / Et cremeras souverainement" [you will love God above all, and fear him exceedingly]; this is countered with, "Honneurs, avoirs, soulas querras, / N'a dieu seras obedient" [you will seek honors, possessions, and comfort; you will not be obedient to God]. At the end of the commandments, God reminds us that we must keep all ten in order to get into Heaven; the devil rests his case by pointing out that he is a much easier master, since we can go to Hell by keeping any one of his. A second double set of commandments, similarly illustrated, appears at the end of the *Rose* excerpts (fol. 274v).

The image of the arrows could be seen as analogous to the arrows of Cupid that the hero of the *Rose* encounters soon after his entry into the Garden of Delight. This passage does not appear in MS *Arr*, but any fourteenth-century reader would be sure to know it. In the *Rose*, Cupid shoots the Lover with five arrows and then delivers a long sermon presenting his commandments. These are later summarized as a series of ten commandments (vv. 10373–82) that the Lover recites "en leu de *Confiteor*" [instead of making a Confession (v. 10366)]. The interpretation of Cupid and his arrows as an image for God and the commandments is attested in the fourteenth-century *Ovide moralisé*:

> Nostre Dieus, nostre Sauvaors,
> Bien nous ama, bien nous ot chiers,
> C'est Cupido, li bons archiers,
> Que bien set ses dars empener,
> Pour les amoureus assener.
> Li dart sont li comandement
> De la loy, qui diversement
> Sont fet et de divers ouvraigne.
>
> (Bk. 1, vv. 3320–27)

Our God, our Lord, loved us well, cherished us; that is Cupid, the good archer, who knows well how to feather his darts, in order to strike the amorous. The darts are the commandments of the law, made diversely and of diverse workmanship.

The juxtaposition of divine and diabolical commandments recalls the dialectical structure of the *Rose*. One is particularly reminded of a passage in which Jean reflects on the mutually defining properties of opposites and on the understanding of good that comes from knowing something of evil, concluding, "Ainsinc va des contreres choses, / les unes sunt des autres gloses." [Thus it goes with opposites: the ones are the gloss of the others (vv. 21543–44).] This passage (vv. 21533–52) appears in MS *Arr*, indicating that the compiler considered it an important element of the philosophy expounded in the *Rose*.

The representation of the archer God with his commandments in MS *Arr* does not imply an interpretation of the *Rose* as religious allegory. Rather, as in the *Pelerinage*, important imagery from the *Rose* is appropriated and invested with religious significance. Nor should the Ten Commandments sequence at the beginning of the codex be seen reductively as exclusively an adaptation of the *Rose*. But the *Rose* is nonetheless an important subtext for this striking image and for the opposing commandments, as it is for much else in the collection.

The excerpts from the *Rose* that appear towards the end of the manuscript reflect an interest in salvaging the moral and religious content of the poem while deleting the rest; the resulting text contains nothing incompatible with the devotional tone of Deguilleville's poem. The narrative framework of the *Rose* is completely lost; it is reduced to a series of didactic tirades, called "capitle" [chapters] and somewhat resembling *dits*. First comes an edited version of the discourse of Reason, combining Guillaume's Reason with that of Jean, and ending with a portion of Faux Samblant's sermon to Male Bouche; then edited versions of the discourses of Faux Samblant and Nature; and then a conglomeration of verses drawn mostly from the discourse of Ami and Genius.

The "Chapter of Reason" opens with an introductory passage drawn mostly from Guillaume de Lorris, expressing the Lover's amorous ills and representing the destructive passions that Reason will correct.[17] The adaptation of v. 1573 follows Deguilleville's implied reading of the Perilous Fountain as an image of visual concupiscence: "Qui en ce miroër se mire" [he who gazes into (or: sees himself in) this mirror] becomes "Ceux qui en fol regard se mire" [he who gazes into (sees himself in) foolish

---

[17] This passage consists of vv. 1573–82, 1605–12, 2589–94, 2949–54, 2939–41, an added line, and 4101–4.

glances (fol. 251r)]. The Lover's lamentation culminates in an expression of regret for his folly. Appropriately, it is at this point that Reason appears, first as portrayed in Guillaume (vv. 2955–3056) and then, with certain modifications, as represented by Jean.

The changes introduced in Jean's Reason as she appears in MS *Arr* pose no great surprise after the other remaniements we have seen. Passages containing or alluding to the word 'coilles" or "viz" have been deleted, as have virtually all references to pagan history, philosophy, or mythology. The allusion to homosexuality (vv. 4311–20) is also omitted. Once again, Reason's discourse has been censored in conformity with linguistic decorum and the ecclesiastical bias against the classical writers. In some cases, portions of deleted passages are retained for their general didactic value. For example, the story of Croesus and Phanie is absent, but Phanie's counsel to shun the honors of Fortune and pursue true nobility and generosity (most of vv. 6525–56) remains as part of Reason's words to the Lover. And while there is of course no trace of Reason's defense of seemingly bawdy language, her condemnation of quarrelsome and slanderous discourse, her statement that she would rather await God's judgment than exact her own vengeance for the Lover's accusations, and her praise of discretion remain (most of vv. 6957–7072). Given the context, it is a natural transition to the fourteen lines on discretion excerpted from Faux Samblant's sermon;[18] placing these lines here solves the problem of explaining their presence in the mouth of an incorrigible liar. The entire section is headed with the rubric, "Response de Raison contre rudes paroles et cetera" [Reason's response against rude words etc. (fol. 258v)]. Possibly this rubric is an allusion to Reason's encounter with Rude Understanding in the *Pelerinage*. There too, Reason had to defend herself; and there too she summoned Rude Understanding to appear before divine judgment rather than attempting to punish him herself.

Be that as it may, at least one fourteenth-century reader of Ms *Arr* was well aware of the charges brought against Reason in the *Rose*: at v. 7040, "Qui fole ribaude m'appelles" [you who call me a foolish bawd (fol. 259r)], is the gloss "Quia dixerat coullz" [because she had said "balls"]. We see here the same impulse to restore deleted passages, or at least to account for them, that is reflected in the added pages and marginal annotations of so many other *Rose* manuscripts. The gloss also shows that this reader, at least, did not peruse MS *Arr* in isolation, but rather brought to it a knowledge of the complete *Rose*. Such a reader would be well equipped to recognize the implicit transformations of the *Rose* in Deguilleville and elsewhere in the

---

[18] The lines in question are vv. 12149–50, 12153–58, 12187–90, 12247–78.

codex. As we have seen, it came naturally to medieval readers to approach the *Rose* as part of an intertextual network, in which numerous texts, both explicitly and implicitly present, could comment on one another. It is only to be expected that the *Rose* itself would, in turn, provide a backdrop against which other works could be read, and that a reader's prior experience with the *Rose* would inform his or her subsequent encounters with different versions of the text.

In addition to being de-paganized and freed of questionable vocabulary, Reason is brought into explicit accordance with Christian faith. MS *Arr* contains the long interpolation, characterized by Langlois as "litany of love," that appears in the *KMN* manuscripts (see Appendix c). This passage, in which Reason is explicitly an agent of grace and stepping-stone to mystical union with God, is certainly appropriate to MS *Arr*. And while the redactor of MS *Arr* cannot be credited with having composed the interpolation on mystical love, he did integrate its spiritual values into Reason's discourse. Jean's Reason advises the Lover to seek a middle ground between love and hate:

> l'en i puet bien trover moien,
> c'est l'amor que j'ain tant et prise,
> que je t'ai por amer aprise.
>
> (ed. Lecoy, vv. 5730–32)

One can certainly find a middle ground; that is the love that I so love and praise, that I have taught you to cultivate.

In MS *Arr*, Reason recommends not "le moien," but love of God and Christian charity. Here, vv. 5667–730 are deleted, and v. 5731 is preceded by four lines:

> Amour carnele ne fortune
> Ne dois tu prisier une prune.
> Mais aime Diex en verité,
> Et chascun par grand carité:
> C'est l'amour que j'aim tant et prise . . .   (fol. 256v)

You should not give a prune for carnal love or fortune, but love God truly, and love everyone in great charity: that is the love that I so love and esteem . . .

This advice echoes the Gospel, where Christian law is summed up in two commandments: to love God completely, and to love one's neighbor as oneself (Matthew 22:37–40).

The redactor of MS *Arr* was, however, mindful of Reason's limitations as well, as revealed in her interactions with Grace in the *Pelerinage*. Reason is an indispensable moral guide and agent of grace, and poses no obstacle to spiritual growth; it is Nature, not Reason, who brings charges against Grace and Sapience. We recall that in the first recension of the *Pelerinage* it is Reason who enables the pilgrim's soul to soar outside his body in a sort of literalized mystical ascent. But Reason is not an end in herself, nor is she divine, in spite of her ability to mediate between the divine and the human. The redactor of MS *Arr* accordingly abridged Reason's offer of herself as "amie," deleting vv. 5783–808. Excised in this way is Reason's characterization of herself as a maiden licensed to love, and her warning to the Lover that it is dangerous to spurn a maiden's advances, as shown by the example of Echo. The redactor may have felt, as Deguilleville apparently did when drafting his second recension of the *Pelerinage*, that such language undermines the dignity of a character such as Reason. But the deleted lines also include Reason's claim to be the daughter of God. Far from being undignified, this assertion, for a reader of the *Pelerinage*, is too exalted: Deguilleville clarifies that God's daughter is not Reason but Grace.

The "Chapter of Reason" is followed by excerpts from the discourse of Faux Samblant. Since the frame narrative has been abolished, no trace remains of Faux Samblant's alliance with the God of Love. His function is simply to speak about ecclesiastical corruption and clerical hypocrisy; to explain that true religion can be found in both clergy and laity; and to discuss mendicancy and labor. All references to Guillaume de Saint-Amour and the University of Paris are omitted, probably because these particulars were of little interest to an audience some hundred years removed from the events in question. As in Ms *Tou*, Faux Samblant's discourse is directly followed by the relevant portion of Jean's Apology (vv. 15221–36, 15239–60), in which Jean asserts that he is attacking not the clergy or religion but fraudulence and corruption. The placing of this passage clarifies the didactic force of the Faux Samblant section.

The description and discourse of Nature are also somewhat abridged. Her interaction with Genius remains, along with Genius' warning about revealing secrets to one's wife. As with the discourse of Reason, pagan references have been deleted from the discourse of Nature, and the argument has been somewhat streamlined; but its overall shape and subject matter remain the same. Nature discusses free will and destiny; dreams and mirrors; celestial signs; nobility; the sins of the human race; and even the nature of God and the Incarnation. The latter is already presented by Jean de Meun as something that Nature does not understand, and the redactor of MS *Arr* felt no need to alter this portion of the text in order to bring it into accordance with the *Pelerinage*. Nature's discourse fits well into Ms *Arr*, echoing many of the themes found in the excerpts from Boethius. Her friendship with Venus and Cupid, and her wish for procreation, are deleted. Still, her association with the body and with reproduction is inescapable, and at the end of her discourse, the redactor appended an eight-line defense of breastfeeding.

The discourses of Genius and Ami have undergone profound transformation. Needless to say, the redactor of MS *Arr* had little interest in Ovidian love teachings, and most such material is deleted. Most of the discourse of Genius is also missing, no doubt because of its overly erotic tenor and its questionable theology. What remains from these two portions of the *Rose* is combined, along with some passages from other parts of the poem, under the heading "Viel amy" ["Old Friend"]. This section begins with a discussion of the fall from the Golden Age, consisting of passages pieced together from Ami and Genius. This is followed by the passage on mutually defining opposites (vv. 21533–52), and then by lines from the beginning and the end of the discourse of Genius.

The lines following the passage on opposites do not relate directly to the topic of the Golden Age, but they do address the issue of virtue and vice in the world of nature. The redactor evidently saw the discourse on the decline of the Golden Age as a formulation of the problem of sin. He then added the passage about opposites as commentary on the question of good and evil, and incorporated the relevant portions of Genius' discourse by way of offering a solution. The description of Nature's divinely ordained role in managing the sublunary world (vv. 19475–96) is followed by a reminder of the need for students to listen to their teachers, taken from Guillaume de Lorris (vv. 2051–4), and by Genius' comment on the virtues of brevity (vv. 20603–4). The section closes with a slightly modified version of Genius' final exhortation to virtuous behavior (vv. 20605–18). The changes introduced here bring the sermon into line with Christian doctrine. First of all, Genius' claim to be offering a complete moral lesson – "tretout quan que vous devez fere" [everything that you should do (v. 20606)] – is prudently replaced by the more modest designation, "Un peu de ce que devés faire" [a little of what you should do (fol. 272v)]. Secondly, Genius' concern with the works of Nature – "Pensez de Nature honorer" [be sure to honor Nature (v. 20607)] – is replaced with a higher concern: "Pensés sur tout Dieu honnerer" [be sure above all to honor God (ibid.)]. And the redactor of MS *Arr* took care to insert an allusion to the importance of divine forgiveness, "Si aura Diex de vous pité" [thus God will have pity on you (ibid., replaces v. 20614)].

The "Chapter of the Old Friend" has a second part to it, headed with the rubric, "Des femes et de leur atour" [concerning women and their ornaments (fol. 272v)]. This section, a true pastiche, is largely drawn from the discourse of Ami, beginning with the material about feminine clothing in the discourse of the Jaloux, and moving on to a consideration of love and marriage. That portion of Jean's Apology addressed to women (vv. 15165–204) is placed between the diatribe on feminine beauty (portions of vv. 8856–9032) and the recommendation of equality in relations between the sexes (portions of vv. 9395–9445). But while this might imply an attenuation of the antifeminist tone of the *Rose*, plenty of antifeminist material follows. Much of it is from Ami (portions of vv. 8197–8214, 9383–86, and 9867–9949). However, we also find lines offering various perspectives on feminine greed and fickleness, extracted from Reason (vv. 4533–36) and La Vieille (vv. 14351–52, 14364–78), as well as from the *Dits et proverbes des sages*.[19] Towards the end, the rubric "De fol regard" [concerning foolish glances (fol. 274r)] introduces a scattering of lines from Genius on the dangers of the Perilous Fountain (vv. 20391–92, 20377–80, 20405–06) and a passage from Richesse on the dangers of erotic passion (vv. 10215–20).

The *Rose* excerpts thus begin and end with a meditation on the dangers of visual concupiscence and erotic desire. Along the way, numerous issues are addressed: vice and virtue, sin and salvation; erotic, material, and mystical love; ecclesiastical corruption; the nature of fortune, free will, and divine providence; the feminine character. The redactor of MS *Arr* knew the *Rose* extremely well, to judge from his ability to piece together thematically related passages from disparate parts of the poem. Like Deguilleville, whom he evidently admired, the redactor of MS *Arr* was impressed by the powerful poetry, the striking images, the range of topics found in the *Rose*. At the same time, also like Deguilleville, he must have been troubled by the presence in the *Rose* of frivolity, of pagan myths and legends, of moral ambiguity. Pleased with Deguilleville's solution – his thorough recasting of the *Rose* as a religious vision – the redactor prepared a splendidly illuminated manuscript of the *Pelerinage* cycle and related devotional texts. And into this he incorporated his own rewriting of the *Rose*, his own transposition of the allegorical, encyclopedic romance into a didactic treatise.

---

[19] As described in Chapter 2, stanzas from the *Dits et proverbes* appear in the margins of MS *Ke*, where it is unclear whether they are intended as gloss or as interpolation. Perhaps the redactor of MS *Arr* was working from a copy of the *Rose* that similarly had lines from the *Dits et proverbes* added, either in the margins or directly incorporated into the text. Nothing in Ms *Arr* indicates that the stanza from the *Dits et proverbes* is not part of the *Rose*; it is both preceded and followed by *Rose* material.

7

Poet of love and nature: Guillaume de Machaut and the *Rose*

Greffes avez, pansez d'escrire.[1]   (*Rose*, v. 19764)

In the preceding chapters we have seen several aspects of fourteenth-century *Rose* reception. The poem was read in monastic, clerical, and court circles. It was variously appreciated as romance, as art and critique of erotic love, as a mirror of human life; as a compendium of poetry and philosophy and as a source of imagery and of allegorical constructs. We have also seen that the *Rose* inspired an active participation on the part of its readers, giving rise to glossing and annotation, textual emendation and modification, interpolation and abridgment, extensive remaniement, and all-out recasting in the form of new texts that explicitly announce their origin in a reading of the *Rose*.

As a monastic writer, Deguilleville naturally approached the *Rose* from the perspective of its compatibility with Christian doctrine, and as a source of spiritually and morally edifying imagery. But the study of anthologies containing the *Rose*, of marginal annotations, and of remaniements shows that the poem was also read in other contexts and from other perspectives. In this chapter, we shall consider a medieval reading of the *Rose* as secular poetry about human love and desire. Guillaume de Machaut, one of the greatest French poets of the fourteenth century, does not cite the *Rose* by name as a source; but it is clear that he knew the poem well.[2] And while it is quite unlikely that Machaut would have viewed Deguilleville's spiritual reading of the *Rose* with either surprise or disapproval, his own interest as a poet working for aristocratic patrons was in the reading and writing of secular literature, devoted to the joys and sorrows of human love. Machaut

---

[1] "You have pens, remember to write."

[2] The *Rose* is briefly alluded to in the *Voir Dit*, but not as a source for the text. Toute Belle, praising Guillaume's letters, tells him that she likes what he writes so much that she would never tire of it even if it was as long as the *Rose* or the prose *Lancelot* (ed. Paris, p. 28). I cite from the following editions of Machaut's works: *Le Livre du voir dit*, ed. Paulin Paris; *Jugement du roy de Behaigne* | *Remede de Fortune*, ed. James I. Wimsatt and William W. Kibler; for all other texts, *Oeuvres*, ed. Ernest Hoepffner.

can be associated with an intellectualization of love poetry: for example, the conflation of amorous and Boethian discourse in the *Remede de Fortune*, and the creation of mythographic models of the love experience and the love poet.[3] The *Rose*, with its complex blend of Neoplatonic and Ovidian materials, its reflections on ancient and contemporary history, and its formulation of the vernacular love poet as heir to the Latin tradition, exerted a profound influence on Machaut.[4]

Viewing Machaut's reception of the *Rose* in the context of the *Rose* manuscript tradition is a twofold process. Not only can Machaut's transformations of the *Rose* material be compared to those effected by the authors of interpolations and remaniements, but he may also have been influenced by particular versions of the text. It is likely, in fact, that he had occasion to read the *Rose* in numerous manuscripts in the libraries of his various friends and patrons. It was not uncommon for wealthy aristocrats to own more than one copy of the poem. The library of Charles V, for example, had four copies of the *Rose* by 1373.[5] One of Machaut's patrons, Jean, duc de Berry, owned four copies of the *Rose* by the early fifteenth century,[6] and probably owned others at other times, since he not only commissioned books, but also gave and received them as gifts. Given the importance of the *Rose*, the number of copies in existence during Machaut's lifetime, and the apparent frequency with which different copies of the text were compared, it is a safe assumption that Machaut had seen more than one copy of the *Rose* and that he was aware of significant discrepancies, such as the presence or absence of major interpolations, among versions. It is likely, for example, that he knew widely disseminated passages from the *K*, *M*, and *N* manuscripts, such as Reason's disquisition on love as a

---

[3] Kelly, for example, states that "Machaut comes closer than any other courtly poet to the expression of *fin' amors* as idea. His love is in fact a sublimation," in *Medieval Imagination*, p. 122. Kelly's ensuing discussion of Machaut develops this point at greater length (pp. 121–54).

[4] Machaut's intimate knowledge of the *Rose* is clear from the numerous implicit allusions to that poem throughout Machaut's works. Palmer, for example, states that the *Jugement Behaigne* contains so many echoes of the *Rose* that it is as though "the reader is being challenged to read Machaut's work in reference to its illustrious predecessor," in "The Metafictional Machaut," p. 28. Brownlee argues that "Machaut viewed the *Rose* as embodying an entire poetic tradition, in whose context he sought authorization for his own artistic endeavor," in *Poetic Identity*, p. 20; in this regard see also Uitti, "From *Clerc* to *Poete*." Calin demonstrates the importance of the *Rose* as a source for Machaut's treatment of the first-person narrator figure in "Problèmes de technique narrative." Badel surveys Machaut's reception of the *Rose* in *"Roman de la Rose" au XIVe siècle*, pp. 82–94.

[5] See Léopold Delisle, "Librairie du Louvre – 1373–1424," *Cabinet des manuscrits*, vol. 3, pp. 114–70. All four *Rose* manuscripts (entries no. 1183–86) appear in the inventory of 1373.

[6] See Delisle, "Librairie du duc de Berry – 1402–1416," *Cabinet des manuscrits*, vol. 3, pp. 170–94. Delisle's no. 275 first appears in the inventory of 1402, and is tentatively identified by Langlois with Bibl. Nat. fr. 12595; his no. 276, now Bibl. Nat. fr. 380, is recorded as having entered the duke's library in 1403; and no. 146 and no. 277 first appear in the inventory of 1413. See Langlois, *Manuscrits*, pp. 5–6, 48–49, 201.

mystical experience; Genius' exhortation to remember Reason; the Medusa interpolation; and the *N* explicit heralding Nature's laughter at the moment of sexual union. Machaut's meditation on the different forms of love presented in the *Rose*, and on the figures of Reason, Nature, and Genius, would thus have been affected by the presence of these passages, whether or not he regarded them as the work of Jean de Meun. It is likely too that he had encountered the *B* text of the *Rose*, given its wide dissemination, and that he had therefore seen the Marsyas interpolation, with its implied association of the God of Love with Apollo, god of music and poetry.

The Marsyas interpolation sheds an interesting light on Machaut's poetic persona and its relationship to that of Jean de Meun. Apollo, the amorous god of poetry, is eminently suited both to the *Rose* and to Machaut's writings. Of the many tragic loves of Apollo recounted in the *Metamorphoses*, a striking number end with Apollo's one-time or would-be lover transformed into a tree, bush, or flower. Such is the fate of Daphne, Clytie, Leucothoë, Cyparissus, and Hyacinthus. As lover, Apollo is associated consistently with unrequited or thwarted desire, with the marking of absence and loss through the creation of leafing and flowering monuments. As poet-musician, he is associated with elevated and inspired verse. And in the *Rose* he is set up as analogous to the patron deity of love poetry. He is thus a most interesting model, both for the composite poetic "I" of the *Rose* and for Machaut, the learned poet and composer of love.[7]

The series of mythological exempla that runs throughout the *Rose*, particularly elaborate in texts that include the various interpolations, highlights the central conflict of love and intellect, posing a kind of riddle.[8] Can the young hero chart a path through this terrain populated by Perseus, Marsyas, Pygmalion – not to mention Narcissus, Adonis, and others? Where, amidst these figures of violence, despair, and folly, is the resolution, where the possibility for a legitimate and fruitful love, or for a learned and respectable love poetry? What sort of literary language and what sort of music are appropriate to the discourse of love? These questions, I submit, were ones in which Machaut was deeply interested. For him, the *Rose* provided a vernacular poetic model of supreme importance; and as he studied the *Rose* in various manuscripts, he could hardly have overlooked

---

[7] For an analogous discussion of the importance of Apollo in the works of Froissart, who was profoundly influenced by both Machaut and the *Rose*, see my "Daisy and the Laurel."

[8] Machaut could even have seen versions of the *Rose* containing both the Marsyas and the Medusa interpolations: both passages appear in manuscripts of the *J* family, as well as in MSS *Bâ*, *Bu*, *Bû*, *Bü*, *Bco*, and *Maz*.

passages, interpolated or otherwise, that contributed directly to the issues that concerned him.

ECHOES OF THE *ROSE* IN THE *FONTEINNE AMOUREUSE*

In the past critics have noted similarities between the *Rose* and the *Fonteinne amoureuse*: the motif of dreams that reveal the truth, the perilous fountain of love, the allusions to Narcissus and Pygmalion, the lover who cannot realize his desire without the help of a clerkly poet, even the names "Guillaume (de Machaut)" and "Jean (de Berry)" – if the commonly accepted solution to Machaut's anagram is indeed correct – attached to the two protagonists.[9] Nonetheless, the *Fonteinne amoureuse* differs from the *Rose* in many ways. It lacks, for example, the lengthy philosophical discourses, the satirical portrayal of marriage, the critique of ecclesiastical corruption, the emphasis on procreation, the erotic climax of the conclusion: in short, most of what we associate with Jean de Meun. Yet to say that the *Fonteinne amoureuse* is based on Guillaume's poem alone is not accurate either, since the *Fonteinne amoureuse* does allow for a resolution of the unhappy lover's frustrated desire.

In assessing the relationship of the *Fonteinne amoureuse* to Guillaume's *Rose*, however, we must be careful to consider just what Machaut may have thought the latter to consist of. Gui de Mori, it must be remembered, knew Guillaume's *Rose* as a poem with a happy ending: after protracted lamentations, the Lover is enabled to spend a night of pleasure with the Rose, and although the two are separated at daybreak, it is with the promise of many more such nights to come. It is true that Gui was writing in 1290, at a time when Jean's continuation was less widely disseminated. But the copyist of MS *Tou*, working in 1330, still saw fit to include the "original" ending of Guillaume's poem, together with Gui's hypothesis about Jean's reasons for replacing that ending with his own. The copyist of MS Bibl. Nat. Rothschild 2800 (MS *Eb*), working in 1329, also included the "original" ending of Guillaume's poem, complete with an illustration of the presentation of the Rose to the Lover; following this preliminary conclusion, he copied Jean's continuation, with the notation "Explicit primus / Incipit secundus" [the first (book) ends, the second one begins (fol. 29v)]. The anonymous conclusion is also found in four other manuscripts spanning the fourteenth century, and even appears in a fifteenth-century manuscript.[10] All but one of these manuscripts also

---

[9] See for example my *From Song to Book*, pp. 296–97; Brownlee, *Poetic Identity*, pp. 195, 198, 200–1; Looze, "Guillaume de Machaut and the Writerly Process"; Ehrhart, *The Judgment of the Trojan Prince Paris in Medieval Literature*, pp. 135–37.

[10] The anonymous conclusion of Guillaume de Lorris' *Rose* is printed by Langlois in his edition of the *Rose*, as a note to v. 4058.

contain Jean's continuation, indicating that the two versions of the poem were transmitted together, sporadically but repeatedly, throughout the period of Machaut's lifetime. It is thus not unreasonable to assume that Machaut could have known Guillaume's *Rose* as a "completed" poem with narrative resolution, existing side by side with Jean's recasting and expansion of the whole. He would of course also have seen Guillaume's portion of the *Rose* without its conclusion, no doubt far more frequently. But whether or not Machaut considered the shorter ending to be "original," his understanding of the *Rose* and his use of it in his own work could still have been affected by this version of Guillaume de Lorris.

If we assume that Machaut was familiar with Guillaume's *Rose* in its longer form, then the question of the relationship of the *Rose* to the *Fonteinne amoureuse* takes on a new light. In the *Fonteinne amoureuse*, the lady is escorted to her distraught lover – in a dream – by Venus; in the *Rose* conclusion, the Rose is smuggled out of the tower through the offices of a feminine "Bone Amor" and delivered to the Lover by Beauty. In the *Fonteinne amoureuse*, Venus states that the lady should be neither "couarde" [fearful (*FA*, v. 2179)] nor "honteuse" [ashamed (*FA*, v. 2181)], alluding thereby to two guardians of the Rose, Fear and Shame, the first of whom is cited in the anonymous conclusion. The lady of the *Fonteinne amoureuse* comforts her lover, embracing him and kissing him "plus de cent fois" [more than a hundred times (*FA*, v. 2497)]; Venus then spirits her away before he can awaken. In the *Rose* conclusion, the Lover and his Rose pass a night "A grant solaz, a grant deduit" [in great comfort, in great delight (ed. Langlois, note to line 4058, v. 49)]; at dawn, Beauty arrives to return the Rose to its tower. Both the Lover of the *Rose* and the aristocratic hero of the *Fonteinne amoureuse* are left feeling hopeful about the future: the former is assured that he will always be "dou boton maistre" [the master of the rosebud (ed. Langlois, v. 73)], while the latter is given a ruby ring that remains on his finger after he wakes up, proof of the veracity of his dream. In the *Fonteinne amoureuse*, finally, the parting of lover and lady is doubled in the parting, at the end of the poem, of the poet-narrator from his aristocratic patron. The poem closes on this note of separation, while simultaneously recalling the dream:

> Einsi parti. Je pris congié.
> Dites moy, fu ce bien songié? (*FA*, vv. 2847–48)

Thus he left. I bid farewell. Tell me, was that nicely dreamed?

The closing couplet echoes the closing lines of the *Rose* conclusion:

Atant m'en part en pren congié.
C'est li songes que j'ai songié.

(ed. Langlois, vv. 76–77)

At that I leave and bid farewell. This is the dream that I dreamed.

In its portrayal of the erotic dream and its final dénouement, then, the *Fonteinne amoureuse* more closely echoes the "long form" of Guillaume's *Rose* than that of Guillaume and Jean combined. Machaut may be revealing that, for all his admiration of Jean as a poet, his own rarefied courtly allegories are in many ways more closely allied with the delicate poem of Guillaume than with the digressive, satirical, and sometimes bawdy work of Jean. Even with its brief conclusion, moreover, Guillaume's *Rose* is still more open-ended than that of Jean, closing as it does on a note of hopeful separation rather than on one of total possession; and as such, it shows a closer affinity with Machaut's portrayal of love than does Jean's poem. Nonetheless, Machaut owes much to Jean's *Rose* as well. The fountain with its image of Narcissus, of course, most directly recalls Guillaume's perilous fountain of love. But the added information that the image of Narcissus was sculpted by Pygmalion makes this artifact a locus for the conflation of both Guillaume and Jean; and, as I have argued elsewhere, the very relationship of Pygmalion the artist and Narcissus, his amorous subject, recalls that of Jean de Meun and Guillaume de Lorris, as well as that of Machaut and his amorous patron.[11] The representation of the abduction of Helen, portrayed as inflamed by Venus' firebrand, echoes both interventions of Venus in the *Rose*: in Guillaume, her torch moves Bel Acueil to grant the Lover a kiss, while in Jean her burning arrow routs the guardians of the Rose and leaves the way clear for the Lover to pluck the Rose. The fountain itself, finally, is said to have been jointly sponsored by Venus, Jupiter, and Cupid, each of whom contributed certain materials for its construction and for the landscaping of the area. The location, we are told, was once the abode of Cupid and the amorous trysting place of Venus and Jupiter, who met there to enjoy "le deduit ou nature / Mist plus son entente et sa cure" [that delight in which Nature most places her attention and her concern (*FA*, vv. 1387–88)]. This emphasis on the sexual relations of Venus and Jupiter, closely associated with Cupid, recalls the latter's own reflections, in the *B* text of the *Rose*, on his begetting by Jupiter:

Mes bons peres, puis monta seur
Venus, tout fust ele sa seur,

---

[11] I have discussed Machaut's use of Narcissus and Pygmalion in the *Fonteinne* in *From Song to Book*, pp. 296–97.

> Et firent leur joliveté:
> De la vint ma nativité.
>
> (ed. Langlois, note to lines 10830–31, vv. 7–10)

My good father [Jupiter] then mounted Venus, even though she was his sister, and they took their pleasure. From that came my birth.

These lines always accompany the story of Marsyas, which, as we have seen, appears not only in *B* manuscripts, but in a number of others besides. Machaut could easily have known the passage. The description of the amorous fountain thus carries resonances, through shared mythological motifs, with the beginning, midpoint, and end of the conjoined *Rose* of Guillaume and Jean.

The Judgment of Paris is the principal mythological set-piece of the *Fonteinne amoureuse*, and others have noted its relevance to the poet-patron relationship on which the poem is structured.[12] The distinction of Juno's "tresors amassés" [piled-up treasures (*FA*, v. 2130)], Pallas' "scens" and "clergie" [wisdom and learning (*FA*, v. 2131)], and Venus' "chevalerie" [chivalry (*FA*, v. 2132)] contributes to the clear delineation of the roles of Machaut, the clerkly poet who labors the point of his own lack of chivalric prowess, and the unnamed lord, an amorous aristocrat of noble character. The *Fonteinne amoureuse* echoes the *Rose* in its portrayal of the debate before Paris. Pallas' statement that "richesse estoit vileinne" [wealth was ignoble (*FA*, v. 1758)] recalls the Lover's dismissal, at the end of the *Rose*, of "Richece la vileine" [ignoble Wealth (*Rose*, v. 21732)], while her attempts to win Paris over recall Reason's courtship of the Lover. Venus explains that she argued her supremacy on the basis of her power to conquer even the wisest and wealthiest of people, claiming that

> N'avoit si riche ne si sage,
>
> . . .
>
> Que ne li face, se je vueil,
> Son scens, sa richesse et son vueil
> Tout mettre en ma subjection.
>
> (*FA*, vv. 1794, 1797–99)

There was no one so rich or so wise . . . that I could not make him, if I wished, place his wisdom, his wealth, and his will entirely in my power.

These lines echo Reason's statement in the *Rose* (vv. 4305–10) that no one is sufficiently wise or of such noble lineage that he can resist the power of

---

[12] The Judgment of Paris in the *Fonteinne amoureuse* has been discussed by Calin, *A Poet at the Fountain*, pp. 146–66 *passim*, and "*La Fonteinne amoureuse* de Machaut," pp. 78–80; Ehrhart, *Judgment of the Trojan Prince Paris*, pp. 130–41; Brownlee, *Poetic Identity*, pp. 201–2; J. Cerquiglini, "*Un Engin si soutil*", pp. 124–25.

love. And Venus' statement that even the wise and the powerful will, for the sake of love, give up "Le scens, l'avoir, le corps, les ames" [wisdom, possessions, body, and soul (*FA*, v. 1841)] repeats Reason's warning that love deprives one of "sens, tens, chatel, cors, ame, los" [wisdom, time, belongings, body, soul, and reputation (*Rose*, v. 4598)]. Finally, the association of Venus with "l'estat de chevalerie" [the estate of chivalry (*FA*, v. 2132)] echoes Genius, who uses the term "chevalerie" to refer to the act of procreation (*Rose*, v. 19757).

In spite of Venus' professed ability to drive men mad, however, the lover of the *Fonteinne amoureuse* is greatly comforted after encountering her in a dream. He expresses a new-found lack of concern with Fortune, stating that "des dangiers de Fortune / Ne donroit jamais une prune" [he would never give a prune for the assaults of Fortune (*FA*, vv. 2735–36)]. His equanimity matches that which Reason, in the *Rose*, attributes to her own disciples: love me, she tells the Lover, "et ne priseras une prune / toute la roe de Fortune" [and you will not give a prune for the whole wheel of Fortune (*Rose*, vv. 5815–16)]. The model of the Judgment of Paris shows us that Wisdom and Love have at least this much in common: neither concerns itself with the pursuit of wealth and power; both are inclined to regard Richesse as *vilaine*.

In spite of the explicit attention to the Judgment of Paris, Machaut is representing something more complicated than the simple choice of love over wisdom or riches. He is, rather, exploring the possible alliance of love, the summation of aristocratic cultural values, with wisdom in the medium of learned poetry about love, written for an aristocratic audience.[13] There can be no doubt that the amorous fountain is presented as a locus of dangerous passion, determined by its associations with the lascivious sporting of Jupiter and Venus, with the desperate loves of Narcissus, Pygmalion, and Troilus, with the fall of Troy. It is clearly to be identified with the fountain in the Garden of Delight, not that in the Heavenly Park.[14] Yet we are shown that this encounter with the potentially damaging passions of eros need not prove fatal. Even after his fateful experience at the

---

[13] The conjoining of love and wisdom in the *Fonteinne* is noted by the various critics cited in note 12. Calin, for example, comments in *Poet at the Fountain* that "to the extent that the Lover and Narrator become friends and share (or exchange) traits, the two estates are brought into synthesis" (p. 151), and that, since the Lover is cast as a poet and singer, in the course of the narrative "he also becomes a master of *sapientia*, a devotee of Pallas as well as of Venus" (p. 165).

[14] Ehrhart points out in *Judgment of the Trojan Prince Paris* that Machaut makes a clever pun in portraying Jupiter as having supplied the gold from which the serpentine spouts in the fountain were made, since Jupiter is also the figure who corrupted the original Golden Age: as she suggests, it is ironically implied that "when he deprived the world of its golden age . . . he transmuted the 'gold' into this tempting fountain" (p. 137).

Perilous Fountain, the Lover of the *Rose* still has the option of fruitfully channeling or sublimating his passion. Likewise, the aristocratic lover of the *Fonteinne amoureuse* can – and actually does – bring his own despairing passions under control. Integral to this process is the collaboration of the clerk. It is he who gives written poetic shape to the nobleman's lamentations; apparently he who makes the wished-for dream possible; and certainly his presence in the dream – his unspoken question about the golden apple – that occasions the elaborate explication of the Judgment of Paris. The learning of the clerkly poet and the amorous desire of the nobleman are the two necessary elements of Machaut's allegorical *dit*.

The *Fonteinne amoureuse* offers a variation on the mise-en-scène of poetic election outlined in Machaut's *Prologue*, where the poet is endowed with *scens*, *rhetorique*, and *musique* in order to compose poetry and songs about love. On the one hand, the non-noble poet is peripheral to the rituals of love. The use of the term "chevalerie" to designate the service of Venus stresses that love cannot be separated from the fabric of aristocratic culture, which it informs and of which it is an expression. Yet by placing "chevalerie" in rhyme position with "clergie," Machaut suggests that the values and behavior patterns of aristocratic culture are not only differentiated from, but also complemented by, the intellectual culture of the educated class. It is in poetry that *chevalerie* and *clergie* meet. As Venus argues in the *Fonteinne amoureuse*, she holds sway over all of humankind: her sphere of influence subsumes the wealthy, the powerful, the learned.

Within the *Fonteinne amoureuse*, a model for the love poet is provided in the figures of Orpheus and Apollo, both of whom also appear in other of Machaut's works. Venus places Apollo and Orpheus together at the wedding banquet of Peleus and Thetis, describing them as playing a duet on harp and lyre. She also notes that Pan performed separately on the flute; this provides the occasion for a brief summary of the musical contest of Pan and Apollo and the ill-fated judgment of Midas. Orpheus, the bereaved lover whose song granted him a fleeting glimpse of Eurydice, but not a permanent reunion; Apollo, the poet-god who repeatedly must content himself with images of a lost beloved: these figures are perfectly appropriate to the *Fonteinne amoureuse*. Perhaps most fitting is the story sung by Orpheus about Apollo in the *Metamorphoses* (10:161–219): that of Hyacinthus, accidentally killed by Apollo and transformed into the hyacinth, whose leaves bear the written record of Apollo's lament, "Ai." Similarly, the lover of the *Fonteinne amoureuse* is separated from his lady and left with a written record of his lament. The figures of Apollo and Orpheus simultaneously reflect both the poet and the protagonist of the *Fonteinne amoureuse*, conjoined in a single poetic entity.

247

Machaut has an obvious source for the association of the judgment of Midas and the judgment of Paris, as well as the tale of Ceyx and Alcyone that figures so prominently in the *Fonteinne amoureuse*: although the judgment of Paris does not appear in the *Metamorphoses*, it does appear, along with the two other above-mentioned stories, in Book 11 of the *Ovide moralisé*. There, however, the two judgments are seen as parallel. According to the *Ovide moralisé* commentary, Midas makes the same decision as Paris, choosing the voluptuous over the spiritual or intellectual life. In the *Fonteinne amoureuse*, however, Venus clearly sides with Apollo against Midas, whom she calls "Midos li sos" [Midas the fool (*FA*, v. 1693)]. Machaut's source for this reversal is most likely the Marsyas passage in the *Rose*, where Cupid sided with Apollo. In other respects, Machaut has followed the *Metamorphoses* – or the *Ovide moralisé* – rather than the *Rose*. He restores Midas' identity as judge of Pan rather than Marsyas, and also correctly portrays Midas as judging against Apollo rather than for him. Nonetheless, the insertion of this story into a speech by Venus, and Venus' preference for Apollo, point to the *Rose* passage as an intertext for Machaut's treatment of the motif.

We have already seen that the allusion of the sexual escapades of Venus and Jupiter suggest Machaut's knowledge of the Marsyas interpolation. His treatment of the judgments of Midas and Paris supports this hypothesis. It is certainly not hard to imagine that Machaut, whose authorial self-consciousness as composer of love poetry and music is so elaborately expressed throughout his oeuvre, would be struck by an allusion in the *Rose* to the god of poetry and music and his victory over a lesser musician, especially given the close proximity of this passage to the important discussion of the *Rose* poets and their status as successors to the Latin poetic tradition. Moreover, if Machaut knew the Marsyas interpolation, then he probably knew the brief interpolation that usually accompanies it, in which the God of Love explains that Venus grieved more for Tibullus than for Adonis. In a version of the *Rose* containing these *B* interpolations, Machaut would have found clustered together the enunciation of a poetic tradition linking Latin and French poets; an elaboration on the distinction of lover and love poet, granting pre-eminence to the poet; the explanation of the collaboration between lover – also a poet – and poet – also a disciple of love – that resulted in the creation of one of the masterpieces of medieval French literature; a story about the artistic supremacy of Apollo; and the God of Love's professed enmity with Juno, with Richesse, with Reason.

From this rich configuration Machaut drew the germ of his own poem about the relationship between lover and love poet, in which the former produces a poem and dreams a dream, but relies on the latter to write it down and shape it into a text. He also drew on the major mythological exempla from the beginning and end of the *Rose* respectively, the stories of Narcissus and Pygmalion; and he combined these in such a way as to reiterate the collaboration of artist and lover. From Book 11 of the *Ovide moralisé*, in turn, he drew material for the expansion of the motifs of dream, as both work of art and prophetic revelation; of poetry and music; of the conflicting and complementary values of wealth, wisdom, and love. And for the overall narrative framework, he adapted the "long form" of Guillaume de Lorris, a version of the *Rose* that strikes a balance between the uncertainty and despair of Guillaume's own conclusion, and the finality and climactic fulfillment of Jean's: a version ultimately more suited to Machaut's own preoccupation with the relief of erotic desire through the mediation of artifice, of imagination, of pleasurable thoughts, hopes, and memories.

THE RECONCILIATION OF LOVE AND REASON IN THE *REMEDE DE FORTUNE*

Machaut's interest in the conjoining of love and wisdom as a means of combating the assaults of Fortune did not begin with the *Fonteinne amoureuse*. A similar thematics can be found in the *Remede de Fortune*, composed perhaps twenty years earlier. Here Machaut presents his youthful self, very much in the guise of the Lover of the *Rose*: victim of *jeunesse, folie, enfance*, and *oiseuse*. Having matured to the point of being able to explain himself to his lady, the hero of the *Remede* sums up his failings in these words:

> J'estoie joines et petis,
> Nices, enfés, et enfantis,
> Nus de sens et plains d'ignossence,
> D'assez petite congnoissance,
> D'estre en oyseuse coustumiers.   (*RF*, vv. 3573–77)

I was young and immature, a kid, foolish and childish, devoid of wisdom and full of innocence, of little knowledge, accustomed to idleness.

This list of epithets recalls Reason's chastisements of the Lover of the *Rose*. Guillaume's Reason attributes the Lover's problems to "folie et enfance" [folly and childishness (*Rose*, v. 2982)] and to the influence of Oiseuse [Idleness (vv. 2987–94)]; in Jean de Meun, she criticizes his "povre connoissance" [poor knowledge (*Rose*, v. 4232)] of love and lectures him on the dangerous follies of youth. From this we might guess that the

Remede de Fortune outlines an alternative to the *Rose*: the means by which a young man can continue to serve love without succumbing to the follies that the *Rose* so graphically represents.

Somewhat like the Lover of the *Rose*, Machaut's young hero reveals his love to his lady – or fails to prevent her from seeing it – and then, covered with confusion, retreats and indulges in lengthy poetic lamentations. He receives consolation and instruction about love and fortune, as well as about love poetry, from Hope. Thus armed, he is able to return to the lady's castle and establish a relationship with her, albeit a nebulous one. In its broad outlines, then, the narrative structure resembles that of the conjoined *Rose*: love initially problematical, an unsuccessful encounter with the lady, lamentation, consolation and instruction, a fresh approach to the lady that is considerably more successful. Machaut introduces many variations, however, and ultimately presents a different view of love. He shows that the obstacles to success in love are entirely located within the Lover: it is his own fear, his own inappropriate desire, his own confusion and immaturity, that cause his despair and the ensuing rupture between him and his lady. The lady of the *Remede* does nothing to prevent her admirer from approaching her, talking to her, even entering her castle. As long as the lover tailors his desire and expectations to fit the circumstances, Bel Acueil will not be replaced by Dangier.

The restraining of desire did not come easily to the Lover of the *Rose*, surely one of the most single-minded of all literary heroes. Such, however, was the advice of Reason, spurned by the Lover. Machaut suggests, in effect, what sort of love – and love poetry – might be possible if the Lover did take Reason's advice, while still remaining a disciple of love.[15] The figure that Machaut introduces as the avatar of his new, rational love is Hope. Her discourse, as others have shown, draws on both Jean's Reason and Boethius' Philosophy.[16] Hope warns against attachment to the goods of fortune, and explains that erotic desire is the source of misery in love. Of those who find love painful and arduous, she states:

> Je ne puis ymaginer
> Qu'il aiment sans decevance
> Et qu'en euls trop ne s'avance

---

[15] In *Poet at the Fountain*, Calin points out that Boethius' Philosophy and Jean's Reason are major sources for Machaut's Hope (pp. 57–58), and argues that in the *Remede de Fortune*, "Machaut attempts to resolve conflicts exposed in *Le Roman de la Rose* between the Boethian and courtly philosophies" (p. 61). See also Kelly's discussion of the *Remede de Fortune* in *Medieval Imagination*, pp. 130–37.

[16] In addition to Calin and Kelly, cited in note 15, the relationship between the *Remede de Fortune* and the *Consolation of Philosophy* is also discussed by Brownlee, *Poetic Identity*, pp. 45–46, 50–52, and was first analyzed by Hoepffner in the Introduction to his edition of Machaut's *Oeuvres*, vol. 2, pp. xix–xxx.

> Desirs. Pour ce sont ainssi,
> Qu'il l'ont deservi.   (*RF*, vv. 2016–20)

I cannot imagine that they love without deceit, and that Desire has not taken them over; they suffer so because they deserve it.

In words that echo those of Reason in one recension of the *B* text, Hope comments on the blindness of Love's followers: "Mais Amour qui maint cuer aveugle / D'eus et de cuer te fist aveugle" [but Love, who blinds many a heart, made you blind in eyes and in heart (*RF*, vv. 2711–12; cf. Appendix B, 2, A:13–14)]. Also like Reason, however, Hope insists that she is not against love:

> Je ne vueil mie que tu penses
> Que d'amer te face desfances;
> Ains vueil et te pri chierement
> Que tu aimmes tres loyaument.   (*RF*, vv. 2797–800)

I certainly don't want you to think that I forbid you to love; in fact, I want and warmly urge that you love very loyally.

These lines recall Reason's similar statement of acceptance for loyal, sincere lovers: "Ne cuides pas que jes dessemble: / je veille bien qu'il aillent ensemble" [don't think that I want to separate them: I do want them to come together (*Rose*, vv. 4559–60)].

Reason, however, does not really follow up on her professed sympathy for lovers. She acknowledges procreation as a legitimate motivation for sexual love, but does not pursue the topic. Instead, she argues for asexual friendship and the love of wisdom. In this respect Machaut's Hope differs from Jean's Reason; her attitude recalls the acceptance of "pure" love expressed by the Reason of MS *Mor*. Hope proposes a love that is heterosexual and in some sense erotic. The *joie*, the sweet thoughts, the *plaisance* of which she speaks and sings have little to do with Ciceronian friendship; these derive from the courtly lyric tradition. At times, Hope's advice about love even echoes that of Ami, as she instructs her young charge on the proper means of addressing a lady and cites the value of tears as indices of sincerity. Her advice differs from that of Ami, of course, in that Hope is concerned with explaining the differences between true lovers and false ones, interested only in sexual fulfillment. Ami's tactic of describing the external signs of a true lover so that his young friend can better simulate sincerity, like his other suggestions about techniques of seduction, is quite foreign to Hope. Still, in a curious manner, Hope is a conflation of Jean's Reason and Ami. She preaches against material attachment and lascivious desire; and she explains how to establish a satisfactory relationship with the beloved lady.

Hope even compares herself to Nature. She describes the effects of sunlight on the earth in a lengthy evocation of the proliferation of growth and color that takes place in springtime: Nature decks the earth in a "robe nouvelle / De la couleur d'une pantere" [new gown, the color of a panther (*RF*, vv. 2208–09)], and there is no root that does not burst forth in "Fleur, fruit, fueilles, graine ou verdure" [flower, fruit, leaves, grain or greenery (*RF*, v. 2216)]. Similarly, says Hope, she herself illuminates lovers, giving them "Joye, plaisance en leur amour" [joy and pleasure in their love (*RF*, v. 2240)], and lights up their hearts such that "dedens leur cuer d'amours germe / Fleur, fueille, fruit, et nouvel germe" [in their hearts, there germinates from love flower, leaf, fruit, and new growth (*RF*, vv. 2245–46)]. Hope thus appropriates the language of natural growth and fecundity, but applies it entirely to the affective experience of love: it is not procreation, but optimistic cheerfulness that she fosters. The pleasure of which she speaks results from *dous pensers*, not from sexual contact.

In this way, Hope short-circuits Genius' promises of heavenly bliss as a reward for sexual activity. Under her guidance, the lover can participate in the works of Nature without actually having sex, experiencing love as a sort of inner garden of spiritual delight. Just as the inhabitants of the Heavenly Park sing "motez, conduiz et chançonnetes" [motets, conductus and little songs (*Rose*, v. 20627)], so Hope teaches her followers to sing graceful, optimistic songs of love. At the same time, of course, Hope is a refiguration of Boethius' Philosophy, who also sings songs to her pupil, refreshes his spirits, and teaches him not only about Fortune, but also about the love that governs the cosmos. Philosophy's remarks in Book 2, Meter 8 and Book 4, Meter 6 are especially relevant to Hope's discourse about natural cycles of death and rebirth, darkness and light. Machaut is a careful reader of Jean's transformations of Boethian material in the *Rose*. Jean first effected the fusion of Philosophy and Nature – of the divine love that moves the spheres of heaven and regulates the elements, with the natural urge to procreation – and presented this as the framework within which human erotic desire takes place. Machaut reworks this delicate nexus, reinfusing the vision of love with the spirit of courtly lyricism, and shifting the emphasis from natural procreation to cosmic harmony. One is reminded again of Gui de Mori's work as preserved in MS *Mor*, where we find a Reason who, while preaching Christian charity, also approves of love as celebrated in *bel chant amoureux*; and a God of Love who echoes Reason in arguing that love should be a process of ongoing service, characterized by affection and respect and in no way subjugated to the desire for sexual gratification as an end in itself. There is no evidence that Machaut knew

Gui's remaniement; but like Gui, he was clearly fascinated by the synthesis of amorous and intellectual traditions in the *Rose*.

Hope's effects on the unhappy lover resemble Philosophy's illumination of her troubled protégé. Boethius states that at Philosophy's touch, "me discussa liquerunt nocte tenebrae / Luminibusque prior rediit uigor" [night was over, the darkness left me and my eyes regained their former vigor (Book 1, Meter 3)]; he invokes the image of storm clouds blotting out the sky, then dispelled by winds, and states, "Haud aliter tristitiae nebulis dissolutis hausi caelum" [similarly, with the clouds of sorrow dispersed, I gazed upon the heavens (Book 1, Prose 3)]. Similarly, Machaut tells us that Hope shone so resplendently that she dispersed the "tenebres" and the "nuit obscure" [shadows and dark night (*RF*, v. 1521)] of his sorrow, and "de son ray perchoit la nue" [with her ray pierced the cloud (*RF*, v. 1523)] that had troubled his heart. The light issuing from Hope is compared to the medicine used for cataracts which, when applied to the eye, "li rent sa clarté premiere" [restores its original brightness (*RF*, v. 1539)]: the sight of Hope "me rendoit lumiere / De cuer, de memoire, et de l'ueil" [restored to me the light of heart, memory, and eyesight (*RF*, vv. 1540–41)]. At the same time, however – given the strong presence of the *Rose* in the *Remede de Fortune* – Machaut's description recalls Genius' account of the Fountain of Life. We recall that those who gaze into this fountain gain self-knowledge and enlightenment. And Genius describes the carbuncle in the fountain, whose light cannot be dimmed: "ne ses rais ne peut desvoier / ne vanz ne pluie ne nublece" [nor can its rays be blocked by wind, rain, or clouds (*Rose*, vv. 20504–5)]. Furthermore, Genius asserts that the light of the heavenly carbuncle is so pure that, far from blinding those who gaze into it, it acts to restore their vision, "et revigourer leur veüe / par sa bele clarté veüe [and to reinvigorate their sight with its beautiful visible brightness (*Rose*, vv. 20555–56)]. Finally, Genius notes the scent of the heavenly light, "qui par merveilleuse valeur / tout le parc d'oudeur replenist / par la grant douceur qui en ist" [which by marvellous vigor fills the entire park with odor, through the great sweetness that issues from it (*Rose*, vv. 20558–60)]. Hope is similarly aromatic:

> Et aussi venoit une oudour
> De sa douçour tant precieuse
> . . .
> Si que li pourpris ou j'estoie
> En estoit plains . . .
>
> (*RF*, vv. 1544–45, 1553–54)

And also there came forth an odor of her most precious sweetness . . . such that the area where I was, was filled with it.

Genius' Heavenly Park, itself a recasting of the erotic Garden of Delight with its bewitching images and alluring Rose, is recast once again in Machaut's Hope, in whom Reason, Nature, and Love are fused: a vernacularization of Boethius' Philosophy, as seen through the refracting lens of the *Rose*.

The result of this carefully constructed allegorical personification is a figure that is at once amatory, sensual, worldly, fructifying; and intellectual, detached from the fluctuations of Fortune, free of erotic passion. Hope encourages her pupil to cultivate his devotion to the lady he has chosen, herself a focal point of ethical and aesthetic values: it is from her that the young lover learns to appreciate wisdom, courtesy, and beauty. This devotion is quite remote from the overt eroticism of the *Rose*. It bears fruit in the form of inner joy, courteous behavior, and, of course, the composition and performance of poetry and music. Again, poetry is the medium in which beauty, love, and intellect come together: in his creative act, the poet simultaneously serves Nature, Love, Reason, and his lady. Machaut thus draws on Genius to create a vision in which love and virtue are integrated, in which desire is transfigured; at the same time, he divests this vision of its erotic orientation.

Machaut's recasting of the "work of Nature" and of the discourse of Genius is of great importance; its ramifications reach beyond any individual *dit*, touching on his concept of himself as love poet. We will explore this topic below, in a reading of two of Machaut's last compositions: the *Voir Dit*, a work in many ways related to the *Remede de Fortune*, and the *Prologue*. But before leaving the *Remede*, let us first look briefly at a prose treatise that appears in a fifteenth-century manuscript of the *Remede* (Pepys Library, Magdalene College, Cambridge, MS 1594) and which sheds some light on a medieval reading of Machaut's poem.[17]

The treatise in the Pepys manuscript is untitled and anonymous. There is certainly no reason to think that Machaut might have written it, or that he had read it. But it does raise certain issues reminiscent of his works, and its inclusion in the manuscript suggests that it was seen by at least one fifteenth-century reader as relevant to the *Remede de Fortune*, the main – and only other – text in the codex. The treatise begins, interestingly enough, with an allusion to *De arrha animae*:

---

[17] The Pepys manuscript is briefly described by Wimsatt and Kibler in the Introduction to their edition of the *Jugement du roy de Behaigne and Remede de Fortune*, p. 44. I am grateful to Professors Wimsatt and Kibler for generously loaning me their microfilm of the Pepys manuscript.

Hughe de Saint Victor dit ou livre que l'en appelle *Arraste* pour ce que nulz ne puet vivre senz amour; et que amour est la vie de l'ame. Et vraiement il dit voir, quar amours est la vie de l'aime, le confort du cuer, la plaisance et le delit du corps.

(fol. 38r)

Hugh of Saint Victor says in the book that is called *De arrha animae* that no one can live without love; and that love is the life of the soul. And truly he speaks the truth, for love is the life of the soul, the comfort of the heart, the pleasure and the delight of the body.

The opening reference to *De arrha animae*, followed by the rapid descent from spiritual love to physical pleasure, recalls Gui's prologue to the *Rose*. One cannot help wondering if the author of "Hughe de Saint Victor" could have known Gui's *remaniement*. There is no conclusive evidence for this, but the possibility certainly cannot be ruled out.

"Hughe de Saint Victor" goes on to establish three kings of love: "une mercheande, une villainne, et une loyal, bonne, et certainne" [one mercantile, one villainous, and one loyal, good, and certain (ibid.)]. The first two are dealt with fairly quickly: neither false love for the sake of material gain nor lustful passion is worthy of much discussion. The third variety, corresponding to what is sometimes called "courtly love," is treated at some length:

Or est ainsi que je pense a parler de la bonne amour qui doit en nous regner. Et celle-ci ne faut ne a vie ne a mort. C'est quant le cuer gentil qui tant est noble et franc par douce amour est pris. (fol. 38v–39r)

Now it's time for me to talk about the good love that should reign in us. And this one never falters in life or death. It is when the gentle heart that is so noble and frank is captured by sweet love.

The qualities of this love are what we have come to expect from love treatises in the tradition of Andreas Capellanus. Love is blind to social class, making it appropriate for a man to fall in love with a lady who would not otherwise be considered his social equal; love must be free and unconstrained, and hence operates independently of the institution of marriage. The lover swears to love, serve, and obey his lady, pledging heart, body, and soul.

This all sounds quite conventional, but the text does hold another surprise for us: he who pursues this "good love" is named "Adventereus d'amours" [Adventurer in Love], and he is aided by "un escuier secré qui moult l'aimme, qui Raison est nommez" [a secret squire who greatly loves him, named Reason (fol. 39r)]. At some point since we last saw her in the *Rose*, it seems, Reason has entered the service of Love. It is she who interrogates Adventurer in Love, quizzing him on such matters as social class and marriage; and she approves heartily of his answers. The treatise closes with her warm wishes for the Adventurer's success:

Par foy, sire, ce dit Raisons, vous estes sages sur tous. Et si n'arez plux a non fors li Bieneureuz d'amours. Alez par tout ou vous vouldrez, quar vous arez bien a planté. Et je pri Amours qui vous gart, et vous en doint tréz bone part.

(fol. 44r)

By faith, sir, says Reason, you are wise above all others. And thus you will have no other name any more except Fortunate in Love. Go wherever you want to, for you will have good aplenty. And I pray Love that he guard you, and that he grant you good fortune.

This curious little treatise sets up a tripartite division of love that corresponds more or less to that outlined by Reason in the *Rose*, particularly as reorganized by Gui: love as human affection, love as carnal desire, and love as material greed. The Reason who counsels Adventurer in Love, approving his optimistic spirit and whole-hearted devotion, is kin both to Machaut's Hope and to the Reason of the *Rose*; she is particularly close to the Reason of MS *Mor*. We can neither prove nor disprove the tantalizing possibility that the treatise was written by someone who had read a redaction of Gui de Mori: – perhaps someone who perceived affinities between Gui's Reason and Machaut's Hope, and composed the text as a response to the *Remede*. But the fifteenth-century scribe or patron responsible for the Pepys manuscript must in any case have seen "Hughe de Saint Victor" as a humorous follow-up to the *Remede de Fortune*, in which the teachings of Reason are made to harmonize with an art of love.

RELIVING THE *ROSE*: ALLEGORY AND IRONY IN THE *VOIR DIT*

In the *Voir Dit* Machaut continues to draw on the *Rose* as a source of imagery for the love experience. Allusions to the *Rose* heighten the eroticism of the love story; at the same time, the use of a sacralizing language suggests an attempt to infuse the love relationship with a deeper meaning. But there always remains an ironic disjunction between the experience that is being portrayed and the character of its participants, and the language and literary models with which it is evoked. Guillaume, Machaut's persona in the *Voir Dit*, casts his love in terms of both sacred and erotic allegory, as myth, as chivalric romance; in the end, these models are proved to be effective only in the imaginative space of the literary work. The *Voir Dit* offers a critique, both humorous and enlightening, of the conflicting poetic registers operating in the *Rose*.

The tendency to transfigure the love relationship is initiated at the

beginning of the story, when Guillaume, delighted at having received
Toute Belle's first rondeau, declares:

> Or faisons une trinité
> Et une amiable unité;
> Que ce soit uns corps & une ame,
> D'Amours, de moy & de ma dame.
>
> (ed. Paris, vv. 252–55)

Now let us make up a trinity and a loving union; may it be one body and one
soul, consisting of Love, myself, and my lady.

The rhyme pair *trinité*/*unité* unmistakably points to the triune God of
Christianity; these rhymes appear, for example, in Nature's discussion of
the Trinity in the *Rose* (vv. 19111–12). No sooner does the love affair begin,
in other words, than the possibility arises of its allegorization: the
configuration of the wise poet, the wilful and strangely powerful lady, and
the love that binds them reflects the conjoining of divine wisdom, power
and love. The allegory never quite comes into focus, but the impulse to
recast the love for Toute Belle in sacred terms informs the rhetoric of both
the narrative and the letters. Toute Belle is capable of performing "belles
miracles" [beautiful miracles (*VD*, v. 814)]; indeed her curative powers
surpass those of the saints, for "onques nul miracle ne vi / Si grant com d'un
amant ravi" [never did I see a miracle as great as that of a ravished lover
(*VD*, vv. 819–20)]. She is described in terms evocative of the Virgin: she is
the carbuncle, the diamond that bestows grace, the ruby that cures all ills,
the pole star (*VD*, vv. 95–106).[18] The initial list of Toute Belle's attributes
culminates in an image that perfectly unites the registers of erotic and
sacred allegory: 'Briefment, c'est la rose vermeille / Qui n'a seconde ne
pareille" [in short, she is the red rose, unique and without peer (*VD*, vv.
107–8)].

As the amorous correspondence gets under way, the interplay of sacred
and erotic registers and the appropriation of literary models continues. In
the tenth letter in Paulin Paris's edition, Guillaume assures Toute Belle that
he will love and serve her forever, not only in the chivalric manner of
romance heroes such as Lancelot and Tristan, but also as a deity: "&
aourray comme Dieu terrien & comme la plus precieuse & glorieuse
relique que je véysse onques en lieu où je fuisse" [and I will worship (you)
as an earthly god, and as the most precious and glorious relic that I ever saw
anywhere (*VD*, p. 68)]. The sacred and chivalric dimensions of the love
relationship are equally present in Guillaume's promise, a few lines later, to

---

[18] J. Cerquiglini comments on the use of imagery associated with the Virgin Mary in the descriptions of
Toute Belle, in *"Un Engin si soutil"*, pp. 80–82.

visit Toute Belle by Pentecost. Pentecost, starting point of so many Arthurian adventures, will provide the time frame for the initiation of Guillaume's amorous quest; at the same time, the meeting will be a holy visitation, a descent of poetic inspiration, a loosening of the tongue – or at least of the pen – in preparation for the poetic undertaking to follow.

Let us consider the dense clustering of highly charged terminology and literary allusions in this letter. Lancelot and Tristan, to begin with, are ambiguous models at best. Both loved with an unwavering and whole-hearted devotion, it is true; and both were paragons of chivalry. Both compensated for the absence of the beloved lady through art: Tristan by composing and performing *lais*, Lancelot by writing and painting the story of his love for Guinevere on the walls of his chamber.[19] As a pair, Tristan and Lancelot thus reflect both Guillaume's poetico-musical activity on behalf of Toute Belle, and his fascination with her portrait, enshrined at his bedside. Nonetheless, Tristan and Lancelot are not exactly wholly positive models, for both were involved in adulterous love affairs that brought dishonour on both themselves and their ladies, and ultimately brought about serious disruption of the social order; and however one may wish to interpret the moral tone of the prose romances from which Machaut would have known these stories, it must at the very least be agreed that love is shown to have fierce and powerful enemies, and that these enemies can sometimes get the upper hand. A similar ambiguity clings to the third example mentioned along with Tristan and Lancelot in one of Guillaume's earlier letters (ed. Paris, no. 2): the love of Paris for Helen, the disastrous consequences of which are all too well known. As Jacqueline Cerquiglini has shown in such detail, the *Voir Dit* is, on one level, the story of the clerk who would be a knight; by associating himself with Paris, in particular, Guillaume blurs the distinction, so carefully drawn in the *Fonteinne amoureuse* through the very example of the Judgment of Paris, between chivalric lovers and clerkly love poets.[20] In his eagerness to cast himself as

[19] Lancelot's murals, accompanied by written captions, are described in *Le Livre de Lancelot del Lac*, part 3, ed. Sommer, p. 217–18; and *La Mort le roi Artu*, ed. Frappier, pp. 61, 64. In Thomas's version of the *Roman de Tristan*, Tristan compensates for Iseut's absence during his marriage to Iseut aux Blanches Mains by making statues of Iseut and Brangain that are so lifelike that they can scarcely be distinguished from the real thing. But this episode does not appear in the prose *Tristan*, which was most likely Machaut's source for the story. The prose *Tristan* does, however, contain a number of Tristan's *lais* as lyric insertions.

[20] See J. Cerquiglini, *"Un Engin si soutil"*, pp. 107–38. The failure of the poet's attempt to cast himself as a noble lover is also discussed by Poirion, *Poète et le prince*, and is an important theme in Brownlee's detailed analysis of the *Voir Dit* in *Poetic Identity*, pp. 94–156. In *Poet at the Fountain*, Calin notes Guillaume's "inability to conform to Arthurian romance in a post-Jean de Meun world" (p. 181). In a *complainte*, Guillaume claims that Toute Belle affords a resolution of the Judgment of Paris conflict by subsuming the attributes of the three rival goddesses and transcending all of them: Venus, Juno, and Pallas, he says, will serve her (*VD*, vv. 5867–71).

the hero of a romance, Guillaume ignores the problematical aspects of his literary models. One might well say that he has little understanding of what he is in for, of the potential obstacles and dangers inherent in the experience of passionate love and its commemoration in art and verse.

Moving from knightly models to the promise to worship Toute Belle as god and relic, Guillaume attempts to transpose this chivalric model into a sacred register. Yet here too, the undercurrents of his words work against the overt message. Not only is the precise meaning of "earthly god" somewhat unclear; but the various meanings of the term "relics" are, shall we say, all too clear. The word does have undeniable significance in the context of religious worship; but in the context of love poetry, it has a rather different sense, one illustrated nowhere more vividly than in the *Rose*. In fact, Guillaume's letter clearly echoes the Lover's final approach to the Rose, cast in terms of a great desire to "aourer / le biau saintuaire honourable" [worship the beautiful, honorable sanctuary (*Rose*, vv. 21562–63)] and to approach the "relics" contained therein.

The Lover's conquest of the Rose is also described rather elaborately as a pilgrimage; and so is Guillaume's approach to Toute Belle. The pretext for the lovers' first meeting is Toute Belle's presence in an area to which Guillaume can go on pilgrimage; and the space of sacred devotion quickly becomes a context for amorous devotion as well:

> Si alay à l'église: mais
> Tantost com le piet mis dedens,
> Je fis un veu entre mes dens,
> Que tant comme laiens seroie,
> Tous les jours de nouvel feroie,
> Pour l'amour de ma dame douce. (*VD*, vv. 1514–19)

Thus I went to the church; but as soon as I set foot inside, I made a vow under my breath that as long as I was there, I would compose new poetry every day for the love of my sweet lady.

The ballade that follows duly reiterates Guillaume's veneration of Toute Belle: "Mon Dieu terrien est & fu & sera" [she is, always was, and will continue to be my earthly god (*VD*, v. 1546)]. At a later point, the two lovers actually meet in a church, where the Mass provides the occasion for a surreptitious kiss:

> Mais trop richement m'echéy,
> Que quant on dist: *Agnus dei*,
> Foy que je doy à saint Crapais,
> Doucement me donna la pais,
> Entre .ii. pilers du moustier. (*VD*, vv. 2663–67)

But what happened to me was truly wonderful: at the *Agnus dei*, by the faith of Saint Crapais, she sweetly gave me the kiss of peace, between two pillars of the church.

In this brief image, Machaut truly outdoes himself. For in this Holy Mass that is really an amorous tryst, we can recognize the conclusion of the *Rose*, as Guillaume replays the Lover's worshipful approach to the erotic sanctuary. In the detail that the kiss – at once chaste and erotic, contributing to both religious ritual and seduction – took place "entre .ii. pilers," Machaut links this moment to that in the *Rose* when the Lover, an eager pilgrim, kneels down "entre les .ii. biaus pilerez" [between the two beautiful pillars (*Rose*, v. 21559)] that support the "sanctuary." As the elements of the scene take on their allegorical significance, we even begin to wonder about the Mass itself – could Genius be the priest officiating? Is the *Agnus dei* not the figure designated by Genius as the one who will lead Love's followers into the Heavenly Park?

Allusions to the *Rose* in fact characterize Guillaume's every meeting with his lady. When he sees Toute Belle for the first time, he finds her wearing a hood embroidered with a design of parakeets – a distant echo of the Garden of Delight filled with birds, and even of the God of Love himself, described in the initial encounter as "toz covers d'oisiaus" [completely covered with birds (*Rose*, v. 899)]. And later, seated in a lush garden, he gazes longingly at Toute Belle's lips as she sleeps in his lap; the secretary, covering her lips with a leaf, tempts Guillaume to kiss the leaf, then removes it as the trembling lover bends down. Awakening, Toute Belle teasingly accuses her lover of being "outrageus" [overly bold (*VD*, v. 2289)]. In the red lips partially covered by the leaf, one cannot help seeing the *rose vermeille*, itself surrounded by leaves. And in the ruse employed to bring about the lovers' first kiss, one is reminded that Bel Aceuil's first gift to the Lover was in fact a leaf, plucked from beside the rosebud; and that it was upon receiving this leaf that the Lover was emboldened to ask for the Rose itself, a request that frightened Bel Acueil and resulted in the first appearance of Dangier. Nonetheless, it was not long thereafter that the Lover managed to kiss the Rose. Machaut has conflated the two episodes of leaf and kiss, heightening the erotic tension of the scene.

Who would have thought that Machaut, generally credited with a non-erotic representation of love, would have drawn on precisely the most erotic, and even the most audacious, moments in the *Rose*? Who would imagine that this aging would-be lover, shy and fumbling, might be modeled on the young and virile character who holds nothing back in his repeated attempts on the Rose? Yet it is so. Let us consider another important passage in the *Voir Dit*, the arrival of Toute Belle's portrait. One obvious source for this scene is the Pygmalion episode in the *Rose*, as will be discussed below. Aside from its associations with the Pygmalion story, the scene in which Guillaume receives the portrait acquires a highly charged eroticism from its echoes of the closing section of the *Rose*. The very word *ymage* recalls the final avatar of the lady in the *Rose*, the feminine image supported by the infamous two pillars, at whom Venus fires her burning arrow, and whose chief function appears to be as a vehicle for the erotic "sanctuary":

> Cil pilerez d'argent estoient,
> mout gent, et d'argent soutenoient
> une ymage en leu de chaasse
> . . .
> mes plus oulanz que pome d'ambre
> avoit dedanz un saintuaire,
> couvert d'un precieus suaire.
>
> (*Rose*, vv. 20767–69, 20776–78)

These pillars were of silver, very lovely, and they supported a silver image used as a reliquary . . . but more aromatic than an apple of amber was the sanctuary within, covered with a precious cloth.

It is this figure that occasions the digression about Pygmalion. The "ymage" recurs as the Lover approaches the "relics"; and this passage is an important intertext for the portrait scene. First, Guillaume unwraps the portrait:

> Je pris cest ymage jolie,
> Qui trop bien fu entortillie
> Des cuevrechiés ma douce amour,
> Si la desliay sans demour. (*VD*, vv. 1358–61)

I took that pretty image, which was thoroughly wrapped with the kerchiefs of my sweet love; so I untied it without delay.

The Lover of the *Rose* similarly unveils the object of his desire:

> Trés an sus un po la courtine
> qui les reliques ancourtine;
> de l'ymage lors m'apressai
> que du saintuaire pres sai. (*Rose*, vv. 21569–72)

I lifted the curtain a little, that shielded the relics; then I approached the image, drawing near to the sanctuary.

Guillaume then renders homage to the portrait, "A genous & à jointes mains" [on bended knee and with clasped hands (*VD*, vv. 1368)]; the

Lover of the *Rose* similarly tells us that "m'agenoilli san demourer" [I got down on my knees without delay (*Rose*, vv. 21561)]. Just as the Lover of the *Rose* adopts a worshipful attitude toward the image and relics before him, so Guillaume vows to adore his image "Com ma souveraine déesse" [as my sovereign goddess (*VD*, vv. 1376)]. And Jean's Lover expresses his desire "au reliques touchier" [to touch the relics (*Rose*, vv. 21555)]; Guillaume places the precious portrait beside his bed, "Pour li véoir & atouchier, / A mon lever & au couchier" [to see and touch it upon rising and upon going to bed (*VD*, vv. 1390–91)]. It is clear on even a first reading of the *Voir Dit* that Guillaume's religious veneration of the portrait is decidedly and comically idolatrous; a reading of the passage in tandem with the *Rose* brings out the covert eroticism of the scene, preparing for the amorous pilgrimage to follow.

The centrality of the portrait in the *Voir Dit* has obvious parallels with the story of Pygmalion. Guillaume, like Pygmalion – especially Jean's Pygmalion – dresses and ornaments his image: "Je la vesti, je la paray" (*VD*, v. 1392). At a much later point, he describes a dream in which the image speaks to him, and at the end of which he expresses amazement at the idea of a talking image, which he knows can only have been an illusion. We recall that it was when his image spoke that Jean's Pygmalion knew she was truly alive. Similarly, Guillaume's dream of a talking portrait marks the extent to which his image has taken on a life of its own, to such an extent that it now complains of having been punished for Toute Belle's offences – as if the portrait was somehow utterly independent of the person it supposedly represents. The portrait indeed displaces Toute Belle from Guillaume's life: his relationship is less and less with Toute Belle herself, more and more with her image in portrait, letters, and songs.

A similar series of allusions to the closing section of the *Rose* marks the culminating episode in the erotic dalliance of Guillaume and Toute Belle, the encounter in the scented cloud of Venus. The occasion is, once again, a pilgrimage, arranged expressly so that the lovers can be together. When it is time to separate, Guillaume goes to the room where Toute Belle is sleeping, and opens a small window ("fenestrelle," *VD*, v. 3674). Already the alert reader may recall the "archiere" of the *Rose*: that small opening, at once architectural and anatomical, at which Venus aimed her arrow and into which the Lover, with some effort, inserted his staff. True to his model, Guillaume then unveils the opening: "Si tiray un po la cortine" [then I pulled aside the curtain a little (*VD*, v. 3676; cf. *Rose*, v. 21569)]. Like the Rose, which is accompanied by Bel Acueil, Toute Belle is not alone; she is accompanied by the "pucellette" who, Machaut reminds us, had previously been gathering flowers in the garden: "Qui, el vergier vert & feuilli, / Les fleurs dou chapelet cueilli" [who, in the green and leafy garden, gathered flowers for a garland (*VD*, vv. 3680–81)]. This seemingly gratuitous comment, remarkably enough, enables Machaut to introduce a crucial rhyme pair that occurs both at the end of the *Rose* and at the midpoint, in the God of Love's prophetic citation of the end:

> jusqu'a tant qu'il avra coillie
> seur la branche vert et foillie
> la tres bele rose vermeille   (*Rose*, vv. 10569–71)

until he will have gathered the beautiful red rose on the green and leafy branch;

and

> par grant joliveté cueilli
> la fleur du biau rosier fueilli.
> Ainsint oi la rose vermeille.   (*Rose*, vv. 21747–49)

With great joy I gathered the blossom of the beautiful leafy rosebush. Thus I had the red rose.

The double association of this rhyme pair with the climax of dream and poem alike greatly strengthens its power to evoke the moment of erotic and poetic consummation. This, coupled with a repeated insistence on Toute Belle's red lips – in which "vermeille," then "vermillette" appear in rhyme position (*VD*, vv. 3704, 3707) – unmistakably identifies Guillaume's encounter with Toute Belle as a living out of the allegory of the *Rose*. Even the time of day is appropriate: daybreak, at the moment of waking.

It is at this point that, like the Lover of the *Rose*, Guillaume gets down on his knees (*VD*, v. 3709; *Rose*, v. 21561). His purpose is to deliver a prayer to Venus; and here he takes on aspects of Pygmalion, praying to Venus that she help him consummate his love for the statue. The cloud is hailed, three times in rapid succession – Guillaume is an excitable narrator – as a "miracle," further recalling the vivification of Pygmalion's statue, described by Jean de Meun as "miracles apertes" [manifest miracle (*Rose*, v. 21130)]. Its perfumed aroma in turn recalls the odor of the Rose that infused the Lover on the occasion of the kiss; while its darkness, assuring that "riens goute n'i véoit" [nothing whatsoever could be seen (*VD*, v. 3793)], is a distant echo of the Lover's much more lascivious allusion to the usefulness of his staff for feeling about "es fosses ou je ne voi goute" [in ditches where I can see nothing (*Rose*, v. 21372)]. On the surface, it is unclear just what takes place inside the cloud; indeed, one cannot help suspecting that Guillaume may have concentrated chiefly on the composition of a *virelai*.[21] But the subtext of the *Rose* – the gathering of the bud, Pygmalion's consummated desires – imbues the scene with a subtle but pronounced eroticism; if we are not shown precisely what Guillaume and Toute Belle do, at least we are reminded of what he would like to think they are doing.

Guillaume's repeated insistence on the "miracle si apertes" [such a manifest miracle (*VD*, v. 712)] of his resuscitation as a result of Toute Belle's attentions likewise recalls the central event in the story of Pygmalion. Yet here we encounter a curious reversal, since in the *Voir Dit* it is not the woman but the man who is miraculously given life; and this reversal alerts us to the complex network of mythological allusions that Machaut has created.

In some versions of the *Rose*, the story of Pygmalion is not the only place that a "miracle" occurs. The Medusa interpolation – located, we recall, immediately preceding the Pygmalion story, and occasioned by the same motif of the tower "ymage" – opens with an allusion to miraculous power:

> Tel ymage n'ot mais en tour;
> Plus avient miracle entour
> Qu'onc n'avint entour Medusa.
> (ed. Langlois, note to vv. 20810–11: vv. 1–3)

No tower ever had such an image; more miracles take place around it than ever took place around Medusa.

The "miracles" effected by the feminine tower image are, specifically, the restoration of life to those who have been turned to stone, the resuscitation of the dead, and the restoration of sanity, or "droit sen" (v. 44). These curative transformations are remarkably similar to those that Guillaume ascribes to Toute Belle. As he states it in an early letter (ed. Paris, no. 4):

Je estoie assourdis, arrudis, mus, impotens, par quoy joie m'avoit de tous poins guerpi & mis en oubli; mais vos douces escriptures me font oÿr & parler, venir & aler, & m'ont rendu joie.
(p. 41)

I was deaf, rough, mute, impotent, whereby joy had completely abandoned and forgotten me; but your sweet writings make me hear and speak, come and go, and have restored my joy.

From Guillaume's description of his previous state, one might well say that he had, metaphorically, been turned to stone, and that he had lost his

---

[21] In *From Song to Book*, I argue that Machaut portrays Guillaume as having occupied himself within the scented cloud of Venus by composing a *virelai* (pp. 285–86). Calin, following a different line of argument, shows that Machaut strongly implies that Guillaume did not actually consummate his relationship with Toute Belle; see *Poet at the Fountain*, pp. 190–91.

senses. His repeated claims that Toute Belle "resuscitated" him similarly echo the assertion in the Medusa interpolation, with regard to the tower image, that "ceste resouscite" [this one resuscitates (ed. Langlois, v. 36)]. The language with which Guillaume describes his malady and cure further recalls the characterization of works of art in the *Rose*. Jean stresses the immobility and muteness of art, stating that no art works could ever "par eus aler, / vivre, mouvoir, santir, paler" [go by themselves, live, move, feel, speak (*Rose*, vv. 16034–35)]. And Pygmalion reflects sadly that "J'aime une ymage sourde et mue, / qui ne se crole ne se mue" [I love a deaf and mute image that neither shifts nor moves (*Rose*, vv. 20821–22)].

The deafness, muteness, and immobility with which Guillaume characterizes his life before Toute Belle, and the ability to hear, speak, and move about that he has gained from corresponding with her, thus have roots in both of the mythological exempla tied to the appearance of the "ymage" in the *Rose*. The dangers associated with these myths also invade Guillaume's life. At a later, less idyllic stage of the affair, as Guillaume pours forth poetry and songs for a distant and curiously unresponsive Toute Belle, he begins to resemble Pygmalion, singing and dancing for his lifeless statue; or again, as Toute Belle's behavior finally reduces Guillaume to silence and stasis, making him afraid to visit her and unable to write, there is a suggestion of the effect of Medusa on those who behold her.[22] In all cases Toute Belle is the agent of miraculous or lethal power, Guillaume the recipient. Through her he acquires once again a poetic voice, an ear for music; the joyous disposition needed for the pursuit of his craft; the energy to launch himself into an imagined knightly adventure in which human love will take on a sacred aura, or, in turn, to embark on a pilgrimage that he hopes to infuse with eroticism. Through her he is reduced to despair, the fate of so many literary lovers.

Insofar as Toute Belle's acquaintance has given Guillaume a new life, we may say that this life is itself a revival, an incarnation, of literary models, and in that sense, a bringing to life of art. At the same time, it is through the ultimate failure of these models – the resolutely non-allegorical nature of his pilgrimage, the non-mythic status of the portrait he adores – that Guillaume is forced finally to abandon his amorous and heroic pretentions. In his role as the image of Machaut the poet, Guillaume is supremely successful at transposing life into art; but in his role as lover, he has finally proved incapable of transposing art into life. He is, in fact, no Pygmalion;

---

22 Indeed, Guillaume is sometimes reduced to silence and immobility by Toute Belle's presence as well. For reflections on the possible analogies between Toute Belle and Medusa, see Leupin, "The Powerlessness of Writing," pp. 144–46.

Toute Belle is no saint sent by Heaven. When near the end of the book he receives a visitor, it is no Genius, fresh from the tearful confession of Nature herself, armed with an extravagant vision of the sanctity of erotic love: no, it is only an ordinary human priest, confessor of Toute Belle, bearing a reproachful letter soaked in her tears. The priest does deliver a flowery sermon complete with an elaborately worked-out allegory that responds, point by point, to Guillaume's own earlier poem; its purpose, however, is not to empower Guillaume to perpetuate the species, but rather to remind him of his failings. Indeed, the priest chides Guillaume for having "maniere de fame" [a feminine manner (*VD*, v. 8743)], as though he were one of the *escoilliez* who, according to Genius, have "meurs femenins" [feminine traits (*Rose*, v. 20030)]. In the end the literary models that Guillaume had hoped to live out have turned against him.

We have seen that earlier, there was a decisive dissociation of Toute Belle herself from the portrait that inspires Guillaume and haunts his dreams. By the end of the book, the disjunction between life and art has become even greater. As people in the "real world," Guillaume and Toute Belle can continue an affectionate exchange of poems and letters. But the allegorical and mythical dimensions of their love, the miracles, the erotic encounters within scented clouds, the sacred and secret love of the romance knight and lady: all of this is recognized to be a literary construct, viable only in the space of the book. It is part of the genius of the *Voir Dit* – and a principal reason why so many readers, at least since Paulin Paris, have ascribed to it an autobiographical veracity – that it contains within itself this distinction between the real event and its literary recasting. The very failure of the story to adhere to its literary models seems to confirm its truth. Is it not a marvel when a fictional character can be forced to abandon his pretentions to literariness?

In this strange work written near the end of his career, Machaut plays with and undercuts literary language at the same time that he demonstrates its power to create an enduring work of fiction. Jean de Meun had already created a text in which allegory is taken to an extreme, indeed allowed to run wild. He gave us an amorous hero who fancies that the entire divinely ordained natural order somehow depends on the success of his own erotic foray, who manages to seduce and even impregnate a metaphor, and who conceives of his sexual conquest as a replay of Hercules' conquest of Cacus. While writing a type of poetry that is in many ways very different from the *Rose*, Machaut nonetheless learned a great deal from his study of Jean's poetic strategies, which he appropriated, suitably transformed, into his own frequently humorous poetry.

But is the *Voir Dit* a purely comic work, does Machaut draw on the *Rose* only for ironic purposes? What of the representation of an edifying love, free of sexual passion, in the *Remede*? The attempt to experience human love as an allegory for divine love, in effect to live out the Song of Songs, might even be seen as a noble effort; certainly it makes for interesting poetry. Part of Guillaume's problem is that he does not seem to know whether the allegory in which he casts himself should be the Song of Songs or the *Romance of the Rose*: will he have erotic adventures with a spiritual significance, or spiritual adventures with an erotic significance? His ambivalence can be traced back to that moment in the *Rose* where erotic and sacred registers are most problematically juxtaposed: the discourse of Genius, which medieval readers alternatively saw as serious moral teaching – surely not without some appreciation of its humor as well – or as sacrilege. As attentive a reader, as great a poet as Machaut must have been aware of these different possibilities, and may even have felt himself torn between them. Let us then turn to an examination of Machaut's relationship to Jean's enigmatic priest of Nature.

WRITER OF LOVE AND NATURE: MACHAUT AND GENIUS

Machaut's reception of Genius was twofold. On the one hand, Genius can be seen as the final poet figure in the *Rose*.[23] He reads, and rewrites, Guillaume de Lorris' allegory; more generally, he stands for the very process of writing as the supreme creative act. In his praise of procreation, Genius elaborates an extended metaphor of fruitful sexual coupling as an act of writing; at the same time, as priest of Nature, he engages in a form of writing himself that sustains – one might say "underwrites" – the great chain of being. In this respect Genius is a potent model for the figure of the writer, and for writing as a creative process that mediates between the sacred and the erotic. Yet this last point also accounts for what is problematic in Genius: his vision of an absolute concordance of the natural and the divine, his strange equation of sexual fulfillment and spiritual salvation. Here I will first examine Machaut's use of Genius as a writer figure, and then turn to his treatment of love as a meeting ground for the sacred, the natural, the erotic.

Machaut most explicitly presents himself as poet in the *Prologue* that appears in the later manuscripts of his collected works, and the stance that he adopts is in many ways related to the figure of Genius in the *Rose*. He portrays himself, first, as specially selected by Nature to compose love

---

[23] See Brownlee, "Jean de Meun and the Limits of Romance."

poetry: the opening rubric explains that Nature wished to "reveler et faire essaucier les biens et honneurs qui sont en Amours" [reveal and exalt the benefits and honours that are in Love (ed. Hoepffner, *Pr.*, p. 1)], while in the opening *ballade*, Nature expressly commands Guillaume to make "Nouviaus dis amoureus plaisans" [pleasant new love poems (*Pr.*, v. 5)]. Nature explains that she who presided over Machaut's birth has endowed him with special skills: intellect, rhetoric, and music. In this respect, Machaut casts himself in the guise of Genius, also sent as Nature's emissary to address the amorous: "Alez, amis, au dieu d'Amors / porter mes plainz et mes clamors" [go, friend; bear my plaint and my lamentation to the God of Love (*Rose*, vv. 19339–40)].

In the second pair of *ballades*, Machaut portrays himself as receiving subject matter from the God of Love. It is noteworthy that Cupid's participation here is not to inflame the poet with amorous desire, as at the beginning of Ovid's *Amores*, but rather to provide him with hopeful and pleasant thoughts: as the rubric states, "pour lui donner matere a faire ce que Nature li a enchargié" [to give him material to do what Nature commanded (*Pr.*, pp. 3–4)]. Machaut claims to write under the dual auspices of Nature and Love, but by no means necessarily as a lover in his own right. Similarly, Jean's Genius is welcomed by the God of Love and crowned as a bishop: his sermon is partially authorized by Cupid. Of course the relationship of Genius to Nature or Cupid cannot be exactly the same as that of a human poet; and Machaut also models his persona on that of Jean de Meun. The scene of poetic election is based in part on the midpoint passage of the *Rose*, where Jean's birth is assured by Lucina, a Natura figure, and his poetic inspiration provided by the God of Love. But by having Nature take the initiative in his own formation as a poet, Machaut reverses Jean's priorities and strengthens the parallel between himself and Genius.

An important aspect of Machaut's strategy in placing Nature as the highest authority behind his poetic and musical compositions is the implied analogy between natural and artistic creation. The first three *ballades* make repeated use of the words *fourmer* (and its derivatives *enfourmer, confourmer*), *ordener*, and *faire* to refer alternately to the creation and endowment of Machaut the poet, and to Machaut's own literary and musical creativity.[24] Poetry and music participate actively in formative processes fundamental to the natural order. Indeed, by operating in the service of both Nature and Love, "rhetorique" and "musique" provide an interface between natural

---

[24] I have noted Machaut's emphasis on form and order in natural and creative processes in *From Song to Book*, p. 237. See also Lukitsch, "The Poetics of the 'Prologue'."

creative processes and the affective realm of desire. Through poetry and music, as Machaut elaborates in the remainder of the *Prologue*, dark passions are tamed, spirits raised; desire is intellectualized, sublimated; love bears fruit in the form of poetic and musical composition.

The association of love with the creation of poetry and song, if particularly powerful in the works of Machaut, is nothing new in the Old French tradition. But although Machaut could have had any number of sources for this idea, I would argue that the figure of Genius in the *Rose* is one of the most important. Writing is fundamental to Genius' identity. In both the *Rose* and *De planctu Naturae*, it is he who inscribes the ever-changing natural world in a mysterious book:

> en audience recordait
> les figures representables
> de toutes choses corrumpables
> qu'il ot escrites en son livre,
> si con Nature les li livre.   (*Rose*, vv. 16250–54)

In [Nature's] presence he recorded the presentations of all corruptible things, which he had written in his book, as Nature transmitted them to him.

The natural world, then, is a metaphorical book, written by Genius in collaboration with Nature. Genius also assumes the role of scribe in recording Nature's message for Love's troops: "Lors escrit cil, et cele dite" [then he wrote and she dictated (*Rose*, v. 19376)]. When Nature asks Genius to communicate to the followers of Love the rules written in her book (*Rose*, v. 19354), we must assume that the book in question is that metaphorical record of natural creation and procreation; and that the rules cover both the avoidance of sin and the imperative to increase and multiply. Finally, it is in his address to the Love's barons that Genius elaborates his extended metaphor of the phallus as pen, the female body as tablets. To engage in the act of procreation is to participate in writing the great book of nature. Machaut has appropriated this metaphor and literalized it: he participates in the work of nature by writing actual books – and Machaut makes it clear that he is the writer, involved in book production – explicitly about the "rules" and effects of love.[25]

Machaut also addresses the divine nature of music in his *Prologue*, commenting that this "science" is not only an important aspect of the divine offices, but is even practiced in Heaven, by "li angles, / Li saint, les

---

[25] I have discussed Machaut's self-presentation as writer and author of books, as opposed to singer or simple maker of poems, in *From Song to Book*, pp. 232–38, 242–301. As I show there, writing is fundamental to Machaut's concept of himself as a poet, especially by the time he wrote the *Voir Dit* or the *Prologue*.

saintes, les archangles" [the angels, the male and female saints, the archangels (*Pr.*, vv. 115–16)]. The poet-musician thus not only participates in the work of Nature, but also imitates that of the angels. Music can soothe the spirits of humans and of God alike: it spreads joy, comforts the sorrowful, and was used by David to appease the wrath of God. Machaut attributes miraculous, resuscitative powers to music, asserting that Orpheus – identified as a *poetes* (*Pr.*, v. 138) – removed Eurydice from Hell, "Par sa harpe et par son dous chant" [with his harp and his sweet singing (*Pr.*, v. 137)]. Machaut does not mention Orpheus' ultimate failure. By focusing exclusively on the moment of Orpheus' triumph, Machaut exalts poetry and music to the level of "miracles apertes" [manifest miracle (*Pr.*, v. 145)]. What is more, he presents the amorous poet-musician in the image of Christ as Harrower of Hell – a standard interpretation of Orpheus in the medieval mythographic tradition – and leaves out those parts of the story that would make Orpheus a figure for human depravity. For Machaut, poetry and music are not only the interface between Eros and Nature, but also between Eros, Nature, and God.

This three-way mediation between the sacred, the natural, and the erotic is fundamental to the figure of Genius. As priest of Nature, Genius presides over the joining of soul and body – the collaboration of God and Nature – in the moment of conception. In *De planctu Naturae*, he chastises those who have veered too far in the direction of erotic pleasure for its own sake, recalling them to the rightful purpose for which sex was intended. Natural procreation does provide the matrix within which sexual activity can be legitimized and even blessed by the sacrament of marriage. Nonetheless, the balance is always a delicate one, since excessive erotic desire violates the marriage sacrament and can, if pursued for its own sake, equally violate the principle of procreation; procreation in itself does not legitimize fornication; and nothing can ever sanctify sexuality to the point where it equals chastity. The very act whereby a new soul is conjoined to a new body also constitutes the transmission of Original Sin.

It is this last point that is conveniently overlooked in the *Rose*, not by Jean himself but by his characters. For Genius, procreation is sufficient to sanctify sexuality in an absolute sense, allowing for the transposition of erotic love from the Garden of Delight – a figure for desire, for the postponement of sexual consummation, hence for death – to the Heavenly Park, a figure for the fulfillment of desire and for eternal life. Machaut recasts the three-way meeting of the sacred, the natural, and the erotic through a transformation of the elaborate metaphoric construct. Procreation – the realization of natural creativity – is replaced by poetic creation, in a literalization of Genius' exhortation, "greffes avez, pansez d'escrire" [you have pens, remember to write (*Rose*, v. 19763)]. It is thus through the power of poetry that eros can be sanctified: that a language can be forged capable of mediating directly between the registers of nature, eros, and divinity – indeed, capable of expressing any one in terms of any other. We saw that in the *Remede* it is the intellectualization of love as respectful and non-erotic adoration, as the impetus to virtuous behavior, and ultimately as poetic inspiration, that transports the lover from lamentation to joyous tranquility: a transformation that parallels the move from Garden of Delight to Heavenly Park.

The *Voir Dit* is in many ways a rewriting of the *Remede*. In both poems Machaut portrays himself as an anxious lover plagued by uncertainty, who learns – or attempts to learn – that his love can survive and flourish only when it is free of erotic desire; in both his persona composes lyric poetry, including a lament about Fortune; in both he receives instruction about the nature of love; in both he encounters the personification of Hope. In both poems Machaut draws on the *Rose* as a source for the narrative setting, and in both cases his persona is modeled to a certain extent on the Lover of the *Rose*. In the *Voir Dit*, however, Machaut treats his persona with a greater degree of irony: it is now an ailing cleric in his sixties who emulates the twenty-year-old hero – himself a comic figure – of an erotic allegory. Moreover, Machaut's portrayal of Guillaume suggests that the latter does not fully grasp the literary conventions that he wishes to enact. Guillaume, filled with a longing that he can name only as "desir," hopefully and even obsessively writes, embarks on pilgrimages, thinks about relics, dresses up an image; he expectantly watches for miracles, declares himself "resuscitated"; he attempts to inscribe his love for Toute Belle in the context of sacred devotion, earthly paradise, eternity. In the end, he experiences everything except the one thing he wanted, the one thing that all of these activities are meant to be figures for: a fully consummated sexual relationship. It is as though the proliferation of metaphors in the *Rose* has clouded his understanding of what is really at stake. The sexual desire that spurs him on blocks any possibility of a true sacralization of his love for Toute Belle; his inability to decode the allegory prevents him from experiencing true erotic fulfillment.[26]

But if the bedazzled Guillaume is ultimately caught in the intricate web

---

[26] For a discussion of Chaucer's somewhat similar treatment of the *Rose* and the conventions of courtly poetry as an obstacle to sexual fulfillment, see Wetherbee, *Chaucer and the Poets*, pp. 53–86. Commenting on *Troilus* and the *Rose*, Wetherbee states: "In both cases a combination of genuine innocence, sexual timidity, and the deceptive euphemisms of courtly rhetoric creates a barrier, verbal and psychological, that prevents any open acknowledgment of the physical realities of the quest" (p. 69). This important insight is equally applicable to the *Voir Dit*.

of metaphor, Machaut the poet has succeeded in orchestrating a poetic *tour de force* that rivals the *Rose* itself. Both the power and the limitations of poetic language are masterfully demonstrated in the *Voir Dit*. Poetry cannot transform erotic love into divine Grace – cannot, to return to the language of the *Rose*, turn genitals into sacred relics, or relics into genitals, simply by a transfer of names. Machaut's ironic use of the *Rose* in the *Voir Dit* shows that he appreciated the comedy and the audacity of Jean's erotic allegory, his brilliant distortions of such authors as Boethius and Alain de Lille, his merciless lampooning of the pretentions of courtly diction. At the same time, the very success of such an enterprise, the real force of the satire, is bound up in the fact that, in a different sense, poetry *can* transform the erotic into the sacred, through the power of allegory. In confronting these complex poetic and philosophical issues, Machaut offers no easy solutions. Commenting on the *Remede* and the *Voir Dit*, Calin notes that "while seemingly proclaiming communication, community, success, and the process of writing, Machaut also makes a place for noncommunication, solitude, failure, and the process of reading," and that in these poems "love and art are more complex, more ambivalent than they first appear."[27] But in the *Voir Dit*, as in the *Remede de Fortune* and the *Prologue*, Machaut affirms the potency of writing and interpretation, of poetic discourse, to create a literary space for the interplay and mutual glossing of the many registers – sacred and erotic, chivalric and clerkly, mythic and historic – of language and experience.

[27] Calin, "Medieval Intertextuality," p. 8.

8

Sacred and erotic love: The visual gloss of MS Bibl. Nat. fr. 25526

> Il chantoient un chant autel
> con fussent angre esperitel;
> . . .
> ainz le peüst l'en aesmer
> au chanz des seraines de mer.
>
> (*Rose*, vv. 661–62, 669–70)[1]

Conflicting signals creating a sense of vacillation between sacred and erotic registers are present from the very beginning of Guillaume's *Rose*. Immediately upon entering the garden, the dreamer feels himself to be in "paradis terrestre" [earthly paradise (v. 634)], declaring that "tant estoit li leus delitables, / qu'i sembloit estre esperitables" [so delightful was the place, that it seemed spiritual (vv. 635–36)]. Yet this seeming equation of sensual pleasure with spirituality is swiftly undercut with the odd statement that "il ne fet en nul paradis / si bon estre com il fessoit / el vergier" [there is no paradise where it is as good to be as in the garden (vv. 638–40)]. One cannot help feeling that the narrator may be saying more than he realizes: if the Garden of Delight is so pleasurable that it cannot even be compared to Heaven, perhaps that is because, quite simply, it is not Heavenly. The pattern of spiritual comparisons and undercuttings continues in the description of the birds, compared within less than ten lines to both "spiritual angels" and "sirens of the sea" (vv. 661–62, 669–70); and culminates in the comparison of Cupid, a pagan deity and the embodiment of erotic desire, to a heavenly being: "Il sembloit que ce fust uns angres / qui fust tot droit venuz dou ciel" [it seemed that he was an angel that had just come from heaven (vv. 902–3)]. And of course this conflation and contrast of the spiritual and erotic is brilliantly exploited by Jean de Meun, most notably in the discourse of Genius and the concluding episode of the poem.

---

[1] "They [the birds in the Garden of Delight] sang such a song that it was as though they were spiritual angels; [. . .] thus one could compare it to the song of the sirens of the sea."

As we have seen in the preceding chapters, this aspect of the *Rose* was clearly perceived, if not always clearly understood or appreciated, by medieval readers. Some attacked it or edited it out of their copies of the poem; others expanded on it. Gui de Mori introduced an allusion to Hugh of Saint Victor's *De arrha animae*; both he and the author of the "litany of love" inserted discussions of divine love and mystical union with God. Deguilleville transformed the erotic quest of the *Rose* into a spiritual pilgrimage; Machaut borrowed the poem's spiritual metaphors, exploiting them for their erotic overtones and ironic humor. For all their very real differences, one common ground that unites all of these responses is their fascination with the *Rose* as a global art of love, exploring the interface of the erotic, the natural, the rational, the divine.

In this chapter I turn to a different sort of response to the *Rose*, that of the manuscript illuminator. Since a complete survey of the *Rose* iconographic tradition would far exceed the scope of the present study, I will focus on a single example, the marginal images that appear throughout MS Bibl. Nat. fr. 25526 (MS *Mi*).[2] MS *Mi* was copied and illustrated in Paris, probably during the 1330s, and is the work of Jeanne and Richard de Montbaston.[3] It is not a typical *Rose* manuscript. The marginalia are an idiosyncratic response to the poem, unlike the illustrations in any other *Rose* manuscript that I have seen. Nonetheless, they can be shown to fit into the larger picture of the *Rose* reception as it has been outlined in the previous chapters.

THE NOTION OF A VISUAL GLOSS: ANALOGS FOR MS *MI*

Ms *Mi* is not unique in surrounding a text with visual images that illustrate and comment upon it.[4] I have seen no other *Rose* manuscript that has

---

[2] This chapter incorporates material from my earlier brief analysis of MS *Mi*, "Vignettes marginales comme glose marginale."

[3] This dating was confirmed by François Avril, Curator of Manuscripts at the Bibliothèque Nationale, in a private consultation. For the information that MS *Mi* is the work of the Parisian illuminators Jeanne and Richard de Montbaston I am indebted to Richard Rouse of the University of California, Los Angeles. The Montbastons are discussed briefly by Richard and Mary Rouse in "Commercial Production of Manuscript Books," p. 110; the Rouses are preparing a more detailed study of the Montbastons as part of the 1992 Lyell Lectures in Bibliography. Michael Camille has also identified MS *Mi* with the Montbastons; see his *Image on the Edge*, p. 114. At present, I do not possess sufficient evidence to distinguish the respective contributions of Jeanne and Richard to the illumination of MS *Mi*; nor can I be certain who designed the iconographic program, which did not necessarily originate with the artist(s) who executed it. I will therefore refer to "the artist" and to "the designer of the marginalia," without attempting to identify the individuals responsible for each aspect of the work.

[4] For background on medieval marginalia, see the catalogue by Randall, *Images in the Margins of Gothic Manuscripts*. Randall's inventory includes some images from MS *Mi*. MS *Mi* has also been mentioned by Fleming, *"Roman de la Rose"*, p. viii; Kolve, *Chaucer and the Imagery of Narrative*, pp. 245–46, fig. 116; and Camille, "Book of Signs," pp. 142–43, fig. 10. For discussion of the function of marginalia

marginal images on every page, but it is not unusual to find marginalia on the opening page of the *Rose*, as of other texts both Latin and vernacular. Often this opening page imagery is the standard stuff of marginalia, such as hounds pursuing rabbits or elegant hunts for rabbit or stag. This imagery is appropriate to the *Rose*, of course; Jean himself uses the metaphor of love as a hunt on more than one occasion. Still, similar marginalia are so common on the opening pages of medieval codices that one hesitates to see them as having been selected specially for the *Rose*. In certain cases, however, the *Rose* opens with somewhat more unusual marginalia that surely were intended to reflect on the text. The MS British Library Stowe 947 (MS *Lm³*) opens with a two-part miniature representing the dreamer in bed, and Oiseuse seated inside the garden wall, holding her mirror and comb and surrounded by the rosebush (Pl. 8). This image tells us, first of all, that the poem will be the story of a dream.[5] The conflation of the rose, object of desire, with the sensuality and self-absorption of Oiseuse – a feminine figuration of Narcissus, in whose mirror the rose is first glimpsed – tells us that the dream is inspired by and focused upon erotic love.[6] In the lower margin, however, are two animal figures: a lion, and a beaver biting off its own testicles. These two animals represent the possibility of a corrective antidote to erotic impulses. The lion is an ambivalent symbol, but here probably represents the nobility of heart that is often invoked in the *Rose*, and which the Lover seems never to approach. The beaver, according to bestiary tradition, knew that it was hunted for its testicles, and would bite them off when pursued in order to save its life; similarly, the man pursued by the devil should cast off temptations of the flesh.[7] The Lover is, of

---

in different kinds of manuscripts, see Rieger, " 'Ins e.l cor port, dona, vostra faisso'," pp. 395–415; Sandler, "Bawdy Betrothal in the Ormesby Psalter"; Randall, "Games and the Passion in Pucelle's Hours of Jeanne d'Evreux." As these scholars have demonstrated, marginal images often did provide a visual gloss on the text; those in troubadour chansonnier *N*, catalogued by Rieger (*op. cit.*), are even cued to specific words by means of geometric signs.

[5] The majority of *Rose* manuscripts open with an image of the dreamer in bed, either alone or in conjunction with other scenes; see Kuhn, "Illustration des *Rosenromans*."

[6] For a discussion of Oiseuse and the rosebush as a sign of sensual love in opening-page miniatures, see Dahlberg, "Love and the *Roman de la Rose*." Dahlberg also addresses the possible ironic overtones of the use of Nativity iconography in representations of the dreamer. One must always be careful in such interpretations, since artists could have drawn on familiar patterns in designing new iconography without intending the new scenes to be associated with those on which they were modeled.

[7] Bestiary imagery, though common in marginalia, is particularly relevant to the *Rose*, given that the *Bestiaire d'amours* is sometimes paired with the *Rose* in anthology manuscripts. Langlois identifies four such manuscripts in his *Manuscrits*, making this the most popular choice after Jean's other verse compositions and the *Consolation of Philosophy*; Gui cites the *Bestiaire d'amours* in the opening lines of his prologue. In addition, MS *Eb* includes the bestiary of Guillaume le Clerc. On the beaver see Guillaume le Clerc, *Bestiaire*, ed. Reinsch, vv. 1477–1566; Philippe de Thaün, *Bestiaire*, ed. Walberg, vv. 1135–76. Fournival's use of the beaver is less appropriate to the interpretation of this marginal image. For him, the beaver giving up its testicles teaches the lady that she should give over her heart to her lover; see *Bestiaires d'amours*, ed. Segre, pp. 57–59.

Plate 8 Opening page of the *Rose*, with an image of a beaver castrating itself in the lower margin. London, British Library MS Stowe 947, fol. 1r.

course, uninterested in doing so, although he does try to cast off the word "coilles." Castration is a motif running through the *Rose*, associated with the birth of erotic desire (the castration of Saturn); with the destructive effects of marriage on a man's personal freedom and peace of mind (the castration of Abelard); with sterility and nonprocreative sexuality (castration in general, according to Genius); and with a misguided literalization of Biblical exhortations to virtue (the castration of Origen). The beaver motif participates in this important thematics while adding yet another layer of meaning: continence, the allegorical castration that Origen, not to mention the Lover, ought to have pursued.

A second example of an opening page marginal image that comments on the text appears in MS Bibl. Nat. fr. 1561 (MS *Lb*). Again, the small opening miniature represents the dreamer in bed; in the lower margin, two rabbits and a man extending a phallic staff express the erotic impulses that motivate the dream. Off to the side is an asp, its tail plugging its ear. Bestiary tradition teaches that the asp prevented itself from being lulled to sleep by placing one ear against the ground and stopping up the other with its tail. In Christianizing bestiaries, the asp is a figure for the obstinate sinner who closes his ears to chastisement, certainly an appropriate image for the Lover. However, it is possible that the image in MS *Lb* was inspired by Richard de Fournival's *Bestiaire d'amours*, a text sometimes bound with the *Rose* in anthology manuscripts, in which the asp represents a refusal to be seduced by the sweet appearance of the lady. Given the importance of aural seduction in the opening stages of the dream – the Lover is attracted first by birdsong, then by the song of the carolers – and the importance of verbal deception and manipulation in the erotic conquest, this asp closing its ears to the world could certainly be seen, like the beaver of MS *Lm³*, in opposition to the Lover.[8]

Sometimes readers and even scribes themselves were moved to visualize their reactions to the texts they read or copied. In Chapter 1, I mentioned the scribal doodles of MS Bibl. Nat. Rothschild 2800 (MS *Eb*), some of which illustrate the particular word to which they are attached, and some of which reflect the mood of the poem through motifs of love or sorrow. In the MS Arras, Bibl. Mun. 897 (MS *Bê*), the margins hold several drawings of male and female heads, labeled "Amant" and "Raison," during the discourse of Reason. These images are less a comment on the text than an effort to represent its dialectic structure; they show, again, the extent to which medieval readers would visualize the text. Even scholarly books

---

[8] On the asp, see Guillaume le Clerc, *Bestiaire*, ed. Reinsch, vv. 2553–88; Philippe de Thaün, *Bestiaire*, ed. Walberg, vv. 1615–80; Richard de Fournival, *Bestiaires d'amours*, ed. Segre, pp. 31–33.

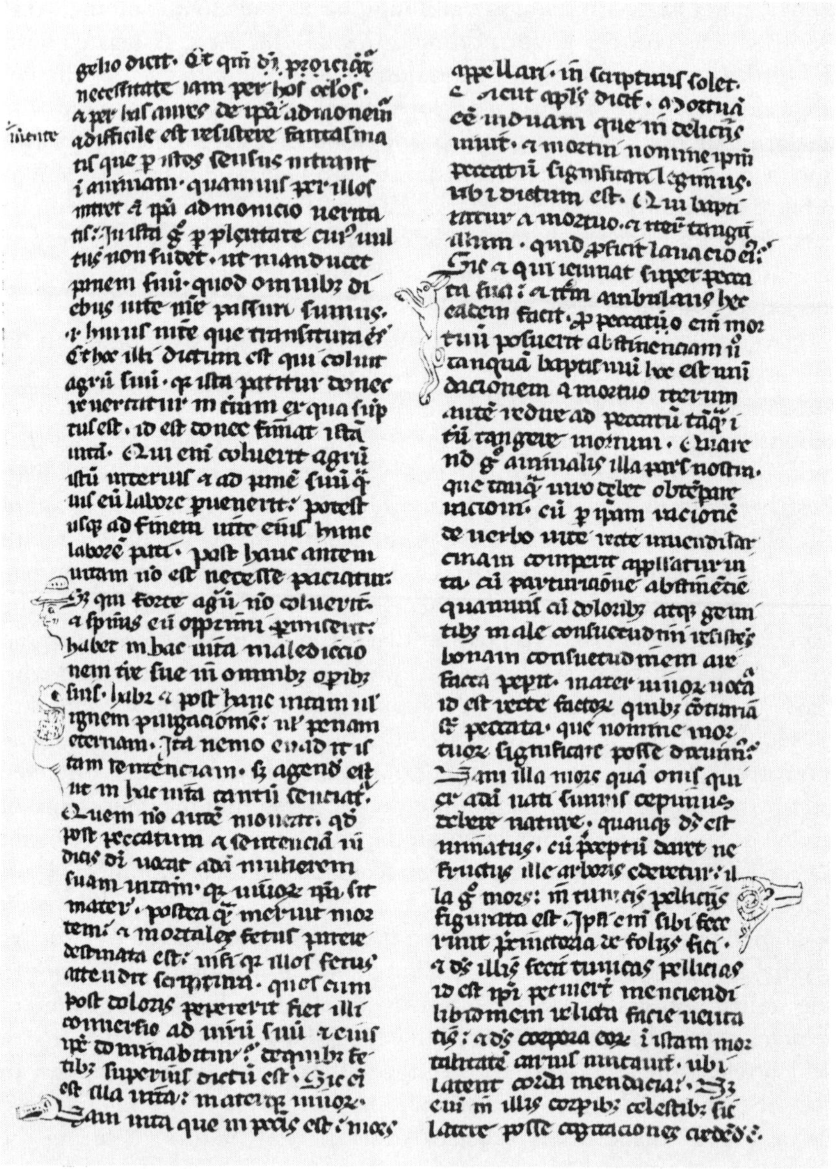

Plate 9 Marginal doodles in Augustine's *De Genesi adversus Manicheos*. Dijon, Bibliothèque Municipale MS 139, fol. 148r.

could be ornamented in this way. A portion of the thirteenth-century codex Dijon, Bibl. Mun. MS 139, a collection of the works of Augustine, is elaborately ornamented with scribal doodles. These begin as abstract, vaguely floral designs part way through the *Liber adversus Maximinum* (fol. 118v) and soon develop into profuse figural drawings that continue until the end of *De Genesi adversus Manicheos* (fol. 159r), responding to the content of the texts (Pl. 9). The discussion of prelapsarian sexual relations in *De Genesi*, for example, is illustrated with a drawing of a man and a woman kissing (fol. 137r; Book 1, ch. 18; *PL*, 34:187); the citation of God's decision to create Eve, "Non est bonum esse hominem solum" [it is not good for the man to be alone (Genesis 2:18)] is accompanied by a drawing of a woman (fol. 141r; Book 2, ch. 1; *PL*, 34:195). The discussion of Eve's punishment – pain in childbirth – is illustrated with the face of a baby wearing a bonnet (fol. 147v; Book 2, ch. 19; *PL*, 34:211); the citation of Wisdom 9:15, introduced with the phrase "Sicut enim Salomon dicit" [for as Solomon said] is accompanied by the head of a king (fol. 147v; Book 2, ch. 20; *PL*, 34:211). At the assertion that "post hanc vitam habebit, vel ignem purgationis vel poenam aeternam" [after this life, [humanity] will have either the fire of purgation or the eternal torment], the scribe drew the gaping jaws of Hell (fol. 148r; Book 2, ch. 20; *PL*, 34:212). In other cases, the drawing is not a literal illustration of the text, but does relate to it metaphorically, as when a grotesque, a ram, and a rabbit are used in quick succession to illustrate the discussion of sin as a state of spiritual death (fol. 148r; Book 2, ch. 21; *PL*, 34:212; Pl. 9).

Clearly, the scribe of Dijon MS 139 read the text as he copied it, and his imagination was stimulated by it. In this case, the scribe's drawings do not imply any particular interpretation of the text in question. But they do serve as a stunning reminder that, in the thirteenth century, reading an Augustinian treatise on Original Sin could be an intensely visual experience; and that the act of writing and that of drawing were scarcely distinguishable, words flowing into images in an integrated process of reading, visualizing and recording. MS *Eb*, in turn, shows that the *Rose* – a poem that addresses some of the same issues – could have a similar effect on its copyist, who might be moved to record his reactions in a similar blend of words and images.

The fourteenth-century *Rose* manuscript BN fr. 9345 (MS *Lq*) has both scribal doodles and marginal drawings. During Nature's discussion of divine justice, for example, the scribe drew angels to ornament the initial letters at the tops of the columns (fol. 54v). In two places, colored drawings in the margins – now somewhat faded – present a caricature of the text. On the page where Venus comes to inflame Bel Acueil into granting the Lover a kiss, there are three figures in the lower margin: a spotted animal body with the head of a man; a second spotted animal with the crowned head of a woman; and a mermaid holding a mirror and comb (fol. 11v). Surely the two grotesques represent Venus and the Lover, partners in seduction; the mermaid recalls Oiscuse, identified by Reason as the condition that leads directly to erotic passion, and represented here in her aspect as siren. The second example illustrates the Lover's rejection of Reason; in the lower margin an animal body with a bearded human head expresses the Lover's descent from Reason into a bestial state (fol. 17r). These marginal drawings were not necessarily executed at the time that the manuscript was being copied; but whoever did them was recording his or her response to key moments in the poem. The representation of Oiseuse as a siren, presiding over the Lover's first major victory in the seduction of the Rose, is in essence a visualization of the idea expressed as a rubric in MS *Lw*: "Comment Oeseuse qui n'est pas sage / A mal fere donne passage" [how Oiseuse, who is not wise, gives passage to evil-doing (fol. 5r)]. And the representation of the Lover as a hybrid, no longer quite human, echoes the rubric of MS *Arr*: "Amator noluit credere rationi" [the lover didn't want to believe reason].

An especially elaborate series of marginal drawings illustrates the *Rose* in the fifteenth-century MS Bibl. Nat. fr. 12592. The drawings are often in the lower margins, although some appear in the side and upper margins as well. They are executed in pen and ink, largely in red and black, though with some use of blue and green, especially towards the end of the manuscript; I cannot tell whether they are the work of the scribe or of a later reader. The drawings are limited to Jean de Meun's portion of the poem, beginning with the drawing of a face at the Lover's request that Reason explain to him what sort of love it is that she approves (fol. 14r, vv. 4634–39). This face, with its red cheeks, prominent teeth, and protruding tongue, expresses the overwrought passions of the Lover as he struggles against Reason's advice. From this point on, almost every page has at least one drawing.

Many of the drawings illustrate events in either the frame narrative or the exemplary tales contained in the various discourses. In the discourse of Reason, we find illustrations of the deaths of Virginia (fol. 16v), Seneca (fol. 18v), and Nero (fol. 19r). For the former, we are shown Virginius beheading his daughter and offering her head on a platter; Seneca is shown with bleeding wrists stepping into a tub of bloody water, while Nero, crowned and holding an orb and a sword, looks on; and on the facing page Nero is beheaded by one man and stabbed by another, while his body is in flames. Other illustrated exempla are the stories of Dido and Medea (fol. 39r); Venus and Adonis (fol. 47r); the couple in Genius' warning tale about

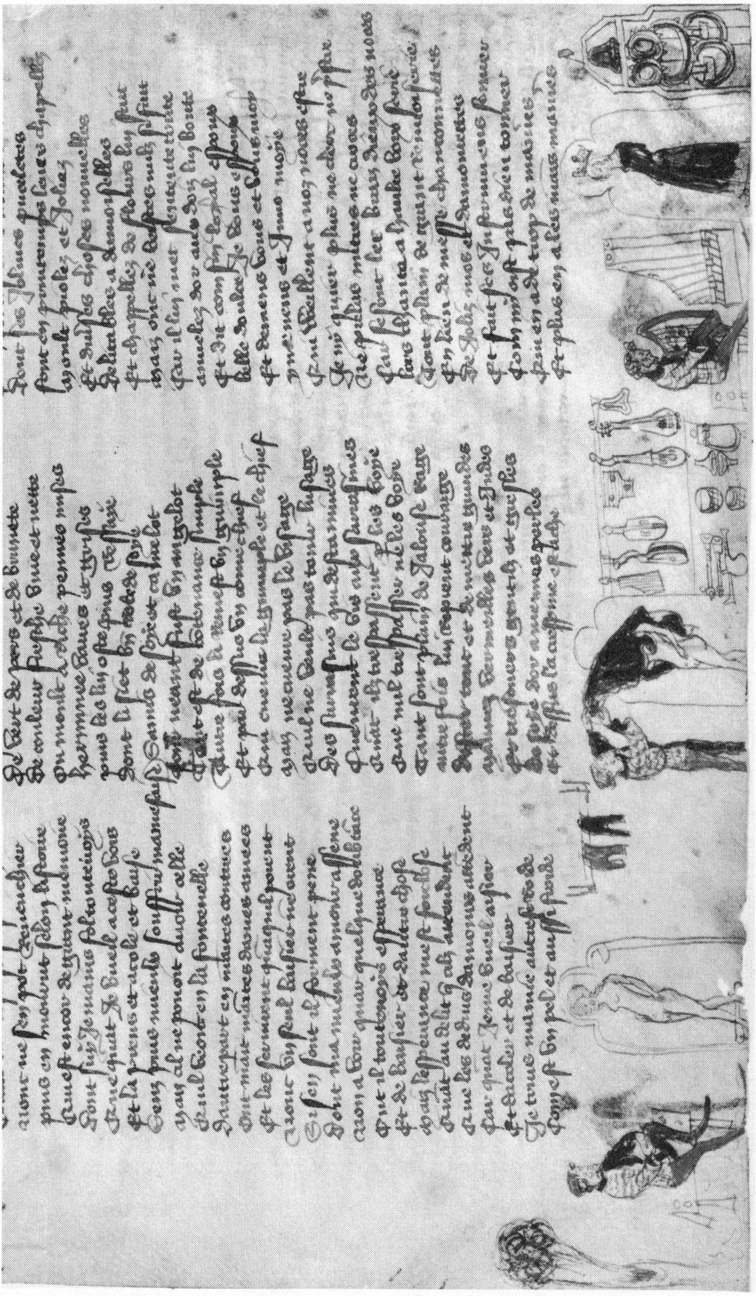

Plate 10 Marginal illustration of the story of Pygmalion. Paris, Bibliothèque Nationale MS fr. 12592, fol. 62v.

revealing secrets to women (fol. 49r); Alexander assaulting the gates of Hell (fol. 56v); Cadmus (fol. 59r); and Pygmalion, whose story is represented in no less than seven scenes (fol. 62r, 62v, 63r) (Pl. 10). Illustrated events of the frame narrative include the death of Male Bouche (fol. 36v); the Lover's conversation with La Vieille (fol. 43v); his subsequent encounter with Fear, Shame, and Dangier (fol. 49v); the battles between the forces of Love and those of Jealousy (fol. 45v, 46r, 46v); Nature's confession and absolution (fol. 50v, 58r); Genius crowned as bishop by Cupid and addressing Love's troops (fol. 58v); the assault on the tower (fol. 62r); and the final conquest of the Rose (fol. 63v, 64r, 64v). The illustrations at the end of the poem preserve the allegorical imagery of the text. The Lover approaches the Rose as a pilgrim, with a staff and a pouch marked with a scallop shell (at v. 21375); he kneels between two pillars and lifts up a curtain in front of a small shrine (at v. 21565); he plucks the rosebud (at v. 21698).

Many other images, while they cannot be described as narrative, do bear directly on the thematics of the text. Sometimes the image is a comment on a character in the poem. For example, the statement that "Male Bouche est trop coverz, / il n'est pas anemis overz" [Male Bouche is too covert, he is not an open enemy (vv. 7791–92)] is illustrated with the image of a rat peering out of its hole (under v. 7794, fol. 23r). The diabolical hypocrisy of Faux Samblant, in turn, is nicely represented in a drawing attached to the high stem of the "l" in the line "tu ne seras pas le prumiers" [you will not be the first (v. 10968, fol. 32r)]. This line is at the top of the textual column in which Faux Samblant begins his sermon (v. 10976), so that the image serves as a marker of his self-revelation. Facing out from the left side of the letter "l" is the head of a monk; facing out from the right side is a hooded head with red horns, raising a finger in a gesture commonly used to represent speech (Pl. 11). The outer and inner nature of Faux Samblant could not be more clearly depicted. And at the top of the column (vv. 11197–243, fol. 33r) where Faux Samblant begins the second instalment of his sermon, prompted by the God of Love's questioning, is the face of a monster, with an open mouth, sharp teeth, and a large tongue. Again, Faux Samblant's vicious character, his verbal sowing of discord, is visually rendered.

In other cases, the drawings may be the visualization of a textual motif. Richesse's description of Hunger, for example, is illustrated with the image of a face covered with red splotches (fol. 29v). This drawing appears at the top of the column that begins with v. 10133, the opening line of the description of Hunger; it draws its inspiration from the statement that Hunger has "joes de roïlle entechees" [splotchy cheeks (v. 10138)]. And Richesse's characterization of her followers as "plus renvoisiez que papegaus" [more gay than parrots (v. 10068)], though seemingly a

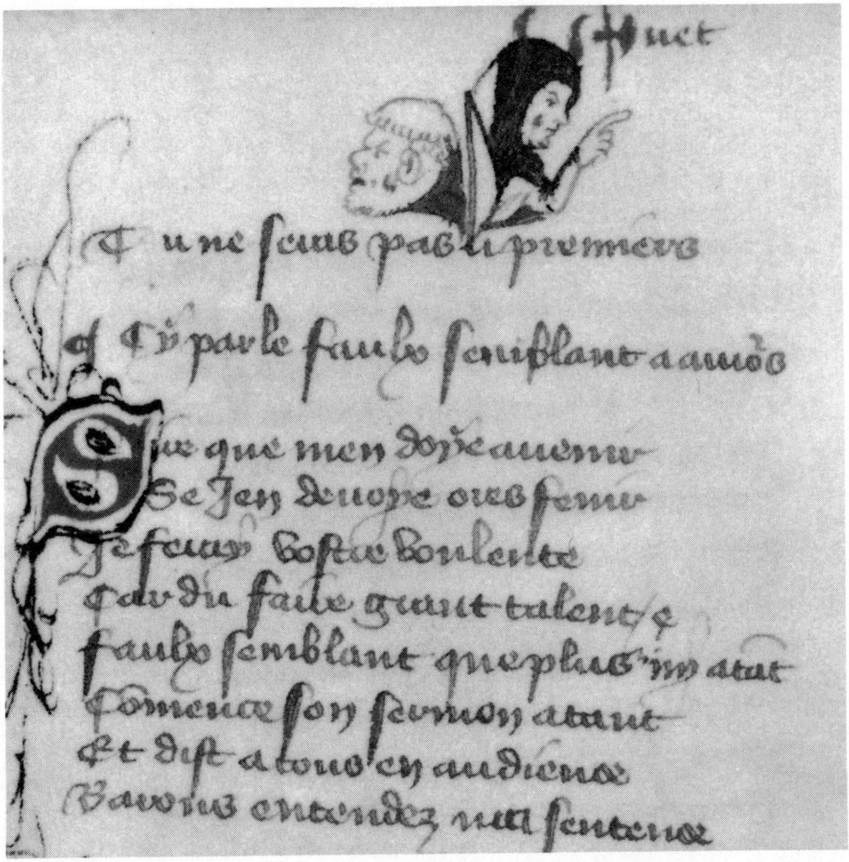

Plate 11 Marginal doodle (upper margin) representing the character of Faux Samblant. Paris, Bibliothèque Nationale MS fr. 12592, fol. 32r.

throw-away comparison, is illustrated with a green parrot that is even labeled with a scroll reading "petit parrotin" [little parrot (under v. 10068, fol. 29r)]. Nature's allusion to insects is illustrated with a drawing of a fly and three crawling insects at the bottom of the column containing vv. 17764–832 (fol. 53v). Her account of divine omniscience, expressed in terms of the mirror in which God beholds past, present, and future (vv. 17434–60), is illustrated in the upper margin with a young male figure beholding his face in a mirror (above v. 17447, fol. 52v). Somewhat surprisingly, a figure of the nimbused face of Christ appears in the discourse of the Jaloux, at the bottom of the column containing vv. 8976–9039 (fol. 26v). The topic of these lines is the assault on chastity and the dissatisfaction of women with their natural beauty, and God is invoked several times: the disquisition on chastity begins, "Dom je jur Dieu, le roi celestre" [wherefore I swear by God, the heavenly king (v. 8983)]; and the discussion of beauty alludes repeatedly to the fact that since natural beauty is God-given, replacing it with artificial beauty constitutes sacrilege. The topos is standard in devotional literature and *contemptus mundi* treatises; in spite of the questionable authority of the Jaloux, it was possible for this particular reader to respond directly to the theological imagery of the text.

The marginal drawings in MS fr. 12592 sometimes illustrate more extended developments in the text. Ami's evocation of the simple life enjoyed during the Golden Age, for example, finds visual expression in the image of a man digging a hole in front of a cottage whose coziness is implied by its smoking chimney (fol. 24v). This image illustrates the last lines of the column under which it appears:

> Covertes erent de genestes,
> de foilliees et de rameaus
> leur bordetes et leur hameaus,
> et fesoient en terre fosses.   (vv. 8360–63)

> Their little cabins and cottages were covered with broomplants, with leaves and branches, and they dug ditches in the earth.

The advent of civilization, in turn – characterized by Ami as a time when people began to travel, to sail the seas, to own property and to engage in power struggles – is illustrated by a castle and fortified tower next to a bridge, with a small boat in the water (under vv. 9434–94, fol. 27v). Genius' description of the reign of Jupiter, characterized by hedonism, violence, and discord, is also illustrated: a king is shown first using hawks to hunt birds (fol. 60v, under vv. 20097–157) and then hunting rabbits (ibid., under vv. 20158–218). These latter images associate the age of Jupiter with the rise of the aristocracy, twice identified by Nature as those who hunt (vv. 18628, 18722). The artist thus links Genius' account with that of Ami, who states that princes and governors came into being as a result of the competition for wealth and property at the end of the Golden Age.

Aside from the myth of Cadmus, the other illustrations in the discourse of Genius pertain to the *biaus parc* that he promises to those who follow Nature. The first appears at the initial description of the "parc du champ joli" [park of the pretty field (v. 19905)], and depicts a flock of sheep under a tree, with a bagpipe-playing shepherd (under v. 19921, fol. 59v). The second appears under the column of vv. 20217–77 (fol. 60v), and depicts the circular park with its fruit-bearing tree, sheep, and shepherd; outside the enclosure a wolf carries off a sheep, and a devil tends the flames of Hell: a detailed representation of the text's account of the Good Shepherd, the danger to the sheep of being eaten by the wolf if they stray from the path, and the depiction of Hell on the exterior of the park's wall. Finally, the review of the two fountains is illustrated with a scene of Narcissus kneeling before a square fountain beneath a tree, surrounded by grass and flowers and enclosed by a flowering hedge (under vv. 20335–95, fol. 61r). Clearly, both the account of the Golden Age and its fall, and the comparison of the worldly and heavenly gardens, made a vivid impression on our reader.

In addition to illustrating the narrative and thematic developments of the poem, the marginalia sometimes also visualize its extended metaphors. In his celebrated antifeminist diatribe, Genius cites Virgil's *Eclogue* 3:92–93 – "Qui legitis flores et humi nascentia frage, / Frigidus, o pueri, fugite hinc, latet anguis in herba" [O youths who gather flowers and strawberries growing along the ground, flee, a cold serpent hides in the grass] – and develops its thematics at some length (vv. 16552–86). The warning to flee is illustrated by three youths running away from a serpent with a forked tongue (under v. 16578, fol. 49v); at the top of the facing page, the danger is illustrated by a serpent devouring a naked man (at v. 16575, fol. 50r). The only other illustration for this portion of Genius' discourse is his exemplary couple in bed, with the wife embracing her husband as he tries to turn away from her (under v. 16406, fol. 49r). The three drawings, one on each page, crystallize the antifeminist doctrine in three memorable images: the blandishments of women; the need for men to turn away or, better yet, flee this monster altogether; the dire consequences if they fail to do so.

I have dwelt at some length on MS fr. 12592 because it allows us to study one reader's visual reaction to the *Rose*. Some of the illustrations correspond to scenes frequently found in miniatures, but many are idiosyncratic; the artist responded directly to the text. The marginalia of MS fr. 12592 include a range of responses to the poem: they illustrate its narrative action, its metaphors, its thematic developments, and sometimes even seemingly random motifs; they comment on the various characters and on their teachings. Like the Dijon Augustine anthology, and like *Rose* MSS *Eb* and *Lq*, MS fr. 12592 is a vivid reminder of the medieval tendency to visualize both narrative and expository writing. Visual images, real or imagined, play a crucial role in the medieval science of memory; the visualization of abstract concepts is fundamental to allegory itself.[9] Illustrations were an important element of a reader's experience of a text, and could be used, like rubrics, verbal glosses, and textual interpolations, to record impressions or to expand upon the text. With this in mind, let us turn now to the marginalia of MS *Mi*, a most unusual visual response to the *Rose*.

---

[9] In the prologue of the *Bestiaire d'amours*, for example, Fournival explains that seeing and hearing are the two gates to memory; hence, his text should include both words and illustrations (ed. Segre, pp. 4–7). See my discussion in *From Song to Book*, pp. 138–40, 164–71.

THE MARGINALIA OF MS *MI*: AN OVERVIEW

The marginalia of MS *Mi* are a varied mix. They relate in different ways, and to a varying extent, to the text that they surround. On many pages, it would have to be said that the marginalia are simply ornamental. Much of the discourse of Nature, for example, is decorated with scenes of animals pursuing one another; while it could be argued that such images represent the world that Nature presides over, it must also be said that such images are the standard fare of marginalia. Other typical marginalia that do not seem to illustrate the text in any way include birds and various human, animal, and angelic musicians. Such images can be regarded as "filler," used to complete the decoration of the codex in sections where the designer of the marginalia did not choose to develop a visual gloss on the text.

In cases where the marginal images do relate to the text, the nature of this relationship is varied. On some pages, we find examples of *Wortillustration*: the visual representation of a particular word or phrase, often one appearing near the top or bottom of a textual column. On fol. 75v, for example, at the beginning of the Lover's encounter with Richesse, is a drawing of a fountain flowing under a tree on a grassy hillside. This no doubt illustrates the line "Jouste une clere fontenele" [next to a clear little fountain (v. 10021)], which appears just five lines up from the drawing. It is beside this fountain that the Lover finds Richesse and her paramour. However, the characters do not appear in the marginal drawing; it is less a representation of the narrative setting than a direct response to an isolated textual motif. A similar example appears on fol. 124r, where we find the image of a pelican stabbing its breast to feed its babies. This is a figurative illustration of the two lines immediately above the drawing: "Jhesucrist, que pas ne trouvames / de sa grace aver ne echar" [Jesus Christ, whom we did not find grudging or sparing in his grace (vv. 16406–7)]. But this reference to divine grace is only a passing reference in the tirade of the wife in Genius' antifeminist scenario, as she reminds her husband of their wedding vows in an effort to disarm him. The allegorical representation of Christ as a pelican is a decontextualized response to the invocation of God, exactly like the image of Christ that appeared in the margin of the discourse of the Jaloux in MS fr. 12592.

Even if such images imply a reading of individual words rather than of the poem as a whole, they do nonetheless show that the marginalia are not random images; they were executed with at least some concern for the text. On other pages, the marginalia visualize more important textual metaphors. The images of a girl playing a ball game with a group of boys in the discourse of Reason (fol. 38v, 48r), for example, are surely inspired by

Plate 12   Marginal representation of fox and wolf as emblematic of Faux Samblant. Paris, Bibliothèque Nationale MS fr. 25526, fol. 115r.

Phanie's characterization of Fortune's caprice: "ainceis s'en geue a la pelote / conme pucele nice et sote" [thus she plays pelote, like a silly and foolish maiden (vv. 627–28)]. Faux Samblant's allusions to the satirical *Ysengrinus* (vv. 11038–40, 11093–98), in turn, are exploited in the image of a fox bearing off a rooster (vv. 11908–73, fol. 91r), illustrating Faux Samblant's final boasts of hypocrisy. The image is repeated on fol. 115r, which contains a portion of Jean's Apology, including the opening lines of his defense of the Faux Samblant section (vv. 15213–25): here we find a fox carrying off a chicken and a wolf carrying of a sheep (Pl. 12). The textual conflation of the corruption of the Church and of love is represented in this standard image of the friar as thieving fox or wolf.[10]

Animals performing human activities are common in marginalia, and MS *Mi* is no exception. Often these humanized animals relate parodically to the text where they appear, and are not just marginal decoration. On fol. 94v, for example, Faux Samblant and Contrainte Astenance arrive to speak with La Vieille, assuring her of the Lover's honorable intentions. Their conversation is represented in a miniature (at v. 12371): the two false clerics on the left, the crafty woman on the right. In the lower margin, three animals standing on their hind legs face off: a lion and a dog playing a vielle on the left, a rabbit holding two large bells on the right (Pl. 13). This little scene humorously recreates the miniature: the voracious character of Faux Samblant and his companion, beguiling La Vieille with their sweet talk, is expressed in the two predatory animals with their instrument, while La Vieille's sexuality and her garrulity are expressed in the bell-ringing rabbit, an animal with strong erotic associations. A similar use of an animal musician appears on fol. 25v, where we see a boar playing the vielle for a stag. On this page the Lover displays his grief before Dangier, and there is

---

[10] For more examples of Renart as an image for the hypocritical friar, both in literary texts and in marginalia, see Robertson, *Preface to Chaucer*, pp. 251–52, and plates 78, 79, 101.

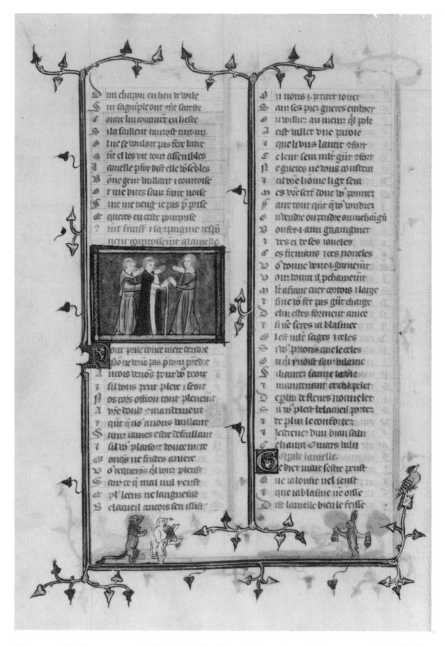

Plate 13   Miniature representing Faux Samblant, Contrainte Astenance, and La Vieille; these figures are parodied by the animals in the lower margin. Paris, Bibliothèque Nationale MS fr. 25526, fol. 94v.

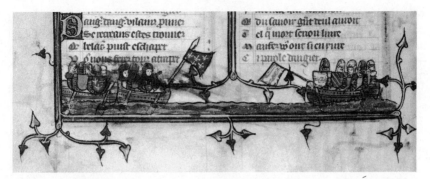

Plate 14   Marginal representation of a naval battle during the storming of the tower of Jealousy. Paris, Bibliothèque Nationale MS fr. 25526, fol. 116v.

an ornamented initial at the line "Forment me plaing, forment souspir" [I lament profoundly, I sigh profoundly (var. of v. 3219)]. It is also on this page that Franchise and Pity arrive to plead with Dangier on the Lover's behalf. The boar vielle-player thus represents the self-pitying lamentations of the Lover, who attempts to lull the object of his hunt with a show of sorrow and sincerity.

Sometimes, though not often, the marginalia illustrate the literal events of the narrative. In the account of the battles to win the Rose, for example, we find in the margins a mixture of battle scenes and animals. The battles begin with the foray of Franchise against Dangier (v. 15273, fol. 115v). This passage is headed with a miniature showing a confrontation between armed knights; in the lower margin, representing the actual nature of these supposedly heroic battles, a dog pursues a hare. As the battles continue on the next page, however, the lower margin contains two young men armed with sword and targe. The battle of Boldness and Surety against Fear is illustrated in the margins with knights riding to battle (fol. 117v); the remainder of the battle of Surety and Fear is illustrated with the image of a hound pursuing a fox (fol. 118r).

The most elaborate marginal response to the battles is the naval battle that illustrates the confrontation of Pity and Dangier (fol. 116v): two boats full of armed knights bearing a blue banner with a white emblem resembling the fleur-de-lis face a boatload of knights flying a banner with two white leopards on a red field, very nearly the arms of the Duke of Normandy (Pl. 14).[11] This scene is a fanciful rendering of the battle as described in the text. The enemies of Love have already been associated

---

[11] Ordinarily the fleur-de-lis and the leopards would both be gold, but no gold leaf is used in the marginalia of MS *Mi*. In any case the artist did not necessarily mean to represent literally the arms of Normandy or of the French royal house, but only humorously to suggest them.

with Normandy through the identification of Male Bouche's soldiers as Normans. The association is reinforced in the statement that Dangier "se deffent con uns liesparz" [defends himself like a leopard (v. 15374)]. And the idea of a battle on water is suggested by the references to Pity's copious tears:

> Mes quant ele ot bien arousé
> de lermes l'ort vilain housé,
> si le convint amoloier;
> vis li fu qu'il deüst noier
> an un fleuve, touz estourdiz.

(vv. 15375–79)

But when she had thoroughly sprinkled the filthy booted peasant with tears, he couldn't help softening; it seemed to him that he was being drowned in a river, all overwhelmed.

Dangier, ally of the late Norman Male Bouche and one who fights like a leopard, heraldic emblem of Normandy, combats Pity, from whom flows a river of tears: our artist has transformed this allegorical construct into a naval battle between forces identified respectively with Normandy and with an indeterminate other branch of the French royal house.

If one examines the layout of the marginal images, a very interesting pattern emerges. In many cases the artist devoted one or even both sides of a bifolium to a single motif. One finds entire bifolia decorated with scenes of children's games, or with hybrids, or with knights riding to battle. In Guillaume de Lorris, for example, saints appear here and there in the margins during the description of the carol participants. The martyrdom of Saint Laurence appears on fol. 9r, where the description of Richesse begins; on fol. 9v, where the description of Richesse continues, one finds the martyrdom of Saint Catherine; on fol. 16v, where the God of Love locks up the Lover's heart, we find an image of Saint Catherine preaching to a group of scholars. The images of Catherine, seemingly far apart, turn out on closer examination to be on opposite sides of the same bifolium, the outer leaf of the gathering. In fact, if we imagine the unbound leaf, we find that one side of it holds folios 16v and 9r: it is decorated with the two saints, Catherine and Laurence. The death of Catherine follows at once, on the other side of the leaf.

Even long narrative cycles are laid out in this fashion. The marginalia of MS *Mi* include several series of images representing the life of Christ, as well as a complete cycle of images representing the life of Saint Margaret. Seemingly contrary to all logic, these images are disposed, in order, across the face of each bifolium in turn. Margaret's martyrdom, for example, appears in the seventh gathering, during the closing sections of the discourse of Reason and the very beginning of the discourse of Ami (see below, Fig. 7). The outer leaf is decorated on one side with her arrest (fol. 49r) and flagellation (fol. 56v), and on the other side with scenes of her imprisonment (fol. 49v, 56r). One side of the third leaf is illustrated with her execution (fol. 51v) and the ascent of her soul to Heaven (fol. 54r). The result, of course, is that the images no longer appear in narrative order when the book is bound: following her death, we still encounter representations of her torments in prison and her flagellation. It is only natural that the artist would work with unbound leaves; that he should design his program of marginalia on the basis of unbound leaves rather than in accordance with the order the pages will assume in the bound volume, is quite unusual. This is a point to which I shall return.

The layout by bifolium does raise the question of just how closely the marginalia relate to the text where they appear. This question can only be answered on a case-by-case basis. Even where the artist did choose to execute a particular motif across an entire bifolium, he could still have adapted the motif to fit the text on each page; if, for example, he had decided to prepare an entire leaf of hybrids or of saints, he could have arranged the figures in poses appropriate to the passage where each appears. A series of images or a narrative cycle might also be inspired generally by the content of a particular section of the poem, without each image necessarily having to correspond precisely to its page; the series might be initiated because of the text on one particular page, and then continued over the rest of the bifolium. In some cases, it even appears that the artist was inspired by the fortuitous juxtaposition of textual passages from different parts of the poem on a given bifolium. These various possibilities will be illustrated below.

The following analysis of MS *Mi* will focus primarily on two large categories: erotic images and sacred images. These are the two poles of the *Rose* itself, particularly in the *M* text, as outlined in Chapter 5. In MS *Mi*, Reason speaks both of mystical love and of kissing testicles on an altar; Faux Samblant's abuse of power is intensified through his added disquisition on the privilege granted him to hear confession – something he soon does, using the sacrament as a pretext for murder. Perseus and Pygmalion appear as alternative role models for the Lover, who in turn proclaims the life-giving powers of his beloved in contrast to Medusa, using language recalling Genius' descriptions of Heaven; and the text is surrounded by marginal images ranging from the obscene to the everyday to the divine. Here, truly, grotesques and angels, fabliau and hagiography are the framework within which the encyclopedic *Mirror of Lovers* unfolds.

THE ICONOGRAPHY OF EROTIC PASSION IN MS *MI*

The marginalia of MS *Mi* include a number of images that are explicitly erotic, as well as numerous others that participate in the metaphoric register of eros; scenes of the hunt, of mermaids, of various characters – human, mermaid, and ape – holding the mirror and comb of Oiseuse. I will begin with explicitly erotic scenes, focusing on a few specific examples rather than attempting to provide an exhaustive catalogue of the manuscript's hundreds of marginalia. The first such examples occur, appropriately enough, in the discourse of La Vieille, and are limited to a single bifolium, entirely decorated with the lascivious sporting of a nun and a monk (Fig. 2). On one side of the bifolium, the nun leads the monk by a leash attached to his phallus, and in a second scene she stands at the top of a tower which the monk scales with a ladder (fol. 106r); on the facing page the two copulate on a grassy hillside, next to a pack mule loaded with a basket of phalluses (fol. 111v) (Pl. 15). On the other side of the bifolium we find nuns gathering the fruit of a tree that bears phalluses (fol. 106v) (Pl. 16); on the facing page, the monk kneels to the nun, and then the two begin to disrobe (fol. 111r). These vignettes clearly illustrate the nature of the "love" taught by La Vieille, and are the visual equivalent of the rubrics found in some manuscripts identifying La Vieille as "maquerelle" [procuress], "pute" [whorish], or "orde" [filthy].

Although the artist grouped his erotic scenes on a single bifolium, it is clear that he did also coordinate them with the text. The consummation of the erotic play coincides with the rendezvous of the Lover and Bel Acueil; in fact, the scene of copulation occurs on the same page as a miniature representing the conversation between the two young men (Pl. 15). In this way, the marginalia reveal the real desire that lies barely hidden beneath the Lover's courtly gallantry and Bel Acueil's coquettish replies. This purpose determined the placement of the final image; the rest of the bifolium was decorated with similar scenes, which of course are appropriate to any part of La Vieille's discourse. Still, the artist evidently noted the text on the page where the first erotic scenes occur (fol. 106r). It is here that La Vieille addresses the regrets of those who take a vow of chastity (vv. 13937–48); this allusion probably determined the decision to use a monk and a nun as the amorous couple. Other details relate to the text in a more general way. The motif of the tower recalls the narrative situation of the *Rose*; and the tree of phalluses, in addition to vividly expressing the rampant sexuality of La Vieille – who declares that she had always wanted "d'estre de touz homes amee" [to be loved by all men (v. 14076)] – is a brilliant and audacious parody of the increasingly erotic rosebush sought by the Lover.

The iconography of erotic passion in MS *Mi*

106r (vv. 13927–98): Nun leads monk by leash; monk scales tower

106v (vv. 13999–14068): Nun at phallus tree; nun and monk embrace

111r (vv. 14630–92): Monk kneels to nun; couple undressing

111v (vv. 14693–753): Copulation; mule loaded with phalluses

Figure 2 Layout of bifolium with marginalia showing the lascivious sporting of a nun and a monk, and a phallus tree.

Plate 15 Miniature representing the meeting of the Lover and Bel Acueil after the discourse of La Vieille; marginal representation of copulation. Paris, Bibliothèque Nationale MS fr. 25526, fol. 111v.

The pages surrounding the explicitly erotic scenes bear images that participate in the generally erotic tenor of the text. For example, the conclusion of La Vieille's story of her unhappy love affair with a pimp is illustrated with a human couple and a pair of mermaids, both embracing

293

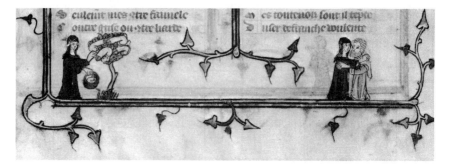

Plate 16 Marginal image of phallus tree during the discourse of La Vieille. Paris, Bibliothèque Nationale MS fr. 25526, fol. 106v.

(fol. 110r). Here La Vieille's sexual escapades are first visualized, then glossed as the dangerous allure of the sirens; the mermaid couple could even be seen as the allegorical representation of the two qualities La Vieille attributes to her lover, "oiseuse" and "delit" [idleness and pleasure (v. 14502)]. On the page facing the phallus tree, to give another example, are two scenes of combat (fol. 107r; vv. 14069–138). In the upper margin, a man and a woman battle one another; the woman is armed with tongs and a large ring, the man with bellows and a large club or bat (Pl. 17). In the lower margin, two young men – recalling the Lover and Bel Acueil – face off in a similarly armed combat: one holds a bellows and a large spoon, the other a pitcher and a pair of tongs. These battles metaphorically represent the erotic battle of the sexes, which La Vieille discusses on that page with examples from her own youth. In both of the illustrated combats, the figure on the left holds a phallic symbol, and the figure on the right – in one case a woman – holds a feminine symbol; the other weapons are the instruments used by Nature at her forge in the ongoing process of procreation. Indeed, the allusion to Nature as the impetus to erotic activity appears twice on this very page. Describing the natural tendency towards total promiscuity, La Vieille comments that "Nature ausinc les demeine" [Nature spurs them on thus (v. 14072)]; and after a digression concerning the many loves of her youth, she concludes, "Ainsinc Nature nos joutise, / qui noz queurs a deliz attise" [thus Nature, who drives our hearts to pleasure, governs us (vv. 14127–28)].

The explicitly erotic scenes with which La Vieille's discourse closes contrast pointedly with the scenes represented on its opening pages: the Visitation and Annunciation to the Shepherds (fol. 97r), the Nativity (fol. 97v), and the Annunciation to Mary (fol. 104v). Once again the artist

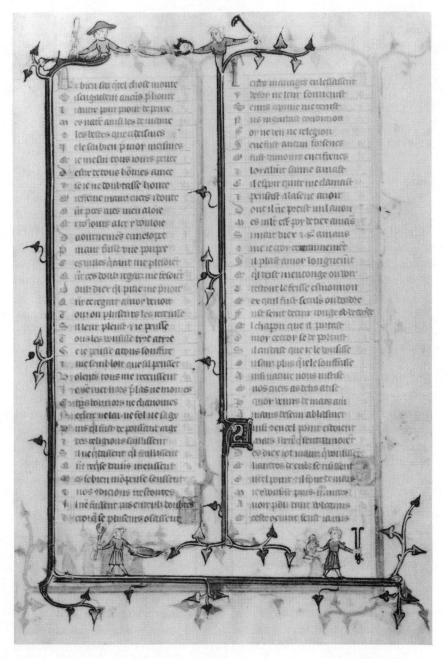

Plate 17 Marginal representation of combat during the discourse of La Vieille. Paris, Bibliothèque Nationale MS fr. 25526, fol. 107r.

97r (vv. 12689–746): Visitation, Annunciation to Shepherds

97v (vv. 12747–816): Nativity

104r (vv. 13647–716): Hound pursues boar

104v (vv. 13717–86): Annunciation to Mary

Figure 3   Layout of bifolium showing scenes from the Nativity.

worked by bifolium (Fig. 3). At the point where La Vieille's sermon begins in earnest (fol. 97r, v. 12731), the artist placed a miniature representing her conversation with Bel Acueil, and across the lower margin of this entire bifolium, he illustrated the scenes of announcement and revelation associated with the birth of Christ, placing that birth itself on the other side of the leaf. La Vieille's "enlightenment" of Bel Acueil, her instructions concerning a young girl's initiation into love and – given the ending of the poem – pregnancy, are thus first contrasted with sacred models of love and pregnancy: the encounter of the young Mary and the aging Elizabeth, the submission of Mary to the dictates of a higher love. And at the end of her discourse, the sordid quality of her teachings is fully unveiled. The marginalia quite clearly provide the parameters for the discussion of love, establishing the all-encompassing framework of sacred history and fabliau.

The amorous nun and monk next appear during the discourse of Nature, where they illustrate the myth of Deucalion and Pyrrha: on the left, the two embrace, while on the right, standing before a chapel, the monk exposes his erect phallus and hands the nun a crosier and a pouch, very nearly the same erotic symbols used by Jean himself at the end of the poem (fol. 133v, vv. 17544–613). The story of Deucalion and Pyrrha was given various interpretations in medieval mythography, but one standard reading of the myth was as an allegory for sexual intercourse. Since Deucalion and Pyrrha are taught to regenerate their lineage by divine oracle, this passage could be read as contributing to a praise of the sacrament of marriage and the divine command to be fruitful and multiply. However, the illustration indicates that such was not the reading favored by the designer of the marginalia. Deucalion and Pyrrha are glossed with an image of concupiscence that associates them with the teachings of La Vieille; it is suggested, indeed, that the pagan temple in which they receive the oracle is a sort of chapel of sexual freedom. I will return below to this idea of a "religion" of love and sexuality.

The phallus tree that we found in the margins of La Vieille reappears

153r (vv. 20382–451): Hound pursuing hare

153v (vv. 20452–521): Boys' game

160r (vv. 21283–350): Nuns at phallus tree; monk gives phallus to nun

160v (vv. 21351–420): Hound pursuing fox

Figure 4   Layout of bifolium containing hunting scenes and a phallus tree.

towards the end of the poem. The castle has been taken; Bel Acueil agrees that the Lover may pluck the Rose. On fol. 160r (vv. 21283–350), we find two images: the infamous tree, with two nuns gathering its fruit; and a monk handing a disembodied phallus to a nun. The marginalia provide an amusing gender-reversed visualization of the text. The image of the tree additionally recalls the context where this image first appeared, during La Vieille's discourse on free love as vestige of the lost Golden Age. The phallus tree is in effect the sign of this nostalgia for a Golden Age of unrestricted lovemaking; it is not surprising that it should reappear at the moment that the lover realizes his own wish for love unhampered. Moreover, it was under the auspices of La Vieille that he had his last meeting with Bel Acueil; we are reminded here that for all his flowery language, the Lover is in fact availing himself of an opportunity for seduction provided by the intervention of an aging procuress.

Let us now examine the entire bifolium where the second phallus tree appears (Fig. 4). Facing fol. 160r with its tree is part of the discourse of Genius (fol. 153v, vv. 20452–521): a description of the Heavenly Park with its Tree of Life, which "porte le fruit de salut" [bears the fruit of salvation (v. 20493)]. This juxtaposition is surely more than mere coincidence. Genius' idea of immortality is closely tied to the immortality of the species, hence to procreation; and his notion of spiritual salvation is intimately tied to that of sexual fulfillment. And of course the Lover himself, in his final assault on the Rose, portrays himself as a pilgrim worshiping sacred relics. The designer of the marginalia, with the open bifolium before him, would have read on the left about the naturalistic heaven for the sexually active with its fruit-bearing tree of life, and on the right about the supposedly sacred rosebush. This fortuitous textual juxtaposition informed his choice of the phallus tree as gloss for the rosebush. Tree of procreation, tree of sexual knowledge: this image mediates between the Tree of Life, symbol both of Christ and of natural fecundity, and the Rose, at once holy relic and feminine genitalia. The marginal image renders explicit the erotic significance of the text's spiritual metaphors.

Indeed, one would have to say that the designer of the marginalia interpreted the *Rose* as presenting a parodic religion of erotic love, to be contrasted with real religion. In this respect, the marginalia suggest a reading of the *Rose* close to that outlined by John Fleming:

> In the *Roman de la Rose* love is a religion . . . The religion of love has a god, a mother of god, a revealed law, a sacramental system, and so forth. The religion so established clearly parodies Christianity . . . It does not discredit the religious system which it apes; it ridicules the idolatry of the Lover.
>
> ("*Roman de la Rose*", pp. 205–6)

It is with the appearance of Genius, priest of Nature and bishop of Love, that the religion of love becomes most fully evident. Interestingly, MS *Mi* lacks the interpolated couplet normally appearing in *M* manuscripts in which Genius tells his audience to remember Reason; possibly the designer of the codex wished to suppress any such link between Genius and Reason. And the marginalia of MS *Mi* capitalize on the figure of Genius to express this idea of the erotic conquest as a parodic holy war. Images of the clergy have recurred throughout the manuscript, as they often do in marginalia; but there is a particularly heavy concentration in the closing pages of Genius' discourse and during the final assault on the Rose. Once again, the images are disposed largely by bifolium, yet not without careful attention to the coordination of image and text.

Three of the pages on one leaf are devoted to scenes representing the alliance of Love and Genius, represented allegorically as one involving ecclesiastical and royal forces (Fig. 5). The ecclesiastics convene towards the end of Genius' discourse (fol. 154r, vv. 20522–91): here we find cardinals arriving on horseback, greeted by a bishop and two clerics standing in front of a church (Pl. 18). But this is no ordinary bishop: instead of a crosier he holds a pen, whose feathery tip conveniently also recalls Cupid's arrows. The bishop is clearly Genius, wielding the instrument of his procreative function. On the other side of the bifolium, the cardinals continue to ride, now accompanied by a group of young men, apparently not clerics; here, Genius concludes his sermon (fol. 154v, vv. 20592–661). The other page appearing on this side of the bifolium holds the end of the Pygmalion digression and the renewed assault on the tower (fol. 159r, vv. 21144–213). This renewed fighting on behalf of the Lover is illustrated by the alliance of Genius' ecclesiastics with Love's barons: we see a tonsured cleric and two cardinals at the left, conversing with a king and two young men on the right. One could imagine this king as representing Cupid, who

154r (vv. 20522–91): Cardinals arrive; bishop with pen outside chapel

154v (vv. 20592–661): Cardinals and young men on horseback

159r (vv. 21144–213): Cardinals and young men before king

159v (vv. 21214–282): Hare and grotesque

Figure 5   Layout of bifolium depicting ecclesiastical and royal forces in an allegorical representation of the alliance of Love and Genius.

Plate 18   Marginal representation of Genius as a bishop holding a pen instead of a crosier. Paris, Bibliothèque Nationale MS fr. 25526, fol. 154r.

is always portrayed in MS *Mi* – as in many other fourteenth-century manuscripts – with a crown, and whom the Lover recognizes not only as a god but also as his feudal lord; the ground is clearly being laid for sexual conquest. That the artist was not simply amusing himself by drawing pictures of clerics is indicated by the fact that the motif is not used for the final page of the bifolium: here, the confrontation between Venus and Dangier is illustrated by the opposition of a rabbit, a standard image for feminine sexuality, and a grotesque with a large beak (fol. 159v, vv. 21214–82).

The tower is illustrated three times in the marginalia of this gathering: an image of a tower with a face peering out through a barred window illustrates Venus' defiance of Shame (fol. 155, vv. 20662–730); knights storming a tower that is defended by other knights illustrates the continuation of this passage, on a page that also holds a miniature in which Venus shoots her flaming arrow at the tower (fol. 155v, vv. 20731 – "Medusa" passage, v. 11); and we see a knight riding to the tower during the opening section of the Pygmalion story (fol. 156v, vv. 20802–72).

Interestingly, the marginalia make no attempt to illustrate the Pygmalion or Medusa stories themselves. The Medusa passage is too short to have required illustration, for it does not take up even one full page. But the Pygmalion episode lasts for several pages; and one can only say that, for the most part, it is treated as a digression, illustrated with images that provide a brief respite from the thematics of the frame text: birds and animals, children playing. There is one exception, however, which suggests what the designer of the marginalia must have seen as the importance of the Pygmalion story: where Pygmalion repents of his former chastity and prays to Venus, we find the image of a cardinal watching while a cleric kneels to offer a book to the pope (fol. 158r, vv. 21013–85). Not only does this scene continue the thematics of love's ecclesiastics; it is also a repetition of the image that illustrated the story of Narcissus (fol. 12v, vv. 1441–1516). We recall that this story also contains a prayer, that of Echo for the punishment of Narcissus (vv. 1455–66). The designer of the marginalia clearly worked from a global view of the poem. This pope – or antipope – presides over the religion of love, punishing the chaste or those disdainful of love and rewarding the amorous.

If we examine the marginalia in the order that they assume in the bound volume, the "holy war" for the Rose is clear. First the cardinals convene at the church of procreation, then ride off with the secular forces; there follow several scenes of the battle for the tower; there is the appeal to the pope, then to the king; and the end result is expressed with the reappearance of the phallus tree, tended by nuns. Not only is love a religion, it is one that preaches its own crusade.

As we have seen, not all readers of the *Rose* appreciated Jean's elaborate juxtaposition of the sacred and erotic registers of his poem. Part of what troubled the critics of the *Rose* was its reversal of the normal system of allegory. A sensual language used for spiritual allegory would not have been surprising; this, after all, can be found in the Bible itself, in the Song of Songs. But in the *Rose*, spiritual language carries an erotic sense. The play of registers – the sacred, the rational, the natural, the erotic – operates throughout the poem. Whether they were pleased or scandalized by it, medieval readers recognized it as essential to the poetics of the *Rose*; as Jean himelf said, "Ainsinc va des contreres choses, / les unes sunt des autres gloses" [thus it is with opposites: one is the gloss of the other (vv. 21543–44)]. The version of the text in MS *Mi* is, as we have seen, one in which the parameters of this play of discourses are even more widely drawn than in Jean's original text. It is to this aspect of the poem that the visual gloss brilliantly responds. Let us now turn to the manuscript's sacred and hagiographic images, in order to complete the picture we have begun to form.

THE ICONOGRAPHY OF DIVINE PASSION IN MS *MI*

As is appropriate to a text populated by Love's preceptors and his suffering disciples, the saints portrayed in MS *Mi* include both confessors and martyrs. In some cases the haloed figure preaching or being beheaded lacks specific features that would allow us to identify it with a particular saint, but it remains nonetheless clear that the sufferings of the Lover and the precepts offered by his advisers are being contrasted with a very different kind of suffering, a very different art of love. In many cases, however, the saint can be identified; and then it is clear that the choice was not arbitrary. For example, the marginal representation of the martyrdom of Saint Laurence appears, as we have seen, during the description of the carol participants (fol. 9r, vv. 953–1022). Much of the page is taken up with the description of Beauty, but the visual gloss probably refers to the figure of Richesse, named in the closing lines of the page. According to the legend, Saint Laurence was put to death in part for the crime of having emptied the imperial treasury by distributing everything to the poor; in the *Pelerinage de vie humaine*, the first recension of which predates MS *Mi* by no more than a few years, the personification of Avarice specifies that Saint Laurence is her special enemy: speaking of her love of wealth, she states, "Jadis Lorens sur le charbon / Je rosti pour ce quë osté / Il le m'avoit et destourné" [long ago I roasted Laurence over the coals because he had stolen and diverted it from me (*PVH*, vv. 10202–4)]. The designer of the marginalia thus suggests an ironic reading of Richesse: aristocratic opulence is not a virtue but a vice. As the description of Richesse continues on the next page, stressing her worldly power and enumerating the jeweled splendor of her garments, the margins respond with the martyrdom of Saint Catherine: a very different image of the female body, mortified and delivered to death so that the soul can be resplendent in heaven (fol. 9v, vv. 1023–92). And once again, the artist continued his theme across an entire bifolium side. The page across from fol. 9 holds a portion of the Lover's encounter with Cupid, who locks up his heart with a key and prepares to explain his commandments (fol. 16v, vv. 1981–2050). In the margin we find Saint Catherine preaching to a group of clerks, an illustration of the legend that her divinely inspired wisdom confounded the sages of the pagan king. In this way the bodily beauty and opulent garments of Love's followers are contrasted with the bodily mortification of the followers of God; and Love's precepts are contrasted with those of revealed religion.[12]

The same thematics of contrasting the teachings, and torments, of erotic love with those of divine love continues throughout the God of Love's sermon. While many of its pages are decorated with typical genre scenes, such as animals, a windmill, a knight tilting at a quintain – images that might have an erotic significance, or might be more purely decorative – one does find two martyrs, one of them a bishop and hence a confessor of the faith, on the page where Cupid forbids the uttering of unclean words and explains the need for elegant dress and appearance (fol. 17v, vv. 2100–73). Once again, physical beauty and stylishness is contrasted with the mortification of the flesh; given the large "Nota" written by the scribe next to the "clean speech" commandment (vv. 2101–2), it is likely that religious confession and preaching is being contrasted with Cupid's much more worldly notion of proper – i.e. euphemistic, hence deceptive – speech. And a cluster of saints appears at the end of the sermon, once more disposed on three pages of a single bifolium. The description of lovesickness is glossed with the image of a female martyr's soul being borne aloft by angels (fol. 20r, vv. 2458–527); the Lover's anxious questions as to how he is to bear the pain of lovesickness, by the beheading of a crowned female saint (fol. 20v, vv. 2528–95); and the conclusion of the sermon, with a male saint addressing a group of men (fol. 21v, 2670–741). Cupid's precepts are thus framed by scenes of saintly preaching; his preoccupation with physical beauty and with the torments of sexual desire is contrasted with saintly martyrdom.

A second cluster of saints appears near the midpoint of the poem, on the third leaf of the tenth gathering (Fig. 6). One side of the bifolium is devoted to Saint Nicholas: his gift of dowries to three poor girls glosses Ami's closing diatribe about feminine inconstancy (fol. 75r, vv. 9883–956), while his miraculous resurrection of three murdered clerks illustrates the God of

---

[12] The disposition of the saintly figures on this leaf shows that the artist did take into account the particular pages in question, rather than merely decorating a randomly selected bifolium with images of saints. He did not place the two images of Catherine together, nor the two martyrdoms; rather, he arranged his images such that Saint Laurence marks the appearance of Richesse; the image of female martyrdom continues the description of feminine splendor; and the image of preaching illustrates the God of Love's sermon.

75r (vv. 9883–956): Saint Nicholas and three maidens

75v (vv. 9957–10025): Martyr with angels; fountain

78r (vv. 10301–60): Saint Christopher; two rams

78v (vv. 10361–425): Saint Nicholas reviving the three clerks

Figure 6   Layout of bifolium showing Saint Nicholas and Saint Christopher.

Love's consolation of the unhappy Lover and his efforts to aid in his quest (fol. 78v, vv. 10361–425). The saint's charity and his commitment to lawful marriage contrast with Ami's cavalier advice to win women through bribery and deception, while also preparing a corrective to the Lover's upcoming attempt to win the favor of Richesse so that he can purchase sexual favors. Nicholas's identity as patron and protector of clerks, in turn, contrasts with Cupid's pretensions to the same position. On the other side of the leaf, a martyr flanked by angels continues the contrast with the lovesick disciple of Cupid (fol. 75v, vv. 9957–10025); and the figure of Saint Christopher, protector of real pilgrims, provides a telling contrast to the God of Love, patron of the "pilgrimage" that here gets under way (fol. 78r, vv. 10301–60).

Other saintly figures appear from time to time throughout the poem; the most important of these is Saint Margaret. As virgin martyr and patron of childbirth, she does have a particular relevance to the *Rose*. The most complete cycle of the life of Saint Margaret appears in the discourse of Reason, where the scenes are interspersed with scenes from the life of Christ. These images take up part of the sixth and all of the seventh gatherings of the manuscript. The infancy of Christ appears in the sixth gathering, together with a representation of Margaret as a shepherdess – her occupation at the time that an imperial legate abducted her and, when she spurned his sexual advances, had her imprisoned and executed. The first three sacred images – the Annunciation, the Visitation, and Saint Margaret – are on the pages where Reason tells the story of the young girl Virginia, who accepted death in order to avoid a life of sexual abuse (fol. 43v [vv. 5517–92] and fol. 44r [vv. 5593–5660]) (Pl. 19). Reason tells the story to illustrate her discussion of justice, but the marginalia respond more to the character of Virginia. Like Mary, she submitted wholly to the will of a father; like Margaret, she was martyred in the name of chastity. We are reminded of Gui's insertion of the story of Susannah at this point in the

303

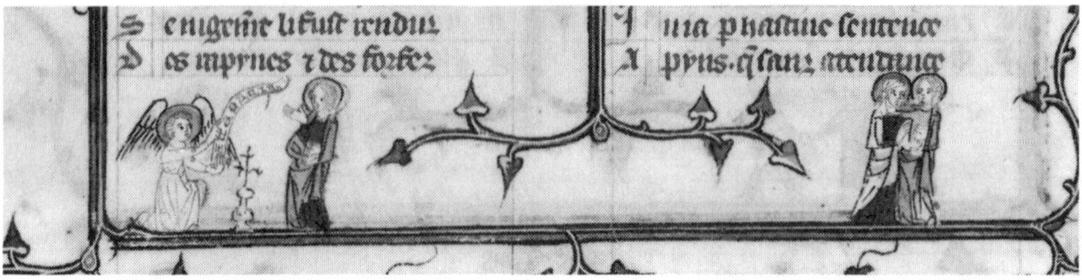

Plate 19   Marginal representation of the Annunciation and the Visitation in the discourse of Reason. Paris, Bibliothèque Nationale MS fr. 25526, fol. 43v.

poem. Whereas Gui offered the counter-example of a Biblical heroine miraculously spared both rape and death, the artist chose to glorify the notion of sexual purity, humility, and martyrdom; both responded strongly to the exemplary tale of a chaste maiden's tragic death.

It is also in this part of the poem – during the marginal representation of the infancy of Christ – that Reason advises the Lover that he should give up his foolish love for the Rose and love her instead. The daughter of God, rival for the Lover's affections, is thus juxtaposed with the Son of God, Bridegroom of all humanity. This juxtaposition continues throughout the next gathering, where, in the margins, the Passion of Christ is interwoven with the Passion of Saint Margaret on alternating bifolia (Fig. 7). In this way the artist stresses Margaret's identity as imitator and bride of Christ. The imagery of suffering and death is appropriate to the general tenor of the text, where Reason discusses the ravages of Fortune and recounts the deaths of such figures as Nero, Seneca, Croesus, and Manfred, stressing that worldly wealth and power offer no security to those who love them. Again, pagan and contemporary examples are expanded by the examples from sacred history and hagiography.

What does this juxtaposition imply? Do the marginalia suggest an assimilation of Reason and Christ, an equation of rational love with mystical love? Reason does state that her lovers, free from worldly desires, accept misfortune and death with tranquility; and in MS *Mi*, she does not hesitate to speak of divine love. Or do the steadfast sufferings of Margaret and Christ, conjoined through love of God, correspond to the torments which the Lover and Bel Acueil suffer for the sake of the God of Love? The Lover too has declared himself ready to undergo whatever suffering is necessary to prove his loyalty to Love, while Bel Acueil, like Saint Margaret, languishes in prison.

The system of contrasts is especially apparent on the first leaf of the seventh gathering; given the artist's habit of working with entire bifolia, it

49r (vv. 6275–6344): Arrest of Saint Margaret

49v (vv. 6345–414): Margaret led to prison

50r (vv. 6415–74): Arrest in Gethsemane

50v (vv. 6475–6532): Christ bearing the Cross

51r (vv. 6533–90): Hound pursuing fox

51v (vv. 6591–660): Margaret blessed in prison; Margaret beheaded

52r (vv. 6661–730): Crucifixion

52v (vv. 6731–802): Entombment of Christ

53r (vv. 6803–71): Resurrection of Christ

53v (vv.6872–941): Descent from the Cross

54r (vv. 6942–7011): Margaret's soul carried to Heaven

54v (vv. 7012–81): Hound pursuing fox

55r (vv. 7082–145): Flagellation of Christ

55v (vv. 7146–206): Mocking of Christ

56r (vv. 7207–77): Margaret in prison, tormented by devil

56v (vv. 7278–347): Flagellation of Margaret

Figure 7 Layout of gathering juxtaposing scenes from the Passion of Christ and the Passion of Saint Margaret.

is likely that he appreciated this fortuitous textual juxtaposition, even if he did not expect subsequent readers of the manuscript to notice it. Half of each side of this leaf is taken up with the discourse of Reason – here given over to Fortune and the death of Nero – and half to the initial exchange between the Lover and Ami. Thus the contrast between rational and carnal love is heightened through the juxtaposition of Reason and Ami; and of the death of Nero, disciple of Fortune, with the Lover's plaintive request for Ami's advice: "Mort sui, se n'i metez conseil" [I am dead, if you do not advise me (v. 7230; fol. 56r). The disposition of Saint Margaret's arrest, torture, and imprisonment across both sides of the leaf frames the dialectic of the poem with this third sort of love and suffering. Her arrest illustrates Reason's discussion of Fortune and honors (fol. 49r, vv. 6275–344); facing that, her flagellation illustrates Ami's initial advice (fol. 56v, vv. 7278–347).

On the verso side, a visibly wounded Margaret is led to prison while Reason narrates the death of Nero (fol. 49v, vv. 6345–414); facing that, Margaret is tormented in prison by the devil, while the Lover tells his sad story to Ami (fol. 56r, vv. 7207–77). The thematic nexus is particularly close knit on the verso side. The imprisonment of Margaret contrasts with the Lover's account on that page of Bel Acueil's imprisonment; the textual references to death, real or imagined, create a three-way configuration of the Lover, the saint, and Nero. And the scene of Margaret's encounter with the devil plays off two textual references to metaphoric devils: on fol. 56r, the Lover refers to Fear, Shame, and Dangier as "ly deable" [devils (v. 7240)], while on fol. 49v, Reason terms the forces of love "li vif deable" [living devils (v. 6361)].

Following this statement of contrasts on the opening leaf of the gathering, the two passion narratives are disposed alongside the text in which Reason argues for rational love and discourse over erotic love and discourse. To the textual triangle of Reason, the Rose, and the Lover there is thus juxtaposed the mystical marriage of Margaret and Christ: erotic passion and passionless reason are both contrasted with spiritual passion. It is not immediately easy to know how to read such a juxtaposition. Who, we may well ask, is the real "deable"? This interpretive difficulty points up the duality of perspective embodied in the text: we read the visual gloss one way through the eyes of Reason, another way through the eyes of the Lover. Ultimately, the images of sacred passion point up the limitations of the perspectives of both the Lover and Reason. What is represented in the margins is not simply the denial of passion, but rather its sublimation in mysticism – which, in the end, is just as "irrational" as sexual passion. The difference, of course, is that sexual passion is inferior to reason, while the mystical union of the soul with God – often described in quasi-erotic terms – transcends reason. But if Reason is revealed not to be the final goal of love, she is certainly shown to be superior to the Lover. In MS *Mi*, she reminds the Lover of the need to devote himself to God and to the Virgin. Listening to the voice of Reason is a first step towards spiritual enlightenment.

But the story of Christ is not only one of love; it is also the story of the redemption of a fallen humanity. The motif of the Fall is evoked in the discourse of Reason when she recounts the myth of the castration of Saturn, the act which caused the end of the Edenic Golden Age and the birth of Venus, goddess of sexual love and desire. The incarnation on earth of erotic love marks the beginning of the temporal world, governed by fickle Fortune. Reason acknowledges that humans have lost their original innocence; and in MS *Mi*, she speaks briefly of the redemptive powers of

43r (vv. 5453–516): Bagpipe-dance

43v (vv. 5517–92): Annunciation; Visitation

44r (vv. 5593–660): Saint Margaret as shepherdess; emperor on horseback

44v (vv. 5661–726): Slaughter of the Innocents

45r (vv. 5727–96): Adoration of the Three Magi

45v (vv. 5797–864): Flight to Egypt

46r (vv. 5865–934): Nativity

46v (vv. 5935–6006): Annunciation to the Shepherds

Figure 8 Layout of two bifolia showing scenes from the Nativity, Saint Margaret as shepherdess, and Venus' bagpipe-dance.

Christ. In this way too the marginalia, perhaps inspired by the "litany of love," expand on the thematics of the text: the Incarnation of divine love marks a new era, one in which spiritual redemption is possible. In fact, the marginal representations of the life of Christ begin on the page directly following the allusion to the birth of Venus. The marginalia stress that the doctrine of love – erotic, rational, divine – cannot be separated from the doctrine of Fall, of the partial redemption achieved by pagan philosophers with the light of Reason and the spiritual redemption offered by Christ.

Once again, the intricate play of text and visual gloss cannot be fully appreciated without a consideration of the layout by bifolium. The myth of Venus is illustrated in the margin of that page with a dance led by a bagpipe-player (fol. 43r, vv. 5453–516). The bagpipe dance is strongly associated with Venus in this manuscript, for the same image appears later on when La Vieille continues the story of Venus, telling of her adultery with Mars (fol. 107v, vv. 14143–212). But that is not its only significance. If we examine the entire bifolium, we find that the myth of Venus and the bagpipe-dance are next to the marginal representation of the Annunciation to the Shepherds (fol. 46v, vv. 5935–6006) (Figure 8). This is a most interesting juxtaposition. Medieval shepherds are commonly depicted as playing bagpipes, and bagpipe-players and dancers often appear in representations of the Annunciation to the Shepherds. This bagpipe-dance is at once the celebration of the incarnation of erotic love, and a pendant to the celestial celebration of the Incarnation of divine love. The motif was not chosen haphazardly; it contributes to the opposition of Fall and Redemption, each associated with a different type of love. A reader of the

Plate 20 Marginal representation of Saint Margaret in prison, as the Lover approaches the Rose. Paris, Bibliothèque Nationale MS fr. 25526, fol. 161v.

bound codex would have to be extraordinarily curious to discover this; it may have originated as a private joke on the part of the artist and the other artisans involved in making the book. But even if it was not meant for the eyes of later readers of the volume, this juxtaposition of images is an important clue to the ways in which the designer of the marginalia read the poem and conceived the book.

While the discourse of Reason contains the most complete cycle of illustrations of the lives of both Christ and Saint Margaret, both figures do reappear elsewhere in the manuscript. Margaret recurs in two further places; and both cases support the interpretation of the saint as a gloss on the spiritual blindness of the Lover and the sordidness of his tactics. Margaret as shepherdess appears on the page where La Vieille, after speaking with Faux Samblant, agrees to advance the Lover's case with Bel Acueil (fol. 95r, vv. 12421–84): the young maiden about to fall victim to abduction and sexual violence is thus offered as an analogy to the young lady represented by Bel Acueil, who is about to be betrayed and, in effect, sold to the Lover by La Vieille. Margaret's third appearance is at the end of the poem, as the Lover makes his final approach to the Rose (fol. 161v, vv. 21491–560). Here we see once more the double image of Margaret in prison: first tormented by the devil in the form of a dragon, then blessed by the Holy Spirit in the form of a dove (Pl. 20). This dual image of suffering and reward is surely a comment on the textual statement on the same page that "qui mal essaié n'avra / ja du bien guieres ne savra" [one who does not try evil will never know good (vv. 21533–34)], and that opposites have an effect of mutual glossing. The imagery of martyrdom and grace reveals that the concept of coming to know joy through the experience of sorrow has a far more elevated meaning than simply the intensified pleasure of a long-deferred orgasm. The visual gloss illustrates both the Lover's folly and the greater truth of his remarks – a truth that he himself cannot see.

The life of Christ recurs at many other points in the codex, with at least one scene appearing during each of the major discourses. Interestingly, the story, represented in its entirety during the discourse of Reason, is retold in fragmented form in the marginalia of Reason's three major opponents: Ami, Faux Samblant, and La Vieille. In general, the evocation of sacred history serves to point up the problematic nature of each character and his or her abuse of an authoritative discourse. Ami, arguing for love affairs outside of marriage, paints the horrors of marriage through the violent ravings of the Jaloux. At the beginning of this section (fol. 65r, vv. 8459–528) is the marginal image of Saint Paul, who in 1 Corinthians 7 specifically recommends marriage as the only acceptable context for sexual relations, and describes the sacred bond between husband and wife. The negative portrayal of marriage is thus implicitly countered by the presence of the Apostle. During the tirade of the Jaloux, the events of Christ's Passion are interlaced with representations of Hell, of monkey-priests, of animals. The mixture of images recalls the interlacing of the Passions of Christ and Margaret during the discourse of Reason. If Reason's advice might ultimately have led to mystical love, as exemplified by the saint, the advice of the cynical seducer and the abusive husband is more likely to lead to damnation.

As we survey the disposition of marginalia in the major discourses, a very interesting pattern emerges. In the discourse of Reason, the two-way opposition of the text – reason versus eros – gave way to the new opposition of reason *and* eros, as alternatives contained within this world, to otherworldly martyrdom; in the discourse of Ami the seeming opposition of "free love" and marriage, of courtly paramours and abusive husbands, gives way to a new opposition of worldly attachment versus attachment to the spiritual Bridegroom, and ultimately to one of damnation as opposed to salvation. A similar effect obtains in the discourse of La Vieille. There, that portion of the Gospel narrative concerned with feminine purity and humility provides a point of contrast both with the affected courtliness of Bel Acueil, and with the cynical worldliness of La Vieille; the poles of the contrast are ultimately defined as those of celestial purity and wanton sexual abandon. In all cases, the visual gloss expands the parameters of the text, redefining its system of "contreres choses," of "mal" and "bien."

The system of contrasts is particularly elaborate in the discourse of Faux Samblant. Faux Samblant represents, among other things, the abuse of justice and political power; and the scenes from the Gospel that gloss his discourse are the Flight to Egypt – Christ's escape from corrupt political authorities – and the arrest in Gethsemane. Once again, it is instructive to

81r (vv. 10694–761): Slaughter of the Innocents

81v (vv. 10762–832): Flagellation of Christ

82r (vv. 10833–900): Mocking of Christ

82v (vv. 10901–68): Couple conversing; nude man

87r (vv. 11366–422): Almsgiving; animal

87v (vv. 11423–92): Arrest in Gethsemane

88r (vv. 11493–558): Praying figures

88v (vv. 11559–625): Flight to Egypt

Figure 9   Layout of two bifolia showing scenes from the life of Christ in the discourse of Faux Samblant.

examine the complete bifolia where these images appear (Fig. 9). Two leaves contain scenes from sacred history, one on both sides; in all cases, the bifolium juxtaposes a page of text from Faux Samblant's sermon with one from the God of Love's address to his troops. In the first leaf of the gathering, the Slaughter of the Innocents illustrates Cupid's discussion of his mother (fol. 81r, vv. 10694–761), while, facing that, the Flight to Egypt illustrates Faux Samblant's revelations of his own hypocrisy (fol. 88v, vv. 11559–625). On the verso side, the Flagellation of Christ glosses Cupid's continued discussion of his mother and of the relative value of poor and wealthy lovers (fol. 81v, vv. 10762–832); and two praying figures gloss Faux Samblant's words about taking confession as a means of despoiling the wealthy (fol. 88r, vv. 11493–558). On the next leaf, finally, the Mocking of Christ accompanies Cupid's discussion of fleecing wealthy lovers (fol. 82r, vv. 10833–900), and the arrest in Gethsemane glosses Faux Samblant's explanation of the exile of Guillaume de Saint-Amour, caused by Faux Samblant's mother, Hypocrisy (fol. 87v, 11423–92).

The designer of the marginalia, studying these unbound pages, would thus have found a sustained juxtaposition of Cupid and his mother Venus with Faux Samblant and his mother Hypocrisy; in both cases the mother–son team is devoted to combating and routing their enemies and to despoiling the wealthy. In one place the text even cites the Gospel of Matthew (fol. 88v, vv. 11559–625). The visual gloss that frames the text draws on the Gospel, representing the abuse of Christ and of the Jewish innocents and twice using scenes that involve the mother–son relationship. The seeming opposition between the courtly, noble God of Love and the corrupt Faux Samblant dissolves as both figures are opposed to the embodiment of true love. We realize, in fact, that Faux Samblant can be seen as a parodic doubling of Cupid, generated directly from the context that has been established for erotic love: idleness, deception, and the abuse of wealth and power. Faux Samblant is a figure for desire run amok: as he says, "En aquerre est toute m'entente" [I think only of acquisition (fol. 88r; v. 11535)]. The close relationship between Cupid and Faux Samblant becomes explicit in the text when Cupid makes Faux Samblant an officer at his court, the *roi des ribauds*. The king and deity of erotic love and his officer in charge of regulating – or perhaps corrupting – sexual mores are thus both placed in opposition to the King of Heaven.

A further textual detail links the figures of Cupid and Faux Samblant and heightens their opposition to Christ. Reason and Ami respectively offer mythological and allegorical accounts of the fall of the Golden Age, and the marginalia consistently gloss these accounts with imagery of redemption. In Reason's version, the end of the Golden Age is associated with the birth of Venus; in that of Ami, with the appearance of Barat [Fraud]. These figures are none other than the mother of Cupid and the father of Faux Samblant respectively: the God of Love and his ghostly double represent two visions of desire and dissimulation in a fallen world, one considerably more grotesque than the other. It is thus fitting that both should be contrasted with the Redeemer. Both can also be associated with the fallen language that was problematized in the Lover's debate with Reason over obscenity and euphemism. Cupid, proponent of courtly diction and erotic poetry, represents the displacement of sign and referent through euphemism, obscurity, and seductive "douz parler." Faux Samblant, embodiment of mendacity, represents the complete dissociation of sign and referent: as shape-shifter and seducer, he is an endless generator of signs with no referent at all. Faux Samblant is thus the polar opposite of Christ, Incarnation of the Word and embodiment of absolute truth; indeed, he is closely identified with the Antichrist (vv. 11683, 11815, 14713–15). The God of Love, generator of poetic truth, mediates between the two poles of *mensonge* and *verité*, partaking of both.

Only a few images of sacred history appear in the discourse of Nature. The Annunciation is found at the top of fol. 137r, where Nature discusses optical allusions (vv. 18175–244). The image does not seem immediately appropriate to the topic at hand, but may be meant as a reminder of Nature's limitations: she does admit at a later point that the Virgin Birth surpasses her understanding. The Circumcision of Christ and the Adoration of the Magi appear on another bifolium (fol. 139v, vv. 18259–600; fol. 142r, vv. 18881–951). On these pages, Nature discusses nobility and the interpretation of celestial signs. The image of earthly kings worshiping the infant Jesus stresses that, in the face of divinity, all worldly rank and nobility is meaningless. It also reminds us of the most important celestial sign in history, the Star of Bethlehem that the three kings followed; and suggests that while the heavens can indeed be read and interpreted, we must remember that all such signs come from God. As in the other sections of the poem, the marginalia expand on the seeming opposition set up by the text: upper and lower classes, princes and clerks, are equal before God.

Just one sacred image appears in the discourse of Genius: as he begins his comparison of the Heavenly Park with the Garden of Delight, we find the Visitation represented in the upper margin, contrasting with two animal musicians, a fiddler and a drummer, in the lower margin (fol. 151v, vv. 20184–253). The marginalia on this page clearly express the system of oppositions elaborated by Genius. At the same time, the image of the Visitation stresses that the divine realm to which Genius alludes exists outside the realm of natural procreation, for we see here two images of miraculous pregnancy: the conception of John the Baptist was brought about by divine intervention, while that of Christ occurred through the sole agency of the Holy Spirit. The contrast set up by Genius is one of sterility – sexual abstinence or homosexuality – as opposed to the fertility of heterosexual activity; the visual gloss, here as throughout the codex, restates the poem's fundamental binarism in terms of purity and grace, whether virginal or conjugal, as opposed to sensual pleasure-seeking.

The recurring imagery of hagiography and the life of Christ establishes the contrast between the "religion of love" and the Christian religion as a motif running throughout the entire poem. Faux Samblant, the false friar, is the first explicitly ecclesiastical figure to ally with the forces of love; his abusive relationship to the sacraments of the Church is textually represented through his distortion of confession, and visually glossed with the image of a priest celebrating the Eucharist near the beginning of his sermon (fol. 83r, at v. 10969). The same gloss is applied to Genius, Love's other priestly figure. A miniature represents Genius addressing the troops at the beginning of his sermon (fol. 146r, at v. 19475); the preaching figure of Genius reappears in the upper margin, and in the lower margin we see a priest celebrating the Eucharist, accompanied by an angel. The ecclesiastical saints that recur in the margins likewise contrast with Cupid's officers. Saint Nicholas in particular, as a bishop who presides over marriage and the regeneration of life, is a corrective to Genius.

The foregoing discussion has amply demonstrated the relevance of the marginal images to the text, their function as a visual gloss. But although we have touched on points of similarity between the marginalia and other medieval responses to the *Rose*, the discussion has largely focused on MS *Mi* as an isolated phenomenon. Let us turn now to a consideration of the place of the marginalia in the larger context of medieval *Rose* reception.

THE LITERARY CONTEXT OF MS *MI*

One interesting analog for MS *Mi* is Jean de Condé's *Messe des oisiaus*, which dates from the first half of the fourteenth century and is thus not far removed from our manuscript.[13] This peculiar poem relates a dream-vision in which the narrator witnesses a Mass worthy of Genius himself. The service is celebrated by birds in honor of Venus; the priest is a nightingale, the bird most closely associated with erotic love in the vernacular tradition; the Eucharistic Host is a rose. Following the service, Venus presides over a banquet in which the menu consists entirely of such allegorical dishes as "sighs and plaints" (*MO*, ed. Ribard, v. 475), "hugs and kisses" (v. 600), and "jokes and games" (v. 623). An intoxicating beverage, consumed in large quantities, soon drives the banqueters into a frenzy, much to Venus' pleasure: she loves best those who drink the most. The feast is followed by a dispute between nuns and canonesses; the latter feel that, being of nobler birth, they have a greater right to love, and should not have to compete for lovers with the lower-born nuns. Venus declares that all living things are under her sway, that all are equal before Nature, and that all are therefore entitled to the pursuit of love.

At this point, Jean de Condé breaks off his narrative and offers an exposition of the poem, explaining that the first part is an allegory for the Mass; that the drunken, orgiastic banquet of Venus represents the transports of those who are filled with the Holy Spirit; and that the dispute and judgment are meant to remind us that all humans are equal in the eyes of God, and all have equal access to his love. Condé further adds that erotic love, in spite of its place in the natural order, poses a danger to spiritual salvation:

> Car Amours, dont Venus est dame,
> Ele est du tout contraire a l'ame
> Et dampnation li enorte,
> Ja soit che Nature l'aporte.
>
> (*MO*, vv. 1533–36)

For Love, whose mistress is Venus, is completely contrary to the soul and leads it to damnation, even if Nature does urge it.

---

[13] I cite from the edition by Ribard. For a discussion of the *Messe* in the context of fourteenth-century *Rose* reception, see Badel, *Roman de la Rose au XIVe siècle*, pp. 117–23. The poem and its gloss are discussed by Lepage, with attention to parodic and satirical elements, in "Dislocation de la vision allégorique."

He stresses that no one who has taken religious orders should pursue erotic love, for they are committed to "la vraie amour" [true love (v. 1564)], i.e. that of God. The laity, however, are free to pursue love within the legitimizing context of marriage: "Une amour y a raisounable, / Laqueile amour maintenir puelent / Tout cil qui mariier se vuelent" [there is a reasonable love, which can be maintained by all those who wish to marry (*MO*, vv. 1543–45)]. Marital love was ordained by God and is sanctified by the Church: "Par sainte Eglise est confermeis / Mariages" [Marriage is confirmed by Holy Church (*MO*, vv. 1548–49)].

If we take the *Messe des oisiaus* as an interpretent for MS *Mi*, certain aspects of the marginalia do become clearer. We find, for example, an explicit literary portrayal of a parodic religion of erotic love, one that contains overt allusions to the *Rose*. The mass and the ensuing banquet present an erotic Pentecost: as Ribard explains in his edition of the *Messe*, the service that is described is modeled on that used to celebrate the Pentecost, and the intoxicating drink, glossed as possession by the Holy Spirit, completes the motif. That this is a parodic infusion of spirits rather than Spirit is stressed by the effects of the drink, which, far from imparting to its imbibers the linguistic plenitude of the real Pentecost, actually deprives them of linguistic use: as the narrator comments, "Si buch un si grant trait aprés / Que je ne seu tiés ne romans" [so then I drank such a great draught that I knew neither Germanic nor Romance vernacular (*MO*, vv. 507–8)].

The seeming conflation of divine and erotic love that operates during the narrative proper is dismantled in the narrator's gloss on his poem, where it is made clear that the sexual liaisons of nuns are to be condemned and that the pursuit of erotic pleasure is in opposition to spiritual salvation and the love of God; erotic love is permissible only within the framework of holy matrimony. In these respects the *Messe des oisiaus* can be related not only to MS *Mi* but also to MS *Tou*, which was made within a few years of MS *Mi*. Gui's use of *De arrha animae* provides a similar point of contrast between erotic and divine love, as does the inclusion of the discourse of Genius in MS *Tou*; the designation of marriage as the appropriate locus of sexual love, though not a feature of the marginalia of MS *Mi*, does emerge from the more favorable representation of marriage in Gui's remaniement. MSS *Tou* and *Mi*, along with the *Messe des oisiaus*, bear witness to a fourteenth-century interest in the *Rose* as a text that problematizes the seeming sanctification of erotic love through the divine command to procreate, as well as the poetic sacralization of erotic love as an allegory for divine love. Both Gui de Mori and Jean de Condé remind us that not procreation, but the sacrament of marriage legitimizes sexual activity. Gui, Condé, and the designer of MS

Mi, as well as Machaut, demonstrate in different ways that the existence of an allegorical language signifying at once erotic and sacred love does not imply the actual equation of these two moral registers.

Do the marginalia of MS *Mi* operate in the same manner as Jean de Condé's gloss, suggesting that the *Rose* is ultimately to be read as an allegory for divine love or spiritual enlightenment? Such a reading would place the *Rose* in a well-established literary tradition whose most notable example, for medieval readers, was the Song of Songs. Nor was it impossible for pre-modern readers to approach the *Rose* from this perspective. Clément Marot, in the preface to his early sixteenth-century edition of the *Rose*, acknowledges that some of his contemporaries considered the *Rose* a dangerous work conducive to moral corruption; he suggests that it can be more profitably read if the Rose is understood as Divine Sapience, as Divine Grace, as the Virgin Mary, or as the Beatific Vision. Jean Molinet's late fifteenth-century prose redaction of the *Rose* includes an elaborate – and, to the modern eye, bizarre – interpretation of the text as religious allegory.[14] Some of Molinet's allegorizations do recall the juxtapositions of MS *Mi*. He identifies the God of Love with the Christian God, and the Lover with the human soul seeking its Lord; La Vieille as the Virgin Mary, mediatrix between the human soul and divine grace; the Jaloux as the Heavenly Bridegroom, disciplining the errant soul.

Still, as Rosemund Tuve has argued, such readings are inescapably at odds with the text; moreover, Molinet's work post-dates MS *Mi* by some 150 years, and so cannot reliably be used as a guide to the interpretation of the marginalia. Marot's edition is later still; and Marot himself evidently felt certain doubts about the authenticity of his suggested reading, for, having proposed that the author of the *Rose* may have intended a covert moral or allegorical sense, he adds, "Je ne veulx pas ce que je dis affermer, mais il me semble qui'il peult ainsi avoir faict" [I do not want to insist on the truth of what I said, but it seems to me that he could have done it that way (ed. Baridon, p. 90)]. The allegorization of the *Rose* as developed by both Molinet and Marot shows that the interpretation of the poem remained problematic and controversial into the sixteenth century. We see that medieval and Renaissance readers continued to interrogate the text for its moral and spiritual teachings, to explore the possible depths of its allegory, and to examine the erotic quest against the backdrop of the spiritual quest. The expositions of Molinet and Marot thus participate in

---

[14] Molinet's *Romant de la rose moralisie cler et net* was probably composed ca. 1482, and was published in 1500 (Vérard), in 1503 (Lyon), and in 1521 (Paris). See Tuve, *Allegorical Imagery*, pp. 237—46 and *passim*.

the general context in which we must read MS *Mi*; but these texts do not prove that the *Rose* of MS *Mi* is to be read as sacred allegory. La Vieille's discourse opens with marginal imagery of the Virgin Mary; but it closes with scenes of wanton depravity. In all, the contrasts between the saints depicted in the margins and the members of Cupid's entourage, and the carefully disposed scenes from the life of Christ, provide a far more coherent commentary on the text if they are understood as underscoring the opposition of erotic and divine love: the former is a parody or a debasement, not an allegory, of the latter.

Indeed, one cannot help feeling that even the gloss of the *Messe des oisiaus* is offered with more than a touch of irony. By constructing a vision of erotic love that closely parodies the Christian religion, Jean de Condé does make it possible to move from one register to the other with relatively little effort; because the rites of Venus form a sort of anti-Church, they allow for speculation on the structures and revealed truths of Christianity. Yet it would be difficult to admit that they contain these truths in any real sense. Condé leaves many details of his text unexplained, inviting the reader to supply the gloss. In this way he encourages his audience not to dwell on the representation of erotic love in and of itself, but rather to use it as a springboard for meditation on spiritual love and Christian doctrine. The gloss ultimately serves less to illuminate the events of his narrative than to redirect entirely the reader's reception of the poem. Much the same point can be made concerning Gui's prologue allusion to *De arrha animae*: the thoughtful reader realizes that the *Rose* is indeed not about the kind of love treated by Hugh and, by considering this opposition, may be led to a deeper understanding of earthly and heavenly love alike. And it is by studying the pattern of contrasts between the text and the sacred figures that surround it that the reader of MS *Mi* can be led to a similar understanding.

A second important analogue for MS *Mi*, virtually contemporary with the codex, is the first recension of the *Pelerinage de vie humaine*. Here too, the erotic quest is implicitly contrasted with the quest for spiritual salvation. Deguilleville even invokes some of the same saints that appear in MS *Mi*: Saint Laurence is opposed to Avarice (*PVH*, vv. 10202–4), Saint Nicholas is identified as the protector of clerks (*PVH*, vv. 8489–91). If we take the *Pelerinage* as an interpretent for MS *Mi*, we must conclude again that the sacred images in the marginalia are an implicit critique of erotic love, providing a corrective to the text. Deguilleville reveals the hazards that await those who enter the path of Oiseuse; he demonstrates both the wisdom and the limitations of Reason, and firmly establishes the subservience of Nature to divine wisdom and grace. He rewrites the *Rose*, transforming erotic allegory into spiritual allegory. The visual gloss of MS *Mi* operates in much the same manner, embedding the erotic quest in a larger framework that reveals the limitations of Reason and Nature and the blindness of the Lover, laying bare the machinations cloaked by the courtly allegory and also mapping out the alternative path of spiritual salvation.

Yet another literary analog for MS *Mi* is the vernacular polyphonic motet. With its use of multiple voices, the motet lends itself more than any other literary genre to the simultaneous juxtaposition of moral and poetic registers. Motets vary in degree of poetic complexity, and in many cases the two or three texted voices belong to a single register, be it devotional, courtly, or pastoral. In a significant number of cases, however, the texted voices are in a relation of contrast or opposition, as amorous, antifeminist, and devotional texts are placed in various combinations. In "Qui voudroit feme esprover" (ed. Raynaud, no. 14), for example, the juxtaposition of an antifeminist diatribe in the quadruplum with a love monologue in the triplum and an evocation of springtime in the duplum recalls the *Rose*, with its contrast between the antifeminist song of Male Bouche and the Lover's amorous lament, or between Bel Acueil and La Vieille. In the motet, the accompaniment of these voices by a tenor drawn from the liturgy suggests that the backdrop for these various views of love and of women, these various models for relations between the sexes, is the overarching framework of religious devotion: a similar effect to that created in MS *Mi* with the representation of the Virgin in the margins of La Vieille, or of the Ascension of Christ at the increased activity of Male Bouche following the Lover's kiss.[15]

A second example, even more relevant to the *Rose*, is Machaut's motet "Amours qui a le pouir / Faux Samblant m'a deceü / Vidi dominum" (ed. Chichmareff, no. 15). As Kevin Brownlee has shown, the duplum and triplum elaborate an opposition between Love, who acts on a person's inner being, and Faux Samblant, identified with the outward appearance of the lady.[16] The seductive beauty of the lady seems to offer hope to her lover, but she ultimately betrays such hope in her unwavering resistance to love; Love, who would be capable of moving the lady to receive her lover, has thus far refrained from doing so. This opposition is undercut by the tenor, whose text ultimately derives from Genesis 32:30: "Vidi dominum facie ad faciem; et salva facta est anima mea" [I have seen the Lord face to face, and my soul is saved]. Both the God of Love and Faux Samblant are thus contrasted with the Christian God as the ultimate embodiment of truth and source of salvation, in a move that closely parallels the effect created by the marginalia in MS *Mi*. Furthermore, Brownlee points out that a similar

---

[15] On the juxtaposition of voices in the Old French motet, including remarks on the relationship between certain motets and the *Rose*, see my "Polyphonic Poetry."
[16] Brownlee, "Machaut's Motet 15 and the *Roman de la Rose*."

strategy is used by Machaut in other motets: the motet "De Bon Espoir de /
Puis que la douce / Speravi" (ed. Chichmareff, no. 4) contrasts amorous and
spiritual hope; and the motet "Qui es promesses de Fortune / Ha! Fortune /
Et non est qui adjuvat" (ed. Chichmareff, no. 8) opposes Fortune and
divine Grace, an opposition created in MS *Mi* by the marginal representation of Margaret and Christ during Reason's discussion of Fortune. The
vernacular motet thus provides a generic analog for MS *Mi*, again
supporting a reading of the visual gloss as a means of setting the dialectics
of Eros, Reason, and Nature against the backdrop of divine love and truth.

Although the visual gloss of MS *Mi* is clearly the work of one who loved
the *Rose*, and presumably one who read it as a poem that carried a moral
teaching – a most elaborate art and remedy of love – the reading that is
implied by the marginalia is ultimately different from that outlined by either
Gui de Mori or Pierre Col. For example, Gui's lengthy focus on marriage
and on the possibility of a constructive love relationship – one that might
not even include sexual consummation – has no counterpart in the
marginalia, where erotic dalliance and saintly martyrdom, damnation and
salvation, are the two alternatives. In this respect the marginalia follow the
text of Guillaume and Jean, where – as Christine de Pizan was quick to note
– marriage is not offered as a viable alternative, and where the two choices
faced by the Lover are the pursuit or the renunciation of erotic pleasure.
Pierre Col's reading of the discourse of Genius as a serious contrasting of
the follies of *fol' amour* with the celestial joys of spiritual salvation is not
entirely foreign to MS *Mi*, which arranges for this contrast to be played out
on a large scale throughout the entire poem. Yet it is difficult to believe that
the designer of the marginalia read the discourse of Genius as an orthodox
sermon. Like Deguilleville, the designer of MS *Mi* was undoubtedly
inspired by the explicit evocation of divine love in the discourses of Genius
and – given the presence of the *M* text – the discourse of Reason; but also
like Deguilleville, the designer of the marginalia set out to do the job right.
Nothing in the marginalia suggests the valorization of heterosexual
activity, whether for the purpose of procreation or for that of avoiding
homosexuality, that is put forth by Genius and accepted in Pierre Col's
reading of the *Rose*. Instead, the marginalia suggest a reading of Genius'
sermon as parody, to be taken in the same vein as the spiritual metaphors
with which the poem concludes: the juxtaposition of sacred and erotic
registers is indeed meaningful and telling, but not in the manner imagined
by Genius or by the Lover.

In spite of its idiosyncratic nature in the context of *Rose* iconography, the
visual gloss of MS *Mi*, while retaining its own distinctive character, does fit
into the general context of fourteenth-century *Rose* reception as exempli-

fied in literary responses and remaniements. The interpretive issues that it raises were important ones for medieval readers of the *Rose*, however unusual it may have been to explore these issues through the medium of marginal illustrations. In order to complete our understanding of this remarkable visual gloss, we must now return to the manuscript and examine once more the disposition of the images by bifolium.

THE CODICOLOGICAL ROSE: THE CONCENTRIC STRUCTURE OF MS *MI*

In the foregoing discussion I have stressed the importance of examining not just pages, but bifolia in MS *Mi*. The layout of images across bifolia and the resulting play of textual passages and visual commentary occurs too frequently to be coincidental; the marginalia were clearly designed and executed as a response to this copy of the poem, with its particular gathering structure and juxtaposition of passages on individual bifolia. Such a disposition of marginalia is extraordinary. I have been unable to find another manuscript of any kind in which such a high proportion of the marginalia – much less narrative sequences of images – are executed by bifolium. While other such manuscripts may nonetheless have existed, it is safe to say that MS *Mi* is quite unusual; the overall layout of the marginalia must be included in our analysis of the visual gloss.

In the bound book, the disposition of the marginalia by bifolium results in a concentric framing of episodes and motifs. In the seventh gathering, for example, the concentric disposition of episodes of the two Passions is striking. This effect of *emboîtement* creates a pronounced rhythm throughout the manuscript. At the center of the fourth gathering, for example, is the Ascension and Christ in Majesty, framed by pages of apes and beasts. The Pentecost appears at the center of the fifth gathering, framed by scenes of daily life and by hybrids. In the eleventh gathering, scenes from the life of Christ frame genre scenes and animals, with the torments of Hell at the center. In the seventeenth gathering, genre scenes frame pages of obscenities, which in turn frame more genre scenes, with a sexual encounter at the center. Many of the gatherings in the first half of the book have sacred scenes at the center. In the second half the number of sacred images diminishes sharply; erotic and violent images increase.

The concentric disposition of the marginalia is analogous to the rhetorical *emboîtement* practiced by Jean de Meun. This concentric style is particularly pronounced in the discourses of Ami, La Vieille, and Nature.[17]

---

[17] On Jean's use of *emboîtement*, see Poirion, Le *"Roman de la Rose"*, pp. 125–26; Patterson, " 'For the Wyves love of Bathe'," pp. 669–74.

Each of these characters repeatedly digresses from one topic to another until finally, in the second half of the speech, each unfinished topic is completed, beginning with the most recent and working backwards to the topic with which the speech began. We have seen that Gui de Mori sought to restructure the major discourses of the poem, imposing a linear order both by deleting entire trains of thought, and by relocating passages from the second half to the first half of the discourse. But no doubt other readers appreciated the concentric structure as an important aspect of Jean's poetics. Nature, digressing and at times virtually free-associating from topic to topic, produces a discourse whose structure is of a complexity to match the cycles and epicycles of the Ptolemaic cosmos. La Vieille, expert on seduction, builds slowly to a climax, revealing ever more of her art of erotic conquest, ever more of her own sexual escapades; she tantalizingly dangles Mars and Venus before us, ensnared in amorous embrace, and leaves them suspended while she digresses on the topic of the natural sex drive. Aside from creating the ironic effect aptly noted by Fleming – La Vieille discourses about sexual freedom at precisely the moment that her exemplary couple is caught in a trap – Jean's digressive style is essential to the endless deferral of the poem's ending, the protracted pleasure of the text.[18] The poem as a whole is constructed around a midpoint passage that includes a description of the climax with which the poem will end and even a quotation of its closing verses, which will not reappear for another ten thousand lines. As La Vieille herself says: "Geus d'amours est, quant plus demeure, / plus agreable par demeure" [the game of love is all the more pleasant the more it is delayed (vv. 14289–90)].

The effect of poetic dilation and digression is matched in the marginal images in much of the codex. The antics of the couple introduced in the margins of La Vieille's discourse are interrupted by other motifs and do not reach their climax until several pages later, at the end of her discourse. The martyrdom of Margaret, the entombment and Resurrection of Christ, are enshrined at the center of their joint story, concentrically framed by episodes split between the first half and the second half of the gathering. Only through a vision of the entire series of images does the complete narrative fall into place. Possibly the designer of the marginalia was inspired by the structure of the *Rose*. The kaleidoscopic flow of the marginalia, the interlace of themes, certainly does parallel Jean's digressive and encyclopedic poetics.

---

[18] Fleming discusses La Vieille's use of Mars and Venus in *"Roman de la Rose"*, pp. 179–81. Patterson discusses poetic dilation and *emboîtement* as a strategy for deferring the poem's ending in " 'For the Wyves love of Bathe.' "

The concentric disposition of the marginalia has a further consequence, whether by chance or by design, for the reader of the bound book. The sequence of images invites a reading independent of that of the written text, which of course follows the normal progression from page to page. To follow the narrative sequence of the marginalia or to match up the pages decorated with the same motifs, one would have to read this book gathering by gathering, leaf by leaf, reading each gathering from the outside towards the center. To return to the example of gathering seven: one can follow the narrative sequence of the marginal images by beginning with fol. 49r and 56v, then 49v and 56r; fol. 50r and 55v, then 50v and 55r; and so on (see p.305, Fig. 7). The concentric structure of the gathering corresponds to that of the Rose, formed of concentric petals and located at the center of a series of concentric frameworks and fortifications that multiply dizzyingly throughout most of the poem.[19] The reading of the marginalia, a process of opening and of movement towards the center of the leaves of the gathering, continuously re-creates the central action of the poem: the unfolding of the rose and the movement towards its center. Did the author of the marginalia conceive the book in the image of the Rose? One could hardly give a definitive answer to this question. But such a conception would explain the peculiar system of the marginalia.

If the book is indeed conceived as a series of symmetrical framings, then it is important to investigate the image found at the center of the whole – at the center of the central gathering. It is of course at the midpoint of the text that Jean reveals the dynamics of the poem's joint authorship, a strategy picked up by Gui de Mori when he inserted his own name and portrait into the text. We might expect, then, that the designer of the marginalia would also take advantage of this important structural point. As it happens, the midpoint of the poem does not quite correspond to the center of the book, or of a gathering; the text covers twenty gatherings plus an additional three folios. But the center of the tenth gathering falls very close to the midpoint discussion of authorship, coinciding with the arrival of the God of Love to console the Lover. And here, we do in fact find a very interesting series of figures. A woman working at a table – possibly preparing ink or pigments – and a male scribe at his desk appear at the end of the discourse of Richesse (fol. 77r, vv. 10163–232). And on the next page, at the arrival of the God of Love (fol. 77v, vv. 10233–300), we find a man and a woman – presumably the same couple – seated each at a desk, entering decorative initials on to

---

[19] On the accumulation of frames and layers around the Rose, see Verhuyck, "Guillaume de Lorris *ou* la multiplication des cadres."

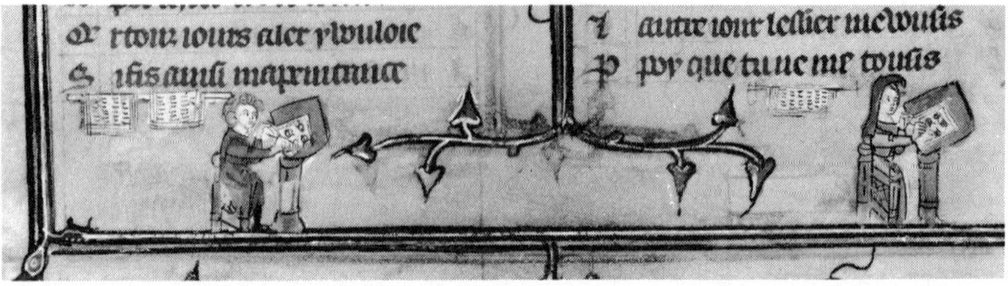

Plate 21 Marginal representation of illuminators. Paris, Bibliothèque Nationale MS fr. 25526, fol. 77v.

sheets of parchment with more pages of text hanging on racks behind them (Pl. 21).

This portrait of the book-makers is most remarkable. It is hard to escape the conclusion that they represent the Montbastons, the artisans who made MS *Mi*. As designers and makers of the codex, their images appear at the codicological center of the poem, just as the verbal portraits of the poem's authors appear at the textual center. It is certainly intriguing that this poetic mirror of love and eros, in which writing becomes an important metaphor for sexual intercourse and in which the book itself is seemingly modeled on the Rose, should be represented as resulting from the joint efforts of man and woman.

The marginalia of MS *Mi* play a complex and subtle role. As an iconographic code, they comment upon and expand the dialectic play of the poem. This response to the text, though idiosyncratic in many ways, has elements in common with other medieval reactions to the *Rose*. But the marginalia are more than just a simple series of visual glosses. The marginal program has its own coherence, follows its own internal law. It unfolds alongside the poem, providing a counterpoint to the text. This brief analysis of MS *Mi* has shown above all the extent to which the book subsumes all textual and visual elements – poems, rubrics, miniatures, marginalia – to become a work of art in and of itself.

9

Conclusion: the protean *Rose*

Pectoribus mores tot sunt, quot in orbe figurae;
  Qui sapit, innumeris moribus aptus erit,
Utque leves Proteus modo se tenuabit in undas,
  Nunc leo, nunc arbor, nunc erit hirtus aper.[1]
(*Ars amatoria*, 1:759–62)

The *Romance of the Rose* is a protean text, as difficult to grasp and to interpret, and as prone to modification, as the shape-shifting god himself. The art of love originally offered by Guillaume is revised and reinterpreted from a variety of perspectives in the course of Jean's continuation, and his principal motifs transposed into the most diverse contexts. The figure of Oiseuse comes to be identified not only with the leisure time stipulated by Ovid as a prerequisite for amorous pursuit, but also with the idleness of the mendicants and with the irresponsibility of those who fail to procreate. Franchise, originally a figure for the open expression of amorous affection, gives rise to La Vieille's vision of sexual freedom as opposed to marriage and to Nature's doctrine of free will unhampered by divine omniscience. Gui de Mori reveals that the art of seduction itself is too multifarious for simple codification. Echoing Ovid, Gui's Ami explains to the Lover that "par nule general rieule / Amors de feme ne se rieule / . . . / Car eles ont les coers muables" [the love of women cannot be regulated by any general rule, for they have changeable hearts (MS *Tou*, fol. 80r)]. It is necessary for the would-be lover to adapt to the particular character of the woman he pursues. While ostensibly attributing the principle of protean mutability to the feminine nature, Gui thus implicitly claims this principle for the male lover as well: he who would love must be able to modify his behavior at will.

---

[1] "Hearts have as many fashions as the world has shapes; the wise man will suit himself to countless fashions, and like Proteus will now resolve himself into light waves, and now will be a lion, now a tree, now a shaggy boar" (transl. Mozley).

Conclusion

The *Rose* contains the very embodiment of Proteus in the persona of Faux Samblant, who declares,

> car Protheüs, qui se soloit
> muer en tout quan qu'il voloit,
> ne sot onc tant barat ne guile
> con je faz . . .
> (vv. 11151–54)

For Proteus, who was accustomed to change himself into whatever he wanted, never knew such fraud or guile as I practice.

This enigmatic figure of falseness, of seeming rather than being, appears at the midpoint of the poem, in the same passage where the poem's two authors are named; his intervention marks the turning point of the Lover's enterprise. As the embodiment of fiction, Faux Samblant is the link between poetry and seduction, the problematic mendacity that lies at the heart of both the literary and the erotic quest. The *Rose* is haunted by a search for truth: for the meaning hidden in obscure dreams and fables, for an unproblematical relationship of word and thing, for the unmasking of hypocritical promises and ruses. At the same time, it warns against the dangers of proceeding too openly. The husband must conceal his secrets, the wife her adultery, the lover his desire. The woman adorns her body, making of it a work of art: La Vieille characterizes her own youthful self as "d'aournemenz envelopee, / por neant fust une popee" [enveloped in adornments, such that a doll was nothing in comparison (vv. 14081–82)]. The poet expresses himself in fictions and allegorical figures, compelling and at times disturbing, and never easy to decipher. The *Rose* grants its readers a totalizing vision of love and desire in a social, a natural, and a spiritual context. Yet the vision that comes to us is not unmediated: gazing into the *Miroër aus amoreus*, we glimpse the truth *per speculum in aenigmate* rather than face to face.

Christine de Pizan based her criticism of the *Rose* in part on its very difficulty of interpretation: in her opinion, it would never be possible to arrive at a definitive understanding of the poem, "car la matiere en est tres deshonneste" [for the material is very deceptive (ed. Hicks, p. 126)]. She compared the *Rose* to an alchemical treatise, a form of literature that seems to have definite ties to the physical world and to prescribe specific operations, yet is so obscurely written that it cannot be deciphered:

Sés tu comment il va de celle lecture? Ainsy come des livres des arguemistes: les uns les lisent et les entendent d'une maniere, les autres qui les lisent les entendent tout au rebours. (Ibid.)

Do you know how this reading is going? Just like with the books of the alchemists:

some read them and understand them in one way, others who read them understand them in the opposite manner.

As Christine saw it, the attempt to extract meaning from the *Rose* was an undertaking as doomed to failure as that of the alchemist who attempts to "fere de fiens or" [make gold from dung (ibid.)]. For Christine, deeply concerned with the role played by literature in social reform, as for a monastic writer like Deguilleville, the enigmatic, protean quality of the *Rose* was troubling. A similar desire to simplify the text or to clarify its didactic import appears, as we have seen, in various abridgments and remaniements of the thirteenth and fourteenth centuries.

Nonetheless, the multitude of perspectives contained within the *Rose*, the plethora of mythographic and allegorical exempla that reflect and refigure its themes, must also be held responsible for its unparalleled success in the field of medieval French literature. The many texts that are incorporated into Jean's *Rose* in particular, and the transformations wrought on the canonical texts of the university curriculum – such as the successive recasting of Philosophy and Natura in Reason, La Vieille, and Nature – are both a source of delight and a rich field for interpretation. As Badel showed in his study of the reception of the *Rose*, and as we have seen in the analysis of the *Rose* manuscript tradition – and as Christine asserted from a somewhat different perspective – this was a poem that was susceptible to the most varied readings. For this very reason, the *Rose* appealed to a wide and diverse audience. Moreover, the open-ended quality of the text with its unfulfilled promises of glossing and exposition, its kaleidoscopic review of such themes as love, sexuality, and language, and its explicitly multiple authorship, invited the participation of subsequent poets in the continuing process of shaping and reshaping the poem.

The different approaches of the various poets of the *Rose* can be illustrated by comparing their treatment of specific passages. For example, both Gui de Mori and the redactor of MS *κυ* reworked the story of Narcissus in Guillaume de Lorris. Gui rewrote the passage entirely, omitting all reference to Echo and inserting the story of Narcissus' mother, Liriopé, who was raped by Floris in female disguise.[2] Several points emerge from the analysis of Gui's Narcissus. First, although Gui deleted Guillaume's warning to women not to follow the example of Narcissus in rejecting their suitors, he incorporated this message into the fabric of the tale. With Echo gone, the story contains no positive female figure.

---

[2] Gui's version of the Narcissus passage has been published by Jung, "Gui de Mori et Guillaume de Lorris," pp. 120–22.

Narcissus' crime, resistance to appropriate sexual love, is a replay of his mother's similar failing; and just as Liriopé was tricked and overpowered, so Narcissus is taken by surprise and assaulted by love's arrow. Feminine pride and resistance, embodied in the mother and passed along to her unfortunate son, lie explicitly at the basis of the exemplum. Gui thus develops the story in accordance with the overall framework of the *Rose* as he understood it, an exposition of erotic love and the power it exercises on the human psyche, devoted in large part to an explication of the means by which feminine resistance can be overcome. While we cannot know whether Gui produced this version of Narcissus before or after having read Jean's continuation, it is interesting to note that this view of sexual relations – that resistance is to be overcome by force and guile – fits very well with Ami's recommendations to the Lover and with the conclusion of the quest, and is more fully appropriate to the *Rose* of Jean de Meun than to that of Guillaume de Lorris.

In addition, Gui's treatment of Narcissus emphasizes the youth's complete lack of interest in all women. Ovid's Narcissus is uninterested in amorous attachments with either men or women; Guillaume's Narcissus is simply uninterested in Echo. Gui's Narcissus, however, specifically rejects heterosexual involvement: "Et si fu ses coers embramis / D'orgoel, c'ainc ne volt estre amis / A dame ne a damoisiele" [and thus his heart was so consumed with pride that he did not want to be beloved of any lady or maiden (MS *Tou*, fol. 18v)]. For this reason, it is all the more significant that the figure that Narcissus does fall in love with is masculine: "il cuida tout ciertainement / Vëoir .i. emfant proprement" [he thought with certainty that he clearly saw a young boy (fol. 19r)]. In effect, Narcissus rejects heterosexual love in favor of a homoerotic attachment that is also a form of self-love. Although Gui deleted explicit references to homosexuality from both Reason and Genius, he did retain Genius' exhortation to procreate, and he would certainly have known that the condemnation of sodomy was a theme of *De planctu Naturae*. Reason, for her part, reminds the Lover in MS *Mor* that self-love is a form of idolatry – preferring the creature to the creator – and spiritual death. Gui's reworking of Narcissus results in a double parable of the irresistible power and supremacy of heterosexual, procreative love and the lethal effects of homoerotic attraction and self-love. Again, one cannot help wondering to what extent Gui may have revised his Narcissus episode in the light of Jean's continuation.

The treatment of Narcissus in MS κυ reflects very different concerns. As we have seen, the primary innovation in this version of Narcissus is the insertion of the comparison between the mirror of love and that crafted by Virgil (Appendix E, 1). The contrast between homoerotic and heterosexual attraction is not important here; instead, the contrast is between eros and wisdom, between abandonment to passion and the discipline of political and military rule. This contrast is elaborated in terms of two kinds of vision represented by the two mirrors, establishing a theme that will remain important throughout the poem. Reason attributes sexual desire to "vision desordenee" [disordered vision (v. 4352)]; Nature discusses mirrors, visions, and optical illusions; Genius explains that whereas the perilous mirror drives mad those who gaze into it, the fountain of life reveals the truth about oneself and God. And of course Perseus appears in MS κυ with his mirror of wisdom and prowess, protection against the dangerous feminine allure.

In keeping with its emphasis on the motif of vision, the Narcissus story in MS κυ manifests certain other variants that appear in none of the manuscripts collated by Langlois, but that are shared by MS Pierpont Morgan M 132, which contains the same version of Guillaume de Lorris as MS κυ. The cause of Narcissus' death, for example, is no longer love but the obsessive gaze itself. The standard text states that "il ama son ombre demainne, / si en fu morz" [he loved his own shadow, and thus he died (vv. 1492–93)]; the text of MS κυ reads, "Et vit tant son ombre demaine / Qu'il en fu mors" [and he saw his own shadow so much that he died from it (fol. 12v)]. MS M 132 goes one step further, attributing the death simply to the fatal vision of a human figure: here, we learn that Narcissus died because he "vit tant cel umbre humaine" [saw that human shadow so much (fol. 13v)]. The motif of sight dominates the account of Narcissus' death, even more than in other manuscripts. The standard text explains that when Narcissus saw that he could not have what he desired, "il perdi d'ire tot le sen / et fu morz en poi de termine" [from rage he completely lost his senses and was soon dead (vv. 1500–01)]. Both MSS κυ and M 132 insert here an additional allusion to deranged vision: "Tant qu'il en perdi tout son senz / Et fu mort; car les ieus de chief / Le volerent a grant meschief" [until he completely lost his senses from it and died; for his eyes burst from his head in despair (MS κυ, fol. 12v)]. Narcissus' disordered vision, narrow, self-absorbed, and ultimately self-destructive, is associated with the lethal effects of erotic obsession and contrasted with the revelatory vision of Virgil's mirror and its service to the empire: in this way the Narcissus story is adapted to fit into the ethical framework of MS κυ. Unlike Gui, the redactor of the text in MS κυ did not significantly expand or modify the poem's art of love or its exposition of courtship and sexuality. His contribution lay primarily in the development of a moral program stressing the responsibilities of rulers and the lessons of history.

It is equally illuminating to compare the treatment of Reason, Nature, and Genius in different textual versions, for these important figures take on very different guises. Reason's use and defense of obscenity, for example, is deleted by Gui de Mori; modified by the *B* remanieur; expanded in the *KLMN* manuscripts; and expanded even more in MS *κυ*. Gui modified Jean's elaborate exploration of the dynamics and the subversion of allegory. Gui wanted the poetic text to present an attractive, decorous surface; and he admired the *Rose* as an allegorical art of love. He suppressed the entire discussion concerning the difference between euphemism and *integumentum*, as if preferring not to raise the issue. For Gui there was nothing irrational or hypocritical about a refined and intellectualized love poetry; we recall that in his text Reason, far from condemning such discourse, actually praises *bel chant amoureux*. Gui does, however, implicitly identify the Lover as an irrational reader by having him cite Hugh of Saint Victor and 1 John in defense of love: the Lover clearly has not grasped the distinction between different kinds of love, and misunderstands Hugh's allegory of betrothal and amorous embrace as referring to the sort of love he feels for the Rose. In his own way, then, Gui does portray the Lover as a perversely literal reader, one incapable of understanding the realm of the spirit; but he does so in a way that leaves intact the possibility of decorous poetry about human love.

Both the *B* and the *KMN* versions of the *Rose* also, in different ways, expand on the Lover's literalization of that which should be understood figuratively or spiritually, showing that the only kind of "hidden meaning" he understands is an erotic one. The *B* remanieur is still somewhat cautious in his approach to the issues of euphemism and obscenity, treating the hypocrisy of euphemism in a playful manner while nonetheless avoiding "plain speech." But the author of the *KLMN* interpolation extending Reason's comments about the consequences of calling relics "testicles" was clearly exploiting the link between Reason's discussion of allegory and euphemism, and the concluding episode of the poem. Copies of the *Rose* containing this passage present even more explicitly the conflict between two allegorical systems, one incarnating spiritual and intellectual concepts through bodily images and one figuring the erotic by means of the spiritual.

Gui's *Rose* does resemble the *KMN* manuscripts, however, in its addition of a theological dimension to Reason's teachings – a feature lacking both from the *B* text and from the original poem. Among the various versions of the *Rose* one can discern two quite different concepts of Reason. Reason as presented by Jean and as developed in the *B* text is, in Wetherbee's words, "*only* 'reason' . . . and the love she asks is in effect a renewal of man's sense of participation in the natural order."[3] Reason does

---

[3] Wetherbee, "Literal and the Allegorical," p. 271.

not cast the Lover's problem in theological terms, does not speak of Grace: she proposes rational, moral behavior. Deguilleville, who probably encountered the *Rose* in a recension of the *B* text, followed this view of Reason's capacities and limitations in his opposition of Reason and Grace. But in certain other versions of the *Rose*, we find a Reason who does speak in theological terms, one who better fits Fleming's characterization of Reason as an image of Divine Sapience. In these texts Reason still offers advice about moral behavior in this world; but she also refers to the love of God, to mystical illumination and to the Incarnation, urging her young charge to embrace a love that is supra-rational and spiritually uplifting.

If Gui expanded Reason's role, however, he considerably reduced Nature's discourse. In this he resembles the redactors of MSS *Bi* and *Lm*. Yet these approaches to the abridgment of Nature are again independent, reflecting quite different concerns. Gui created a Nature who more closely resembles a combination of Alain de Lille's Natura and Boethius' Philosophy: she teaches about free will and laments the sins of the human race, without digressing very far from these themes. In MS *Lm*, on the other hand, Nature has little to say about free will; but she does discourse about optics, dreams, and nobility, as well as touching on the mystery of the Incarnation. The contrast between Gui and the *Lm* remanieur continues in the discourse of Genius. Gui's Genius resembles the Genius of Alain de Lille: he is neither theologian nor social philosopher, but simply reiterates the dependence of natural law on divine authority and voices the need for humankind to uphold Nature's work. The Genius of MS *Lm* is no longer described in terms that link him to Alain's Genius. He is, however, both social philosopher and theologian; his fixation on sexual intercourse having been greatly decreased, it is easier to see him as voicing the poem's moral and spiritual message of sexual activity within the bounds set by God and Nature, and of the ultimate frivolity of erotic passion and dalliance. Gui was guided by his knowledge of Jean's medieval Latin sources, the *Consolation of Philosophy* and *De planctu Naturae*. The redactor of MS *Lm* was guided by his interpretation of the principal themes of the *Rose*: visions, images, and dreams that deceive or enlighten; the delineation of social values and of true nobility; the many faces of love, both sacred and human. The distinction between homoerotic and procreative sexuality and the exhortation to further the work of Nature were accepted by both Gui and the *Lm* redactor; but each in his own way rendered this message far less erotically explicit. And the redactor of MS *Bi* deleted Nature and Genius entirely: for him, neither science, philosophy, nor theology – nor any allusion to homoeroticism – had any place at all in the art of love.

We have seen that the marginalia of MS *Mi* reflect an acceptance and appreciation of Jean's interweaving of Christian theology, Chartrian naturalism, and Ovidian love psychology. For such a reader, Genius is a parodic figure, perhaps even the key to the entire poem. In effect, Genius' discourse figures the paradoxical status of sexuality in a fallen world. As Thomas Hill has stated, Genius' discourse is both comic and pathetic: comic by virtue of the absurdity of his claims, but pathetic in that "there was a time which man has lost, but not altogether forgotten, in which there was no conflict between moral imperatives and man's natural desire to perpetuate himself."[4] So powerful indeed is this post-lapsarian conflict that many medieval readers of the *Rose* could not tolerate Jean's graphic portrayal of its consequences. For example, Gui and the redactors of MS *Fa* and *Fe* – possibly the B remanieur as well[5] – did agree on one thing: Nature's acceptance of Faux Samblant could not remain. Jean's ironic portrayal of a Nature so eager for procreative activity that she can even temporarily forget her distress over human sin was not appreciated by these medieval readers of the *Rose*. Similarly, many readers found it necessary to fit Genius' sermon into a recognizable category. The possibilities were many, given the complexity of the original text. For Pierre Col, whose reading is most suited to the *KMN* text, Genius is speaking in defense of conjugal relations, reasonably conducted for procreative purposes, with post-coital confession and penance: all perfectly compatible with Christian doctrine. For other readers, the essence of Genius' sermon was his projection of spiritual rewards as superior to worldly pleasure (for example, MS *Lm*); or his projection of procreation as superior to lust, particularly homoeroticism (for example, Gui's remaniement). Still others perceived Genius as a spokesman for active sexuality, aware of the need for confession and prayer but otherwise limited to sublunary considerations (for example, MS *Lk*). What we find here is a dismantling of Jean's dense construct. Genius speaks either in favor of spiritual values, or for the sanctity of procreation, or for the indulgence of the natural sex drive: but not for all three at once.

The model that Badel formulated to describe the different currents of literary reception of the *Rose* can be equally well applied to the history of the poem itself. Not all fourteenth-century readers were prepared to undertake a consideration of the *Rose* as a whole, to search for an overall meaning that would account for every textual detail. No doubt a significant portion of the medieval audience experienced the poem through the oral presentation or private perusal of particular sections, rather than through a

---

[4] Hill, "Narcissus, Pygmalion, and the Castration of Saturn," p. 423.
[5] Nature's acceptance of Faux Samblant's participation in the erotic quest is deleted from MS *Eb*, which frequently agrees with the B text.

sustained reading of the entire poem. As we saw in Chapter 1, the distribution of marginal "Nota bene" signs in individual manuscripts strongly suggests that readers concentrated their attention on selected passages; and a few manuscripts even contain explicit notices warning against the public diffusion of the Faux Samblant section. In such texts as the *Echecs amoureux* and its commentary or the *Chevalier errant*, one does find evidence for an interest in the all-embracing quality of Jean's *Rose* and a tolerance for, even a fascination with, the complexities and ambiguities of the text.[6] The elaborate index appearing in MS Paris, Bibl. Mazarine 3874 (*Maz*) must also have been compiled by a reader interested in making sense of the poem as a whole: in this detailed guide the many topics covered in the *Rose* are grouped by subject so as to follow each theme or motif throughout the poem.[7] Many writers, however, borrowed from the *Rose* selectively, using it as a source of maxims, vivid images, or narrative vignettes. We have seen such a contrast in the works of Machaut and Deguilleville respectively.[8] Deguilleville rewrote the allegory of the *Rose* to eliminate moral ambiguity, subordinating all elements of the text to the orthodox representation of spiritual conversion. Machaut, on the other hand, manifests a far greater degree of receptivity to the quest for meaning as an open-ended poetic process. His works reflect both a parodic representation of love as self-delusion or idolatry, and a serious belief in the power of poetry to subsume the sacred, the moral, and the erotic.

The various abridgments, interpolations, and remaniements of the *Rose* reflect a similar variety of approaches. The *KLMN* manuscripts parallel the *Echecs amoureux* or the works of Machaut in treating the *Rose* as an open-ended meditation on the psychological, social, natural and cosmic contexts in which human love exists, at once humorous and edifying. The marginalia of MS *Mi* strikingly illustrate this delight in the complexities of the *Rose*, this sense of play in a text at once humorous, irreverent, and morally edifying. MS *κυ* likewise presents a diverse text; and with its emphasis on political history and social responsibility, this version of the *Rose* is particularly close to the *Chevalier errant* or the *Echecs amoureux*, a mirror of human life crafted for the aristocracy. But as we have seen, other versions of the *Rose* reflect a more reductive approach, a selective reading that makes the poem more simply an art of love or more clearly a learned and edifying treatise. Because of the very complexities and tensions that

---

[6] Badel discusses the *Echecs* and its commentary in *Roman de la Rose au XIV siècle*, pp. 263–315; on the *Chevalier errant*, see pp. 315–30.

[7] For a description of MS *Maz*, see Langlois, *Manuscrits*, pp. 84–85, 509–10.

[8] Badel makes a similar point with his comparison of Gilles li Muisis, Machaut, and Deschamps as readers of the *Rose* in *"Roman de la Rose" au XIVe siècle*, pp. 74–114.

exist within the *Rose*, these efforts to resolve or to reduce the text led to quite different results.

No less protean than the text of the *Rose* is its first-person authorial voice. Of the various poets who worked on the *Rose* subsequent to Jean de Meun, Gui is the only one known to have inscribed himself and his project of remaniement in the text, informing us of his name and his love for the *Rose* and carefully marking his interpolations and deletions. As we have seen, Gui even inserted himself into the God of Love's discourse as the poem's third author. Aside from Gui, only the Dutch and Italian translators, rewriting the *Rose* entirely in a new language, inserted their names in this way; and both of these poets simply took on the first-person voice of the text.[9] For both Heinric and Durante, the fictional identity of lover, narrator, and author is preserved throughout the poem: the distinction between Guillaume and Jean disappears, and the first-person protagonist is given a new name that identifies him directly with the author of the new text. Gui is thus the only known *Rose* poet who preserved the distinction between Guillaume and Jean while still creating his own explicit presence in the text, not as protagonist but solely as co-author. The study of *Rose* manuscripts shows that from a very early period in the tradition, scribes distinguished between the voice of the Lover, rubricated "l'Amant," and that of the authorial narrator, rubricated "l'A[u]cteur."[10] This strategy helps to bridge the transition from one author to the next by suggesting that the *je* of the poem, rather than being identified with either Guillaume or Jean, embodies two distinct fictional personae, narrator and protagonist, whose voices could be appropriated as easily by Jean as by Guillaume. Gui's recognition of the composite nature of the narrative voice of the *Rose*, and his ready acceptance of the poem as having more than one author and more than one possible version, enabled him to insert himself as an authorial figure and to participate in the poetic process without eclipsing the original authors or completely effacing the original text.

It is probably because of his strong presence in the text that Gui has been accepted as something akin to an author by modern critics. Langlois,

---

[9] The Dutch poet Heinric translates the line "Vez ci Guillaume de Lorriz" [see here Guillaume de Lorris (v. 10496)] as "Siet hier van Brusele Henrecke" [see here Heinric of Brussels (cited by Van der Poel, *De Vlaamse "Rose" en "Die Rose" van Heinric*, p. 16)]. Heinric does not indicate that the poem ever had more than one author; for a full discussion, see Van der Poel, *Vlaamse "Rose"*, pp. 16–19. The Italian poet Durante similarly omits any reference to the poem's dual authorship, and inserts his name into the God of Love's discourse to his barons: "Chè pur convien ch'i' soccorra Durante" [for I must help Durante (ed. Marchiori, sonnet 82, v. 9)].

[10] On rubrication of the first-person voice in *Rose* manuscripts, see my *From Song to Book*, pp. 91–95, 99–103; and my "'Ci parle l'aucteur'." Braet analyzes iconographic evidence for the distinction of the dreamer-narrator and the protagonist in "Roman der Rose, Raum im Blick."

whose concern was with establishing the text, deplored Gui's intrusions into an early and probably very good copy of the poem.[11] Still, Langlois considered it worthwhile to publish an article in the *Bibliothèque de l'Ecole des Chartes* containing extracts from Gui's work and a list of manuscripts containing his interpolations.[12] In more recent years, Jung and Hult have published work on Gui, Jung concentrating on Gui's reworking of Guillaume de Lorris and, in particular, his attitude towards love, and Hult addressing the question of whether or not Gui can be considered an author.[13] Gui's reworking of the poem is extensive, and his presence is powerful in his prologue, in the passage composed to tie together Guillaume's poem and Jean's continuation, and in his self-portrait; one is strongly encouraged to conclude that the remanieur is something very close to an author, and that in the Middle Ages, the rewriting of previously existing text takes its place, along with other forms of adaptation, translation, and *conjointure*, as a type of literary creation.

Yet Gui was not, as one might think from the body of secondary literature, the only medieval remanieur to fall in love with the *Rose*. Perhaps because other versions of the *Rose* do not come equipped with a self-proclaimed author, the tradition of *Rose* studies has treated them as manuscripts or manuscript families endowed with variants rather than as new texts. Langlois does not give Gui's alterations among his variant readings, nor does he describe them in his study of the *Rose* manuscript tradition. These are not part of the *Rose* textual tradition; they are the work of an independent writer, addressed in a separate article. On the other hand, his study of *Rose* manuscripts does include a detailed account of the B, K, L, M, and N families. In his edition, however, Langlois gives variants for the B and L texts, but not for K, M, or N. Variants appearing in only one or two manuscripts, such as MSS *κυ* or *Lm*, are scarcely documented anywhere, since these were seen as contributing neither to the establishment of the text, to the identification of a manuscript family, nor to the understanding of an identifiable medieval author. And none of the anonymous remanieurs have been studied as Gui has: past critics have devoted no articles to the analysis of the B remaniement or the KMN interpolations, to the remanieurs' ideas about love and poetry, or to their status as authorial figures. Gui's self-conscious and explicit stance as remanieur at once denies him a place in *Rose* textual history while granting

---

[11] Of MS *Tou*, Langlois states it is of little use in establishing the text because it has lost numerous leaves and also, "pis encore, son texte a été en beaucoup d'endroits modifié par Gui de Mori" (*Manuscrits*, p. 425).   [12] Langlois, "Gui de Mori et le *Roman de la Rose*."
[13] Jung, "Gui de Mori et Guillaume de Lorris"; Hult, "Gui de Mori, lecteur médiéval"; this material also appears in Hult's *Self-fulfilling Prophecies*, pp. 35–55.

him a certain status as a medieval writer; the anonymity, the self-effacement of the other remanieurs has the opposite effect, enshrining their work as the basis of *Rose* manuscript families while at the same time reducing their status from literary creator to that of producer of variants and "common errors."

Interestingly, it is Gui, the quasi-author, whose version of the Rose retains the most information about the poem's "real" authors and about its textual history in general; whereas the *B* remanieur, remembered only as an agent of *mouvance*, suppresses information about the poem's authorship and textual history. Gui's system of marginal annotations enables the reader or copyist to distinguish at a glance between original text and remaniement, and to reconstruct the original, in part or in whole, if he or she so desires. Thus Gui's work, in spite of his prominent role in the God of Love's discourse as the third *Rose* poet, is not fully integrated into the *Rose* text: his remaniement remains self-consciously, explicitly, a version, bearing within itself the instructions whereby the changes wrought can be undone and the original restored. And Gui takes care to proclaim the pre-eminence of the two original *Rose* poets, and to clarify their relationship. Not only did he retain the God of Love's discourse; he also gave his own explanation for Jean's continuation, which he believed to have replaced Guillaume's original ending: Jean felt that Guillaume had boasted improperly of winning his lady too easily, and wanted to draw the process out longer. Jean himself becomes, for Gui, something of a remanieur: like Gui, he deleted certain lines and added (a great many) others. The distinction between author and remanieur is indeed interestingly blurred in Gui's understanding of literary history. And just as Gui marked the changes he made in the text, so he also left what he considered to be Guillaume's original ending, allowing the reader to choose between the different versions of the text. In his hands, the *Rose* becomes a complex palimpsest of versions and rewritings, the collaborative effort of three different poets.

The *B* remanieur, on the other hand, was interested in preserving the integrity of Guillaume's *Rose*. The *Bi* redactor in particular, by deleting so much of the material in Jean de Meun that had no precedent in Guillaume de Lorris, created a much more unified, much less digressive poem. Even the discourse of Faux Samblant, though somewhat of an aberration, might be explained as a continuation of Guillaume's description of Papelardie, as well as a response to the figure of Male Bouche. If one had only the *B* text to go on, the *Rose* would appear to be the work of a single anonymous poet. In MSS *Bi*, *Be*, and *Lz* (which follows the *B* text in large portions) the poem is seamless: an allegorical account of falling in love and eventually winning the lady's consent, cast as a dream, including an exposition of love, friendship, and seduction, and narrated by the young man who had the dream. It is not that the *B* remanieur had no interest at all in the figure of the poet or in poetic tradition. As we have seen, two models for the poet do appear in his *Rose*: Tibullus and Apollo. The poetic discourse fostered by Love and exemplified in the *Rose* is presented as heir to the classical tradition. But the identities of the *Rose* poets are effaced, as is the fact that there were two – indeed, now three – of them.

Both Gui and the *B* remanieur encountered the *Rose* at a time when Guillaume's poem still circulated independently of Jean's contribution, and affected people's understanding of what the *Rose* was. Like the *B* remanieur, and like the redactor of MS *Lm*, Gui suppressed passages that violated the spirit of the *Rose* as he understood it, and sought to reduce the digressiveness of the poem. But while Gui altered Jean's contribution, he did not seek to shorten it; he rather liked the idea of extending the erotic quest, making it the vehicle for philosophical teachings and social commentary. He delighted in the play of versions and poetic voices, emphasizing the identities of the poem's authors, now three in number, and the contribution each had made. The *B* remanieur and the redactor of MS *Lm*, on the other hand, were interested in preserving the *Rose*'s character as a dream-narrative teaching of love, punctuated by exemplary mythological figures who variously resisted or served love and art: Narcissus, Adonis, Pygmalion, and, in the *B* manuscripts, Marsyas. These remanieurs aimed for unity, not plurality, of theme and voice.

The various remaniements fared somewhat similarly in the subsequent manuscript tradition, contributing passages that circulated to varying degrees. The tendency in the *Rose* manuscript tradition was towards the accumulation of text. The poem easily absorbed interpolations, be they those of Gui de Mori or of the anonymous remanieurs, while deletions tended to be restored. Such a process is implied in Gui's marginal annotations, which identify interpolations for easy – and selective – borrowing, and mark deletions so that these can, if desired, be restored from another manuscript. But the names of the remanieurs did not accompany their added verses. It was Gui's interpolations about such topics as pride or friendship that entered the manuscript tradition, and not those in which he names himself; and if other poets of the *Rose* named themselves, those passages have not survived at all. Not until Molinet's late fifteenth-century prose redaction would a French reworking of the *Rose* once again have a known author. The *Rose* was known throughout the Middle Ages as a poem by Guillaume de Lorris and Jean de Meun, even when it contained hundreds of lines that did not derive from either of these two poets. If it accumulated text, it did not accumulate authors; but neither were the names of the two primary authors effaced, the *B* remanieur's efforts notwithstanding. Guillaume, and most of all Jean, acquired an authority that was never achieved by later poets of the *Rose*.

As Badel has shown so well, the *Rose* was a major source of inspiration for generations of medieval French authors, providing them with a basis for the formulation of their own poetic authority; indeed, it played an important part in the emergence of the very notion of French literature.[14] The *Rose* even came to be seen as having played a formative role in the creation of Second Rhetoric. An anonymous treatise on "Les Règles de la seconde rhétorique," written between 1411 and 1432, posits a literary lineage of canonical authors, stating that if anyone wishes to compose poetry, "il convient que on les face selon ce que donnerent les premiers rethoriques, dont aucuns s'ensuyvent" [it must be done according to what was laid down by the first rhetoricians, some of whom follow (ed. Langlois, p. 11)].[15] The first poet named turns out to be Guillaume de Saint-Amour, "lequel ou parvis de Paris fist destruire Heresie, Ypocrisie et Papelardie, la mere de Faulz Semblant" [who in the public square in Paris destroyed Heresy, Hypocrisy and False Holiness, the mother of Faux Semblant (ibid.)], and who is credited with having composed poetry in honor of the Virgin.[16] The second is Guillaume de Lorris, "lequel commencha le Rommant de la Rose" [who began the *Romance of the Rose* (p. 12)]; the third is Jean de Meun, credited with completing the *Rose* and with writing other books as well. There then follow Philippe de Vitry, Guillaume de Machaut, Brisebarre de Douai, and numerous others, such as Jean Le Fevre, Eustache Deschamps, and Jean Froissart.

The poetic tradition configured here thus begins with two authors whose work was received and continued by Jean de Meun, Guillaume de Saint-Amour and Guillaume de Lorris, representing two very different kinds of poetry. The former, as understood by the author of the treatise, was committed to social and ecclesiastical reform, using poetic language for didactic and devotional purposes: "en l'onneur de Nostre Dame, mist les figures de la Bible et les appliqua a la vierge Marie" [in the honor of Our

---

[14] Badel asserts that throughout the fourteenth-century the *Rose* was the object of an admiration "assez grande pour que . . . naisse obscurément à son sujet, autour de 1400, la notion même de littérature française" (*Roman de la Rose au XIVe siècle*, p. 502). Aside from Badel, other critics have noted the formative influence of the *Rose* in the self-presentation of late medieval French authors. See, for example, Uitti, "From *Clerc* to *Poète*"; Brownlee, *Poetic Identity*, pp. 12–21 and *passim*; and Brownlee's "Discourses of the Self."

[15] The treatise is published by Langlois, *Recueil d'arts de seconde rhétorique*.

[16] The poem attributed here to Guillaume de Saint-Amour appears in manuscripts with an attribution to either Nicole Bozon or Rutebeuf, and is variously titled "Les Propriétés Nostre Dame" or "Les .ix. Joies Nostre Dame"; see Langlois, *Recueil d'arts*, p. 11, n. 3.

Lady, he set down Biblical allegories and applied them to the Virgin Mary (p. 11)]. The latter wrote in a secular framework, producing an erotic allegory characterized by lyrical subjectivity. Jean brought these two very different strands together in a masterful synthesis, which then gave rise to the most diverse authors, including lyric as well as narrative poets; love poets and satirists; court poets and clerics. Such a view is the logical outgrowth of the first century and a half of *Rose* reception. The importance of the *Rose* as a crowning achievement of French literature is expressed in the colophon of MS Bibl. Nat. fr. 1566, copied in 1351:

Anima magistri Johannis Medunensis per misericordiam Dei requiescat in pace; quia ad laudem, circumspectionem et honorem tocius gentis hunc libellum gallicis verbis intellective et proficue composuit. (fol. 129r)

May the soul of Master Jean de Meun rest in peace through the mercy of God; for with discernment and to good effect he composed this little book in the Gallic language for the praise, admonition, and honor of all people.

In the *Rose*, French verse composition was elevated to the status of literature, worthy of being read by all, providing a framework that could absorb literary interpolations of the most varied sort; and ultimately coming to be seen as quite literally a matrix for subsequent French poetry.

Appendix A

The remaniement of Gui de Mori

The following passage, appearing only in MS *Mor*, is part of a long description of love as distinct from sexual desire, following v. 1952.

[fol. 17r]

> **A**ucun sage et bien enparlé
> Ont maintes fois d'amours parlé
> Comment on doit amer amie;
> Et maint sont qui ne cuident mie   4
> Que nulle femme soit amee
> Se n'est pour la fin desvëe
> De vouloir aveuc lui gesir
> Et faire son charnel desir.   8
> En ceste opinion se fierent
> Cil qui fors ce fait riens ne quierent,
> Que tout cil a celle fin tendent
> Qui a amer femmes entendent.   12
> Mais cil qui au pui ont chanté,
> Et qui mon mestier ont hanté,
> Sevent bien tenir le contraire;
> Et je t'en vueil ci preuve faire.   16
> **T**u dois amer une personne
> Pour ce qu'elle est, ou belle ou bonne.
> Ce sont li doy commencement
> Dont viennent tout acointement.   20
> Au mains en doivent il venir,
> Car bien puis pour voir soustenir
> Que biautés et bontés avoient
> Cuers a amours, ou quelles soient.   24
> Mais se tu aimes vraiement
> Tu ameras certainement
> Aussi bien comme toy meïsme,

Dont tu pues sans soffime   28   [−2]
Par toy apertement savoir
Quelle amour tu y dois avoir.
Car tu t'aimes en tel maniere
– C'est a prouver chose legiere –   32
Que tout ce dont tu pues cuidier
Qui te puist valoir ne aidier
A honnours, los, et pris conquerre:
Tu le quiers ou tu le dois querre,   36
Et t'i desires atenir.
Ce dont deshonnours puet venir
Qui puet faire vergongne ou blasme,
Ou empire ta bonne fame,   40
On en autre maniere nuyre:
Tu le fuis ou tu le dois fuire.
Cilz qui en lui tel chose quiert,
Droiture et vraie amour requiert   44
Qu'i le quiere en celui qu'il aime,
Puis que il vray amant se claime;
Dont ne doit nuls querre en s'amie
Deshonnesté ne vilonnie.   48

Notes

13: The *puy* was a regular gathering of jongleurs and *trouvères*, where songs were performed in competitions. It is particularly associated with the regions of Picardy and Artois.

17–24: Gui's interpolation on the arrows of love also includes a disquisition on outer beauty and inner goodness as the two causes of love.

25–27: Interestingly, Gui applies the Biblical notion of loving one's neighbor as oneself (Matthew 22:39) to the exposition of erotic love.

2. REASON'S DESCRIPTION OF LOVE

This passage, appearing only in MS *Mor*, is part of an amplification of Reason's definition of love following v. 4346. After explaining that God manifested true love in the Incarnation and that the love of God transcends human love and friendship, Reason offers to explain the origins of love:

[37r]   Dieux manans en la trinité,
          Parfais en pure deité,
          Qui de nullui besoing n'avoit,

Car tout povoit et tout savoit;   4
N'au deffors lui n'avoit riens nee,
Ains contenoit tout en son ydee;   [+1]
Cilz Dieux qui tout fist et crea
Par amour tant s'umelia,   8
Car la grant amour pure et monde
Et li grans biens qu'en li habonde,
Qui sont d'espandable nature,
Li firent faire creature   12
Qui fust de ses biens recevable.
Et pour memoire pardurable,
Que par amours faicte l'eüst
– Et pour ce amer l'en deüst –   16
Il fist el cuer une fontaine
De dilection toute plaine,
Siques celle fontaine livre
Au cuer de creature vivre,   20
Que li cuers ne puet vivre une heure
Que celle fontaine ne queure.
   Ceste fontaine a .ii. ruissiaux
Qui moult font deux divers essiaux,   24
Car li uns va par virlence   [−1]
La dont il avoit pris naiscence,
Car a Dieu dont il vint retourne
Quant aucune personne atourne   28
Son cuer et embrase et enflame
A amer Dieu de toute s'ame,
Et que riens ne li puet tant plaire
Com fait la voulenté Dieu faire.   32
Cy ruissiaux cy esperités
Est proprement dit charités.
Et qu'est charités? Amours fine,
Qui de Dieu naist et en Dieu fine.   36
Dieu seul aime, Dieu seul desire,
Et li fait toute riens despire
Qui de Dieu amer le destourne.
[37v]   Qui son cuer a ceste amout tourne   40
Du tout bien puet asseür estre
Qu'il ara le gloire celestre.
De li Sainte Escripture compte
Que sans charité riens ne monte: 44

Biens c'om face, maulx c'om despite,
N'aumosne noient ne pourfite,
Ne son corps a martire offrir,
Ne tourmens que nulz puist souffrir   48
Ne vault a ce que soit sauvee
Ame sans charité trouvee.
Charités, c'est chose certaine,
Est des vertus la souveraine.   52
Car elle est la somme et la riulle
Qui toutes autres vertus riulle,
Et les met a ordennement
D'amer Dieu tout premierement,   56
Et puis son proisme en tel maniere
Que l'amour Dieu soit la premiere.
Car pour lui doit on Dieu amer,
Et son proisme pour Dieu clamer   60
Frere et ami, et ensement
Faire com a soy proprement.
Et c'est charités ordennee,
Sans cui ame n'ert ja sauvee;   64
C'est un des ruis de la fontaine
Dont l'iaue est douce, clere, et saine.
    Li autres ruis queurt d'autre part,
Et par cest monde cy s'espart   68
Par desir de choses mondaines,
Dont les amours fausses et vaines
Viennent, et qui petit pourfitent
A l'ame, quant cuers s'i delitent: 72
Quant on aime la creature
Et on n'a du createur cure,
Ou quant on a amour greignour
Au monde qu'a nostre seignour.   76
Et cy ruis que je cy devise
Est proprement dit convoitise.
    Or esgar la diversité
De convoitise a charité: 80
Car quant charité surhabonde,
Elle fait les choses du monde
Amer selon ce qu'elles valent.
Et pour ce que elles deffalent,   84
Et qu'il y a paine et moleste,

Charités point ne s'i arreste,
Ains tent aux choses souveraine
Qui sont durables et certaines.   88
Convoitise fait le contraire,
Car en cest monde a son repaire.
   Or t'ay la diffinicion
D'amours ditte, et ostencion   92
Faitte que ce est et dont vient,
Et quelle amour tenir convient
Qui veult avec Dieu part avoir.
Or te vueil je faire savoir   96
Des autres manieres d'amours,
Car ceste generaulx clamours,
Amours, ou que elle se rue,
Pour bien ne pour mal ne se mue   100
Que elle adés ne se confourme
A ce a cui amer s'enfourme,
Car amours si est confourmable
Del amant a la chose amable.   104
Augustins [dit], ne le vueil taire,   *MS omits 'dit'*
Se tu terre aimes, tu es terre.
Se tu aimes Dieu, que seras?
Dieux? Ne l'os dire! Ains trouveras   108
Que par David, se l'oeil y prestes,
Dist Dieux, "Je di que vous dieu estes."
Par quoy tu pues assés savoir
Que tu ne pues a Dieu avoir   112
Amour vraie, fine, ne pure,   *MS: A.v.p.n.f.*
Tant con tu aimes creature
Plus que le createur ne faces.

At this point Reason proceeds to distinguish the various types of "convoitise." After treating familial love (a reworked version of vv. 5741–48, 5753–64), she moves on to sexual love and desire, introduced by means of vv. 4347–54. This form of love is of two kinds:

[38r]   Ce sont les fins a quoy entendent   116
          Cil qui a tel amour entendent.
          Mais c'est auques diversement.
          Aucun aiment si purement
          Que riens qui tourt a vilonnie   120
          Il ne quierent en leur amie,

N'il ne li voudroient trouver.
Et pour ceste amour approuver
Sont fait li bel chant amoureux   124
Que li amant ont fait pour eulx.
Et c'est auques raisons et drois
Que vrais amans en tous endrois
Eschieut tout ce qu'il puet le fame   128
Empirer, ou acueillir blasme
Ou deshonneur ou villenie
De celle qu'il tient pour amie.
  Li aucun aiment proprement   132
Pour avoir leur delitement
Charnel; n'autre riens il ne veulent,
Combien qu'il dient qu'il se deulent.
C'est la propre amour delitable,   136
A laquelle sont enclinable
Li plus, ce te di sans mentir,
Pour le delit charnel sentir.
C'est li fins que tes amans chace   140
Qui tel amour en ses las lace.

There follow a slightly reworked version of vv. 4355–98 and 4517–98, and then a greatly expanded version of the discussion of youth and old age, beginning with v. 4399.

Notes

21–22: Gui makes a similar formulation in the prologue to MS *Tou* where, citing *De arrha animae*, he states that it is impossible "Que nus coeurs sans amours demeure, / Ki a vivre couvoite une hoeure" (MS *Tou*, fol. 5r).

43–52: This development derives from 1 Corinthians 13, the famous Pauline discussion of charity that also forms a basis for an interpolation in the discourse of Reason in the *K*, *M*, and *N* manuscripts; see Appendix C.

56–62: An allusion to the two great commandments formulated by Jesus (Matthew 22:37, 39). On the latter point, cf. the God of Love's remarks above, section 1, vv. 25–27.

62: A restatement of the Golden Rule (Matthew 7:12).

99–104: The notion of love as a conforming of the soul to the thing loved is a fundamental tenet of medieval thought. It is developed at length in Augustine's *Confessions*.

105–10: "Terram diligis? Terra eris. Deum diligis? Quid dicam? Deus eris? Non audeo dicere ex me, scripturas audiamus: 'Ego dixi, dii estis, et filii altissimi omnes'" [Do you love the earth? You will be earth. Do you love God? What shall I say? Will you be God? I dare not say it on my own, but let us listen to Scripture: "I have said, you are all gods, and sons of the most high" (Augustine, *Tractatus in Epistulam Iohannis ad Parthos* 2.14)]. The Biblical passage cited here and repeated by Gui (vv. 109–10) is Psalm 81 [82]: 6, interpreted in medieval exegetical tradition as a divine rebuke to corrupt judges and rulers who, through their sins, have relinquished the eternal joys of salvation and embraced spiritual death. I am grateful to James J. O'Donnell of the University of Pennsylvania for his help in identifying this passage.

112–15: A standard tenet of medieval thought, deriving from Saint Paul's characterization of the sinful who "servierunt creaturae potius quam Creatori" [served the creature rather than the Creator (Romans 1:25)] and were thus led into a multitude of crimes, including sexual depravity.

119: Gui's use of the word *purement* is an allusion to the *amor purus* described by Andreas Capellanus in *De amore*, Book 1, Dialogue 8: a form of love, also identified as "sapiens" [wise], that stops short of full sexual consummation.

119–31: Reason's words here closely parallel those of the God of Love given above, section 1, vv. 44–48.

123–25: Reason's citation of love songs – presumably those of the *trouvères* – as expressions of a noble form of human love parallels Cupid's citation of the *puy* participants as virtuous and true lovers.

3. EXEMPLARY TALES OF JUSTICE AND INJUSTICE (FOLLOWING v. 5628)

Text of MS *Tou*; variants from MSS *He*, *Mor*, and *Ke* (vv. 1–100).

In MS *Ke*, the first hundred lines appear in the margins of fol. 40r—40v, to be inserted after v. 5628; a note indicates that the passage continued on a now lost page at the beginning of the manuscript. A marginal note also states that an interpolation following v. 5632 was to be found on that same page, presumably the disquisition on justice and corruption that appears in the same location in MSS *Tou* and *Mor*.

In MS *He*, the discussion of justice precedes the passage given below, and the whole is inserted after v. 5558 (fol. 45v—47v).

In MS *Mor* (fol. 51r—52r) the passage appears in the same location as it does in MS *Tou*.

[f. 58r]   **N**e fisent pas grant mesprison
             Li juge de cui nous lison,
             Qui par faus tesmoing accuserent
             Susanne, et a mort le jugerent,   4

3–4 *Mor inv.*

Por ce que il souspris estoient
De s'amour, et si ne pooient
De li faire lor volenté,
De coi il estoient tempté.   8
S'en fu ele asprement requise,
Si com li letre nous devise.
Mais ele, com vaillans et sage,
N'avoit cure de tel outrage;   12
Ains se complainst en ytel guise,
"Lasse! de toutes pars m'ont prise
Angoisses; mais a la parsome,
Mieus vaut que je caie en mains d'ome,   16
Que je la loy Dieu relenquisse,
Ne contre son voloir feïsse."
Quant chil virent qu'il ne poroient
Faire de li che k'il queroient,   20
Si disent, oyant tout le peule,
Qu'il l'avoient trouvëe seule
Dedens son jardin emfermee
Avoec .i. varlet esseulee,   24
Et que il les virent jesir
Ensamble par carnel desir.
Cascuns d'iaus ensi l'accusoit,
Et ele point ne s'escusoit;   28
Car s'ele point s'en escusast,
Cascuns son escus refusast,
Car cil qui ensi l'accusoient
Juge et meneur dou peule estoient.   32
Pour ce ne s'en escusoit mie,
Mais com dolente et esmarie
Prioit Dieu moult devoctement,
Que il feïst demoustrement,   36
Par aucun singne veritable,
Que dou fait n'estoit pas coupable.
[f. 58v]   Et Dieus li envoia secours:
Car Danïel i vint le cours,   40
Qui soutieument l'en delivra,

---

4 *He* a m. livrerent *Ke* a m. condempnerent   10 *Mor* la l. le d.
16 *He* Vaut mieus   20 *He* vorroient   21 *He* S. d. devant   36 *He* Qu'il i.
39 *He* y envoia   41 *He* Et s.

Et les juges com faus livra
Au peuple, pour prendre justice
Et vengance de lor malisce.   44
Et chil les faus jugeors prisent,
Et tout erramment les occisent,
Ensi lor loiier emporterent
De ce que faussement jugerent.   48

Par coi li jugement sont perverty

Ky .i. tel Danÿel trouver
Poroit, qui seüst esprouver
Les juges ki sont orendroit,
Je croi que souvent en prendroit   52
De tels ki moult mauvaisement
Ont tost rendut .i. jugement.
Et se tels cas ne vient en place,
Maint autre souvent en yglace,   56
Qui ausci grant mestier eüscent,
Que selonc droit bien jugié fuscent.
Et nonporquant cascuns se gart
Et comment il li est regart;   60
Car cist dont fu vengance prise
Furent dechut par convoitise,
Qui as juges a moult grant canle
Au jour d'uy, si com il me sanle,   64
Et les dechoit vilainement.
.II. coses sont souvrainement,
Qui les juges font consentir
A lor jugemens pervertir: 68
C'est ire et si est convoitise.
Convoitise les coers atise
A estre negligent et lasce,
Et ire fait jugier entasce.   72
Coers ki en convoitise est mis
Fait les juges estre remis;
Et ire les fait trop tost prendre
A jugier sans raison entendre.   76

42 *He* l. j. confus l.   43 *Mor* p. faire j.   46 *He* t. maintenant *Ke* caramment
50 *He* P. q. peüst e.   61 *He* fust   64 *Mor* si c. m. s.   70 *He* C. l. gens

Nous trouvons d'un roy Avenir,
Quant il ot fait a lui venir
Celui que tant amer soloit,
Pour çou que de çou se doloit   80
Que laissié avoit s'acointance
Et renoïë sa creance.
Raison l'en voloit demander;
Pour ce le fist a luy mander.   84
Quant li preudom i fu venus,
Qui estoit por saiges tenus,
"Sire roys, dist il, je vous prie,
Avant que nule riens vous die,   88
Que vous ostés .ii. anemis
Qui sont en vo pretoire mis;
Car tant com je les i saroie,
Riens dire ne vous oseroie;   92
Ne ne dirai, bien le sachiés,
Se vous hors ne les encachiés."
Un petit a li rois pensé,
Et puis si a dit son pensé: 96
"Et ki sont cil doy anemy,
Que vous volés sevrer de my?"
Chieus li respondi, "Biaus dous sire,
Saciés, c'est convoitise et ire.   100
Quar convoitise en vous habite:
Delectatïons i excite,
Et delectatïons afulent
Raison, si que toute l'anulent,   104
[f. 59r]   C'a paines poés vous entendre
Fors au delit convoitiét prendre.
Et ire ne fait fors destruire.
Cil doy vous beent a souduire.   108
Ce sont doy anemy mortel,
Qui en vo coer ont pooïr tel
Que tant quierent de vo maisnie,
Tant en sera raisons banie,   112
Et verités tout ensement.

79 *Mor* qui   82 *He* renvoié ot   83 *He* le   96 *He* li a d.
101 *He Mor* Quant c.   106 *He* Fors qu'a   107 *He* sousduire.
108 *He* destruire   110 *Mor* ont pris hostel

Ostés les viguereusement,
Et en lor lieus soit equités,
Raisons, prudence, et verités."   116
Li rois ensi li octroia,
Et chieus löes contee li a
L'occoison de sa departie:
Qu'il avoit en mescreandie   120
Toute sa vie demouré,
Et les ydoles aouré,
Conme caitis et mescheans.
Or voloit estre en Dieu creans,   124
Car la loys Dieu trop miex valoit.
Pour ce d'entor lui s'en aloit.
Maintes coses li prist a dire,
Dont li roys fu moult espris d'ire,   128
Et le fist ariere bouter,
Que plus ne le pot escouter;
Et dist au preudome souvent,
S'il ne li eüst en couvent   132
Qu'il en eüst fait ire fuire,
Il l'euïst fait tantost destruire.
Mais ire, ki estoit banie,
Ly avoit sauvëe la vie.   136
Bien doit on proiier cascun juge,
Que ces .ii. anemis fourjuge,
Que ire nel puist empirier,
Ne par nul mauvais desirier   140
Le puist convoitise malmetre.
Tels juges se doit entremetre
De faire les grans jugemens
Qui ne sieut pas les mouvemens   144
De coer, ki souvent les meurs blecent,
Et droit jugement empeecent.
Mais se il voit ou povre ou riche,
En le verité si se fiche,   148
Que l'un et l'autre jugera
Selonc ce que raisons sera.

135–36 *Not in Mor*   137 *He* Si d.   139 *He* Qu'yre ne les   144 *Mor* sont
150 *He* Selonc çou que cescuns sera.

Appendix A

Notes

13–18: "Ingemuit Susanna, et ait: Angustiae sunt mihi undique . . . Sed melius est
mihi absque opere incidere in manus vestras, quam peccare in conspectu
Domini" [Susannah sighed and said: I am surrounded by tribulations . . . But it
is better for me to fall, innocent, into your hands than to sin in the eyes of God
(Daniel 13: 22–23)].
48: The rubric following this line appears in MS *Tou* only.
77–136: The story of King Avenir is taken from the legend of Barlaam and
Josaphat, which circulated in various Latin and vernacular versions.

4. THE DISCOURSE OF GENIUS

Gui's version of the discourse of Genius appears in MSS *He* and *Mor*. In
MS *Tou*, the deleted lines are completely restored, and marked with the sign
of a "subtraction reprise." I give here the text of MS *He* with variants from
MS *Mor* and, for those lines shared by all three manuscripts, MS *Tou*.

19475	**D**el auctorité de nature,	[fol. 147r]
	Qui de tout le mont a le cure,	
	Comme vicaire et connestable	
	Del empereour pardurable,	4
19479	Qui siet en la tour souverainne	
	De la noble citté mondainne,	
	Dont il fist nature ministre,	
	Qui tous les biens y aministre	8
19483	Par l'influance des estelles,	
	Car tout est ordené par elles	
	Selonc les drois emperiaus,	
	Dont nature est officiaus,	12
19487	Qui toutes coses a fait naistre,	
	Puis que cils mons devint en estre;	
	Et lor donna terme ensement	
	De grandour et d'acroissement;	16
19491	N'onques ne fist riens pour noiant,	
	Sous le ciel qui va tournoiant	
	Entour le tierre sans demeure,	
	Si haut desous comme deseure,	20
19495	Ne ne ciesse ne nuit ne jour,	

4 *Tou Mor* A l'e.   9 *Tou* Par i.
14 *Tou* mondes vint *Mor* monde vint a naistre.   16 *Tou* D'engenrer

349

	Mes tous jours tourne sans sejour,	
	Soient tout escumeniyét	
	Li desloial, li renoyiét,	24
19499	Et condampné sans nul respit,	
	Qui les oevres ont en despit,	
	Par qui nature est soustenue,	
	Soit de grant gent ou de menue;	28
19503	Et cils qui de toute sa force	
	De nature garder s'esforce,	
	Et qui de bien amer se painne	
xxx	Et d'essauchier lingnie humainne,	32
19507	U qui loiaument y travaille,	
19508	Floris em paradis s'en aille.	
19724	Signour, assauver vos linnages,	
19723	Avés .ii. moult grans avantages.	36
19725	Se li tiers iestre ne volés,	
	Mout avés les sens affolés.	
	Si n'avés c'un seul nuisement,	
	Deffendés vous tout prousement:	40
19729	D'unne part iestes assali.	
	.III. campion sont moult fali,	
	Et bien ont desiervi le batre,	
	S'il ne pueent le quart abatre.	44
19733	.III. sereurs sont, se n'el savés,	
	Dont les .ii. a secours avés;	
	La tierce seulement vous grieve,	
	Qui toutes les vies abrieve.	48
19737	Saciés ke moult vos reconforte	[fol. 147v]
	Clato qui le kenoulle porte,	
	Et Lathesis qui le fil tire;	
	Mais Atropos ront et descire	52
19741	Canques ces .ii. pueent filler.	
	Atropos vos bee a ghiller:	
	Celle qui parfont nos fora	
	Tous vos linnages enfoura,	56
19745	Et vait espiant vous meïsmes.	

27–28 *Tou inverted.*   28 *Tou* soit de m.   32 *Tou* Sans nule pensee vilaine
33 *Tou* Mais q.   34 *Mor* en aille.   50 *Mor* Cloto   51 *Mor* Lachesis.
52 *Mor* trestout descire.   55 *Tou Mor* ne fora.

350

	Ains pire bieste ne veïsmes,	
	N'avés nul anemi grignour.	
	Signour, mierci; mierci, signour,	60
19749	Souviengne vous de vos boins peres,	
	Et de vos anciiennes meres.	
	Selonc lor fais les vos lingnies	
	Gardés que vous ne fourlingnies.	64
19753	C'ont il fait? Prendés vous y garde,	
	S'il est qui leur proeeche esgarde.	
	Il se sont si bien deffendu,	
	Qu'il vous ont cest estre rendu.	68
19757	Se ne fust lor chevalerie,	
	Vous ne fuissiés pas or en vie.	
	Moult orent de vous grant pitié,	
	Par amours et par amistié.	72
19761	Pensés des autres qui venront,	
	Et vos linnages maintenront.	
	Ne vous laissiés pas desconfire:	
	Graffes avés, pensés d'escrire;	76
19765	N'aiiés pas les bras enmoufflés,	
	Martelés, forgiés, et soufflés.	
	Aidi[é]s Clato et Lathesis,	
	Si que de ses fius cope .vi.	80
19769	Atropos, qui tant est vilainne,	
	Qu'il en resaille une dousainne.	
	Pensés de vous multepliier,	
	Si porés ensi cunchiier	84
19773	La felonnesse, larenesse,	
19774	Atropos, qui tout empeece.	
19855	Pensés de mener boinne vie,	
	Voist cescuns embracier s'amie,	88
	Et son ami cescunne embrace,	
	Et jue et festoie et sollace.	
19859	Se loiaument vous entramés,	
19860	Ja n'en devés iestre blasmés.	92
20601x	Et pour vous plus legierement	
20602x	Retenir mon ensengnement,	

70 *He Tou* ore pas e. v.   74 *Tou Mor* Qui v. l. m.   79 *Mor* Cloto e. Lachesis.
85 *Mor* L. f. la nuiesce   88 *Tou* Aut c. e.   90 *Tou Mor* Et baise et f.
93–94 *Tou* Et pour tout mon ensengnement / Retenir plus legierement.

20605	Je vous voel ci brieument retraire	
	Cou que devés fuïr et faire:	96
	Pensés de nature honnourer	
	Par bien siervir et labourer;	
20609	Se vous del autrui riens avés,	
	Rendés le se vous le savés,	100
	Et se vous rendre ne poés	
	Les biens despendus ou joés,	
20613	Aiiés ent boinne volenté,	
	Quant vous en arés a plenté.	104
	D'occision nuls ne s'aproce;	
20616	Tenés nettes et mains et bouce.	
xxx	Je vous abandon tous delisces,	
xxx	Et commanch a fuïr les visces,	108
19837	Que nature vostre mestresse	
	Me vint hui conter a ma messe:	
	Tous les mesdist, ains puis ne sis,	
19840	Vous en y trouverés .xx.vi.,	112
xxx	Trestous contraires a nature,	
xxx	Plains de malvaistié et d'ordure.	
20617	Mais soiiés loiaus et piteus,	
20618	S'irés el biel lieu deliteus,	116
xxx	Ou Diex apries le mort envoie	
xxx	Ciaus qui chi tiennent droite voie.	
	Je voel chi mon siermon finnir,	
20633	Car trop vous poroie tenir.	120
20635	Or y parra que vous ferés	[fol. 148r]
	Quant en haut encroé serés,	
	Pour preechier a la bretesce.	
20638	Genius ensi leur preece.	124

95 *Tou* J. v. revoel b.   96 *Tou* Trestous canques vous devés faire
98 *Tou* Servés le par bien labourer   99 *Tou* Et se d. a.
102 *He* despendus et ycels; *I have amended according to Tou, Mor.*
104 *Tou* Q. des biens a.   106 *Tou* Nettes aiiés.   107–8 *Not in Tou.*
113–14 *Not in Tou.*   115–16 *Tou* Soiiés l. soiiés p. Lors irois ou camp deliteus.
117—18 *Not in Tou.*   119–20 *inverted in Tou.*   119 *Tou* Chi vous voel m. s. f.
120 *Tou* Trop v. p. huimais t.   123 *Tou* sor le b.

Appendix B

The *B* remaniement

1. DISCOURSE OF REASON, BIBL. NAT. FR. 25524 (*BI*)

MS *Bi* was copied by a careless scribe, who seems not to have understood the text very well. Obvious errors resulting in nonsense or disrupted rhyme have been corrected with recourse to *B* variants when these exist; otherwise, from Lecoy's edition. All rejected readings are given in notes.

4195	**Lors** vi droit a moi revenent	[fol. 66r]
	Raison la bele, la vaillent,	
	Qui de la tour jus descendi	
4198	Quant mes complaintes entendi;	4
xxx	Car selonc ce qu'ele pourroit,	
xxx	Moult volentiers me secouroit.	
4199	"Biaus amis, dit Raisons la bele,	
	Commant se porte cil querele?	8
	Seras tu ja d'amours lassés?	
	N'as tu pas ancor mal assés?	
	Que te samble des maus d'amer?	
4204	Sunt il trop dous ou trop amer?	12
	Sez en ou le millor eslire	
	Qui te puist aidier et soufire?	
	As tu [or] bon signour servi,	
4208	Qui si t'a pris et asservi	16
	Et te tourmente sans sejour?	
	Il te meschaï bien le jour	
	Que tu homage li feïs.	
4212	Fos fus, quant a ce te meïs.	20
	Mais sans faille tu ne savoies	
	A quel seignour servi avoies,	
4215	Car se tu bien le cogneüsses,	
4216	Jamais, certes, ses hons ne fusses:	24

14 aidier a soufire   15 or *omitted*

4221	Son homage li reniasses,	
	Ne jamais par amour n'amasses.	
	Cognois le tu point? – Oïl, dame.	
4224	– Non fais. – Si fais. – De quoi, par t'ame?	28
	– De tant qu'il me dit: 'Tu dois estre	[fol. 66v]
	Moult liés quant tu as si bon mestre	
	Et signour de si grant renom.'	
4228	– Cognois le tu de plus? – Je non,	32
	Fors tant qu'il me bailla sa regle,	
	Puis s'en fuï plus tost c'une egle,	
	Et je remeis en la balence.	
4232	Certes, c'est povre connoissence.	36
4216	Jamais, certes, ses hons ne fusse	
xxx	S'oumage fait ne li aüsse.	
4233	– Or voil je que tu le cognoisses,	
4234	Qui tant en as aü d'angoisses,	40
4237	Ne pues fors aprenre grignor.	
	Bon fait cognoistre son signor.	
4239	Et se tu bien le cognoissoies,	
xxx	Jamais nul jour nel serviroies,	44
xxx	Car trop malement en ampires.	
4242	– Dame, voir, puis qu'il est mes sires,	
	Et je ses hons liges antiers,	
	Moult i antendit volentiers	48
4245	Mes cuers, et plus i en preïst,	
	S'i fust qui l'art l'an apreïst.	
	– Par mon chief, or t'en voil aprendre,	
4248	Puis que tes cuers i viaut entendre.	52
xxx	Si sauras miex toi contenir,	
xxx	A ton signour tres bien servir.	
4249	**O**r te demonstrerai sans fable	
	Chose qui n'est pas demontrable.	56
	Si savras trestout sans science,	
4252	Et cognoistras la cognissence.	
4259	Lors t'aurai le neu desnöé	
4260	Que tous jours trouveras nöé.	60
	Or i met bien l'antention.	[fol. 67r]
	Vois ici la division:	

36 contenence   55 s. faille   56 demetable   59 veu   61 Or i vois

Amours si est pais anuieuse,
4264   Amours est haïne amoureuse;   64
C'est loiautez la desloiaus,
C'est la desloiautez loiaus;
C'est poor toutë asseüree,
4268   Esperence desesperee;   68
C'est raisons toute forsenable;
C'est forcenerie resnable;
Peri[l]s de noier agreable,
4272   Gries fais sans nuisence parable;   72
Ce est Caldis la perilleuse,
La sade, la delicïeuse;
Ce est languors toute santive;
4276   C'est santez toute maladive;   76
C'est fains saous en habundance;
C'est convoiteuse soufisence;
C'est la soif qui tous jours est yvre,
4280   Yvresce qui de soif s'enivre;   80
C'est faus delis et courtoisie;
C'est leesce la courrecie[e],
Douz mal, douceur malicïeuse,
4284   Douce savour mal savoureuse;   84
Entechiez de pardon pechiez,
De pechiez pardon antechiez;
C'est poine qui trop est joieuse;
4288   C'est felonie la piteuse;   88
C'est li ri[e]ns qui n'est pas estables,
Ains est trop fiers et trop muables;
Force enferme, enfermeté fors
4292   Qui tout esmuet par ses esfors;   92
C'est fos sens, c'est sage folie;   [fol. 67v]
C'est pesance triste et jolie;
C'est ris plains de plours et de lermes,
4296   Repos travaillens an touz termes;   96
Ce est enfers li doucereus,
C'est paradis li douleureus,
Chartre qui prisonier solace,

---

67 pais   70 Ce est fois et honours r.   78 convoitise   80 sans ivre
81   C'est sans   83 De mal de cuer m.   86 Pechiez de pardon a.
91 F. et ferme et fermeté f.   96 et de termes

4300	Printens et plains de froit rimage;	100
	C'est taigne qui rien ne refuse;	
	Les porpres et les buiriax use,	
	Car ausinc bien sont amoretes	
4304	Sous buiriax commc sous burcttcs.	104
	Que nul n'est de si haut lignage,	
	Ne nul ne treve l'en si sage,	
	Ne de force tant esprouvé,	
4308	Ne nul si bel n'a l'en trouvé,	108
	Ne qui tant ait autres bontés,	
	Que par Amour ne soit dontés.	
	Tous li mondes vat cele voie,	
4312	C'est li diex qui tous les desvoie.	112
4321	**M**ais se tu viaus bien eschever	
	Qu'Amours ne te puisse grever,	
	Se tu viaus issir de tel rage,	
4324	Ne pues boire si bon beuvrage	116
	Comme panser de le foïr;	
	Tu n'en pues autrement joïr.	
	Se tu le suis, il te cuira,	
4328	Se tu t'en fuis, il s'en fuira."	120
	Quant j'oi Raison bien entendue,	
	Qui pour noiant s'est debatue,	
	"Dame, dis je, de ce me vant,	
4332	Je n'en sai pas plus que devant,	124
	A ce que m'en puisse retraire.	[fol. 68r]
	En ma leçon a trop contraire	
	Car je n'en puis nul mot entendre,	
4336	Si la sai je bien par cuer rendre.	128
	Onques mes cuers rien n'oblia.	
	Bien sai trestout quancqu'il i a,	
	Pour lir[e] en tout communement,	
4340	Ne mes a moi tant solement.	132
xxx	Si croi qu'a grant [tort] me blasmez,	
xxx	Dont Amours est par moi amez.	
4615	Bien me volés ore trahir.	
	Doi je donques les gens haïr?	136

100 Brun tens   104 bevettes   119 fuis i. t'en c.   127 je n. voit
132 N. m. asmai

	Donc harrai je toutes persones?	
	Puis qu'amours ne sunt mie bones,	
	Jamais n'amerai d'amours fines,	
4620	Ains vivrai tous jours en haïnes?	140
	Lors si serai mortiex pechierres,	
4622	Voire, par Dieu, pires que lierres!	
4629	Bon conseil m'avés or donés,	
4630	Qui tous jours consoillié m'avés	144
	Que je doie d'amours recroire!	
4632	Or est fos qui ce ne viaut croire!	
xxx	– Biaus amis, tu ne m'antens gueres.	
4650	Amours sunt de plusors menieres.	148
4655	Amistés est nomee l'une:	
	C'est bone volenté commune	
	Des gens, antre aus, sans descordance,	
4658	Selon la Dié benivolence.	152
4717	Par la foi de ceste amistié	
	Dit Tulles en un sien dit[i]é,	
	Que bien devons faire [re]queste	
4720	A nos amis, s'ele est honeste,	156
	Et lor requeste referom,	[fol. 68v]
	S'ele contient droit et raison.	
	Ne doit pas estre autrement fete,	
4724	Fors en .ii. cas qu'il en excepte:	160
	S'en les voloit a mort livrer,	
	Panser devons d'aus delivrer;	
	Se l'en assaut lor renome[e],	
4728	Garde que ne soit diffamee.	164
	En ces .ii. cas l'estuet deffendre,	
4730	Sans droit et sans raison entendre.	
4733	Ceste amour que ci te propos	
	N'est pas contraire a mon propos.	168
	Ceste voil je bien que tu sives,	
4736	Et l'autre voil que tu eschives.	
	Ceste a toute vertu sans mort,	
4738	Mais l'autre met les gens a mort.	172
5341	Ansorquetout trop te voi nice,	
	Qui m'as mis a sus tel malice	
	Que je haïne te commant:	

152 Se non   155 Car b.

357

5344	Di moi en quel lieu, ne commant.	176
	– **V**ous ne finastes hui de dire	
	Que je doi mon signour despire,	
	Pour ne sai quele amour sauvage.	
5348	Qui cercheroit jusqu'a Cartage,	180
	[Et d'Orient en Occident,]	
	Et bien queïst tant que li dent	
	Li fussent chaü de viellece,	
5352	Et queïst tous jours sans peresce,	184
xxx	Les pans laciés a la sainture,	
xxx	Tant come tous li mondes dure,	
5355	Jusqu'il aüst trestout veü,	
	N'avroit il pas aconsseü	188
	Ceste amour que ci dit m'avez.	
	Bien en fu il mondes lavez,	[fol. 69r]
	Des lors que li dieu s'en foïrent,	
5360	Quant li jaient les assaillirent,	192
	Et Drois et Chastëe et Fois	
	S'en foïrent tuit a lor fois.	
	Cele amour fu si esperdue,	
5364	Qu'el s'en foï tout espendue.	196
	Justice qui plus pesans iere	
	Si s'en foï la darreniere.	
	Il ne porent soffrir le[s] guerres,	
5368	Si laissierent toutes les terres,	200
	Es cieux firent lor habitacles.	
	Ains puis, se ne fu par miracles,	
	N'oserent ça jus devaler.	
5372	Baras les en fist tous aler,	204
	Qui tient en terre l'eritage	
5374	Par sa force et par son oultrage.	
5391	Tele amour donques ou querroie,	
5392	Quant ça jus ne la trouveroie?	208
	Puis je voler avec les grues,	
	Voire saillir outre les nues,	
	Com fist li cignes Tocratés?	
5396	Ne quier plus parler, je la tes.	212
	Ne sui pas de si fol espoir.	

180 Q. ce croiroit   181 *omitted*   201 Et tuit f.   211 li c. qui ert T.
213 fui

	Li dieu cuideroient espoir	
	Que j'assaillisse paradis,	
5400	Con firent li jaiant jadis;	216
	S'en porroi[e] estre foudroiés.	
	Ne sai se vous le voudroiés.	
	Si n'en doi je pas estre en doute.	
5404	– Biaus amis, dit el, or m'escoute.	220
xxx	Ja voler ne te convendra,	
xxx	Mais voloir a chascun vaudra.	[fol. 69v]
5781	Pour quoi, sans plus, creés mes ouevres?	
5782	Ja ne convient qu'autrement ouevres.	224
5772	Et se te voil a moi tenir,	
5771	Je voil t'amie devenir.	
5767	Met, s'il te plait, a moi t'entente.	
	Ne suis je bele dame et gente,	228
	Digne de servir un prodome,	
5770	Et fust emperieres de Rome?	
xxx	Lors ameras et si garras,	
xxx	Ne jamais nullui ne harras.	232
5699	Nepourquant il ne s'ensuit mie,	
5700x	Se l'en deffent une folie,	
5701x	Que l'en commant a faire graindre;	
	Nepourquant se je voil estaindre	236
	La fole amor a quoi tu bees,	
5704	Ne commant je pas que tu hees;	
5711	N'amours ne voil je pas deffendre	
	Que l'en n'i doie bien entendre,	240
	Fors a cele qui les gens blesce.	
	Pour ce se je deffen yvresce,	
5715	Si ne deffen je pas le boivre.	
5716	Ce ne vaut pas un grain de poivre;	244
5721	Je ne fais pas tiex argumens.	
	– Si faites voir. – Certes, tu mens.	
	Ja ne te quier de ce flater,	
5724	Tu n'as pas bien pour moi mater	248
	Cerché les livres ancïens.	
	Tu n'ies pas bons logicïens.	

216 Que   220 dit il   227 Mais   232 nul leu ne charras [*em. from B*î]
236—37 Nepourquant je ne voil estraindre / La folie a moi que tu bees
248 bon

Je ne lis pas d'amours ansi.
5728　Onques de ma bouche n'issi　　　　252
Que nule rien haïr doie on.
On i puet bien trouver moion.　　　[fol. 70r]
C'est l'amour que j'ains tant et prise,
5732　Que je t'ai par amour aprise.　　　256
5813　Par amour devien mes amis,
5814　Et lais le dieu qui ci t'a mis.
6871　　– Dame, dis je, ce ne puet estre.
6872　Il me convient servir mon mestre.　　260
6883　Tenir li voil son convenent,
Car il est drois et avenent.
S'en enfer me devoit mener,
6886　Ne puis je mon cuer refrener.　　　264
xxx　D'autre part, se je vous amoie,
Autres amours avec le moie
Averiez vous plus de .c. mile.
Il n'est hons a bourc ne a vile,　　　268
Puis que tenir le poïssiés,
Que vous ne le receüssiés,
Et vouroiés qu'il vous amast,
Puis que s'amie vous clamast.　　　272
Trestout le mondë averiés!
Trop vous abondoneroiés.
Je ne voil pas, ne vous poist mie,
Approprier commune amie.　　　276
J'en voil une avoir moie quite."
Quant j'oi ceste parole dite,
Raisons respont a escïent,
Un petitet en sus rient,　　　280
"De noiant te mes en esmai.
Seroies tu jalous de moi,
Que pechiés en moi se meïst?
Certains seras, se Diex m'aïst,　　　284
Que ja n'i aras vilenie,
Quant de t'amour m'aras saisie.　　[fol. 70v]
Miex fust ma chars livree a lous,
Que tu fusses cous ne jalous,　　　288
Puis qu'a moi te seras donez.

251 d'a. ansin　264 rafermer　276 De prier si communement　281 nes

xxx	– Dame, de noiant sermonez,	
6887	Puis que mes cuers n'es[t] pas o moi;	
	N'onques ancore n'antammai,	292
	Ne n'ose pas a antamer	
6890	Mon testament pour autre amer.	
6895	Si ne vouroie pas la rose	
6896	Changier a vous pour nule chose,	296
xxx	Tant me saüssiés bien flater.	
xxx	Ne je ne voil plus desputer,	
xxx	Ne je ne vous en croirai pas:	
xxx	Or avez gastés tous vos pas."	300
7199	Quant Raisons m'ot, si s'en retourne,	
7200	Et me laise pansis et morne.	

2. PASSAGES FROM REASON IN MS BE

MS *Be* is Turin, University Library L.III. 22. Due to damage from the fire of 1904, portions of the text are lost or illegible. In those cases, I have supplied the missing words from Lecoy's edition, placing such text between brackets. For interpolated lines, illegible text is supplied from Langlois's critical notes.

A. Trace of an original abridgment of the second half of Reason's discourse

5809	["Or] me dites donques ainçois,	[fol. 44r]
	[N]on en latin mais en françois,	
	[D]e [qu]oi volés vos que je serve?	
5812	[– S]ueffre que je soie ta serve,	4
	[Et] tu li mien loiaux amis.	
	[L]e dieu lairas qui ci t'a mis,	
5815	[Et] ne priseras pas une prune	[+1]
5816	[T]oute la force de Fortune.	8
xxx	[Et] laisse ta pensee fole,	
xxx	[Et] le faux dieu qui si t'afole.	
xxx	[A]mours qui [te fa]it en li croire	
xxx	Te tolt ton [sens] et ta memoire,	12
xxx	[Et] de ton cuer les iex avugle,	
xxx	[S]i te fait on tenir pour bugle.	
6871–7161	[– Dame, fis je,] les metafores	
7162	[Ne bé] je pas a gloser ores.	16
	[M]ais se je puis estre garis,	

7164	Et li service m'iert meris,
	Dont si grant guerredon atens,
	Bien les gloserai tout a tens, 20
	Au mains ce qu'il en aferra,
7168	Si que chascuns clers i verra.
7175	Mais je vos cri, pour Dieu merci,
7176	Ne me blasmés plus d'amer ci. 24
7169	Et je vos tieing a escusee
7170	De la parole ensi usee.
7177	Se je sui folx, c'est mes damages.
	Mais au mains fui je lors bien sages, 28
	De ce cuic je bien estre fis,
7180	Quant homage a mon mestre fis.
	Se je sui fox, ne vos en caille.
	[J]e vuel amer, comment qu'il aille, 32
7183	[L]a rose ou je me sui vöés,
xxx	Et m'en ostés, se vos pöés.
xxx	Tous li pourfis que vous me dites
xxx	De vos amer soit vostre quites. 36
xxx	– **Or** biaux amis, de dit Raison,
xxx	Puis que j'ai gasté ma saison
xxx	A toi enseignier et aprendre,
xxx	Je ne te vueill or plus desfendre 40
xxx	Que tu ta volenté ne faches.
xxx	Mais [une] chose vueill que saches,
xxx	Que [se tu m]on conseill cre[üss]es,
xxx	L[oial] amour et bone e[ü]sses. 44
5817	A [Socratés] fusses samblables,
5818	Qui tant [fu] fors et tant [estables.] . ."

B. Reworking of part of the discussion of plain speech

6913	Lors [se prist] Resons a sousrire,	[fol. 51v]
	[En] sousriant me prist a dire:	
	"Biaux amis, je puis bien nommer,	
6916	Sans moi faire mal renommer, 4	
	Apertement, par propre non,	
	Chose qui n'est se bone non.	
	Vaire, dou mal seürement	
6920	Puis je parler bien proprement, 8	
6922	S'est chose qu'a pechié ne monte;	

xxx	Je n'ai pas de voir dire honte
xxx	Se verité n'est si cuisant
xxx	Qu'el fust contre vertu nuisant. 12
xxx	[M]ais quant le verité doit nuire
xxx	[Contre] vertu, bon le fait fuire.
xxx	Sans faille bien l'as oï dire:
xxx	Tout voir ne sunt pas bon a dire. 16
6917x	L'en doit nommer par propre non
6918	Chose qui n'est se bone non.
xxx	Mais qui vuelt mal[vestié] confondre,
xxx	Verité n'est pas a repondre. 20
xxx	Tiex verités n'est pas a tai[re]:
xxx	Cele doit on tous jours [retraire],
xxx	Car verité quant vous la [dites]
xxx	Pour connoistre les ypocrites 24
7135	La verités dedans repose.
7136	Clere seroit s'ele iert e[sposte].
	Bien l'entendras, se bien re[petes],
	Les enseingnements [aus pöetes]. 28
	La verras une g[rant partie]
7140	Des secrés de [philosophie],
7145	Car en lor gieus [et en leur fables]
7146	Gisent delit [moult profitables,] 32
7141	Ou moult te vou[dras deliter]
7142	[. . .] te po[rras mout profiter].
7143	En delitant pourfiteras, [fol. 52r]
7144	En pourfitant deliteras, 36
7147	Cex qui lor pensees couvrirent
	Quant le voir des fables vestirent.
	Si te convendroit a ce tendre,
7150	Se bien vues la parole entendre. 40
7123	[Si] dit on bien a ces escoles
7124	Maintes choses par paraboles,
	Qui moult sunt beles a entendre.
	Si ne doit on mie tant prendre 44
	En la lettre quanc'on i ot.
7128	En ma parole autre sens n'ot,
	Au mains quant des coullons parloie,
	Quant si briément parler voloie, 48
	Que celui que tu i vues mestre.
7132	Et qui bien verroit en la lestre,

	Le sens verroit en escriture,	
7134	Qui esclarcist la fable oscure.	52
xxx	Mes peres plus que nus les blasme,	
xxx	N'il ne het tant nul autre blasme.	
6925x	[Et] je qui onques ne pechié	
xxx	Ne hé tant rien com tel pechié;	56
6923	Ne chose ou pechié se meïst	
6924	N'est nus qui faire me feïst.	
xxx	Je ne tiens autre chose a lede;	
xxx	Qui plaidier en voudra, s'en plede.	60
6927	Bien puis nomer la noble chose	
	Par plain texte, sans metre glose,	
	Que mes peres en paradis	
6930	Fist de ses propres mains jadis . . ."	64

Lines 7123–50 are not repeated later. Following v. 7122 are vv. 7103–4, after which the text continues from v. 7151 on.

Appendix C

The "litany of love" in the discourse of Reason

This interpolation in Reason's description of love follows v. 4370 in twenty-eight of the 116 manuscripts collated by Langlois. It appears in most manuscripts of the second group: the families *K*, *M*, and *N* and their descendants. I give the text from MS *Mi*, with variants from MSS *Arr* (fol. 252r–252v), *Ke* (fol. 31v–32r), and **Npr* (fol. 32r–32v).

[fol. 34r]   **Me**[e]smement de ceste amour:
Li plus sage n'i scevent tour.
Mais or entent, je te dirai,
Une autre amor te descriprai.   4
De celle veil je que pour t'ame
Que tu aimes la douce dame.
Si com dit la Sainte Escripture,
Amors est fors, amour est dure,   8
Amors soustient, amor endure,
[fol. 34v]   Amour revient et toujours dure,
Amour meit en amer sa cure.
Amour loial, amour seüre,   12
Sert et de service n'a cure.
Amour fait de propre commun,
Amour fait de divers cuers un.
Amour enchasce, ce me semble.   16
Amour depart, amour assemble,
Amour joint divers cuers ensemble,
Amour rent cuers, amour les emble.
Amour despiece, amour refait,   20

1 *Ke M.* en
2 *Arr adds* Amour carnele et fausse et vaine / N'est pas comme tainture en graine / Puisque delis a fait sen cours / Amours est tournee en decours
3 *Arr* que te d.   5–6 *Not in Arr*   6 *Ke* Aimes tu la trés d. d.
7 *Arr* Si que   11 *Arr Ke *Npr* en amour   15 *Arr* A. si fait de .ii. cuers un
16 **Npr* A. enchante   16–17 *reversed Arr*   17 *Arr* A. de par   20 *Arr* defait

Amour fait pais, amour fait plait.
Amour [fait] bel, amour fait lait,
Toutes heures quant il li plait.
Amors atrait, amor estrange,   24
Amour fait de privé estrange;
Amour seurprent, amor enprent,
Amour reprent, amor esprent.
Il n'est riens qu'amors ne face.   28
Amour tost cuer, amour tost grace.
Amour deslie, amours en lace,
Amour occist, amour efface,
Amour ne craint ne pic ne mace.   32
Amour fist Dieu venir en place,
Amour fist Dieu devenir cendre,
Amour li fist nostre char prandre,
Amour le fist devenir mendre,   36
Amour le fist le monde prandre,
Amour le fist en la croiz pandre,
Amour le fist illec estendre,
Amour li fist le costé fendre,   40
Amour li fist les maulx reprandre,
Amour li fist les bons aprandre;
Amour le fist a nous venir,
Amour nous fait a lui tenir.   44
Si com l'escripture racompte:
Il n'est de nulle vertu conte
S'amour ne joint et lie ensemble.
Il m'est avis et voir resemble   48
Que pou vaut foi ne esperance,

---

23 *Not in Ke; Arr* T. h. que boin lui est   24 *Ke* A. acroit
26 *Arr* A. sousprent, a. esprent
26–27 *Ke* A. esprent a. reprent / A. aprent a. esprent   27 *Not in Arr*
28 *Ke* Amours n'est riens qu'ele ne face
29 *Arr* et donne grace *Ke* a. taint face   31 *Not in Arr; Ke* a lasche
32 *Ke* A. ne vaint *Npr* ne pie ne menace *Ke adds:* Amour ne craint ne chaut ne
    glace   37 *Ke* aprendre   38 *Npr* prendre
41 *Ke* aprendre *Npr* les mains r.   41 *Arr* fait   42 *Arr Ke* fait
44 *Arr adds:* Amours nous fait les biens avoir / Qui valent miex que nul avoir
46 *Mi* Il es de toute v. c.   47 *Mi* nous j. *Arr* nel j.   48 *Arr Ke* me semble
49 *Arr* et esperance *Ke* Po vault f. po vault e.

Justice, force, n'atrempance,
Qui n'a finë amour o soi.
L'apostre dit et je l'otroi   52
Qu'amosne faite, ne martire,
Ne bien que nullui sache dire,
Ne vault riens s'amor y deffaut:
Sanz amour trestout bien deffaut.   56
Sanz amour n'est nulz homs parfait,
Ne par parole ne par fait.
Ce est la fin, ce est la somme:
Amour fait tout le parfait homme.   60
Amours les enserrez desserre,
Amour si na cure de guerre.
Fine amor qui ne cesse point
A Dieu les met, a Dieu les joint.   64
Loial amor fait a Dieu force,
Quar amour de l'amer s'efforce.
Quant amor devotement ore
En .i. moment et en pou d'ore,   68
Quant amor parfaitement pleure,
Li vient tresgrant douceur en l'eure.
Et fine amor d'amer est yvre,
Car grant douceur fait amour yvre.   72
Lors la convient dormir a force,
Quant en dormant d'amer s'efforce;
Car amor ne puet estre oisive,
Tant com el soit et saine et vive.   76

---

50 *Arr Ke* et atrempance   51 *Arr* avoec s.   53 *Ke* Qu'a une feite
54 *Arr* Ne nulz biens qu'aulcuns   55 *Arr adds:* Li homs sans amour riens ne vault
56 **Npr* S. a. ce est b. d. *Not in Arr*
60 *Arr Ke *Npr add:* Amours commence, amours assomme | Sans amours n'est
    mie fait homme [*Ke:* S. a. n'est nul parfet homme; *follows v. 60*]
61 *Arr *Npr* A. les enserre et d.   62 *Arr* A. si nature deguerre
62 *Ke* A. qui n'a c. d. g. | A Dieu tret les cuers et les serre   67 *Ke* oeure
68–69 *Reversed in Ke*   70 *Ke* douceur desseure
71–72 *Arr* Qui fine a. d'amer enivre | Adont puis que d'amer est ivre *Ke* Quant
    grant d. d'amer enyvre | Et quant a. est d'amer yvre
72 **Npr:* g. d. amor enyvre   74 *Ke* Mes en d.   75 *Arr* oyzeuse
76 *Arr* T. qu'elle *Arr Ke *Npr* s. ne v.

Lors dort en meditation,
Puis monte en contemplacion;
Ilec s'aboivre, ilec s'esveille,
[fol. 35r]   Ilec voit mainte grant merveille,   80
La voit tout bien, la voit tout voir,
La treuve tout son estouvoir,
La voit quanque on puet veoir,
La sent quanque on puet avoir;   84
La aprent quanqu'on puet aprendre,
La prent du bien quanqu'on puet prendre.
Mais quant plus prent et plus aprent,
Et plus son desirier la prent,   88
Toujours li croit son apetit,
Et tient son assez a petit.
En amor n'a point de clamour,
Chascun puet amer par amour.   92
Quant d'amours ne te pues clamer,
Par amour te convient amer:
De tout ton cuer, de toute t'ame,
Veil que aimes la douce dame.   96
Quant amor amer la t'esmuet,
Par amour amer la t'estuet.
Donc aime la vierge Marie,
Par amour a li te marie.   100
T'ame ne veult aultre mari,
Par amour a lui te mari,
Aprés Jhesu Crist son espous:
A lui te donne, a lui t'espous,   104
A lui te donne, a lui t'otroi,
Sanz desotrier t'i otroi.
       De l'autre amour dirai la cure
Selon la devine Escripture.   108
4371   Et mesmement en ceste guerre,
4372   Ou nulz ne scet le moien querre . . .

---

79 *Ke* I. s'ahurte   82–83 *Not in Arr*   83 *Ke* savoir   85–86 *Reversed in Arr*
85 *Arr Ke* La prent quanques on p. a.   87 *Arr* M. que   88 *Arr* esprent
90 *Arr* Tant com en celle joye vit   93 *Arr* oster   95 *Arr* De tout c.
96 *Arr* Aime Dieu et la d. d.   98 **Npr* amer l'estuet
99 *Ke* Veil amer la v. M.   100 *Ke* Par amour a a non Marie
103 *Arr* Que J. C. son doulc espeus   109–10 *K MSS omit vv. 4371–74*

Appendix D

Discourse of Genius in MS *Lm* (partial)

In MS *Lm* (Rennes, Bibl. Mun. MS 15963), the first part of the discourse of Genius is heavily abridged, while the rest is complete. It is possible that at one time there were more abridgments or other alterations, for the gathering that begins with v. 20637 was evidently made at a different time from the preceding, and may have been copied from a different model (see Chapter 5). However, it is clear that the original state of Genius' sermon did include at least some of the material outlining the comparison of the Garden of Delight and the Heavenly Park, since this section begins well within the original portion of the manuscript. Here, I give the text of Genius' sermon up to v. 20067. From v. 20067 to the end of the gathering (v. 20636), only the following lines are missing: vv. 20105–8, 20120–34, 20233–36, 20269–70, and 20337–38. The portion of Genius' sermon appearing in the new gathering is complete except for vv. 20577–78.

19475	**D**el auctorité de Nature,	[fol. 109v]
	Qui de tout le monde a le cure,	
	Comme vicaire et connestauble	
	A i'empereour pardurable,	4
19479	Qui siet en la tour souverainne	
	De la noble cité mondainne,	
	Dont il fist Nature ministre,	
	Qui tous les biens i aministre	8
19483	Par l'influance des esteles,	
	Car tout est ordené par eles,	
	Selonc les drois emperiaus	
	Dont Nature est officiaus,	12
19487	Qui toutes choses a fait nestre,	
	Puis que cis mondes vint en estre,	
	Et leur donna terme ensement	
	De grandeur et d'acroissement,	16
19491	N'onques ne fist riens pour noiant	
	Sous le ciel qui va tournoiant	
	Entour la terre sans demeure,	
	Si haut desous comme deseure,	20
19495	Ne ne cesse ne nuit ne jour,	
	Mais tous jours tourne sanz sejour,	
	Soient tuit escommenié	
	Li desloial, li renoié,	24

19499	Et condampné sans nul respit,	
	Qui les oevres ont en despit,	
	Soit de grant gent, soit de menue,	
	Par cui Nature est soustenue.	28
19503	Et cis qui de toute sa force	
	De Nature garder s'efforce,	
	Et qui de bien amer se painne,	
	Sans nule pensee vilainne,	32
19507	Mais qui loiaument i travaille,	
	Flouris em paradis s'en aille.	
	Mais qu'il se face bien confes,	
	J'en prent seur moi trestout le fes	36
19511	De tel pooir com je puis rendre,	
	Ja pardon n'en avera mendre.	
	Mar lor ait Nature donné,	
	Les fox dont j'ai ci sermonné,	40
19515	Greffes, taublés, martiaus, enclumes,	
19516	Selonc les lois et les coustumes,	
19547	Que Diex de sa main entailla,	
19548	Quant a ma dame les bailla.	44
19669	Metes tous vos martiaus en oevre,	
19670	Assez eschauffe qui bien oevre.	
19765	N'aiés pas les bras en moufflés,	
19766	Martelés, forgiés, et soufflés.	48
19855	Pensés de mener bonne vie,	
	Voit chascuns embrachier s'amie,	
	Et son ami chascuns embrace,	[MS: soit]
	Et baise et festie et soulace.	52
19859	Se loiaument vous entr'amez,	
	Ja n'en devrés estre blasmés.	
	Et quant assez avez joué,	
19862	Si com je vous ai ci loé,	56
19865	Reclamés Dieu le roi celestre,	
	Que Nature reclaimme a maistre.	
	Cis en la fin vous secourra,	
	Quant Atropos vous enfaurra.	60
19869	Cis est salus de cors et d'ame,	
	C'est li biaus mireoirs ma dame.	
	Ja ma dame riens ne seüst,	
	Se tel bel mireoir n'eüst.	64
19873	Cis le gouverne, cis la regle,	[fol. 110r]
	Ma dame n'a point d'autre regle.	
	Canqu'ele set il li aprist,	
19876	Quant il a chambriere le pris.	68
20065	Jupiter qui le monde regle,	
	Commande et estaubli pour regle	
	Que chascuns peust de soi estre aise . . .	

Appendix E

The *Rose* of Cambridge, University Library Add. MS 2993

1. INTERPOLATION OF THE MIRROR OF VIRGIL IN MS *KU*

The following passage appears between vv. 1576 and 1577 (fol. 13r).
Variants are given for Pierpont Morgan Library, MS M 132 (fol. 14v).

> Foi que doi S. Pere de Romme,
> Le mirouer que fist a Romme
> Virgiles li nobiles clers
> Ne par fu onques aussi clers,   4
> Ne tant de choses ne vit on,
> Car celi n'estoit achoison
> Fors que de garder son païs
> Pour la dombte des anemis,   8
> Si comme li acteur recordent,
> Et les escriptures s'acordent.
> En veoit par ce mirouer
> .VII. liues: et neïz arrer   12
> Veoit en purement les terres,
> Et apercevoit en les guerres,
> Et veoit en les chevauchiees
> Des anemis, et les marchiees   16
> Qui sus eulz vouloient venir,
> Dont se povoient il garnir,
> Et garder et combatre a eulz
> Et eulz garantir tout par eulz.   20
> Mes de ce mirouer sauvage,
> Il n'a u monde homme si sage,
> Si s'abesse pour soi mirer,
> Qu'il ne la face souspirer,   24
> Et amer ou il vueille ou non.

4 si tres clers   6 n'avoit   7 le païs   10 Qui as escriptures
23 S'il s'i a. p. m.

Pour ce a il d'amours le non,
Car li diex d'amours en tous temps
N'a en nul senz autre pourpens   28
Qu'a espier ceulz qui se mirent,
Et qui du regarder s'atirent.
Et quant les a mis en ces las,
Li amoureus n'ont mes soulas   32
De riens fors d'entendre a amer.
Illec leur convient entamer
Leur conscience souveraine
Pour eulz mirer a la fontaine.   36

27 son temps   28 en nul lieu   29 s'i mirent   31 ses las

2. INTERPOLATION ON ANCIENT HEROES IN MS *KU*

Follows v. 6747. Variants and emendations from BN fr. 24392, fol. 55r–57r
(follows v. 6844).

Encore te vueil je moustrer,   [fol. 52r]
Ce dit Reson, et menistrer
Mes parolles; et retenir
Les dois, qu'il t'en puist souvenir.   4
Encor te vueil ramentevoir
Des grans fes, si qu'apercevoir
Te puisses de celle Fortune:
Ne vault une pourrie prune.   8
Leüs tu onc des Troyians,
De leur seigneur le roy Prians,
Que li Griiois mistrent a fin;
Que Fortune commë or fin   12
Afina; et fu si trés hault
Qu'avis li ert qu'en ciel en hault
Deüst voler par grant richesce,
Mes puis aprés par grant destresce   16
Vit il Hector son chier enfant
Trainer vilment par .i. enfant
De son sanc mesmes, qu'Achilés
L'avoit occis a .i. eslés.   20

2 Dit R. et aministrer   5 Et si   7 Les puisses car c. F.
10 *KU* E de leur sires   17 *KU* Vit il entour

Et tous ses autres filz perdi.
Si les te nomme. Je te di:
L'un fu Paris, Deïphebus,
Et Elenus et Troïlus.   24
Tous ces .v. furent chevaliers
Preus et hardiz et haulz parliers.
Et ses .iii. filles reperdi.
Entent leurs nons, je les te di: 28
L'unë ot a non Creüssa,
Et la seconde Crassandra,
Et la tierce Polixenan.
Et perdi au disemë an   32
Famë et enfanz et cité,
Et mesmes son corps fu gité
Aus grans champs ou fu devoré
Des bestes et du mal oré.   36
Et la vile mist a ardoir
.vii. ans, ainsi le dit pour voir   [fol. 52v]
Li escript anciennement
Escript, se malement ne ment.   40
   D'Alixandre te vueil parler,
Que Fortune fist tant aler
Par .x. ans conquerre le monde,
Car si com est en la rëonde,   44
Tout fu a son comandement;
Puis fina il mauvesement.
Car en Babiloine la grant,
Onques ne fu homme si grant   48
Que il ne fust jus amené.
Par poison fu envenimé,
Car .ii. freres l'enpoisonnerent
Qui eulz mesmes mal se boisierent,   52
Car il en furent puis malmis,
Et a la mort a la fin mis.
Mais cil grans hons dont je te conte,
Qui par traistres fu mis a honte,   56
Si dist .i. trop grant vilain mot:

21 *κυ* ces   22 te nommeray je di   28 les noms   29 ot nom   33 Femmes
39 L. e. qui a.   44 Que si c.   47 Car puis B.   50 fust   52 se boulerent
56 *κυ om.* mis

"Onques Diex, dit il, chier ne m'ot
Qui si petit monde fourmer
Volt, ou je ne puis pas esmer   60
Mon pueple ne moi contourner."
Mais pour cest orgueil ramener
A humilité basse et vile,
Qui tous les orgueilleus avile,   64
Consenti Diex, li roys poissant,
Qu'il fust puis homme nonpoissant,
Si qu'il fu puis en terre mis,
Et son corps a grant honneur mis.   68
Neïs sa mere, Olimpias –
Sachiés que il ne heoit pas,
Ains l'amoit sus tretoute rien,
Ne il n'avoit cure de rien   72
Qu'el n'en eüst la premeraine –
Souffri aprés moult trés grant paine,
Car elle fu mortë a glaive,
Aus champs mise en une falaise.   76
Illecques fu si devouree
D'oisiaus, de bestes atournee,
Qu'il n'i remaint ne pel ne char.
Et tous ces pers, par grant eschar,   80
Se desconfirent et a mort
Se mistrent tous aprés sa mort.
Ainsi Fortune en eulz ouvra,
Qui premier pour eulz bien ouvra,   84
Et au derrenier en la boe
Les mist a mort tous par sa roe
Qu'elle fist tourner fierement
Contr'eulz, s'escripture ne ment.   88
    Je te vueil de Cezar conter,
Que Fortune volt tant monter
Que sires du monde l'eslut,
Par enging que premier eslut.   92
Premierement li senateur

64 trestous les orgueilz   69 ᴋᴠ Mais esmere O.   71 sur toute riens
74 aprés lui moult grant   76 ᴋᴠ om. Et   80 ses pers   84 bien pour eulz
90 fist   91 seigneur

De Romme, comme bienfecteur,
L'envoierent France conquerre.
.v. ans dut demourer en guerre,   96
Et .x. en demoura et plus.
Par ce s'accorderent le plus
De Romme riches et moiens,
Qu'en prison fust et en lïens.   100
Mais il ne le volt consentir,
Ains les sot tous bien aastir,
Et les guerria malement,
Et moult trés vertueusement,   104
De quoi, quant Romme vit le fet,
Il eslurent tuit par un fet
.i. homme qui maintaint la guerre:
Ce fu Pompee, qui par terre   108 [fol. 53r]
Se combati a son serourge

. . . .

Car Pompee ot eü la fille
Cezar. Pour ce maintint la ville   112
Plus hardiement contre li.
Cezar tant ala contre li
Que il le fist si reculer
Qu'il l'en convint par force aler.   116
    Entent, dit Reson, douz amis,
La guerre de ces .ii. amis,
Comment elle fu aspre et dure,
Sans reson, sans nulle mesure.   120
Tant ala la bataille male
En .i. champ qui ot nom Thesale,
Ou Pompee ot le pieur,
Et Cezar en ot le meilleur,   124
Qui de fort ferir bien s'esforce.
Pompee en fet foïr par force,
Car il ot paour d'estre occis.
Si s'en ala mat et pensis,   128
Et prist sa fame et si enfant,
Et lessa ses hommes en sanc

96 dust   102 A. le sceut bien tost   107 mena l. g.   114 C. ala tant
117 Or enten dit Raison amis   121 T. ala a la b.   122 κυ Chessable
126 fist f.   129 print   130 aus champs

Gesans moilliez, mors et occis,
Et il s'en eschaperent vis.   132
    Quant Pompee vit que victoire
Ne pot avoir, en li memoire
Ot de s'en foïr en Egipte.
Il s'en ala a .i. mar gipte.   136
Cesti la trivier le mena,
Tant qu'au port Cressus l'atourna.
Il mist sa fame et si enfant
En une ille illec devant,   140
Que il vouloit avant savoir
Se il pourroit repos avoir.
Mais Tholonis li faux traïstrez,
Par conseil des ses faux menistres,   144
I envoia .ii. faux gloutons
Qui y vindrent com .ii. moutons,
Et s'en issirent con serpens
Aus caintures noez les pens,   148
Et l'occirent u bastelet
Com l'en occist .i. angnelet.
Car quant il sot et entendi
Que la mort li vint, je te di,   152
Qu'il ne mourut pas con garçon,
C'onques de sa bouche plainçon
Ne mot ne demi ne gemi,
N'onques ne dit ne laz ne mi,   156
Ains prist son mantel a .ii. mains,
Si en couvri son chief au mains,
Et la rendi son esperit.
Ainsi mouru et sans respit.   160
Mes tous ses enfans et sa fame,
Qui moult par estoit bonne dame,
Le vit mourir, si s'escria,
En dueil sans joie lermoia.   164
    Un Rommain estoit en Egipte,
Qui de Romme ot esté legite,
Si fu baniz pour ne sai quoi.
Moult amoit Pompee a ce quoi.   168

---

139 cil enfant   143 Tholomer   155 mot de d.   156 Ne il n. d.   157 print
158 aux mains   161 ĸ⋁ ces   164 Et en parfont deuil l.   165–204 *omitted*

De ce port vit faire ce murtre.
Aussi loiaus fu comme turtre
Envers son mestre, au dire voir.
Il atendi tretout pour voir   172
Jusques au soir, bien tart par nuit,
En l'iaue se mist sans deduit
Tout nuz et noa ça et la,
Tant que le corps qui avala   176
Aval l'iaue li vint devant.
Il le saisi en son devant,   [fol. 53v]
Tout en plorant a chiere mate.
Sus la rive le mist sanz nacte   180
Et sans coisin, sans oreillier,
Lez lui; ne volt pas sommeillier,
Que il ne fust aperceüs,
Car s'il i feüst conceüs,   184
Il feüst livrez a martire.
Ice ci osai je bien dire.
Adont prist .ii. quaillos bises,   [−1]
Et de l'estrain moult fectises,   188   [−1]
De buissons, de haies, d'espines,
Aluma feu, que serpentines
Ne manjassent le corps son mestre,
Qui aucune fois le seult pestre,   192
Et l'ardi a ce petit feu.
S'il feüst a Romme, .i. grant feu
Eüst esté bien alumez,
Illec fust son corps amenez.   196
A petite honneur recevoir
Sus celle rive, tout pour voir,
Fu ars Pompee, tout son corps.
Mes le chief en fu porté hors   200
Au faux roy Tholonis, l'enfant,
Qui en vourra faire .i. present
A Cezar, l'enpereur de Romme,
Qui a fet mal a maint preudomme.   204
    Nouvelles qui partout s'espendent,
Qui secrez a paroles mandent,
Alerent tant qu'a Julius

171 κυ Est vers   206 et paroles

377

Cezar vindrent. Titulius,   208
Un hons de Romme, vint a li,
Et dit que Pompee et li
Estoient alés vers Egipte,
Mais il y trouva moult mal giste, 212
Car le chief si lui est osté,
Et son corps en l'iaue gieté.
Quant le leu felon entendi,
Ravissable il dit, "Je te di,   216
J'amasse miex avoir perdu
Tout mon pooir et esperdu
Fusse .x. ans en essil mis,
Et perdu parans et amis,   220
Qu'il ne l'eüssent sain rendu.
Tholonis en sera pendu."
Ainsi disoit li desloiaus,
Qui en son temps juga tous maulz, 224
Mais il ne vousist pour riens nee
Que la chose ne fust tournee
Ainsi com elle se tourna,
Dont puis a mauvés chief tourna. 228
 A ce temps ot avant a Romme,
Si com en tesmoigne, .i. sage homme,
Qui nommez estoit en son temps
Chaton. Onc plus sage nulz temps 232
Ne fu, ne qui miex esgardast
Comment franchise se gardast.
Quant il vit a guerre si grant,
Et aperçut que si trés grant 236
Devenoit Cezar Julius,
Si prist son filz Titulius,
Sa fame et sa mesnie aussi,
Et en Libe s'en ala, si   240
Que nulz hons, au sien cuidement,
N'en seust noiant; mais malement
Se repont qui est encusez,
Car ceulz qui sont a mal usez, 244
Et qui portent fausses parolles,

---

211 en Egipte 215 l'entendi 216 *om.* il 222 Tholomer 229 En c. t.
230 un prudomme 236 apparut 238 print 240 ala cy 243 qu'il ert

Si vindrent sans autres frivolles
A Cezar en Egipte droit,
Et li distrent ou il estoit.   248 [fol. 54r]
Et quant Cezar si se parti
D'Egipte, adont departi
Son ost, et partie en lessa,
Et l'autre o li si s'eslessa   252
Tant que en Libe s'en alerent.
Et tantost nouvelles alerent
Au preudomme que Cezar vient,
Quant il oï, si dit qu'avient   256
Aucune fois par grant meschief
Que maint preudomme est a meschief.
"Je ne vueil perdre ma franchise.
Avant feray de moi justise   260
Que vif me conviengne servir,
Ne plus vilain de moi servir."
Dont but du venin, si mourut.
Mais avant sa mort acourut   264
Sa fame a lui, et li pria
Pour Dieu qui le monde crea,
Qu'a son filz vousist ensaignier
Aucun sens a li espargnier.   268
Si fist il, mais po en retint.
Aprés, quant il fu mors, se tint
Cezar li grans a engigniez.
La fu aaisiez et saigniez,   272
Et demoura .i. po de temps.
A Romme s'en revint a tans,
Et se fist clamer enperiere,
Dont au derrain li fu amere   276
L'empire, si com tu orras.
Entent bien, aprendre pourras.
    Entent folz, et si le retien.
Je t'aprendrai sans riens du tien   280
Mectre don il te vendra preu.
Cezar cuida faire son preu
Quant il entra en son païz,

252 si le laissa   254 Et quant les n.   256 Q. il l'oï   κυ dit savient
262 N'a

Dont il estoit enfes naïz, 284
Et li bourgois, li citoien
Virent que il ne valut rien,
Et qu'il escouvenoit par force
Qu'il fust leur sires. Une escorce 288
Ne donnoit d'eulz tous. Si manderent
Toute l'empire, et assamblerent
Leur gent de par tout le païs.
Si s'est chascun a li sousmis, 292
Et il en reçut les hommages,
Sans rendre leur cous ne dommages
Qu'ilz eüssent par lui eüz.
Dont fu a force esleüz 296
Et receüz a roy sus eulz,
Et couronne porta entr'eulz.
Et fu sires du mont clamez,
Et fu plus doubtez que amez, 300
Car il se fist doubter et craindre.
En la ville fist il sans faindre
Places a gieus, esbatemens,
Luites fors dont il vint tourmens 304
Et maulz, plus c'on ne puet penser.
Ne se fesoit que pourpenser
De faire choses enuieuses,
Pesans, chargans, et venimeuses. 308
Tant se fist partout redoubter,
Que neïs aus oiseaus douter
De l'air se feïst, s'il peüst,
Aus bestes, a quanqu'il sceüst, 312
Qui souz les nues posseïssent,
Tout volt qu'a li honneur feïssent.
Or l'ot bien Fortune essausé.
Mais aprés, le ra menasé, 316
Dont il ne se donnoit regart.
Or escoutes, se Dieux te gart. [fol. 54v]
   Or esgardes com grant honneur
Avint a ce desvé seigneur. 320

285 b. et c.   286 valoit   288 seigneur   289 de tous   292 *κʋ* Si scet
293 reprent   294 S. r. ne cour   299 Si fu   305 tant com pourroit penser
308 *κʋ* cerchans   312 et q.

T'est il avis que par grant fainte
Li ot s'amour Fortune atainte,
Et monstree par biau samblant?
Aprés li avint que tramblant   324
Devint .i. jour, et si ne sot
Dont tel chose avenir li pot,
Par songes et par fantasies.
Car Fortune amis et amies   328
Li presentoit chascun jour tant
Que il s'i fia du tout tant,
Qu'il s'abandonna tant a eulz,
Qu'il se sont assemblez entr'eulz.   332
A conseil se sont assemblé,
Tout bellement et en emblé,
Tant que d'entre'eulz ont esleü
Un jones hons bien conneü.   336
Bructus ot nom, et fu neveu
A Cezar, qui leur fist .i. veu
A tous, qu'au premier jour de plet
L'occirroit, et chascun le let   340
Atant, et .iiii. autres avec,
Chascun .i. greffe lonc avec.
Dont quant le jour fu assamblé,
Cezar ne vint pas en emblé;   344
Ains s'asist en la grant chaiere –
Plus grant fu que apotiquere –
Pour tenir plez, et fu asis
Plus hault que li autres. Pensis   348
Estoit, de ce n'en doutes ja,
Car le cuer li disoit desja.
Mais s'aventurë i gesoit
A ce que avenir devoit.   352
Bructus u braz si le feri,
Et l'autre u costé li couvri
Son greffë, et l'autrë u col.
A tart se pot tenir pour fol.   356
Adont chascun si l'a feru,

322 sa mort   330 Qu'il se f. d. t. et t.   331 tant   332 Et s'assemblerent
334 a emblé   337 si fu n.   338 Cesar lequel   344 a emblé
351 M. aventure

Que de nulz ne fu secouru.
Ainsi vint a sa mort Cezar.
Onc Melchion ne Baltazar,   360
Ne Jaspar ne cil d'Alemaigne,
Les .iii. roys qui de terre estraigne
Vindrent offrir a Jhesucrist,
Si com l'en le treuve en escrist,   364
Ne furent si bien espié
De Erodes li renoié   ·
Com fu Cezar dont je te conte.
Or puez oïr comme grant honte   368
Avint a ce grant païsant,
Et aus autres qui bien fesant
Furent, que Fortune nourrit
En leur vie et si seignorit,   372
Que il en pristrent si grans cures,
Qu'il en orent mal aventures.
Tout ce t'ai je retret pour toi.
Je te deprie, repens toi.   376

371 nourrist   372 seignourist   373 prinrent   376 rapaise toy

Notes

126–27: The battle in Thessaly and Pompey's flight are recounted in *Pharsalia* 7 and *Fet des Romains* 3.12.

138: Cressus: Probably a corruption of Casius, the scene of Pompey's murder. The confusion may result from the discussion of the death of Crassus directly preceding that of Pompey in *Fet des Romains* 3.13.

139–40: In all other sources Pompey leaves his family on the island of Lesbos for their safety during the battle. The poet seems to be conflating this passage with the one where Cornelia is forced to remain behind in the main boat while Pompey goes to meet the envoys of Ptolemaeus. The confusion may derive from an inaccurate memory of the *Fet* passage where Cornelia, left in the boat, alludes to having been left at Lesbos during the battle (3.13.21).

143: Tholonis: A corruption of Ptolemaeus.

143–64: The account of Pompey's death is consistent with that in *Pharsalia* 8 or *Fet des Romains* 3.13.

167: In other sources Pompey is buried by one of his followers, not by a banished citizen.

169–204: The account of Pompey's funeral follows that of Lucan or the *Fet des Romains*, except that in both of those sources the fire for the pyre is taken from another untended pyre rather than being struck from flint.

208: Titulius: This name seems to have been invented by the medieval poet.

238: Titulius: There is no tradition of Cato having a son named Titulius.

240–42: Cato's journey in Libya is described in *Pharsalia* 9 and *Fet des Romains* 3.14.

293–95: The statement that Caesar failed to compensate his men is in direct contradiction with the *Fet des Romains* (4.1.2), which, following Suetonius, states that Caesar did reward his men with both booty and land.

297–98: Caesar was often accused of having aspired to kingship (see e.g. Suetonius, *Lives of the Caesars* 1:79); but of course he never was crowned king. The *Fet des Romains* uses the title *emperor*. The poet's use of the term *roy* may indicate that his words about Caesar are intended to reflect on the French king; given the date of the manuscript (1354) this would probably be either Philip VI (reigned 1328—50) or John II (reigned 1350–64), both of whom were frequently in conflict with the French nobility.

309–15: Caesar's arrogance is described in *Fet des Romains* 4.2.32–35, which follows Suetonius, *Lives* 1:76–79. However, the poet has invented his own details.

337–59: This account of the assassination of Caesar does not closely follow that of Suetonius (1:80–84) or the *Fet des Romains* (4.3).

361: The phrase "cil d'Alemaigne" refers again to the Three Kings just named, whose relics were kept at Cologne. The comparison of Caesar to the Magi is not clearly motivated, and is, as far as I know, unique to this text. For advice concerning this passage I am grateful to Richard Trexler of the State University of New York, Binghamton.

Bibliography

ABBREVIATIONS

CFMA   Classiques Français du Moyen Age
PL   *Patrologiae cursus completus: Series latina.* Ed. J.-P. Migne. 221 volumes. Paris: Migne, 1844–64.
SATF   Société des Anciens Textes Français
TLF   Textes Littéraires Français

PRIMARY SOURCES

Abelard. *Historia calamitatum.* Ed. Jacques Monfrin. Bibliothèque des Textes Philosophiques. Paris: Vrin, 1959.

Alain de Lille. *Anticlaudianus.* Ed. R. Bossuat. Paris, 1955.

De planctu Naturae. Ed. Nikolaus M. Häring. *Studi Medievali* 19 (1978): 797–879.

Arnulf of Orleans. *Arnolfo d'Orléans, un cultore di Ovidio nel secolo XII.* Ed. Fausto Ghisalberti. Memorie del R. Istituto Lombardo de Scienze e Lettere, 24, fasc. 4. Milan, 1932.

Augustine. *Confessions.* Transl. John K. Ryan. Garden City, NY: Image Books, 1960.

De Genesi adversus Manicheos. PL 34 (1841). Col. 173–220.

Boethius. *The Consolation of Philosophy.* With the English translation of "I.T." (1609), rev. by H. F. Stewart. Loeb Classical Library. Cambridge, MA: Harvard University Press, 1918. Rpt. 1962.

Bolton-Hall, Margaret, ed. "A Critical Edition of the Medieval French Prose Translation and Commentary of *De Consolatione Philosophiae* of Boethius contained in MS 2642 of the National Library of Austria, Vienna." Dissertation, University of Queensland.

Cato. *Disticha.* In *Poetae Latini Minores.* Ed. Aemilius Baehrens. Vol. 3. Bibliotheca Scriptorum Graecorum et Romanorum Teubneriana. Leipzig: B. G. Teubner, 1881. Rpt. The Garland Library of Latin Poetry. New York: Garland Publishing, 1979.

Chaucer, Geoffrey. *Works.* Ed. F. N. Robinson. Boston: Houghton Mifflin, 1957.

Chrétien de Troyes. *Le Chevalier de la Charrette (Lancelot).* Ed. and transl. Alfred Foulet and Karl D. Uitti. Classiques Garnier. Paris: Bordas, 1989.

Christine de Pizan. *The Book of the City of Ladies.* Trans. Earl Jeffrey Richards. New York: Persea Books, 1982.

Les Diz et proverbes des sages (Proverbes as philosophes). Ed. Joseph Morawski. Université de Paris, Bibliothèque de la Faculté des Lettres, ser. 2, 2. Paris: PUF, 1924.

Evrart de Conty. Commentary on the *Echecs amoureux*. Bibl. Nat. fr. 9197.

Li Fet des Romains. Ed. L.-F. Flutre and K. Sneyders de Vogel. 2 vols. Paris: Droz, and Groningen: Walters, 1938.

Il Fiore e Il Detto d'amore. Ed. Claudio Marchiori. Genoa: Tilgher, 1983.

Gautier de Coinci. *Les Miracles de Nostre Dame*. Ed. V. Frederic Koenig. TLF. 3 vols. Paris: Minard, and Geneva: Droz, 1961.

Gervais de Bus. *Le Roman de Fauvel*. Ed. Arthur Långfors. SATF. Paris: Firmin Didot, 1914–19.

Glossa Ordinaria. PL 113 (1852).

Gratian. *Decretum*. In *Corpus Iuris Canonici*. Ed. Emil Ludwig Richter and Emil Friedberg. Leipzig, 1879; rpt. Graz, 1959. Vol. 1.

Gui de Cambrai. *Barlaam und Josaphat*. Ed. Hermann Zotenberg and Paul Meyer. Bibliothek des Litterarischen Vereins, 75. Stuttgart: Litterarisches Verein, 1864.

Guillaume de Deguilleville. *Le Pelerinage de la vie humaine*. Ed. J. J. Stürzinger. Roxburghe Club Publications, 124. London: Nicholson and Sons, 1893.

Guillaume de Lorris and Jean de Meun. *Le Roman de la Rose*. Ed. Ernest Langlois. SATF. 5 vols. Paris: Champion, 1914–24.

Le Roman de la Rose. Ed. Félix Lecoy. CFMA. 3 vols. Paris: Champion, 1965–70.

Le Roman de la Rose. Ed. D. Méon. 4 vols. Paris: Didot, 1814.

Le Roman de la Rose. Ed. Daniel Poirion. Classiques Garnier. Paris: Flammarion, 1974.

Le Roman de la Rose dans la version attribuée à Clément Marot. Ed. Silvio F. Baridon. Introduction by Antonio Viscardi. 2 vols. Milan: Istituto Editoriale Cisalpino, 1957.

Guillaume le Clerc. *Le Bestiaire*. Ed. Robert Reinsch. Altfranzösische Bibliothek, 14. Leipzig: O. R. Reisland, 1892.

Hicks, Eric, ed. *Le Débat sur le Roman de la Rose*. Bibliothèque du XVe siècle, 43. Paris: Champion, 1977.

Horace. *Satires, Epistles, and Ars Poetica*. Transl. Rushton Fairclough. Loeb Classical Library. Cambridge, MA: Harvard University Press, and London: William Heinemann, 1961.

Hugh of Saint Victor. *De arrha animae*. PL 176 (1854). Col. 951–70.

Soliloquy on the Earnest Money of the Soul. Transl. Kevin Herbert. Milwaukee: Marquette University Press, 1956.

Innocent III. *See* Lotario dei Segni.

Jean de Condé. *La Messe des oiseaux et le Dit des Jacobins*. Ed. Jacques Ribard. TLF. Geneva: Droz, 1970.

Jean de Meun. "Boethius' *De Consolatione* by Jean de Meun." Ed. V. L. Dedeck-Héry. *Mediaeval Studies* 14 (1952): 165–275.

Langlois, Ernest, ed. *Recueil d'arts de seconde rhétorique*. Paris: Imprimerie Nationale, 1902.

Bibliography

Le Livre de Lancelot del Lac: Part 3. Ed. H. Oskar Sommer. *The Vulgate Version of the Arthurian Romances,* vol. 5. 1912; rpt. New York: AMS Press, 1969.

Lotario dei Segni (Pope Innocent III). *De miseria condicionis humanae.* Ed. and transl. Robert E. Lewis. The Chaucer Library. Athens: University of Georgia Press, 1978.

Machaut, Guillaume de. *Jugement du roy de Behaigne and Remede de Fortune.* Ed. James I. Wimsatt and William W. Kibler. The Chaucer Library. Athens: University of Georgia Press, 1988.

   Le Livre du Voir-Dit. Ed. Paulin Paris. Paris: Société des Bibliophiles Français, 1875.

   Oeuvres. Ed. Ernest Hoepffner. SATF. 3 vols. Paris: Firmin Didot, 1908–21.

Macrobius. *Commentary on the Dream of Scipio.* Transl. William Harris Stahl. New York: Columbia University Press, 1952.

Marie de France. *Lais.* Ed. Jean Rychner. CFMA. Paris: Champion, 1973.

Marot, Clément. *See* Guillaume de Lorris and Jean de Meun. *Le Roman de la Rose dans la version attribuée à Clément Marot.*

Matthew of Vendôme. *Ars versificatoria.* In Edmond Faral. *Les Arts poétiques du XIIe et du XIIIe siècle.* Paris: Champion, 1924. Rpt. 1971: 106–93.

La Mort le roi Artu. Ed. Jean Frappier. TLF. Geneva: Droz, 1964.

Ovid. *The Art of Love and Other Poems.* Transl. J. H. Mozley. Loeb Classical Library. Cambridge, MA: Harvard University Press, and London: William Heinemann, 1969. [Includes *Ars amatoria, Remedia amoris,* and *Ibis.*]

   Tristia / Ex Ponto. Transl. Arthur Leslie Wheeler. 2d edn rev. by G. P. Goold. Loeb Classical Library. Cambridge, MA: Harvard University Press, and London: William Heinemann, 1988.

Philippe de Thaün. *Le Bestiaire.* Ed. Emmanuel Walberg. Lund and Paris, 1900. Rpt. Geneva: Slatkine, 1970.

Raynaud, Gaston, ed. *Recueil de motets français des XIIe et XIIIe siècles.* Bibliothèque Française du Moyen Age. 2 vols. Paris: Vieweg, 1881. Rpt. New York and Hildesheim: Georg Olms, 1972.

Richard de Fournival. *Li Bestiaires d'amours e la response du Bestiaire.* Ed. Cesare Segre. Milan and Naples: Riccardo Riccardi, 1957.

Roman des sept sages de Rome. Ed. Mary B. Speer. Edward C. Armstrong Monographs on Medieval Literature, 4. Lexington, KY: French Forum, 1989.

The Romaunt of the Rose and Le Roman de la Rose. Ed. Ronald Sutherland. Berkeley and Los Angeles: University of California Press, 1968.

Walther, Hans, ed. *Proverbia Sententiaeque Latinitatis Medii Aevi / Lateinische Sprichwörter und Sentenzen des Mittelalters in alphabetischer Anordnung.* Carmina Medii Aevi Posterioris Latina, 2:1–5. Göttingen: Vandenhoeck and Ruprecht, 1963–69.

Werner, Jacob. *Lateinische Sprichwörter und Sinnsprüche des Mittelalters aus Handschriften gesammelt.* Heidelberg: Carl Winter, 1912.

Bibliography

SECONDARY SOURCES

The Astor Collection of Illuminated Manuscripts. Twenty Manuscripts from the Celebrated Collection of William Waldorf Astor (1848–1919) . . . Day of Sale: Tuesday, 21 June 1988. London: Sotheby's, 1988.

Atkinson, J. Keith, and Cropp, Glynnis M. "Trois Traductions de la *Consolatio Philosophiae* de Boèce." *Romania* 106 (1985): 198–232.

Badel, Pierre-Yves. "Raison 'Fille de Dieu' et le rationalisme de Jean de Meun." *Mélanges Frappier.* Textes Littéraires Français, 112. Vol. 1. Geneva: Droz, 1970: 41–52.

——. *Le "Roman de la Rose" au XIVe siècle: Étude de la réception de l'oeuvre.* Publications Romanes et Françaises, 153. Geneva: Droz, 1980.

Baird, Joseph L., and Kane, John R. "*La Querelle de la Rose*: In Defense of the Opponents." *The French Review* 48 (1974): 298–307.

Baumgartner, Emmanuèle. "De Lucrèce à Héloïse, remarques sur deux exemples du *Roman de la Rose* de Jean de Meun." *Romania* 95 (1974): 433–42.

——. "The Play of Temporalities; or, The Reported Dream of Guillaume de Lorris." In *Rethinking the "Romance of the Rose": Text, Image, Reception.* Ed. Kevin Brownlee and Sylvia Huot. Pp. 21–38.

——. "Temps linéaire, temps circulaire, et écriture romanesque (XIIe–XIIIe siècles)". in *Le Temps et la durée dans la littérature au moyen âge et à la Renaissance.* Ed. Yvonne Bellenger. Paris: Nizet, 1984: 7–21.

Bouché, Thérèse. "L'Obscène et le sacré, ou l'utilisation paradoxale du rire dans le *Roman de la Rose* de Jean de Meun". *Le Rire au moyen âge dans la littérature et dans les arts.* Ed. Thérèse Bouché and Hélène Charpentier. Bordeaux: Presses Universitaires de Bordeaux, 1990: 83–95.

——. "Ovide et Jean de Meun." *Le Moyen Age* 83 (1977): 71–87.

Braet, Hermann. "Der Roman der Rose, Raum im Blick." *Träume im Mittelalter: Ikonologische Studien.* Ed. Agostino Paravicini Bagliani and Giorgio Stabile. Stuttgart and Zürich: Belser Verlag, 1989: 183–92, colour plates 20–23.

Brownlee, Kevin. "Discourses of the Self: Christine de Pizan and the *Rose.*" *Romanic Review* 79 (1988): 199–221.

——. "Jean de Meun and the Limits of Romance: Genius as Rewriter of Guillaume de Lorris." In *Romance: Generic Transformation from Chrétien de Troyes to Cervantes.* Ed. Kevin Brownlee and Marina Scordilis Brownlee. Hanover, NH: University Press of New England, 1985: 114–34.

——. "Machaut's Motet 15 and the *Roman de la Rose*: The Literary Context of *Amours qui a le pouir/ Faux Samblant m'a deceü / Vidi Dominum.*" *Early Music History* 10 (1991): 1–14.

——. "Orpheus's Song Resung: Jean de Meun's Reworking of *Metamorphoses,* x." *Romance Philology* 36 (1982): 201–9.

——. *Poetic Identity in Guillaume de Machaut.* Madison: University of Wisconsin Press, 1984.

Brownlee, Kevin, and Huot, Sylvia, eds. *Rethinking the "Romance of the Rose": Image, Text, Reception.* Philadelphia: University of Pennsylvania Press, 1992.

Bibliography

Burton, Rosemary. *Classical Poets in the "Florilegium Gallicum".* Lateinische Sprache und Literatur des Mittelalters, 14. Frankfurt a. M. and Bern: Peter Lang, 1983.

Calin, William. *"La Fonteinne amoureuse* de Machaut: Son or, ses oeuvres-d'art, ses mises en abyme." *L'Or au moyen âge (monnaie, métal, objets, symbole). Senefiance* 12. Aix-en-Provence: CUER-MA, 1983: 77–87.

"Medieval Intertextuality: Lyrical Inserts and Narrative in Guillaume de Machaut." *The French Review* 62 (1988): 1–10.

A Poet at the Fountain: Essays on the Narrative Verse of Guillaume de Machaut. Lexington, KY: University of Kentucky Press, 1974.

"Problèmes de technique narrative au Moyen Age: Le *Roman de la Rose* et Guillaume de Machaut." *Mélanges Pierre Jonin. Senefiance* 7. Aix-en-Provence: CUER-MA, 1979: 125–38.

Camille, Michael. "The Book of Signs: Writing and Visual Difference in Gothic Manuscript Illumination." *Word and Image* 1/2 (1985): 133–48.

Image on the Edge: The Margins of Medieval Art. Cambridge, MA: Harvard University Press, 1992.

Cerquiglini, Bernard. *Eloge de la variante: Histoire critique de la philologie.* Paris: Seuil, 1989.

Cerquiglini, Jacqueline. *"Un Engin si soutil": Guillaume de Machaut et l'écriture au XIVe siècle.* Bibliothèque du XVe Siècle, 42. Paris: Champion, 1985.

Cohen, Jeremy. *"Be Fertile and Increase, Fill the Earth and Master It": The Ancient and Medieval Career of a Biblical Text.* Ithaca: Cornell University Press, 1989.

Dahlberg, Charles. "Love and the *Roman de la Rose." Speculum* 44 (1969): 568–84.

"Macrobius and the Unity of the *Roman de la Rose." Studies in Philology* 58 (1961): 573–82.

Dean, Ruth. "Un Manuscrit du 'Roman de la Rose' à Jersey." *Romania* 65 (1939): 233–37.

Delisle, Léopold. *Le Cabinet des Manuscrits de la Bibliothèque Nationale.* 3 vols. Paris: Imprimerie Nationale, 1881.

Dragonetti, Roger. *Le Gai Savoir dans le rhétorique courtoise: "Flamenca" et "Joufroi de Poitiers".* Connexions du Champ Freudien. Paris: Seuil, 1982.

Le Mirage des sources: L'Art du faux dans le roman médiéval. Paris: Seuil, 1987.

Dwyer, Richard A. *Boethian Fictions: Narratives in the Medieval French Versions of the Consolatio Philosophiae.* Cambridge, MA: The Medieval Academy of America, 1976.

Ehrhart, Margaret J. *The Judgment of the Trojan Prince Paris in Medieval Literature.* Philadelphia: University of Pennsylvania Press, 1987.

Faral, Edmond. "Guillaume de Digulleville, moine de Chaalis," *Histoire Littéraire de la France.* Vol. 39. Paris: Imprimerie Nationale, 1962: 1–132.

Les Jongleurs en France au moyen âge. 1910. Rpt. New York: Burt Franklin, 1970.

Fawtier, R. "Deux manuscrits du *Roman de la Rose." Romania* 58 (1932): 265–73.

Fleming, John V. "The Moral Reputation of the *Roman de la Rose* before 1400." *Romance Philology* 18 (1964–65): 430–35.

Reason and the Lover. Princeton: Princeton University Press, 1984.

The "Roman de la Rose": A Study in Allegory and Iconography. Princeton: Princeton University Press, 1969.

Foulet, Alfred, and Speer, Mary Blakely. *On Editing Old French Texts*. Edward C. Armstrong Monographs on Medieval Literature, 1. Lawrence, KS: Regents Press of Kansas, 1979.

Fourez, Lucien. "Le *Roman de la Rose* de la Bibliothèque de la ville de Tournai." *Scriptorium* 1 (1946–47): 213–39, plates 21–24.

Frappier, Jean. "Variations sur le thème du miroir, de Bernart de Ventador à Maurice Scève." *Cahiers de l'Association Internationale des Etudes Françaises* 11 (May 1959): 134–58.

Ghisalberti, Fausto. "Medieval Biographies of Ovid." *Journal of the Warburg and Courtauld Institute* 9 (1946): 10–59.

Guichard-Tesson, Françoise. "La *Glose des Echecs amoureux*: Un savoir à tendance laïque: Comment l'interpréter?" *Fifteenth-Century Studies* 10 (1984): 229–60.

Ham, Edward Billings. "The Cheltenham Manuscripts of the 'Roman de la Rose'." *Modern Language Review* 26 (1931): 421–35.

Harris, Kate. "John Gower's *Confessio Amantis*: The Virtues of Bad Texts." In *Manuscripts and Readers in Fifteenth-Century England: The Literary Implications of Manuscript Study*. Ed. Derek Pearsall. Cambridge, UK: D. S. Brewer, 1983: 27–40.

Hassell, James Woodrow, Jr. *Middle French Proverbs, Sentences, and Proverbial Phrases*. Subsidia Mediaevalia, 12. Toronto: Pontifical Institute of Mediaeval Studies, 1982.

Hawkins, Richmond Laurin. "The Manuscripts of the 'Roman de la Rose' in the Libraries of Harvard and Yale Universities." *Romanic Review* 19 (1928): 1–28.

Hill, Thomas J. "Narcissus, Pygmalion, and the Castration of Saturn: Two Mythographical Themes in the *Roman de la Rose*." *Studies in Philology* 71 (1974): 404–26.

Hillman, Larry H. "Another Look into the Mirror Perilous: The Role of the Crystals in the *Roman de la Rose*." *Romania* 101 (1980): 225–38.

Hult, David F. "Gui de Mori, lecteur médiéval." *Incidences*, n.s. 5 (1981): 53–70.

——— "Reading it Right: The Ideology of Text Editing." *Romanic Review* 79 (1988): 74–88.

——— *Self-fulfilling Prophecies: Readership and Authority in the First "Roman de la Rose"*. Cambridge, UK: Cambridge University Press, 1986.

Huot, Sylvia. "Authors, Scribes, Remanieurs: A Note on the Textual History of the *Roman de la Rose*." In *Rethinking the "Romance of the Rose": Text, Image, Reception*. Ed. Kevin Brownlee and Sylvia Huot. Pp. 203–33.

——— " 'Ci parle l'aucteur': Rubrication of Voice and Authorship in *Roman de la Rose* Manuscripts." *SubStance* 17.2 (1988): 42–48.

——— "The Daisy and the Laurel: Myths of Desire and Creativity in the Poetry of Jean Froissart." *Yale French Studies*, special issue (1991): 240–51.

——— *From Song to Book: The Poetics of Writing in Old French Lyric and Lyrical Narrative Poetry*. Ithaca: Cornell University Press, 1987.

——— "Medieval Readers of the *Roman de la Rose*: The Evidence of Marginal Notations." *Romance Philology* 43 (1990): 400–20.

"The Medusa Interpolation in the *Romance of the Rose*: Mythographic Program and Ovidian Intertext." *Speculum* 62 (1987): 865–77.

"Notice sur les fragments poétiques dans un manuscrit du *Roman de la Rose*," *Romania* 109 (1988): 119–21.

"Polyphonic Poetry: The Old French Motet and Its Literary Context," *French Forum* 14 (1989): 261–78.

"The Scribe as Editor: Rubrication as Critical Apparatus in Two *Roman de la Rose* Manuscripts." *L'Esprit Créateur* 27 (1987): 67–78.

"Seduction and Sublimation: Christine de Pizan, Jean de Meun, and Dante." *Romance Notes* 25 (1985): 361–73.

"Vignettes marginales comme glose marginale dans un manuscrit du 'Roman de la Rose' au XIVe siècle (B.N. fr. 25526)." In *La Présentation du livre*. Ed. Emmanuèle Baumgartner and Nicole Boulestreau. Littérales: Cahiers du Département de Français, 2. Nanterre: Centre de Recherches du Département de Français, 1987: 173–86.

Ivy, Robert H., Jr. *The Manuscript Relations of Manessier's Continuation of the Old French "Perceval"*. Philadelphia: University of Pennsylvania Press, 1951.

Jung, Marc-René. "Gui de Mori et Guillaume de Lorris." *Vox Romanica* 27 (1968): 106–37.

"Jean de Meun et l'allégorie." *Cahiers de l'Association Internationale des Etudes Françaises* 28 (1976): 21–36.

Kahane, Henry and Kahane, Renée. "The Hidden Narcissus in the Byzantine Romance of *Belthandros and Chrysantza*." *Jahrbuch der Österreichischen Byzantinistik* 33 (1983): 199–219.

Kaske, Carol V. "Getting around the *Parson's Tale*: An Alternative to Allegory and Irony." In *Chaucer at Albany*. Ed. Rossell Hope Robbins. New York: Burt Franklin, 1975: 147–77.

Kelly, Douglas. "'Li chastiaus . . . Qu'Amors prist puis par ses esforz': The Conclusion of Guillaume de Lorris's *Rose*." In *A Medieval Miscellany*. Ed. Norris J. Lacy. University of Kansas Publications: Humanistic Studies, 42. Lawrence, KS: 1972: 61–78.

"Courtly Love in Perspective: The Hierarchy of Love in Andreas Capellanus." *Traditio* 24 (1968): 119–47.

Medieval Imagination: Rhetoric and the Poetry of Courtly Love. Madison: University of Wisconsin Press, 1978.

Kelly, Thomas and Ohlgren, Thomas. "Paths to Memory: Iconographic Indices to *Roman de la Rose* and *Prose Lancelot* Manuscripts in the Bodleian Library." *Visual Resources* 3 (1983): 1–15.

Kennedy, Elspeth. "The Scribe as Editor." *Mélanges de langue et de littérature du Moyen Age et de la Renaissance offerts à Jean Frappier*. Geneva: Droz, 1970: 523–31.

Kleinhenz, Christopher, ed. *Medieval Manuscripts and Textual Criticism*. Studies in Romance Languages and Literatures, Symposia, 4. Chapel Hill: University of North Carolina, Dept. of Romance Languages, 1975.

Kolve, V. A. *Chaucer and the Imagery of Narrative: The First Five Canterbury Tales*. London, 1984.

Bibliography

König, Eberhard. *Der Rosenroman des Berthaud d'Achy: Codex Urbinatus Latinus 376.* With an Appendix by Gabriele Bartz. Facsimile and commentary, 2 vols. Codices e Vaticanis selecti, 71. Zurich: Belser Verlag, 1987.

Kuhn, Alfred. "Die Illustration der Handschriften des *Rosenromans.*" *Jahrbuch der Kunsthistorischen Sammlungen des allerhöchsten Kaiserhauses* 31.1 (1912): 1–66.

Langlois, Ernest. "Gui de Mori et le *Roman de la Rose.*" *Bibliothèque de l'École des Chartes* 68 (1907): 249–71.

    Les Manuscrits du "Roman de la Rose": Description et classement. Lille: Tallandier, and Paris: Champion, 1910.

Lepage, Yvan G. "La Dislocation de la vision allégorique dans la *Messe des oiseaux* de Jean de Condé." *Romanische Forschungen* 91 (1979): 43–49.

Leupin, Alexandre. "The Powerlessness of Writing: Guillaume de Machaut, the Gorgon, and *Ordenance.*" *Yale French Studies* 70 (1986): 127–49.

Lewis, C. S. *The Allegory of Love.* Oxford: Oxford University Press, 1936.

Looze, Laurence de. "Guillaume de Machaut and the Writerly Process." *French Forum* 9 (1984): 145–61.

Lukitsch, Shirley. "The Poetics of the 'Prologue': Machaut's Conception of the Purpose of His Art." *Medium Aevum* 52 (1983): 258–71.

Lynch, Kathryn L. *The High Medieval Dream Vision: Poetry, Philosophy, and Literary Form.* Stanford: Stanford University Press, 1988.

Manuscrits et livres anciens. Sale catalog for Ader, Picard, Tajan, Commissaires-Priseurs Associés. Paris, Hotel George V, 16 September 1988.

Marchello-Nizia, Christiane. *Histoire de la langue française aux XIVe et XVe siècles.* Bordas Etudes: Langue Française. Paris: Bordas, 1979.

Minnis, A. J., ed. *The Medieval Boethius: Studies in the Vernacular Translations of "De Consolatione Philosophiae".* Cambridge, UK: D.S. Brewer, 1987.

Morawski, Joseph. "Fragment d'un *Art d'aimer* perdu du XIIIe siècle." *Romania* 48 (1922): 431–36.

Newton, Francis L. "Tibullus in Two Grammatical Florilegia of the Middle Ages." *TAPA* 93 (1962): 253–86.

Nichols, Stephen G. "Ekphrasis, Iconoclasm, and Desire." In *Rethinking the "Romance of the Rose": Text, Image, Reception.* Ed. Kevin Brownlee and Sylvia Huot. Pp. 133–66.

Nitzsche, Jane Chance. *The Genius Figure in Antiquity and the Middle Ages.* New York: Columbia University Press, 1975.

Novati, Francesco. *Attraverso il medio evo.* Bari, 1905.

    "Un Poème inconnu de Gautier de Châtillon." In *Mélanges Paul Fabre.* Paris: Picard, 1902: 265–78.

Omont, Henri. "Notice sur quelques feuilles retrouvées d'un manuscrit français de la Bibliothèque de Dijon." *Romania* 34 (1905): 364–74.

Ott, Karl August. *Der Rosenroman.* Erträge der Forschungen, 145. Darmstadt: Wissenschaftliche Buchgesellschaft, 1980.

Palmer, R. Barton. "The Metafictional Machaut: Self Reflexivity and Self-Mediation in the Two Judgment Poems." *Studies in the Literary Imagination* 20 (1987): 23–39.

Paré, Gérard. *Les Idées et les lettres au XIIIe siècle: Le "Roman de la Rose".* Université de Montréal Bibliothèque de Philosophie, 1. Montréal: Centre de Psychologie et de Pédagogie, 1947.

Le "Roman de la Rose" et la scolastique courtoise. Publications de l'Institut d'Etudes Médiévales d'Ottawa, 10. Paris: Vrin/Ottawa: Institut d'Etudes Médiévales, 1941.

Patterson, Lee. "' For the Wyves love of Bathe': Feminine Rhetoric and Poetic Resolution in the *Roman de la Rose* and the *Canterbury Tales*." *Speculum* 58 (1983): 656–95.

Payen, Jean-Charles. "Le *Livre de Philosophie et de Moralité* d'Alard de Cambrai," *Romania* 87 (1966): 145–74.

La Rose et l'utopie: Révolution sexuelle et communisme nostalgique chez Jean de Meung. Classiques du Peuple "Critique." Paris: Editions Sociales, 1976.

Pellegrin, E. "Manuscrits de l'abbaye de Saint-Victor et d'anciens collèges de Paris," *Bibliothèque de l'Ecole des Chartes* 103 (1942): 69–98.

Peruzzi, Simonetta Mazzoni. *Il Codice Laurenziano* Acquisti e Doni *153 del "Roman de la Rose".* Società Dantesca Italiana, Quaderno 3. Florence: Sansoni, 1986.

Pickens, Rupert T. "*Somnium* and Interpretation in Guillaume de Lorris." *Symposium* 29 (1974): 175–86.

Pickford, Cedric. "The 'Roman de la Rose' and a Treatise Attributed to Richard de Fournival: Two Manuscripts in the John Rylands Library." *Bulletin of the John Rylands Library, Manchester* 34 (1952): 333–65.

Poirion, Daniel. "Écriture et ré-écriture au moyen âge," *Littérature* 41 (February 1981): 109–18.

"From Rhyme to Reason: Remarks on the Text of the *Roman de la Rose*." In *Rethinking the "Romance of the Rose": Text, Image, Reception.* Ed. Kevin Brownlee and Sylvia Huot. Pp. 67–77.

"Narcisse et Pygmalion dans le *Roman de la Rose*." In *Essays in Honor of Louis Francis Solano.* Ed. Raymond Cormier and Urban T. Holmes. Studies in the Romance Languages and Literatures, 92. Chapel Hill: University of North Carolina Press, 1970: 153–65.

Le Poète et le prince: L'Evolution du lyrisme courtois de Guillaume de Machaut à Charles d'Orléans. Paris: PUF, 1965.

Le Roman de la Rose. Paris: Hatier, 1973.

Polak, Lucie. "Plato, Nature and Jean de Meun." *Reading Medieval Studies* 3 (1977): 80–103.

Quilligan, Maureen. "Words and Sex: The Language of Allegory in the 'De planctu naturae,' the 'Roman de la Rose,' and Book III of 'The Faerie Queen'." *Allegorica* 1 (1977): 195–216.

Randall, Lilian M. C. "Games and the Passion in Pucelle's Hours of Jeanne d'Évreux." *Speculum* 47 (1972): 246–57.

Images in the Margins of Gothic Manuscripts. Berkeley: University of California Press, 1966.

Richards, Earl Jeffrey. *Dante and the "Roman de la Rose": An Investigation into the Vernacular Narrative Context of the "Commedia".* Beihefte zur Zeitschrift für Romanische Philologie, 184. Tübingen: Max Niemeyer, 1981.

"Reflections on Oiseuse's Mirror: Iconographic Tradition, Luxuria and the

Roman de la Rose." *Zeitschrift für Romanische Philologie* 98 (1982): 296–311.

Richter, Otto. *De Vincentii Bellovacensis Excerptis Tibullianis (Dissertatio).* Bonn: Rosenthal, 1985.

Rieger, Angelica. " 'Ins e.l cor port, dona, vostra faisso': Image et imaginaire de la femme à travers l'enluminure dans les chansonniers de troubadours." *Cahiers de Civilisation Médiévale* 28 (1985): 385–415.

Robathan, Dorothy M. "The Missing Folios of the Paris *Florilegium* 15155." *Classical Philology* 33 (1938): 188–97.

Robertson, D. W. *A Preface to Chaucer.* Princeton: Princeton University Press, 1962.

Rosenstein, Roy. "*Mouvance* and the Editor as Scribe: *Trascrittore Tradittore?*" *Romanic Review* 80 (1989): 157–71.

Rouard, —. "D'un manuscrit inconnu du Roman de la Rose." *Bulletin du Bibliophile et du Bibliothécaire.* 14 ser. (1860): 976–87.

Rouse, Richard H. "Florilegia and Latin Classical Authors in Twelfth- and Thirteenth-Century Orléans." *Viator* 10 (1979): 131–60.

Rouse, Richard H., and Rouse, Mary A. "The Commercial Production of Manuscript Books in Late Thirteenth- and Early Fourteenth-Century Paris." *Medieval Book Production: Assessing the Evidence.* Ed. Linda L. Brownrigg. Los Altos Hills: Red Gull Press, and Oxford: Anderson-Lovelace, 1990: 103–15.

"The *Florilegium Angelicum*: Its Origin, Content, and Influence." *Medieval Learning and Literature: Essays Presented to Richard William Hunt.* Ed. J. J. G. Alexander and M. T. Gibson. Oxford: Clarendon Press, 1976: 66–114.

Roy, Bruno. "A la recherche des lecteurs médiévaux du *De amore* d'André le Chapelain." *Revue de l'Université d'Ottawa* 55 (1985): 45–73.

" 'Cristals est glace endurcie par molt d'ans'." In *Le Nombre du Temps: En hommage à Paul Zumthor.* Paris: Champion, 1988: 255–61.

Rychner, Jean. *Contribution à l'étude des fabliaux: Variantes, remaniements, dégradations.* 2 vols. Neuchâtel: Faculté des Lettres, and Geneva: Droz, 1960.

Sandler, Lucy Freeman. "A Bawdy Betrothal in the Ormesby Psalter." In *A Tribute to Lotte Brand Philip, Art Historian and Detective.* Ed. William W. Clark, et al. New York: Abaris Books, 1985: 155–59.

Sanford, Eva Matthews. "The Manuscripts of Lucan: *Accessus* and *Marginalia.*" *Speculum* 9 (1934): 278–95.

"The Use of Classical Latin Authors in the Libri Manuales." *TAPA* 55 (1924): 190–248.

Shonk, Timothy A. "The Scribe as Editor: The Primary Scribe of the Auchinleck Manuscript." *Manuscripta* 27 (1983): 19–20.

Smith, Nathaniel. "In Search of the Ideal Landscape: From *Locus Amoenus* to *Parc du Champ Joli* in the *Roman de la Rose.*" *Viator* 11 (1980): 225–43.

Söderhjelm, Werner. "Un manuscrit du *Roman de la Rose* à la Bibliothèque royale de Stockholm." In *Bok- och Bibliothekshistoriska Studier Tillägnade Isak Collijn.* Uppsala: Almqvist & Wiksells, 1925: 75–90.

Sonet, Jean, S. J. *Le Roman de Barlaam et Josaphat.* Vol. 1: *Recherches sur la tradition manuscrite latine et française.* Bibliothèque de la Faculté de Philologie et Lettres de Namur, 6. Namur: BFPL/Paris: Vrin, 1949.

Speer, Mary B. "Editing the Formulaic Romance Style: The Poetics of Repetition in the *Roman des sept sages*." *L'Esprit Créateur* 27 (1987): 34–52.

"Textual Criticism Redivivus." *L'Esprit Créateur* 23 (1983): 38–48.

"Wrestling with Change: Old French Textual Criticism and *Mouvance*." *Olifant* 7 (1980): 317–23.

Stein, Henri. "La Bibliothèque du connétable d'Albret à Sully-sur-Loire (1409)." *Bibliographe Moderne* 6 (1902): 91–93.

Triaud, Annie. "Une version tardive de l'*Eneas*." In *The Spirit of the Court: Selected Proceedings of the Fourth Congress of the International Courtly Literature Society (Toronto 1983)*. Ed. Glyn S. Burgess and Robert A. Taylor. Asst. eds. Alan Deyermond, Dennis Green, and Beryl Rowland. Cambridge, UK: D. S. Brewer, 1985: 360–72.

Tuve, Rosemund. *Allegorical Imagery: Some Mediaeval Books and Their Posterity*. Princeton: Princeton University Press, 1966.

Uitti, Karl D. "From *Clerc* to *Poète*: The Relevance of the *Romance of the Rose* to Machaut's World." In *Machaut's World: Science and Art in the Fourteenth Century*. Ed. Madeleine Pelner Cosman and Bruce Chandler. *Annals of the New York Academy of Sciences* 314 (1978): 209–16.

ed. *The Poetics of Textual Criticism: The Old French Example. L'Esprit Créateur* 27, 1 (1987).

Ullman, B. L. "Classical Authors in Certain Mediaeval *Florilegia*." *Classical Philology* 27 (1932): 1–42.

Studies in the Italian Renaissance. Rome: Edizioni di Storia e Letteratura, 1955.

"Tibullus in the Mediaeval *Florilegia*." *Classical Philology* 23 (1928): 128–74.

Van der Poel, Dieuwke. "Over gebruikersnotities in het *Rose*-handschrift K.A. XXIV." *De Nieuwe Taalgids* 79 (1986): 505–16.

De Vlaamse "Rose" en "Die Rose" van Heinric: Onderzoekingen over Twee Middelnederlandse Bewerkingen van de "Roman de la Rose" (avec un résumé en français). Middeleeuwse Studies en Bronnen, 13. Hilversum: Verloren, 1989.

Vanossi, Luigi. *Dante e il "Roman de la Rose": Saggi sul "Fiore"*. Biblioteca dell' "Archivium Romanicum," series 1, 144. Florence: Leo S. Olschki, 1979.

Verhuyck, Paul. "Guillaume de Lorris *ou* la multiplication des cadres." *Neophilologus* 58 (1974): 283–93.

Vitz, Evelyn Birge. Review of John V. Fleming, *Reason and the Lover* (Princeton: Princeton University Press, 1984). In *Modern Language Quarterly* 46 (1985): 202–8.

Von Schulte, Johann Friedrich R. "Die Glosse zum Decret Gratians von ihren Anfängen bis auf die jüngsten Ausgaben." *Denkschriften der Kaiserlichen Akademie der Wissenschaften: Philosophisch-historische Classe* 21:2 (1872): 1–97.

Wailes, Stephen L. *Medieval Allegories of Jesus' Parables*. Berkeley: University of California Press, 1987.

Walters, Lori. "Illuminating the *Rose*: Gui de Mori and the Illustrations of MS 101 of the Municipal Library, Tournai." In *Rethinking the "Romance of the Rose": Text, Image, Reception*. Ed. Kevin Brownlee and Sylvia Huot. Pp. 167–200.

"A Parisian Manuscript of the *Romance of the Rose*." *Princeton University Library Chronicle* 51 (1989): 31–55.

"Le Rôle du scribe dans l'organisation des manuscrits des romans de Chrétien de Troyes." *Romania* 106 (1985): 303–25.

Wetherbee, Winthrop. *Chaucer and the Poets: An Essay on "Troilus and Criseyde".* Ithaca: Cornell University Press, 1984.

"The Literal and the Allegorical: Jean de Meun and the 'De Planctu Naturae." *Medieval Studies* 33 (1971): 264–91.

Platonism and Poetry: The Literary Influence of the School of Chartres. Princeton: Princeton University Press, 1972.

Williams, Sarah Jane. "An Author's Role in Fourteenth-Century Book Production: Guillaume de Machaut's 'livre ou je met toutes mes choses'." *Romania* 90 (1969): 433–54.

Wimsatt, James I., and Kibler, William W. "Machaut's Text and the Question of His Personal Supervision." *Studies in the Literary Imagination* 20 (1987): 41–53.

Wright, Steven. "Deguileville's *Pelerinage de Vie Humaine* as 'Contrepartie Edifiante' of the *Roman de la Rose.*" *Philological Quarterly* 68 (1989): 399–422.

Zumthor, Paul. *Essai de poétique médiévale.* Paris: Seuil, 1972.

"Narrative and Anti-narrative: 'Le Roman de la Rose'." *Yale French Studies* 51 (1974): 185–204.

Index of manuscripts

Arras: Bibliothèque Municipale
MS 845: 39, 61, 207–8, 231–38, 280,
365–68
MS 879: 146, 147, 159–61, 277
Brussels: Bibliothèque Royale
MS 11019: 38, 147, 156, 241 n. 8
Cambridge, UK: Cambridge University
Library
Add. MS 2993: 6–7, 195–206, 326–27,
331, 371–83
Cambridge, UK: Magdalene College,
Pepys Library
MS 1594: 254–56
Chantilly, Musée Condé
MS 686: 39–40, 200 n. 33
MS 911: 52 n. 5, 147
Copenhagen, Royal Library (Kongelige
Bibliotek)
MS NKS 63–2°: 147, 241 n. 8
MS GKS 2061–4°: 6, 72, 87, 89, 105,
111, 114, 124–29, 344–52
Dijon, Bibliothèque Municipale
MS 139: 278–79, *plate 9*
MS 525: 75–84, *plate 6*
MS 526: 34
Florence, Biblioteca Laurenziana
MS A. e D. 153: 14
London, British Library
MS Egerton 881: 38
MS Stowe 947: 275, *plate 8*
Lyon, Bibliothèque Municipale
MS 764: 181 n. 18
Maihingen, Öttingen-Wallerstein Library
MS without shelfmark (*Ter*): 86, 115
Montpellier, Faculté de Médecine
MS H 438: 38, 147, 241 n. 8
New York, Pierpont Morgan Library
MS M 132: 29–31, 196, 202, 327,
371–72, *plate 1*

Paris, Bibliothèque de l'Arsenal
MS 2988: 146, 147
MS 3337: 27, 55–58
Paris, Bibliothèque Mazarine
MS 3873: 183
MS 3874: 241 n. 8, 331
Paris, Bibliothèque Nationale
MS fr. 246: 76
MS fr. 378: 37
MS fr. 797: 86–87, 93–100, 109, 111,
116–28 *passim*, 251, 252, 256, 326,
338–52
MS fr. 799: 185, 330
MS fr. 802: 182 n. 18
MS fr. 803: 200 n. 33
MS fr. 1317: 19
MS fr. 1559: 158
MS fr. 1560: 48–55, 61–63, 74
MS fr. 1561: 277
MS fr. 1563: 158–62
MS fr. 1564: 28
MS fr. 1565: 31–32, *plates 2–3*
MS fr. 1566: 183–85, 337
MS fr. 1567: 186–89, 330
MS fr. 1569: 34
MS fr. 1571: 137, 147, 156, 160
MS fr. 1574: 29, 39, 48, 53, 183, 280
MS fr. 1576: 137, 147, 241 n. 8
MS fr. 1946: 166
MS fr. 2195: 146, 147, 159–61
MS fr. 9197: 68 n. 29, 109 n. 27, 148,
213 n. 4, n. 6
MS fr. 9345: 279–80
MS fr. 12587: 133 n. 6, 145–46, 147,
158, 334
MS fr. 12592: 280–85, *plates 10–11*
MS fr. 12594: 34
MS fr. 19154: 146, 147, 152 n. 23,
159–61

Index of manuscripts

MS fr. 19157: 145, 146, 147, 185, 330

MS fr. 24389: 147, 211

MS fr. 24390: 18, 27–28, 63–75, 87, 124, 128–29, 179, 344–48, 365–68, *plate 5*

MS fr. 24392: 196, 372–83

MS fr. 24432: 19

MS fr. 25524: 37, 131, 132–33, 139–45, 147, 149, 150, 151, 154, 159–60, 195, 211, 329, 334, 353–61

MS fr. 25525: 40–46, *plate 4*

MS fr. 25526: 15, 178–79, 274, 286–322, 329, 331, 365–68, *plates 12–21*

MS lat. 1860: 59

MS lat. 3893: 70 n. 32

MS lat. 8758: 74 n. 34

MS lat. 15155: 59, 62–63

MS lat. 16708: 59

MS Rothschild 2800: 28–29, 56, 107

n. 24, 242, 277, 330 n. 5

Princeton, Firestone Library
MS Garrett 126: 365–68

Private collection
MS without shelfmark (**Bü*): 31, 52 n. 5, 147, 156, 241 n. 8

Rennes, Bibliothèque Municipale
MS 15963: 6–7, 39, 189–95, 329, 330, 333, 335, 369–70

Rome, Vatican Library
MS Urb. lat. 376: 14

Suchier fragment
MS without shelfmark (*Bï*) 144, 147

Tournai, Bibliothèque de la Ville
MS 101: 6–7, 85–128 *passim*, 174, 175, 236, 242, 314, 344–52, *plate 7*

Turin, University Library
MS L. III. 22: 35–36, 92, 132, 133 n. 6, 137–39, 145–47, 152–55, 158, 160, 334, 361–64

General index

Abelard, 75, 79, 83; castration of, 277; deleted from *Rose*, 105, 115; in *Rose*, 48, 79–80, 115, *plate 6*

abridgments: in Ami, 136, 140–42, 159–62: in Cupid, 136; in Faux Samblant, 39–40, 140 n. 12, 190, 236; in Genius, 114, 139, 141, 185, 188–89, 193, 194–95, 237, 329–30, 349–52, 369–70; in Nature, 111–14, 117–18, 137–39, 185, 193–94, 236, 329, 330; in Reason, 12, 106–7, 109, 110, 140, 145–47, 153–55, 183, 233–36, 353–62; in Richesse, 139, 142; in Vieille, 137, 190–92; of erotic material, 12, 105, 115, 136–38, 142–43, 192, 194, 237; of mythological material, 105, 109–10, 112, 116–17, 136–38, 191, 194, 234, 236

Adonis, 48, 109, 193; in *B* text, 131, 133–34, 143–44

Advocacie Nostre Dame, 76

Alain de Lille, 22, 25, 171; Genius in, 104, 114, 221, 270; Gui de Mori and, 89, 107, 109, 114; "litany of love" and, 165–66; Nature in, 107–8, 114, 137

Alard de Cambrai, 60

Alexander, 195, 201, 374–75

Ami, 78, 92, 192; in *B* text, 136, 140–42, 159–62; in Gui de Mori, 100–5, 119, 128–29; in Ms *Arr*. 237–38; Machaut and, 251; marginalia in, 284, 302, 305–6, 309; on dreams, 20; readers' annotations of, 36, 44, 56, 57, 65, 67–69, 70, 72; *see also* abridgments; interpolations

Andreas Capellanus, 74; Gui de Mori and, 99–100, 101, 106

annotations, 11, 36–37, 331; Ms *Arr*, 234; MS Arsenal 3337, 55–58; MS *Be*, 35–36, 92; MS *Dij*, 79–83; MS *He*, 72: MS *Ke*, 63–74, 179; MS *Me*, 48–55,

61–63, 74; MS *Tou*, 87–89, 334, 335, *plate 7*; of Michel Alès, 41–44, *plate 4*; *see also individual topics and characters*

antifeminism, 24, 43–44, 79, 92–93, 193, 317; *B* text and, 37, 131, 132, 136, 138, 141–42, 160–62; Gui de Mori and, 100, 102–4, 117, 127–28; marginalia concerning, 285; Ms *Arr* and, 237–38; readers' annotations concerning, 35–36, 43–44, 50, 62, 65, 66; *see also* Christine de Pizan; rape

Apollo, 124, 131, 134–36, 241, 335; in Machaut, 247–48

Aristotle: *Ethics*, 49, 50, 53, 55, 74; in Deguilleville, 222–23; in Gui de Mori, 109, 110, 119 n. 35; *Physics*, 49–50, 54, 62

Augustine, Saint, 74, 97–98, 132, 213, 278–79, 342, 344, *plate 9*; in Deguilleville, 209, 210

authorship: medieval idea of, 1–3, 334–35; of *Rose*, 2, 4, 89, 124, 133, 332–36

Avenir (King), 111, 125–26, 128, 347–48

B remaniement, 6, 163, 195, 328–29, 330, 333–35; Ami in, 136, 140–42, 159–62; authorship in, 133, 334–35; concluding passage of, 142–43; Cupid in, 134–36, 142, 155–56, 244–45; Deguilleville and, 8, 211, 214, 217, 219; Faux Samblant in, 131, 140, 152–53, 334; Genius in, 137, 139; Machaut and, 241, 244–45, 248, 251; manuscript tradition of, 53, 124, 131–32, 145–48, 157–62; Nature in, 132, 137–39; Reason in, 12, 53, 124, 140, 145–56, 167, 211, 219, 328–29, 353–64; Richesse in, 136, 142; Vieille in, 137, 139

Badel, Pierre-Yves, 10–11, 34, 97, 330, 336

Bartholomew of Brescia, 70, 72–73
Bernardus Silvestris, 62
Bible: annotations in *Rose* manuscripts
   and, 49–51 *passim*, 55, 74; dreams and,
   50–51; *Rose* interpolations and, 12, 94,
   96, 97–98, 110–11, 120, 164–65,
   169–70, 235, 339, 342, 343–46
Brisebare, 127
Brownlee, Kevin, 317

Caesar, Julius, 195, 201–2, 374–83
Calin, William, 272
carol, 29, 214, 230, 277, 290
Catherine, Saint, 290, 301–2
Cato, 56, 82, 201, 378–79; French
   translation of, 76, 79, 82
Cerquiglini, Bernard, 3
Cerquiglini, Jacqueline, 258
Charles d'Anjou, 200
Chastelaine de Vergi, 34, 189
Chevalier errant, 331
Chrétien de Troyes, 140, 142
Christine de Pizan, 23, 26, 55, 172;
   critique of *Rose*, 22, 25, 36, 37, 57, 149,
   174, 186, 324–25; Deguilleville and,
   228; Gui de Mori and, 93, 104
Christopher, Saint, 303
Chrystostom, John, 71
Cicero, 109, 110
Circe, 82–83, 84
Col, Pierre, 24–25, 37–38, 84, 172–73,
   178, 206; Gui de Mori and, 93, 123;
   reading of Genius, 25–26, 31, 174–75,
   195, 318, 330
Commens d'amours, 34
Condé, Jean de, 313–16
Consolation of Philosophy: cross-referenced
   with *Rose*, 81–83; French translations
   of, 76–77, 81, 144, 166–67, 231; Gui de
   Mori and, 89, 97, 111–12; "litany of
   love" and, 166–67; Machaut and, 250,
   252–54; Vieille and, 210
Croesus, 43, 111, 140, 200, 234, 304
Cupid, 78, 169, 196, 209–10, 211–12, 273;
   allegoricization of, 232–33; Apollo and,
   134–36; discussion of authorship by,
   52–53, 89–91, 133–34; in *B* text,
   134–36, 142, 155–56, 244–45; in Gui de
   Mori, 93–95, 99, 107, 116, 119, 338–39;
   in Machaut, 268; in MS κυ, 204, 205;
   marginalia in, 298–99, 301–2, 310–11;

readers' annotations of, 56–58; *see also*
   abridgments; interpolations

Daedalus, 58, 109
Dangier, 156; Deguilleville and, 209, 214,
   220; marginalia concerning, 289–90,
   299, *plate 14*
De miseria condicionis humane, 51
Decretum, 70–75
Deguilleville, Guillaume de, 12, 14, 55,
   274, 331; *B* text and, 8, 211, 214, 217,
   219; critique of *Rose*, 226–28; Genius
   and, 220–25; Nature in, 214–15, 217,
   221–24; *Pelerinage de l'ame*, 225, 231;
   Pelerinage de vie humaine (first recension),
   207–25, 226, 228, 229, 231, 301,
   316–17; *Pelerinage de vie humaine* (second
   recension), 208, 225–30, 236; Reason
   in, 211, 214–15, 216–19, 223, 228, 329
Deucalion, 109, 117, 296
Dit de l'Empereur Coustant, 127
Diz et proverbes des sages, 60, 61, 67, 74,
   238
Doctrinal sauvage, 76
Dragonetti, Roger, 2
dreams, 53–54, 74; interpretation of,
   19–20, 49, 50–52, 178–79, 181; *see also*
   eroticism: in dreams; Macrobius

Echecs amoureux, 331; commentary on, 68
   n. 29, 109 n. 27, 148, 213 n. 4, n. 6
Echo, 109, 236; deleted from *Rose*,
   325–26
Enguerrand de Marigny, 200 n. 33
eroticism, 13, 23–25, 28–29, 44–45, 53,
   148–51, 172, 181–82, 209–10, 230; and
   the sacred, 22–23, 114, 118–24, 173–75,
   255, 256–60, 267, 270–72, 273–74,
   294–312, *plates 18–20*; didactic use of,
   107–9, 110, 174–75; in dreams, 19–20,
   50–52; in Machaut, 256–60, 270–72; in
   MS *Lk*, 186–89; in *Rose* illustrations,
   29, 31, 32, *plates 2–3*; marginalia
   concerning, 275–77, 279–80, 292–300,
   plates 8, 15–17; readers' annotations
   concerning, 57–58, 68–69; *see also*
   abridgments: of erotic material; Cupid;
   friendship: erotic love and; love
euphemism, 25, 167–68, 302, 311; in
   Alain de Lille, 107–8; in *B* text,
   148–49, 154–57, 328; in Deguilleville,

euphemism, (cont.)
218–20; in Jean de Meun, 107–8, 148–49, 218–19; in MS κυ, 199–200; see also obscenity; Reason: and language

Faux Samblant, 34, 38–40, 83, 148, 179, 190, 317: Cupid and, 310–11; Deguilleville and, 221, 227; in B text, 131, 140, 152–53, 334; in Gui de Mori, 39, 102, 112, 118, 125; in MS Arr, 39, 233, 234, 236; marginalia, 282, 286–87, 309–10, 312, plates 11–13; Nature and, 112, 172, 185, 194, 330; Nero and, 184–85; Proteus and, 324; readers' annotations of, 68, 71, 74; rubrication of, 39; scribal warnings about, 17–18, 38–39, 77, 190, 331; see also abridgments; interpolations
Fet des Romains, 195, 202, 203, 382, 383
Fleming, John, 11–12, 13, 14–15, 25–26, 97, 107, 110, 170, 298, 320, 329
florilegia, 51–52, 55, 58–63, 73, 75
friendship, 56, 78, 110, 128–29, 141; divine love and, 96, 97, 341; erotic love and, 94, 99–100, 102, 122–23, 170, 338–39

Genius, 92, 96, 104, 106, 171–74, 217, 277; Col's interpretation of, 25–26, 174–75, 195, 318, 330; Deguilleville and, 220–25; Gerson's interpretation of, 22–23; in B text, 137, 139; in Gui de Mori, 96, 103, 114, 115–16, 122–23, 174, 329, 330, 349–52; in KMN text, 170, 172–73, 175, 177; in MS Arr, 236, 237–38; in various L manuscripts, 183–84, 186–89, 193, 194–95, 329, 330, 369–70; Machaut and, 252, 253–54, 260, 266, 267–71; marginalia in, 284–85, 298–99, 312; modern interpretations of, 25–26, 173–74; readers' annotations of, 43–44, 70, 71–72; rubrication of, 29–31; see also abridgments; interpolations
Gerson, Jean, 22–23, 25, 26, 47–48, 97, 130–31, 174; Deguilleville and, 217, 229; Gui de Mori and, 104, 105, 107, 114, 115
Gilles li Muisis, 12
gloss: discussed in Rose, 21, 37, 108,

148–49; Jean's continuation as, 21; see also annotations; euphemism; marginalia
Grace, 315; in Deguilleville, 12, 212–28 passim, 236
Gregory the Great, 97
Gui de Mori, 6, 12, 14, 37, 242, 251, 252–53, 255, 256, 314–15, 318, 320, 323; Ami in, 100–5, 119, 127–28; authorial persona, 89–92, 332–34, 335; compared to other remanieurs, 131–32, 136, 139, 143, 149, 164, 165, 193, 236, 274, 325–35; conclusion of Rose in, 105; Cupid in, 93–95, 99, 107, 116, 119, 338–39; Deguilleville and, 215, 217, 229; Faux Samblant in, 39, 102, 112, 118, 125; Genius in, 96, 103, 114, 115–16, 122–23, 174, 329, 330, 349–52; Guillaume de Lorris and, 68 n. 29, 85–87, 93–95, 109 n. 27, 125, 325–26, 334; manuscript tradition, 63, 66, 74, 86–89, 124–29, 145, 157, plates 5–7; Nature in, 111–14, 117–18, 125, 329; Reason in, 12, 95–103, 106–7, 109, 110–11, 119, 120–21, 125–26, 128, 198, 328, 339–40; Vieille in, 117, 127
Guillaume de Lorris, 335, 336; anonymous continuation of, 17, 85, 86, 95, 242–44; B text and, 131, 136, 139–40; Deguilleville and, 208–10, 211–14, 230; Gui de Mori and, 68 n. 29, 85–87, 93–95, 109 n. 27, 125, 325–26, 334; Machaut and, 242–44, 249, 260; narrator interventions, 16, 69, 178–79; rubrication of, 29; Tibullus and, 52–53; κ text and, 196–98, 371–72; see also authorship: of Rose
Guillaume de Saint-Amour, 190, 236, 310, 336–37

Harris, Kate, 8
Heloise, 75, 79, 83; deleted from Rose, 105, 115; in Rose, 48, 81, 115, 126
Hill, Thomas, 330
homosexuality, 175, 182, 188; Alain de Lille and, 114 n. 32, 171; deletion of references to, 106, 114, 194, 234; Narcissus and, 326; Nero and, 106
Hope: in Machaut, 250–54
Horace, 72

Hugh of Saint Victor, 119–22, 255, 328
"Hughe de Saint Victor" (anonymous
    treatise), 254–56
Hult, David, 2, 3, 89, 333
Hundred Years' War, 43, 45–56

interpolations: anonymous continuation
    of Guillaume de Lorris, 17, 85, 86,
    95, 242–44; concerning Richesse,
    196, 202–3; extended conclusion of
    Jean de Meun, 181–82; in Ami,
    72–73, 100–4, 127–28, 203, 204; in
    Cupid, 93–95, 99, 133–35, 155–56,
    204, 205, 244–45, 338–39; in Faux
    Samblant, 39–40, 118, 125, 131,
    152–53, 195, 203; in Genius, 170–72,
    173, 175, 183–84, 186–89, 195, 204;
    in Nature, 45, 186; in Reason, 12,
    53, 95–100, 110–11, 124, 125–26,
    128, 146–48, 150–54, 164–70, 195,
    196, 198–202, 235, 328–29, 339–49,
    360–64, 365–68, 372–83; in Vieille,
    117, 127; Marsyas, 124, 134–35, 144,
    155–56, 241, 245, 248; Medusa,
    175–77, 195, 197–98, 264–65; mirror
    of Virgil, 196–97, 327, 371–72
Io, 117
Ivy, Robert, 8, 9

Jaloux, 25, 68–69, 315; in B text, 140; in
    Gui de Mori, 103, 127–28;
    marginalia in, 283, 309
Jean de la Mote, 34
Jean de Meun: Apology, 16–17, 35, 38,
    39, 90, 118, 142 n. 13, 180–81, 236,
    238; as glossator, 21; authorial
    reputation, 33, 38, 130–31, 227–28,
    231, 335–37; Codicille, 33, 76;
    Testament, 33, 34, 63, 65, 70, 76, 78,
    84, 231; translation of Boethius,
    76–77, 81, 144; Trésor, 33; see also
    authorship: of Rose
Jeu de Robin et Marion, 34
Jeu des echecs moralisés, 76, 79, 81, 82, 83
Joseph, 111
Jung, Marc-René, 171, 333
Juvenal, 48, 105, 115, 117

Kennedy, Elspeth, 2
König, Eberhard, 14, 15

Kuhn, Alfred, 14

Langlois, Ernest, 5–7, 152, 154, 163, 164,
    332–33
Laurence, Saint, 290, 301, 316
love: as religion, 25, 296, 298–300, 312,
    313–14, plate 18; contrasting varieties
    of, 93–96, 98–99, 119–24, 148,
    150–51, 169–70, 174–75, 182,
    188–89, 252–54, 257–60, 301–12,
    338–43, plates 19–20; in Machaut,
    241, 244–47, 249–54, 256–66,
    268–72; in Michel Alès, 44–45; in
    "Hughe de Saint Victor," 254–56;
    mirror of, 196–97, 213, 233, 326–27,
    371–72; see also Ami; Cupid;
    eroticism; friendship; Reason: love
    and; Roman de la Rose: as love poetry
Lucan, 203; use in Rose interpolation,
    195, 202, 374–83
Lucretia, 83, 110, 126
lyric tradition, 99, 106, 140, 252

Machaut, Guillaume de, 14, 274, 331,
    336; Boethius and, 252–54; Fonteinne
    amoureuse, 242–49, 258; Gui de Mori
    and, 251, 252–53; poet figures in,
    244, 246–48, 258, 265, 267–70;
    Prologue, 247, 267–70; Remede de
    Fortune, 249–54, 271; Voir Dit,
    256–67, 271–72
Macrobius, 20, 47, 49, 50, 54; Gui de
    Mori and, 89, 110
Male Bouche, 36, 140
manuscript families, Roman de la Rose: B
    text, see B remaniement; F text, 185,
    330; H text, 6, 124; J text, 157, 241
    n. 8; K text, 6, 18, 106 n. 23, 128,
    157, 163–79, 183, 185, 195, 196, 206,
    328, 330, 331, 333, 365–68; L text, 6,
    7, 167, 178, 183–95, 328, 333; M
    text, 6, 163–79, 185, 195, 291, 328,
    330, 331, 333, 365–68; N text, 6, 7,
    163–82, 195, 328, 330, 331, 333,
    365–68; κ text, 6–7, 195–206,
    326–27, 328, 331, 333, 371–83; see
    also Gui de Mori: manuscript
    tradition; Roman de la Rose:
    manuscript tradition
Margaret, Saint, 290–91, 303–6, 308, 320,
    plate 20

marginalia (visual): in MS *Bê*, 277; in MS
Dijon, Bibl. Mun. 139, 278–79, *plate
9*; in MS *Lb*, 277; in MS *Lm³*, 275,
plate 8; in MS *Lq*, 279–80; in MS
Mi, 286–322, *plates 12–21*; in MS
Paris, Bibl. Nat. fr. *12595*, 280–85,
plates 10–11; layout by bifolium,
290–91, 292–94, 295–96, 297, 302–3,
304–8, 310–11, 319–22
Marie de France, 21
Marot, Clément, 157, 164, 315
marriage, 22, 78, 98, 309; allegorical
significance of, 119, 122; context for
sexual activity, 25, 119, 122–23, 170,
175, 206, 314; in Gui de Mori, 37,
92, 103–4, 115, 123–24; MS *Tou* and,
118, 123–24; readers' annotations
concerning, 36, 69
Marsyas: *see* interpolations: Marsyas
Matthew of Vendôme, 49, 53, 62
Medusa: *see* interpolations: Medusa
Méon, Dominique, 164
Michel Alès, 40–46, 56, 67, 68
Molinet, Jean, 315, 335
Montbaston, Jeanne and Richard, 274,
322, *plate 21*
Montreuil, Jean de, 23–24, 26, 34, 178
moral reading of *Rose*, 11–13, 78; for
Deguilleville, 210–13, 216, 219–30
passim; for Marot, 315; for Molinet,
315; in Gui de Mori, 93–105, 107,
109, 118–24, 325–26, 328–30; in *K*
text, 18; in *KMN* text, 164–78, 328,
330; in MS *κυ*, 197–200, 202–3,
205–6, 326–27, 331; in MS *Lb*, 277;
in MS *Lm³*, 275; in MS *Mi*, 292–319;
readers' annotations and, 35–36,
49–54, 56–58, 79–84; rubrication
and, 29–31; *see also* Christine de
Pizan; Col, Pierre; Gerson, Jean;
Montreuil, Jean de
Morawski, Joseph, 129
motets, 317–18
mouvance, 3–4, 11, 40, 42
Myrrha, 137

Narcissus, 53, 63, 109, 176–77; in Gui de
Mori, 85, 109, 125, 325–26; in
Machaut, 244; in MS *κυ*, 326–27;
marginalia concerning, 285, 300;
moral implications of, 121, 174,
213–14, 325–27; Oiseuse and, 275
Nature (allegorical personification), 92,
97, 197, 215, 221, 223–24, 267, 269,
320; antifeminism and, 36, 138; Col's
interpretation of, 26; Gerson's
interpretation of, 22; in Alain de
Lille, 107–8, 114, 137; in *B* text, 132,
137–39; in Deguilleville, 214–15,
217, 218, 222, 224; in Gui de Mori,
111–14, 116, 117–18, 125, 329; in
MS *Arr*, 236–37; Machaut and, 252,
267–68; marginalia in, 282, 283, 286,
296, 311–12; modern interpretations
of, 25–26; readers' annotations of,
36, 74, 81; rubrication of, 32; sacred
mysteries and, 114, 138–39, 217, 222,
236; sexual activity and, 31, 32,
170–72, 181–82, 186–88, *plates 2–3*;
see also abridgments; interpolations
Nero, 83, 111, 280, 304, 305; variants
concerning, 106, 140, 184–85, 200
Nicholas of Lyra, 55, 74
Nicholas, Saint, 302–3, 312, 316

obscenity, 12, 22–23, 25, 149, 179–80,
183–84; *B* text and, 140, 151–57; Gui
de Mori and, 106–7, 115;
interpolations concerning, 167–68,
199–200, 328; *see also* euphemism;
Reason: language and
Oiseuse, 15 n. 32, 29, 249, 275, 280,
plate 8; in Deguilleville, 211
Origen, 112, 277
Orpheus, 247, 270
Ovid, 35, 47, 48, 62, 72, 75, 132; *Amores*,
52, 92, 131, 133–34; *Ars amatoria*,
43, 44, 47–48, 55–58, 59, 60, 65, 72,
73, 91–92, 135, 171–72, 190;
authorial persona, 91–92; in
Deguilleville, 228–29; *Metamorphoses*,
49, 50, 57, 68, 134, 241, 247; *Remedia
amoris*, 91–93, 136
Ovide moralisé, 232, 248, 249
owners of *Rose* manuscripts: Anne of
France, 196; Charles d'Albret, 55;
Charles V, 240; Jean de Berry, 203,
240; Jehan de Merville, Frère, 158;
Marie de Sully, 55; Mathias Rivalli,
75–84; Michel Alès, 40–46; Pourrès
family, 118; Robert des Esleu, 34;
Sorbonne, 84

Pallas Athene, 176–77, 197, 245
Pamphilus, 44, 49, 50, 53, 62, 65
Paris: Helen and, 244, 258; Judgment of, 135, 245–46, 248, 258
Paul, Saint, 164–5, 170, 198, 309
Perseus, 176–77, 197, 327
Peruzzi, Simonetta, 14
Plato, 71
Poirion, Daniel, 2, 3, 4
Poissanche d'amours, 34
Pompey, 195, 201, 375–78
poverty, 67–68, 78, 136, 141, 142, 202
Priam, 195, 201, 372–73
Prise amoureuse, 34
procreation, 23–24, 329, 330; Genius and, 25, 32, 172–75, 267, 269, 270–71, 297–98, 312, *plates 2–3*; in Deguilleville, 223–24; in Gui de Mori, 119; Reason and, 98, 169–71, 172–73, 175
proverbs: in readers' annotations, 36, 43, 56–57, 65–66
Purgatoire Saint Patrice, 76, 83
puy, 99, 338, 339
Pygmalion, 48, 176–77, 197, 224; deleted by Gui de Mori, 105, 109; in *B* text, 137, 143–44; in MS *Tou*, 117; Machaut and, 244, 261, 262, 263; marginalia concerning, 280, 300, *plate 10*
Pyrrha, 109, 117, 296

querelle, 22–26, 29, 44, 158; *see also* Christine de Pizan; Col, Pierre; Gerson, Jean; Montreuil, Jean de
Quilligan, Maureen, 156

rape, 102; in *B* text, 136, 141–42, 160–61; readers' annotations concerning, 44, 50, 62, 65; *see also* Lucretia; Susannah
Reason (allegorical personification), 12–13, 92, 172–73; Grace and, 12, 215–17, 235–36; in *B* text, 12, 53, 124, 140, 145–56, 167, 211, 219, 328, 353–64; in Deguilleville, 12, 211, 214–15, 216–19, 223, 228, 329; in Gui de Mori, 12, 95–103, 106–11, 119, 120–22, 125–26, 128, 198, 328, 339–49; in *KMN* text, 164–71, 173, 175, 328, 365–68; in MS *Arr*, 233–36, 365–68; in MS *κυ*, 198–202,

372–83; language and, 12, 23, 24, 106–9, 140, 146–56 *passim*, 167–68, 183, 199–200, 218–19, 234, 328, 362–64; love and, 95–103, 140, 148–51, 164–66, 168–71, 197, 198, 245–46, 249–51, 255–56, 339–44; Machaut and, 249, 250–51; marginalia in, 277, 280, 286–87, 303–8, 309, *plate 19*; readers' annotations of, 35, 36, 50, 53, 56, 58, 66–67, 70, 73, 234; Sapience and, 12, 100, 164, 198; spiritual love and, 95–98, 118–21, 164–67, 235–36, 303–7, 339–44, 365–68; *see also* abridgments: in Reason; interpolations
Reclus de Molliens, 34, 76, 78
Response au Bestiaire, 34
Richard de Fournival, 61, 99; apocryphal works, 34; *Bestiaire d'amours*, 34, 119, 277
Richesse, 68; in *B* text, 136, 142; in Guillaume de Lorris, 142; in MS *κυ*, 196, 202–3; marginalia in, 282, 286, 290, 301; *see also* abridgments: in Richesse; wealth
Robert d'Artois, 200 n. 33
Roman de Fauvel, 34, 76, 78, 83
Roman de la Rose: anthology manuscripts of, 32–34, 75–84, 127, 203, 231–38; as love poetry, 27–29, 34, 56–58, 68–69, 90–104, 118–24, 136, 139–44, 190–95, 242–65 *passim*; Latin tradition and, 12, 13, 47–84, 89, 91–93, 96–98, 100, 106–14, 119–22, 133–36, 165–67, 171–73, 175–77, 200–3; manuscript tradition of, 5–7, 11–12, 124–29, 325–36; translations of, 157, 191 n. 23, 205 n. 38, 332; *see also* authorship: of *Rose*; manuscript families, *Roman de la Rose*; owners of *Rose* manuscripts
Roman de Thebes, 203
Roman de Troie, 203
rubrication, 29–32 *passim*, 48, 76–77, 205, 280, 292, 332
Rude Understanding, 217, 218–20, 234
Rychner, Jean, 3, 9

sacred imagery, 29–31, 188, 198–99, 225, *plate 1*; in Deguilleville, 209, 212–17

sacred imagery, (*cont.*)
  passim; in Gui de Mori, 95–98, 114,
  119–24, 339–44; in Machaut, 256–62,
  267, 269–70; in marginalia, 283–85,
  286, 290–91, 294–96, 301–12, 319,
  320, *plates 18–20*; juxtaposed with
  erotic, 22–23, 114, 118–24, 273,
  294–319 *passim*, *plate 20*; "litany of
  love," 164–67, 365–68
Sallust, 48, 180
Sanford, Eva, 203
Sapience, 12, 198, 315; in Deguilleville,
  222–23
Saturn, 106, 116, 140, 155, 277, 306
scribe: role of, 2–3, 8–9, 38–40, 56–57,
  132, 157–62; doodling by, 28,
  277–79, *plate 9*; marginalia
  concerning, 321–22, *plate 21*; Mathias
  Rivalli, 75–84, *plate 6*; Michel Alès,
  40–46, *plate 4*
Second Rhetoric, 336
Seneca, 65, 109, 110; death of, 83, 111,
  140, 280, 304
Söderhjelm, Werner, 7
Speer, Mary, 9
Suetonius, 110, 184; use in *Rose*
  interpolation, 195, 202
Susannah, 110–11, 125–26, 128, 303–4,
  344–46

Ten Commandments, 231–33
Tibullus, 49–53 *passim*, 61–62, 74, 91, 92,
  335; death of, 52, 131, 133–34, 135,
  144, 248
Triaud, Annie, 9

Tuve, Rosemund, 14, 315

Venus, 94–95, 116–17, 159, 176–77,
  186–88, 189, 224; Adonis and, 48,
  109, 133–34; birth of, 306–7; in
  Deguilleville, 208, 226–28; in
  Machaut, 243–48 *passim*, 263; in
  Messe des oiseaux, 313; Jupiter and,
  156, 244–45; marginalia concerning,
  279–80, 299, 307–8; Mars and, 48,
  109, 117, 137–38, 173, 178, 194, 197,
  320; Tibullus and, 52, 133–34, 248
Vieille, La, 25, 78, 92–93, 150, 179, 210,
  320, 324; antifeminism and, 35–36,
  92; in B text, 136, 137, 139; in Gui
  de Mori, 118, 127; in MS *Lm*,
  190–92; marginalia in, 287, 292–96,
  307, 308, 309, *plates 13, 15–17*;
  readers' annotations of, 35–36, 65,
  66, 67, 73, 82–83, 84, 92; rubrication
  of, 30, 292; *see also* abridgments:
  Vieille; interpolations
Vincent of Beauvais, 60, 61–62, 73
Virgil, 48, 285; mirror of, 196–98,
  326–27, 371–72
Virginia, 110, 125–26, 128, 280, 303

wealth, 35, 36, 56, 66, 140; love and, 142,
  245–46; *see also* Richesse
Wetherbee, Winthrop, 25–26, 97, 328
women: implied readers of *Rose*, 23, 132;
  see also antifeminism; Christine de
  Pizan

Zumthor, Paul, 3, 21